Beginning C# Databases

Scott Allen

Syed Fahad Gilani

Jacob Hammer Pedersen

Ranga Raghunathan

Jon Reid

Wrox Press Ltd. ®

Beginning C# Databases

First Printed in July 2002

Published by Wrox Press Ltd,
Arden House, 1102 Warwick Road, Acocks Green,
Birmingham, B27 6BH, UK
Printed in the United States
ISBN 1-86100-609-8

Trademark Acknowledgments

Wrox has endeavored to provide trademark information about all the companies and products mentioned in this book by the appropriate use of capitals. However, Wrox cannot guarantee the accuracy of this information.

Credits

Authors
Scott Allen
Syed Fahad Gilani
Jacob Hammer Pedersen
Ranga Raghunathan
Jon Reid

Additional Material
Robin Dewson

Managing Editor
Viv Emery

Commissioning Editor
Julian Skinner

Technical Editors
Chris Goode
Victoria Hudgson
Dan Maharry
Dave Mercer

Project Managers
Emma Batch
Claire Robinson

Author Agent
Nicola Phillips

Technical Reviewers
Cristian Darie
Mark Horner
Bill Burris
Helmut Watson
Jeff Gabriel
Phil Powers DeGeorge
Erick Sgarbi
Robin Dewson
Cristof Falk
David Whitney
Thearon Willis

Production Coordinators
Abbie Forletta
Manjiri Karande

Index
John Collin

Proof Reader
Chris Smith

Cover
Natalie O'Donnell

About the Authors

Scott Allen

Scott Allen received a master's degree in computer science from Shippensburg University in Pennsylvania, and began writing real time embedded software, numerical analysis algorithms, and serial communication protocols for a leading manufacturer of near infrared spectroscopy instruments. More recently, Scott has been involved in designing and implementing highly scalable Internet applications. This includes using XML and Web Services to integrate C++ COM components into the J2EE based enterprise application of a Fortune 50 company. Scott currently works with Butterfly.Net, a production studio, online publisher, and technology provider for massively multiplayer games that connect PCs, consoles, and mobile devices.

Scott holds an MCSD certification and regularly serves as an adjunct faculty member at several colleges in the Maryland and Pennsylvania areas. Scott lives in Hagerstown, Maryland with his wife Vicky, and sons Alex and Christopher. You can reach him as bitmask@fred.net.

I'd like to thank Wrox press for giving me the opportunity to work on this project, and a special thanks to Chris Goode, Emma Batch, and Julian Skinner for helping me along the way. I'd like to dedicate this work to the engineering team of the former Ultraprise Corporation, the finest and brightest collection of professionals I've had the pleasure of working with.

I consider those three years a fabulous success based on what I learned about software, and about opportunity, but mostly on the friends I made.

Syed Fahad Gilani

A 21 year old bachelor, Fahad has just started a Masters Program in Computer Engineering at the Australian National University. Living in Pakistan all his life, He's been into the programming scenario for the last thirteen years, managing to sell his first program at the age of ten. Over the years, he has worked in a number of software development companies and on numerous private projects in various roles, which have been a great source of income. His expertise includes anything that's possible and anything that would manage to keep him awake through the night. Currently Fahad is running a small software development company, teaching, training, and writing.
When he's not working, you'd find him playing his guitar, jogging, eating, or back-flipping. Fahad wishes to keep a horse one day.

A bundle of thanks goes to Wrox for bearing with me, listening to me and being supportive.

I've had a great time writing this book. Special thanks goes to my family for being the best, my mom for her love, my friends who haven't been seeing much of me lately, to Adil for the pizzas, and to my pal Hamid for all the encouragement in this world, from childhood to now.

I hope all of you readers out there enjoy reading this book. We've all put in a lot of effort into making it just the right one for you.

Jacob Hammer Pedersen

Jacob Hammer Pedersen is a systems developer at Fujitsu Invia.

He pretty much started programming when he was able to spell the word 'Basic', which, incidentally is the language he's primarily using today. He started programming the PC in the early 90s, using Pascal, but soon changed his focus to C++, which still holds his interest. In the mid 90s his focus changed again, this time to Visual Basic. In the summer of 2000 he discovered C# and has been happily exploring that ever since.

Primarily working on the Microsoft platforms, other expertises include MS Office development, COM, COM+, SQL Server, and Visual Basic.NET.

A Danish citizen, he works and lives in Aarhus, Denmark and can be reached at Author@jham.dk

Ranga Raghunathan

Ranga Raghunathan works with Microsoft Technologies in Dallas, USA. He has a Bachelor's degree in Engineering from Birla Institute of Technology and Science, Pilani, India, and a Master's degree from Virigina Tech, USA. He is currently teaching his two-year old son Vivek to handle a joystick and enjoys playing with him in the park. He dedicates this book to his late father, who would have been proud to hold it in his hand. He would like to thank his wife Radha for her encouragement and support. His special thanks goes to Julian Skinner and Emma Batch of Wrox for their help in this project.

Ranga can be contacted at: ranga1@attbi.com

Jon D. Reid

Jon is the Chief Technology Officer for Micro Data Base Systems, Inc. (www.mdbs.com), maker of the TITANIUM™ Database Engine and GURU® Expert System tool. His primary current activity is developing database tools for the Microsoft .NET environment. He was editor for the C++ and Object Query Language (OQL) components of the Object Data Management Group (ODMG) standard, and has co-authored other Wrox titles including *Fast Track to C# Programming*, *ADO.NET Programmer's Reference*, *Beginning C#* and *Professional SQL Server 2000 XML*. When not working, writing, or cycling, he enjoys spending time with his wife and two young sons. Jon would like to thank his family and the team at Wrox (especially Julian and Emma) for their support and encouragement.

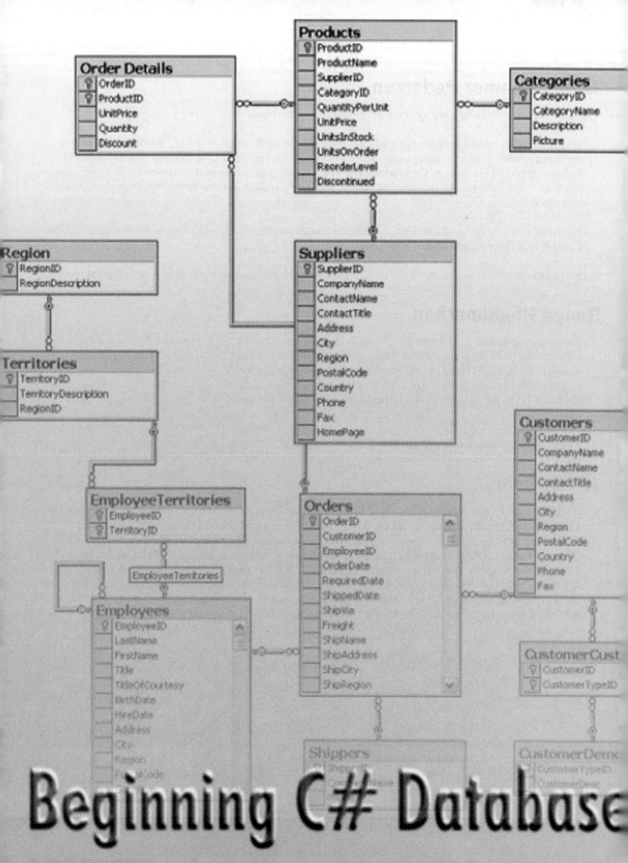

Table of Contents

Table of Contents

Table of Contents

Table of Contents

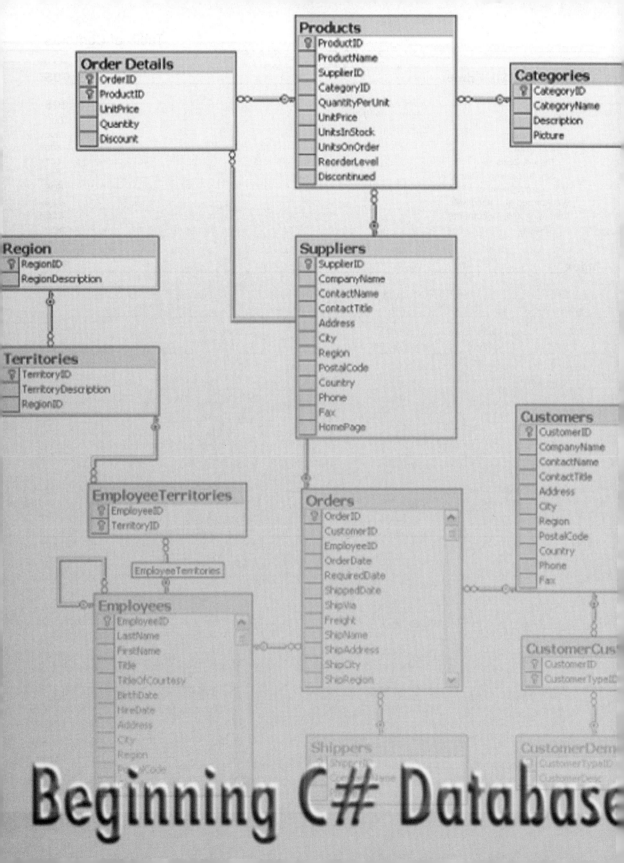

Order Details
- OrderID
- ProductID
- UnitPrice
- Quantity
- Discount

Products
- ProductID
- ProductName
- SupplierID
- CategoryID
- QuantityPerUnit
- UnitPrice
- UnitsInStock
- UnitsOnOrder
- ReorderLevel
- Discontinued

Categories
- CategoryID
- CategoryName
- Description
- Picture

Region
- RegionID
- RegionDescription

Suppliers
- SupplierID
- CompanyName
- ContactName
- ContactTitle
- Address
- City
- Region
- PostalCode
- Country
- Phone
- Fax
- HomePage

Territories
- TerritoryID
- TerritoryDescription
- RegionID

Customers
- CustomerID
- CompanyName
- ContactName
- ContactTitle
- Address
- City
- Region
- PostalCode
- Country
- Phone
- Fax

EmployeeTerritories
- EmployeeID
- TerritoryID

EmployeeTerritories

Orders
- OrderID
- CustomerID
- EmployeeID
- OrderDate
- RequiredDate
- ShippedDate
- ShipVia
- Freight
- ShipName
- ShipAddress
- ShipCity
- ShipRegion

Employees
- EmployeeID
- LastName
- FirstName
- Title
- TitleOfCourtesy
- BirthDate
- HireDate
- Address
- City
- Region
- PostalCode

CustomerCus
- CustomerID
- CustomerTypeID

Shippers

CustomerDem
- CustomerTypeID
- CustomerDesc

Beginning C# Database

Introduction

Every program, no matter what language or environment it is written in, is concerned with manipulating data. At its simplest, this might just involve variables whose initial values are hard-coded into the application. For more complex programs, though, this is almost certain to mean extracting data from an external data source, displaying it to the user, allowing the user to add, delete, and edit parts of that data, and saving changes back to the original data source. The subject of this book is how to achieve those universal tasks using Microsoft's brand-new C# language.

When large amounts of data need to be quickly accessible, the only real option is to store that data in a relational database. A Relational Database Management System (RDBMS for short) is an application that allows us to store data in a tabular format – a relational database consists of any number of tables, which are linked to allow the storage of distinct but related data. These applications can be very powerful and very expensive, but in this book we use the Microsoft Data Engine (MSDE), which can be installed free of charge with Visual Studio .NET, Visual C# .NET Standard Edition, or the full Microsoft .NET Framework SDK. MSDE is a cut-down version of Microsoft's powerful SQL Server database, so this book is also fully compatible with that RDBMS.

This book explains clearly, in easy-to-follow language, the concepts behind relational databases, with concise explanations of how to design databases, and how to optimize their performance, for example by using indexes to reduce the look-up time for frequently accessed fields. We also examine SQL – the Structured Query Language – which is used to communicate with database systems and that allows us to access and update data in the data store, and we see how we can access the database more efficiently by writing precompiled stored procedures in this language.

However, the core of the book is about accessing databases with C#. C# is dependent on the classes defined in the .NET Framework for most of its functionality, and data access and manipulation is no exception. For this, a set of special classes together known as ADO.NET is provided. ADO.NET provides easy and intuitive classes and methods for connecting to databases, retrieving data (by executing SQL commands or stored procedures), and updating the database. We also see how we can display our data to the user in Windows applications and in ASP.NET web applications, and how we can validate the user's input before saving it to the database.

Who Is This Book For?

This book is aimed at anyone who is using, or planning to use, the .NET Framework and the C# language to build Windows applications or ASP.NET web applications that access and manipulate data from a relational database. A basic knowledge of C# is assumed, but prior experience with relational databases is not necessary to get the most out of this book.

> **If you want more information about C#, to complement this book, you may find**
> *Beginning Visual C#* **useful (Wrox Press, ISBN: 1-86100-758-2).**

What Does This Book Cover?

This book is divided into five main sections, plus two appendices. The chapters are designed to provide a graded introduction to database concepts, the SQL language, and ADO.NET.

Getting Started

The first three chapters are designed to provide you with all the information you need to write a simple database-centric application using the wizards provided in Visual Studio .NET or Visual C# .NET Standard Edition. In this section, we look at installing and using the MSDE database engine, the wizards we can use to generate C# code quickly and effortlessly, and the basics of the SQL language.

ADO.NET Basics

Once we've seen how to use the wizards to create simple applications with almost no code, we move on in Chapters 4 to 8 to see how we can create more powerful applications by writing the ADO.NET code ourselves. We look at the classes provided by ADO.NET for connecting to the database, retrieving and updating data, and manipulating data locally on the client.

Displaying the Data

Once we've got our data, we need to do something with it! In Chapters 9 to 11, we look at displaying data in Windows applications and in ASP.NET web applications. In particular, we see how we can bind visual Windows and web controls to a particular data source, so the .NET Framework will handle most of the work to refresh the values in the controls and update the data source for us.

More about Databases

Once we've got a solid understanding of ADO.NET, we can turn to look in detail at some more advanced database concepts. Chapters 12 to 16 cover improving the design of your databases, more advanced SQL statements that allow us to join data from multiple tables, creating views and stored procedures and calling them from C# code, optimizing performance with indexes, and assigning permissions for specific database operations to prevent unwanted access to your data.

Advanced ADO.NET

Next, we turn to look at some of the more advanced features of ADO.NET. Chapters 17 to 21 look at using XML documents with ADO.NET, implementing transactions to ensure that if one operation fails, any related operations will also fail, handling exceptions and events raised by ADO.NET, and retrieving and updating irregular data, such as images stored in the database.

Appendices

Finally, we provide two appendices containing useful background information. The first of these appendices demonstrates how to build a small program in C# that we can use to execute SQL statements against the database; the second is a quick primer of Extensible Markup Language, or XML, a text format that can be read from any platform, and that is rapidly gaining in popularity.

What Do I Need to Use This Book?

This book assumes that you have one of the various flavors of Visual Studio .NET installed. This could be either Visual Studio .NET Professional (or higher), or Visual C# .NET Standard Edition. If you have the Standard Edition installed, it is recommended that you also have Access 2000 or later installed for use as a front end to MSDE. Both of these require installation of the .NET Framework. You will also need either MSDE or SQL Server; however, MSDE can be installed free of charge with the .NET Framework, Visual C# Standard Edition, or Visual Studio .NET.

Conventions

We've used a number of different styles of text and layout in this book to help differentiate between the different kinds of information. Here are examples of the styles we used and an explanation of what they mean.

Code has several styles. If it's a word that we're talking about in the text – for example, when discussing a `for(...)` loop, it's in this font. If it's a block of code that can be typed as a program and run, then it's also in a gray box:

```
SqlConnection cn = new SqlConnection(connectString);
cn.Open();
```

Sometimes we'll see code in a mixture of styles, like this:

```
SqlConnection cn = new SqlConnection(connectString);
cn.Open();
SqlCommand cmd = new SqlCommand("SELECT FirstName, LastName FROM Employees");
```

When this happens, the code with a white background is code we are already familiar with; the line highlighted in gray is a new addition to the code since we last looked at it.

Advice, hints, and background information come in this type of font.

> **Important pieces of information come in boxes like this.**

Bullets appear indented, with each new bullet marked as follows:

- **Important Words** are in a bold type font.
- Words that appear on the screen, or in menus like File or Window, are in a similar font to the one you would see on a Windows desktop.
- Keys that you press on the keyboard like *Ctrl* and *Enter*, are in italics.

Customer Support

We always value hearing from our readers, and we want to know what you think about this book: what you liked, what you didn't like, and what you think we can do better next time. You can send us your comments, either by returning the reply card in the back of the book, or by e-mail to feedback@wrox.com. Please be sure to mention the book title in your message.

How to Download the Sample Code for the Book

When you visit the Wrox site, http://www.wrox.com/, simply locate the title through our Search facility or by using one of the title lists. Click on Download in the Code column, or on Download Code on the book's detail page.

When you click to download the code for this book, you are presented with a page with three options:

- If you are already a member of the Wrox Developer Community (if you have already registered on ASPToday, C#Today, or Wroxbase), you can log in with your usual username and password combination to receive your code.
- If you are not already a member, you are asked if you would like to register for free code downloads. In addition you will also be able to download several free articles from Wrox Press. Registering will allow us to keep you informed about updates and new editions of this book.
- The third option is to bypass registration completely and simply download the code.

Registration for code download is not mandatory for this book, but should you wish to register for your code download, your details will not be passed to any third party. For more details, you may wish to view our terms and conditions, which are linked from the download page.

Once you reach the code download section, you will find that the files that are available for download from our site have been archived using WinZip. When you have saved the files to a folder on your hard drive, you will need to extract the files using a de-compression program such as WinZip or PKUnzip. When you extract the files, the code is usually extracted into chapter folders. When you start the extraction process, ensure your software (WinZip, PKUnzip, etc.) is set to use folder names.

Errata

We've made every effort to make sure that there are no errors in the text or in the code. However, no one is perfect and mistakes do occur. If you find an error in one of our books, like a spelling mistake or a faulty piece of code, we would be very grateful for feedback. By sending in errata you may save another reader hours of frustration, and of course, you will be helping us provide even higher quality information. Simply e-mail the information to support@wrox.com, where your information will be checked and, if correct, posted to the errata page for that title, or used in subsequent editions of the book.

To find errata on the web site, go to http://www.wrox.com/, and simply locate the title through our Advanced Search or title list. Click on the Book Errata link, which is below the cover graphic on the book's detail page.

E-mail Support

If you wish to directly query a problem in the book with an expert who knows the book in detail then e-mail support@wrox.com, with the title of the book and the last four numbers of the ISBN in the subject field of the e-mail. A typical e-mail should include the following things:

- ❑ The **title of the book**, **last four digits of the ISBN (6098)**, and **page number** of the problem in the Subject field

- ❑ Your **name**, **contact information**, and the **problem** in the body of the message

We **won't** send you junk mail. We need the details to save your time and ours. When you send an e-mail message, it will go through the following chain of support:

- ❑ Customer Support – Your message is delivered to our customer support staff, who are the first people to read it. They have files on most frequently asked questions and will answer anything general about the book or the web site immediately.

- ❑ Editorial – Deeper queries are forwarded to the technical editor responsible for that book. They have experience with the programming language or particular product, and are able to answer detailed technical questions on the subject.

- ❑ The Authors – Finally, in the unlikely event that the editor cannot answer your problem, they will forward the request to the author. We do try to protect the author from any distractions to their writing; however, we are quite happy to forward specific requests to them. All Wrox authors help with the support on their books. They will e-mail the customer and the editor with their response, and again all readers should benefit.

The Wrox Support process can only offer support to issues that are directly pertinent to the content of our published title. Support for questions that fall outside the scope of normal book support, is provided via the community lists of our http://p2p.wrox.com/ forum.

p2p.wrox.com

For author and peer discussion join the P2P mailing lists. Our unique system provides **programmer to programmer™** contact on mailing lists, forums, and newsgroups, all in addition to our one-to-one e-mail support system. If you post a query to P2P, you can be confident that it is being examined by the many Wrox authors and other industry experts who are present on our mailing lists. At p2p.wrox.com you will find a number of different lists that will help you, not only while you read this book, but also as you develop your own applications. Particularly appropriate to this book are the **aspx** and **aspx_professional** lists in the .NET category of the web site.

To subscribe to a mailing list just follow these steps:

1. Go to http://p2p.wrox.com/

2. Choose the appropriate category from the left menu bar

3. Click on the mailing list you wish to join

4. Follow the instructions to subscribe and fill in your e-mail address and password

5. Reply to the confirmation e-mail you receive

6. Use the subscription manager to join more lists and set your e-mail preferences

Why This System Offers the Best Support

You can choose to join the mailing lists or you can receive them as a weekly digest. If you don't have the time, or facilities, to receive the mailing list, then you can search our online archives. Junk and spam mails are deleted, and your own e-mail address is protected by the unique Lyris system. Queries about joining or leaving lists, and any other general queries about lists, should be sent to listsupport@p2p.wrox.com.

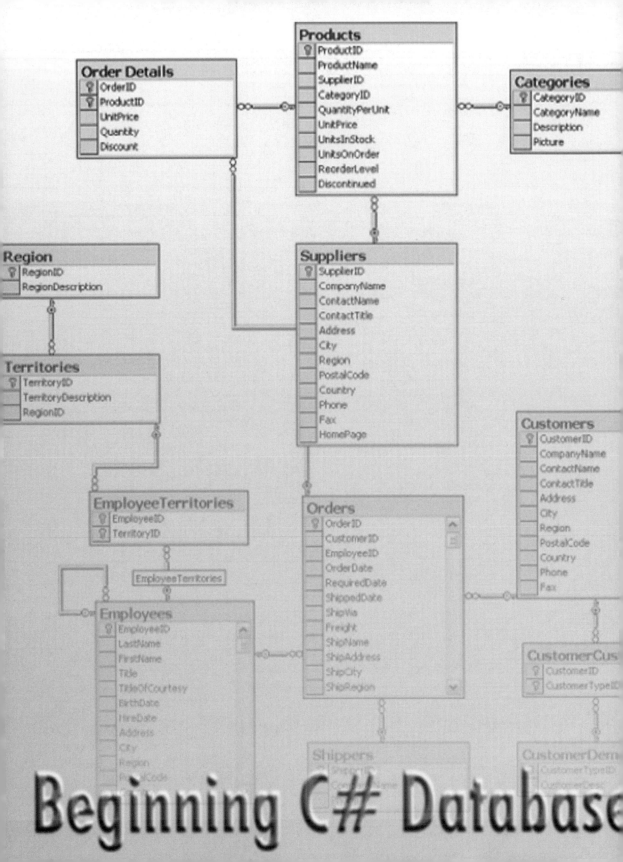

Installing MSDE

Before reading this book, the chances are that you're already familiar with the term "data", and you'll have some understanding of the fact that data can be stored in many formats. We could store data in a text file as a comma separated list, or we could store it in a database like SQL Server or Oracle. We can even store data as XML files, which is probably one of the biggest innovations of data storage in recent years. We can then work with this data and present it to end users in many different formats, from an application running on your local machine, to a web application that can be viewed with a browser.

Throughout this book we're going to discuss how to work with data when using the C# language, but in order to present a common set of samples that you can work through, we need to set up some kind of data store that you can refer to. We're therefore going to start this book by getting you properly set up with a database engine and sample data, all of which is provided free of charge by Microsoft. Specifically, in this chapter we will cover the following topics:

❑ Installing the .NET Framework

❑ Installing MSDE (**M**icro**S**oft **D**ata **E**ngine)

❑ Connecting to MSDE using Access

❑ Authentication types

❑ Databases, and the Server Explorer

For the purpose of this book we've chosen to work with the database called the Microsoft Data Engine. The MSDE can be described as a scaled-down version of Microsoft SQL Server – in fact you'll see that except for the fact that MSDE only comes with a five user license, and therefore isn't particularly interesting for the enterprise, it is a very good tool for you to learn on, before switching to the full-scale product when you need to be able to scale the application you are creating. If you already have an instance of SQL Server installed, feel free to use it instead of MSDE, but look through the section below entitled *Installing MSDE and the Sample Databases* anyhow to see how to install the sample databases used in this book if they are not already installed.

You can get MSDE thorough a number of commercial products and by download. Some of the products that include the MSDE are:

❑   Microsoft Office XP

❑   Microsoft Visual Studio.NET

❑   .NET Framework SDK (can be downloaded free of charge)

At the very least you should have a final release version of the .NET Framework SDK, as it is the basis for all .NET development. Included in that package are the .NET samples and a version of the MSDE. As we're going to be using the databases found in the samples, let's start by installing these and, in the process, MSDE as well. After that we'll take a quick look at the installation process if you are using Visual Studio.NET.

Installing MSDE with the .NET Framework

If you haven't installed the .NET Framework SDK, this is the time to do so. You can download the SDK from http://msdn.microsoft.com/downloads/default.asp (in the tree to the left, select Software Development Kits and then Microsoft .NET Framework SDK) – a download of about 131 MB, so if you're not on a fast connection, you may want to think about getting the framework on CD. This can, at a small price, be obtained from another Microsoft site:

http://microsoft.order-2.com/trialstore/. Click the Developer Tools link and then the .NET Framework SDK link.

At the time of writing this book, there is currently one service pack to the .NET Framework available from Microsoft. You should download the latest service pack and install it – it can probably be found by following a link on the page described above under the Related Information section.

Installing the .NET Framework

To install the .NET Framework SDK and the samples, follow these instructions:

1.   Run the file setup.exe.

2.   The first screen you'll see is a welcome screen. Click Next.

3.   The second screen is a license agreement screen. Read the license and then, as long as you agree to the terms, check the "I accept the agreement" radio button, and click Next.

4.   The third screen lets you select what you want to install. We want both the SDK and the samples, so we leave the screen unchanged and click Next.

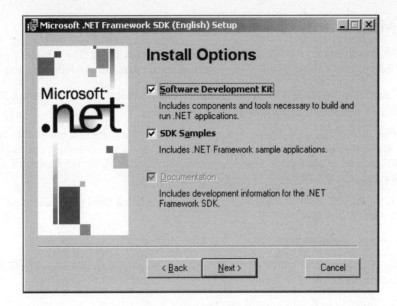

5. The next screen lets you choose the destination folder. Change the folder if needed and click Next.

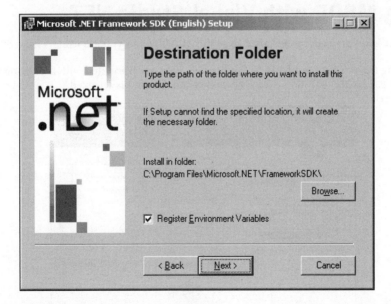

6. The .NET Framework SDK is now installed.

Installing MSDE and the Sample Databases

When the installation finishes, you're still not quite ready to begin as yet. The samples haven't been properly installed yet, and neither has MSDE. To install these, perform the following steps:

1. Click Start, then locate and open the group named Microsoft .NET Framework SDK and click the entry named Samples and QuickStart Tutorials.

2. Read the instructions on the page that opens, and then click the link Install the .NET Samples Database and select Open when prompted to open the installation file from its current location, instead of saving it to a new location. Microsoft SQL Server Desktop Engine is now installed.

3. To start the MSDE service, open a command prompt (click Start | Run and type cmd and press enter). Then type:

   ```
   > net start MSSQL$NetSDK
   ```

4. Back on the Samples and QuickStart Tutorials page, go to step two and click Set up the QuickStarts, and then click Open.

That's it! You are now ready to begin using the database.

Installing MSDE with Visual Studio.NET

There are a lot fewer steps to the installation of the MSDE when you are using Visual Studio.NET:

1. During the installation of Visual Studio.NET, you are presented with the dialog shown below. Make sure that the option SQL Server Desktop Engine is checked.

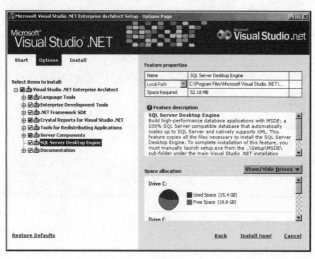

2. Choose the remaining options you wish to install, and allow Visual Studio.NET to install by clicking Install now!

3. The above dialog stated that we should install MSDE from a folder in the Visual Studio.NET installation. However, we want to install the samples from the SDK, and the easiest way to do this is to follow the instructions shown above for *Installing MSDE and the Sample Databases*.

> **We recommend that you install your samples as shown in the section named** *Installing MSDE and the Sample Databases***. Following the Visual Studio setup steps will install the samples correctly, but they will be installed into a different instance name of MSDE, (local)\VSDotNet, instead of (local)\NetSDK. This will affect all of the code examples in the book, and if you install the Visual Studio way, you'll end up having to alter the server name in the connection details for every sample in the book.**

You are now ready to begin using the databases.

Connecting to MSDE using MS Access

You should now have a running instance of Microsoft SQL Server Desktop Engine on your machine, and you are therefore ready to connect to it for the first time. We are going to do this with MS Access, which should give you a good idea of how connections are made as well as allowing us to examine some of the common tasks when connecting to MSDE or SQL Server.

If you do not own a copy of MS Access, don't worry, we'll switch to Visual Studio .NET shortly. Access is, however, a nice way to check that our database server is up and running, as well as a nice tool for displaying data visually.

1. Open Microsoft Access and cancel the first dialog that is displayed.

2. Select File | New and create a new database of the type Project (Existing Database). On the following dialog name the project Test Project and click OK.

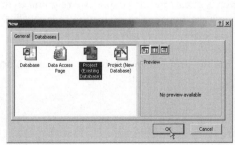 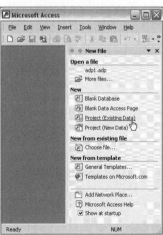

Office 2000 **Office XP**

3. Access now displays the Data Link Properties dialog. There are rather a lot of options on this dialog, but for the time being you only need to concern yourself with the tab labeled Connection.

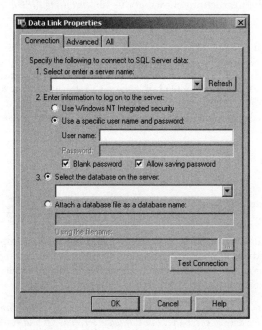

The first step is to select the server to be used. From the drop-down list at the top of the dialog, select the server that you just installed. If you have just installed MSDE as described above, you can type the following name:

```
(local)\NetSDK.
```

If you are accessing a different named instance, or if you are using a SQL Server running on another machine, you will need to select the appropriate server from the list.

4. The next step is to select the mode with which we are going to log on to the server. We've got two choices: Use Windows NT Integrated security and Use a specific user name and password. These two options represent what are known as "Windows NT Authentication" and "SQL Server Authentication" respectively. Later in this chapter we're going to discuss the differences between the two, but for now we'll change the selection to Use Windows NT Integrated security.

5. Finally we can select the database from the drop-down list. Select the name Northwind and then click Test Connection.

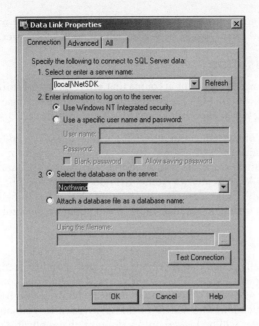

6. Click OK and Access will now import the Northwind sample database into the project.

Authentication Types

Before we continue to look at what Access is now displaying to us, let's talk a bit about the two types of authentication that were mentioned in Step 5 above. SQL Server, and therefore MSDE as well, have two distinct methods for users to connect to the database. These are:

❑ Windows Authentication

❑ SQL Server Authentication

Because the features being discussed in the following sections are particularly relevant to SQL Server we are going to use the term "SQL Server" to mean both SQL Server and MSDE. Remember that MSDE can be thought of as a scaled-down version of SQL Server that only runs locally, and that has no visual front-end tools supplied out of the box.

As a rule you should select SQL Server Authentication only when you are not connected to a network domain, for example, when you are working at a home PC or similar.

Windows Authentication

When a database uses "Windows Authentication", it means that SQL Server validates account names and passwords by making calls to the Windows security features. This means that to log on to a database with this type of authentication you must be logged into a Windows NT or Windows 2000 domain. In most enterprise settings this will probably not be a problem, but a personal user on a single computer running Windows 98, or earlier, or for that matter some other operating system, this possibility simply doesn't exist. For these users, SQL Server Authentication as explained below is the only possibility.

The benefits of using Windows Authentication are that only an account name and password are needed to log into the Windows domain and SQL Server, which makes for easier administration.

SQL Server Authentication

SQL Server Authentication makes use of accounts that are created and stored in SQL Server itself. When using SQL Server authentication, SQL Server maintains the accounts, meaning that a user logging on to the database will be using two accounts: their Windows account and a SQL Server account.

The benefits of this kind of authentication are that the user doesn't need to be logged into a Windows NT/Windows 2000 domain, and so personal users can gain access. Another benefit is that SQL Server authentication makes it much easier for a programmer to change the name and password they are using to connect to a database. With Windows Authentication the user must be logged into the domain with the account to use, but with SQL Server Authentication all that has to be changed is the name and password in a connection string. We'll hear much more about connection strings in later chapters.

Mixed Mode

What's this? We specifically stated that there are two types of authentication, and here's a third? Not really; if you are running a full scale SQL Server you will probably encounter the option to create databases using mixed mode. This simply means that the database will be able to use both Windows and SQL Server Authentication. The benefit of this is obvious: In a situation where we do not know whether the user/developer will be logged onto a domain, the application can take advantage of the Windows Authentication features when needed, and use SQL Server Authentication when it's not. Also, this allows a developer to easily change the account used to log into the database programmatically.

Exploring the Database

Let's return to the database project we created in Access a little earlier. Access should now be done importing the Northwind database, and you should see a window like the one shown below:

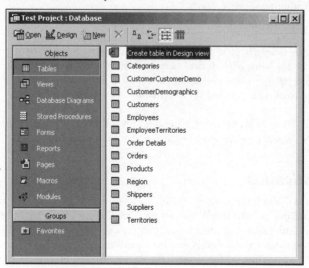

Now that we have everything set up and ready to use, let's look briefly at the structure of the database we are using. To begin with, we'll discuss some of the fundamental items found in any relational database, namely: tables, columns, and rows.

Tables, Columns, Rows, and Relationships

In the above picture the Tables tab is selected in the left pane. In the right window, thirteen tables are displayed. These thirteen tables contain all the information that is stored in the database. Each table consists of a number of columns and rows. Try double-clicking some of the tables. Access will display a grid that shows the data currently stored in the table.

You may have heard the word record used in place of row and field instead of column. Row and record hold the same meaning but the word "row" appears to be the one most commonly used today. Column and field will be used interchangeably in this book, but column will be used primarily when referring to an entire column in a table and a field primarily when referring to a specific entry in a row.

The grid consists of a number of columns, each with a name that acts as a label for the content of the column, for example FirstName and LastName are two columns in the Employees table whose content should be self evident. Together all the columns in a table form a row. Each row contains one complete entry in the table.

Let's continue this discussion by taking a closer look at some of the tables in the database.

Never worry about changing anything in the Northwind database. It is a sample database and can be reinstalled simply by returning to the page under Framework SDK from which it was originally installed. You must then go to the configuration details section and following instructions on that page. In addition to that, the database is also distributed with Access.

1. Right-click the Employees table and select Design View. If you are warned that you do not have exclusive access to the database, just ignore this and click OK. You should then see something like this:

Column Name	Datatype	Length	Precision	Scale	Allow Nulls	Default Value	Identity	Identity Seed	Identity Increment	Is RowGuid
EmployeeID	int	4	10	0			✓	1	1	
LastName	nvarchar	20	0	0						
FirstName	nvarchar	10	0	0						
Title	nvarchar	30	0	0	✓					
TitleOfCourtesy	nvarchar	25	0	0	✓					
BirthDate	datetime	8	0	0	✓					
HireDate	datetime	8	0	0	✓					
Address	nvarchar	60	0	0	✓					
City	nvarchar	15	0	0	✓					
Region	nvarchar	15	0	0	✓					
PostalCode	nvarchar	10	0	0	✓					
Country	nvarchar	15	0	0	✓					
HomePhone	nvarchar	24	0	0	✓					
Extension	nvarchar	4	0	0	✓					
Photo	image	16	0	0	✓					
Notes	ntext	16	0	0	✓					
ReportsTo	int	4	10	0	✓					
PhotoPath	nvarchar	255	0	0	✓					

Employees : Table

2. Access now displays each of the columns in the table as a row, with the name of the column in the first column, and the properties of that column in the following columns.

Let's take a look at some of the properties that you can set on each of the columns:

Property Name	Description
Column Name	The name of the column.
Datatype	There are a great number of different data types to choose from, ranging from integers to char strings and date/time types. Some of the most common types are:
	❑ int, tinyint, smallint, ...: Integer values
	❑ varchar, nvarchar: Used to represent variable length strings
	❑ datetime: Used to represent a data and time
	❑ bit: Used to represent a boolean value
Length	The length of the data type in bytes.
Allow Nulls	This value can either be true or false. If the value is true it means that this column can be left empty when you are inserting data into the table. When data is inserted into a row in the database, and a field is not given a value, the database will mark the value to be NULL. This is not the same as 0 (zero). Please refer to Chapter 3 for more information about this special value.
Default Value	Setting this value means that, should you omit the column when you insert data into the table, SQL Server will automatically insert the default value rather than Null.
Identity	Setting this property to true means that this column will always contain unique values. Setting this to true also prohibits the Allow Nulls property. You should never, or at least very rarely, set the value of an Identity column yourself – SQL Server will insert a unique value for you.

Also note the BirthDay column. If you try to enter anything other than a valid date in this column, you'll get an error message telling you that the value isn't valid. In other words, SQL Server enforces the data types.

The final column I'll draw your attention to is one that looks slightly boring but really is the most exciting of all the columns in the table: the ReportsTo column. This column shows what the word *relational* in relational databases means! At a glance the values in ReportsTo doesn't seem to make any sense (2, 5, and empty), at least until you realize that the employee with:

EmployeeId 6 (Michael Suyama) reports to the employee with:

EmployeeId 5 (Steven Buchanan) who in turn reports to the employee with:

EmployeeId 2 (Andrew Fuller) who must be the big boss, because he doesn't report to anybody!

The values found in ReportsTo are relations to another field. You could describe the values found in the ReportsTo column as a kind of pointer. In this case it points to another row in the same table, but it might just as easily have pointed to a row in another table altogether. A relation never explicitly describes what it is pointing to. What this means is that neither the number in the ReportsTo column nor the information we saw about it told us it was in fact a reference to the EmployeeID column, so naming the columns in a way that the name allows others to realize what the related table and column is, is strongly encouraged. Names such as IdOrders for a column that represents a relationship to an order is easily understood, but name the same column Relation, and for all we know, the value could point to anything. This would make it much more difficult to understand the table.

> It is possible to create something in the database that is called a relationship. When this is done, you explicitly tell the database that two columns, possibly in the same table, possible in different tables, are related. Doing this lets the database enforce certain rules, for example the database can enforce that if there is an order containing a certain EmployeeID, then there must be an Employee with that ID.

So what have we gained by using this relationship? Imagine what the same table would have looked like if a relationship had not been used. In order to be able to obtain the same information as the relationship provides, we would have had to replicate the data found in the row to which the relation points. In other words, for each column in the table we would need another column with the same name, but with the prefix ReportsTo. This would lead to a lot of replicated data, which at best is a waste of space and at worst, a nightmare to maintain. We'll look at relationships in a lot more detail in Chapter 12, *Tables and Relationships*.

Connecting using the Server Explorer

Before we move on to creating a small application that uses the Northwind database in the next chapter, we are going to abandon Access and move our attention to Visual Studio .NET, and in particular to the Server Explorer.

When we open Visual Studio .NET, the Server Explorer is collapsed on the left pane in the Window (if not, you can press *Ctrl-Alt-S* to display it). You may see one of two things, depending on the version of Visual Studio .NET being used. When using an Enterprise version, it expands to display a tree from which we can control just about anything on the local computer as well as any remote computers we have access to. For people using Visual C# Standard edition, you do not have the ability to connect to other servers.

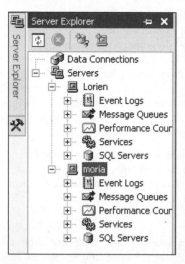
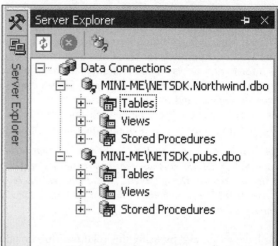

The picture to the left is a screenshot from a computer with the Enterprise version VS.NET and shows the Server Explorer with the two servers **Lorien** and **Moria** expanded. The other screenshot displays the Server Explorer on a computer with the Standard Edition of VS.NET. As you can see, only the data connections are displayed. This, however, is exactly what we are interested in, so the you should find that the cut-down server explorer provided with Visual C# Standard Edition will do just fine for viewing our database details.

> Note that one big difference between Visual Studio Professional (and higher) and Visual C# Standard Edition is that VC# only lets you connect to databases and view database details. In the full version of Visual Studio .NET you are able to create new databases, add new tables, views, stored procedures, and so on. Users with VC# are forced to use a tool like Microsoft Access to assist with issues like this in a visual environment. Alternatively, SQL statements and ADO.NET code can produce the same results. Readers who work through this book should eventually be comfortable enough to perform tasks like these.

What we are interested in is the **Data Connections** section. Using this, we are able to create and manage connections to any number of databases, located on any number of servers. As if that wasn't enough, you can also create connections and store them here for a large number of different database servers; SQL Server and Oracle to name just a few.

For now, we are going to stick to what we know, which is the MSDE on our local machine and the Northwind database. So let's create the connection:

1. Right-click the **Data Connections** node in the tree and select **Add Connection**.

2. The dialog that is displayed should look familiar to you, because it is in fact the same dialog as Access displayed when we created the connection to the database. Enter the same information on the **Connection** tab as you did before. To spare you the shuffling through the pages, here is the data:

Server name: (local)\NetSDK
Authentication: Use Windows NT Integrated Authentication
Database: Northwind

3. There is one major difference from this dialog to the one we saw in Access: The **Provider** tab.

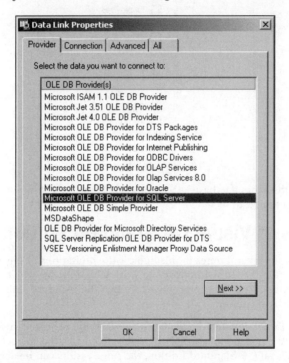

On this tab you can select which provider to use when you connect to the database. The selected provider is Microsoft OLE DB Provider for SQL Server, which is excellent as this is the database server we wish to connect to. However, should we want to connect to a database on Oracle, we would simply select the Microsoft OLE DB Provider for Oracle, and continue in exactly the same way.

4. Click **OK**. A new node is added to the tree below the **Database Connections** node.

5. Click on the plus in front of the new node to expand it.

6. Click on the plus in front of the **Tables** node to view the tables in the database:

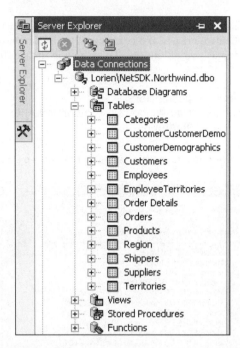

As you can see, this is the same database as we saw earlier; the only difference is the way in which the information is being presented to us.

The Limitations of Visual C# Standard Edition

An issue that will come up several times in this book is the limitations of the Visual C# Standard Edition product. When it comes to writing code to work with data, we won't be seeing many differences at all. The main differences, from our perspective, are that the Standard Edition restricts the functionality of our Server Explorer.

In Visual Studio .NET Professional and above, the Server Explorer can be used to add tables, stored procedures, and more to our databases simply by right-clicking in the correct place and following some wizards. When using Visual C# Standard Edition, the same results can be achieved by using raw SQL statements. Essentially, we're forced to "do it by hand" (we'll see how we can do this in Chapter 3). As a result, in many places in this book, we'll point out differences between the two products, and provide SQL statement alternatives for the visual tool. We'll also look at a couple of applications, written in C#, which can be used to issue SQL commands against our database and that will help to further our understanding of using C# to work with data. One of these will be used in Chapter 3, and we'll show the code for that application in Appendix A. The other application will be introduced and explained in Chapters 12 and 13.

If you own a copy of Visual C# Standard Edition, and you'd prefer to work more visually, a copy of Microsoft Access is a very useful thing to have around. It has the ability to connect to MSDE and SQL Server databases using data projects, which give us the ability to add tables, diagrams, and so on.

There is another tool, currently a technology preview (a very early release that's not quite in Beta yet) called the ASP.NET Web Matrix Project that is designed for creating ASP.NET pages and sites.

The Web Matrix has its own version of a Server Explorer, however, unlike Visual C# Standard Edition, you can use it to create new databases, tables, and so on, all using mouse clicks and minimal typing. It's available for free download from http://www.asp.net/webmatrix/ where you can also find out a lot more information about this interesting and useful tool.

Summary

In this first chapter we've installed the Microsoft SQL Server Desktop Engine and the example databases that we'll use in the following chapters, as well as this one. We've seen how to connect to a database in MSDE from Microsoft Access and with the Server Explorer in Visual Studio.NET.

Finally we've taken our first look at tables, rows, columns, and relations, which are the foundations of database theory. These concepts will be explored in more detail in Chapters 12 to 16, where we get deep and dirty into database theory.

In the next chapter we'll leap straight into a sample application that will introduce some of the tools that Visual Studio (of all varieties) offers us when developing data applications. We'll concentrate mostly on getting results, leaving theory of how the code under the covers works to later chapters.

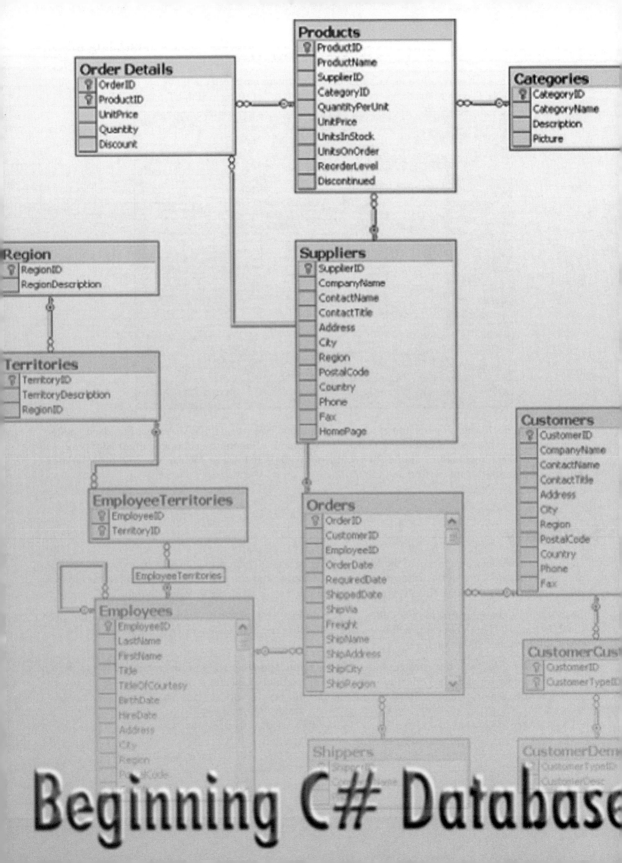

A Simple Data-Driven Application

Now that we've installed our database server and had a look at what's in the Northwind database, we're going to walk through the series of steps needed to create a basic data-driven application, using some of the powerful functionality provided by Visual Studio. We're not going to look too hard at what is going on behind the scenes; instead, we'll concentrate on getting comfortable with using Visual Studio's built-in shortcuts and wizards. In the later chapters, we'll be spending more time talking about the code that's generated for us by Visual Studio, and how we can work with that code to improve and refine our applications.

Working through this chapter, you'll learn:

❑   How to build a Windows Form application that connects to the Northwind database and displays selected data from it

❑   How to edit the data and update the database

Creating the Application

The application we're going to create will be able to perform some simple, but very common tasks on a single table from the Northwind database. Once complete, we'll be able to use the application to:

❑   Display a list of the last names of the employees in the Northwind database

❑   Display the address information of an employee selected in the list and allow the user to edit the information

❑   Update the edited address information in the database

> Note that for all of the examples in this book, we will simply tell you to "create a new solution/project" – where these solutions are stored is up to you. However, we recommend creating a folder called **BegCSharpDb** on your system, then creating each new solution within this folder. That way you'll end up with a neat hierarchy of code folders for the whole book. This is the way the code that is available for download from **http://www.wrox.com** is stored. All the code for this book is available for download from the Wrox site.

So, it's time to get started! In this section, we'll just create the project, and then we can add to it later on in the chapter.

Try It Out: Creating the Foundations

We are going to create a Windows Forms application, so fire up Visual Studio .NET and follow the steps below:

1. Create a new blank solution by selecting the **New Project** link on the **Start** page, or by selecting **File | New | Blank Solution...** from the main menu. In the dialog that appears, name your solution `Chapter2_Examples`, save it within your `BegDSharpDB` folder, and click **OK**:

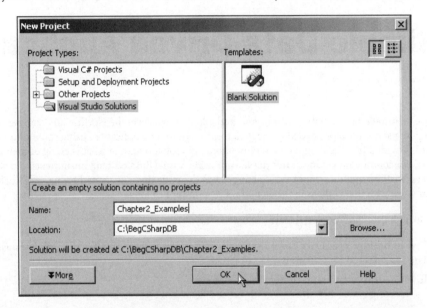

> This structure will be used throughout this book for examples, and is mirrored in the code download. The code for each chapter will consist of one or more example projects, each contained within one chapter solution.

2. Not a lot appears to happen when you click **OK**. However, if you hover your mouse pointer over the Solution Explorer (normally found on the right of the Visual Studio environment) you will see our solution listed in there. Right-click on the solution and select **Add | New Project** from the context menu. Create a new **Visual C# Windows Application** project and give it the name `Employees`.

3. Open up the Solution Explorer window, click the **Show All Files** button at the top of the Solution Explorer, and then expand all the nodes. You should see something like this:

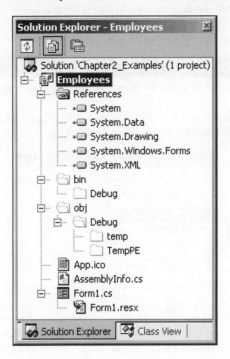

How It Works

The simple action of creating a new project has created several default files and directories. Inside all of these files, we can see that Visual Studio has inserted some starter code.

The items in the list you're likely to become acquainted with include:

❑ The `Form1.cs` file, which is the default file for a Windows Form. This is where our form code resides.

❑ The **References** section, which contains a series of namespaces. By default, Visual Studio .NET has guessed that we may need to use classes contained within namespaces relating to graphical elements, and to data applications, simply because these are the most common scenarios. As applications become more complex, we may need to add to this list.

These two sections – along with the parent **Project** and **Solution** sections – are likely to be the ones you use most when creating a Windows Form application. Other types of application create slightly different files. For example, a Web Form application will include files that relate to configuration details, global application settings, and references to plenty of namespaces with the word "web" in them (`System.Web`, `System.Web.UI`, and so on). In contrast, when creating a simple console application, we see a lot less files in the Solution Explorer, since we're not concerned with a visual front end.

Let's continue with our application and see how we can connect to our database.

Establishing Contact with the Database

In order to be able to work with the database, we need to connect to it from our C# Windows Form application. In Chapter 1, we saw how to manually create a connection to the Northwind database from the Server Explorer, but that is not the same thing as creating a connection programmatically.

Try It Out: Creating a Connection

To be able to get data into our application, we must now add the connection to it:

1. Click on the form to select it and then examine the properties panel to the right. Find the entry named (DataBindings). Expand this by clicking the + sign to the left:

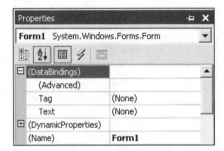

2. Leaving the (Advanced) section for later, you can see two properties of the form – Tag and Text – that can be bound to data. However, if you try to assign something to them, you will see that you cannot. The reason for this is that there is currently no contact with any data – we've not yet connected our application to our database.

3. In the Server Explorer, click and drag the connection to the Northwind database (which we created in the last chapter) on to the form:

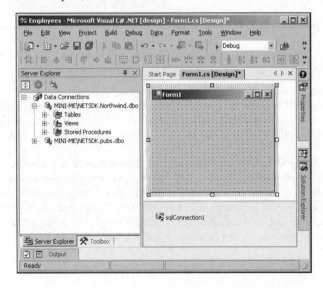

Rather than placing the connection on the form itself, Visual Studio .NET opens a tray below the form and places the connection in the tray. This is because the connection isn't represented visually.

4. Right-click the `sqlConnection` object in the tray and select **Properties**:

5. Change the name of the connection to sqlConnectionNorthwind.

One of the other properties in the list is the `ConnectionString` *property. A **connection string** describes how to connect to a given database, security parameters, and many other things. For now we are not going to concern ourselves too much with this, as the Server Explorer has generated it for us, but we'll see how to write our own connection strings in Chapter 5.*

6. The next step is to specify which data to get from the database. Open the Server Explorer and expand the **Tables** node. Select and drag the `Employees` table onto the form.

This creates a `sqlDataAdapter`. Select it, and change its name to `sqlDataAdapterEmployees` in the same way as we changed the name of the connection in Steps 4 and 5 above.

The `DataAdapter` specifies how to select, edit, and update data. It does not, however, hold the data itself – this job is performed by another ADO.NET object, namely, the `DataSet`.

7. Select the `sqlDataAdapterEmployees` in the tray and view its properties. Just below the properties panel you'll see three links:

These links are:

❑ **Configure Data Adapter...** used to configure what data to work on. This was done for us when we dragged the table onto the form, so we'll leave this option alone.

❑ **Preview Data...** clicking this link displays a dialog where you can preview the data.

❑ **Generate DataSet...** this is the option we are interested in. It will allow us to generate a `DataSet` object, which is the object that will contain the actual data from the tables.

8. Click the **Generate DataSet...** link.

9. On the dialog that is displayed, change the name of the `DataSet` to `DataSetEmployees` and click OK:

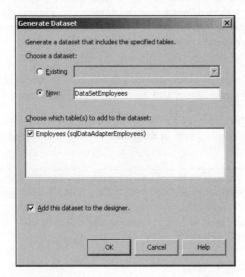

How It Works

All we appear to have done so far is a lot of double-clicking and a bit of dragging and dropping, but don't worry, Visual Studio .NET has actually been busy writing code for us with each step. Behind the scenes, we now have the ability to connect to a database, select specific data, and work with that data using a `DataSet`. We'll be looking at `DataAdapters` and `DataSets` in Chapter 8, where we'll learn how to code them and how to use them.

Note that although we named our `DataSet DataSetEmployees`, the design-name for our dataset is actually `dataSetEmployees1`, so when we refer to our `DataSet` in our code later on, we'll refer to `dataSetEmployees1`.

Data Binding

Now let's take some of the data from our database and display it using some controls on a Windows Form – this is what we mean by data binding. There are two ways to bind data to controls: complex and simple data binding. Complex data binding is only supported by a few Windows Forms controls, such as the `DataGrid` and `ListBox`, and allows the control to display lists of data. Simple data binding is supported by most other Windows Controls, and, unlike complex data binding, it only allows the control to bind to a single value at a time.

We'll use complex data binding only once in our application – to bind the data for the list of names. The rest of the controls are textboxes that use simple data binding. Let's start putting our form together.

Try It Out: Creating a User Interface

We need to create the front end for our data application, which involves a certain amount of dragging and dropping. We also need to tell our user interface controls what data to display in each box.

1. From the Visual Studio environment, you should have the form displayed in the design pane. To the left is a tab for the toolbox. This toolbox contains a list of controls that we can place on our form. We're going to use thirteen textbox and label controls, and one listbox. The layout of the form is shown in the screenshot:

The large box numbered 1 on the diagram is the listbox. The controls numbered 2-14 are textboxes. The text next to each control is in a corresponding label control. You can add and position the controls according to the picture by dragging and dropping them from the Toolbox onto the form.

2. Using the properties panel, set the properties of the textboxes like this:

Number	Property	Value
2	Name	textBoxNotes
2	MultiLine	True
3	Name	textBoxFirstName
4	Name	textBoxLastName
5	Name	textBoxTitle
6	Name	textBoxTitleOfCourtesy
7	Name	textBoxBirthday
8	Name	textBoxHireDate
9	Name	textBoxAddress
10	Name	textBoxCity
11	Name	textBoxPostalCode
12	Name	textBoxCountry
13	Name	textBoxHomePhone
14	Name	textBoxExtension

3. For each of the textboxes, clear the `Text` property.

4. For each of the label controls, set the `Text` property as shown in the previous screenshot.

5. Set the properties of the `ListBox` (number 1 on the form) like this:

Property	Value	Description
Name	listBoxNames	This is the name of the control.
DataSource	dataSetEmployees1.Employees	This identifies the `DataSet` and table containing the data to display.

Property	Value	Description
DisplayMember	LastName	This tells the control to display the value of the LastName field.
ValueMember	EmployeeID	If we were to ask the control for the value of the selected item in the list, the control would use EmployeeID as the value, rather than LastName.

6. Select the TextBox marked as 2, and look at the top of the Properties panel. There you'll find an entry named (DataBindings):

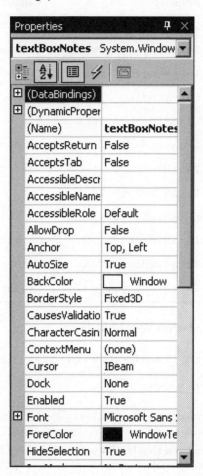

7. Expand this node, and then drop down the Text property. Select the Notes field as shown here:

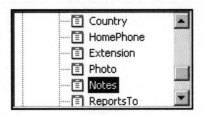

8. Repeat Steps 6 and 7 for the remaining textboxes, assigning the following fields to the numbered controls:

Number	Property	Value
3	DataBindings.Text	FirstName
4	DataBindings.Text	LastName
5	DataBindings.Text	Title
6	DataBindings.Text	TitleOfCourtesy
7	DataBindings.Text	BirthDate
8	DataBindings.Text	HireDate
9	DataBindings.Text	Address
10	DataBindings.Text	City
11	DataBindings.Text	PostalCode
12	DataBindings.Text	Country
13	DataBindings.Text	HomePhone
14	DataBindings.Text	Extension

9. Right-click the form and select **View Code**.

10. Locate the method Form1() and insert the code below

```
InitializeComponent();

sqlDataAdapterEmployees.Fill(dataSetEmployees1);
```

11. Run the application, and you should now see the data from the Northwind database displayed in your Windows Form, like this:

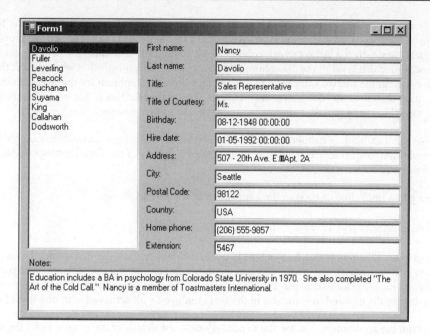

How It Works

We started out by adding three ADO.NET objects to our application by dragging and dropping them from the Server Explorer to the form.

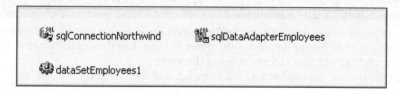

- ❑ `sqlConnection`
- ❑ `sqlDataAdapter`
- ❑ `sqlDataSet`

We are going to see a lot of these objects during the course of the book, and in later chapters we are going to go into much more detail about them.

Note that ADO.NET uses the prefix `sql` before each of the object names (for example, `sqlConnection`). These prefixes indicate that we are working with the SQL Server data provider that can be used to access Microsoft SQL Server or MSDE. Had we performed all of the above steps, but with an Access database as the backend, say, the objects would have been prefixed `OleDb` (for example, `OleDbConnection`). We'll see more about the different data providers in Chapters 4 and 5. Aside from the way they connect to databases, and their prefixes, the objects are essentially interchangeable.

After some cosmetic steps where we added the controls to the form and set some of their values, we bound the listbox to the `LastName` column in the `Employees` table of the Northwind database.

First we set the `DataSource` property. This tells the listbox where it should look for its data. Remember that the `dataSetEmployees1` is the ADO.NET object that stores the data. The second property we set, `DisplayMember`, tells the listbox which column to use to fill itself. The third property we set is `ValueMember`, which is set to the ID column, `EmployeeID`. This means that when we ask the listbox for the selected item in the list, we want the value of the `EmployeeID` column for the selected employee to be returned rather than the entry for `LastName` column. The reason for this is that more than one employee may have same last name, but each and every employee must have a unique `EmployeeID`.

Next, we set the data binding properties of all of the textboxes. Since these controls use simple data binding, they are somewhat simpler to set; we simply set the `Text` property of the **DataBindings** section to the column of the data we want the textbox to display.

Finally, we add a single line of code to the constructor of the `Form1` class:

```
sqlDataAdapterEmployees.Fill(dataSetEmployees1);
```

The data adapter is the object that knows how to get at the data, but it is the dataset that holds the data. To get the data into the dataset, we call `Fill()` on the data adapter, passing in the dataset as a parameter. When the application runs, the listbox displays the last names of the employees in the `Employees` table and the textboxes display the detailed information of the first employee – all achieved with one line of code!

When you run the application, you see the expected result: the details of the employee by the name Davolio are displayed in the textboxes to the right. However, when you click select another employee from the list box, nothing happens! The reason for this is, that there is no link between the information displayed in the listbox and what is displayed in the textboxes. We will need to add this link to our code.

Try It Out: Making the Form Dynamic

1. Return to the design view. Go to the **Properties** panel for the listbox and click the yellow lightning icon at the top to display the possible event handlers of the control. Locate the `SelectedValueChanged` event, enter the name `listBoxNames_SelectedValueChanged`, and then hit *Enter*.

2. Enter the following code in the event handler:

```
// Clear the databindings on the TextBoxes
textBoxAddress.DataBindings.Clear();
textBoxBirthday.DataBindings.Clear();
textBoxCity.DataBindings.Clear();
textBoxCountry.DataBindings.Clear();
textBoxExtension.DataBindings.Clear();
textBoxFirstName.DataBindings.Clear();
textBoxHireDate.DataBindings.Clear();
textBoxHomePhone.DataBindings.Clear();
textBoxLastName.DataBindings.Clear();
textBoxNotes.DataBindings.Clear();
textBoxPostalCode.DataBindings.Clear();
textBoxTitle.DataBindings.Clear();
textBoxTitleOfCourtesy.DataBindings.Clear();
```

```
// Add a new binding, with a new data source: the selected row.
textBoxAddress.DataBindings.Add(
    "Text",
    dataSetEmployees1.Employees.Rows[listBoxNames.SelectedIndex],
    "Address");

textBoxBirthday.DataBindings.Add(
    "Text",
    dataSetEmployees1.Employees.Rows[listBoxNames.SelectedIndex],
    "BirthDate");

textBoxCity.DataBindings.Add(
    "Text",
    dataSetEmployees1.Employees.Rows[listBoxNames.SelectedIndex],
    "City");

textBoxCountry.DataBindings.Add(
    "Text",
    dataSetEmployees1.Employees.Rows[listBoxNames.SelectedIndex],
    "Country");

textBoxExtension.DataBindings.Add(
    "Text",
    dataSetEmployees1.Employees.Rows[listBoxNames.SelectedIndex],
    "Extension");

textBoxFirstName.DataBindings.Add(
    "Text",
    dataSetEmployees1.Employees.Rows[listBoxNames.SelectedIndex],
    "FirstName");

textBoxHireDate.DataBindings.Add(
    "Text",
    dataSetEmployees1.Employees.Rows[listBoxNames.SelectedIndex],
    "Hiredate");

textBoxHomePhone.DataBindings.Add(
    "Text",
    dataSetEmployees1.Employees.Rows[listBoxNames.SelectedIndex],
    "HomePhone");

textBoxLastName.DataBindings.Add(
    "Text",
    dataSetEmployees1.Employees.Rows[listBoxNames.SelectedIndex],
    "LastName");

textBoxNotes.DataBindings.Add(
    "Text",
    dataSetEmployees1.Employees.Rows[listBoxNames.SelectedIndex],
    "Notes");

textBoxPostalCode.DataBindings.Add(
    "Text",
```

```
        dataSetEmployees1.Employees.Rows[listBoxNames.SelectedIndex],
        "PostalCode");

textBoxTitle.DataBindings.Add(
        "Text",
        dataSetEmployees1.Employees.Rows[listBoxNames.SelectedIndex],
        "Title");

textBoxTitleOfCourtesy.DataBindings.Add(
        "Text",
        dataSetEmployees1.Employees.Rows[listBoxNames.SelectedIndex],
        "TitleOfCourtesy");
```

Run the application again. When you select an item in the listbox, the personal details in the textboxes change:

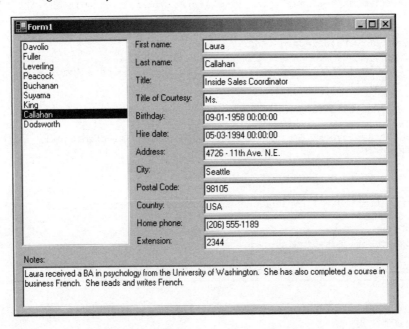

How It Works

We created an event handler for the `SelectedValueChanged` event of the listbox. This is fired whenever the active selection in the listbox is changed by, for example, a user clicking a mouse.

The event handler may look complex, but in essence it only contain two lines of code. These are repeated for each of the textboxes on the form:

```
textBoxAddress.DataBindings.Clear();
...
textBoxAddress.DataBindings.Add(
        "Text",
        dataSetEmployees1.Employees.Rows[listBoxNames.SelectedIndex],
        "Address");
```

The first line of code tells the textbox to remove any current data bindings. The second line of code then reinserts the data binding, but this time with data from the currently selected row. The first parameter of the Add() method is the name of the property we want to bind data to, namely the Text property. The second parameter is the actual data the control should use. We know that the index of the selected item in the ListBox is the same as the row we are interested in, and so we select this index from the rows in the Employees table. The third and final parameter is the name of the column the control should use.

Editing Data

Now that we are able to display and move around in the data, we have one last task: to edit and update the data in the database. The edit part is simple as we are using textboxes for the data. We will update the data on the database every time the Validated event is fired by one of the textboxes. This happens whenever a textbox loses focus to another control that has the CausesValidation property set to true. This is the default for all of the controls we've used in this chapter.

Try It Out: Adding Edit Functionality

1. Go to the design view of Visual Studio, and select the textbox named textBoxNotes. In the **Properties** panel, click the lightning icon and select the Validated entry. Enter the name TextBox_Validated and hit *Enter*.

2. Repeat this for the remaining textboxes.

3. Add the following code to the event handler:

```
private void TextBox_Validated(object sender, System.EventArgs e)
{
    // Open the connection
    sqlConnectionNorthwind.Open();

    // Update
    sqlDataAdapterEmployees.Update(dataSetEmployees1, "Employees");

    // Refresh the data in the dataset
    sqlDataAdapterEmployees.Fill(dataSetEmployees1);

    // Close the connection again
    sqlConnectionNorthwind.Close();
}
```

4. Run the application and try to change the last name of one of the employees and then hit the *Tab* key to leave the textbox. This will update the data:

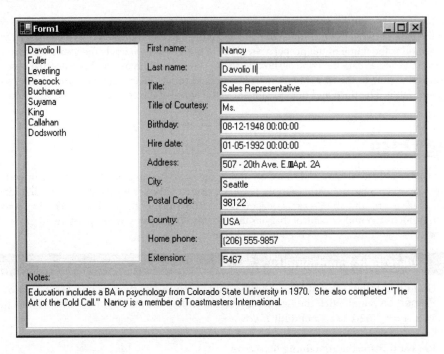

How It Works

We created a single event handler, `TextBox_Validated()`, which is called by all of the textboxes whenever the `Validated` event is fired. The first line opens the connection to the database:

```
sqlConnectionNorthwind.Open();
```

You may be surprised to learn that the connection to the database has actually been closed ever since we first called the `Fill()` method on the `DataAdapter` in the constructor of the `Form1` class. The data is said to be **disconnected** from the database. This has a number of advantages over connected data, and we'll look at this in more detail in later chapters. For now, we simply reconnect to the database in order to be able to transmit the changes to it.

The second line updates the data in the database.

```
sqlDataAdapterEmployees.Update(dataSetEmployees1, "Employees");
```

We call `Update()` on the data adapter. The first parameter of the `Update()` method is the dataset containing the data we wish to update and the second parameter specifies the table we want to update.

The third line is not actually needed to refresh the data in the dataset, but whenever the update is called, the listbox seems to forget a line, so in order to refresh the listbox easily, we need to refresh the content of the dataset.

Finally we call the `Close()` method on the `Connection` object to close it again.

Summary

In this chapter, we've built up a simple application, but we've not looked in detail at how the code works. Instead, we've relied heavily on using the features provided for us by Visual Studio. With just a few clicks and a minimal amount of typing we can create some quite powerful functionality. As we worked through the chapter we saw:

❑ How to create a blank solution and add a Windows Form application to the solution

❑ What Visual Studio .NET creates for us when we create a blank application

❑ How to add data connectivity to our application using the Server Explorer, and following a similar process, create a `DataAdapter` and a `DataSet`

❑ How to create a user interface by using controls, and binding data to those controls

❑ How to make our application update dynamically

❑ How to make it possible to update the data in the database

We'll learn more about the ADO objects from Chapter 4 onwards, but before we dive in to ADO.NET, we need to look at an important tool in the data-driven application developer's toolkit – SQL, the language of data.

Exercises

1. Modify the application to work on the `Products` table instead of the `Employees` table.

2. Change the application so that the data is only updated when the selection in the list box changes.

3. Change the list box to display the ID of the employee instead of the last name.

Solutions to these exercises are available for free download from http://www.wrox.com/ from the code download page for this book.

There's also an online discussion forum for this book that you can use to discuss the solutions, or any other problems you may be having at http://p2p.wrox.com/list.asp?list=beginning_c_sharp_database

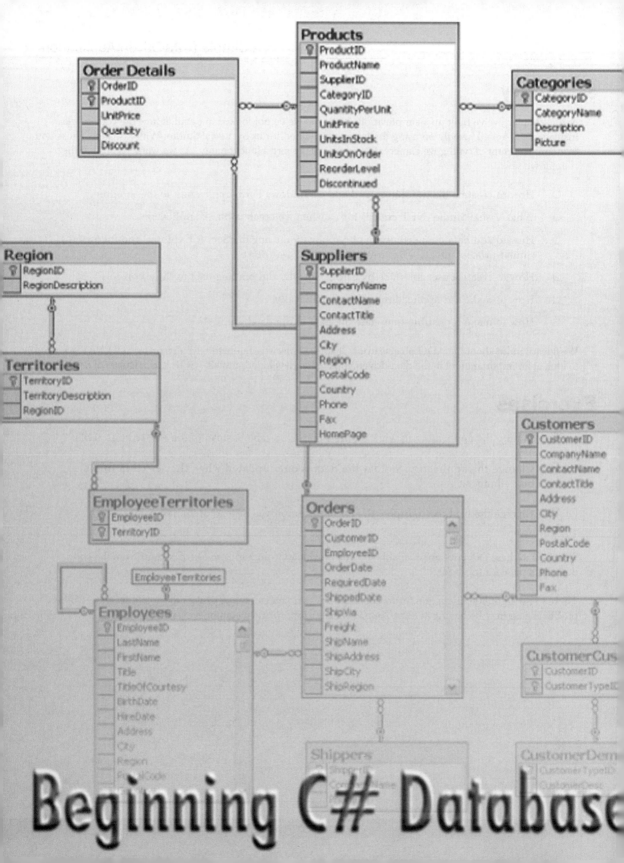

Introducing SQL

In the previous chapter we saw how easy it is to build a simple application using C# and Visual Studio .NET that displays and modifies data in a database. In this chapter we're going to take a step back from the application approach and look at SQL (Structured Query Language).

In this chapter we'll look at some of the most common elements of the SQL Language:

- ❑ The SELECT query
- ❑ The INSERT command
- ❑ The UPDATE command
- ❑ The DELETE command
- ❑ SQL data types

What is SQL?

If you've ever worked with databases much in the past, you'll have probably seen some SQL. SQL is the language we use to communicate with databases. We can write SQL statements that we can use to create, read, change, or delete data. SQL in itself is purely a language with no front end; however, many database tools exist that can provide a visual element that shows what our SQL statements are doing to our data. It's also quite simple to show these working using a simple C# application, which we'll look at shortly.

When you read through this book, you may see SQL and T-SQL used interchangeably. T-SQL is shorthand for Transact SQL and is the brand of SQL used by SQL Server and thus by the MSDE. As this book works with MSDE we are focusing on Transact SQL here, rather than ANSI SQL. ANSI SQL is the 'pure' SQL format, which defines the set of methods, datatypes, operators, and so on that should be included in an implementation of SQL. There are, however, several different implementations of SQL, which don't always completely adhere to the specification and often add to it. Transact SQL does just that, and some of the operators and methods found later in this chapter may not work if you try the SQL with another database server than MSDE and SQL Server.

Let's briefly return to familiar territory, and look at the application presented in the previous chapter so we can see SQL in action.

If you display the properties of the `sqlDataAdapterEmployees`, you'll see four properties named `DeleteCommand`, `InsertCommand`, `SelectCommand`, and `UpdateCommand`.

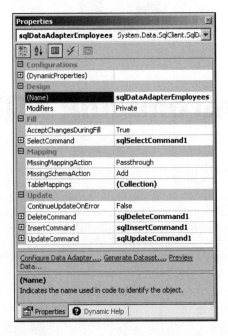

In the example in Chapter 2 we saw how the `DataAdapter` was used to retrieve and update data, but not store the data.

The four commands mentioned here represent the `SELECT` query and the `DELETE`, `UPDATE`, and `INSERT` commands in SQL. These are what are needed to create, read, update, and delete from/to a database, also known as the CRUD functions. In this chapter we are going to examine these four types of SQL statements and look a bit more at SQL data types.

Using SQL

To execute SQL statements, we need to use some kind of tool that can pass on the SQL to the database. There's several options available to us:

- ❑ Visual Studio's built-in SQL tool
- ❑ The OSQL command-line tool
- ❑ The SQL Server Query Analyser
- ❑ A custom tool

Since the minimum requirements for this book are that you are running MSDE and Visual C# Standard Edition, we'll look at the all of the above methods with the exception of the SQL Server Query Analyser, since not all of you will have a copy of this. One of the tools we'll look at is a custom tool that we've supplied along with the code download for this book, which is explained in Appendix A.

If you have a full version of SQL Server installed, you will find the SQL Server Query Analyser tool under **Program Files** / **Microsoft SQL Server**. *We won't be looking at this tool in detail in this book, but if you want more information, you might be interested in reading* Beginning SQL Server 2000 Programming, *Wrox Press, ISBN: 1-86100-523-7.*

Running SQL Statements from Visual Studio .NET

There's a tool available to us, whether we're running full Visual Studio .NET, or whether we're only running just the cut-down version Visual C# Standard Edition, which we can use to enter SQL statements. It's not that easy to find, so let's look at how we can start it up.

Try It Out: Running SQL Statements from Visual Studio .NET

1. Fire up Visual Studio and navigate straight to the Server Explorer utility. In Chapter 1 we created a connection to the Northwind database in our MSDE database, so let's look at that connection now. Click to expand the Tables node and double-click on the Employees table:

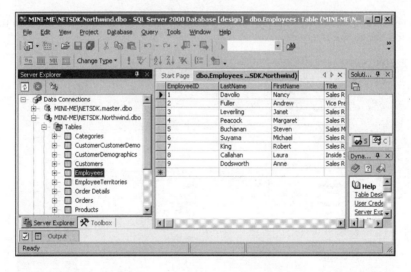

2. If you position your cursor anywhere within the grid of data, the SQL button on the toolbar becomes enabled, so click this button and you should see the following screen:

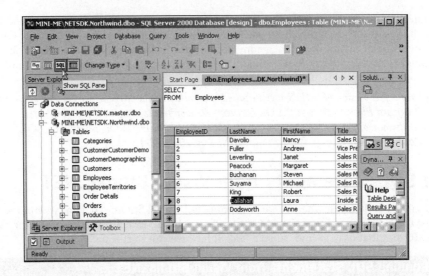

You should now see a window above your data, which represents the query fired under the covers to generate the data in the table. We'll look at what this query statement means in this chapter.

3. To test out the window, change the word Employees to Products, and click on the ! icon on the toolbar to run the query:

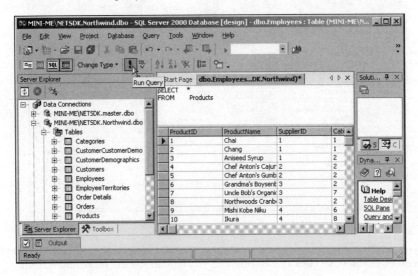

How It Works

The tool available with Visual Studio .NET is quite powerful and lets us execute all kinds of queries and commands against our database using SQL. Since we've not looked at how SQL works yet, we won't look into this in too much detail here, but it's worth remembering that this facility exists.

Running SQL from the Command Line

If you ever find yourself needing to run T-SQL statements without a visual tool, there's a nifty command-line tool that is simple to use that comes along with MSDE and SQL Server, called `osql.exe`. To use this tool, all T-SQL that you need to execute has to be entered one line at a time in a command prompt, or placed into a flat file and then executed. This is a simple tool with no graphics but it's useful to be aware of its existence.

To use `osql`, you need to get a command prompt instantiated within your system. You can then enter `osql` followed by a number of parameters. The range of parameters is listed in the following section, and has been taken by using `osql /?` within the command prompt.

It is not our intention to go through all of these options, however, we will demonstrate the essential options to execute the T-SQL within this book.

Try It Out: Executing SQL Using the OSQL Tool

1. To log in to the local MSDE database, we firstly need to enter the -S switch, followed by our server name, then we use the switch -E to indicate we want to use Windows Authentication.

```
osql -S (local)\NetSDK -E
```

To log on to a server rather than a server on your local machine, simply change (local) to the name of the server. We'll find out more about connections in Chapter 5

2. Now that we are logged in to the server you can enter the T-SQL commands one line at a time delimited by pressing the *Enter/Return* key. Once all the commands are entered, then simply type in GO to execute the code. Enter the following code line by line:

```
osql -S(local)\NetSDK -E
USE Northwind
GO
SET ROWCOUNT 2
GO
SELECT * FROM Products
GO
```

You should see the following output:

3. To close our connection and exit, type EXIT and press *Enter*.

How It Works

As you can see, it isn't exactly the prettiest of tools to use, and the output doesn't tend to be the easiest to read as it is; however, it is a utility that will save the day when you need to quickly interrogate some crucial item within your database. You can also save your output to a file using the -o switch.

In our brief example, we used the osql tool to log in to our server using Windows authentication, and the instance NetSDK that we have created for the MSDE database for this book. We then executed some simple T-SQL code to return just 2 lines of output from a table within the Northwind database. Don't worry too much about the actual T-SQL code listed as this is simply to demonstrate the tool and we will be covering most of this code in a few moments.

Another method to execute T-SQL code is to place it in a flat file, and then define the name of the flat file as well as the folder location if required, by using the -i option. You would tend to do this for more complex or repetitive commands rather than single, one-off T-SQL commands that you will be performing within this book. For example, you could have placed all of the code from Step 2 of our example into a file called SelectSql.txt, renamed the file to SelectSql.sql, then typed the following:

```
osql -E -S (local)\NetSDK -i SelectSql.sql
```

The Custom Query Tool

As an additional exercise in working with C# and databases, we've created a custom query application that we can use to execute the queries in this chapter. The code and explanation of how to create this query are available in Appendix A, but the working application is available in the Chapter 3 code available for download from the Wrox web site, at http://www.wrox.com. Once you've worked through some more of the chapters in this book and feel more comfortable with writing C# code for connecting to and working with databases, you may want to look through this code and create your own version of the application.

All the SQL statements in this chapter can, of course, be run using any of the tools we've mentioned, but we'll use our custom tool for all the examples in this chapter.

It's now time to move on and start to take a look at the first set of SQL code for working with data within tables.

Reading Data

In the previous chapter we used a `DataAdapter` that read data from the database for us. The `DataAdapter`, however, as with all other objects that access the data in a database, uses SQL code behind the scenes. If you look at the properties for the `DataAdapter` and expand the node named `SelectCommand` in the properties panel, you'll see an entry named `CommandText`:

SelectCommand	sqlSelectCommand2	▼
⊞ (DynamicProperties)		
(Name)	sqlSelectCommand2	
CommandText	SELECT OrderID, CustomerID, EmployeeID, OrderDate, Requir(	
CommandTimeout	30	
CommandType	Text	
⊞ Connection	sqlConnectionEdit	
Modifiers	Private	
Parameters	(Collection)	
UpdatedRowSource	Both	
TableMappings	(Collection)	

This property is the SQL statement that is used to select all the rows that was used in the application – or rather, all the rows that exist in the `Orders` table. Let's look at this statement in more detail.

The SELECT Statement

The `SELECT` statement retrieves data you specify from your database tables. In its simplest form, it consists of two parts:

- ❑ A `SELECT` part, where the columns that we are interested in are specified
- ❑ A `FROM` part, where the table or tables we are interested in are specified

I've written select and from in capital letters in the above listing, because tradition requires the SQL keywords to be written in capitals. The purpose of writing the keyword in capital letters is to distinguish SQL keywords from other parts of the query. This makes it much easier to read large queries, something that you will find very helpful when you start to create complex data applications.

Using the two statements, `SELECT` and `FROM`, we are able to create the simplest possible statement that will get data from the `Orders` table. If we assume that we are connected to the Northwind database, we could enter the following query:

```
SELECT *
FROM Employees
```

The asterisk (*) is a wildcard character, which means we want to select all the columns in the table. Knowing this fact makes the SQL statement a fairly straightforward read: Select all data from all columns from `Employees`. If you run this against the Northwind database, you get all of the rows and all of the columns returned that are in the table `Employees`.

Try It Out: A Simple SELECT Statement

To try the `SELECT` query described above, open up the `Chapter3_Examples` solution that comes in the code download from http://www.wrox.com, and run our query application. Hit *F5* to run our application and we are now ready to run our code.

1. In the `RichTextBox` at the top of the dialog, enter the following `SELECT` query:

```
SELECT *
FROM Employees
```

2. In order to execute the query, you can hit *F5* or select **Actions | Execute** from the menu.

3. The resulting dialog should look something like this:

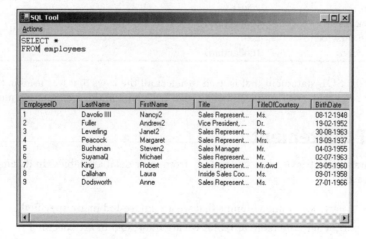

In the screenshot, I've run the Format Statements method by hitting F12. This has colored the SELECT and FROM statements, as well as converted them to uppercase.

How It Works

We asked the database to return all data from all columns, which is exactly what has happened. If you scroll to the right, you will find all of the columns in the `Employees` table listed.

If you are still not convinced, you can open the Server Explorer and select the Northwind database. (You will have to close the running application first). Then expand the **Tables** node and double-click the **Employees** node. This will also return all data in all columns of the `Employees` table, and you should be able to verify that our simple application is working as expected.

You'll find that most of the time you are not really interested in all of the columns of a table, and whenever that happens, you should limit the query as much as possible. The reason for this is that when you select data from columns that you're not going to use, you put unnecessary strain on the network and database. In order to explicitly select the columns you want, you enter the names of each of them after the `SELECT` keyword:

```
SELECT EmployeeID, FirstName, LastName
FROM Employees
```

The above statement selects all rows from the `Employees` table but only the `EmployeeID`, `FirstName`, and `LastName` columns are selected:

Try It Out: Selecting Specific Column Data

1. Run our SQL Tool application and enter the following statement:

```
SELECT EmployeeID, FirstName, LastName
FROM Employees
```

2. Hit *F5* to execute the query.

If you still have the application running and have some text in the `RichTextBox`, you don't have to delete it. Instead enter the above text in the `RichTextBox` below the old text. Then select the text you have just entered and hit F5. Whenever there is text selected in the `RichTextBox`, only that will be sent to the database. If nothing is selected, everything in the `RichTextBox` will be sent to the database.

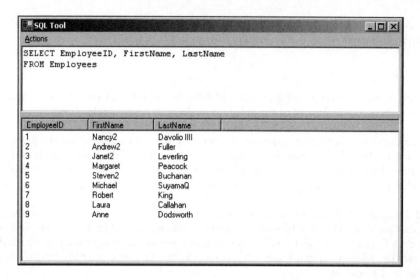

How It Works

The screenshot shows the application after the query has been run. Note that only the three columns `EmployeeID`, `FirstName`, and `LastName` are selected:

The WHERE Clause

The third part of a select query is the `WHERE` clause. This part of the query allows you to specify criteria for the data that you want the database to return. This part of a select query can become very complex indeed, but we'll stick to the simple usage for now. These uses can for the most part be described as:

```
WHERE <Column 1> <Operator> <Column 2>
```

where `<Operator>` is a comparison operator (for example =, !=, >, <, etc). A list of the operators is included after this example.

Try It Out: Refining our Query

1. Enter the following text into our application:

```
SELECT FirstName, LastName, Country
FROM Employees
WHERE Country = 'USA'
```

2. Run the code by pressing *F5* and you should see the following:

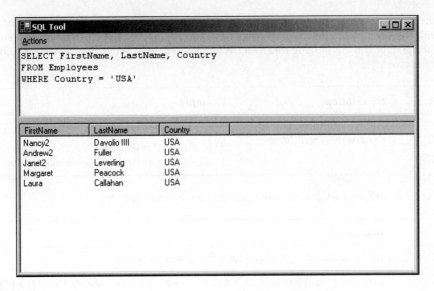

How It Works

The above statement could be formulated in clear text as: *Return all the data from the columns FirstName, LastName, and Country from the Employees table, but only the rows where the data in the Country column equals USA.*

The Operators of the WHERE Clause

You can use a number of different comparison operators in place of the = in the above example:

Operator	Description	Example
=	Equals	`EmployeeID = 1`
<	Less than	`EmployeeID < 1`
>	Greater than	`EmployeeID > 1`
<=	Less than or equal to	`EmployeeID <= 1`
>=	Greater than or equal to	`EmployeeID >= 1`
!=, <>	Not equal to	`EmployeeID!= 1`
!<	Not less than	`EmployeeID!< 1`
!>	Not greater than	`EmployeeID!> 1`

As mentioned earlier, there are several different implementations of SQL. This section is specific to T-SQL (Transact SQL) and will not be accurate on other implementations of SQL. If at some point you will find yourself working with another implementation of SQL, please refer to the documentation of the product you are using to find the differences in the SQL.

Besides the above operators there is one that you will find useful when the column you are working on is of a string type. The LIKE operator allows you to specify that the information you are entering is pattern for the data you are looking for. Note: When you are specifying text the text should be enclosed in quotation marks ('):

Operator	Description	Example
LIKE	Allows you to specify a pattern to search for	WHERE Title LIKE 'Sales %' This selects all rows where the Title column contains a value that starts with the word Sales and a space.

You can use four different wildcards in the pattern you are searching for:

Wildcard	Description
%	Any combination of characters. See above example.
_	Any one character. WHERE Title Like '_ales' selects all rows where the title column equals 'aales', 'bales', ...
[]	A single character within a range [a-d] or set [abcd]. WHERE Title like '[bs]ales' selects all rows where the Title column equals either the word 'bales' or 'sales'.
[^]	A single character not within a range [^a-d] or set [^abcd].

Sometimes it is useful to select the rows where a value is not set. When no value has been set for a column, it contains a NULL value. NULL is the value that is assigned to a column when it doesn't contain any data. This is not the same as a column that contain the value 0 (zero) as that column actually holds a value with some kind of integer type. To select a row with a column with no value, use the IS operator:

Operator	Description	Example
IS NULL IS NOT NULL	Allows you to select rows where a column has no value. The reverse is true if NOT NULL is used.	WHERE Region IS NULL returns all rows where Region has no value. WHERE Region IS NOT NULL returns all rows where Region has a value.

*Note: The IS NULL and IS NOT NULL must be used to select NULL or non-NULL fields respectively. The following is valid but always produces zero rows as the result: SELECT * FROM Employees WHERE Region = NULL. If you change the = to IS you will find that the query suddenly returns rows.*

To select values in a range or in a set, the BETWEEN and IN operators can be used:

Operator	Description	Example
BETWEEN	True if a value is in a range.	WHERE Extension BETWEEN 400 AND 500 returns the rows where Extension is between 400 and 500.
IN	True if a value is in a list. The list can also be an entire new query	WHERE City IN ('Seattle', 'London') returns the rows where City is either Seattle or London.

Combining Filters

Quite often you'll need to use more than one statement to filter your data. You can use the following logical operators:

Operator	Description	Example
AND	Combines two expressions, evaluating the complete expression to true only if both are true	WHERE (Title LIKE 'Sales%' AND LastName = 'Peacock')
OR	Combines two expressions, evaluating the complete expression to true if either is true	WHERE (Title = 'Peacock' OR Title = 'King')

When you are using these operators, it is often a good idea to include parentheses to clarify the query and in complex queries they are absolutely necessary.

Sorting the Data

After we've filtered the data we want, the final task we can set the SELECT statement is to sort the data on one or more criteria and in a certain direction. Sorting the data isn't just to make the result friendlier to the eye, but having data sorted in a specific order is an immense help in many common programming tasks. To sort the data we use the ORDER BY clause:

```
ORDER BY <Column name> [ASC | DESC] {, n}
```

The Column name is the column that should be used to sort the result. The {,n} part means that you can specify any number of sort expressions. They will be evaluated in the order you specify them.

There are two sort directions:

❑   ASC: Ascending (1, 2, 3, 4, ...).

❑   DESC: Descending (10, 9, 8, 7, ...). If you omit the ASC or DESC part, the sort order defaults to ASC.

Now we've seen all of the common parts of the select statement. Writing it formally in all its glory is a bit long-winded, but the essence of it is this:

```
SELECT <Column Names>
FROM <Table Names>
WHERE <Expression>
ORDER BY <Column Name> ASC | DESC
```

Let's see this in an example.

Try It Out: An Enhanced SELECT Statement

Putting this to the test, let's create one query that uses some of all this. This is what we'll do:

❑ We want to select all of the orders in the `Orders` table that has been handled by the Employee with `EmployeeID` = 5.

❑ We only want to select the orders that were shipped to either France or Brazil.

❑ We are only interested in the columns `OrderID`, `EmployeeID`, `CustomerID`, `OrderDate`, and `ShipCountry`.

❑ We want to view the orders ordered by the destination country and then by the date the order was placed!

Sounds complicated? Let's try it out.

1. Fire up our Query tool application, and once it's loaded, enter the following SQL code:

```
SELECT OrderID, EmployeeID, CustomerID, OrderDate, ShipCountry
FROM Orders
WHERE EmployeeID = 5 AND (ShipCountry IN ('Brazil', 'France'))
ORDER BY ShipCountry ASC, OrderDate ASC
```

2. Hit *F5* to run the application and you should see the following output:

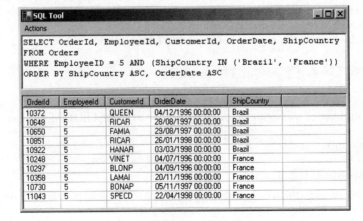

How It Works

Let's look at the lines individually. The first line specifies which columns we want to use:

```
SELECT OrderID, EmployeeID, CustomerID, OrderDate, ShipCountry
```

While the second line specifies that we want to use the `Orders` table:

```
FROM Orders
```

The third line is a bit more complicated. It consists of two expressions that individually state that

- ❑ The `EmployeeID` column of the selected rows must be 5
- ❑ The `ShipCountry` must be in the list 'Brazil' and 'France'

As the two expressions are combined with an `AND`, they both must evaluate to true for a row to be included in the resulting set of rows. Here is the third line we used to achieve this:

```
WHERE EmployeeID = 5 AND (ShipCountry IN ('Brazil', 'France'))
```

The fourth line specifies the order in which the rows are sorted. In fact it does more than that. We stated that we wanted the rows to be ordered by the country to which the order were shipped, and by specifying that the rows should be sorted by the `ShipCountry` first, and then the `OrderDate` we achieve just that.

```
ORDER BY ShipCountry ASC, OrderDate ASC
```

When you look at the result as shown above, the `OrderDate` field appears to be unsorted. If, however, you look closely you will see that the `OrderDate` is sorted for all rows with Brazil as the `ShippingCountry` and then for all rows with France. This means that the column isn't sorted in its entirety, but only within the blocks created by the first `ORDER BY` criterion.

Inserting Data

The second important task we should be able to perform is to insert new rows into the tables. This is done with an `INSERT` statement. The `INSERT` statement is much simpler to look at than the select statement, particularly because the `WHERE` and `ORDER BY` clauses have no meaning when inserting data, and therefore are not used.

INSERT INTO Statement

A normal `INSERT INTO` statement has these parts:

```
INSERT INTO <Table name>
(<column 1>, <column 2>, ... <column n>)
values (<Value column 1>, <Value column 2>, ... <value column n>)
```

Using the above formula, let's insert a new row in the `Shippers` table of the Northwind database. Before we insert, let's look at the table. Our table contains three rows:

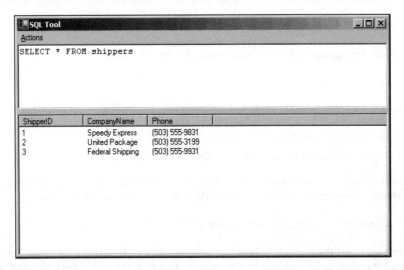

The first column, `ShipperID`, is an Identity column, and as such we can't insert values into it explicitly – MSDE will make sure a unique value is inserted for us. Therefore the insert statement will look like this:

```
INSERT INTO Shippers
(CompanyName, Phone)
Values ('We shred them before you get them', '555-123456')
```

The result will look like this:

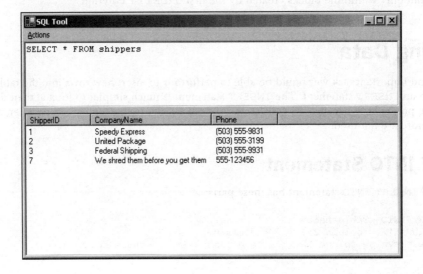

When you insert into columns, you should be careful to insert data of the correct data type. In the above example, both the columns have a character type and we therefore inserted characters. If we had used a column with an integer data type we should have inserted an integer in stead. Please refer to the end of this chapter for a list of SQL data types.

Updating Data

The third task we are often set when working with data is to update one or more columns in one or more rows. As we saw in Chapter 2, this task was easily performed when using the `DataSet` and `DataAdapter` of ADO.NET (which we'll look at in more detail in some of the upcoming chapters), and there was little reason for concern as we performed the update. That, however, is a completely different story when working with SQL directly. In the following section you should be careful when you try the examples as it is quite easy to suddenly update all the rows in a table where you only wanted to change one. This will happen if you forget to enter the `WHERE` part of the `UPDATE` statement, so be careful to enter all of the text before hitting *F5*!

The UPDATE Statement

Now that we are well aware of the danger that lurks when using the `UPDATE` statement, let's take a good look at it.

> *Should it happen that you change something on the Northwind database that you regret, remember that you can simply restore it using the procedure described at the end of this chapter.*

In essence this is a simple and powerful statement that allows you to update one or more rows and columns based on a criterion:

```
UPDATE TableName
SET <Column 1> = value 1, <Column 2> = value 2, ... <Column n> = value n
WHERE <criterion>
```

As an example, let's imagine that the company we added earlier, 'We Shred Them Before You Get Them' has realized that, though probably true, name doesn't do business any good, and this is therefore changing it to 'Speed of Light Delivery'. In order to make this change on our database we first need to locate a column with a value that is unique to the company in question. Theoretically there could be more than one company with the same name, so we shouldn't use the `CompanyName` column as the unique identifier. Instead we locate the correct row and make a note of the `ShipperID` identity column value:

7	We shred them before you get them	555-123456	

The unique ID of the row is seven, and we can now update the column:

```
UPDATE Shippers
SET CompanyName = 'Speed of Light Delivery'
WHERE ShipperID = 7
```

Executing this update returns the nice result: 1 row(s) affected. If you select the row again, you'll see that the CompanyName has changed:

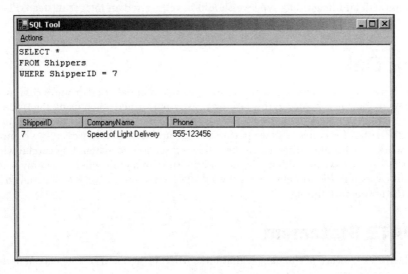

When you are updating more than one table, you only write the SET clause once. In other words, to update both the name and the Phone of the company above, the following statement could be used:

```
UPDATE Shippers
SET CompanyName = 'Speed of Light Delivery',
    Phone = '555-654321'
WHERE ShipperID = 7
```

Deleting Data

Deleting data holds the exact same perils as does the UPDATE statement – it is all too easy to delete everything in a table by forgetting the WHERE clause – so be careful when you enter the text. In 'real-world' databases you will often find that rows aren't actually deleted. Instead a column named Deleted, or something to that effect, marks a row as deleted. This row is then used when selecting from the table to exclude the rows that are marked as deleted. This is obviously a safer approach, and it also allows for recovery of deleted rows. Whether or not you choose to use this approach, it is highly recommended that you create a backup of your real-life databases from time to time.

At a glance, the DELETE statement looks a bit odd, which is because there seems to be something missing at the very beginning of it. You use the DELETE statement to remove entire rows, and it is therefore not necessary to specify any columns to use, which means that the FROM part of the statement is situated right next to the DELETE keyword:

```
DELETE FROM <Table name>
WHERE <expression>
```

If the company we have used for our previous examples has finally given up and gone out of business, we would need to remove it from the Shippers table. As with the UPDATE statement, we should locate the unique value of the Identity column of the row we wish to remove, and use that in our statement:

```
DELETE FROM Shippers
WHERE ShipperID = 7
```

If you select everything from the Shippers table now, you will see that the company in question is no longer there:

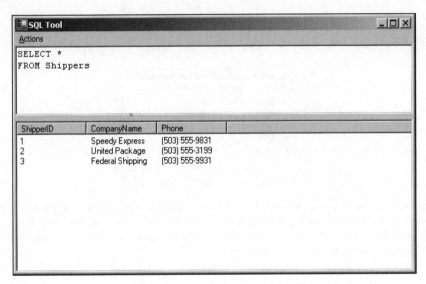

If you were to attempt to delete one of the three other shippers, you would get an error returned from the database. The reason for this is that the Shippers are used in the Orders table, and there is a relationship between those tables. We'll examine this in more detail in Chapter 12, but for now, the result is that you are not allowed to delete these rows.

Deleting Every Row

Obviously there may be times where you'll actually want to remove every single row in a table. Though this is probably not something that happens often, when it happens you shouldn't use the DELETE statement, but rather the TRUNCATE TABLE statement, which will perform the task faster than the DELETE statement. The reason for the speed difference is that the TRUNCATE TABLE statement doesn't perform any logging. As it is, you shouldn't be allowed to perform the following on the Northwind database, because of the ties between the tables, but in theory, to delete every row in the Shippers table you could do the following:

```
TRUNCATE TABLE Shippers
```

This concludes our tour of the basic SQL statements used to select, update, insert, and delete data in the database. In the next section of this chapter, we'll look the SQL data types.

SQL Data Types

In Chapter 2 we used the values of some of the columns in the Orders, Products, and Order Details tables. The reason we were able to do so relatively effortlessly is that the Server Explorer had already mapped the data types of the columns in the database to C# data types. This mapping can be found if you open the project again.

1. Open our Chapter2_Examples solution.

2. In the Solution Explorer to the right, click the Show all files icon.

3. Double-click the file DataSetEmployees.xsd. This will open this window:

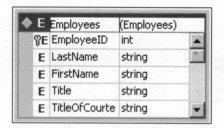

In the box above you can see that the data we are working with in our C# application all has types that C# knows and can work with. These are, however, not the same data types as are used in the database itself. The following tables show the data types that are available to us in SQL and how they map to C# data types:

Numeric Data Types

SQL Data Type	C# Type	Description
BIT	bool	A bit value can either be 0 or 1, which is equivalent to a boolean value
DECIMAL	decimal	A fixed or floating-point value
FLOAT	float	A floating-point value
INT	int	A 32-bit integer
REAL	float	A 32-bit floating-point value
SMALLINT	short	A 16-bit integer
TINYINT	byte	An 8-bit integer

String Data Types

All of the SQL string-related data types convert into a string in C#, hence the single entry in the table below:

SQL Data Type	C# Type	Description
CHAR	string	A fixed-length string from 1-255 chars long.
NCHAR		This type of chars are used to represent Unicode characters.
NVARCHAR VARCHAR		Variable length strings. A VARCHAR can contain up to 8,000 chars, while an NVARCHAR can contain 4,000 chars. The reason for this is, that a Unicode character is 2 bytes long, while a normal character is only 1 byte long.
TEXT		Variable length string.

Date and Time Data Types

All of the SQL date and time types convert into the type `System.DateTime` in C#, hence the single entry in the table below:

SQL Data Type	C# Type	Description
DATE	System.DateTime	A Date value
DATETIME		A DateTime value

Binary Data Types

Binary data types cannot uniquely be mapped to a single data type in C#, as content of a field of any of these type can be, well, anything.

SQL Data Type	C# Type	Description
BINARY VARBINARY	N/A	BINARY is a fixed-length binary value of up to 8,000 bytes. VARBINARY is the variable-length equivalent

Before we finish this chapter, let's revisit the OSQL tool and discover how we can restore our Northwind database, just in case we've accidentally deleted too much data!

Restoring the Northwind Database

As we work through this book we'll probably be spending a fair amount of time adding, editing, and removing data from the Northwind database. This procedure, which is relatively simple, can be used to restore our Northwind database to its original state. When we installed MSDE, the installation script actually ran this utility for us behind the scenes, but the SQL script that restores the database remains on our database should we need to use it. We'll be using the OSQL command-line tool that we discussed earlier to run this script. All we need to do is open a command prompt and navigate to the directory containing a restoration SQL script provided for us. We then execute the script using the OSQL tool.

Try It Out: Restoring the Northwind Database

1. Open up a command prompt window and type the following command:

```
cd C:\Program Files\Microsoft.NET\FrameworkSDK\Samples\setup
```

2. Now enter the following statement to run the restoration script:

```
osql -E -S (local)\NetSDK -i instnwnd.sql
```

you should see the following output:

... and about 2-3 minutes and a lot of scrolling later:

How It Works

The first command we type changes the active working directory to be the same directory as the script file:

```
cd C:\Program Files\Microsoft.NET\FrameworkSDK\Samples\setup
```

The next command runs the OSQL tool on the SQL script in the folder:

```
osql -E -S (local)\NetSDK -i instnwnd.sql
```

The first switch in our statement indicates that we're using a trusted connection to connect to our database. The second switch, -S, followed by our server name, (local)\NetSDK, indicates the server that we're going to be working on. The final switch, -i, precedes the name of the input .sql file.

The SQL in the instnwnd.sql script checks to see if we've already got an existing instance of the Northwind database, and if we have, it recreates the database exactly as it was when it was first installed.

We'll be looking at more advanced SQL statements in some of the later chapters, so you may want to look at the actual SQL code in this script (by opening it in Visual Studio or even in Notepad) to see some more complex statements in action.

Summary

In this chapter we have seen how to use SQL statements to perform the four most common tasks on a database: UPDATE, SELECT, INSERT, and DELETE data. Understanding how to create these statements is going to be of great help to you later, when you examine and manipulate data with the ADO.NET objects.

We examined the data types of SQL and saw how they mapped to the data types used in the C# language.

Finally, we saw how we could restore our Northwind database to its original state after having added and deleted lots of data.

Exercises

1. Insert a new row into the Customers table. Insert it so that the Region and Fax columns are empty.

2. Update the row you created in Exercise 1 so that the Fax number equals '555-654321' and the Region column equals 'CA'.

3. Delete the row that you created in Exercise 1.

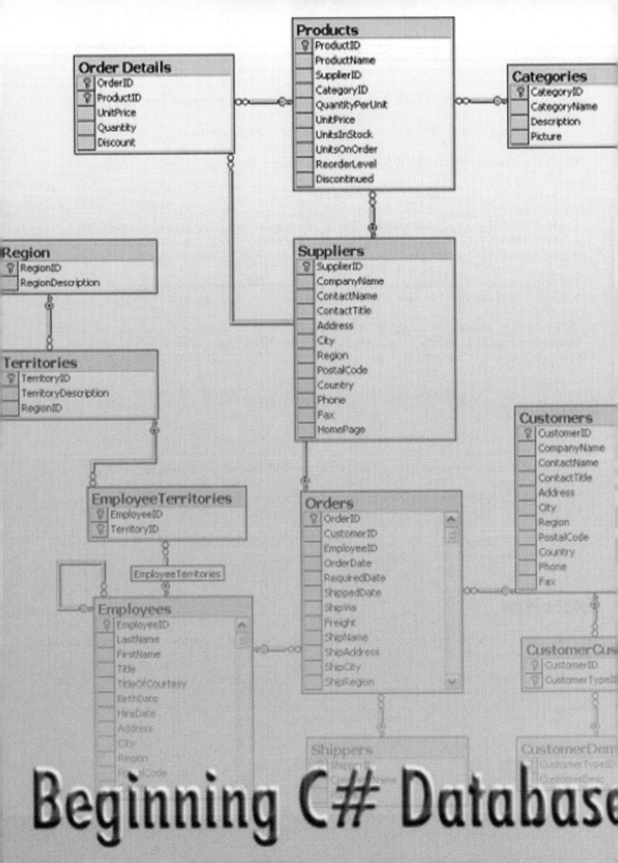

What's ADO.NET?

Now that we've talked about SQL, MSDE, and the Visual Studio .NET wizards used in creating simple data-driven `applications`, let's now meet the final piece in the puzzle: ADO.NET. When we created our simple application in Chapter 2, we used Visual Studio .NET extensively to connect to our data and to work with our data. What we didn't really look at in detail was what Visual Studio .NET created for us behind the scenes. Underneath all the drag-and-drop functionality, VS was using ADO.NET objects to access and display our data. Understanding these objects is the key to understanding how to build powerful data-driven applications. Before we start weaving applications and samples together, we'll start by looking at ADO.NET from the ground up. In this chapter, we'll be looking at:

- ❑ What is ADO.NET
- ❑ The architecture of ADO.NET
- ❑ .NET data providers and their components
- ❑ The role of `DataSet` in ADO.NET

Let's now begin by looking at what ADO.NET is, and how it works.

Why ADO.NET?

Almost all applications require some data access in one way or another. Up until recently, developers have been using established data access infrastructures such as ODBC, OLEDB, and ADO. With the introduction of the .NET Framework, Microsoft created a new way to work with data, which it termed ADO.NET. Before we find out about ADO.NET in detail, we'll take a brief look at some of the older data access technologies, since terms like OLEDB and ODBC still exist in ADO.NET.

Moving on from ADO

The name ADO (an acronym for **A**ctiveX **D**ata **O**bjects) may sound familiar to some of you who've worked with data access technologies before .NET. ADO is a collection of ActiveX data access objects that are designed to work in a **connected** environment (where a constant connection is maintained to the data source). It was built around existing OLEDB data providers (which we'll look at later in this chapter) for accessing data sources. OLEDB provided support for accessing data from non-SQL data stores as well as standard SQL-type data stores, and ADO introduced methods that were designed to make it easier to work with these OLEDB providers, and make it simple to manipulate data.

However, accessing data using ADO with OLEDB under the hood meant that you had to walk through several layers of connectivity before you'd even reach the data source. Just as OLEDB was there to connect to a large number of data sources, an older data access technology, ODBC, was there to connect to more obscure and older data sources like dBase and Paradox. To access ODBC data sources using ADO, you'd use an OLEDB provider for ODBC (since ADO only works directly with OLEDB), thus adding more layers to an already multi-layered model.

Acknowledging the problems in maintaining constant connections to data sources, a disconnected data access model was introduced, which was termed RDS (Remote Data Services). Although this worked reasonably well in storing locally-cached data, you were restricted to using Internet Explorer version 4 or above as it worked using DHTML. Also, updating the original data source proved troublesome, and as a result, many developers would stick to the connected data access model.

With the multi-layered data access model and the constantly connected nature of ADO, you could easily end up sapping server resources and creating a performance bottleneck. ADO has served us well, but we've now been introduced to ADO.NET, which has some great features that make it a superior data access technology in many ways.

From ADO to ADO.NET

ADO.NET is a completely new data access methodology – a new technology, a new design, and built entirely from scratch. First of all, let's get this cleared up, ADO.NET does not stand for ActiveX Data Objects .NET. Why? Because:

❑ ADO.NET resides *inside* the .NET Framework and is not an external entity

❑ ADO.NET is *not* a collection of ActiveX components

The name ADO.NET is analogous to ADO for a very obvious reason: since Microsoft designed the new technology in a similar fashion to ADO (functionality wise) and since ease of use and basic ground-level functionality was the same, Microsoft wanted developers to feel at home using ADO.NET and didn't want them to think that they'd need to 'learn it all over again'.

As the specifications for the .NET Framework were laid out, it was realized that ADO wasn't going to fit in. ADO was accessible to data applications as an external package and followed a very non-.NET-compliant model – it was a COM interface (an external component that could be used by any application), which required the application attempting to use its services to explicitly include a reference to it. In contrast, .NET applications are designed to share a single model, where all libraries, methods, and classes are integrated into one single framework, organized into logical namespaces, and declared public to any application that wishes to use them. This approach was pragmatic and considered easily adaptable, so it was decided that the data access technology in .NET would take on a new guise, and it was named ADO.NET.

ADO.NET has been designed to accommodate a connected, as well as a disconnected internet world – a world that ADO was not designed to handle. Also, the design of ADO.NET sought to embrace the widely accepted XML standard (We'll cover more on this in Chapter 17), much more than ADO did, since the explosion of interest in XML only really came about after ADO was created. Not only can you use XML as a transfer medium between two applications, you can now export data from your application into an XML file, store it locally in you system and retrieve it later when you need to.

They say performance comes with a price. In the case of ADO.NET, the price is definitely good. Unlike ADO, ADO.NET no longer wraps around OLEDB providers, instead it uses managed data providers (we'll be talking about managed providers later in the chapter in the *.NET Data Providers* section) that are designed specifically for a certain type of data source, thus leveraging their true power and adding to the overall speed and performance of your application.

ADO.NET also works in both a connected and a disconnected environment. We can connect to a database, and remain connected to that database while simply reading data, then closing our connection, which is a very similar process to that of ADO. Where ADO.NET really begins to shine is in the disconnected world. If we need to make edits and amends to the data in our database, maintaining an open connection as in ADO would be costly, since the server has to maintain each connection continuously. ADO.NET gets round this problem by moving this side of data access to the disconnected model. The data we wish to edit or amend is sent from the server to the client and cached locally on the client's machine. Edits can then be made, and when we're ready to update the database, we can send the data back to the server, where any conflicts are managed for us.

In ADO.NET, when we are reading data, we use an object known as a `DataReader`. When we're working with disconnected data for edits and updates, the data is cached locally in a relational data structure called a `DataSet`.

ADO.NET and the .NET Framework

A `DataSet` can hold large amounts of data in the form of tables (as a `DataTable` object), their relations (as a `DataRelation` object), and constraints in an in-memory cache, which can then be exported to an external file or to another `DataSet` object for that matter. With XML as an integral part of ADO.NET, you're also allowed to produce XML schema (We'll cover this in Chapter 8 when we learn more about `DataSets`) from tables in a data source or transmit and share data using XML as a medium.

Coming back to the framework, you should already be aware that the .NET Framework groups related classes, used day to day in all kinds of applications, into namespaces. The ADO.NET classes are grouped into the following namespaces:

Namespace	Description of its contents
`System.Data`	Consists of classes that constitute the ADO.NET architecture
`System.Data.Common`	Contains classes shared by other classes (the .NET data providers) used to access a data source
`System.Data.OleDb`	Classes that make up the .NET data provider for OLEDB-compatible data sources
`System.Data.SqlClient`	Classes that make up the .NET data provider for SQL Server, optimized specifically for SQL Server 7.0 and above
`System.Data.SqlTypes`	Provides classes for native data types within SQL Server as a better alternative to other data types

XML support has been closely integrated into ADO.NET, so it's worth mentioning that the ADO.NET classes, found in the `System.Data` namespace, are linked to the XML classes found in the `System.Xml` namespace. Thus, when compiling your data access code using the Visual Studio C# editor, you need to make sure you have the following two namespaces under the **References** title in the **Solution Explorer** of the IDE:

```
System.Data
System.XML
```

Actually, these are references to assembly files, and are needed for compilation. If you create a new **Console Application** project using the **New Project** dialogue from the main menu, these two references should already be there, along with `System`. However, if for any reason they're not present, you can simply perform the following few steps to add references to these namespaces into your project:

1. Right-click on the **References** title in the **Solution Explorer** and click **Add Reference**.

2. A dialogue box with a list of available references will be displayed. Select `System.Data.dll`, `System.XML.dll`, and `System.dll` (if not already present) one by one and click on the **Select** button.

3. Now click **OK** and your references will be added to the project.

For those of you interested in working from the command line, you can use the following line command to produce the same result:

```
> csc /r:System.dll /r:System.Data.dll /r:System.XML.dll <file name>
```

Looking at the namespaces the Framework offers, it can be clearly seen that ADO.NET has the capacity to work with older technologies, as the .NET Framework offers classes for connection to OLEDB-compatible data sources and separates out classes that provide connection to the SQL Server version 7.0 and above. The SQL Server classes are designed to communicate directly with SQL Server, which makes for a very efficient connection. Performance figures produced by Microsoft highlight the fact that these SQL-specific classes are far faster for connecting to SQL Server than going via OLEDB, giving .NET + SQL Server an edge in the performance wars. We'll look at this in more detail later in the chapter.

Clearly, this type of classes-in-a-nutshell approach of ADO.NET was needed so that developers could feel at home while they code, and not worry about messy details of COM and its associated dilemmas. In contrast to other programming languages and data access techniques, ADO.NET can safely claim to be a technology that fits well in all kinds of scenarios, connected or not, and a technology that will go a long way.

Architecture of ADO.NET

We've talked so much about the pros and cons (well, not really the cons) of ADO.NET that it's about time we perform an x-ray on our new friend and see what it looks like from the inside. The following diagram should give you a clear view:

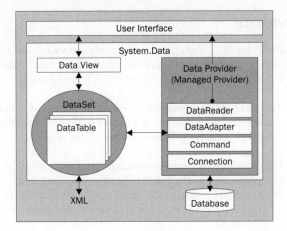

We can classify the ADO.NET classes into two layers (of classes); for your understanding, these are shaded in the diagram above. The first layer would consist of those essential objects that establish the actual connection with the data source. These can be classified as the **data provider** classes. A data provider performs the actual connection to the data source for reading and writing.

The second layer can be defined as the independent `DataSet` object, available to work in a disconnected fashion, caching data locally and updating the data source as required. A `DataSet` is capable of storing multiple `DataTable` objects at one time. A single `DataTable` object represents one complete physical table from a database, for instance you can store the whole of the `Employees` table from the Northwind database into a `DataTable` and manipulate the data at will.

However, to update a data source using a `DataSet`, some external help from a data provider is needed, since it's completely cut off from connection details. It can also use its available methods to read and write data in XML files. We'll look more into this when we come across `DataSets` later in the chapter, and specifically, later in the book (Chapter 8 – *The DataSet and the DataAdapter*).

In the previous diagram, you can see the use of a `DataView` class. This class is primarily used when binding data to both Windows Forms and Web Forms (Data binding is discussed thoroughly in Chapter 9) and does not hold data itself. It can be used with a `DataSet`, optionally, for filtering and selecting data that the `DataSet` contains since a `DataView` can be used for creating different views of data stored in a `DataSet`, which can be changed dynamically.

Furthermore, as indicated by the arrows in the figure, the two classes, the `DataSet` and the `DataReader`, can be used for *reading* from the data source. `DataReader` provides a fast, forward-only cursor (the cursor in the database can move in one direction only, reading each record once as it travels through) for reading from a *connected* data source only, whereas a `DataSet` reads all data available in the data source all at once, and can then work in a *disconnected* fashion.

If you're curious, you've probably tried looking for the `Connection` or the `DataAdapter` class in the `System.Data` namespace, as shown in the diagram, and by now you're probably wondering why they aren't there. As it shows, these fundamental objects are wrapped by a specific data provider. In other words, every managed provider (that's another term for data provider in the .NET Framework) supplies its own implementation of these objects and has a different name altogether (We'll cover this in the next section). For instance, a `Connection` class in the SQL Server Provider namespace is named `SqlConnection`, whereas it's named `OleDbConnection` in the OLE DB Provider namespace.

.NET Data Providers

We've heard so much about the .NET data providers already, and we know for a fact that these are a set of objects designed to communicate with a particular data source, and fetch data in an abstract manner, unless it's SQL Server on the backend, the provider for which fetches data in a very provider specific way.

Picture a managed provider as being a component that handles the conversation between your program and the data source. Each set of classes that belong to a specific data provider, are grouped under a different name and are available in a specific namespace all together.

In contrast to earlier OLEDB and ADO providers, each .NET data provider provides specific data access architecture and routines, and so they differ slightly from each other. In spite of their diminutive differences, all .NET data providers seem to be similar in their functionality, outcome, and method calls. This is a great feature of ADO.NET since you can now easily port from one provider to another by only making a few changes to your code.

Below is a list of available .NET data providers (at present):

Data provider namespace	Description
System.Data.SqlClient	As we saw earlier, this is a data provider for SQL Server 7.0, and above.
System.Data.OleDb	Data provider for OLEDB-compatible data sources, for example, this includes Microsoft Access, and earlier versions of SQL Server.
Microsoft.Data.Odbc	Used for direct access to native Microsoft Open Database Connectivity (ODBC) drivers. This namespace is not shipped with the Framework by default, but is downloadable from the Microsoft web site (available from http://msdn.microsoft.com/downloads) and can be added to the Microsoft .NET Framework. We'll look at this in more detail later in this chapter.
System.Data.OracleClient	At the time of writing, a Beta 1 release of the .NET Framework data provider for Oracle is currently available. Not shipped with the Framework, this is an add-on component to the .NET Framework that provides access to an Oracle database using the Oracle Call Interface (OCI). This provider is available from http://msdn.microsoft.com/downloads.

As mentioned earlier, different data providers have been created so that you may efficiently utilize the full power of the specific database your program is designed to work with. For instance, if you choose SQL Server for your backend database, intending to use version 7 or greater, you should use the SQL Server (SqlClient) data provider as it provides the most efficient way to work with SQL Server and is specially designed for these versions. These classes communicate natively with SQL Server, bypassing many of the layers that OLEDB connections have had to use.

The .NET OLEDB Provider exists to provide access to older versions of SQL Server and other databases, such as Access (or indeed any data source for which there is an OLEDB provider). It interacts with a couple of abstract layers, namely OLEDB Service Component and the OLEDB Provider, before reaching the data source, which means it's a bit slower than the SQL-specific provider.

The following figure shows the interaction between a SQL Server 7.0, or later, database and the two data providers.

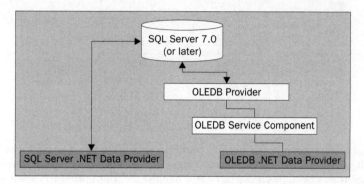

If your application connects to an older version of SQL Server, SQL Server 6.5 or earlier for example, or if it connects to more than one databases (other than SQL Server 7.0 or above) at the same time (also known as multiple database connectivity), for example an Access and an Oracle database connected simultaneously, only then should you choose to use the .NET OLEDB Provider. We will see why this is the case later on in the chapter.

Note there are no hard and fast rules; you may decide to use the .NET OLEDB Provider for SQL Server 7.0 and the available data provider for Oracle (System.Data.OracleClient) if you wish, but it's important that you choose the right provider for your purpose. Given the performance benefits of the SQL Server-specific classes, if you use SQL Server or MSDE, 99% of the time you should be using the SQL classes.

Before we look at what each provider does and how it's used, we need to take note of a few important functionality details. Each .NET data provider is designed to perform two functions very well. They must:

❑ Provide access to data with an active connection to the data source
❑ Provide data transmission to and from the independent DataSet object through a DataAdapter class

Active connections with databases are established by using the provider's internal Connection object. Other objects such as the DataReader, Command, and DataAdapter are there to assist you in reading, executing commands, and reading or writing to a DataSet object respectively.

As we've seen, each provider is prefixed with the type of data source it connects to, for instance, the SQL Server provider is prefixed with 'Sql', and so its connection object has been named SqlConnection. In the case of an OLEDB provider, it's been named OleDbConnection. Let's now have a look at the object model of both of these providers. We'll work simultaneously with two separate databases (Access and SQL Server 2000) in order to show to you how easy it is to switch between data providers and what, if any, their main visible differences are.

Note that this diagram also presents the concept of 'multiple database connectivity', as I spoke of earlier, and shows how two data providers work in a single application, sharing a single `DataSet` object for storage and retrieval of data.

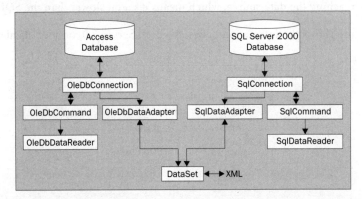

The two .NET providers can be seen working simultaneously, sharing a single `DataSet` object. Notice that the OLEDB provider belongs to the namespace `System.Data.OleDb`, whereas the SQL Server provider belongs to `System.Data.SqlClient` namespace. Both providers seem to have a similar (external) architecture, yet are completely different from the inside.

Let's go into a little depth and examine individually how each of these providers can be put to work.

SQL Server .NET Data Provider

As we saw in the previous section, the .NET data provider classes for SQL Server 7.0 or later are located in the `System.Data.SqlClient` namespace. This provider performs a root-level connection; instead of traveling through a number of layers (the way OLEDB does), it directly connects to SQL Server on a one-on-one basis, and uses its own, specially designed, architecture to communicate and retrieve data.

The following table lists some classes from the `SqlClient` namespace, with their respective descriptions, which we will come across in the course of the book:

Class	Description
SqlCommand	Used for execution of Transact-SQL statements or stored procedures
SqlConnection	Represents a connection to a SQL Server data source
SqlDataAdapter	Represents a bridge between the `DataSet` and the data source
SqlDataReader	Provides a forward-only cursor to read from a SQL Server data source
SqlError	Holds information about errors and warnings that are returned by the SQL Server
SqlParameter	Represents a parameter to a `SqlCommand`
SqlTransaction	Represents a Transact-SQL transaction to be made in a SQL Server data source

If you look at the .NET Framework namespace hierarchy, you'll notice another namespace, `System.Data.SqlTypes`, which has been provided to go hand in hand with the SQL data provider and SQL Server. This namespace enables us to make use of native SQL Server data types as an alternative to conventional data types, resulting in increased efficiency and making developers' lives a lot easier when it comes to designing cross-back-end data resources. Recall that we looked at SQL data types in Chapter 3.

Let's start looking at some code. We're going to implement the SQL Server data provider in an example. This example will not be covering connections and data retrieval in detail; it's simply designed to familiarize you with what you'll experience and learn in upcoming chapters.

Try It Out: A Simple Console Application Using the SQL Server Provider

We're going to create a simple console application that opens a connection and runs a SQL query, using the `SqlClient` namespace against our MSDE database, which is the sample Northwind database that comes with VS.NET. (For more information on how to install this database, you may want to refer back to Chapter 1.) We're going to write some code that accesses data stored in that database, and display the data in the console window.

1. Open up Visual Studio .NET and create a new solution, called `Chapter4_Examples`, which we'll use to contain all of the projects for this chapter. Recall that we looked at how to do this in Chapter 2.

2. Right-click on the solution in the Solution Explorer and select **Add | New Project** from the menu. In the **Add New Project** dialog, create a new Console Application project, and call it `SQLServerProvider`. Within the project, rename the main file `SQLServerProvider.cs`.

3. Since we will be creating our example from scratch, select all the code in the code window and delete it. This will clear the window and you can now enter the following code:

```csharp
using System;
using System.Data;          // Includes some essential ADO.NET classes
using System.Data.SqlClient; // Includes the SQL Server Provider classes

class SQLServerProvider
{
  static void Main(string[] args)
  {
    // Tell the connection object where to find the Database
    string ConStr = @"server=(local)\NetSDK;" +
                    "Integrated Security=true;database=Northwind";

    // Pass connection string to the SqlConnection object
    SqlConnection sqlConn = new SqlConnection(ConStr);

    try
    {
      // Open Connection to start reading
      sqlConn.Open();

      // SQL query string that we'll use to get data from the database
      string SQL = "SELECT * FROM Employees";
```

```
        // Pass query string and connection object to the SqlCommand object
        SqlCommand sqlComm= new SqlCommand(SQL,sqlConn);

        // Read through each record returned
        SqlDataReader sqlReader = sqlComm.ExecuteReader();
        Console.WriteLine("This program demonstrates the use of" +
                        " SQL Server .NET Data Provider");
        Console.WriteLine("Querying database '{0}' with query" +
                        "'{1}'\n", sqlConn.Database, sqlComm.CommandText);
        Console.WriteLine("First Name\tLast Name\n");

        // Advance the cursor to the next record
        while(sqlReader.Read())
        {
          // Retrieve values from the SqlReader
          Console.WriteLine("{0} | {1}",
                            sqlReader["FirstName"].ToString().PadLeft(10),
                            sqlReader["LastName"].ToString().PadLeft(10));
        }
      }
      catch(Exception ex)
      {
        // Catch an exception thrown, if any, and display
        Console.WriteLine("Error: " + ex.Message);
      }
      finally
      {
        // Close active connection
        sqlConn.Close();
        Console.ReadLine();
      }
    }
}
```

4. Save the project, and hit the *F5* key to start debugging. A console window should appear with the following output.

How It Works

Let's take a look at the code we've just run and see how it works, starting with the `using` statements at the top of the file:

```
using System;
using System.Data;          // Includes some essential ADO.NET classes
using System.Data.SqlClient; // Includes the SQL Server Provider classes
```

Our code starts by importing some namespaces, giving us a short cut to accessing the classes contained within these namespaces in our code. Adding these references to our code enables us to use the classes directly, without having to specify the namespace they reside in each time. For example, we can refer to a `SQLConnection` object, instead of a `System.Data.SqlClient.SQLConnection` object.

After including the namespaces, we open an active connection to the database using the following lines of code:

```
string ConStr = @"server=(local)\NetSDK;" +
                "Integrated Security=true;database=Northwind";

// Pass connection string to the SqlConnection object
SqlConnection sqlConn = new SqlConnection(ConStr);
```

> *Remember, an '@' sign preceding the string indicates a string literal in C# so that escape prefixes for the backslash characters are not needed.*

We pass the new `SqlConnection` object a connection string, which comprises the server name, security authorization information, and the database name.

If we look at our connection string, we'll see the following statement:

```
Integrated Security=true;
```

This enables us to log in to our local SQL Server account using the current Windows login and password as the security authorization, rather than using a separate SQL Server-specific password. Also, in the upcoming examples and chapters, you might come across the term SSPI, for example:

```
Integrated Security=SSPI;
```

You can consider this to mean the same thing as our statement above, where we set it to `true`. SSPI, an acronym for Security Support Provider Interface, links SQL Server's security with Windows Security.

Up to this point, we haven't activated our connection to the database, and until that happens, our code wouldn't be of much use since we can't query a database without an open connection. We need to explicitly call the `Open()` method of the `SqlConnection`:

```
try
{
  // Open Connection to start reading
  sqlConn.Open();
```

You'll probably notice the inclusion of a `try` block in our code. A `try` and `catch` block is used as a 'standard' way of handling exceptions in ADO.NET. Any code that will not throw exceptions is placed outside the `try` block. In contrast, opening the connection to the database is an action with a relatively high probability of throwing an error (server not running, network connection problems, incorrect password, etc.), so we include this in the `try` block.

Next, to start reading records from the database, we need to first obtain the data we require by passing a SQL query string to `SqlCommand`, which also holds a reference to the connection object used for querying. In this case, we're requesting the database for all available records in its `Employees` table:

```
string SQL = "SELECT * FROM Employees";

// Pass query string and connection object to the SqlCommand object
SqlCommand sqlComm= new SqlCommand(SQL,sqlConn);
```

The following lines of code use available properties of the `SqlConnection` and the `SqlCommand` objects to display information about the name of the database we're dealing with and the SQL query string that we passed to the `SqlCommand` object:

```
Console.WriteLine("This program demonstrates the use of" +
                  " SQL Server .NET Data Provider");
Console.WriteLine("Querying database '{0}' with query" +
                  "'{1}'\n", sqlConn.Database, sqlComm.CommandText);
Console.WriteLine("First Name\tLast Name\n");
```

We retrieve records from the database with the help of a populated `SqlDataReader` object, by executing the `ExecuteReader()` method of `SqlCommand`. It's worth mentioning that we didn't explicitly instantiate a `SqlDataReader` object since it's an abstract class and can only be instantiated by calling the `ExecuteReader()` method of `SqlCommand`, which returns an instance of a `SqlDataReader`:

```
SqlDataReader sqlReader = sqlComm.ExecuteReader();
```

We then display each record, one by one, on the console, padding each returned string to the left purposely, so that the output is neatly displayed. The `Read()` method, from the `SqlDataReader` class, advances the `DataReader` to the next record and returns `true` if there are more rows or `false` otherwise:

```
while(sqlReader.Read())
{
  // Retrieve values from the SqlReader
  Console.WriteLine("{0} | {1}",
                    sqlReader["FirstName"].ToString().PadLeft(10),
                    sqlReader["LastName"].ToString().PadLeft(10));
}
```

Next we make sure that we handle any exceptions that may occur when we run our code:

```
catch(Exception ex)
{
  // Catch an exception thrown, if any, and display
  Console.WriteLine("Error: " + ex.Message);
}
```

Finally we close the connection by executing the `Close()` method of `SqlConnection`. As a general rule, you should close the connection in the `finally` block (even if we close it in the `try` block too); this way we can be sure it will be closed no matter what happens within the `try` block:

```
finally
{
  // Close active connection
  sqlConn.Close();
  Console.ReadLine();
}
```

Note that we used a `Console.ReadLine()` method call after we closed the connection. This is there so that the Console window doesn't disappear, after it executes the program, until you press the *Enter* key.

OLEDB .NET Data Provider

OLEDB can safely be claimed as a standard for accessing both relational and non-relational data. This means that it can be used to access data stored in any format, or queried via any method! OLEDB has been out in the open for quite a while now and has been the staple diet of ADO programmers, whenever it was necessary to connect to a data source for which an appropriate OLEDB Provider exists. It's still a source of high-performance data access methods for ADO.NET.

The OLEDB .NET provider classes can be found in the namespace `System.Data.OleDb`. Following are some of the classes that reside in the namespace, with their descriptions:

Class	Description
OleDbCommand	Used for execution of SQL statements or stored procedures against an OLEDB data source
OleDbConnection	Represents an open connection to an OLEDB data source
OleDbDataAdapter	Creates a bridge between the `DataSet` and the data source
OleDbDataReader	Provides a forward-only cursor (term explained earlier in the book) to read from an OLEDB data source
OleDbError	Holds information about errors and warnings that are returned by the data source
OleDbParameter	Represents a parameter to an `OleDbCommand`
OleDbTransaction	Represents an SQL transaction to be made at an OLEDB data source

You may have noticed the similarity between the two .NET provider classes, `SqlClient` and `OleDb`. As mentioned earlier, this may be explained by the fact that each of these classes implements a common interface, which is already defined and available in the namespaces, `System.Data` and `System.Security`. This also means that you can actually implement available interfaces and create your very own data provider, should you really want to!

OLEDB .NET data provider has been tested with, among others, the following providers, but note that it can be made to work with any data source that has an available OLEDB provider.

Provider	Description
SQLOLEDB	Microsoft OLEDB Provider for SQL Server
MSDAORA	Microsoft OLEDB Provider for Oracle
Microsoft.Jet.OLEDB.4.0	OLEDB Provider for Microsoft Access (which uses the Jet engine)

Let's implement the OLEDB .NET data provider, using the exact same code as we looked at earlier with a few minor changes.

Try It Out: A Simple Console Application Using the OLEDB Data Provider

In this example, we'll connect once again to our MSDE database, but using a different method this time – implementing the OLEDB .NET data provider instead of the SQL Server data provider. Note that it is encouraged that you use the SQL Server data provider for your real-world applications when dealing with SQL Server 7 and above. This example is just to show you how it's possible using OLEDB for comparison purposes.

1. Following the same steps as we did for our last example, create a new Console Application project called OleDbProvider in the chapter solution. Next, remove the auto-generated code from the code window and enter the code below. Name this file OleDbProvider.cs:

```
using System;
using System.Data;      // Includes some essential ADO.NET classes
using System.Data.OleDb; // Includes the OLEDB Provider classes

class OleDbProvider
{
  static void Main(string[] args)
  {
    // Our connection details
    string ConStr = @"server=(local)\NetSDK;provider=SQLOLEDB;" +
                    "Integrated Security=SSPI;database=Northwind";

    // Pass connection string to the OleDbConnection object
    OleDbConnection OleDbConn = new OleDbConnection(ConStr);
    try
    {
      // Open Connection to start reading
      OleDbConn.Open();

      // OleDb query string that we'll use to get data from the database
      string SQL = "SELECT * FROM Employees";

      // Pass the SQL query and Connection object to the OleDbCommand object
      OleDbCommand OleDbComm= new OleDbCommand(SQL,OleDbConn);

      // Read through each record returned
      OleDbDataReader OleDbReader = OleDbComm.ExecuteReader();
      Console.WriteLine("This program demonstrates the use of" +
```

```
                              " OLEDB .NET Data Provider");
        Console.WriteLine("Querying database '{0}' with query: " +
                    "'{1}'\n", OleDbConn.Database, OleDbComm.CommandText);
        Console.WriteLine("First Name\tLast Name\n");

        // Read() advances the cursor to the next record
        while(OleDbReader.Read())
        {
          // Retrieve values from the OleDbReader one record at a time
          Console.WriteLine("{0} | {1}",
                              OleDbReader["FirstName"].ToString().PadLeft(10),
                              OleDbReader["LastName"].ToString().PadLeft(10));
        }
      }
      catch(Exception ex)
      {
        // Catch an exception thrown, if any, and display
        Console.WriteLine("Error: " + ex.Message);
      }
      finally
      {
        // Close active connection
        OleDbConn.Close();
        Console.ReadLine();
      }
    }
  }
}
```

2. As one final step, we now need to make this project the default start-up project for our application so that this is the application that starts when we hit *F5*. Right-click on the project name, `OleDbProvider`, in the Solution Explorer, and select **Set as St*a*rtUp Project** from the menu.

3. Save and run your application again by pressing *F5*. Your code should produce the following output:

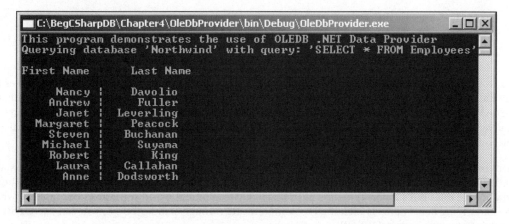

How It Works

Since the code is exactly the same as it was for our last example on the SQL Server data provider, we'll only discuss the major changes presented in the code.

You might notice mention of a new namespace, shaded below. This is the OLEDB .NET provider namespace and holds classes, which we can use directly in our code:

```
using System;
using System.Data;
using System.Data.OleDb;
```

The following code snippet is our connection string for the database. The only new thing here is that we've used the clause 'provider=SQLOLEDB'. This suggests that we'll be using the OLEDB data provider for SQL Server. Without this clause our application will not execute:

```
string ConStr = @"server=(local)\NetSDK;provider=SQLOLEDB;" +
                    "Integrated Security=SSPI;database=Northwind";
```

The rest of the code is identical to that which we saw in our previous example, except for the obvious differences in class names, for example `OleDbConnection`, `OleDbCommand`, and `OleDbDataReader` instead of the `Sql...` equivalents. This can be justified by the fact that each data provider follows a similar class name convention in the form xxxConnection, xxxCommand, xxxDataReader and so on, thus making developers' life much easier when it comes to porting from one data provider to another (for any reason there might be).

ODBC .NET Data Provider

ODBC .NET is a successor to the old faithful, native ODBC data provider. In the real world, ODBC still is widely used by a large number of developers; developers who make small applications that use minimal data access or developers who need to connect to older, more obscure data sources. For this reason, Microsoft decided to provide the ODBC .NET data provider, not as part of the Framework, but as an add-on component, downloadable from the Microsoft website.

This provider fills the need of connectivity to native ODBC drivers, which currently includes the following:

❑   SQL Server ODBC Driver

❑   ODBC Driver for Oracle

❑   Access ODBC Driver

It's worth mentioning that for a fact, you can use OLEDB to reach the above-mentioned databases just the way ODBC can. So where's the difference? The main difference between the two is the fact that ODBC works primarily with relational data, accessible through SQL only (even though you can read simple text files with it), whereas OLEDB can be used with any type of data source and communicate via any method (data sources like e-mail, spreadsheets, documents, and so on).

Because of ODBC's strict dependency on the physical structure of the data source, ODBC targets all underlying databases with the same layer of (SQL) code, decreasing efficiency in certain cases where the data source does not support the same SQL language (true in real-world scenarios); but in cases where the underlying data source is identified to communicate through standard SQL, you can use ODBC for a much faster access than OLEDB.

You should only use ODBC when it's necessary, for example you can choose to use ODBC if you're planning to use an old database for which an OLEDB provider is not available. Where an OLEDB provider exists, you're likely better off to use OLEDB over ODBC.

Once downloaded, the data provider classes for ODBC .NET can be found in the `Microsoft.Data.Odbc` namespace. This namespace should be included for any code that connects to an ODBC data source. Also, if you are using Visual Studio .NET, you will need to add a reference to the `Microsoft.Data.Odbc.dll` file from the Solution Explorer, as we learned earlier. In contrast, if you intend to compile your code using the command line outside of Visual Studio .NET, you must include a reference to the `.dll`, for example:

```
> csc /r:Microsoft.Data.Odbc.dll <file name>
```

Like other .NET data providers, ODBC .NET provider classes follow the same convention, and so classes within its namespace have the prefix `Odbc`. The following table lists some of the classes contained in the ODBC.NET namespace:

Class	Description
OdbcCommand	Used for execution of SQL statements or stored procedures against an ODBC data source
OdbcConnection	Represents an open connection to an ODBC data source
OdbcDataAdapter	Creates a bridge between the `DataSet` and the data source
OdbcDataReader	Provides a forward-only cursor to read from an ODBC data source
OdbcError	Holds information about errors and warnings that are returned by the data source
OdbcParameter	Represents a parameter to an `OdbcCommand`
OdbcTransaction	Represents a SQL transaction to be made at a data source

Let's take a look at the ODBC .NET data provider in the very same example we've been looking at previously.

Note that to run this next example you must firstly have the ODBC Data Provider installed on your system. In addition, you need to have created a new system DSN to connect to the SQL data source using your local instance, plus setting the default database to Northwind. If you're not familiar with the process, you should be able to follow the code without running it, because creating ODBC DSNs are beyond the scope of this book.

Try It Out: A Simple Console Application Using the ODBC Data Provider

Once again, we use the same MSDE database that we've been using for the last two examples in the chapter; only this time, we'll cover connecting to the database, using the ODBC .NET data provider.

1. Follow the same steps, as per the previous couple of examples, for creating a new Console Application project as part of the chapter solution and name this project OdbcProvider.

2. Clear all and enter the code below into the main file, renamed to OdbcProvider.cs:

```csharp
using System;
using System.Data;          // Includes some essential ADO.NET classes
using Microsoft.Data.Odbc;  // Includes the ODBC Data Provider classes

class OdbcProvider
{
  static void Main(string[] args)
  {
    // Our connection details
    string ConStr = "DSN=SQLODBC";

    // Pass connection string to the OdbcConnection object
    OdbcConnection OdbcConn = new OdbcConnection(ConStr);
    try
    {
      // Open Connection to start reading
      OdbcConn.Open();

      // Odbc query string that we'll use to get data from the database
      string SQL = "SELECT * FROM Employees";

      // Pass the SQL query and Connection object to the OdbcCommand object
      OdbcCommand OdbcComm= new OdbcCommand(SQL,OdbcConn);

      // Read through each record returned
      OdbcDataReader OdbcReader = OdbcComm.ExecuteReader();
      Console.WriteLine("This program demonstrates the use of" +
                        " ODBC .NET Data Provider");
      Console.WriteLine("Querying database '{0}' with query: " +
                        "'{1}'\n", OdbcConn.Database,
                        OdbcComm.CommandText);
      Console.WriteLine("First Name\tLast Name\n");

      // Read() advances the cursor to the next record
      while(OdbcReader.Read())
      {
        // Retrieve values from the OdbcDataReader one record at a time
        Console.WriteLine("{0} | {1}",
        OdbcReader["FirstName"].ToString().PadLeft(10),
        OdbcReader["LastName"].ToString().PadLeft(10));
      }
    }
    catch(Exception ex)
    {
      // Catch an exception thrown, if any, and display
      Console.WriteLine("Error: " + ex.Message);
    }
    finally
```

```
    {
        // Close active connection
        OdbcConn.Close();
        Console.ReadLine();
    }
}
}
```

3. We need to perform two more steps before we can run our application. Firstly, you need to add a reference to `Microsoft.Data.Odbc.dll` so that our code can compile. In the solution explorer, right-click on the **References** section in our project, and select **Add Reference**. In the dialog that appears, select the `Microsoft.Data.Odbc.dll` component from the **.NET** tab, click the **Select** button to the right, then click on **OK**:

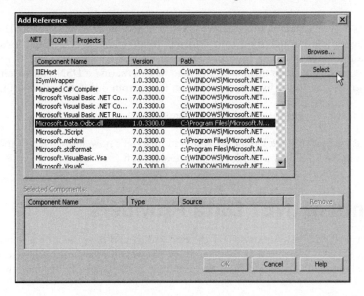

4. Right-click on the name of the project in the Solution Explorer and set it to be the default startup project, as we did for the `OleDb` example.

5. Hit *F5* to run the application and you should see the following output:

How It Works

Let's look quickly at the changes that are important. The first to mention would be the addition of the following namespace:

```
using Microsoft.Data.Odbc;
```

This line includes the ODBC .NET Provider classes. In order to run the application, we also needed to make sure we had a reference to `Microsoft.Data.Odbc.dll` in the project.

The second obvious change in the code is the connection string. We have added the following new clause to it.

```
DSN=SQLODBC;
```

This indicates the use of a Data Source Name (DSN), created by using the ODBC Data source Administrator (accessible through the Control panel), by the name **SQLODBC**. Consider a DSN to be something like a reference or a path to a specific database and the server ((local)\NetSDK for server and Northwind for database, in this case). Because while creating a DSN you specify a specific server and a database to use, the following clause has been taken from our connection string:

```
"server=(local)\NetSDK;database=Northwind"
```

Having looked at each of the .NET data providers in turn, let's now study each of the individual components that make up a data provider in our next section.

Components of .NET Data Providers

So far, we've covered quite a lot about .NET data providers and have seen code samples making use of different provider classes, objects, and their methods. However, only four of these objects represent the core fundamental elements needed to form the dynamic .NET data provider model. These objects are:

- ❑ Connection
- ❑ Command
- ❑ DataReader
- ❑ DataAdapter

You've probably noticed that all of the .NET providers we came across implement their own version of these objects with their respective prefixes attached. In reality, all of these objects implement a set of common interfaces, provided by the .NET Framework, and further customize them by adding their respective provider-specific details. Let's now study each of these objects in a little detail as a preview of what to expect in some of the upcoming chapters.

The Connection Object

A `Connection` object is primarily used to establish an active connection with a data source. Once the connection has been made, other objects that are independent of connection details – yet dependent on an active connection, such as the `Command` object, may use the connection to run commands on the data source.

Every .NET data provider has its own provider-specific version of the connection class that you can instantiate, which implements the IDbConnection interface available through the System.Data namespace. For instance, SqlConnection and OleDbConnection both implement the IDbConnection interface. This interface represents a unique session with a data source and provides basic connection operations that allow users to close, open, or change connections at will.

A connection is usually established by an explicit call made to the Open() method. Once it has served its purpose, like populating a DataSet object with relational data from a data source, a call made to the Close() method explicitly closes the connection. It's good practice to ensure you always explicitly close a connection when it's not being used to eliminate any excess drain on server resources.

If for any reason you do not explicitly close the connection yourself, the Garbage Collector finds the unreferenced Connection object and collects it. However, it is preferable to close the connection explicitly when it's not needed as it makes sure all changes made to the database are persisted.

The Command Object

The Command object is responsible for querying the data source, among other things, by using SQL statements. Our commands can take many forms; we can attempt to update, modify, or retrieve data from the data source through a simple SQL query string or through a stored procedure. If a result is returned after issuing a command to the database, the Command object can populate it in a DataReader, return it as a scalar value (for instance, the numbers of rows affected), or return the result as parameters.

All .NET data provider Command classes implement the IDbCommand interface. The three default functions available for executing commands are:

❑ ExecuteReader, which returns a populated DataReader object

❑ ExecuteScalar, which returns a scalar value

❑ ExecuteNonQuery, which returns the number of rows affected by the command that was executed

The DataReader Object

The DataReader object is probably one of the most important, when it comes to retrieving data from the database. As the name suggests, it reads through every record from a database and provides fast, unbuffered, read-only, sequential access to the database. In addition, the DataReader has a very tidy way of accessing data; it considers the incoming stream of data as a collection, so it loops through the data and loads one row at a time, just as you might through an array perhaps, thus reducing system overhead and resulting in an increase in application performance. We'll find out more about the DataReader object in Chapter 7.

The DataAdapter Object

The DataAdapter serves as a gateway to the disconnected world from the .NET Provider model by bridging between the DataSet and the data source, and providing methods for retrieving and saving data.

The `DataAdapter` object fits well in a connected or disconnected environment because it exposes two very useful methods, namely the `Fill()` and the `Update()` methods. The `Fill()` method synchronizes the data held in the data source with that in the `DataSet`. Calling the `Update()` method updates the data source with the modified data within the `DataSet`; this could be anything from a single row to an addition of a new table. We'll find out more about the `DataAdapter` in conjunction with the `DataSet` in Chapter 8.

The DataSet

The `DataSet` is the heart of ADO.NETs offline scenario. This class represents an in-memory, offline container for relational data, originated by any type of an external data source (an XML file, an Access database etc.).

It's more of a glutton of a container; keep filling it with data and it'll happily devour it, unless you eventually run out of system memory or local disk space, since it's an in-memory relational data structure.

At one time, it can represent many tables, in the form of `DataTable` objects, which can further represent any number of columns, rows, constraints, and relationships as `DataColumn`, `DataRow`, `Constraint`, and `DataRelation` objects respectively. We'll cover more on this in Chapter 8, *The DataSet and the DataAdapter*.

A `DataSet` can hold data that provides a relational data model independent of the data source and, in addition, exposes itself as a hierarchical representation of relational data while disconnected from the data source. Because the `DataSet` has no perception of what data source it's linked to, it can work as effectively with data local to the application and can thus store it in an external source or file.

The following diagram can better express the hierarchical object model of a `DataSet`, its origin, and the relational data model it can contain. You can also see how neatly it arranges and holds relational data:

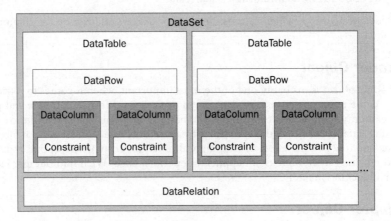

We'll find out a lot more about the `DataSet` in Chapter 8.

Summary

In this chapter, we saw why ADO.NET is gaining stature in the data access world, especially with its support for the disconnected Internet world. Also, we spent time going over legacy technologies and their support in ADO.NET. We shuffled through the available .NET data providers and saw how their constituent components unleash their power and effectively accomplish tasks when they get down to business. In addition, we saw each of the .NET data providers work using basic examples to contrast between their available methods and functionalities.

In this chapter we have connected to a SQL Server database using three different methods:

❑ Using the `System.Data.SqlClient` classes

❑ Using the `System.Data.OleDb` classes

❑ Using the `Microsoft.Data.Odbc` classes that are an additional download from the Microsoft site

By connecting to the same database using three different methods we've seen how similar our code can be, even though the methods we use to connect to the data are quite different.

Finally, we introduced some of the core components of .NET data access, including:

❑ The `Connection` object

❑ The `Command` object

❑ The `DataReader`

❑ The `DataAdapter`

❑ The `DataSet`

In the next chapters we'll look at these in more detail, starting with the `Connection` object in the next chapter.

Exercises

1. What object in ADO.NET supports working with data while disconnected from the data source?

2. What are the four fundamental objects in the .NET Provider model?

3. Write a Console application using the SQL Server provider with our MSDE Northwind database and retrieve the `CompanyName` and `ContactName` column values from the `Customers` table.

For further investigation, you might want to look through the .NET documentation and look at the .NET Framework class reference. Browse through the Data classes and look through some of the properties and methods. This will give you more of an idea of what to expect when working with data in .NET

Solutions to these exercises are available for free download from http://www.wrox.com/ from the code download page for this book.

There's also an online discussion forum for this book that you can use to discuss the solutions, or any other problems you may be having at http://p2p.wrox.com/list.asp?list=beginning_c_sharp_database

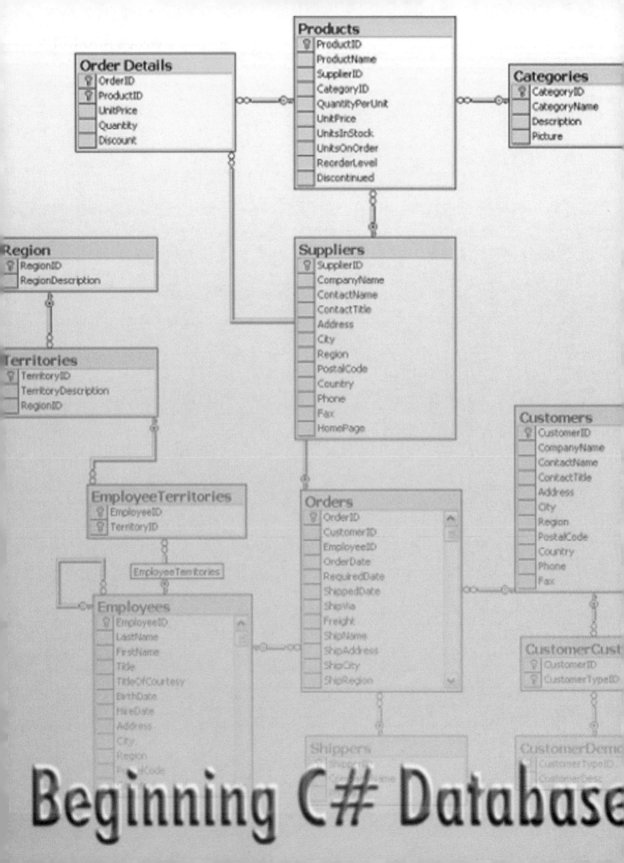

5

Connecting to the Database

Before we can do anything useful with the data in our database, we need to establish a connection to it. The first step in connecting to a database is to create a `Connection` object from the appropriate .NET data provider. In this chapter, we'll focus on the different .NET data providers available, and examine in detail how to establish a connection using them, what problems you might come across along the way, and how to go about solving them.

By the end of this chapter, you will have learned how to:

❑ Use `Connection` objects with each of the major .NET data providers

❑ Build connection strings to specify options when opening the connection

❑ Use the different clauses within connection strings

❑ Understand and solve common connection problems

❑ Specify users and passwords

❑ Work with the most common methods and properties of the `Connection` object

Connection Objects in .NET Data Providers

As we saw in the last chapter, each .NET data provider has its own namespace and its own `Connection` object. These are summarized in the table below:

.NET Data Provider	Namespace	Connection object name
SQL Server	`System.Data.SqlClient`	`SqlConnection`
OLE DB	`System.Data.OleDb`	`OleDbConnection`
ODBC	`Microsoft.Data.Odbc`	`OdbcConnection`
Oracle	`System.Data.OracleClient`	`OracleConnection`

The Oracle .NET data provider referred to here is a Microsoft product in beta release at the time of writing. See the OracleClient example at the end of this chapter for more details.

As you can see, the names follow a similar convention, using Connection but starting with a prefix specific to the .NET data provider. Each .NET data provider Connection object inherits a common set of methods and properties from the IDBConnection interface, so the use of each one follows a similar pattern, with differences only in detail. Each one adds methods and properties that provide additional functions specific to a particular database. Let's look at the use of one of these objects, SqlConnection, with a simple example.

Connecting to MSDE with SqlConnection

We'll connect to the MSDE database that we discussed in Chapter 1. Because MSDE is a desktop version of SQL Server, we'll use the SqlConnection object in the SQL Server .NET data provider for the connection.

Try It Out: Using SqlConnection

1. In Visual Studio .NET, create a new Solution and call it Chapter5_Examples.

2. Within your solution, make a new Visual C# console application project and give it the name Connection_Sql. Name the main file Connection_Sql.cs and enter the following code:

```
using System;
using System.Data;
// use SQL Server .NET Data Provider namespace
using System.Data.SqlClient;

namespace Wrox.BeginningCSharpDatabases.Chapter05
{
  class Connection_Sql
  {
    static void Main()
    {
      // create SqlConnection object
      SqlConnection thisConnection = new SqlConnection();

      // Set connection string to connect to .NET SDK MSDE
      thisConnection.ConnectionString =
      // server instance name - may also be (local)\VSdotNET
      @"Server=(local)\NetSDK;" +
      // use Windows login
      "Integrated Security=SSPI;" +
      // wait only 5 seconds
      "Connection Timeout=5;" ;

      try
      {
        // Open connection
```

```
      thisConnection.Open();
      // report success
      Console.WriteLine("Connection Successfully Opened!");
      // close connection
      thisConnection.Close();
      // close was successful
      Console.WriteLine("Connection Successfully Closed!");
    }
    // catch exception if Open failed
    catch (SqlException ex)
    {
      // Display details of error
      Console.WriteLine(ex.ToString());
    }
  }
}
}
```

3. Now build the example and run it without debugging (Debug | Start without Debugging or *ctrl-F5*). If the connection is successful, you'll see this output appear in the program's console window:

If the connection failed, you will see an error message much like the following:

Bear in mind that connections fail all the time for reasons that have nothing to do with your code. It may be because a server wasn't started, a password is wrong, or some other configuration problem. We'll look at common problems with setting up database connections in detail shortly in *Debugging Connections to SQL Server*.

How It Works

Let's go through the example code in `Connection_Sql.cs` to understand the steps in the connection process. The first thing we need to do is specify the namespaces for ADO.NET and the SQL Server .NET data provider, so we can use these system classes without having to specify the full namespace along with the class name each time:

```
using System;
using System.Data;
using System.Data.SqlClient;
```

Next, we create the namespace, class, and `Main()` function definitions for this program:

```
namespace Wrox.BeginningCSharpDatabases.Chapter05
{
  class Connection_Sql
  {
    static void Main()
    {
```

Because this example is so small, we do all of our work in the `Main()` function; let's look at it line by line. The first thing we do here is create the `Connection` object. In this case the actual class we create is a `SqlConnection` object, because we are using the SQL Server .NET data provider:

```
SqlConnection thisConnection = new SqlConnection();
```

This creates an uninitialized `SqlConnection` object, so before using it we must set its properties. The most important property of a `Connection` object is `ConnectionString`, which specifies the name of the database server and any other information needed to make the connection. A **connection string** is a quoted character string, containing a list of clauses of the form:

```
name=value;
```

Each clause may appear in any order in the string. In our example, the connection string contains three clauses: the server, security, and timeout clauses, each of which ends with a semicolon (;):

```
thisConnection.ConnectionString =
    @"Server=(local)\NetSDK;" +
    "Integrated Security=SSPI;" +
    "Connection Timeout=5;" ;
```

The semicolon is a separator and is optional at the end of the last clause. It's a good idea to include one at the end anyway, in case you want to tack on another option to the list later. Each clause is specified on a separate line for clarity, but we could easily have put them together in one line.

If you have worked with ADO, the use of connection strings may be familiar. Actually, you'll find that the `Connection` *object in ADO.NET is the closest match to ADO in any part of ADO.NET, so don't expect to see this similarity in other areas.*

Let's briefly examine each of the connection clauses in this example. The server clause specifies the name of the SQL Server instance we want to connect to:

```
@"Server=(local)\NetSDK;"
```

For SQL Server instance names, `(local)` means a SQL Server located on the same machine as the client program, so we specify it as `(local)\NetSDK`. We'll cover connections to non-local servers soon. (The `@` is needed to indicate a literal string constant, since there is a backslash (\) in the instance name, which is a C# escape character.) We want to connect to the MSDE instance from Visual Studio .NET, which is called `NetSDK`, and it is located on the machine where we are using Visual Studio .NET.

If you installed the `(local)\VSdotNET` instance of MSDE that comes with Visual Studio .NET, then you should use that name in the server clause instead.

The next clause indicates that we should use our Windows login as the login and password to SQL Server:

```
"Integrated Security=SSPI;"
```

Recall that SSPI stands for Security Support Provider Interface, and links the security system of SQL Server with Windows security, so that we can log in to the SQL Server database using the current Windows login. We could alternatively use `True` instead of `SSPI`, as they both have the same effect.

SQL Server must be set up so that your Windows login has access; this is the default for the MSDE instance that comes with Visual Studio .NET, but may not be true for another SQL Server. We'll talk about this in more detail later in this chapter in *Security and Passwords in SqlConnection*.

Finally, the timeout clause sets the connection timeout to 5 seconds:

```
"Connection Timeout=5;"
```

This controls how long our program waits before returning an error when trying to connect to a non-existent server. We would have omitted this clause, but the default is 15 seconds, which is a bit long to wait for a connection to the local machine; maybe just long enough for you to type *Ctrl-C* or do something else rash! For a non-local connection, a longer timeout may be appropriate.

Before we continue, we should quickly look at another important clause, which we omitted in this example – the database clause:

```
"Database=Northwind;"
```

Now we've got our connection string, we still need to activate the connection to the database by calling the `Open()` method on our `SqlConnection` object. If an error happens during connection, this is where the exception from the error will be thrown, so we must put the operation in a `try ... catch` block:

```
try
{
  thisConnection.Open();
```

If there is no error, then the connection was opened successfully. We print a message after calling `Open()` to show that it worked:

```
Console.WriteLine("Connection Successfully Opened!");
```

Sometimes, when debugging a program with more complex logic, your code may never call `Open()`, even though you think it should, so it's always a good idea to print a message like this when first developing a database program.

At this stage in the code, we would normally issue a query or do some other database operation to use the open connection. However, we'll look at that in the following chapters, so for now, we'll concentrate on the connection and won't actually issue any database commands.

When we're finished with the connection, we call `Close()` to deactivate it:

```
thisConnection.Close();
```

It is very important to always call the `Close()` method.

> Connections are expensive; they take up memory space on both the client and server machines. Garbage collection happens only for memory on the client machine where the C# program is running, and does not get rid of open connections to the server. Too many open connections can slow a server down or prevent new connections from being made.

Now we print a message to show that the `Close()` method call was successful:

```
Console.WriteLine("Connection Successfully Closed!");
```

It's very rare for `Close()` to fail or generate an error. We can call the `Close()` method several times with no exception being generated, even if the connection was already closed. We display the message for the purpose of this example simply to show that the `Close()` method was indeed called.

If a connection error occurred, we do not see the close message because an exception is thrown. We have an exception handler to handle the case of the failure to open:

```
catch (SqlException ex)  // catch exception if Open failed
{
  Console.WriteLine(ex.ToString());  // Display details of error
}
```

Each .NET data provider has a specific exception class for its error handling; `SqlException` is the class for the SQL Server .NET data provider. The `ToString()` method of the exception handler returns a SQL Server-specific error message and the location of the error.

That's it! We are finished with our first connection example. Since, however, we are on the subject of errors, let's look at how to find the cause of these errors.

Debugging Connections to SQL Server

Writing the C# code to use a `Connection` object is usually the easy part of getting a connection to work. Problems often lie not in the code, but rather in a mismatch in the connection parameters between the client (your C# program) and the database server. All the connection parameters have to match. Even experienced database professionals often have problems getting a connection to work the first time.

The diagram below illustrates some of the connection parameters:

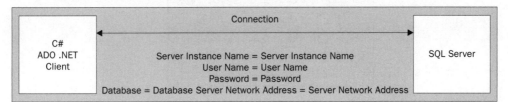

There are more parameters than shown here, but you get the idea. A corollary of Murphy's Law applies to connections: if several things can go wrong, surely one of them will. Our goal is to check both sides of the connection to make sure all of your assumptions are correct and that everything the client program specifies is matched correctly on the server.

Often the solution is on the server side, not the client side. If SQL Server is not running, then the client will be trying to connect to a server instance that does not exist. If the user name and password on the client do not match the name and password of a user who is authorized to access the SQL Server database, then the connection will be rejected. If the database requested in the connection does not exist, there will be an error. If the client's network information does not match the server's, then the server may not receive the client's connection request, or the server response may not reach the client.

For connection problems, using the debugger to locate the line of code where the error occurs usually doesn't help – the problem almost always occurs on the call to the `Open()` method. The question is why? We need to look at the error message.

A typical error is:

```
Unhandled Exception: System.ArgumentException:
  Unknown connection option in connection string: user.
```

The most likely cause for this is a simple typographical error in one of the clauses in your connection string. Make sure you have entered what you really meant to.

Probably the most common message when trying to connect to SQL Server is this one:

```
System.Data.SqlClient.SqlException:
 SQL Server does not exist or access denied.
   at System.Data.SqlClient.SqlConnection.Open()
   at Wrox.BeginningCSharpDatabases.Chapter05.Connection_Sql.Main() in
C:\BegCSharpDB\Chapter5\Connection_Sql.cs:line 23
```

In this case, most likely SQL Server (or MSDE) is not running. Go to the SQL Server Service Manager and make sure that the server is running. It should look like this screen:

You should be able to find SQL Server Service Manager in the system tray at the bottom right-hand corner of your Windows Desktop, or from the Start menu under Programs | MSDE | Service Manager. *If you have a full version of SQL Server 2000, the service manager is located in* Start | Programs | Microsoft SQL Server | Service Manager.

If the green arrow is not displayed on the server icon on the left, press Start/Continue to start the server. You may also want to check the box to ensure that the server is started automatically when Windows is started. When the green arrow appears, try running the example program again.

You can also start the MDSE NetSDK instance from the command line by typing the following command:

```
> net start MSSQL$NetSDK
```

Other possible causes of this message are:

❑ The SQL Server instance name is incorrect – we typed (local)\NetSDK, but your machine might use (local)\VSdotNET instance instead. It's also possible that SQL Server was already installed as (local) with no instance name, or is on another machine (see the next section). Correct the instance name if this is the case.

❑ The MSDE program has not been installed – go back to Chapter 1 and follow the instructions there for installing MSDE.

❑ A security problem – your Windows login and password do not match the ones on the server side. This is unlikely to be the problem when talking to a (local) SQL Server, unless you installed MSDE under a different Windows login from the one you are using to write C# programs. We'll talk more about this in the *Security and Passwords in Sql Connection* section later on.

❑ A hardware problem – again unlikely since in this case we are trying to connect to a server on the same machine.

Maybe you didn't install MSDE because you have access to SQL Server on another machine in your office LAN. Let's talk about how to connect in that situation.

Connecting to a SQL Server on Another Server Machine

Note that on the Service Manager window shown previously, the actual machine name of the server is shown instead of (local). My machine is called CT57709-A, so the full SQL Server instance name is \\CT57709-A\NetSDK. We could have also specified the machine name when specifying the connection, for example:

```
@"Server=CT57709-A\NetSDK;"
```

However, this would only work on my machine, not yours! (local) is more universal. However, to connect to a SQL Server instance located on another machine in your network, you must specify the actual machine name as part of the instance name, as shown above.

The instance name may be different as well, depending on how SQL Server has been set up by your database administrator. If only one SQL Server is running on a server machine, in many cases it is set up so that no separate instance name is needed – the name of the SQL Server instance is the same as the machine name. For example, to connect to a SQL Server running on a machine named ORION where no separate instance name has been setup, simply specify ORION as the data source:

```
@"Server=ORION;"
```

If you're accessing the SQL Server over a TCP/IP network, you can just specify the IP address of the server machine, as in:

```
@"Server=123.123.123.123;"
```

This also works with an instance name; simply add the instance name to the IP address separated by a backslash, as with the machine name:

```
@"Server=123.123.123.123\NetSDK;"
```

See your database administrator if you are not sure which of these variations is right in your situation.

To check the SQL Server parameters, the database administrator can use the SQL Enterprise Manager to check the server configuration to make sure the server network information, database name, and security (login/password) information on the server are what you think they are.

Security and Passwords in SqlConnection

As we saw in the first chapter, there are two ways of logging in to SQL Server. The first, preferred way is to use Windows integrated security, as we did in the first example. The SQL Server uses your Windows login to access the database. Your Windows login must exist on the machine where SQL server is running, and your login must be authorized to access the SQL Server database, or be a member of a user group that has that access.

If you don't include the "Integrated Security = SSPI" (or "Integrated Security = True" clause in the connection string, the connection defaults to SQL Server security which uses a separate login and password within SQL Server.

If you forget the integrated security clause you'll most likely see this message:

```
Unhandled Exception: System.Data.SqlClient.SqlException: Login failed for
user '(null)'. Reason: Not associated with a trusted SQL Server connection.
    at System.Data.SqlClient.SqlConnection.Open()
```

To correct this, add the `"Integrated Security = SSPI"` clause to the connection string

How to Use SQL Server Security

If you really did intend to use SQL Server security because that is how your company or department has set up access to your SQL Server (perhaps because some clients are non-Microsoft), then you need to specify a username and password in the connection string, as shown here:

```
thisConnection.ConnectionString =
    @"Server=(local)\NetSDK;" +  // server instance name
    "user id=sa;" +              // Default SQL Server administrator user name
    "password=x1y2z3;" +         // SQL Server password
    "Connection Timeout=5;"      // wait only 5 seconds
```

The `sa` user name is the default system administrator account for SQL Server. If a specific user has been set up, such as `george` or `payroll`, then specify that name. The password for `sa` is set when SQL Server is installed. If the user name you use has no password, you can omit the password clause entirely or specify an empty password as follows:

```
password=;
```

However, a blank password is bad practice that should be avoided, even for a test setup.

Connection String Clauses in SqlConnection

The allowable clauses within the connection string are summarized in the table below:

Name	Example	Aliases	Default Value	Allowed Values	Description
Data Source	Data Source= (local)\Net SDK	Server Address Addr	None	Server name, instance name, server address	Name of the target SQL Server Instance
Integrated Security	Integrated Security=SSPI	Trusted_ Connection	false	True False Yes No SSPI	Tells if the Windows login is used to access SQL Server
Connect Timeout	Connection Timeout=5	Connection Timeout	15	0-32767	How long to wait for connection

Name	Example	Aliases	Default Value	Allowed Values	Description
Database	`Database= Northwind`	`Initial Catalog`	`master`	Any database that exists on server	Which database you wish to use
User ID	`User ID=sa`	`UID`		Any valid SQL Server user	User name if not using Windows security
Password	`Password= x1y2z3`	`PWD`		Password for SQL Server user	Password if not using Windows security
Workstation ID	`Workstation ID=machine999`		Network name of this machine	Any string	

The 'aliases' column in this table shows alternative names for each clause. For example you can specify the server using any of these clauses:

```
"Data Source=(local)\NetSDK"
"Server=(local)\NetSDK"
"Address=(local)\NetSDK"
"Addr=(local)\NetSDK"
```

Each of these variants has exactly the same meaning. I prefer to use `Server` when connecting to SQL Server because it helps me remember that it is the server instance that goes in that place in the connection string. `Data Source` is a more generic term that works in `SqlConnection` and also all the other .NET data providers, but it means different things within each provider.

The clauses listed here are the ones used for basic database operations. There are many other clauses that can be specified in the connection string for `SqlConnection`. You can see the complete list in the Visual Studio .NET online documentation under the topic *SqlConnection.ConnectionString Property*. (You can view the documentation either by clicking the link from the Visual Studio .NET program group on your **Start** menu, or over the web, at http://msdn.microsoft.com.) Most of these additional clauses specify low-level details of the network connection, such as network protocol, network packet size, size of the connection pool, and so on. Most applications do not need to change these low-level implementation details and should use the default values.

Connection Pooling

One low-level detail that is worth noting – even though you should not change it – is **connection pooling**. Recall that creating connections is expensive in terms of memory and time. With pooling, a closed connection is not immediately destroyed but is kept in memory in a pool of unused connections. If a new connection request comes in that matches the properties of one of the unused connections in the pool, then the unused connection is retrieved from the pool and used as the new connection.

Creating a totally new connection over the network can take seconds whereas reusing a pooled connection can happen in milliseconds; it is much faster to used pooled connections. The connection string has clauses that can change the size of the connection pool or even turn off connection pooling; my advice is don't mess with these clauses; it will hurt performance unless you are an expert and really know what you are doing. The default values (for example, connection pooling is on by default) are good for 99% of applications. See the Visual Studio .NET online help under the topic *Connection Pooling for the SQL Server .NET Data Provider* for complete details.

Improving Your Use of Connection Objects

The code in the first sample program was very simple so we could concentrate on how a `Connection` object works. Now we're going to improve this program to make a better model for you to follow when creating and using `Connection` objects in the future.

Using the Connection String in the Connection Object Constructor

We have seen how to create of the `SqlConnection` object and specify the connection string in separate steps. Since you always have to specify a connection string when using a connection object, `SqlConnection` (as well as the connection objects for other .NET data providers) has another overloaded constructor that takes the connection string as a parameter:

```
// create SqlConnection object
SqlConnection thisConnection = new SqlConnection(
    @"Server=(local)\NetSDK;" +
    "Integrated Security=SSPI;" +
    "Connection Timeout=5;" );
```

This constructor sets the `ConnectionString` property immediately on creating the `SqlConnection` object, and is a more common way to initialize connection strings, so we'll stick to this method from now on.

Use finally for Closing Connections

Now we want to talk about a better way to ensure that the connection to the database is always closed. We have seen it very briefly already; it involves putting the `Close()` method call in a `finally` block in the exception handling logic of the function that opens the connection.

Try it Out: Using finally to Close a Connection

1. Create a new application within the chapter solution, and call it `Finally`. Name the main file `Finally.cs`.

2. Copy over the code from the previous example, and add the following highlighted code to `Main()`:

```
static void Main()
{
  // create SqlConnection object
  SqlConnection thisConnection =
  new SqlConnection(
    @"Server=(local)\NetSDK;" +      // server instance name
    "Integrated Security=SSPI;" +    // use Windows login
    "Connection Timeout=5;" );       // wait 5 seconds for server
  try
  {
    // open connection
    thisConnection.Open();
    // open was successful
    Console.WriteLine("Connection Successfully Opened!");
  }
  catch (SqlException ex)
  {
    Console.WriteLine(ex.ToString());
  }
  finally
  {
    // close connection
    thisConnection.Close();
    // close was called
    Console.WriteLine("Finally Block: Connection Closed.");
  }
}
```

3. Right-click on the Finally project in the solution explorer and select "Set as StartUp Project" from the context menu.

4. Try running this program without debugging (*Ctrl-F5* in Visual Studio .NET). If the SQL Server service is running, the program produces this output:

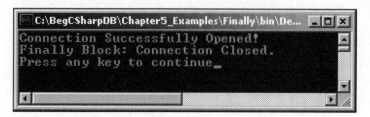

Try stopping the SQL Server service and running the program again to see what happens if there is an exception:

How It Works

Within the `finally` block, `Close()` is called before the `Main()` method exits, whether an exception occurs or not, so the `finally` block executes in both cases to close the connection. This is a good pattern to follow, since it ensures a closed connection in all cases. Suppose an exception occurs after the connection is made, for example, when reading data from the database. In this case, a call to `Close()` that is placed in the regular logic would never be made. Placing it in the `finally` block ensures that it is called.

Although it does not hurt to call `Close()` twice – it would not throw an exception – we have removed the `Close()` method call from the `try` block, where it was placed in our first example.

As an aside, there is a case where multiple calls to `Close()` make sense. ADO.NET is set up to do offline processing of data, even when the connection to the .NET data provider has been closed. The `try` block for this pattern looks like this:

```
try
{
   thisConnection.Open();   // open connection for initial query

   /* do online processing of data here - SQL queries,
   read data, load in-memory structures, etc. */

   thisConnection.Close();   // close connection

   /* do offline processing here - change data in memory,
   read & write XML, etc. */

   thisConnection.Open();   // re-open connection for update

   /* do update of data here - SQL UPDATE/INSERT/DELETE operations,
   write data, etc.*/

   thisConnection.Close();   // close connection
}
```

Because SQL connections are expensive to keep open, it is good practice to open the connection, load data into the program with database queries, and then close the connection to do offline processing of the data. If we need to update the database after offline processing, we then re-open the connection to perform the update.

The `finally` block still contains a `Close()` call that is called twice if no exceptions are encountered, but this doesn't cause a problem. Whether this is worth the complexity it adds to our code depends on the extent of the in-memory processing being done. Many programs just hold the connection open while doing the processing, and then use the connection to update the database. However, with connection pooling, re-opening a closed connection is cheaper than one might think.

Displaying Connection Information

The `Connection` object has several properties that contain information about the connection. Most of these properties are read-only, since their purpose is to display rather than set information. (Connection values are set in the connection string.) These properties are often useful when debugging connections, in order to verify that the connection properties at run time are what we expect them to be.

Here, we'll describe the connection information properties common to most .NET data providers. The complete list of properties and methods is available in the Visual Studio .NET online documentation under the heading *SqlConnection Members*. Later in the chapter, we'll see some of the properties specific to other .NET Data Providers.

Try It Out: Displaying Connection Information

We're going to copy and modify our `Finally.cs` example program to display these properties, and then we'll explain what each change means.

1. Create a new console application and call it `Display`. Call the main file `Display.cs`.

2. Copy over the code from the previous example, then modify the example program shown previously by adding the following lines to the `try` block after the connection is opened:

```
try
{
  // open connection
  thisConnection.Open();
  // close was successful
  Console.WriteLine("Connection Successfully Opened!");

  // Display connection properties
  Console.WriteLine("Connection Properties:");
  Console.WriteLine("\tConnection String: {0}",
                    thisConnection.ConnectionString);
  Console.WriteLine("\tDatabase: {0}", thisConnection.Database);
  Console.WriteLine("\tDataSource: {0}", thisConnection.DataSource);
  Console.WriteLine("\tServerVersion: {0}", thisConnection.ServerVersion);
  Console.WriteLine("\tState: {0}", thisConnection.State);
  Console.WriteLine("\tWorkstationId: {0}", thisConnection.WorkstationId);
}
```

When you execute this program, the output is as follows:

How It Works

The `ConnectionString` property can be both read from and written to. Here we display it (`\t` is the tab character and is used to indent the display a bit):

```
Console.WriteLine("\tConnection String: {0}",
                thisConnection.ConnectionString);
```

We are basically printing out the value we just assigned to it when creating the `Connection` object:

```
Connection String: Server=(local)\NetSDK;Integrated Security=SSPI;Connection
Timeout=5;
```

What is the point in that, you might ask? Well, it is handy when debugging connections to verify that the connection string really contains the values we believed we assigned. For example, if we're trying out different connection options we may have different connection string clauses inserted in the program. We may have commented out one intending to use it later but forgotten about it – printing out the `ConnectionString` property helps to see that a clause is missing.

> Note that in a Windows Forms or other non-console program you can use the
> `System.Diagnostics Trace` and `Debug` classes to display this information in a way that does
> not interfere with your program's main user interface.

The next line displays the `Database` property. Since a SQL Server instance has several databases, this property shows which one we are initially using when we connect:

```
Console.WriteLine("\tDatabase: {0}", thisConnection.Database);
```

In our program it displays:

```
Database: master
```

We did not specify a database in our connection string, so it connects to the default database, which is usually the `master` database (it will always exist in any SQL Server instance). If we wanted to connect to the `Northwind` sample database, for example, then we need to specify that in the connection string:

```
// create SqlConnection object
SqlConnection thisConnection = new SqlConnection(
  @"Server=(local)\NetSDK;" +
  "Database=Northwind;" +
  "Connection Timeout=5;" );
```

Again, this is a handy property to display for debugging purposes. If you get an error message saying that a particular table doesn't exist, often the root of the problem is not the table, but that you are connecting to the wrong database. Displaying the `Database` property helps you to find that kind of error more quickly.

If you specify a database in the connection string that does not exist on the server, you may see the error:

System.Data.SqlClient.SqlException: Cannot open database requested in login 'Northwind'. Login fails.

This can happen if you didn't run the script to create the Northwind sample database when installing MSDE.

We can change the database currently used on a connection with the `ChangeDatabase()` method. We'll see a good use for that method in the next chapter.

The next line displays the `DataSource` property, which gives the server instance name for SQL Server database connections:

```
Console.WriteLine("\tDataSource: {0}", thisConnection.DataSource);
```

In our example it displays the same SQL Server instance name we have been using in all the examples so far:

```
        DataSource: (local)\NetSDK
```

The utility of this again is mainly for debugging purposes.

Continuing looking through our example, the `ServerVersion` property displays, as you would expect, the server version information:

```
Console.WriteLine("\tServerVersion: {0}", thisConnection.ServerVersion);
```

In our example it shows the SQL Server 2000 version for MSDE as included with Visual Studio .NET (SQL Server 2000 came after SQL Server 7.0, so it is considered version 8.x of SQL Server):

```
        ServerVersion: 08.00.0384
```

The version number is useful for debugging. This piece of information actually comes from the server, so it shows that information has flowed across the connection from the server.

Our next line is as follows:

```
Console.WriteLine("\tState: {0}", thisConnection.State);
```

The `State` property indicates whether the connection is open or closed. Since we display this property after the `Open()` method call, it shows that the connection is open:

```
State: Open
```

We have been printing a message indicating that the connection is open, but this property indicates that information directly. If the connection is closed, then the `State` property contains the string `Closed`.

The `WorkstationId` property is specific to SQL Server, but is very handy for debugging, so it deserves a mention:

```
Console.WriteLine("\tWorkstationId: {0}", thisConnection.WorkstationId);
```

The workstation ID is a string identifying the client computer. It defaults to the computer name as shown in the Network Identification section of the properties of the system. Recall that my computer was named `CT57709-A`, and that is the name that displays in the workstation ID on my system:

```
WorkstationId: CT57709-A
```

What makes this useful for debugging is that the SQL Server tools on the server can display which workstation ID issued a particular command. If we don't know which machine is causing a problem we can modify our programs to display the `WorkstationId` property and compare them to the workstation IDs displayed on the server.

We can also set this property with the workstation ID connection string clause as shown below, so if we want all the workstations in, say, Building B to show that information on the server you can indicate that in the program:

```
// create SqlConnection object
SqlConnection thisConnection = new SqlConnection(
    @"Server=(local)\NetSDK;" +              // server instance name
    "Integrated Security=SSPI;" +        // use Windows login
    "workstation ID=Building B Machine 75;" +  // identify machine
    "Connection Timeout=5;" );            // wait 5 seconds for server
```

This modification to the program produces this output:

```
Connection Successfully Opened!
Connection Properties:
        Connection String: Server=(local)\NetSDK;Integrated Security=SSPI;
        workstation ID=Building B Machine 75;Connection Timeout=5;
        Connection Timeout: 5
        Database: master
        DataSource: (local)\NetSDK
        ServerVersion: 08.00.0384
        State: Open
        WorkstationId: Building B Machine 75
Finally Block: Connection Closed.
```

That finishes off the basic `SqlConnection` properties section of this chapter. Now we've explored `SqlConnections` fully, let's look at connection objects in other data providers.

Connecting to Microsoft Access with OleDbConnection

As we saw in the previous chapter, the OLE DB .NET data provider is used to work with any OLE DB-compatible data store. Microsoft provides OLE DB providers for SQL Server, Microsoft Access (Jet), Oracle, and a variety of other database and data file formats.

If a native .NET data provider is available for a particular database or file format (such as the SqlClient provider for SQL Server), then it is generally better to use it, rather than the generic OLE DB data provider. This is because OLE DB introduces an extra layer of indirection that affects performance, as illustrated in the diagram below:

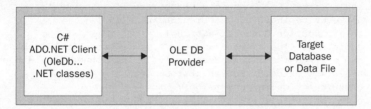

One common database format for which there is no native .NET data provider is the Microsoft Access database file format (.mdb file), also known as the Jet database engine format, so in this case we need to use OLE DB .NET data provider.

Try It Out: OLE DB Connection

We're going to create a C# program to connect to a Microsoft Access Jet database (.mdb) file with the OLE DB .NET data provider. The pattern of this program is very similar to the SQL Server example, the main differences being the namespace for the .NET data provider – System.Data.OleDb – and the use of OleDb instead of Sql as a prefix to the Connection and Exception classes. Also, the connection string clauses for OLE DB are slightly different.

1. Create a new C# console application called Connection_OleDB and name the main file ConnectionOleDB.cs

2. Enter the following code into our file.

```
using System;
using System.Data;

// use OLE DB .NET Data Provider namespace
using System.Data.OleDb;

namespace Wrox.BeginningCSharpDatabases.Chapter05
{
  class ConnectionExample3
  {
    static void Main()
    {
      // create OleDbConnection object
      OleDbConnection thisConnection = new OleDbConnection(
```

```
            @"Provider=Microsoft.Jet.OLEDB.4.0;" +
            @"Data Source=" +          // Data Source = path name of .mdb file
            @"C:\Program Files\Microsoft Visual Studio .NET\FrameworkSDK" +
            @"\Samples\QuickStart\aspplus\samples\portal\data\portal.mdb");

    try
    {
      // open connection
      thisConnection.Open();
      // open was successful
      Console.WriteLine("OLE DB Connection Successfully Opened!");
      Console.WriteLine("Connection Properties:");
      Console.WriteLine("\tConnection String: {0}",
        thisConnection.ConnectionString);
      Console.WriteLine("\tDatabase: {0}", thisConnection.Database);
      Console.WriteLine("\tDataSource: {0}", thisConnection.DataSource);
      Console.WriteLine("\tServerVersion: {0}",
        thisConnection.ServerVersion);
      Console.WriteLine("\tState: {0}", thisConnection.State);
      // OLE DB-specific properties
      Console.WriteLine("\tProvider: {0}", thisConnection.Provider);
    }
    catch (OleDbException ex)
    {
      Console.WriteLine(ex.ToString());
    }
    finally
    {
      // close connection
      thisConnection.Close();
      // close was closed by finally block
      Console.WriteLine("Connection Closed.");
    }
  }
 }
}
```

3. Compile this program and execute it. If you have the .NET sample files installed, you will see
this output:

If you don't have the Visual Studio .NET sample files installed or perhaps have a different version that does not have this file in exactly the same location, you may get an error message. If you do not have the file in this location, you could search your system to see if you can find another `.mdb` file on your system to try this with. Either way, you can see how the program tries to find the file in the given path.

How It Works

We're going to concentrate on the differences between this example and the previous examples. Where the code is the same, we'll just mention that and move on.

Naturally, the first step is to reference the `System.Data` namespace and our provider as we saw before. The OLE DB provider uses a different namespace within `System.Data`:

```
using System.Data.OleDb;
```

Next, we need to create a `Connection` object and open the connection to the data source.

Just as with SQL Server we create a connection object, `OleDbConnection`, specifying a connection string as input to the constructor:

```
OleDbConnection thisConnection = new OleDbConnection(
  @"Provider=Microsoft.Jet.OLEDB.4.0;" +
  @"Data Source=" +        // Data Source = path name of .mdb file
  @"C:\Program Files\Microsoft Office\Office\Samples\Northwind.mdb"
  );
```

The `OleDbConnection` string is a little different from the `SqlConnection` string, but is similar in concept. We must specify the OLE DB provider that we wish to connect to; there is a `Provider` connection clause specific to the `OleDbConnection` object for this purpose. For Microsoft Access databases, the OLE DB provider is always the following name ("Jet" is the name of the database engine included in Access):

```
"Provider=Microsoft.Jet.OLEDB.4.0;"
```

If you are using a different OLE DB provider for a different data store, then specify the name of that provider in the `Provider` clause. In the previous chapter, we saw an example using the SQL Server provider whose name is SQLOLEDB. Another commonly used provider is MSDAORA for Oracle databases (we'll look briefly at that, just ahead). Each of these OLE DB providers comes with Visual Studio .NET; they are installed with the Microsoft Data Access Components (MDAC) in the Windows Update that accompanies VS.NET.

A handy trick for obtaining an OLE DB connection string is to use the Universal Data Link (UDL) program included with Windows. Simply create a new document on the desktop with the extension `.udl` (assuming you have file extensions showing and not hidden for known types). You may then open this connection and enter the parameters to connect to an OLE DB data source. Then, close it and change the file extension back to `.txt` (or open the UDL file with Notepad). The file now contains a valid OLE DB connection string you can cut and paste for your C# program.

The second part of the connection string is the `Data Source` clause, and in the OLE DB/Microsoft Access case, this simply specifies the path name of the Microsoft Access database file (`.mdb` file) we are going to open:

```
@"C:\Program Files\Microsoft Office\Office\Samples\Northwind.mdb"
```

No user and password is specified, because this `.mdb` file is not password protected; if it were, we would specify user and password as with SQL Server security:

```
"user id=myusername;pass=password"
```

The remainder of the program is very similar to the `SqlConnection` example. We open the connection, display its properties, and close it in the `finally` block of the exception handler.

There is, however, one informational property that is unique to the `OleDbConnection` object, and that is the `Provider` property:

```
        // OLE DB-specific properties
        Console.WriteLine("\tProvider: {0}", thisConnection.Provider);
```

This shows the OLE DB Provider as specified in the connection string:

```
        Provider: Microsoft.Jet.OLEDB.4.0
```

Let's now look at a snippet of code that also uses the OLE DB .NET provider, but with a different OLE DB provider.

Connecting to Oracle with OleDbConnection

Besides accessing `.mdb` files, another common use of the OLE DB .NET data provider is for accessing Oracle databases. This just requires changing the connection string appropriately for Oracle, specifying the MSDAORA OLE DB provider instead of Jet, and adding login information:

```
OleDbConnection thisConnection = new OleDbConnection(
   @"Provider=MSDAORA;" +
   @"Data Source=testdb; User ID=scott; Password=x1y2z3"
   );
```

When this program executes against an Oracle database named `testdb`, we see this output:

```
OLE DB Connection Successfully Opened!
Connection Properties:
    Connection String: Provider=MSDAORA;Data Source=testdb; User ID=scott;
    Database:
    DataSource: testdb
    ServerVersion: 09.00.0000 Oracle9i Release 9.0.1.1.1 - Production
    State: Open
    Provider: MSDAORA
Connection Closed.
```

You may have noticed that the `Database` property appears blank in both the Jet and Oracle examples. Oracle has a separately named server instance for each database so it does not make sense to distinguish this concept. In the case of Jet, the data file is in effect the server instance. When using the SQLOLEDB provider, as shown in the previous chapter, then the `Database` property would contain the name of the database being accessed, just as with the native SQL Server provider.

Connecting to MySQL with OdbcConnection

ODBC (Open DataBase Connectivity) has been around since the early 1990s and literally hundreds of types of databases have ODBC drivers to allow access from any ODBC client program. The ODBC .NET data provider is used to work with any ODBC-compatible database.

> **The ODBC .NET data provider is not included in Visual Studio .NET, but is available for free as a download from http://msdn.microsoft.com/downloads.**

The ODBC .NET data provider is a good alternative when neither a native .NET provider nor an OLE DB provider is available for the database you are trying to access. It is also good to use when connecting to more than one RDBMS (perhaps to move data between databases); even though we would still need a separate ODBC connection for each database, the code for each would be very similar.

ODBC is well known for supporting many databases and formats but it does not have a good reputation for performance. It is a 'generic' layer like OLE DB, but because it uses a 'driver manager' layer in addition to the database-specific ODBC driver itself, it requires even more intermediate layers between your client program and the database, as shown here:

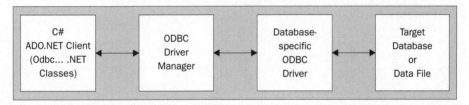

Each intermediate layer needs to be set up correctly for the entire path from the client to the server to function, which can lead to many possible errors, as well as reduced performance. If a native .NET provider is available, then you should use that instead.

If you were moving code from another database to SQL Server, you might use the SQL Server ODBC driver when first doing the conversion, as this would allow you to get something working with minimal code changes. The conversion to a native driver could come later when optimizing for performance.

Nevertheless, there are many other databases with well-optimized ODBC drivers where ODBC is a perfectly good API for accessing the database. The example data source we use is the popular open-source MySQL database, for which the `MyOdbc` driver is available.

Try It Out: ODBC Connection

As with the OLE DB provider, the namespace for the ODBC .NET data provider is different –
`Microsoft.Data.Odbc` – and the prefix to the `Connection` and `Exception` classes is `Odbc`
instead of `Sql` or `OleDb`. Also the connection string clauses for ODBC are slightly different.

1. Create a new Console application called `Connection_MySQL`. Name the main file
`Connection_MySQL.cs`.

2. Enter the following code into `Connection_MySQL.cs`, which is our C# program that
connects to MySQL via ODBC:

```
using System;
using System.Data;

// use ODBC .NET Data Provider namespace
using Microsoft.Data.Odbc;

namespace Wrox.BeginningCSharpDatabases.Chapter05
{
  class ConnectionExample4
  {
    static void Main()
    {
    // create OdbcConnection object
    OdbcConnection thisConnection = new OdbcConnection(
      "DRIVER={MySQL ODBC 3.51 Driver};" +
      "SERVER=localhost;" +
      "DATABASE=test;" +
      "UID=root;" +
      "PASSWORD=;"
      );

      try
      {
        // open connection
        thisConnection.Open();
        // open was successful
        Console.WriteLine("ODBC Connection Successfully Opened!");

        Console.WriteLine("Connection Properties:");
        Console.WriteLine("\tConnection String: {0}",
          thisConnection.ConnectionString);
        Console.WriteLine("\tDatabase: {0}",
          thisConnection.Database);
        Console.WriteLine("\tDataSource: {0}",
          thisConnection.DataSource);
        Console.WriteLine("\tServerVersion: {0}",
          thisConnection.ServerVersion);
        Console.WriteLine("\tState: {0}", thisConnection.State);
        // odbc-specific properties
        Console.WriteLine("\tDriver: {0}", thisConnection.Driver);}
```

```
     catch (OdbcException ex)
     {
       Console.WriteLine(ex.ToString());
     }
     finally
     {
       // close connection
       thisConnection.Close();
       // close was closed by finally block
       Console.WriteLine("Connection Closed.");
     }
   }
 }
}
```

3. Once you have downloaded and installed the ODBC provider, you must add a reference to the `Microsoft.Data.Odbc.dll` library to your project for the ODBC.NET data provider, since this is not in the standard .NET system directories. We can do this by right-clicking on the **References** section in solution explorer, and selecting **Add Reference**, as we saw in the last chapter. This dialog is also available under the **Project** menu.

4. Now compile and link the example. When it runs we see the connection properties as shown here:

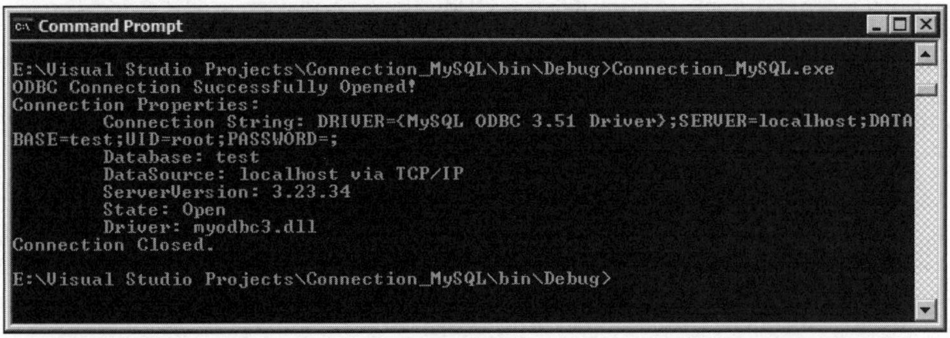

```
Command Prompt                                                      _ □ ✕
E:\Visual Studio Projects\Connection_MySQL\bin\Debug>Connection_MySQL.exe
ODBC Connection Successfully Opened!
Connection Properties:
     Connection String: DRIVER=<MySQL ODBC 3.51 Driver>;SERVER=localhost;DATA
BASE=test;UID=root;PASSWORD=;
     Database: test
     DataSource: localhost via TCP/IP
     ServerVersion: 3.23.34
     State: Open
     Driver: myodbc3.dll
Connection Closed.

E:\Visual Studio Projects\Connection_MySQL\bin\Debug>
```

How It Works

Once again, we'll just concentrate on the differences between this example and the previous examples.

The first step is to reference the `System.Data` namespace and our provider as we saw before. The ODBC provider uses a `Microsoft` namespace, because it is not part of the .NET Framework:

```
using Microsoft.Data.Odbc;
```

Next, we create a `Connection` object and open the connection to the data source, specifying a connection string as input to the constructor:

```
// create OdbcConnection object
OdbcConnection thisConnection = new OdbcConnection(
    "DRIVER={MySQL ODBC 3.51 Driver};" +
    "SERVER=localhost;" +
    "DATABASE=test;" +
    "UID=root;" +
    "PASSWORD=x1y2z3;"
```

The ODBC connection string differs only slightly from the OLE DB case. Instead of an OLE DB provider, we must specify the ODBC driver using the `DRIVER` clause.

You can see what ODBC drivers are available on your system in the ODBC component of the Control Panel of your Windows system (on Windows 2000 & XP this tool is in the Administrative Tools submenu of the Control Panel).

The ODBC driver for MySQL is named as shown below:

```
"DRIVER={MySQL ODBC 3.51 Driver};"
```

If you are using a different ODBC driver for a different database or data format, then specify the name of that driver. Because so many different ODBC drivers exist, there is a lot of variation in the way each driver interprets the connection string information; check the documentation for the particular ODBC driver you are using.

With MySQL's ODBC driver, we use the server connection string clause to specify the server instance; for MySQL, `localhost` is the server running on the current machine, similar to `(local)` for SQL Server `root` is the system administrator account, similar to `sa` for SQL Server.

The remainder of the program is very similar to the `Connection_OleDB` example. We open the connection, display properties of the connection, and close it in the `finally` block of the exception handler. We display the `Driver` property of the connection, which is similar to the `Provider` property in OLE DB.

Connecting to Oracle with OracleConnection

In April 2002, Microsoft released a beta version of a native Oracle .NET provider, compatible with Oracle 8i and above clients, and Oracle 7.3 and above servers. When the final version of this driver is released, it will be the preferred way of accessing the Oracle database from ADO.NET. While it is in beta, the OLE DB provider will still be the proven, reliable way of accessing Oracle.

> **The Oracle provider is not included with Visual Studio .NET; you must download it from Microsoft's web site at http://www.microsoft.com/downloads/release.asp?ReleaseID=37805. An updated version may have appeared by the time you read this. You will also need to have the Oracle client tools installed and configured to connect to your server for this example to run.**

The architecture of Oracle is a direct connection client-server model similar to SQL Server. Let's look at a program that uses this provider.

Try It Out: Connecting to Oracle

The namespace for the Oracle provider is `System.Data.OracleClient`. The prefix to the `Connection` and `Exception` classes is `Oracle`.

As with the ODBC provider, you must first download and install the Oracle .NET provider on your system, and then add a reference within the project to the `System.Data.OracleClient.dll` assembly.

Let's look at the C# code called `Connection_Oracle.cs` that connects to Oracle, shown here:

```
using System;
using System.Data;

// use Oracle .NET Data Provider namespace - may change in final release
using System.Data.OracleClient;

namespace Wrox.BeginningCSharpDatabases.Chapter05
{
  class ConnectionExample5
  {
    static void Main()
    {
      // create OracleConnection object
      OracleConnection thisConnection = new OracleConnection(
        "SERVER=testdb;" +
        "UID=scott;" +
        "PASSWORD=x1y2z3;"
        );
      try
      {
        // open connection
        thisConnection.Open();
        // open was successful
        Console.WriteLine("Oracle Connection Successfully Opened!");
        Console.WriteLine("Connection Properties:");
        Console.WriteLine("\tConnection String: {0}",
          thisConnection.ConnectionString);
```

```
     // database property not in OracleConnection
     Console.WriteLine("\tDataSource: {0}",
       thisConnection.DataSource);
     Console.WriteLine("\tServerVersion: {0}",
       thisConnection.ServerVersion);
     Console.WriteLine("\tState: {0}", thisConnection.State);
   }
   catch (OracleException ex)
   {
     Console.WriteLine(ex.ToString());
   }
   finally
   {
     // close connection
     thisConnection.Close();
     // close was closed by finally block
     Console.WriteLine("Connection Closed.");
   }
  }
 }
}
```

If you compile and run this code, you should see the following output when connection to an Oracle 9i server:

You'll need to change your login details as appropriate. In the above screenshot, we ran the code against a server called `nineaye`, instead of `testdb`.

How It Works

As with the other providers described in this chapter, the Oracle provider has its own namespace:

```
// use Oracle .NET Data Provider namespace
using System.Data.OracleClient;
```

The `Connection` object and connection string are similar to previous examples:

```
  // create OracleConnection object
  OracleConnection thisConnection = new OracleConnection(
    "SERVER=testdb;" +
    "UID=scott;" +
    "PASSWORD=x1y2z3;"
    );
```

We specify a specific user and password to connect to Oracle, as with the OLE DB connection.

The Oracle .NET provider also supports integrated security if you are connecting to the Enterprise version of Oracle. To use integrated security with Oracle, specify `"Integrated Security=yes;"` *as one of the connection string clauses.*

There are no special properties for `OracleConnection` provider at the moment – its connection string clauses and server properties are the same base set that is present in all the other .NET data providers.

This completes our demonstration of Oracle connections and indeed of connections with all .NET data providers.

Summary

In this chapter, we looked at the `Connection` object within the various .NET data providers. We learned about connection strings and connection string clauses, and saw how to open and close connections.

We examined the different security options for SQL Server and other data sources and also saw how to display information about the connection after it is established, using the properties of the `Connection` object. Understanding all the different parameters in your connection is very important when debugging connection problems.

We saw how to handle exceptions generated by connection errors, and learned to close the connection in the `finally` block of the exception handler to ensure that the connection is closed in all cases.

Finally, we looked at specific examples of connecting to different data sources, including:

❑ SQL Server

❑ Microsoft Access

❑ Oracle

❑ MySQL

In the next chapter, we'll move on to look at the ADO.NET `Command` object, and how we can use it to retrieve the data we require from a data source.

Exercises

1. Which ADO.NET data providers provide a direct client-server connection to the data source?

2. Which .NET data providers go through an intermediate layer to connect?

3. Write an ADO.NET C# program to connect to a SQL Server database named SQLHERE running on the same machine as your program.

4. Write an ADO.NET C# program to connect to the `grocertogo.mdb` file that is included in the samples for Visual Studio .NET. (Hint: use the Search function in Windows to find this file.)

5. Describe two different methods of connecting to an Oracle database. What are the pros and cons of each method?

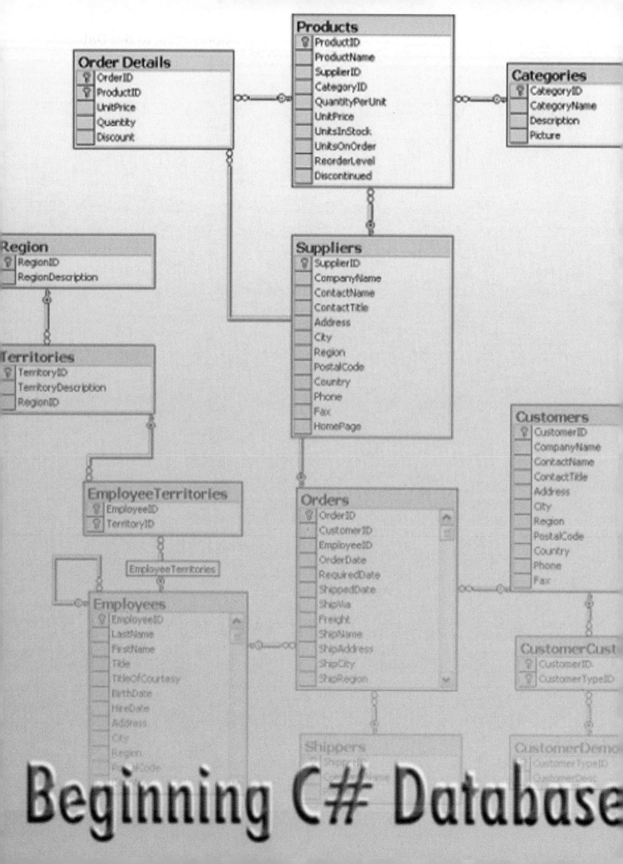

Order Details
- OrderID
- ProductID
- UnitPrice
- Quantity
- Discount

Products
- ProductID
- ProductName
- SupplierID
- CategoryID
- QuantityPerUnit
- UnitPrice
- UnitsInStock
- UnitsOnOrder
- ReorderLevel
- Discontinued

Categories
- CategoryID
- CategoryName
- Description
- Picture

Region
- RegionID
- RegionDescription

Suppliers
- SupplierID
- CompanyName
- ContactName
- ContactTitle
- Address
- City
- Region
- PostalCode
- Country
- Phone
- Fax
- HomePage

Customers
- CustomerID
- CompanyName
- ContactName
- ContactTitle
- Address
- City
- Region
- PostalCode
- Country
- Phone
- Fax

Territories
- TerritoryID
- TerritoryDescription
- RegionID

EmployeeTerritories
- EmployeeID
- TerritoryID

EmployeeTerritories

Orders
- OrderID
- CustomerID
- EmployeeID
- OrderDate
- RequiredDate
- ShippedDate
- ShipVia
- Freight
- ShipName
- ShipAddress
- ShipCity
- ShipRegion

CustomerCust
- CustomerID
- CustomerTypeID

Employees
- EmployeeID
- LastName
- FirstName
- Title
- TitleOfCourtesy
- BirthDate
- HireDate
- Address
- City
- Region
- PostalCode

Shippers

CustomerDemo

Beginning C# Database

Getting the Data

Once we've established a connection to the database as demonstrated in the previous chapter, we need to start interacting with it and getting it doing something useful for us. We might need to add, update, or delete some data, or perhaps modify the database in some other way. Whatever the task, it will inevitably involve a command of some kind.

In this chapter then, we'll introduce the Command object in the ADO.NET data provider. It's this object that encapsulates the database command associated with whatever action it is you want to perform. Typically, these commands are written as SQL statements, as SQL is the command language used by almost all relational databases. Indeed, we've already seen how to construct simple SQL statements in Chapter 3 so the actual commands won't be a new thing for us.

> Note that most relational databases actually use a particular **dialect** of SQL, which is specific to that particular database or family of databases rather than the actual standard SQL language. For example, Microsoft SQL Server, MSDE, and Access all use Transact-SQL – T-SQL for short.

Similarly, ADO.NET does not require that your commands are written in (a dialect of) SQL, but SQL is the language that most .NET data providers support. In fact, it will work with any command language as it doesn't try to interpret the command itself but simply passes it on to the database for execution, using the Command object as the envelope in which to send the command.

In this chapter we'll see how this process works, and also learn how to:

❑ Create a Command object

❑ Associate the command with a connection

❑ Use connection methods that apply to commands

❑ Use Command object properties and methods

❑ Set the text of the command statement

❑ Execute the command at the database

❑ Process the results returned from the database having executed the command

❑ Learn how to use the Command object in different .NET data providers

We'll use the SQL Server .NET data provider (`System.Data.SqlClient` namespace) in most of our examples; the `Command` object in this provider is called `SqlCommand`. Then, at the end of the chapter, we'll touch on the use of the `Command` object in other .NET data providers.

So then, let's get started by learning how to create a `Command` object.

Creating a Command Object

We can create a `Command` object using either the `SqlCommand` constructor or by using methods that create the object for us. Let's look at the first of these alternatives.

Try It Out: Creating a Command Object with a Constructor

In this example we're going to take our `SqlConnection` example that we worked with in the previous chapter and add some code to it to create a `Command` object.

1. Open Visual Studio.NET and create a new blank solution called `Chapter6_Examples`.

2. Within the new solution, create a new C# console application project called `CommandExampleSql`. Rename `Class1.cs` to `CommandExampleSql.cs`.

3. Open the last `SqlConnection` example (`Finally.cs`) in the previous chapter and copy the code. Delete all the code in `CommandExampleSql.cs` and paste in the code from `Finally.cs`.

4. Now, modify or add the following highlighted lines of code:

```csharp
using System;
using System.Data;          // use ADO.NET namespace
using System.Data.SqlClient; // use SQL Server .NET data provider namespace

namespace Wrox.BeginningCSharpDatabase.Chapter06
{
  class CommandExampleSql
  {
    static void Main()
    {
      // create SqlConnection object
      SqlConnection thisConnection =
        new SqlConnection(
        @"Server=(local)\NetSDK;"   +   // server instance name
        "Integrated Security=SSPI;" +   // use Windows login
        "Connection Timeout=5;"     );  // wait 5 seconds for server

      // create SqlCommand object
      SqlCommand thisCommand = new SqlCommand();
      Console.WriteLine("Command object created.");

      try
```

```
    {
      // open connection
      thisConnection.Open();
    }
    catch (SqlException ex)
    {
      Console.WriteLine(ex.ToString());
    }
    finally
    {
      thisConnection.Close();   // close connection
      Console.WriteLine("Connection Closed.");
    }
   }
  }
}
```

5. Build the program and run without debugging; you can do this in Visual Studio .NET or
Visual C# with the key combination *Ctrl-F5*. When the program is run you will see this output:

How It Works

Let's take a look at the lines of code that we added to this example and look at what they do in a bit more
detail. The first block of code declares the new namespace that we'll be using in this chapter and sets the class
name to reflect what we're doing.

```
namespace Wrox.BeginningCSharpDatabase.Chapter06
{
  class CommandExampleSql1
```

The second block of new code creates a `SqlCommand` object using the default constructor, and prints a
message indicating we have created it:

```
      // create SqlCommand object
      SqlCommand thisCommand = new SqlCommand();
      Console.WriteLine("Command object created.");
```

In this example, the `SqlCommand` object is empty; it is not associated with a connection nor does it have a
command set. We can't do much with it here, so let's move on and look at how we can associate it with
our connection.

Associating a Command with a Connection

For our commands to be executed against the database of our choice, each `Command` object must be associated with a connection to that particular database. This is done by setting the `Connection` property of the `Command` object, and in order to save resources, multiple `Command` objects may use the same connection. There are a couple of different ways to set this association up, so let's try them out in our program.

Try It Out: Set Connection Property

1. Modify the `try` block of our previous example program, `CommandExampleSql.cs`, as follows:

```
// create SqlCommand object
SqlCommand thisCommand = new SqlCommand();
Console.WriteLine("Command Object created.");

try
{
  // open connection
  thisConnection.Open();

  // connect command to connection
  thisCommand.Connection = thisConnection;
  Console.WriteLine("Created Command Object on this connection.");
}
catch (SqlException ex)
{
  Console.WriteLine(ex.ToString());
}
finally
{
  thisConnection.Close();    // close connection
  Console.WriteLine("Connection Closed.");
}
```

2. Compile and run. Now we see:

How It Works

As we saw in the previous example, we start our code by creating our `Connection` and `Command` objects.

```
// create SqlConnection object
SqlConnection thisConnection = new SqlConnection( ... );
// create SqlCommand object
SqlCommand thisCommand = new SqlCommand();
```

At this point, both the `Connection` and `Command` objects exist but they are not associated with each other in any way. It's only when we assign the `Connection` object to the `Command` object's `Connection` property that they are associated.

```
// connect command to connection
thisCommand.Connection = thisConnection;
```

The actual assignment occurs after the call to `thisConnection.Open()` in this particular example, but we could have done it before calling `Open()`; the connection does not have to be open in order for the `Connection` property of the `Command` object to be set.

As mentioned earlier, there is a second way to associate a connection to a SQL Server or MSDE database with our commands; calling the `Connection` object's `CreateCommand()` method will return a new `Command` object with the `Connection` property already set to that connection.

```
// create SqlCommand object
SqlCommand thisCommand = thisConnection.CreateCommand();
```

This block of code is exactly equivalent to the previous one; in both cases we end up with a `Command` object associated with our connection. It also takes fewer lines of code, because you don't have to assign the `Connection` property.

We still need one more thing within the `Command` object in order to use it, and that is the text of the command itself. Let's see how to set that next.

Assign a Command Text to a Command Object

Every `Command` object has a property, `CommandText`, which is where we set the SQL statement we intend to execute against the database. You can assign to this property directly or specify it when constructing the `Command` object. Let's look at these alternatives.

Try It Out: Set CommandText Property

1. Modify the `try` block of the previous example program, `CommandExampleSql.cs`, as follows:

```
// create SqlCommand object
SqlCommand thisCommand = new SqlCommand();
Console.WriteLine("Command Object created.");

try
{
  // open connection
  thisConnection.Open();

  // connect command to connection
  thisCommand.Connection = thisConnection;

  // associate SQL command to command object
  thisCommand.CommandText = "SELECT COUNT(*) FROM Employees";
  Console.WriteLine("Ready to execute SQL command: {0}",
                    thisCommand.CommandText);
}
```

2. Compile and run the program again. This time you should see the following output:

```
E:\Visual Studio Projects\Chapter6_Examples\CommandExampleSql\bin\Debug\CommandExampleSql...
Command Object created.
Ready to execute SQL command: SELECT COUNT(*) FROM Employees
Connection Closed.
Press any key to continue
```

How It Works

The `CommandText` is just a string so we can print it out with `Console.WriteLine()` just like any other string. The command we specified, `"SELECT COUNT(*) FROM Employees"`, will return the number of employees in the Northwind `Employees` table when we're ready.

> Note that you must set both the `Connection` and the `CommandText` properties of the `Command` object before the command itself can be executed.

Both of these properties can be set when the `Command` object is created with yet another variation of its constructor, as shown here:

```
// create SqlCommand object for SELECT command on thisConnection
SqlCommand thisCommand =
            new SqlCommand("SELECT COUNT(*) FROM Employees", thisConnection);
```

Again, this way takes even fewer lines of code, but is exactly equivalent to the above code that assigns each property explicitly. This is the most commonly used variation of the `SqlCommand` constructor, and we will use this one for the rest of the chapter.

Executing Commands

Commands aren't much use unless we can execute them, so let's look at that now. The `Command` object provides several different `Execute` methods for executing SQL commands. The differences between these methods depend on the results you expect from the command. Some commands, such as queries, return multiple rows of data, whereas others may return no rows at all. We determine which `Execute` method to use by considering what we expect to be returned. Have a look at the following table to get an idea of it all.

If the command is going to return	You should use
Nothing : the statement isn't a query	ExecuteNonQuery
A single value	ExecuteScalar
One or more rows	ExecuteReader
XML (More on this in Chapter 17)	ExecuteXmlReader

The SQL statement we just used in our example, "SELECT COUNT(*) FROM Employees", should return one value, the number of employees. Looking at the table, we can see that we should use the ExecuteScalar() method of SqlCommand to execute the command and return this one result. Let's try it.

Try It Out: The ExecuteScalar Method

1. Add a new C# console application project called CommandExampleScalar to our open solution, Chapter6_Examples. Rename Class1.cs to CommandExampleScalar.cs.

2. Copy the code from CommandExampleSql.cs and paste it into CommandExampleScalar.cs replacing the automatically generated code already there.

3. Now modify the code to look like the following; blocks with changes are highlighted:

```
using System;
using System.Data;              // use ADO.NET namespace
using System.Data.SqlClient;    // use SQL Server .NET data provider namespace

namespace Wrox.BeginningCSharpDatabase.Chapter06
{
  class CommandExampleScalar
  {
    static void Main()
    {
      // create SqlConnection object
      SqlConnection thisConnection =
        new SqlConnection(
        @"Server=(local)\NetSDK;"   +    // server instance name
        "Integrated Security=true;" +    // use Windows login
        "Connection Timeout=5;"     +    // wait 5 seconds for server
        "Database=Northwind;");          // connect to Northwind database

      // create SqlCommand object
      SqlCommand thisCommand =
        new SqlCommand("SELECT COUNT(*) FROM Employees", thisConnection);

      try
      {
        // open connection
        thisConnection.Open();

        // execute query to return number of employees
        Console.WriteLine("Number of Employees is: {0}",
          thisCommand.ExecuteScalar());
      }
      catch (SqlException ex)
      {
        Console.WriteLine(ex.ToString());
      }
      finally
      {
        thisConnection.Close();    // close connection
        Console.WriteLine("Connection Closed.");
```

```
                }
              }
            }
          }
```

4. Compile and run. Now we see:

```
E:\Visual Studio Projects\Chapter6_Examples\CommandExecteScalar\bin\Debug\CommandExecteSc...
Number of Employees is: 9
Connection Closed.
Press any key to continue
```

How It Works

`ExecuteScalar()` takes the `CommandText` and sends it to the database (MSDE) using the connection from the `SqlCommand` object's `Connection` property. It returns the result (the number 9) as a single object, which we print out with `Console.WriteLine()`.

This is pretty simple to follow but it's worth noting this really is simpler than you'll usually have it because `Console.WriteLine()` will take any kind of object as its input. In fact, `ExecuteScalar()`'s return type is an `object`, the superclass of all types in the .NET Framework, which makes perfect sense when you remember that a database may hold any type of data. So, if you want to assign the returned `object` to a variable with a specific data type (`int`, for example), you must cast the object to convert it to the specific data type. If the object types do not match, then the system will generate a run-time error indicating an invalid cast.

Here is an example that demonstrates this idea. In it, we store the result from `ExecuteScalar` in the variable `count`, having cast it to the specific data type `int`:

```
thisCommand.CommandText = "SELECT COUNT(*) FROM Employees";
int count = (int) thisCommand.ExecuteScalar();
Console.WriteLine("Number of Employees is: {0}", count);
```

If you're sure the type of the result will always be an `int` (a safe bet with `COUNT(*)`) then the above code is safe. However, if we left the cast to `(int)` in place and changed the `CommandText` of the command to read:

```
SELECT FirstName FROM Employees WHERE LastName='Davolio'
```

then `ExecuteScalar()` would return the string "Nancy" instead of an integer and we would get this exception:

Unhandled Exception: System.InvalidCastException: Specified cast is not valid.

because you can't cast a `string` to an `int`.

Another problem may occur if your SQL command actually returns multiple rows where you thought it would return only one; for example, what if there were multiple employees with the last name of "Davolio" in the example I just gave? In this case, `ExecuteScalar()` just returns the first row of the result and ignores the rest. If you use `ExecuteScalar()`, do make sure you are expecting a single value to be returned.

Executing Commands with Multiple Results

For queries where you're expecting multiple values to be returned, the `Command` object provides the `ExecuteReader()` method. If then, we wanted to see all the data in the `Employees` table we'd definitely be expecting more than one result to be returned and should use this method to execute our query.

`ExecuteReader()` returns a `SqlDataReader` object, which is an instance of the `DataReader` class that we'll read about in the next chapter. It provides methods that allow us to read successive rows of data should more than one be returned in our resultset, and to retrieve individual data values from those rows as well.

We'll leave the details of the `DataReader` object to be explained in the next chapter but for comparison's sake, we will show a brief example here of using the `ExecuteReader()` method to create a `SqlDataReader` from a `Command` object and displaying the results it contains.

Try It Out: ExecuteReader Method

1. Add a new C# console application project called `CommandExampleReader` to our open solution, `Chapter6_Examples`. Rename `Class1.cs` to `CommandExampleReader.cs`.

2. Add the following code to `CommandExampleReader.cs`.

```csharp
using System;
using System.Data;            // use ADO.NET namespace
using System.Data.SqlClient;  // use SQL Server .NET data provider namespace
namespace Wrox.BeginningCSharpDatabase.Chapter06
{
  class CommandExampleReader
  {
    static void Main()
    {
      // create SqlConnection object
      SqlConnection thisConnection =
        new SqlConnection(
        @"Server=(local)\NetSDK;"    +   // server instance name
        "Integrated Security=SSPI;" +   // use Windows login
        "Connection Timeout=5;"     +   // wait 5 seconds for server
        "Database=Northwind;" );        // connect to temp database

      SqlCommand thisCommand =
        new SqlCommand("SELECT FirstName, LastName FROM Employees",
        thisConnection);
```

```
    try
    {
      // open connection
      thisConnection.Open();

      SqlDataReader thisReader = thisCommand.ExecuteReader();

      while (thisReader.Read())
      {
        Console.WriteLine("Employee name: {0} {1}",
          thisReader.GetValue(0),
          thisReader.GetValue(1));
      }

    }
    catch (SqlException ex)
    {
      Console.WriteLine(ex.ToString());
    }
    finally
    {
      thisConnection.Close();  // close connection
      Console.WriteLine("Connection Closed.");
    }
  }
 }
}
```

3. Now build and run the program. It will display the first and last names of all nine employees:

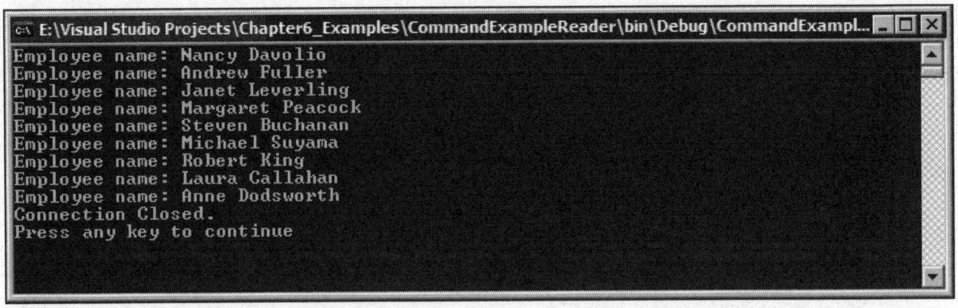

How It Works

In this example we've used the `ExecuteReader()` method to retrieve and then output the first and last names of all of the employees in the `Employees` table to the screen. As with `ExecuteScalar()`, `ExecuteReader()` takes the `CommandText` and sends it to the database using the connection from the `SqlCommand` object's `Connection` property.

When we used the `ExecuteScalar()` method we only produced a single scalar value. In contrast, using `ExecuteReader()` returned a `SqlDataReader` object:

```
SqlDataReader thisReader = thisCommand.ExecuteReader();

while (thisReader.Read()) {
  Console.WriteLine("Employee name: {0} {1}",
      thisReader.GetValue(0),
        thisReader.GetValue(1));
}
```

The `SqlDataReader` object has a `Read()` method, which gets each row in turn, and a `GetValue()` method, which get the value of each column in the row. The particular column whose value it retrieves is given by the integer parameter indicating the index of the column. Note that `GetValue()` uses a zero-based index, so the first column is column zero, the second column is column one, and so on. Since our query asked for two columns, `FirstName` and `LastName`, these are the columns numbered 0 and 1 in this query result.

As promised, `SqlDataReader` will be explained in much more detail in the next chapter, but for now we need to move on.

Executing Non-Query Commands

Although it's most intuitive to think of a command as a SQL statement that queries a database and returns some information, there are several cases where we'll need to issue commands and expect no results at all. For example, while the `SELECT` statement is a **query** command that returns a resultset of zero or more rows, other SQL commands, such as `INSERT`, `UPDATE`, and `DELETE` are **non-query** commands; they do not return a resultset but instead make changes to the database.

The `ExecuteNonQuery()` method of the `Command` object is designed to execute these non-query commands. Let's try it.

Try It Out: The ExecuteNonQuery Method

1. Add a new C# console application project called `CommandExampleNonQuery` to our open solution, `Chapter6_Examples`. Rename `Class1.cs` to `CommandExampleNonQuery.cs`.

2. Add the following code to `CommandExampleNonQuery.cs`:

```
using System;
using System.Data;          // use ADO.NET namespace
using System.Data.SqlClient; // use SQL Server .NET data provider namespace


namespace Wrox.BeginningCSharpDatabase.Chapter06
{
  class CommandExampleNonQuery
  {
    static void Main()
    {
      // create SqlConnection object
      SqlConnection thisConnection = new SqlConnection
          (@"Server=(local)\NetSDK;"     +   // server instance name
           "Integrated Security=SSPI;" +   // use Windows login
           "Connection Timeout=5;"     +   // wait 5 seconds for server
```

```
                    "Database=Northwind;");          // connect to Northwind database

        // create SqlCommand objects
        SqlCommand selectCommand =
          new SqlCommand("SELECT COUNT(*) FROM Employees", thisConnection);
        SqlCommand nonqueryCommand = thisConnection.CreateCommand();

      try
      {
        // open connection
        thisConnection.Open();

          // execute query to return number of employees
          Console.WriteLine("Before INSERT: Number of Employees is: {0}",
            selectCommand.ExecuteScalar() );
          nonqueryCommand.CommandText =
            "INSERT INTO Employees (Firstname, Lastname) " +
            "VALUES ('Zachariah', 'Zinn')";
          Console.WriteLine(nonqueryCommand.CommandText);
          Console.WriteLine("Number of Rows Affected is: {0}",
            nonqueryCommand.ExecuteNonQuery() );
          Console.WriteLine("After INSERT: Number of Employees is: {0}",
            selectCommand.ExecuteScalar() );
          nonqueryCommand.CommandText =
            "DELETE FROM Employees WHERE Firstname='Zachariah'" +
            "AND Lastname='Zinn'";
          Console.WriteLine(nonqueryCommand.CommandText);
          Console.WriteLine("Number of Rows Affected is: {0}",
            nonqueryCommand.ExecuteNonQuery() );
          Console.WriteLine("After DELETE: Number of Employees is: {0}",
            selectCommand.ExecuteScalar() );
      }
      catch (SqlException ex)
      {
        Console.WriteLine(ex.ToString());
      }
      finally
      {
        thisConnection.Close();  // close connection
        Console.WriteLine("Connection Closed.");
      }
    }
  }
}
```

3. Compile and run the program, and we see its output as follows:

```
E:\Visual Studio Projects\Chapter6_Examples\CommandExampleNonQuery\bin\Debug\CommandExa...
Before INSERT: Number of Employees is: 9
INSERT INTO Employees (Firstname, Lastname) VALUES ('Zachariah', 'Zinn')
Number of Rows Affected is: 1
After INSERT: Number of Employees is: 10
DELETE FROM Employees WHERE Firstname='Zachariah'AND Lastname='Zinn'
Number of Rows Affected is: 1
After DELETE: Number of Employees is: 9
Connection Closed.
Press any key to continue
```

How It Works

In this program we actually create and use two Command objects. The first is selectCommand, which encapsulates a SELECT COUNT(*) SQL command to count the rows in the Employees table as we did we did in an earlier example. We will use this command several times to monitor the number of rows as we INSERT and DELETE employees. The command text of selectCommand stays constant, so we initialize the command text using the overload of the SqlCommand constructor that sets its CommandText and Connection properties at the time we create selectCommand itself:

```
// create SqlCommand objects
SqlCommand selectCommand =
  new SqlCommand("SELECT COUNT(*) FROM Employees", thisConnection);
```

Next, we create another Command object named nonqueryCommand. This will be used for executing the INSERT and DELETE commands. Since the command text of this object will not remain constant (we'll change the text when we switch from INSERT to DELETE), we'll set the command text for these commands just before we execute the commands; the only property we'll initialize when constructing nonqueryCommand is the Connection property; the CreateCommand() method of the Connection object is an easy way to do this:

```
SqlCommand nonqueryCommand = thisConnection.CreateCommand();
```

The first operation performed after we open the connection is an INSERT to add a row to the table. First we need to Open() the connection, and then we use the selectCommand object to display the number of rows in the table before we modify anything:

```
// open connection
thisConnection.Open();

// execute query to return number of employees
Console.WriteLine("Before INSERT: Number of Employees is: {0}",
  selectCommand.ExecuteScalar() );
```

Note that we called ExecuteScalar() to execute the SELECT command, using the command text and connection as initialized when selectCommand was created. Next we create the command text for the INSERT command and assign it to the CommandText property of nonqueryCommand, then display the command on the console:

```
nonqueryCommand.CommandText =
  "INSERT INTO Employees (Firstname, Lastname) " +
  "VALUES ('Zachariah', 'Zinn')";
Console.WriteLine(nonqueryCommand.CommandText);
```

Note that we haven't executed the command yet. We do this in the next line with a call to ExecuteNonQuery():

```
Console.WriteLine("Number of Rows Affected is: {0}",
  nonqueryCommand.ExecuteNonQuery() );
```

ExecuteNonQuery() returns an int indicating how many rows were affected by the command. Since we want to display the number of affected rows, we put the call to ExecuteNonQuery() within the call to Console.WriteLine() so we don't have to store the result in a temporary variable but instead we display it directly. Again we use our select command to display the number of rows, this time after the INSERT operation:

```
Console.WriteLine("After INSERT: Number of Employees is: {0}",
 selectCommand.ExecuteScalar() );
```

Now we want to restore the table back to its original state, so we need a DELETE statement to delete the employee we just inserted. We'll reuse the nonqueryCommand object and modify the CommandText property to hold a DELETE statement instead of INSERT:

```
nonqueryCommand.CommandText =
  "DELETE FROM Employees WHERE Firstname='Zachariah'" +
  "AND Lastname='Zinn'";
Console.WriteLine(nonqueryCommand.CommandText);
```

Now we execute the DELETE statement with ExecuteNonQuery the same way we executed the INSERT, and again use the selectCommand to display the results afterwards:

```
Console.WriteLine("Number of Rows Affected is: {0}",
  nonqueryCommand.ExecuteNonQuery() );
Console.WriteLine("After DELETE: Number of Employees is: {0}",
  selectCommand.ExecuteScalar() );
```

As we said, when INSERT, UPDATE, or DELETE are executed, they affect some number of rows in the database; the return result from ExecuteNonQuery() indicates how many rows were changed.

If this number comes back zero when you didn't expect it to, then maybe the WHERE clause of the SQL command was specified incorrectly. For example, if we had mistyped the WHERE clause for the DELETE command in the above program, we might see this output:

We misspelled Zinn as Xinn and so did not find any row to delete. The number of employees remaining after the DELETE is 10, and not 9 as expected. If we fix this error and re-run the program, we insert one more row but then delete 2:

```
E:\Visual Studio Projects\Chapter6_Examples\CommandExampleNonQuery\bin\Debug\CommandExa...
Before INSERT: Number of Employees is: 10
INSERT INTO Employees (Firstname, Lastname) VALUES ('Zachariah', 'Zinn')
Number of Rows Affected is: 1
After INSERT: Number of Employees is: 11
DELETE FROM Employees WHERE Firstname='Zachariah'AND Lastname='Zinn'
Number of Rows Affected is: 2
After DELETE: Number of Employees is: 9
Connection Closed.
Press any key to continue
```

This is because the second row was left behind when the previous DELETE failed to find it.

Creating Tables

Of course, adding and removing data in our tables are not the only non-queries we'll end up sending to our server. Often we'll need to create a table or other database object from our program, such as when we create a temporary table to hold some data as part of our application processing on the server.

Such operations use the CREATE command in SQL and are called **DDL** (Data Definition Language) commands. These are distinguished from Data Manipulation Language (**DML**) commands such as INSERT, UPDATE, and DELETE that we used in the previous example.

You can use ExecuteNonQuery() to execute DDL commands as well as DML commands. Let's check it out.

Try It Out: Using the ExecuteNonQuery() Method with CREATE TABLE

The aim of this example is to create a table called MyTmpTable and insert some data into it by executing a non-query command on the tempdb database.

1. Add a new C# console application project called CommandExampleCreate to our open solution, Chapter6_Examples. Rename Class1.cs to CommandExampleCreate.cs.

2. Copy and paste the code from our previous example, CommandExampleNonQuery.cs, into CommandExampleCreate.cs and edit it as shown below; blocks showing the lines that differ from the previous example are highlighted:

```csharp
using System;
using System.Data;              // use ADO.NET namespace
using System.Data.SqlClient;    // use SQL Server .NET data provider namespace
namespace Wrox.BeginningCSharpDatabase.Chapter06
{
  class CommandExampleCreate
  {
    static void Main()
    {
      // create SqlConnection object
      SqlConnection thisConnection = new SqlConnection
        (@"Server=(local)\NetSDK;"    +   // server instance name
```

```
                  "Integrated Security=SSPI;"    +    // use Windows login
                  "Connection Timeout=5;"        +    // wait 5 seconds for server
                  "Database=tempdb;");                // connect to tempdb database

         // create SqlCommand objects
         SqlCommand nonqueryCommand = thisConnection.CreateCommand();

         try
         {
           // open connection
           thisConnection.Open();

           // execute non-query to create temporary table
           nonqueryCommand.CommandText = "CREATE TABLE MyTmpTable (COL1 integer)";
           Console.WriteLine(nonqueryCommand.CommandText);
           Console.WriteLine("Number of Rows Affected is: {0}",
             nonqueryCommand.ExecuteNonQuery() );

           // execute non-query to insert some data
           nonqueryCommand.CommandText = "INSERT INTO MyTmpTable VALUES (37)";
           Console.WriteLine(nonqueryCommand.CommandText);
           Console.WriteLine("Number of Rows Affected is: {0}",
             nonqueryCommand.ExecuteNonQuery() );

         }
         catch (SqlException ex)
         {
           Console.WriteLine(ex.ToString());
         }
         finally
         {
           thisConnection.Close();  // close connection
           Console.WriteLine("Connection Closed.");
         }
      }
    }
  }
```

3. Compile and run the program. We see the output of the program as follows:

```
E:\Visual Studio Projects\Chapter6_Examples\CommandExampleCreate\bin\Debug\CommandExampl...
CREATE TABLE MyTmpTable (COL1 integer)
Number of Rows Affected is: -1
INSERT INTO MyTmpTable VALUES (37)
Number of Rows Affected is: 1
Connection Closed.
Press any key to continue
```

How It Works

We repeat the style from the previous example, using `CreateCommand()` to create a `Command` object named `nonqueryCommand` associated with the connection at create time:

```
SqlCommand nonqueryCommand = thisConnection.CreateCommand();
```

We've two tasks to do in this example – creating the table and then filling it with some data – so that's two commands we need to issue. As before, we'll need to change the `CommandText` property for each of these tasks before we execute the commands. First we execute the `CREATE TABLE` command:

```
// execute non-query to create temporary table
nonqueryCommand.CommandText = "CREATE TABLE MyTmpTable (COL1 integer)";
Console.WriteLine(nonqueryCommand.CommandText);
Console.WriteLine("Number of Rows Affected is: {0}",
  nonqueryCommand.ExecuteNonQuery() );
```

`ExecuteNonQuery()` returns minus one (`-1`) when executing any DDL command such as `CREATE TABLE`, since creating a new table does not affect any rows of existing tables. So we see the `CREATE TABLE` being executed, and the return value is `-1`.

Next, we execute the `INSERT` command to put some data into the newly created table:

```
// execute non-query to insert some data
nonqueryCommand.CommandText = "INSERT INTO MyTmpTable VALUES (37)";
Console.WriteLine(nonqueryCommand.CommandText);
Console.WriteLine("Number of Rows Affected is: {0}",
  nonqueryCommand.ExecuteNonQuery() );
```

The `INSERT` into the table after its creation does affect one row so `ExecuteNonQuery()` returns plus one (`1`).

`ExecuteNonQuery()` also returns `-1` if you give it a `SELECT` command to execute. This is because `SELECT` does not change any rows, it just reports on the data contained within existing rows. However, don't use `ExecuteNonQuery()` for `SELECT` commands; you'll want to look at the results of a `SELECT` command and `ExecuteScalar()` or `ExecuteReader()` are better methods to use for this purpose as these both return the means to look at results.

> *Note that because we created `MyTmpTable` in the `tempdb` temporary database, it will disappear the next time SQL Server is restarted. That's OK for this table; we were just using it as an example. However, don't use the `tempdb` database for any data that you really want to be permanent.*

Creating Databases

The previous example created a table in the `tempdb` database, which is always present in SQL Server and MSDE for temporary tables. This is a handy trick for incidental work, but it's often more convenient to create a whole database for your application rather than a few new tables in a database that already exists.

As it turns out, this is easy enough to program in ADO.NET; you just execute the SQL command CREATE DATABASE. There is a chicken-and-egg problem, however, in that you can't access the database in your SqlConnection until the database exists. This is one reason why the Connection class has a ChangeDatabase() method. Let's see how it is used.

Try It Out: Creating a Database and Using It

1. Add a new C# console application project called CommandExampleCreateDB to our open solution, Chapter6_Examples. Rename Class1.cs to CommandExampleCreateDB.cs.

2. Copy and paste the code from our previous example, CommandExampleCreate.cs, into CommandExampleCreateDB.cs, change the class name to CommandExampleCreateDB and edit the try block as shown below:

```
try
{
    // open connection
    thisConnection.Open();

    // create new database called MyDatabase
    nonqueryCommand.CommandText = "CREATE DATABASE MyDb";
    Console.WriteLine(nonqueryCommand.CommandText);

    // always returns -1, no need to display return value
    nonqueryCommand.ExecuteNonQuery();
    Console.WriteLine("Database created, now switching");
    thisConnection.ChangeDatabase("MyDb");

    // execute non-query to create temporary table
    nonqueryCommand.CommandText = "CREATE TABLE MyTmpTable (COL1 integer)";
    Console.WriteLine(nonqueryCommand.CommandText);
    nonqueryCommand.ExecuteNonQuery();

    // execute non-query to insert some data
    nonqueryCommand.CommandText = "INSERT INTO MyTmpTable VALUES (37)";
    Console.WriteLine(nonqueryCommand.CommandText);
    Console.WriteLine("Number of Rows Affected is: {0}",
        nonqueryCommand.ExecuteNonQuery() );

}
```

3. Compile and run. We see this output:

```
CREATE DATABASE MyDb
Database created, now switching
CREATE TABLE MyTmpTable (COL1 integer)
INSERT INTO MyTmpTable VALUES (37)
Number of Rows Affected is: 1
Connection Closed.
Press any key to continue
```

How It Works

This example works in a very similar way to the previous one. The new addition is the creation of the database and switching to the newly created database within C# without having to open a new connection. When the database is created, the current database is the one specified when you opened the connection, in this case `tempdb` since we didn't change that part of the code:

```
SqlConnection thisConnection = new SqlConnection
    (@"Server=(local)\NetSDK;"    +    // server instance name
    "Integrated Security=SSPI;"    +    // use Windows login
    "Connection Timeout=5;"        +    // wait 5 seconds for server
    "Database=tempdb;" );               // connect to Northwind database
```

If you don't specify the `Database=` or `Initial Catalog=` clause in the connection string, the default database, `master`, becomes the current database. However, the current database is irrelevant when you issue the `CREATE DATABASE` command, as the new database resides on the server, not in a particular database:

```
// create new database called MyDatabase
nonqueryCommand.CommandText = "CREATE DATABASE MyDatabase";
Console.WriteLine(nonqueryCommand.CommandText);
```

If you are creating this on your local machine, you can actually see the program pause and hear your disk drive work as it creates the new file to contain the new database. Immediately after creating the database we switch to the newly made database:

```
Console.WriteLine("Database created, now switching");
thisConnection.ChangeDatabase("MyDatabase");
```

Now when the `CREATE TABLE` command is executed to create `MyTmpTable`, the table is created in `MyDatabase`, not `tempdb`:

```
// execute non-query to create temporary table
nonqueryCommand.CommandText = "CREATE TABLE MyTmpTable (COL1 integer)";
Console.WriteLine(nonqueryCommand.CommandText);
nonqueryCommand.ExecuteNonQuery();
```

For temporary tables, just use the `tempdb` database. If you need to create permanent set of tables, however, it is a good idea to put them in their own database.

Command Parameters

When a SQL command is executed by the server, all the information needed by the server must be contained within the string in the `CommandText` property. So if we want to insert some numbers into a column, we must specify the numbers as part of the string for the `INSERT` command:

```
INSERT INTO MyTmpTable VALUES (1)
INSERT INTO MyTmpTable VALUES (2)
INSERT INTO MyTmpTable VALUES (3)
INSERT INTO MyTmpTable VALUES (4)
```

It would get very tedious very quickly if we had to issue a separate `INSERT` for every value, so it would be great if we could do it with a program. The `CommandText` is only a string though, so we could build the string for the command by converting the variable containing the value we wish to insert into the database into a string, like this:

```
try
{
  // open connection
  thisConnection.Open();

  int i;
  for (i=1; i<=4; i++)
  {
    nonqueryCommand.CommandText =
      "INSERT INTO MyTmpTable VALUES (" + i.ToString() + ")";

    Console.WriteLine(nonqueryCommand.CommandText);
    Console.WriteLine("Number of Rows Affected is: {0}",
      nonqueryCommand.ExecuteNonQuery() );
  }
}
```

This approach of building the command text with normal string conversion operations and string addition works just fine for simple `INSERT` statements, and does the job with relatively few lines of code as well. However, it can get complicated to maintain, especially if you need to insert values into multiple columns, each of different types. Also, for irregular data types (for example, byte arrays containing binary data) this method does not work correctly (`ToString()` returns the name of the data type rather than the data itself for many object data types).

A better way to handle these more complex cases is to use **command parameters**, which have the following advantages:

❑ The mapping between the variables in your code and the place where they are used in the SQL command is clearer and more readable with parameters.

❑ The data type conversion between C# types and SQL data types is cleaner and more correct with parameters. As we will see, parameters let you use the data type definitions that are specific to a particular ADO.NET provider to ensure that your program variable is mapped to the correct back-end SQL data type.

❑ Parameters let you use the `Prepare()` method, which makes your code run faster. This is described in more detail in the explanation of the following example.

❑ Parameters are used extensively in more advanced programming techniques, such as stored procedures (which we'll cover in Chapter 14) and working with irregular data (Chapter 21).

A parameter for a SQL command is a placeholder in the command text that marks a place where a value will be substituted. In SQL Server **named parameters** are used; these begin with an @ sign followed by their name with no space. So then, in the following `INSERT` statement @MyName and @MyNumber are both parameters:

```
INSERT INTO MyTable VALUES (@MyName, @MyNumber)
```

Note that some other .NET data providers used unnamed parameters using the question mark (?) as a substitution placeholder. We'll look at these when we look at other .NET provider Command *objects, just ahead in this chapter.*

Try It Out: Using Command Parameters and the Prepare() Method

1. Add a new C# console application project called CommandExampleParameters to our open solution, Chapter6_Examples. Rename Class1.cs to CommandExampleParameters.cs.

2. Copy and paste the code from our previous example, CommandExampleCreateDB.cs, into CommandExampleParameters.cs, change the class name to CommandExampleParameters, and edit the try block as shown below:

```
try
{
  // open connection
  thisConnection.Open();

  // execute non-query to create temporary table
  nonqueryCommand.CommandText =
    "CREATE TABLE MyTable (MyName VARCHAR (30), MyNumber integer)";
  Console.WriteLine(nonqueryCommand.CommandText);
  nonqueryCommand.ExecuteNonQuery();

  // create INSERT command with named parameters
  nonqueryCommand.CommandText =
    "INSERT INTO MyTable VALUES (@MyName, @MyNumber)";

  // add parameters to Command object Parameters collection
  nonqueryCommand.Parameters.Add("@MyName", SqlDbType.VarChar, 30);
  nonqueryCommand.Parameters.Add("@MyNumber", SqlDbType.Int);

  // prepare INSERT command for repeated execution
  nonqueryCommand.Prepare();

  // data to be inserted
  string[] names = { "Enrico", "Franco", "Gloria", "Horace" } ;
  int i;
  for (i=1; i<=4; i++)
  {
    nonqueryCommand.Parameters["@MyName"].Value = names[i-1];
    nonqueryCommand.Parameters["@MyNumber"].Value = i;
    Console.WriteLine(nonqueryCommand.CommandText);
    Console.WriteLine("Number of Rows Affected is: {0}",
      nonqueryCommand.ExecuteNonQuery() );
  }
}
```

3. Compile and run. We see this output:

```
E:\Visual Studio Projects\Chapter6_Examples\CommandExampleParameters\bin\Debug\CommandEx...
CREATE TABLE MyTable (MyName VARCHAR (30), MyNumber integer)
INSERT INTO MyTable VALUES (@MyName, @MyNumber)
Number of Rows Affected is: 1
INSERT INTO MyTable VALUES (@MyName, @MyNumber)
Number of Rows Affected is: 1
INSERT INTO MyTable VALUES (@MyName, @MyNumber)
Number of Rows Affected is: 1
INSERT INTO MyTable VALUES (@MyName, @MyNumber)
Number of Rows Affected is: 1
Connection Closed.
Press any key to continue
```

How It Works

The general outline of this example is similar to our first example that created a table in `tempdb` and inserted a row into the table. Other than the fact that we created a table with two columns instead of one and changed class names, all the code up to setting the text for the first `INSERT` command is the same as in previous examples. Here is where we first specify the parameters named `@MyName` and `@MyNumber` inside the text of the `INSERT` command:

```
// create INSERT command with named parameters
nonqueryCommand.CommandText =
    "INSERT INTO MyTable VALUES (@MyName, @MyNumber)";
```

Next we need to add these parameters to the `Parameters` collection of the `Command` object. `Parameters` is a property of the `SqlCommand` object; it is a C# collection of `SqlParameter` objects. We use the collection's `Add` method to add new members to the collection here:

```
// add parameters to Command object Parameters collection
thisCommand.Parameters.Add("@MyName", SqlDbType.VarChar, 30);
thisCommand.Parameters.Add("@MyNumber", SqlDbType.Int);
```

Each `SqlParameter` object has a name that must match a name used in the command text, and a type that is specified by the `SqlDbType` enumeration. `SqlDbType` lets us specify a SQL-specific data type that exactly matches the column in the database. This helps ensure correct type conversion when variables from your C# program are substituted for the parameters. Next we call the `Prepare()` method. `Prepare()` lets the database server know that a command with parameters is going to be repeated several times, so it can pre-compile the command at the server, resulting in faster execution and less memory usage:

```
// prepare INSERT command for repeated execution
nonqueryCommand.Prepare();
```

The `Prepare()` method is not a requirement for using parameters, but it is a good idea if you are going to execute the same command multiple times with the only change to the command being different values for the parameter variables. Be aware that not every back-end database and provider support the prepared execution of statements, but SQL Server and the `SqlClient` provider do.

With our parameters set up, it's just a matter of inserting the various data values as required. We have four names in an array, so that names[0] is "Enrico", names[1] is "Franco", and so on. We do a `for` loop and set the @MyName parameter to a name from the names[] array and the @MyNumber parameter to an integer from the `for` loop index for each iteration through the loop. By assigning the `Value` property of the parameter we tell the system to convert the value from the variable in our program to the appropriate text to substitute into the INSERT command.

```
// data to be inserted
string[] names = { "Enrico", "Franco", "Gloria", "Horace" } ;
int i;
for (i=1; i<=4; i++)
{
    nonqueryCommand.Parameters["@MyName"].Value = names[i-1];
    nonqueryCommand.Parameters["@MyNumber"].Value = i;
```

Next we print out the command text:

```
Console.WriteLine(nonqueryCommand.CommandText) ;
```

Notice that it prints out the parameter name rather than the actual substituted value. For each iteration of the loop, we get:

INSERT INTO MyTable VALUES (@MyName, @MyNumber)

This is because the parameter substitution does not actually change the command text string; instead the parameters are substituted at the time the command is executed at the server, which is the next step:

```
Console.WriteLine("Number of Rows Affected is: {0}",
    nonqueryCommand.ExecuteNonQuery() );
}
```

When the command is actually executed, the server substitutes "Enrico" for @MyName and 0 for @MyNumber on the first iteration, "Frances" for @MyName and 1 for @MyNumber on the next iteration, and so on. Each of the four times the command is executed 1 row is affected. The result is the same as if we had executed the literal commands:

```
INSERT INTO MyTable VALUES ("Enrico", 0)
INSERT INTO MyTable VALUES ("Frances", 1)
INSERT INTO MyTable VALUES ("Gloria", 2)
INSERT INTO MyTable VALUES ("Horace", 3)
```

After we finish inserting the data, we close the connection. This example finishes our look at how the Command object is used with the SQL Server\MSDE provider. The SqlCommand class has a few more methods and properties but they are beyond the scope of this book. We'll finish this chapter then with a look at how the Command object is used with other .NET data providers.

Using Command Objects in Other .NET Data Providers

Both the OLE DB and ODBC data providers have their own `Command` objects, `OleDbCommand` and `OdbcCommand`, and both act very much the same as the `SqlCommand` object we have been using up until now. (Likewise the Oracle provider has one too, but as it was still in beta as we went to press, it's not covered here.) Let's look at a couple of examples.

Try It Out: Using the OleDbCommand Object

This sample is based on our previous `CommandExampleReader` example but rather than access the Northwind database, we will use OLE DB to access a Microsoft Access (Jet) `.mdb` sample file located in the Visual Studio .NET sample data.

> *Note: the file used, `GrocerToGo.mdb`, is included in the Quickstart samples that are installed by default by Visual C# Std Edition or Visual Studio. NET. If you selected an install option to not to install the Quickstart samples, this sample will not work. To correct this and run the example, you can install the sample files or change the code to reference another `.mdb` file located on your system (the `Northwind.mdb` file included in the Microsoft Office sample directory, for example).*

1. Add a new C# console application project called `CommandOleDbQuery` to our open solution, `Chapter6_Examples`. Rename `Class1.cs` to `CommandOleDbQuery.cs`.

2. Copy and paste the code from our `CommandExampleReader.cs` example into `CommandOleDbQuery.cs` replacing the previous code there. Edit the code to look like the following example. The changes to the code are highlighted:

```csharp
using System;
using System.Data;              // use ADO.NET namespace
using System.Data.OleDb;        // use OLE DB .NET data provider namespace
namespace Wrox.BeginningCSharpDatabase.Chapter06
{
  class CommandOleDbQuery
  {
    static void Main()
    {
      OleDbConnection thisConnection = new OleDbConnection(
        @"Provider=Microsoft.Jet.OLEDB.4.0;" +
        @"Data Source=" +          // Data Source = path name of .mdb file
        @"C:\Program Files\Microsoft Visual Studio .NET\FrameworkSDK\Samples" +
        @"\QuickStart\aspplus\samples\grocertogo\data\grocertogo.mdb"

      OleDbCommand thisCommand =
        new OleDbCommand("SELECT ProductID, ProductName FROM Products",
        thisConnection);

      try
      {
        // open connection
        thisConnection.Open();
```

```
        OleDbDataReader thisReader = thisCommand.ExecuteReader();

    while (thisReader.Read())
    {
      Console.WriteLine("Product ID and Name: {0} {1}",
        thisReader.GetValue(0),
        thisReader.GetValue(1));
    }

  }
  catch (OleDbException ex)
  {
    Console.WriteLine(ex.ToString());
  }
  finally
  {
    thisConnection.Close();   // close connection
    Console.WriteLine("Connection Closed.");
  }
    }
  }
}
```

3. Compile and run. We see this output:

```
E:\Visual Studio Projects\Chapter6_Examples\CommandOleDbQuery\bin\Debug\CommandOleDbQuer...
Product ID and Name: 1001 Chocolate City Milk
Product ID and Name: 1002 Bessie Brand 2% Milk
Product ID and Name: 1003 Funny Farms  Milk
Product ID and Name: 2001 Fruity Pops
Product ID and Name: 2002 U.F.O.s Cereal
Product ID and Name: 2003 Healthy Grains
Product ID and Name: 2004 Super Sugar Strike
Product ID and Name: 3001 Purple Rain
Product ID and Name: 3002 Extreme Orange
Product ID and Name: 3003 Kona Diet Cola
Product ID and Name: 3004 Fizzy Fizzing Drink
Product ID and Name: 1005 Marigold Whole Milk
Connection Closed.
Press any key to continue
```

How It Works

The code in this example is exactly the same as our first `ExecuteReader()` example, except for the name and location of the of sample data, the text and formatting of the query output, and the fact that the objects in the OLE DB .NET data provider have different names prefixed with `OleDb` – `OleDbConnection`, `OleDbCommand`, `OleDbException`, and so on. The differences in the `Connection` object and connection string between different .NET data providers were explained in the previous chapter. The `OleDbCommand` object itself is constructed in the same way as with `SqlCommand`, specifying a command text and connection:

```
OleDbCommand thisCommand =
    new OleDbCommand("SELECT ProductID, ProductName FROM Products",
    thisConnection);
```

The SQL commands accepted by the Microsoft Access (Jet) engine are slightly different compared to SQL Server's commands, but the basic commands are still the same.

Now let's try an example with the ODBC .NET data provider. We'll discover that once again there are only a few differences between it and the SQL Server .NET data provider.

Try It Out: Using the OdbcCommand Object

For this example, we'll base our sample code on the command parameters example we created earlier (`CommandExampleParameters.cs`).

> *As noted in Chapter 5, the ODBC .NET data provider is a separate download not included with Visual C# Standard Edition or Visual Studio.NET. See the instructions for the `OdbcConnection` example in Chapter 5 and/or the description of the ODBC .NET data provider in Chapter 4 for download instructions. Also, MySql and the MyOdbc ODBC driver for MySql, which is used in this project is a separate database product (see www.mysql.com for more information); while we show MySql since it is one of the more common databases accessed via ODBC, any ODBC driver and data source that you have available can be used instead.*

1. Add a new C# console application project called `CommandOdbcExample` to our open solution, `Chapter6_Examples`. Rename `Class1.cs` to `CommandOdbcExample.cs`.

2. Copy and paste the code from our `CommandExampleParameters.cs` example into `CommandOdbcExample.cs` replacing the previous code there. Edit the code to look like the following example. The changes to the code are highlighted:

```
using System;
using System.Data;              // use ADO.NET namespace
using Microsoft.Data.Odbc;      // use ODBC .NET data provider namespace
namespace Wrox.BeginningCSharpDatabase.Chapter06
{
  class CommandOdbcExample
  {
    static void Main()
    {
```

```
// create OdbcConnection object
OdbcConnection thisConnection = new OdbcConnection
  ("DRIVER={MySQL ODBC 3.51 Driver};"    +
  "SERVER=localhost;" +
  "DATABASE=test;"       +
  "UID=root;" +
  "PASSWORD=;");

// create OdbcCommand objects
OdbcCommand nonqueryCommand = thisConnection.CreateCommand();

try
{
  // open connection
  thisConnection.Open();

  // execute non-query to create temporary table
  nonqueryCommand.CommandText =
    "CREATE TABLE MyTable (MyName VARCHAR (30), MyNumber integer)";
  Console.WriteLine(nonqueryCommand.CommandText);
  nonqueryCommand.ExecuteNonQuery();

  // create INSERT command with ? unnamed parameters
  nonqueryCommand.CommandText =
    "INSERT INTO MyTable VALUES (?, ?)" ;

  // add parameters to Command object Parameters collection
  nonqueryCommand.Parameters.Add("@MyName", OdbcType.VarChar, 30);
  nonqueryCommand.Parameters.Add("@MyNumber", OdbcType.Int);

  // prepare not supported by current version of myODBC and mySQL
  // nonqueryCommand.Prepare();

  // data to be inserted
  string[] names = { "Enrico", "Franco", "Gloria", "Horace" } ;
  int i;
  for (i=1; i<=4; i++)
  {
    nonqueryCommand.Parameters["@MyName"].Value = names[i-1];
    nonqueryCommand.Parameters["@MyNumber"].Value = i;
    Console.WriteLine(nonqueryCommand.CommandText);
    Console.WriteLine("Number of Rows Affected is: {0}",
      nonqueryCommand.ExecuteNonQuery() );
  }

  // check to see the data we inserted
  nonqueryCommand.CommandText = "SELECT MyName, MyNumber FROM MyTable";
  OdbcDataReader thisReader = nonqueryCommand.ExecuteReader();

  while (thisReader.Read())
  {
    Console.WriteLine("Name and Number: {0} {1}",
      thisReader.GetValue(0),
```

```
                   thisReader.GetValue(1));
            }
      }
      catch (OdbcException ex)
      {
        Console.WriteLine(ex.ToString());
      }
      finally
      {
        thisConnection.Close();   // close connection
        Console.WriteLine("Connection Closed.");
      }
    }
  }
}
```

3. The `Microsoft.Data.Odbc.dll` is a separate download and install not included in Visual Studio.NET. After installation you must add an explicit reference to it in your project. To do this, select **Project | Add References** and select `Microsoft.Data.Odbc.dll` from the list of available .NET references. See the `OdbcConnection` example in Chapter 5 for a more detailed explanation of this.

4. If it doesn't exist already, add a database called `test` to your mySQL server.

5. Build and run the program. We see this output:

```
ET E:\Visual Studio Projects\Chapter6_Examples\CommandOdbcExample\bin\Debug\CommandOdbcExa...  _ □ X
CREATE TABLE MyTable (MyName VARCHAR (30), MyNumber integer)
INSERT INTO MyTable VALUES (?, ?)
Number of Rows Affected is: 1
INSERT INTO MyTable VALUES (?, ?)
Number of Rows Affected is: 1
INSERT INTO MyTable VALUES (?, ?)
Number of Rows Affected is: 1
INSERT INTO MyTable VALUES (?, ?)
Number of Rows Affected is: 1
Name and Number: Enrico 1
Name and Number: Franco 2
Name and Number: Gloria 3
Name and Number: Horace 4
Connection Closed.
Press any key to continue
```

How It Works

Again we see the differences in the names of the ADO.NET data provider objects: `OdbcConnection`, `OdbcCommand`, `OdbcType`, and so on. The connection object differences were described in the previous chapter.

Command parameters are an area where there are several differences between the .NET data providers. The ODBC provider does not support named parameters; instead it uses unnamed parameters indicated in the text of the command by a question mark:

```
// create INSERT command with ? unnamed parameters
nonqueryCommand.CommandText =
   "INSERT INTO MyTable VALUES (?, ?)" ;
```

Unnamed parameters are position dependent; the first parameter added will be associated with the first question mark, and so on in order. Here we do the `Add` operation; note that names are used here but they are ignored when substituting into the command text:

```
// add parameters to Command object Parameters collection
nonqueryCommand.Parameters.Add("@MyName", OdbcType.VarChar, 30);
nonqueryCommand.Parameters.Add("@MyNumber", OdbcType.Int);
```

Note we use the `OdbcType` enumeration that lists the ODBC data provider types; the `SqlDbType` we used in the previous example is specific to SQL Server, even though the same basic types are supported – differences are at the fine detail level.

```
// prepare not supported by current version of myODBC and mySQL
// nonqueryCommand.Prepare();
```

The `Prepare()` method is not supported by the back-end database (mySQL) in this case, so we do not call it here; as stated earlier, it is optional. This is an optimization issue; it does not affect the program except potentially in performance. Carrying on, the insertion loop is exactly the same as the SQL example:

```
// data to be inserted
string[] names = { "Enrico", "Franco", "Gloria", "Horace" } ;
int i;
for (i=1; i<=4; i++)
{
  thisCommand.Parameters["@MyName"].Value = names[i-1];
  thisCommand.Parameters["@MyNumber"].Value = i;
  Console.WriteLine(thisCommand.CommandText);
  Console.WriteLine("Number of Rows Affected is: {0}",
     thisCommand.ExecuteNonQuery() );
}
```

We added a `DataReader` execution to check on the data we inserted; note that it is an `OdbcDataReader`, keeping with the naming convention for all ODBC .NET data provider objects.

```
// check to see the data we inserted
nonqueryCommand.CommandText = "SELECT MyName, MyNumber FROM MyTable";
OdbcDataReader thisReader = nonqueryCommand.ExecuteReader();
```

That finishes the ODBC example and also the chapter. Let's summarize.

Summary

In this chapter we learned:

❑   What the ADO.NET data provider `Command` object is and does

❑   How to create a `Command` object (`SqlCommand`)

❑   How to associate a `Command` object with a `Connection`

❑   How to set the command text for a `Command` object

❑   What the different `Execute` methods do within the `Command` object

❑   How to use `ExecuteScalar()` to get a single result back from a query

❑   How to use `ExecuteReader()` to process multiple query results

❑   How to use `ExecuteNonQuery()` to execute data manipulation commands

❑   How to create databases and tables using `ExecuteNonQuery()`

❑   What command parameters are and how to use them

❑   How to use the `Command` object in other .NET data providers, specifically `OleDbCommand` and `OdbcCommand`.

In the next chapter we'll look in more detail at the `DataReader` object.

Exercises

1.   What method can you use to create a `Command` object without calling its constructor? Write a program that shows this method.

2.   What are the four `Execute` methods for the `Command` object? What are the differences between each of them?

3.   Write a program showing the use of `ExecuteScalar` to confirm the results of our `INSERT` statements in the first `ExecuteNonQuery` example.

4.   Add an `ExecuteReader` to the SQL Server `CommandParametersExample` to check that the data inserted is correct.

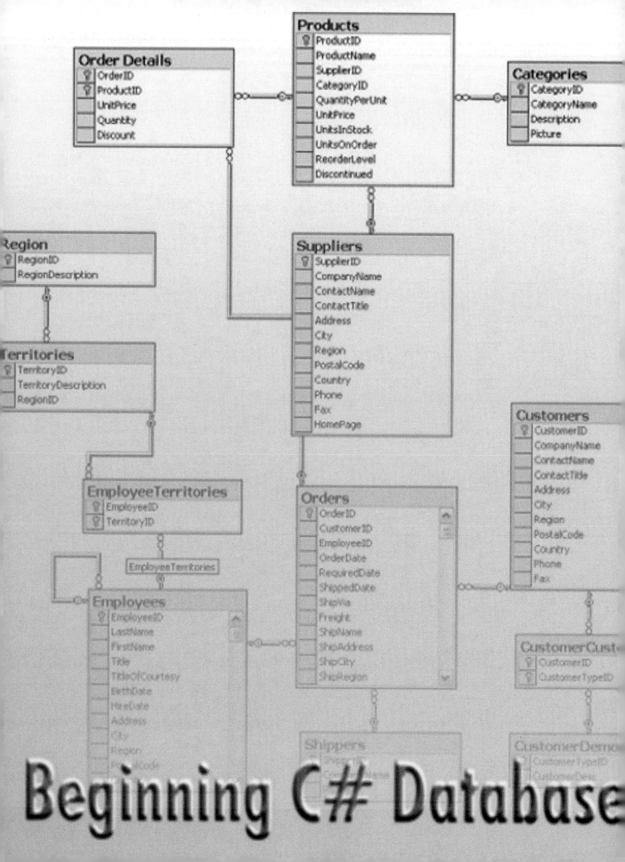

Using the DataReader

Now that we've looked at connecting to a database, and issuing commands to retrieve data from a database using that connection, we need to be able to read in the required data so we can display it in some way. In the previous chapters we've briefly met the ADO.NET `DataReader`, and we've seen that we can use it to read data from a data source in a connected manner, reading through all of the data selected using the `Command` object. In this chapter we'll spend more time looking at the `DataReader` in more detail, learning more about how it works. As we progress through this chapter, we'll gradually learn more about the `DataReader`, how it's used, its limitations, and importance in the .NET programming scenario.

In particular, we will look at:

❑   What's under the hood of the `DataReader`

❑   Using ordinal and column name indexers

❑   More about the dataset

❑   How to get schema information for a `DataReader`

❑   How to use multiple resultsets in a `DataReader`

Let's start by looking at how the `DataReader` works in more detail.

Getting to Know ADO.NET Data Readers

As you'll recall, the .NET Framework is a highly-ordered collection of classes contained within namespaces. The classes within the namespaces relating to ADO.NET contain functionality such as establishing connections wrapped up inside the ADO.NET class framework.

From the data provider namespaces, after the `Connection` and the `Command` objects, the next vital object down the list would certainly be the `DataReader`. Once we've connected to a data source, and queried it with commands, we need some way to read what's returned. It could be a set of columns, a single row, or even an aggregated value, returned by the query run. This is where the `DataReader` comes in.

If you're porting from an ADO background, it would be worth mentioning here that an ADO.NET `DataReader` is a bit like an ADO forward-only `RecordSet`, only this time, as we know, it's not another COM object!

The `DataReader` class is a fast, unbuffered, forward-only, read-only cursor that works while connected to a data source and accesses data on a per-row basis; alternatively we could say that it reads in one row at a time and then loops through them all.

We cannot directly instantiate a `DataReader` class; instead, an instance of it is returned by executing the `ExecuteReader` method of a `Command` object. For example, the code snippet below shows a call made to the `ExecuteReader` method of an `OleDbCommand` object.

```
OleDbDataReader OleDbReader = OleDbComm.ExecuteReader();
```

When we need to query a database for results, for instance if we queried the `Employees` table in the Northwind database for employee details, the `ExecuteReader` method needs to be called in order to get an associated `DataReader` instance returned (in the case shown above, it's an `OleDbDataReader` object). Once at our disposal, we can use it for accessing the desired data.

> One point to note that we'll be coming back to in the next chapter is the issue of **DataReader** versus **DataSet**. The general rule is to always use a **DataReader** for simply reading data. If all you are doing is reading and displaying data, all you'll need to use in the majority of situations is a **DataReader**.

Under the Hood of the DataReader

Knowing enough about the outer shell and the role of a `DataReader` in the ADO.NET class framework, you probably can't wait to get reading some data. Let's get down to business and discover what it's really like under the hood. We'll advance through a couple of examples and passages and learn the different ways in which the `DataReader` can be read. Our first encounter will be with a reader that's looped for records.

Try It Out: Looping Through a DataReader

Let's say that we've successfully established a connection with the database, a query has been executed for results, and everything seems to be going fine – what now? The next sensible thing to do would be to retrieve the records and then possibly display them. We know that the `ExecuteReader()` method returns a `DataReader` instance for us to play around with. So now, we start reading.

Consider the following console application that illustrates the use of an `SqlDataReader` and shows you how to loop through it for records. To begin with, perform the following steps:

1. Open Visual Studio .NET and create a new blank solution, called `Chapter7_Examples`, which we'll use to contain the samples in this chapter.

2. Within our solution, create a new Console Application. Call this `DataLooper` and the main file `DataLooper.cs`

3. You should now be in the code window, and the cursor positioned within some generated code.

4. Select all code and press *Delete*. This should clear the window and allow you to start writing the following code from scratch:

```
using System;
using System.Data;          // Includes some essential ADO.NET classes
using System.Data.SqlClient; // Includes SQL Server Provider classes

namespace Wrox.BeginningCSharpDatabases.Chapter07
{

class DataLooper
{
  static void Main(string[] args)
  {
    // Our connection string
    string ConStr = @"server=(local)\NetSDK;" +
                     "Integrated Security=SSPI;database=Northwind";

    // Pass connection string to the SqlConnection object
    SqlConnection sqlConn = new SqlConnection(ConStr);

    try
    {
      // Open Connection to start reading
      sqlConn.Open();

      // SQL query for getting values from the database
      string SQL = "SELECT ContactName FROM Customers";

      // Pass query string and Connection object to the Command object
      SqlCommand sqlComm= new SqlCommand(SQL,sqlConn);

      /// Get an instance of a SqlDataReader
      SqlDataReader sqlReader = sqlComm.ExecuteReader();

      // Loop through the available records
      while(sqlReader.Read())
      {
        // Print one record at a time
        Console.WriteLine("{0}", sqlReader[0]);
      }

      sqlReader.Close();
    }
    catch(Exception ex)
    {
```

```
                Console.WriteLine("Error Orccured: " + ex.Message);
      }
      finally
      {
        sqlConn.Close();
        Console.ReadLine();
      }
    }
  }
}
```

5. Save and run your project by pressing *F5*. If all has gone well, the above code produces the following output:

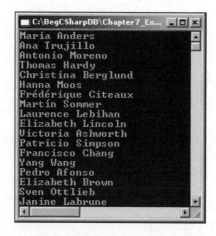

How It Works

Let's walk through the code and see what we've created. We began our program with the usual set of instructions, including importing commonly-used namespaces, setting up our connection details, and creating a query for our database, as shown in the code below:

```
using System;
using System.Data;          // Includes some essential ADO.NET classes
using System.Data.SqlClient; // Includes SQL Server Provider classes

namespace Wrox.BeginningCSharpDatabases.Chapter07
{
class DataLooper
{
  static void Main(string[] args)
  {
    // Our connection string
    string ConStr = @"server=(local)\NetSDK;" +
                    "Integrated Security=SSPI;database=Northwind";
```

```
// Pass connection string to the SqlConnection object
SqlConnection sqlConn = new SqlConnection(ConStr);

try
{
  // Open Connection to start reading
  sqlConn.Open();

  // SQL query for getting values from the database
  string SQL = "SELECT ContactName FROM Customers";

  // Pass query string and Connection object to the Command object
  SqlCommand sqlComm= new SqlCommand(SQL,sqlConn);
```

In our last few chapters, we've gone over the `Connection` and the `Command` object quite extensively. Since we are already familiar with the two objects and their usage, let's get straight down to the intricacies of using a `DataReader`.

Recall from previous chapters, that a `SqlDataReader` class is an abstract class and cannot be instantiated explicitly. For this reason, we obtain an instance of a `SqlDataReader` by executing the `ExecuteReader()` method of `SqlCommand`. This is done by the following line of code:

```
SqlDataReader sqlReader = sqlComm.ExecuteReader();
```

Once we have a reader attached to the active connection, we can loop through each row of the returned resultset, provided that the resultset is not empty, and retrieve values column by column. In order to do this we need to make a call to the `Read()` method of `SqlDataReader`, which returns `true` if there is a 'next' row available and advances the cursor, or it returns `false` if there isn't another row. Since `Read()` advances the cursor to the next available record, we have to call it each time manually. So for this purpose, we use a `while` loop in our example to do the job as shown below:

```
while(sqlReader.Read())
```

Once we call the `Read()` method, the next row is returned as a collection and stored in the `SqlDataReader` object itself. To access data from a specific column, we can use a number of methods (we'll cover these in our next section), but for this application we used the ordinal indexer lookup method; giving the column number to the reader to retrieve values (just as we would give an index to an array of integers perhaps). Since in our case we chose a single column from the `Customers` table while querying the database, only the zeroth indexer is accessible and so we use the following line of code to display each record one by one:

```
Console.WriteLine("{0}", sqlReader[0]);  // The index is zero-based
```

To be able to use the connection for another purpose or to run another query on the database, it is important that we call the `Close()` method of `SqlDataReader` to close the reader explicitly. This is because, once the reader is attached to an active connection, the connection remains busy fetching data for the reader, and remains unusable for another purpose till the reader has been detached from it. The following line shows this being done after we're looped through the resultset and we're done using the `DataReader`:

```
sqlReader.Close();
```

Once the connection has been used, it is closed explicitly in the `finally` clause. If for some reason you don't close the connection, the .NET garbage collector does this for you during the cleanup, but remember, sometimes you might have pending queries or transactions lined up in a queue, and closing the connection explicitly would make sure they're all processed and executed before the application ends – the garbage collector will not; it'll just collect unreferenced objects and you might end up losing some of the changes you made to the data since the queue would not be processed. It is advisable that you close the connection explicitly with the `Close()` method:

```
finally
{
  sqlConn.Close();
  Console.ReadLine();
}
```

The last line in the `finally` block makes sure that the console window does not close as soon as the application finishes after executing.

Using Ordinal Indexers

In the previous example, we mentioned the use of ordinal indexers in retrieving column data from the database. We shall look at the same code snippet again and learn more about it. However, we will only be taking into consideration the piece of code where the actual index has been referenced to avoid any kind of confusion:

```
sqlReader[0]
```

Looks familiar? If you've ever used arrays, this line shouldn't be foreign to you. This is one of the ways we can request a data reader to fetch data, and this method of fetching data is called the ordinal indexer method. The indexer we pass to the `DataReader` object is actually an item property and the return value is an object.

Compared to the field-name indexing method, something we'll learn in a section later in this chapter, this method is faster simply because the reader does not have to *find* the column from the row but jumps right to it with the index provided, saving time, energy, and resources. Let's take a look at another example to demonstrate this more clearly.

Try It Out: Using Ordinal Indexers

Let's compare ordinal indexing to a real-world example; we're standing in a street of fifty houses and we have to find someone named 'John Hook'. All we're aware of is his name and we don't know which house he lives in. To find him, we'll have to individually check each house. Wouldn't it be a lot easier if we knew his address instead and stepped right to it? Sure would! That's just what ordinal indexing is about.

Let's consider a small console application that uses the ordinal indexer lookup method, and later compare our results with those of the field name indexing method, which we'll cover in the next section. To be able to start and execute our program, perform the following steps:

1. Open Visual Studio.NET and create a new Console Application within our chapter solution. Call this `OrdinalIndexer` and the main file `OrdinalIndexer.cs`.

2. Select all code from the main file and press *Delete*. This should clear the window and allow you to start writing the following code from scratch:

```
using System;
using System.Data;          // Includes some essential ADO.NET classes
using System.Data.SqlClient; // Includes SQL Server Provider classes

namespace Wrox.BeginningCSharpDatabases.Chapter07
{
class OrdinalIndexer
{
  static void Main(string[] args)
  {
    // Our Connection string
    string ConStr = @"server=(local)\NetSDK;" +
                    "Integrated Security=SSPI;" +
                    "database=Northwind";

    // Pass connection string to the SqlConnection object
    SqlConnection sqlConn = new SqlConnection(ConStr);

    try
    {
      // Open Connection to start reading
      sqlConn.Open();

      // SQL query for getting values
      string SQL = "SELECT CompanyName, ContactName FROM " +
                   "Customers WHERE ContactName LIKE 'M%'";

      // Pass query string and Connection object to the Command object
      SqlCommand sqlComm= new SqlCommand(SQL,sqlConn);

      // Get an instance of a SqlDataReader
      SqlDataReader sqlReader = sqlComm.ExecuteReader();

      // Print titles
      Console.WriteLine("\t{0}    {1}",
        "Company Name".PadRight(25),
        "Contact Name".PadRight(20));

      Console.WriteLine("\t{0}    {1}",
        "============".PadRight(25),
        "============".PadRight(20));

      // Loop through the available records
      while(sqlReader.Read())
      {
        Console.WriteLine(" {0} | {1}",
```

```
            sqlReader[0].ToString().PadLeft(25),
            sqlReader[1].ToString().PadLeft(20));
    }

    sqlReader.Close();
}
catch(Exception ex)
{
    Console.WriteLine("Error Orccured: " + ex.Message);
}
finally
{
    sqlConn.Close();
    Console.ReadLine();
}
    }
}
}
```

3. Right-click on the `OrdinalIndexer` project in the Solution Explorer, and select **Set as StartUp Project** from the context menu.

4. Save and run the code by pressing *F5*. You should be presented with the following output:

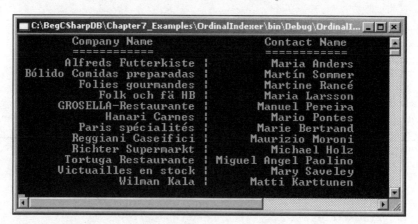

How It Works

Since we've looked at the connection details for examples like this in earlier chapters, we'll not dwell on that here. Let's move on to the `DataReader`-specific code.

For this example, we queried the `Customers` table from the database for columns `CompanyName` and `ContactName`, where contact names begin with the letter 'M'. This can be seen in the line below:

```
string SQL = "SELECT CompanyName, ContactName FROM " +
             "Customers WHERE ContactName LIKE 'M%'";
```

Since two columns were selected by our query, the returned data would also comprise a collection of rows from only these two columns, thus allowing access to only two possible `DataReader` indexers, 0 and 1.

We call on our ordinal indexers in a `while` loop, fetching values of the two columns for us, as the cursor advances to a new row in the dataset every time a call to the `Read()` method is made. Since the returned value is an object, we need to explicitly convert the value into a string so that we may make use of the `PadLeft` function for displaying the output in an organized manner:

```
while(sqlReader.Read())
{
  Console.WriteLine(" {0} | {1}",
    sqlReader[0].ToString().PadLeft(25),
    sqlReader[1].ToString().PadLeft(20));
}
```

After retrieving column values, we explicitly close the reader to free or unbind our connection or any other resource, and close the connection in the `finally` block:

```
    sqlReader.Close();
...
    sqlConn.Close();
```

Using Column-Name Indexers

It's true that most of the time we don't really keep track of column numbers and prefer retrieving values by their respective column names, simply because it's much easier remember them by their names, and also makes your code more self-documenting.

Column-name indexing is done by passing a column name to the `DataReader`, as opposed to the ordinal indexer method. This has many advantages. For instance, it could happen, for whatever reason, that our database changes its schema (schemas are discussed later in the chapter in the section on *Getting Schema Information for a DataReader*), probably by an addition or deletion of one or more columns (though considered drastic in any circumstance), thereby upsetting column ordering and raising exceptions in older code that uses the ordinal indexer look up method. Using column-name indexers could take care of most of these issues, but it is preferred that we use the ordinal look up method for faster results, especially when it comes to accessing hundreds of records from a number of columns and tables.

Let's consider a code snippet that retrieves the same columns (`CompanyName` and `ContactName`) our last example did, using the column-name indexer method as follows:

```
Console.WriteLine("{0} | {1}",
  sqlReader["CompanyName"].ToString().PadLeft(25),
  sqlReader["ContactName"].ToString().PadLeft(20));
```

You can use this code snippet with the example we saw on the ordinal indexer method, by performing the following steps:

1. Open the code for the previous example and search for the following line of code:

```
Console.WriteLine(" {0} | {1}",
  sqlReader[0].ToString().PadLeft(25),
  sqlReader[1].ToString().PadLeft(20));
```

2. Replace this line with the one below:

```
Console.WriteLine("{0} | {1}",
  sqlReader["CompanyName"].ToString().PadLeft(25),
  sqlReader["ContactName"].ToString().PadLeft(20));
```

3. Save the project and execute it. This will produce the same result as we saw for the ordinal indexer method.

Our next section might prove to be a much better approach for most cases.

Using Typed Accessor Methods

You've probably noticed how simple it is to retrieve data from any OLE DB-specific data source using the OLE DB data provider, or even from a SQL Server backend using the SQL Server data provider, but has it occurred to you that the 'string' or the 'integer' values we retrieve would probably not be represented the same way in the database? It could simply be a `varchar`, a `text`, an `nvarchar`, or a `numeric` value stored in the database that we conveniently retrieve and use without knowing what's really going on behind the scenes. SQL supports retrieving column data in various data formats, by simply requesting it in that type.

When a `DataReader` returns a value from a data source, the resulting value is retrieved and stored locally in a .NET Framework type rather than the original data source type. This in-place type conversion feature is a tradeoff between consistency and speed, and so to give some control over the data being retrieved, the `DataReader` exposes typed accessor methods that you can use if you know the specific type of the value being returned.

Typed accessor methods all begin with a `Get`, take an ordinal for data retrieval, and are type safe – C# will not allow you to get away with unsafe casts. These methods turn out to be faster than both the ordinal and the column name indexer methods. Being faster than column name indexing seems only logical as the typed accessor methods take ordinals for referencing, but being faster than ordinal indexing needs to be further explained. This is due to the fact that even though both techniques take in a column number, the conventional ordinal indexing method needs to look up the data type of the result and then eventually go through a type conversion, but the overhead of looking up the schema is avoided in the case of typed accessor calls.

For almost all data types supported by SQL Server or by OLE DB-specific databases (since some databases support data types like Oracle's `VARCHAR2`, in contrast to `VARCHAR` in SQL Server), there are respective .NET Framework data types and typed accessor methods available.

The following table should give you a brief idea of when to use typed accessors and with what data type. We shall first consider SQL Server data types, their corresponding .NET Framework data types, typed accessor and special SQL Server-specific typed accessor methods designed particularly for returning objects of type `SqlTypes` (`System.Data.SqlTypes`).

SQL Server data type	.NET Framework type	.NET Framework typed accessor	SqlType typed accessor
bigint	Int64	GetInt64()	GetSqlInt64()
binary	Byte[]	GetBytes()	GetSqlBinary()
bit	Boolean	GetBoolean()	GetSqlBit()
char	String or Char[]	GetString() or GetChars()	GetSqlString()
datetime	DateTime	GetDateTime()	GetSqlDateTime()
decimal	Decimal	GetDecimal()	GetSqlDecimal()
float	Double	GetDouble()	GetSqlDouble()
image or long varbinary	Byte[]	GetBytes()	GetSqlBinary()
int	Int32	GetInt32()	GetSqlInt32()
money	Decimal	GetDecimal()	GetSqlMoney()
nchar	String or Char[]	GetString() or GetChars()	GetSqlString()
ntext	String or Char[]	GetString() or GetChars()	GetSqlString()
numeric	Decimal	GetDecimal()	GetSqlDecimal()
nvarchar	String or Char[]	GetString() or GetChars()	GetSqlString()
real	Single	GetFloat()	GetSqlSingle()
smalldatetime	DateTime	GetDateTime()	GetSqlDateTime()
smallint	Int16	GetInt16()	GetSqlInt16()
smallmoney	Decimal	GetDecimal()	GetSqlDecimal()
sql_variant	Object	GetValue()	GetSqlValue()
text or long varchar (Also memo long varchar)	String or Char[]	GetString() or GetChars()	GetSqlString()
timestamp	Byte[]	GetBytes()	GetSqlBinary()
tinyint _Short_	Byte	GetByte()	GetSqlByte()
uniqueidentifier	Guid	GetGuid()	GetSqlGuid()
varbinary	Byte[]	GetBytes()	GetSqlBinary()
varchar	String or Char[]	GetString() or GetChars()	GetSqlString()

Chapter 7

Now we look at some available OLE DB data types, their corresponding .NET Framework data types and typed accessor methods:

OLE DB type	.NET Framework type	.NET Framework typed accessor
DBTYPE_I8	Int64	GetInt64()
DBTYPE_BYTES	Byte[]	GetBytes()
DBTYPE_BOOL	Boolean	GetBoolean()
DBTYPE_BSTR	String	GetString()
DBTYPE_STR	String	GetString()
DBTYPE_CY	Decimal	GetDecimal()
DBTYPE_DATE	DateTime	GetDateTime()
DBTYPE_DBDATE	DateTime	GetDateTime()
DBTYPE_DBTIME	DateTime	GetDateTime()
DBTYPE_DBTIMESTAMP	DateTime	GetDateTime()
DBTYPE_DECIMAL	Decimal	GetDecimal()
DBTYPE_R8	Double	GetDouble()
DBTYPE_ERROR	ExternalException	GetValue()
DBTYPE_FILETIME	DateTime	GetDateTime()
DBTYPE_GUID	Guid	GetGuid()
DBTYPE_I4	Int32	GetInt32()
DBTYPE_LONGVARCHAR	String	GetString()
DBTYPE_NUMERIC	Decimal	GetDecimal()
DBTYPE_R4	Single	GetFloat()
DBTYPE_I2	Int16	GetInt16()
DBTYPE_I1	Byte	GetByte()
DBTYPE_UI8	UInt64	GetValue()

OLE DB type	.NET Framework type	.NET Framework typed accessor
DBTYPE_UI4	UInt32	GetValue()
DBTYPE_UI2	UInt16	GetValue()
DBTYPE_VARCHAR	String	GetString()
DBTYPE_VARIANT	Object	GetValue()
DBTYPE_WVARCHAR	String	GetString()
DBTYPE_WSRT	String	GetString()

To see typed accessor methods in action, let's now consider looking at a console application that makes use of them. For this example, we will use the `Products` table from our Northwind MSDE database.

Below is the data design of the table. Note that the data types given in the table below will be looked up for their corresponding typed methods from the tables we saw above, so that we can use them correctly in our application.

Column Name	Data Type	Length	Allow Nulls
ProductID (Unique)	int	4	No
ProductName	nvarchar	40	No
SupplierID	int	4	Yes
CategoryID	int	4	Yes
QuantityPerUnit	nvarchar	20	Yes
UnitPrice	money	8	Yes
UnitsInStock	smallint	2	Yes
UnitsOnOrder	smallint	2	Yes
ReorderLevel	smallint	2	Yes
Discontinued	bit	1	No

Let us now begin with our example.

Try It Out: Using Typed Accessor Methods

1. Open Visual Studio.NET and create a new Console Application within the chapter solution. Call this `TypedMethods` and the main file `TypedMethods.cs`.

2. Select all code from `TypedMethods.cs` and press *Delete*. This should clear the window and allow you to start writing the following code from scratch:

```csharp
using System;
using System.Data;
using System.Data.SqlClient;

namespace Wrox.BeginningCSharpDatabases.Chapter07
{
class TypedMethods
{
  static void Main(string[] args)
  {
    // Our connection string
    string ConStr = @"server=(local)\NetSDK;" +
                     "Integrated Security=true;" +
                     "database=Northwind";

    // Pass connection string to the SqlConnection object
    SqlConnection sqlConn = new SqlConnection(ConStr);

    try
    {
      // Open Connection to start reading
      sqlConn.Open();

      // Our SQL query string
      string SQL = "SELECT ProductName, UnitPrice," +
                   "UnitsInStock, Discontinued FROM Products";

      // Create Command object for executing our SQL query
      SqlCommand sqlCom = new SqlCommand(SQL,sqlConn);

      // Get an instance of a DataReader
      SqlDataReader sqlReader = sqlCom.ExecuteReader();

      // Start fetching data
      while(sqlReader.Read())
      {
        Console.WriteLine("{0}\t {1}\t\t {2}\t {3}",
                          // GetString() for a nvarchar
                          sqlReader.GetString(0).PadRight(30),
                          // GetDecimal() for money
                          sqlReader.GetDecimal(1),
                          // GetIn16 for smallint
                          sqlReader.GetInt16(2),
                          // GetBoolean for bit
                          sqlReader.GetBoolean(3));
      }

      // Close DataReader
      sqlReader.Close();
    }
    catch(Exception ex)
    {
```

```
         Console.WriteLine("Error Orccured: " + ex.Message);
      }
      finally
      {
         sqlConn.Close();
         Console.ReadLine();
      }
   }
}
}
```

3. Save and run the code by pressing *F5*, and you should see something like this:

```
C:\BegCSharpDB\Chapter7_Examples\TypedMethods\bin\Debug\TypedMethods.exe        _ □ x
Chai                             18                39        False
Chang                            19                17        False
Aniseed Syrup                    10                13        False
Chef Anton's Cajun Seasoning     22                53        False
Chef Anton's Gumbo Mix           21.35             0         True
Grandma's Boysenberry Spread     25                120       False
Uncle Bob's Organic Dried Pears  30                15        False
Northwoods Cranberry Sauce       40                6         False
Mishi Kobe Niku                  97                29        True
Ikura                            31                31        False
Queso Cabrales                   21                22        False
Queso Manchego La Pastora        38                86        False
Konbu                            6                 24        False
Tofu                             23.25             35        False
```

How It Works

After establishing a connection with our database, we query it for four columns, namely `ProductName`, `UnitPrice`, `UnitsInStock`, and `Discontinued`. This can be seen by the code snippet below.

```
// Our SQL query string
string SQL = "SELECT ProductName, UnitPrice," +
             "UnitsInStock, Discontinued FROM Products";
```

The reason for our choice of columns was to deal with different kinds of data types and see how relevant typed methods could be used to obtain the correct results. As shown in the data design above, each of these columns has a different type defined in the schema.

After executing the `ExecuteReader` method, we come to the part where we have used the typed accessor methods. The code snippet below shows this being done:

```
...
      while(sqlReader.Read())
      {
        Console.WriteLine("{0}\t {1}\t\t {2}\t {3}",
                        // GetString() for a nvarchar
                        sqlReader.GetString(0).PadRight(30),
                        // GetDecimal() for money
                        sqlReader.GetDecimal(1),
                        // GetIn16 for smallint
                        sqlReader.GetInt16(2),
                        // GetBoolean for bit
                        sqlReader.GetBoolean(3));
      }
...
```

Tallying with the tables, given earlier, for native data types, we can see that an `nvarchar`, a `money`, a `smallint` and a `bit` data type in SQL Server can be accessed by the `GetString`, `GetDecimal`, `GetInt16`, and the `GetBoolean` accessor methods respectively.

This technique is fast and completely type safe. By this I mean, the implicit conversions from native data types to the .NET Framework types are completely safe and handled, thus increasing speed and performance. Also, if a typed method is used incorrectly, for example with a non-compatible data type, an exception is thrown for invalid casts. For instance if we try using the `GetString` method on a `bit` data type instead of using the `GetBoolean` method, a 'Specified cast is not valid' exception will be thrown.

Talking about speed and performance: remember how much we've stressed using the right provider for a specific database. If you're using SQL Server 7.0 or later, there's more that the .NET Framework has to offer. Along with these relatively general typed methods (you can use these typed methods with any version of SQL Server), the Framework offers optimized typed methods specifically designed for SQL Server 7+. These typed methods can be spotted by their addition of 'Sql' in the middle. For instance, the `GetString` method's SQL Server 7+ specific counterpart is `GetSqlString`.

These methods can be used just like other typed methods, but it's worth mentioning that they return a `SqlTypes` object, available through the `System.Data.SqlTypes` namespace. For instance, the `GetSqlString` method returns an object of type `System.Data.SqlTypes.SqlString` and not of type `System.String`, which the `GetString` method returns. These data types are implicitly handled by the Framework for all kinds of type conversions to the native .NET Framework types.

Learning More about the Data

So far all we've learned to do is retrieve data from the data source. Once we have a populated `DataReader` in our hands, there's much more we can do. We're exposed to a number of useful methods that can be used for retrieving schema information or retrieving information directly related to the returned data. The table below shows these functions and properties of the `DataReader` along with their description.

Function or Property Name	Description
Depth	A property that gets the depth of nesting for the current row
FieldCount	A property that gets a value indicating the number of columns in the current row
GetDataTypeName	A method that accepts an ordinal and gets a string containing the name of the column data type
GetFieldType	A method that accepts an ordinal and gets the .NET Framework data type of the object
GetName	A method that accepts an ordinal and gets the name of the specified column
GetOrdinal	A method that accepts a column name and gives the gets the column ordinal

Let's look at a sample application that utilizes some of these methods and properties. Note that we refer to data that is returned as a result of a query being executed on a database as a **resultset**, literally meaning a set of resulting data.

Try It Out: Getting Information from the Resultset using the DataReader

To be able to start and execute our program, perform the following steps:

1. Open Visual Studio.NET and create a new Console Application within the chapter solution. Call this `ResultSetInfo` and the main file `ResultSetInfo.cs`.

2. Select all code in `ResultSetInfo.cs` and press *Delete*. This should clear the window and allow you to start writing the following code from scratch:

```
using System;
using System.Data;
using System.Data.SqlClient;

namespace Wrox.BeginningCSharpDatabases.Chapter07
{
class ResultSetInfo
{
  static void Main(string[] args)
  {
    // Our connection string
    string ConStr = @"server=(local)\NetSDK;" +
          "Integrated Security=true;" +
          "database=Northwind";

    // Pass connection string to the SqlConnection object
    SqlConnection sqlConn = new SqlConnection(ConStr);

    try
    {
      sqlConn.Open();

      // SQL Query
      string Sql = "SELECT ContactName, ContactTitle FROM " +
                   "Customers WHERE ContactName LIKE 'M%'";

      SqlCommand sqlCom = new SqlCommand(Sql,sqlConn);

      SqlDataReader sqlReader = sqlCom.ExecuteReader();

      // Get Column names
      Console.WriteLine("Column Name:\t{0} {1}",
                        sqlReader.GetName(0).PadRight(25),
                        sqlReader.GetName(1));

      // Get Column data types
      Console.WriteLine("Data Type:\t{0} {1}",
                        sqlReader.GetDataTypeName(0).PadRight(25),
                        sqlReader.GetDataTypeName(1));

      Console.WriteLine();

      while(sqlReader.Read())
```

```
    {
      // Read column values
      Console.WriteLine("\t\t{0} {1}",
                           sqlReader.GetString(0).ToString().PadRight(25),
                           sqlReader.GetString(1));
    }

    Console.WriteLine();

    Console.WriteLine("Total Field Count in a single row:" +
                         " {0}", sqlReader.FieldCount);

    // Get info about Dataset
    Console.WriteLine("'{0}' has an ordinal of {1} " +
                         "and the column Field Type is: {2}",
                         sqlReader.GetName(0),
                         sqlReader.GetOrdinal("ContactName"),
                         sqlReader.GetFieldType(0));

    Console.WriteLine("'{0}' has an ordinal of {1} " +
                         "and the column Field Type is: {2}",
                         sqlReader.GetName(1),
                         sqlReader.GetOrdinal("ContactTitle"),
                         sqlReader.GetFieldType(1));

    sqlReader.Close();
  }
  catch(Exception ex)
  {
    Console.WriteLine("Error Orccured: " + ex.Message);
  }
  finally
  {
    sqlConn.Close();
    Console.ReadLine();
  }
}
}
}
```

3. Running the above code by hitting *F5* produces the following output:

How It Works

The following code snippet uses the `GetName` method to get a column name with its ordinal provided. This method, among others, does not require the `DataReader` to move its cursor and so it can be called before the call to `Read()` is made:

```
Console.WriteLine("Column Name:\t{0} {1}",
                  sqlReader.GetName(0).PadRight(25),
                  sqlReader.GetName(1));
```

After retrieving the column names from the table, the next code snippet displays what each column type is interpreted as, against their respective column names. The `GetDataTypeName` method takes the column number and returns the native data type of the column before it goes through the automatic conversion, which is always into a `System.String` type if not explicitly mentioned otherwise. Like the `GetName()` method, this method does not require the cursor to move and so it can be safely used before the call to `Read()` is made:

```
Console.WriteLine("Data Type:\t{0} {1}",
                  sqlReader.GetDataTypeName(0).PadRight(25),
                  sqlReader.GetDataTypeName(1));
```

The `FieldCount` property of the `DataReader` counts the number of columns there are in a single row. This property can be useful; especially to loop through a selected number of columns within a boundary or to retrieve the schema information from the database. The following line of code shows it being used:

```
Console.WriteLine("Total Field Count in a single row:" +
                  " {0}", sqlReader.FieldCount);
```

Finally, in order to display how the `GetOrdinal` and `GetFieldType` methods are used, the following lines of code demonstrate their output and usage:

```
Console.WriteLine("'{0}' has an ordinal of {1} " +
                  "and the column Field Type is: {2}",
                  sqlReader.GetName(0),
                  sqlReader.GetOrdinal("ContactName"),
                  sqlReader.GetFieldType(0));
```

That's it, all done, for obtaining information from the resultset. Let's now have a closer look at schema, as promised earlier.

Getting Schema Information for a DataReader

What really is a schema? We've already heard this word several times and it can be used for a number of different purposes too, but for our purpose the word merely means representation of data structure. So what kind of data? In this context, data could be a vast spectrum of things, not just values out of a database but all that's related to it, and what can values out of a database be better related to than the table that holds the values itself. We know that a table consists of rows and columns, and we also know that each column in a row can have a different value stored, a different field type, a different data type, and can also have a different storage capacity altogether. All of this information and more is what we call a schema – it literally holds all the information that defines a table in a database.

Realizing the need for retrieving this information in a manageable and a painless, effortless way, ADO.NET has introduced a `GetSchemaTable` method that can be called from a `DataReader`. As the name suggests, this method returns a `DataTable` object, which is a representation (schema) of the table queried and contains a collection of rows and columns in the form of `DataRow` and `DataColumn` objects. These rows and columns are returned as collection objects by the properties `Rows` and `Columns` of the `DataTable` class.

However, here's where a slight confusion usually occurs. `DataColumn` objects are not really column values, but simply column schemas (or a column blueprint). These objects represent individual columns and so control the behavior of each of these. The object can be looped through by use of an indexer or a column name and can tell us a lot about the resultset. Let's begin with a practical demonstration of the `GetSchemaTable` method.

Try It Out: Showing Schema Information

To be able to start and execute our program, we need to perform the following steps:

1. Open Visual Studio.NET and create a new Console Application within the chapter solution. Call this `SchemaTable` and the main file `SchemaTable.cs`.

2. Select all code from `SchemaTable.cs` and press *Delete*. This should clear the window and allow you to start writing the following code from scratch:

```
using System;
using System.Data;
using System.Data.SqlClient;

namespace Wrox.BeginningCSharpDatabases.Chapter07
{
class SchemaTable
{
  static void Main(string[] args)
  {
    string ConStr = @"server=(local)\NetSDK;" +
                    "Integrated Security=true;" +
                    "database=Northwind";

    // Pass connection string to the SqlConnection object
    SqlConnection sqlConn = new SqlConnection(ConStr);

    try
    {
      sqlConn.Open();

      string Sql = "SELECT * FROM Employees";
      SqlCommand sqlCom = new SqlCommand(Sql, sqlConn);
      SqlDataReader sqlReader = sqlCom.ExecuteReader();

      // Store the data structure of the Employees table in a DataTable
      DataTable schemaTable = sqlReader.GetSchemaTable();
```

```
    /* Display data structure info of each row in the
     * returned DataTable, which describes
     * one column in the original table */
    foreach (DataRow dRow in schemaTable.Rows)
    {
      foreach (DataColumn dCol in schemaTable.Columns)
        Console.WriteLine(dCol.ColumnName + " = " + dRow[dCol]);
      Console.WriteLine("----------------");
    }

    sqlReader.Close();
  }
  catch(Exception ex)
  {
    Console.WriteLine("Error Orccured: " + ex.Message);
  }
  finally
  {
    sqlConn.Close();
    Console.ReadLine();
  }
 }
}
}
```

The above code produces the following output:

How It Works

Other than connection similarities, our code is quite different from the other examples we've been looking at. When the call to the `GetSchemaTable()` method is made (shown below), a populated instance of a `DataTable` is returned. A `DataTable` can be used to represent a complete table in a database, either in the form of a table that represents its schema or in the form of a table that holds all of its original data for offline use:

```
DataTable schemaTable = sqlReader.GetSchemaTable();
```

This returned schema table offers further breakdown into individual rows and columns as `DataRow` and `DataColumn` objects respectively, thus allowing us to traverse through and get a quick sneak peek at the kind of data structure we're dealing with.

In our example, once we grab hold of a schema table, we retrieve a collection of rows through the `Rows` property of `DataTable` and a collection of columns through the `Columns` property of the `DataTable`. (The `Rows` property can be used to add a new row into the table altogether or remove one, and the `Columns` property can be used for adding or deleting an existing column – we'll cover this in our next chapter):

```
foreach (DataRow dRow in schemaTable.Rows)
// For each row in Rows collection
...

foreach (DataColumn dCol in schemaTable.Columns)
//For each column in Columns collection
...
```

Each row returned by the table describes one column in the original table, and so for each of these rows, we traverse through the column's schema information one by one, using a nested `foreach` loop. This is shown below:

```
foreach (DataRow dRow in schemaTable.Rows)
{
  foreach (DataColumn dCol in schemaTable.Columns)
    Console.WriteLine(dCol.ColumnName + " = " + dRow[dCol]);
  Console.WriteLine("----------------");
}
```

Notice how we used the `ColumnName` property of the `DataColumn` object to retrieve the current schema name in the loop and then retrieved the value related to that schema by using the familiar indexer style method using the `DataRow` object. There are a number of overloaded indexers that the `DataRow` accepts and this is only one of the ways of doing it. The column schema can also be accessed separately if a schema name is given to the `DataRow` object, for example, like this:

```
Console.WriteLine(Null value allowed:  dCol.AllowDBNull);
```

The above line checks whether the column supports null values by checking whether the `AllowDBNull` property of the `DataColumn` returns `true`, if it's allowed, or `false` if not.

Using Multiple Resultsets in a DataReader

There may be times when we really want to get a job done quickly and also want to query the database with two or more queries at the same time. As well as this, we wouldn't want the overall application performance to suffer in any way either by instantiating more than one Command or DataReader object, or by exhaustively using the same objects over and over again, adding onto the code as we go on.

So what does ADO.NET have in store for us now? Is there any way we can get a single DataReader object to loop through multiple datasets without much hassle?

The answer is definitely a *yes* since the ADO.NET DataReader exposes a method similar to the one we've already seen; the Read() method that neatly and efficiently loops through a single resultset has a cousin called NextResult() whose job is to advance the reader onto the next resultset, and so both methods work side by side; Read() places the cursor onto the next record while NextResult() places the cursor to the next resultset and from there Read() takes charge again.

To see both of these methods work together, it would be best if we look at the following code snippet that shows the concept being implemented. You can use the following code in a skeleton console application that imports the SQL Server provider classes and uses the Northwind sample database:

```
...

string SQL = "SELECT CompanyName, ContactName FROM Customers;" +
             "SELECT FirstName, LastName FROM Employees";

SqlCommand sqlCom = new SqlCommand(SQL, con);

con.Open();

SqlDataReader sqlRead = sqlCom.ExecuteReader();

do
{
  Console.WriteLine("{0}\t\t{1}", sqlRead.GetName(0),
                    sqlRead.GetName(1));

  while(sqlRead.Read())
    Console.WriteLine("{0}\t\t{1}", sqlRead.GetSqlString(0),
                      sqlRead.GetSqlString(1));
}
while(sqlRead.NextResult());

sqlRead.Close();
con.Close();

...
```

We supply the Command object with two query strings, each of which access a different table and so returns a different resultset. Notice that we separated the two queries with a semicolon between them:

```
string SQL = "SELECT CompanyName, ContactName FROM Customers;" +
             "SELECT FirstName, LastName FROM Employees;"
```

Next we obtain a populated `SqlDataReader` and start with the chase. However, since we can only read the resultsets one at a time in a sequential order, we use a do...while loop to loop through the first resultset in the waiting line, advancing the cursor through every column, and then moving on to the next one by calling the `NextResult()` method. This can be shown in code below:

```
do
{
  Console.WriteLine("{0}\t\t{1}", sqlRead.GetName(0), sqlRead.GetName(1));

  while(sqlRead.Read())
    Console.WriteLine("{0}\t\t{1}", sqlRead.GetSqlString(0),
                      sqlRead.GetSqlString(1));
}
while(sqlRead.NextResult());
```

This code can be used to obtain data from multiple resultsets by simply adding more queries to the query string and then using the `NextResult()` method to loop through all available resultsets.

Summary

In this chapter, we covered details on one of the most fundamental objects in ADO.NET, the `DataReader`. The main lesson we learned is that the `DataReader` is a fast, sequential, read-only cursor that works in a connected environment and accesses data on a per-row basis, in other words it reads in one row at a time.

Also during the chapter we worked our way through several different examples, and covered important topics about, and relating to, the `DataReader`. We began by looking at the internals of the `DataReader`, and the different ways we can use it to move through a database; we then learned about resultsets and schema information. Finally we saw how to use more than one resultset in a `DataReader`.

Exercises

1. Why is the DataReader the best choice for accessing data in an environment such as the Internet?

2. Why should you choose using typed accessor methods as much as possible?

3. Create a console application using the SqlDataReader to read the Northwind Product table and list all Product Names (native data type is nvarchar) and Unit Price (native data type is money) using the correct accessor methods.

4. Create a console application using an OleDbDataReader that returns a schema table from Northwind's Employees table and loops through each row showing the column data types on the console.

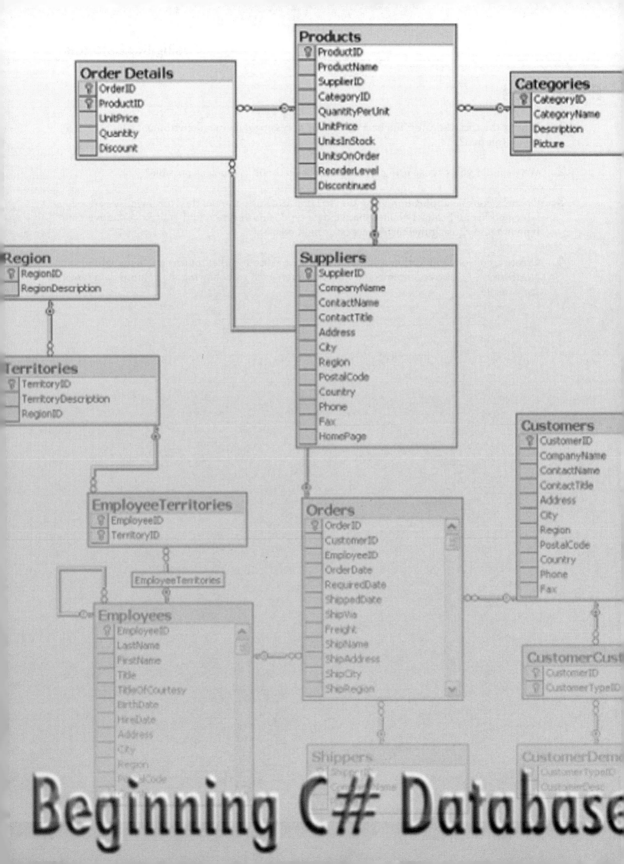

The DataSet and DataAdapter

In the last chapter, we saw how to use a `DataReader` object to access data from our database in a connected, forward-only, read-only fashion. Often, this is all we want to do, and the `DataReader` object suits our purposes perfectly.

In this chapter, we're going to look at a new object for accessing our data – the **DataSet**. Unlike the `DataReader`, the `DataSet` class is an individual, separate component, which is completely unaware of the data source and works disconnected from the data source, and it's not part of the .NET data provider classes. Its primary purpose is to support access to relational data stored in an in-memory cache or a local file for *offline* use.

So, if a DataSet is not connected in any way to a database, then how do we populate it with data, and save its data back to the database? This is where the **data adapter** comes in. You can think of the `DataAdapter` object as a bridge between the DataSet and the data source. Without it, a `DataSet` cannot access any kind of external data source. The data adapter has been designed to take care of all connection details for the DataSet, and is capable of populating it with data and updating the data source with its data.

In this chapter, we're going to be covering:

- ❑ The `DataSet` and `DataAdapter` objects – what they are and how they work together
- ❑ How data is stored in a `DataSet` – the `DataTable`, `DataRow`, and `DataColumn` objects
- ❑ How to get different views of the data in a `DataSet`
- ❑ How to manipulate the data in a `DataSet` – edit and update it, insert and delete data
- ❑ How to persist changes in the `DataSet` back to the original data source
- ❑ Working with `DataSets` and XML
- ❑ Typed and untyped `DataSets`

The Object Model

We'll start off this chapter with a quick look at all the new objects that you'll need to understand in order to work with `DataSets` and data adapters. We'll start with a quick review of the difference between DataSets and the data readers that we saw in the last chapter, and then to move on to look in more detail at how data is structured within a `DataSet`, and how the `DataSet` works in collaboration with the data adapter.

DataSets versus Data Readers

If you simply want to read and display data, then you only need use a data reader, as we saw in the last chapter, particularly if you are working with very large quantities of data. In situations where you need to loop through thousands or millions of records, you want a fast, sequential reader (reading a single row of data at one time), and the data reader does this job in a time effective manner without taking up system resources, or buffering up information, especially when it's not needed.

If you need to manipulate the data in anyway and update the database, then you need to use a `DataSet`. The ADO.NET `DataSet` uses a data reader behind the scenes to get its data, and so in either case, you'd be using a data reader. In the case of the `DataSet`, however, there's additional bulk in saving data to make it available for offline use. If you're using the `DataSet`, you need to think about whether you really *do* need to store data for offline use; otherwise, you'd just be wasting resources. A drawback associated with using the `DataSet` in a connected environment is that it stores data in a local cache, thus building up as data grows. Taking the Internet scenario into account, where bandwidth is an issue, things can get worse if large amounts of data start moving in from both ends. Unless you want to use most of the `DataSet`'s features like reading and writing to XML files, exporting database schema, creating XML views of the database, or updating the data source with modifications made, you should use the data reader wherever possible, as it's simpler to use and is easier on resources.

A Brief Introduction to DataSets

The notion of a `DataSet` in ADO.NET is a big leap in the world of data access, and a big step towards the future of multi-tiered data application modeling. When modifying and retrieving large amounts of data, it's always quite a job keeping track of column schemas or storing relational data models without ending up in a complex web of rambling data, coming in from all ends. The slightest modification requires an active connection to the data source for as long as necessary, which only adds to the overall performance cost, not to mention scalability problems suffered where resources aren't utilized properly.

The `DataSet` really helps us here, because it allows us to store and modify large amounts of structured relational data in an offline local cache.

Let's look at an example. Imagine you're trying to connect to a remote database server over the Internet for detailed information about some business transactions. You search on a particular date for all available transactions, and the results are displayed. Behind the scenes, your application is creating a connection with the data source, traversing through a couple of related tables, and retrieving the results. Suppose you now want to edit this information and add or remove details. Whatever the reason, your application will go through the same cycle over and over again: creating a new connection, looping through tables, and retrieving data. Not only will it be an overhead creating a new connection every time, but it will also slow down your pace in certain cases where the bandwidth is low or the connection breaks, especially if you're dealing with the same piece of data. Wouldn't it be better if you could connect to the data source once, store the data locally in a relational structure that resembles that of the database, close the connection, modify the local data, and then update all changes back to the data source by the end of the day?

This is exactly what the ADO.NET `DataSet` is designed to do. Not only do you save the number of connections to the data source, but you are also able to view and modify your data with speed, and save the data in a local file for later referencing.

The `DataSet` stores relational data in the form of collections of `DataTable` objects. You might recall we met this briefly in the last chapter where a `DataTable` object was used in the retrieval of a database's schema information. In that instance, however, the `DataTable` only contained schema information, whereas in a `DataSet`, the `DataTable` objects contain both metadata describing the structure of the data and the data itself.

The hierarchical object model of the `DataSet` is shown below:

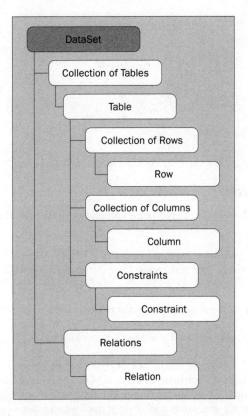

You can see how this object structure reflects the physical representation of a database. We'll be seeing how to use `DataTable`, `DataRow`, and `DataColumn` objects in this chapter, but we'll leave relationships and constraints until later in the book.

Getting Acquainted with the DataAdapter

When we first instantiate a `DataSet`, it contains no data. We obtain a populated `DataSet` object by passing it to a `DataAdapter`, which takes care of connection details and is part of the .NET data provider classes. Being a separate entity and not part of the data provider classes, a `DataSet` is completely unaware of its surroundings. It is like a bucket, ready to be filled with water, but needs an external pipe to put the water in. In other words, the `DataSet` needs a data adapter to populate it with data and to allow any access to the outside world.

Each .NET provider has its own data adapter in the same way that it has its own connection objects and data readers, and it's the data adapter that manages the connection to the database on behalf of the independent `DataSet`.

The diagram below illustrates the relationship between the `DataSet`, the data adapter, and the data source:

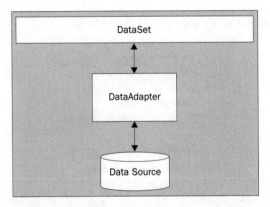

Creating a DataAdapter

We start by defining a SQL query and creating a connection to the database as you have seen in previous examples:

```
string SQL = "SELECT * FROM Customers";
SqlConnection sqlConn = new SqlConnection(@"server=(local)\NetSDK;" +
                        "Integrated Security=SSPI;database=Northwind");
```

To instantiate a `DataAdapter`, we simply pass these two variables to the constructor:

```
SqlDataAdapter da = new SqlDataAdapter(SQL, sqlConn);
```

Here, we're using a `SqlDataAdapter` from the SQL Server provider to connect to our sample MSDE database. The `SqlDataAdapter` constructor takes a SQL query and a `Connection` object as arguments, and internally opens a connection with the database if one is not already open. If you wish to, you may explicitly open a connection and close it once you're done populating the `DataSet`.

We'll see all this working in action shortly. For now, let's move on and look at what the `DataTable`, `DataColumn`, and `DataRow` objects are used for. We'll be using these quite extensively in the upcoming sections.

DataTables, DataColumns, and DataRows

A `DataTable` is a member of the `System.Data` namespace. You can imagine it as an objective representation of a physical table in a database. As you can see from the diagram of the object hierarchy shown earlier, the `DataTable` has nested inside it collections of `DataRows` and `DataColumns`, which in turn contain information about a physical table's schema and the data it contains, respectively. These nested collections can be accessed via the `Rows` and `Columns` properties of the `DataTable` object, and can be manipulated, and updated individually with ease.

A `DataTable` can represent a standalone independent table, either inside a `DataSet` – as we will see in this chapter – or as an object created explicitly by a call to another method, as we saw in the last chapter.

> *We saw an example in the last chapter where a `DataTable` object was returned from a call to `GetSchemaTable()`. In this instance, the object contained only schema information, whereas the `DataTable` objects that make up a `DataSet` contain full representations of the tables, including all the data contained therein.*

The schema of the `DataTable`'s table includes information about a column's data type, its default value, and so on. A `DataColumn` instance can be associated with a single column schema within a `DataTable`, and can then be used to set or get schema properties, such as `AllowDBNull`, `MaxLength`, `DefaultValue`, and so on. For example, we could use it to set the default value of a column by giving a value to the `DefaultValue` property of the instance.

The collection of `DataColumns` is obtained using the `Columns` property of `DataTable`, and a reference to a single `DataColumn` can be obtained using the name of the column:

```
// Here, 'dt' is our DataTable object
DataColumn dc = dt.Columns["ContactName"];
```

or using an ordinal index:

```
DataColumn dc = dt.Columns[2];
```

A `DataRow` represents an actual record in the table, rather than the schema. We can programmatically add rows to an existing `DataTable`, update, or delete them. To be able to retrieve available rows from a `DataTable` object, we call the `Rows` property, or pass an ordinal to the `Rows` property to retrieve a specific row, for example:

```
DataRow dr = dt.Rows[2];
```

That's enough theory for now – it's about time we got down to some coding and see how all of these objects work together in practice!

Working with DataSets and DataAdapters

You can create an empty `DataSet` object with the default constructor:

```
DataSet ds = new DataSet();
```

The `DataSetName` property of a `DataSet` created like this is set to `NewDataSet`. This property describes the internal name of the `DataSet`, which can be used for later referencing. It can also be specified in the constructor, which accepts a name as a string:

```
DataSet ds = new DataSet("MyDataSet");
```

or we can simply set the property:

```
DataSet ds = new DataSet();
ds.DataSetName = "MyDataSet";
```

Populating a DataSet

We can populate our new `DataSet` in one of two ways:

❑   From a database using a data adapter

❑   From an XML file

For most of the examples in this chapter, we'll be using the former method, as the focus of this book is on working with relational data. However, towards the end of the chapter, we'll take a quick peek at the second method, when we look at the facilities the `DataSet` offers for working with XML.

Try It Out: Populating a DataSet with a DataAdapter

In this example, we'll create a `DataSet`, populate it with data using a data adapter, and then display the contents. The steps are outlined below:

1.   Open Visual Studio .NET and create a new blank solution called `Chapter8_Examples`. Add a new Console Application project called `PopDataSet` within the solution.

2.   Delete all the code from the code window and replace it with the following:

```
using System;
using System.Data;
using System.Data.SqlClient;

class PopDataSet
{
  static void Main()
  {
    string conStr = @"server=(local)\NetSDK;" +
                "Integrated Security=true;" +
                "database=Northwind";

    SqlConnection sqlConn = new SqlConnection(conStr);

    try
    {
      sqlConn.Open();

      string SQL = "SELECT ProductName, UnitPrice " +
```

```
                "FROM Products WHERE UnitPrice < 20";

    SqlDataAdapter da = new SqlDataAdapter(SQL, sqlConn);

    // Create a DataSet
    DataSet ds = new DataSet();

    // Populate the DataSet with the Products table
    da.Fill(ds, "Products");

    // Get reference to the DataTable object for the Products table
    DataTable dt = ds.Tables["Products"];

    // Display data stored in the DataTable
    foreach (DataRow dRow in dt.Rows)
    {
      foreach (DataColumn dCol in dt.Columns)
        Console.WriteLine(dRow[dCol]);
      Console.WriteLine("==================");
    }
  }
  catch(Exception ex)
  {
    // Catch an exception thrown, if any, and display
    Console.WriteLine("Error: " + ex.Message);
    sqlConn.Close();
  }
  finally
  {
    // Close active connection object
    sqlConn.Close();
    Console.ReadLine();
  }
 }
}
```

3. Build and run the code. You should see something like the this:

How It Works

We start off by defining a SQL query, creating a connection to the database, and then creating and initializing the data adapter:

```
SqlDataAdapter da = new SqlDataAdapter(SQL, sqlConn);
```

We then create the `DataSet` object:

```
DataSet ds = new DataSet();
```

At this stage, all we have is an empty `DataSet`. The key line is where we use the `Fill()` method of the data adapter to execute the query, retrieve data and then populate the `DataSet`:

```
da.Fill(ds, "Products");
```

The `Fill()` method uses a `DataReader` internally to access data from the database and the schema of the table, and then uses it for populating the `DataSet`.

Note that this method is not just used for filling `DataSet`s. It has a number of overloads and can also be used for filling an individual `DataTable` with records, if needed.

If you do not provide a name for the table in the `Fill()` method, it will automatically be named `Table`*n*, where *n* starts from nothing (the first table name is simply `Table`) and increments every time a new table is inserted into the `DataSet`. Thus, it is recommended that you use user-defined names for tables.

If the same query is run more than once, passing in a `DataSet` that already contains data, then the `Fill()` method updates the data, while skipping the process of redefining schema or creating the table.

It is worth mentioning here that the following code would have produced the same result. The highlighted lines show another way of using the `SqlDataAdapter` by setting its `SelectCommand` property to a `SqlCommand` object. `SelectCommand` can be used to get or set an SQL statement or a stored procedure:

```
SqlDataAdapter da = new SqlDataAdapter();
da.SelectCommand = new SqlCommand(SQL, sqlConn);

DataSet ds = new DataSet();
da.Fill(ds, "Products");
```

With a populated `DataSet` at our disposal, we can now extract individual tables from as `DataTable` objects, which we use to access the actual data. Our `DataSet` currently only contains one table :

```
DataTable dt = ds.Tables["Products"];
```

Finally, we use a nested `foreach` loop and access column data from each row, and output this to the screen:

```
foreach (DataRow dRow in dt.Rows)
{
    foreach (DataColumn dCol in dt.Columns)
        Console.WriteLine(dRow[dCol]);
    Console.WriteLine("==================");
}
```

Filtering and Sorting in the DataSet

In the previous example, we saw how we can extract a `DataTable` object from a `DataSet`. However, if we're working with `DataSets`, then the chances are that we are going to want to do more with our data than simply accessing and displaying it. Often, you will want to dynamically filter or sort the data to your needs. In this section, we'll see how we can use `DataRows` to achieve just that.

Try It Out: Dynamically Filtering and Sorting Data in a DataSet

This example console application will illustrate how to sort and filter results dynamically and how to access individual rows or columns from within a `DataTable` object.

1. Create a new Console Application called `ReadFromDb` within our chapter solution.

2. Remove all the generated code and replace it with the following:

```
using System;
using System.Data;
using System.Data.SqlClient;

class ReadFromDb
{
    static void Main(string[] args)
    {
        string conStr = @"server=(local)\NetSDK;" +
                         "Integrated Security=true;" +
                         "database=Northwind";
        SqlConnection Conn = new SqlConnection(conStr);
        try
        {
            Conn.Open();
            string SQL = "SELECT * FROM customers;" +
                         "SELECT * FROM products WHERE UnitPrice < 10";

            DataSet ds = new DataSet();
            SqlDataAdapter da = new SqlDataAdapter();
            da.SelectCommand = new SqlCommand(SQL, Conn);
            da.Fill(ds, "Customers");

            // Get a collection of Tables from the DataSet
```

```
        DataTableCollection dtc = ds.Tables;

        Console.WriteLine("Results from CUSTOMERS table:");
        Console.WriteLine("CompanyName".PadRight(20) +
                            "ContactName".PadLeft(23));
        Console.WriteLine();

        // Set a filter for query
        string fl = "Country = 'Germany'";
        // Set an ascending sort order
        string Srt = "CompanyName ASC";

        foreach(DataRow myRow in dtc["Customers"].Select(fl, Srt))
        {
          Console.WriteLine("{0}\t{1}",
            myRow["CompanyName"].ToString().PadRight(25),
            myRow["ContactName"]);
        }

        Console.WriteLine();
        Console.WriteLine("----------------------------");
        Console.WriteLine("Results from PRODUCTS table:");
        Console.WriteLine("ProductName".PadRight(20) +
                            "UnitPrice".PadLeft(21));
        Console.WriteLine();

        // Get data from the second table in the collection
        foreach(DataRow myRow in dtc[1].Rows)
        {
          Console.WriteLine("{0}\t{1}",
            myRow["ProductName"].ToString().PadRight(25),
            myRow["UnitPrice"]);
        }
      }
    catch(Exception ex)
    {
      Console.WriteLine("Error Orccured: " + ex.Message);
      Conn.Close();
    }
    finally
    {
      Console.ReadLine();
      Conn.Close();
    }
  }
}
```

3. Right-click on the solution and set this project to run as the start project, then build and run the code by pressing *F5*. You should see the following output:

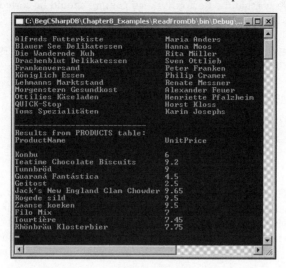

How It Works

We query the database with two SELECT statements, which are bound to the SelectCommand property of SqlDataAdapter for internal use by the Fill() method:

```
string SQL = "SELECT * FROM customers;" +
        "SELECT * FROM products WHERE UnitPrice < 10";
DataSet ds = new DataSet();
SqlDataAdapter da = new SqlDataAdapter();
da.SelectCommand = new SqlCommand(SQL, Conn);
da.Fill(ds, "Customers");
```

The DataSet object is filled with two separate resultsets; each stored internally in the form of a DataTable object.

The Tables property of the DataSet returns an instance to a DataTableCollection, which represents a collection of DataTable objects:

```
DataTableCollection dtc = ds.Tables;
```

In our case, this collection holds data and schema information from both the Customers and the Products tables. Note that the order of precedence in the DataTable collection depends on the order in which queries were made. In this case, results from the Customers table were returned prior to the Products table.

Next we declare two strings:

```
string fl = "Country = 'Germany'";
string Srt = "CompanyName ASC";
```

The first string is a filter, whose contents resemble a WHERE clause you might see in a typical SQL command. We want to filter all rows where the Country column holds "Germany". The second line sets a sorting order and says that the CompanyName column should be sorted in ascending order. If you replace ASC with DESC here, the result will be sorted in descending order.

We now enter a foreach loop for displaying the data extracted from each row, and you can see here how the filter and sorting order strings are used:

```
foreach(DataRow myRow in dtc["Customers"].Select(fl, Srt))
{
  Console.WriteLine("{0}\t{1}",
    myRow["CompanyName"].ToString().PadRight(25),
    myRow["ContactName"]);
}
```

All the interesting stuff is going on in the first line. We obtain a reference to a single DataTable object from the collection of tables (the dtc object) using the table name that we defined previously while creating the DataSet. Next, we use one of the overloaded Select() methods of DataTable and pass two parameters to it: our filter and sort order strings. Select() does an internal search on the DataTable, filters the required data, sorts it in the prescribed order, and finally returns an array of DataRows as a result.

It is worth mentioning that we could have had the same result if we had described a filter and a sort order in our SQL query, as shown below:

```
SELECT * FROM customers WHERE Country = 'Germany' ORDER BY CompanyName ASC
```

This would have saved time and would have proved to be a much faster approach, since the overhead of searching and sorting the resultset again would have been avoided. But then again, if you're using stored procedures or SQL queries that you use repeatedly in your code, and would prefer not to have to pre-define sort orders or filters, then the Select() method is a good choice for setting and changing custom filters and sort orders at will.

Finally, we enter another foreach loop, retrieve a collection of rows, and display each one of them on the console:

```
foreach(DataRow myRow in dtc[1].Rows)
{
  Console.WriteLine("{0}\t{1}",
    myRow["ProductName"].ToString().PadRight(25),
    myRow["UnitPrice"]);
}
```

Note that the data in this DataTable was already filtered by our SQL query, using the WHERE clause (WHERE UnitPrice < 10). However, this could be replaced by using the Select() method, as discussed above.

Using DataViews

In our previous example, we saw how to dynamically filter and sort data contained by a `DataTable` using the `Select()` method. However, ADO.NET has another approach for doing much the same thing and more – DataViews. A `DataView` object enables us to create dynamic views of the data stored in the underlying `DataTable`, reflecting all changes made to its content and ordering. This differs from the `Select()` method, which returns an array of `DataRow` objects whose content reflect only changes made to the physical data and not its ordering.

> A `DataView` is a dynamic view of the contents of a `DataTable` and should not be compared to a `DataTable` object or a physical table. It does not hold actual data.

Try It Out: Refining Data with the DataView Object

We won't be covering all aspects of the `DataView` object here, as it is beyond the scope of this book, but to see how it can be used, we'll look at a quick example that uses a `DataView` to dynamically sort and filter the underlying `DataTable`.

1. Create a new Console Application called `DataViewEx` within our chapter solution.

2. Delete all the generated code and replace it with the code shown below:

```
using System;
using System.Data;
using System.Data.SqlClient;

class DataViewEx
{
  static void Main()
  {
    string conStr = @"server=(local)\NetSDK;" +
                    "Integrated Security=true;" +
                    "database=Northwind";
    SqlConnection Conn = new SqlConnection(conStr);

    try
    {
      string SQL = "SELECT ContactName, Country FROM Customers";
      SqlDataAdapter da = new SqlDataAdapter();
      da.SelectCommand = new SqlCommand(SQL,Conn);

      DataSet ds = new DataSet();
      da.Fill(ds, "Customers");

      DataTable dt = ds.Tables["Customers"];

      DataView myView = new DataView(dt,
```

```
                                "Country = 'Germany'",
                                "Country",
                                DataViewRowState.CurrentRows);

      foreach (DataRowView myDrv in myView)
      {
        for (int i = 0; i < myView.Table.Columns.Count; i++)
          Console.Write(myDrv[i] + "\t");
        Console.WriteLine();
      }
    }
    catch(Exception ex)
    {
      Console.WriteLine("Error Orccured: " + ex.Message);
      Conn.Close();
    }
    finally
    {
      Conn.Close();
      Console.ReadLine();
    }
  }
}
```

3. Set this project to run as the start project, then build and run the code. Here is the output:

How It Works

We create a new `DataView` object and initialize it by passing several parameters to the constructor:

```
DataView myView = new DataView(dt,
                        "Country = 'Germany'",
                        "Country",
                        DataViewRowState.CurrentRows);
```

The first parameter is the `DataTable` we just created, the second supplies a filter to be performed on the contents of the `DataTable`, the third is our sort order, and the final parameter specifies the types of rows to include.

A `DataViewRowState` object represents the different states that rows can have in a `DataTable`. These are summarized in the table below:

`DataViewRowState` member	Description
`Added`	A newly added row
`CurrentRows`	All rows; unchanged, new, modified, and so on
`Deleted`	A deleted row
`ModifiedCurrent`	The current version of a modified row
`ModifiedOriginal`	The original version of a modified row
`None`	None of the rows
`OriginalRows`	All original rows, including unchanged and deleted
`Unchanged`	A row that has not been modified

Every time a row is modified, added, or deleted, it changes its internal state to one of the above. This is useful if you're interested in retrieving, sorting, or filtering specific rows based on their state, for example, all new rows that have been added to the `DataTable` or all rows that have been modified.

Next, we loop through the rows in the `DataView` we have just created:

```
foreach (DataRowView myDrv in myView)
{
   for (int i = 0; i < myView.Table.Columns.Count; i++)
      Console.Write(myDrv[i] + "\t");
      Console.WriteLine();
}
```

Just as a `DataRow` represents a single row in a `DataTable`, a `DataRowView` represents a single row in a `DataView`. We retrieve the filtered and the sorted column data for each `DataRowView` and output it to the console.

As you can see from this simple example, the `DataView` object can provide a powerful and flexible way to dynamically change content views.

Modifying Data in the DataSet

In this section, we'll work through a practical example showing a number of ways to modify and edit `DataTables` programmatically. Note that here we are just changing the data in the `DataSet`, but not modifying the data in the database itself. We'll see in a later section how to persist changes in a `DataSet` to the original data source.

> **Changes you make to the `DataSet` are made offline and are not automatically persisted to the database. In order to save the changes in the database, you need to connect to it again and explicitly make an update.**

Try It Out: Modifying a DataTable from a DataSet

1. Create a new Console Application called `ModifyDataTable` within our chapter solution.

2. Replace the auto-generated code with the following:

```
using System;
using System.Data;
using System.Data.SqlClient;

class ModifyDataTable
{
  static void Main()
  {
    string conStr = @"server=(local)\NetSDK;" +
                "Integrated Security=true;" +
                "database=Northwind";
    SqlConnection Conn = new SqlConnection(conStr);
    try
    {
      string SQL = "SELECT * FROM Employees " +
              "WHERE Country = 'UK'";
      SqlDataAdapter da = new SqlDataAdapter();
      da.SelectCommand = new SqlCommand(SQL,Conn);

      // Create DataSet and fill with available data
      DataSet ds = new DataSet();
      da.Fill(ds, "Employees");

      // Get DataTable from DataSet
      DataTable dt = ds.Tables["Employees"];

      // FirstName column should not accept null values
      dt.Columns["FirstName"].AllowDBNull = false;

      // Modify a single row
      dt.Rows[0]["FirstName"] = "Wrox Press";

      // Add a new row
      DataRow newRow = dt.NewRow();
      newRow["FirstName"] = "Julian";
      newRow["LastName"] = "Skinner";
      newRow["TitleOfCourtesy"] = "Mr.";
      newRow["City"] = "Birmingham";
      newRow["Country"] = "UK";
      dt.Rows.Add(newRow);

      // Display Records
      foreach(DataRow r in dt.Rows)
      {
        Console.WriteLine("{0} {1} {2}",
          r["FirstName"].ToString().PadRight(15),
```

```
                r["LastName"].ToString().PadLeft(25),
                r["City"]);
        }

    // Code for updating the Data Source would come here
    }
    catch(Exception ex)
    {
        Console.WriteLine("Error Orccured: " + ex.Message);
        Conn.Close();
    }
    finally
    {
        /* Close active connection object*/
        Conn.Close();
        Console.ReadLine();
    }
  }
}
```

3. Build and run the code. You should see the following output:

How It Works

As before, we extract a single `DataTable` object from our populated `DataSet`:

```
DataTable dt = ds.Tables["Employees"];
```

Next, we see an example of how we can change column properties in a `DataTable`. We select the `CompanyName` column, which has an `AllowNull` property set to `false` in the data source. Since the `AllowDBNull` property has a default value of `true`, we change it – just to tally with our data source – to `false`:

```
dt.Columns["FirstName"].AllowDBNull = false;
```

Note that we can just as easily select a particular column using an ordinal index as by using a name, for example, `Columns[1]`.

We can modify a record using the same technique. We simply select the appropriate row and set it to whatever value we want to insert, provided that the type of the value matches the column data type. The following line shows the `CompanyName` column of the first row of the resultset being changed to `"Wrox Press"`:

```
dt.Rows[0]["FirstName"] = "Wrox Press";
```

199

The next modification made to our "offline" data is to add a new row (or a record) to the table:

```
DataRow newRow = dt.NewRow();
newRow["FirstName"] = "Julian";
newRow["LastName"] = "Skinner";
newRow["TitleOfCourtesy"] = "Mr.";
newRow["City"] = "Birmingham";
newRow["Country"] = "UK";
dt.Rows.Add(newRow);
```

The `NewRow()` method of `DataTable` returns a `DataRow` instance. We use this newly instantiated `DataRow` object and fill it with values using the simple record modification technique we saw earlier. Finally, we add the new row to the `DataTable`'s `Rows` collection, using the `Add()` method of the `DataTable` object.

Note that we don't set a value for the `EmployeeID` column; if we were to persist the changes to the database, then the database itself would automatically provide a value for this field.

The discussion on updating data sources requires revisiting the `DataAdapter` class and understanding the role of some important methods and properties. Let's take a look at those now.

Persisting Changes to the Data Store

The data adapter is the `DataSet`'s gateway to the connected world and we know that it's responsible for populating a `DataSet` with tables. What we haven't looked at yet is the way that a data adapter updates and synchronizes the data source with the data from the `DataSet`. It has three properties you can use for this:

- ❏ `UpdateCommand`
- ❏ `InsertCommand`
- ❏ `DeleteCommand`

We shall now study each of these properties individually and see them put to work.

UpdateCommand

The `UpdateCommand` property accepts a valid `Command` object and updates the data source with the available SQL `UPDATE` query.

If you attempt to modify the contents of a row in a `DataTable` from a `DataSet`, say, and then wish to synchronize changes with the data source, you need to assign to the `UpdateCommand` property a `SqlCommand` that defines a valid SQL `UPDATE` statement, along with an active connection to the data source. This query has to be self-defined and manually created:

```
da.UpdateCommand = new SqlCommand("UPDATE Customers SET CompanyName = '" +
        dt.Rows[0]["CompanyName"] + "' WHERE CustomerID = '" +
        dt.Rows[0]["CustomerID"] + "'", Conn);

da.Update(ds, "Customers");
```

By calling the `Update()` method on the data adapter, the `DataSet` is checked for any changes made to its contents, and if there are changes, then the modified records are updated in the data source.

InsertCommand

The `InsertCommand` property is used for inserting rows into a table. It is assigned a valid `Command` object that defines a SQL `INSERT` statement along with a reference to an active connection.

Upon calling the `Update()` method, any new row added to the table previously would be searched for and, if any was found, the record would be added to the table in the data source.

The following lines of code add a record to `Customers` table of our sample database:

```
da.InsertCommand = new SqlCommand("INSERT INTO Customers (CustomerID, " +
        "CompanyName, ContactName, ContactTitle, Address, " +
        "City, Region, PostalCode, Country, Phone, Fax) VALUES(" +
        newRow["CustomerID"] + ", '" +
        newRow["CompanyName"] + "', '" +
        newRow["ContactName"] + "', '" +
        newRow["ContactTitle"] + "', '" +
        newRow["Address"] + "', '" +
        newRow["City"] + "', '" +
        newRow["Region"] + "', '" +
        newRow["PostalCode"] + "', '" +
        newRow["Country"] + "', '" +
        newRow["Phone"] + "', '" +
        newRow["Fax"] + "')", Conn);

da.Update(ds, "Customers");
```

DeleteCommand

The `DeleteCommand` property can be used for executing SQL `DELETE` statements for deleting records in a table:

```
da.DeleteCommand = new SqlCommand("DELETE FROM Customers WHERE " +
                    " CustomerID = '" + RowToDelete + "'", Conn);
```

This should result in the deletion of the second row. However, since the `Customers` table is linked with the `Orders` table in the database and has an existing foreign key, deleting a record from this table would require deletion of records from the linked table that holds the same `CustomerID` value. Because of this, the following exception will be thrown:

DELETE statement conflicted with column reference constraint 'FK_Orders_Customers'. The conflict occurred in database 'Northwind', table 'Orders', column 'CustomerID'.

To delete a record whose foreign key exists in a number of tables, you have to delete the record from all linked tables, using a batch SQL statement, such as the one below:

```
da.DeleteCommand = new SqlCommand("DELETE FROM Orders WHERE CustomerID = " +
                    "'" + RowToDelete + "';DELETE FROM Customers WHERE " +
                    " CustomerID = '" + RowToDelete + "'", Conn);
```

201

Note that using this code doesn't work in the Northwind database as is, since the Orders table is linked with another table. For this, you'd have to add more DELETE statements to your string.

Using the CommandBuilder

It can be a bit of a hassle at times to assign SQL statements to UpdateCommand, InsertCommand, or DeleteCommand properties every time you wish to make changes to the DataSet, but ADO .NET helps you out here with the CommandBuilder class. If your DataTable corresponds to a single database table, then you can use this object to automatically generate the appropriate UpdateCommand, InsertCommand, or DeleteCommand properties for your data adapter. This is all done under the hood with a single call made to the Update() method.

Each data provider contains its own CommandBuilder class. For example, the SQL data provider comes with a SqlCommandBuilder class and the OLE DB data provider comes with an OleDbCommandBuilder class.

An instance of this class is obtained by passing a DataAdapter object to it in the call to the class constructor:

```
SqlDataAdapter da = new SqlDataAdapter();
SqlCommandBuilder sqlCb = new SqlCommandBuilder(da);
```

> A **CommandBuilder** will only generate SQL commands for tables with primary key information, and if the **SelectCommand** property of **DataAdapter** has already been set.

To be able to dynamically generate INSERT, DELETE, and UPDATE statements, the CommandBuilder uses the SelectCommand property to extract metadata relevant in creating an SQL statement of its own. If any changes are made to the SelectCommand property after invoking the Update() method, you should call the RefreshSchema() method of the CommandBuilder to refresh the metadata accordingly.

Try It Out: Using SqlCommandBuilder

To see CommandBuilder at work, we shall look at the following console application, which uses code from our previous example and incorporates a SqlCommandBuilder object, for updating the data source.

1. Add a new Console Application to our solution, and call it CmdBuilder.

2. You can copy the code from the ModifyDataTable example and add the lines highlighted below, which are near the bottom of the file:

. . .

```
// Displaying Records
foreach(DataRow r in dt.Rows)
{
  Console.WriteLine("{0} {1} {2}",
    r["CompanyName"].ToString().PadRight(15),
```

```
                    r["ContactName"].ToString().PadLeft(25),
                    r["Phone"]);
            }
            // Code for updating the Data Source comes here
            SqlCommandBuilder sqlCb = new SqlCommandBuilder(da);
            da.Update(ds, "Customers");
        }
        catch(Exception ex)
        {
            Console.WriteLine("Error Orccured: " + ex.Message);
            Conn.Close();
        }
        finally
        {
            Conn.Close();
            Console.ReadLine();
        }
    }
}
```

When executed, this code will update changes to the data source, using automatically generated SQL statements with the help of `SqlCommandBuilder`.

Managing Conflicts

We've seen in this section that it is really quite straightforward to update the database with the data in our `DataSet` using the data adapter. However, in our discussion so far, we have simplified things a little by assuming that no other changes have been made to the database while we have been working with the offline `DataSet`.

Imagine two separate individuals trying to make conflicting changes to the same record in a `DataSet`, and then trying to update those changes to the data source. What happens then? How does the database resolve the conflicts? Which record gets updated first? A simple rule is: the first to update wins. (Note that this rule cannot be applied where updates are made independently on replicated databases.)

Basically, the `DataSet` keeps a record of all added, modified, and deleted records and marks them accordingly. If a modified record is "pushed back" to the database, and someone else has previously modified it since it was retrieved, then it is ignored. This technique can also be referred to as **optimistic** concurrency checking and is the job of a data adapter. We use the `Update()` method of the data adapter to reconcile all changes. This type of checking is different from what is known as **pessimistic** concurrency checking, where records are locked immediately upon editing.

Furthermore, you can implement your own concurrency version checking and conflict resolution programmatically with the help of built-in error handling features exposed by the data adapter. You can catch exceptions if there's a conflict on an `Update()` event and so control how your application responds. However, this topic is beyond the scope of the book.

DataSets and XML

In the world of .NET, XML is the format used for data exchange. Indeed, the `DataSet` class uses XML as its internal storage format and has many methods that allow it to read and write data in XML documents. Working with XML in ADO.NET has been made a lot easier by the `DataSet` object:

- ❏ The structure of a `DataSet` can be imported and exported using XML Schema from an XML file, with the help of the `ReadXmlSchema()` and `WriteXmlSchema()` methods.

- ❏ A user-generated `DataSet` class can be obtained by incorporating a XML Schema file.

- ❏ XML documents can be read from and written to using the `ReadXml()` and `WriteXml()` methods. This can be useful when exchanging data with another application or when storing a local copy of all the tables a `DataSet` contains, after fetching data from the database.

- ❏ Contents of a `DataSet` can be viewed or serialized to an XML document (`XmlDataDocument`). Once an XML view is obtained, the data can be manipulated effortlessly, using the available XML methods.

To populate a `DataSet` with data from an XML file, we can simply call the `ReadXml()` method on the `DataSet` object, passing in the name of the input XML file as a parameter:

```
DataSet ds = new DataSet ();
ds.ReadXml("c:\\MyXmlData.xml");
```

Let's take a look at this in action.

> Note that if you are unfamiliar with XML, there is an XML primer in Appendix B
> that will help to get you up to speed.

Try It Out: Writing Data to XML from a DataSet

We can preserve the contents of a `DataSet` in an XML file using the `WriteXml()` and `WriteXmlSchema()` methods. In this example we'll be using the `WriteXml()` method to store all data in the `DataSet` to an external XML file.

1. Create a new simple console application called `WriteXML` within our chapter solution.

2. Replace all of the code in the file with the following:

```
using System;
using System.Data;
using System.Data.SqlClient;

class WriteXML
{
    static void Main()
```

```
    {
        string conStr = @"server=(local)\NetSDK;" +
                "Integrated Security=true;" +
                "database=Northwind";

        SqlConnection sqlConn = new SqlConnection(conStr);
        sqlConn.Open();

        string SQL = "SELECT ProductName, UnitPrice FROM Products";
        SqlDataAdapter da = new SqlDataAdapter(SQL, sqlConn);
        DataSet ds = new DataSet("MyDataSet");
        da.Fill(ds, "Products");

        // Write all data to an XML file
        ds.WriteXml(@"c:\BegCSharpDB\Chapter8_Examples\ProductsTable.xml");
        sqlConn.Close();
    }
}
```

3. Set the project to run as the start project and press *Ctrl + F5* to run our code. You won't see any output immediately – the console window that appears should simply say "Press any key to continue". We need to open our XML file to verify that this worked.

4. Right-click on our solution, select Add | Existing Item..., and from the list that appears, select ProductsTable.xml and click OK. You should see the following display in your main window:

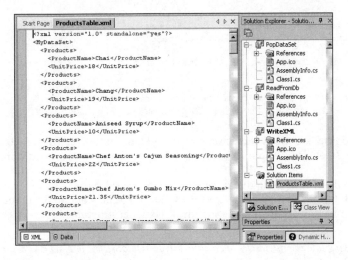

How It Works

If you read through the XML file, you'll realize that our table is now represented as XML, with nodes corresponding to our columns, and our data residing within selected nodes. The ability to generate XML with such ease is one of the biggest innovations in the world of ADO.NET.

Typed and Untyped DataSets

In .NET, a `DataSet` can be one of two types, **typed** and **untyped**. All the `DataSets` we have seen so far in this chapter have been untyped. These have no basic structure whatsoever, and can accommodate `DataTables` irrespective of their schema.

A typed `DataSet`, on the other hand, is closely tied to the structure of the data it holds. The typed `DataSet` class is derived from an ordinary `DataSet` class, and inherits all its methods and properties, but it has additional methods and properties of its own that allow you to access tables and columns by name, rather than using the collections. It does this using an XML Schema file, which is associated with the typed `DataSet`. The XML Schema contains an XML representation of all the `DataTables`, relations, and column schemas contained within the `DataSet`.

> *For more information on XML Schemas, see Appendix B*

Untyped `DataSets` do not expose `DataTables` as class members, but as mere collection objects. For example, to read the `CompanyName` column from the `Customers` table using an untyped `DataSet`, we would need to write this:

```
Console.WriteLine(ds.Tables[0].Rows[0]["CompanyName"]);
```

If we try to do the same thing with a typed `DataSets`, we can access its tables as class members. Following is a code snippet that shows a typed `DataSet` being accessed for a single table.

```
// A typed DataSet created by the XML Schema of the Customers table
CustomersDataSet csDs = new CustomersDataSet();

// Fill DataSet with data from the Customers table
da.Fill(csDs, "Customers");

// Read in the CompanyName from the first row
Console.WriteLine(ds.Customers[0].CompanyName);
```

You can see that this makes the syntax easier to use and more intuitive. To make things simpler, Visual Studio has built-in IntelliSense support for typed `DataSets` and can assist you while you code.

However, you should bear in mind that once you create a typed `DataSet`, you can only fill it with tables that are well-formed and valid, in that they follow the same column data types as defined by the schema, the same rules, and map on to an identical relational structure.

> *We'll skip looking into the intricacies of creating a typed DataSet for now, as it is beyond the scope of this book. For information on creating typed DataSets, you may want to refer to* Professional ADO.NET Programming, *Wrox Press, ISBN: 1-86100-527-X*

Both typed and untyped `DataSets` act as a structure that can hold relational data, allow that data to be accessed and manipulated, and then be transported back to the data source (which could be a database, or even an XML file).

Technically speaking, typed `DataSets` are faster and more efficient than untyped `DataSets`, simply because typed `DataSets` have a defined schema and every time they are populated with data, run-time type identification or conversion isn't necessary. Any similar issues are taken care of at compile time unlike the case of an untyped `DataSet`. Untyped `DataSets` have a lot of work to do every time a resultset is to be created, for example defining a schema every time, handling type conversion issues, and so on.

However, choosing a typed `DataSet` for your application isn't always the best approach. In fact, it can turn out to be quite a pest at times, especially when you really don't have a defined schema ready to be used, or when the data you receive varies from one structure to another. Most of the time, you really don't know what type of schema you're dealing with, and playing safe is always better than getting pesky little run-time exceptions thrown at you from left and right. At times, when you're dealing with a schema that is vulnerable to change, it would be impractical using a typed `DataSet`, which would require regeneration of code every time the schema changes.

In situations like these, or in situations where you need a `DataSet` only for a temporary period of time, you can safely use an untyped DataSet and get your job done.

Summary

In this chapter, we've got well acquainted with the `DataAdapter` and `DataSet` objects. A `DataSet` can be used for storing, reading and modifying relational data from a data source, as well as serializing data into an XML file for later usage or for sharing it with another application.

Through the course of the chapter, we studied techniques to access and modify data in a given `DataSet`, using `DataTables`, and saw data adapter's available properties, `UpdateCommand`, `InsertCommand`, and `DeleteCommand`, at work. Last, but not the least, we saw how a `CommandBuilder` can replace these properties of a data adapter by dynamically generating SQL statements that update a data source with the modified data.

Exercises

1. Why is a data adapter needed with a `DataSet`?

2. If you attempt to modify data in a `DataSet`, what are the many ways of reconciling changes to the data source?

3. What can a `CommandBuilder` do?

4. Create a console application using the `SqlDataAdapter` to read the sample Northwind database and retrieve the three tables, the `Products` table, the `Suppliers` table, and the `Employees` table into an untyped `DataSet` and then display only the first five records of each table, using any number of columns you like.

5. Create a console application using the `SqlDataAdapter` to read the sample Northwind database and retrieve the `Products` table into an untyped `DataSet`. Then add a new table to the `DataSet` and add two new columns to this table by the name 'ID', which should be of type integer, and 'Name' of type string. Now add a new record to this new table and finally add the new table to the `DataSet` table collection. Display only the first five records of the `Products` table using the `Select` method of the `DataTable` and all records of the new table.

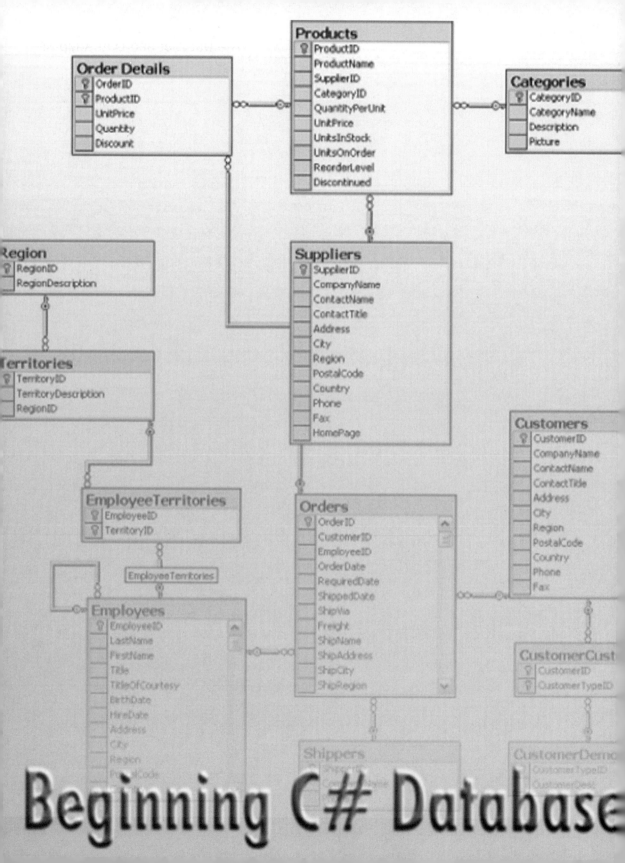

Data and Windows Applications

Cast your mind back to Chapter 2 and you'll recall the simple data-driven Windows Form application that we created. In the subsequent chapters, we've been looking at the theory involved in data access, getting used to terms like connection strings, `DataReaders`, and `DataSets`, and seeing them in use in console applications. We're now going to revisit the visual side of data-driven applications and examine the world of Windows Forms applications.

Generally, there's one goal that every data application aims to achieve, and that's the delivery and reception of data to and from its user. An application can deliver data in a number of ways, but it's important that we consider the most effective way of achieving this, while making it as hassle-free as possible. Our application needs to be able to send and receive data to and from the database transparently. This can all be done using windows forms; they're easy to use, simple to implement, and do all the transparent work of iterating through data objects and loading updated data into the control properties. Better yet, they're better looking than dull console windows.

This chapter will cover the basics of Windows applications and data. We'll see how a number of Windows controls can physically bind themselves to an available data source and allow interaction. During this chapter, we'll look at:

- ❑   Simple data binding
- ❑   Complex data binding
- ❑   How data binding works
- ❑   Different types of data sources, including Arrays, `DataTables`, `DataSets`, and `DataViews`
- ❑   How the `DataGrid` works, and how we can use this powerful control in our applications

Throughout the chapter we'll also show data binding to numerous controls, including the `Label`, `TextBox`, `ListBox`, and `DataGrid`.

Let's get started by taking a closer look at what we mean by data binding.

What is Data Binding?

Data binding has a very literal meaning when it comes to Windows applications. The term 'Data Binding' refers to the technique of interfacing elements of a data source with a graphical interface, such as using a `TextBox` control to bind to a single value from a table.

ADO.NET provides a neat data binding infrastructure for graphical controls, such as the ones mentioned above, to seamlessly bind themselves to almost any structure that contains data. This means that the data source can be anything from an array of values to a set of records in a database, or any object that implements the `IEnumerable` interface (such as the `DataView` object).

Using data binding in our applications essentially reduces the amount of code we have to write for retrieving data from data objects. It's true that using data objects in code provides greater control over data, but data binding can result in the same if implemented properly.

Window controls can be bound to data in two ways:

❑ Simple Data Binding
❑ Complex Data Binding

Simple Data Binding

This type of data binding involves a one-on-one association between an individual control property and a single element of a data source. It can be used for controls that show only one value at a time. An example can be of a `Text` property of a `TextBox` control bound to a column in a `DataTable`. If the underlying data source is modified, a call to the `Refresh` method of the control updates the bound data source, reflecting all changes.

In order to get comfortable with the idea, let's look at a simple Windows Form application that uses the simple data binding technique to bind two `TextBox` controls to two separate columns of the `Employees` table, from our MSDE Northwind database.

*Note that the following code, along with the rest you'll come across in the chapter, is available for download from the Wrox website (*http://www.wrox.com*)*

Try It Out: Our First Simple Data-Bound Application

In this application we're going to bind two values to two textboxes to display the first and last names of an employee in the `Employees` table of the Northwind database.

1. Open up Visual Studio and create a new solution called `Chapter9_Examples`, which will act as a container for all of the applications we produce in this chapter.

2. Within our solution, create a new C# Windows Application. Call this `DataBinding`.

3. You should now be in the form design view. In the Toolbox pane on the left of the Visual Studio .NET workspace, either double-click on the `TextBox` control twice to produce two `TextBoxes` that we can position on our form, or click and drag the two `TextBox` controls onto the form by hand. Your form should look similar to the one shown.

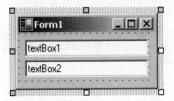

4. Press *F7* to be taken to the code window. Place the following shaded line along with the rest.

```
using System;
using System.Drawing;
using System.Collections;
using System.ComponentModel;
using System.Windows.Forms;
using System.Data;
using System.Data.SqlClient;
```

5. Go back to Design view by clicking on the tab at the top of the workspace, and double-click on the form (not the textboxes – part of the main form surface or the title bar of the form) to be taken to the underlying code. Your cursor should now be positioned in the `Form1_Load` method, which was added when we double-clicked the form. Copy the following code and execute the program.

```
...
      private void Form1_Load(object sender, System.EventArgs e)
      {
        string ConStr = @"server=(local)\NetSDK;" +
          "Integrated Security=SSPI;" +
          "database=Northwind";

        // Get Data from Employees table
        string SQL = "SELECT * FROM Employees";
        SqlConnection Conn = new SqlConnection(ConStr);
        SqlDataAdapter da = new SqlDataAdapter(SQL, Conn);
        DataSet ds = new DataSet();

        // Fill the DataSet with data
        da.Fill(ds, "Employees");

        // Bind to FirstName column of the Employees table
        textBox1.DataBindings.Add("Text", ds, "Employees.FirstName");
        // Bind to LastName column of the Employees table
        textBox2.DataBindings.Add("Text", ds, "Employees.LastName");

      }
...
```

6. Run the code by pressing *F5*, and after the program compiles, you should see the following output:

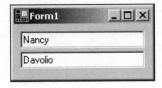

How It Works

When our application is first created, Visual Studio .NET automatically generates a lot of code for us, which exists for the most part to handle all the initialization for us. We are mainly concerned with the `Form1_Load` method that we created when we double-clicked on our form in design view, since that's the method called once the form is ready to be displayed.

Our first task is to establish a connection with the data source and fill a newly created `DataSet` with the resultset. Once we have all the data fetched, we perform the actual bindings with the following lines of code:

```
textBox1.DataBindings.Add("Text", ds, "Employees.FirstName");
textBox2.DataBindings.Add("Text", ds, "Employees.LastName");
```

Each data-bound control in a Windows Form application maintains a list of bindings for all of its data-bound properties. The bindings are maintained in a collection property called `DataBindings`. (It's actually a collection of type `ControlBindingsCollection` and not a 'property'. We'll learn about this later in the chapter.) This collection can contain a number of individual control property bindings, each new binding added using the `Add` method.

Since a `TextBox` control is capable of displaying only one value at a time, we bind its `Text` property to the `FirstName` column from the `Employees` table using the `Add` method. The `Add` method takes the following parameters:

❑ The name of the control property to bind to

❑ The data source

❑ A string literal, the data member, describing the exact location of the value to be bound

Since we're using a `DataSet` as a data source, the data member can only be a path of the form `Table.Column` (or `Table.Relation.Column`). In our example, the last parameter is used to bind ('Employees' is actually a `DataTable` object within the `DataSet`).

Complex Data Binding

Unlike simple data binding, complex data binding is an association between the control and one or more data elements of the data source. This type of binding can be performed with controls that allow more than one value to be displayed at one time, such as the `DataGrid` control or the `DataList` control.

The example below displays a Windows Form application, using a `DataGrid` control, which displays all available columns of the Northwind database's `Customers` table.

Try It Out: Our First Complex Data-Bound Application

1. Open Visual Studio and create a new Windows Application within our chapter solution and call this `ComplexBinding`.

2. You should now be in the form design view. Use the Toolbox to draw a `DataGrid` control on the form. Your form should look similar to the one shown:

3. Press F7 to be taken to the code window. Place the following shaded line along with the rest.

```
using System;
using System.Drawing;
using System.Collections;
using System.ComponentModel;
using System.Windows.Forms;
using System.Data;
using System.Data.SqlClient;
```

4. Double-click on the form and you'll be taken to the underlying code. Your cursor should now be positioned in the Form1_Load method. Copy the following code and execute the program.

```
...

private void Form1_Load(object sender, System.EventArgs e)
{
        string ConStr = @"server=(local)\NetSDK;" +
          "Integrated Security=SSPI;" +
          "database=Northwind";

        // SQL Query
        string SQL = "SELECT * FROM Customers";
        SqlConnection Conn = new SqlConnection(ConStr);
        SqlDataAdapter da = new SqlDataAdapter(SQL, Conn);
        DataSet ds = new DataSet();

        // Fill DataSet with data
        da.Fill(ds, "Customers");

        // Bind the whole table to the DataGrid control
        dataGrid1.SetDataBinding(ds, "Customers");
}
...
```

5. To run our code, right-click on the ComplexBinding project in the solution explorer, and select **Set as StartUp Project** from the context menu. Hit *F5* and our code should produce the following output:

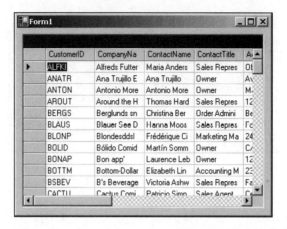

How It Works

Just like the previous example, this example goes through a similar progression, with Visual Studio automatically generating code for us and doing the main initialization for our `DataGrid` control. Our interest, again, lies with the `Form1_Load` method where we insert code to render data from a table, using the `DataGrid` control.

Once a connection with the data source has been established, we populate a `DataSet` with the `Customers` table using a `DataAdapter`. Next, we need to bind the `DataGrid` control to our newly populated `DataSet` object. We do so by using a single line of code, as shown below:

```
dataGrid1.SetDataBinding(ds, "Customers");
```

The `SetDataBinding` method of the `DataGrid` control accepts two parameters, the data source object and a string literal that describes a data member in the data source. Here, a data source can be any object that is capable of holding data, such as an array, or a `DataTable` object. The data member describes what element to bind to the control. In our case, we used a `DataSet` as a data source, and the `Customers` table contained within our `DataSet` as a data member.

A call to the `SetDataBinding` method binds all columns of the `Customers` table to the `DataGrid` control at runtime, which renders our data in the style of a spreadsheet.

We previously used the `DataBindings` collection property to add bindings to our control. We could use this method in our code if we were to bind the `DataSource` property of the control to the `Customers` table. The following line of code is an alternative to using the `SetDataBinding` method:

```
dataGrid1.DataBindings.Add("DataSource", ds, "Customers");
```

This syntax is particularly useful if you need to add more bindings for other individual properties of the control.

We will learn more about the `DataGrid` and the advantage of using a `SetDataBinding` method later in the chapter when we discuss `DataGrids`.

Data Binding – Behind the scenes

In the last few sections, we saw running examples of Windows Form applications using data-bound controls. But how does all of this work? How do controls *really* bind themselves? To answer these questions, we'll begin with some insight into the data-binding mechanism and learn how it works.

The Windows data-bound controls (such as a `Label`, `Button`, or `TextBox`) are able to bind to data because of the functionality made available by the `Binding` class (`System.Windows.Forms.Binding`), which is provided by the .NET Framework. This class is responsible for creating a simple binding between a single control property and a data element in a data source. Have a look at the code snippet below:

```
textBox1.DataBindings.Add("Text", ds, "Employees.FirstName");
```

This line has been taken from our first example in the chapter. Recall that we mentioned that the `DataBindings` property of a control (a control being defined as any object that derives from the `System.Windows.Forms.Control` class) returns a collection of type `ControlBindingsCollection`, which features a collection of `Binding` objects, each of which can be added by using the `Add` method. This means that a data-bound control can have a collection of bindings, each associated with a different property of the control; for example, we could bind the `Text` property of a `Label` control to a single column in a table, and at the same time, bind its `ForeColor` property to an array of different color values, completely unrelated to the table.

The `Add` method has two overloads, one that takes a single `Binding` object and another that implicitly creates an instance of a `Binding` object by calling the `Binding` class constructor (the one we've been using in our previous examples).

The `Binding` class constructor takes three parameters. The first parameter can be the name of a property of a control, like the `Text` property of a `TextBox` control or the `DataSource` property of a `DataGrid` control.

The table below shows a list of a few interfaces with classes that implement these interfaces. The second parameter of the `Binding` class constructor can be an instance of any of the following classes or of classes that implement any of the following interfaces, as a data source.

Interface	Some classes that implement the interface
`ICollection`	`Array`, `BitArray`
`IListSource`	`DataSet`, `DataTable`
`ITypedList`	`DataView`, `DataViewManager`

(We'll look at a number of examples using different data sources later in the chapter.)

The third parameter describes a data member from a data source. It is a string literal that must resolve into a scalar value, such as a column chosen from a table name when using a `DataSet`.

If you'd rather declare a `Binding` object explicitly, the following code is an example of what your code would look like if you were to bind the `Text` property of a `TextBox` control to a data element in a table.

```
Binding newBind = new Binding("Text", ds, "Employees.FirstName");
textBox1.DataBindings.Add(newBind);
```

This approach could be useful in situations where you'd like to bind two or more controls to the same data element. For example, if you have a `Label` and a `TextBox` control in a Windows Form application and you'd like to bind both of these controls to the same column in a table, for whatever reason, you could create one `Binding` object and add that to the `ControlBindingsCollection` of each of the controls by calling the `Add` method.

The code snippet below describes one such scenario of binding the `Text` property of the two controls to the same column in the `Employees` table, assuming that you already have a `Label` and a `TextBox` control on your Windows Form application.

```
...
Binding newBind = new Binding("Text", ds, "Employees.FirstName");
textBox1.DataBindings.Add(newBind);
Label1.DataBindings.Add(newBind);
...
```

Note that when you have a `DataSet` as a data source for binding your control, you are actually binding to a `DataView` object invisibly, behind the scenes. Recall from our discussions in the previous chapter that a `DataView` is specifically designed for providing different views of the data stored in an underlying table (a `DataTable` object), and so is useful when it comes to data binding Windows Form controls.

A `DataView` can allow two or more controls to be bound to the same data source, thus allowing each bound control to have a different view of data altogether. For instance, one control could display all available records in a table (such as a `DataGrid`) while another could display selected data.

Consequently, a single-bound `DataRow` object that you retrieve from the table, a `DataTable` object from within a `DataSet`, is actually a `DataRowView` object providing a customizable view.

Synchronizing Controls with the Data Source

Data binding is a powerful feature, allowing your application to make the most of rendering data dynamically, and making it simple to synchronize bound controls with the underlying data source.

Suppose you build a Windows Form-based application that uses a couple of `TextBox` controls to bind to the same data source, each control bound to a different column in a table. Realistically, the data source will probably have more than one record, just as the `Employees` table in the Northwind database holds a number of records. In our first example of simple data binding, we bound a couple of textbox controls to our data source and displayed only one record (the first record from the resultset to be precise). Most likely, you'd want to allow the user to navigate back and forth through the available records using Next and Back buttons. For this to happen, your controls will need to be synchronized together so that they display the correct data from the current row, as they're currently bound to two different columns.

The .NET Framework provides a "binding manager" for the purpose, which is an instance of a class that inherits from the abstract `BindingManagerBase` class.

The binding manager enables greater control over the data being displayed by bound controls, which are bound to the same data source, by maintaining the 'current' position of the row pointer. This means that whenever a data source evaluates a list of data elements, the binding manager supervises and keeps track of the ordinal position of the current record in the data source. Also, the binding manager fires events to notify the application if the current position in the data source has changed.

The two fundamental properties of a binding manager are `Postion` and `Current`. `Position` is a zero-based integer value that describes an ordinal position of the records being read in the data source. With the `Position` property, you can programmatically advance the row pointer to move on to the next record and vice versa. The `Current` property returns the data object at the current position in the data source.

The two available binding managers are the `CurrencyManager` and the `PropertyManager`, which inherit from the `BindingManagerBase` class. The `CurrencyManager` is specifically designed for data sources that implement the `IList`, `IListSource`, or the `IBindingList` interfaces, such as an `Array`, a `DataSet`, or a `DataTable`. The `PropertyManager`, on the other hand, is returned for a data source that's neither a list nor a collection but a single property of another object or a single value. Note that it can only be used for maintaining the `Current` property of the object. Trying to use the `Position` property will have no effect, since the data source is not a list but a single value.

You cannot create an instance to the `BindingManagerBase` class directly as it is an abstract base class, but can obtain instances of its derived classes by calling the `BindingContext` property of a Windows Form, which returns an instance of an appropriate binding manager type, depending on the type of data source being used.

Every Windows Form groups all bindings defined by its child controls into a collection called `BindingContext`. This collection returns an appropriate binding manager for the specified data source and data member.

Let's now look at a simple example that illustrates the use of a binding manager. Our application will extend beyond the use of a couple of `TextBox` controls, by introducing two `Button`s, "Next" and "Back", which we'll use for navigating through the data source.

Try It Out: A Simple Application that uses a Binding Manager

1. Open Visual Studio and create a new Windows Application within our chapter solution. Call this `MyBindingManager`.

2. You should now be in the form design view. Use the Toolbox to drag two `TextBox`es and two `Button` controls onto the form. Click once on one of the buttons to select it, and in the properties pane, change its `Text` property to say "<< Back". Change the `Text` property of the other button to "Next >>". Your form should look similar to the one shown below.

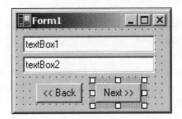

3. In the Properties box, change the `Name` property of each of our buttons, so that they are called `buttonBack` and `buttonNext` respectively.

4. Using the Toolbox, click on the **Data** tab and drag a `DataSet` object on the form. You should see the following dialog box:

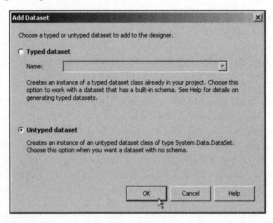

Choose **Untyped DataSet** and click **OK**. This will create a `DataSet` for your application with class scope.

5. Press *F7* to be taken to the code window. Place the following shaded line along with the rest.

```
using System;
using System.Drawing;
using System.Collections;
using System.ComponentModel;
using System.Windows.Forms;
using System.Data;
using System.Data.SqlClient;
```

6. Place the following shaded lines of code along with the rest, under the class declaration.

```
public class Form1 : System.Windows.Forms.Form
{
    private System.Windows.Forms.TextBox textBox1;
    private System.Windows.Forms.TextBox textBox2;
    private System.Windows.Forms.Button button1;
    private System.Windows.Forms.Button button2;
    private System.Data.DataSet dataSet1;

    // Create a BindingManagerBase object with class scope
    BindingManagerBase bManager;
```

7. Press *Shift + F7* to go back to Design mode. Double-click on the form and you'll be taken to the underlying code for the `Form1_Load` method that has just been created. Your cursor should now be positioned in the `Form1_Load` method where you need to place the following code:

```
...
private void Form1_Load(object sender, System.EventArgs e)
{
  string ConStr = @"server=(local)\NetSDK;" +
          "Integrated Security=SSPI;" +
          "database=Northwind";

  // Get Data from Employees table
  string SQL = "SELECT * FROM Employees";
  SqlConnection Conn = new SqlConnection(ConStr);
  SqlDataAdapter da = new SqlDataAdapter(SQL, Conn);
  // Fill DataSet with data
  da.Fill(dataSet1, "Employees");

  // Bind Text property to the FirstName column of the Employees table
  textBox1.DataBindings.Add("Text", dataSet1, "Employees.FirstName");
  // Bind Text property to the LastName column of the Employees table
  textBox2.DataBindings.Add("Text", dataSet1, "Employees.LastName");

  // Return CurrencyManager object for the data source & data member
  bManager = this.BindingContext [dataSet1, "Employees"];
}
...
```

8. Go back to the design mode again and double-click on the button labeled "Next". Your cursor should now be positioned in the buttonNext_Click method. Place the following code there:

```
private void buttonNext_Click(object sender, System.EventArgs e)
{
  // Point to the next row and refresh the contents of the bound TextBox
  bManager.Position += 1;
}
```

9. Again, go back to the design mode and double-click on the button labeled "Back" this time. Your cursor should now be positioned in the buttonBack_Click method. Place the following code there:

```
private void buttonBack_Click(object sender, System.EventArgs e)
{
  // Point to the previous row and refresh contents of the bound TextBox
  bManager.Position -= 1;
}
```

10. Right-click on the project and set it to run as the Startup project, then run the code by pressing *F5* and you should see the following output:

How It Works

This code is very similar to the first example we saw in this chapter, with the exception of the binding manager used to navigate through the data source. Since this example is a mere "upgrade" of the one we saw earlier in the chapter, we can safely skip details regarding simple data-binding techniques and move on to the part where we've actually used the binding manager to do our job.

After declaring a `BindingManagerBase` class object with class scope, the next thing we do is get a suitable binding manager from the `BindingContext` property of the form. This can be seen in the line of code below.

```
bManager = this.BindingContext [dataSet1, "Employees"];
```

'`this`' indicates the active form object being called for an appropriate binding manager from its `BindingContext` property, by specifying the desired data source and a data member. In this case, `BindingContext` returns an instance of a `CurrencyManager` as, if you recall, a `DataSet` implements the `IListSource` interface. With a binding manager at hand, we can now manage all data bindings in our Windows Form application that various controls set on the specified data source.

Our next step is to implement our navigational buttons. The `buttonNext_Click` method is called every time the button labeled "Next" is clicked. The body of the method includes a single line of code, shown below, which basically increments the position of the current record in the data source by incrementing the value returned by the `Position` property of the binding manager.

```
bManager.Position += 1;
```

Similarly, the `buttonBack_Click` method is called every time the button labeled "Back" is clicked. This method uses a single line of code, shown below, to decrement the position of the current record in the data source, by decrementing the value returned by the `Position` property of the binding manager.

```
bManager.Position -= 1;
```

Types of Data Sources

Earlier in the chapter we learned that there is a set of interfaces that can be derived from, and any class that implements any one of these interfaces is eligible for use with bound controls, as a valid data source.

Coming back to the same list of interfaces, we will spend this section studying some available classes that implement these interfaces, and see how they can be used with data that's bound to controls.

Binding to Arrays

In most cases, an `Array` is best suited to storing and retrieving consistent data. Arrays have run-time support for manipulating data, and are easy to work with in our code via the `ICollection` interface.

At times you may want to display the contents of an array in a `TextBox` control. For example, you may have details of cars stored in an array and would like to display the data in a textbox to a potential customer. Let's take a look at a quick example.

Try It Out: A Simple Application that Binds to an Array

1. Create a new Windows Application project called `Arrays` within our chapter solution.

2. Draw a `TextBox` control on the form. Next, double-click on the form to open up the code window with the `Form1_Load` method highlighted, and enter the following code:

```
...
private void Form1_Load(object sender, System.EventArgs e)
{
   String[] carDetails = new String[] {"Mercedez", "Black",
               "E320", "1999", "$1 million"};
   textBox1.DataBindings.Add("Text", carDetails, null);
}
...
```

3. Run the code by pressing *F5*, and you should see the following output:

How It Works

The code shows an array of strings bound to the `Text` property of the `TextBox`. We pass `null` to the `Add()` method since the array does not have data members or a navigation path that could be further resolved into a single scalar value. Ideally, this parameter should be used for a `DataSet` or a `DataTable` since they can be navigated through a set of tables or columns.

To be able to iterate through the array, you can use the `Position` property of the binding manager for the purpose. However, you will have to pass `null` to the data member of the `BindingContext` property since it's an array and has no further break down of member objects. This can be seen in the following line of code:

```
BindingManagerBase bManager = this.BindingContext [carDetails, null];
```

Binding to DataTables

The `DataTable` class implements the `IListSource` interface. As you may recall, a `DataTable` can either be accessed from within a `DataSet` or can exist as an independent object, consisting of rows and columns. We shall consider the latter case for the time being.

A `DataTable` is another good example of a data source, and a typical one too, since it can be used for both simple and complex binding examples. To bind a `DataTable` to a control, you have two options. You can either bind the whole table to a control that supports complex binding (a control that can display more than one record at one time) or you can bind a single column to a control that supports simple binding.

Let's look at an example of an application that implements both simple and complex bound controls.

Try It Out: A Simple Application that Binds to a DataTable

1. Open Visual Studio and create a new Windows Application project within our chapter solution, and call it `DataTableBinding`.

2. You should now be in the form's design view. Use the Toolbox to draw two `TextBoxes` and a `ListBox` control on the form. Your form should look similar to the one shown below:

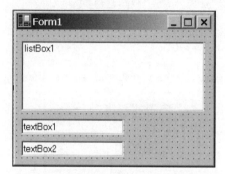

3. Click on the **Data** tab in the Toolbox and drag a `DataSet` object onto the form. In the dialog that appears, choose to create an untyped `DataSet`, and click **OK**. This will create a `DataSet` for your application with class scope.

4. Press *F7* to be taken to the code window. Place the following shaded line along with the rest.

```
using System;
using System.Drawing;
using System.Collections;
using System.ComponentModel;
using System.Windows.Forms;
using System.Data;
using System.Data.SqlClient;
```

5. Press *Shift + F7* to go back to Design mode. Double-click on the form and you'll be taken to the underlying code. Your cursor should now be positioned in the `Form1_Load` method. Place the following code within this method and execute the program.

```
...
private void Form1_Load(object sender, System.EventArgs e)
{
  string ConStr = @"server=(local)\NetSDK;" +
    "Integrated Security=SSPI;" +
```

```
      "database=Northwind";

   // Get Data from Employees table
   string SQL = "SELECT * FROM Employees";

   SqlConnection Conn = new SqlConnection(ConStr);
   SqlDataAdapter da = new SqlDataAdapter(SQL, Conn);

   // Fill DataSet with data
   da.Fill(dataSet1, "Employees");

   DataTable myTable = dataSet1.Tables["Employees"];

   /* Complex-Bind a ListBox control at design time to
    * display values from the FirstName column */
   listBox1.DataSource = myTable;
   listBox1.DisplayMember = "FirstName";
   /* Bind the Text property to the FirstName
    * column of the Employees table */
   textBox1.DataBindings.Add("Text", myTable, "FirstName");
   /* Bind the Text property to the LastName
    * column of the Employees table */
   textBox2.DataBindings.Add("Text", myTable, "LastName");
}
...
```

6. Right-click on the `DataTableBinding` project and set it to run as the start project, then hit *F5* to run our code. Our code should produce the following output:

How It Works

In our example we have a `ListBox` control bound to a `DataTable` object extracted from a populated `DataSet`, as shown in the following code:

```
DataTable myTable = dataSet1.Tables["Employees"];

listBox1.DataSource = myTable;
listBox1.DisplayMember = "FirstName";
```

We bound the `ListBox` control at design time by setting its `DataSource` and `DisplayMember` properties. The `DataSource` property takes a collection object as a data source, such as a `DataTable` or a `DataSet`. The `DisplayMember` property takes a data member from within the data source for filling the `ListBox` with data. In our example, since we have a `DataTable` object as a data source, the `DisplayMember` property takes a column name for binding to the control.

Similarly, the textboxes are bound to the `DataTable` by adding bindings to the `DataBindings` collection and providing the column names from the `DataTable` as data members:

```
textBox1.DataBindings.Add("Text", myTable, "FirstName");

textBox2.DataBindings.Add("Text", myTable, "LastName");
```

Binding to DataSets

The most flexible data source in our toolkit is the `DataSet`. This class implements the `IListSource` interface.

Throughout the rest of this chapter, we'll be looking at code that uses a `DataSet` to navigate through tables and records, not only because it's easier to handle, but also because data binding to a `DataSet` is a quick and straightforward. When we discussed `DataSets` in detail in our last chapter, we discovered that they could be used to store relational data disconnected from a data source. This makes them great candidates for being sources for data-bound controls.

We could bind a `DataSet` to two label controls on a page with the following code, which would be placed inside a `Form_Load` event handler:

```
// Fill DataSet with data
da.Fill(dataSet1, "Products")
```

First, we populate a `DataSet` with data from the `Products` table of the Northwind database. Next, we bind specific fields to the two label controls:

```
// Bind the Label's Text property to the ProductID of the Products table
label1.DataBindings.Add("Text", dataSet1, "Products.ProductName");
// Bind the second label's Text property to the UnitPrice column
label2.DataBindings.Add("Text", dataSet1, "Products.UnitPrice");
```

We've provided an example of this in the code for this chapter, which is available from http://www.wrox.com, as the `DataSetBind` project. This project uses the above code to render the following output:

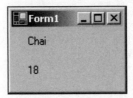

As with our first example, we have no facility to page forwards or backwards through our data, but we could add this functionality using code similar to that used in the `BindingManager` example.

Binding to DataViews

The `DataView` class implements the `ITypedList` interface and presents a customizable view of a `DataTable`. Binding to a `DataView` object is as simple as binding to a `DataTable` object since a `DataView` provides a dynamic view of the contents of a `DataTable`. In fact, using a `DataView` can provide further control over the data you display by implementing custom sorts and filters.

The example below shows a `DataView` bound to two `TextBox` controls:

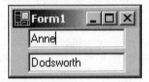

We use the `DataView` to simply filter and sort the contents of a `DataTable`, and then display them on the controls. The above example can be created in a very similar way to the previous examples, and is available in the code download as a project called `DataViewBind` within the `Chapter9_Examples` solution. Let's take a look at the new code:

```
// Fill DataSet with data
da.Fill(dataSet1, "Employees");

DataTable myTable = dataSet1.Tables["Employees"];
// Create a DataView, set a Filter and a Sort order
DataView dv = new DataView(myTable, "Country='UK'",
        "FirstName", DataViewRowState.CurrentRows);
```

As with the previous examples, we first fill a `DataSet` with data. Our next step is to create a `DataTable` to represent the table we are interested in. We then refine our data using our `DataView` object to select from the table in the `DataTable` object the first name column of all employees based in the UK.

The next step is to bind to the textboxes:

```
/* Bind the Text property to the FirstName
 * column of the Employees table */
textBox1.DataBindings.Add("Text", dv, "FirstName");
/* Bind the Text property to the LastName
 * column of the Employees table */
textBox2.DataBindings.Add("Text", dv, "LastName");
```

To see this example for yourself, check out the project in the code download for this chapter.

The DataGrid

The DataGrid is one of the most powerful Windows Forms controls (and indeed it also exists as a Web Form control too, as we'll see in the next chapter). A DataGrid resembles a spreadsheet in its appearance. As the name suggests, it provides you with a scrollable grid of rows and columns, completely customizable for displaying data in a number of ways and accessing data just the way you want to.

To add to the flavor, you can use it with almost any data source as long as it implements either the IList or the IListSource interface, such as an Array or a DataSet. You can provide a modifiable, formatted user interface to a DataSet from the most humble appearance, such as displaying a single table at one time, to the most superior, displaying related tables in a parent-child fashion (we'll find out a lot more about parent-child tables and relationships in detail in Chapter 12).

You can bind the DataGrid to a data source using the DataSource and the DataMember properties at design time or you can use the SetDataBinding method at run time. The difference between run-time and design-time binding is that with design-time data binding, you cannot reset the DataSource and the DataMember properties once they have been set. On the other hand, using the SetDataBinding method, you can set a data source at run time, switching between sources when desired. Also, in most cases, the object to which you want to bind does not exist until run time. This is true for structures such as an Array, which typically needs to be instantiated and populated at run time. For this reason, it's a good idea to bind objects programmatically at run time, rather than binding them at design time.

Previously, we used a DataGrid for data binding in one of our examples. We shall now look at a simple application that binds a DataGrid to a DataSet and displays data in a parent-child fashion, showing related data in two tables.

Try It Out: Binding the DataGrid to Show Tables in a Parent-Child Manner

1. Open Visual Studio and create a new Windows Application within our Chapter9_Examples solution called MultiTableDataGrid

2. You should now be in the form's design view. Use the toolbox to draw a DataGrid control onto the form. Your form should look similar to the one shown below:

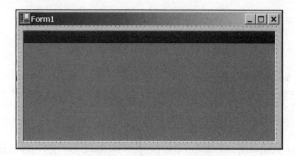

3. Using the Toolbox, click on the Data tab and drag a DataSet object on the form, and again, choose untyped DataSet from the dialog that appears.

4. Press *F7* to be taken to the code window. Place the following highlighted line along with the other namespace imports:

```
using System;
using System.Drawing;
using System.Collections;
using System.ComponentModel;
using System.Windows.Forms;
using System.Data;
using System.Data.SqlClient;
```

5. Press *Shift* + *F7* to go back to Design mode. Double-click on the form and you'll be taken to the underlying code. Your cursor should now be positioned in the Form1_Load method. Place the following code within the method:

```
...
private void Form1_Load(object sender, System.EventArgs e)
{
  string ConStr = @"server=(local)\NetSDK;" +
        "Integrated Security=SSPI;" +
        "database=Northwind";

  // Get Data from multiple tables table
  string SQL = "SELECT * FROM Employees;" +
      "SELECT * FROM Orders";

  SqlConnection Conn = new SqlConnection(ConStr);
  SqlDataAdapter da = new SqlDataAdapter(SQL, Conn);

  // Map default table names to Employees and Orders
  da.TableMappings.Add("Table", "Employees");
  da.TableMappings.Add("Table1", "Orders");

  // Fill DataSet with data from both tables
  da.Fill(dataSet1);

  /* Create a relation between the two distinct tables
   * and add it into the DataSet */
  DataRelation myRel = new DataRelation("EmployeeOrders",
                  dataSet1.Tables[0].Columns["EmployeeID"],
          dataSet1.Tables[1].Columns["EmployeeID"]);
  dataSet1.Relations.Add(myRel);

  // Bind the DataGrid at run time
  dataGrid1.SetDataBinding(dataSet1, "Employees");
}
...
```

6. Set this project to run as the default startup project, and then press *F5* to run the code. You should see the following output:

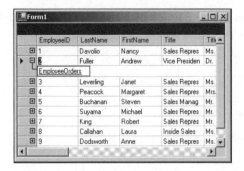

How It Works

Our `DataGrid` can present data from the two tables in a very organized manner. What's good about a `DataGrid` is the fact that it allows us to navigate through related tables with ease. With a single click on the '+' sign on the side of a row that contains related data in a distinct table, a 'hyperlink' appears, leading us to yet another table (the related table) for displaying all available 'related' records. Let's see how our code managed to do so.

In the `Form1_Load` method, we first requested two tables from our database using the following query:

```
string SQL = "SELECT * FROM Employees;" +
    "SELECT * FROM Orders";
```

Next, we filled our `DataSet` with the data from two tables returned by the query, but before calling the `Fill` method, we mapped custom table names to the default table names (`Table`, `Table1`, `Table2`, and so on) provided by the data adapter and added these mapped names to the table mappings collection object of the `SqlDataAdapter`. This ensures that the data filled in the table referred to as 'Table' in the `Dataset` will be referenced as `Employees`, and 'Table1' will be referenced as `Orders`. Note that this is just for our convenience and is not mandatory.

```
da.TableMappings.Add("Table", "Employees");
da.TableMappings.Add("Table1", "Orders");

/* Fill DataSet with data from both tables */
da.Fill(dataSet1);
```

The next two lines of code illustrate a `DataRelation` object being used for relating two distinct tables inside a `DataSet`.

```
DataRelation myRel = new DataRelation("EmployeeOrders",
            dataSet1.Tables[0].Columns["EmployeeID"],
        dataSet1.Tables[1].Columns["EmployeeID"]);
dataSet1.Relations.Add(myRel);
```

In ADO.NET, we use a `DataRelation` object to create a relation between two `DataTables` in a `DataSet`. This relation is established between two common fields (both fields must have the same data type but can have different names) belonging to two distinct tables, which ensures synchronization between the two logically related tables by linking them invisibly and keeping an integrity between the two. We'll cover more on relations and tables in Chapter 12, so you may want to revisit this chapter later on.

After a relation has been defined programmatically, it is added to the `Relations` collection of the `DataSet` where all `DataRelation` objects are grouped and stored together. The next thing we do is bind the `Employees` table from the `DataSet` to the `DataGrid` control.

```
dataGrid1.SetDataBinding(dataSet1, "Employees");
```

Once the `DataGrid` was bound, it automatically searched for all related tables of the bound `DataTable` and presented the data in a scrollable grid form.

A `DataGrid` is a great way of quickly prototyping your applications as it does a lot of work for you. It's also very simple to update the data source using a bound `DataGrid` control, and that's just what we'll explore next.

Updating the Data Source Using a DataGrid

Until now, all we've learned to do is how to "display" data, using data-bound controls. It's time to see how modified data in a bound control can effectively be updated to the data source using very little code.

In our previous chapters we've discovered how to effectively use the `DataCommand`, `DataAdapter`, and `CommandBuilder` objects to update data in the data source, and we've discussed when to use which object. Based on that knowledge, we'll be using a `SqlDataAdapter` and a `SqlCommandBuilder` in a simple application that binds a `DataSet` to a `DataGrid` control. The example will illustrate how easy it is to incorporate the techniques of updating the data source in a console application into a Windows Form-based application.

Try It Out: Updating the Data Source with a Bound DataGrid Control

1. Again, we'll start by creating a new project within out chapter solution. Call this project `DataGridUpdate`.

2. You should now be in the form design view. Use the Toolbox to draw a `DataGrid` and a `Button` control on the form. Change the `Text` property on your button to **Update**, and change the name of the button to `buttonUpdate`. Your form should look similar to the one shown below:

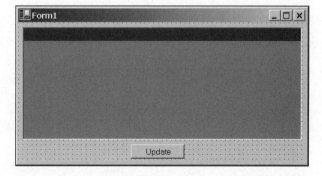

3. Using the Toolbox, click on the **Data** tab and drag a `DataSet` object onto the form, setting it to be an untyped `DataSet` when prompted.

4. Now choose a `SqlCommand` object from the ToolBox and drag it onto the form. This will create a `SqlCommand` object reference in your application with the variable `sqlCommand1`.

5. Press *F7* to be taken to the code window. Add the `System.Data.SqlClient` namespace along with the rest at the top of the file:

```
using System;
using System.Drawing;
using System.Collections;
using System.ComponentModel;
using System.Windows.Forms;
using System.Data;
using System.Data.SqlClient;
```

6. Place the following lines of code into the `Form1` class declaration to create a `SqlCommandBuilder` and a `SqlDataAdapter` reference for the application.

```
...
public class Form1 : System.Windows.Forms.Form
{
  private System.Windows.Forms.DataGrid dataGrid1;
  private System.Data.DataSet dataSet1;
  private System.Windows.Forms.Button button1;
  private System.Data.SqlClient.SqlCommand sqlCommand1;

  private SqlCommandBuilder sqlCb;
  private SqlDataAdapter da;
...
```

7. Press *Shift* + *F7* to go back to Design mode. Double-click on the form and you'll be taken to the `Form1_Load` method, where you should add the following code:

```
private void Form1_Load(object sender, System.EventArgs e)
{
  string ConStr = @"server=(local)\NetSDK;" +
      "Integrated Security=SSPI;" +
      "database=Northwind";

  // Get Data from multiple tables table
  string SQL = "SELECT * FROM Employees";

  SqlConnection Conn = new SqlConnection(ConStr);

  // Create a SqlCommand object
  sqlCommand1 = new SqlCommand(SQL, Conn);

  // Create a SqlDataAdapter object
```

```
da = new SqlDataAdapter();
da.SelectCommand = sqlCommand1;

// Create a SqlCommandBuilder object
sqlCb = new SqlCommandBuilder(da);

// Fill DataSet with data from Employees table
da.Fill(dataSet1, "Employees");

// Bind the DataGrid at run time
dataGrid1.SetDataBinding(dataSet1, "Employees");
}
```

8. Go back to the design mode again and double-click on the **Update** button. Your cursor should now be positioned in the `buttonUpdate_Click` method, where you should add the following code:

```
private void buttonUpdate_Click(object sender, System.EventArgs e)
{
    /* Call the Update method which uses
     * the SqlCommandBuilder to update the data source
     * with modified data */
    da.Update(dataSet1, "Employees");
}
```

9. Make sure that this project is set to run as the startup project and hit *F5* to run the code:

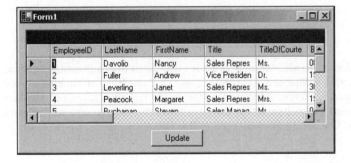

How It Works

To be able to use a `SqlCommandBuilder` object, we create a `SqlCommand` object and pass it to our `SqlDataAdapter` (recall that we learned how to use a `SqlCommandBuilder` in the previous chapter). The code below shows a `SqlCommand` object being created and passed to the `SqlDataAdapter` we created for filling the `DataSet`.

```
sqlCommand1 = new SqlCommand(SQL, Conn);

da = new SqlDataAdapter();
da.SelectCommand = sqlCommand1;
```

We then created a `SqlCommandBuilder` object. We used a `SqlCommandBuilder` so that we don't have to explicitly declare, update, insert, or delete queries, since the `CommandBuilder` will update all modifications made to the data effectively by auto-generating SQL queries for us. This can be seen in the following line of code:

```
sqlCb = new SqlCommandBuilder(da);
```

Next, we filled the `DataSet` with data and bound it to our `DataGrid` control.

```
da.Fill(dataSet1, "Employees");

dataGrid1.SetDataBinding(dataSet1, "Employees");
```

A click on the "**Update**" button updates the data source. The `buttonUpdate_Click` method has only one line of code, which does all the work for us.

```
da.Update(dataSet1, "Employees");
```

This line calls the `Update` method of the `SqlDataAdapter`, which in turn uses the `SqlCommandBuilder` to generate a suitable SQL query from the metadata it collects.

Using the `DataGrid` for modifying tabular data is extremely simply. It has built-in functionality for notifying different events that are launched every time data in the grid changes. We won't be going into `DataGrids` in more detail here since it's a vast topic in itself. For more information you could read *Professional Windows Forms*, Wrox Press, ISBN: 1-86100-554-7.

Summary

There are a number of occasions when you'd want to fetch data automatically from an external data source, be it an array, a database, a `DataSet`, or any data structure capable of storing and retrieving data. In this chapter, we discussed various issues regarding this matter and saw how Windows controls offer built-in support for binding to data sources and retrieving records and allowing ways to modify and update them. The main topics covered in this chapter were:

- ❑ What data binding is
- ❑ Types of data-bound controls (simple and complex binding)
- ❑ Synchronizing controls with a data source
- ❑ Types of bindable data sources
- ❑ Using a `DataGrid` for data binding
- ❑ Updating data sources with a `DataGrid` (or other bound controls)

In the next chapter, we'll meet the web equivalents to a lot of these controls, as we look into ASP.NET and the world of Web Forms.

Exercises

1. What is data binding?

2. How do you obtain a `PropertyManager` or a `CurrencyManager`?

3. Create an application that binds Northwind's `Customers` table to a `ListBox` control. You should have at least two radio buttons that allow you to display different columns by the `ListBox` control.

4. Create an application using two `DataGrid` controls and a populated `DataSet` with two related tables, `Customers` and `Orders` of the Northwind database. Use one control to represent both parent and child tables and the other to display only the child table (`Orders` table). The source code is available in the `Exercise2` directory.

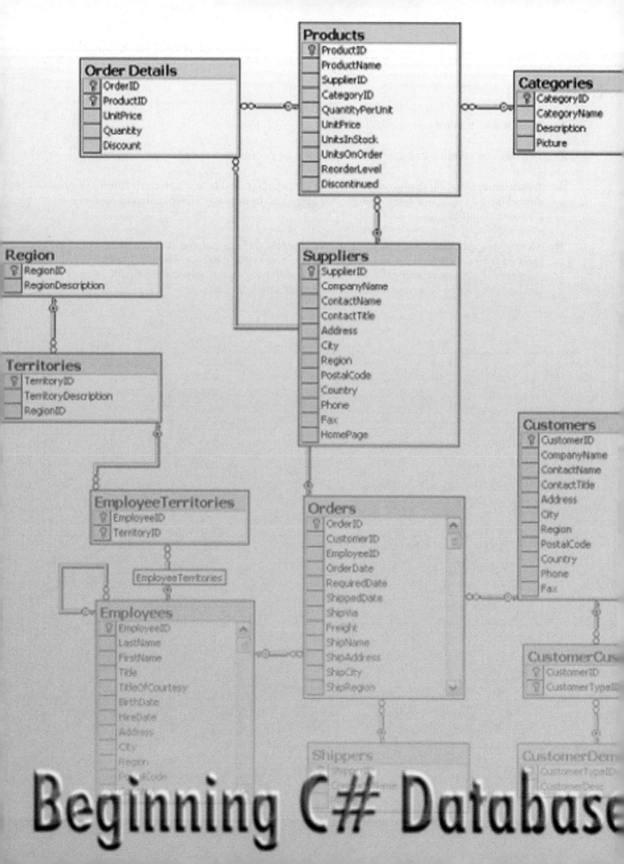

ASP.NET

ASP.NET is the featured Microsoft technology for building web browser applications. You might deploy these applications on a web server for the entire Internet to reach, or perhaps just the co-workers in your department; there is even support for browsers on mobile devices such as cell phones. Indeed, there is such a tremendous amount of functionality in ASP.NET, you couldn't cover it all in a single book let alone a single chapter. Bearing this in mind then, this chapter is going to focus on an important topic for database development: data binding with the `DataGrid` web control. By the end of the chapter we should have a solid understanding of the following `DataGrid` features:

- ❏ Basic data binding
- ❏ Paging records
- ❏ Selecting a record to detail
- ❏ Customizing the column display
- ❏ Editing records
- ❏ Deleting records
- ❏ Sorting records

Along the way we will build up a sample ASP.NET web application, and learn a few of the differences between Windows forms development and web forms development.

The Basics

Before we begin we need to understand some of the basic ground rules for the technology we will be using.

Visual Studio .NET (Standard, Professional, and Enterprise) provides a similar environment for working with ASP.NET as it does for Windows forms programming. These **Web Forms** allow you to drag and drop controls onto a form, double-click to handle events, and right-click controls to set properties with the same results for an ASP.NET page as a Windows application. Indeed, many of the techniques you have already learned in this book for Windows forms are also applicable to web forms for ASP.NET. Underneath the covers, however, web forms work in a slightly different fashion, and being aware of these differences can help you build a better web application.

A web browser will request a web form using the HTTP network protocol. HTTP is a stateless protocol, meaning each request has no knowledge of any of the previous requests or information pertinent to the user's session on the web site. Instead, the web application has the burden of managing the user's session state; for example, it must remember the items in a customer's shopping cart as they move from web form to web form. Managing state yourself makes building web applications a little more complicated than a traditional forms application, but fortunately ASP.NET provides a feature-rich infrastructure to ease the burden.

Web forms also pander their output format to the software and hardware on which they will be displayed. Windows forms render themselves graphically using the native controls and user interface elements of the operating system. Web forms, on the other hand, render themselves using HTML, WML, XML, and script: all text formats. Although a text format might sound limiting, you can actually reach a larger variety of clients using web forms. Web browsers on Linux, Solaris, and cell phones can translate the textual representation of a web form into a graphical display for the host platform.

Web Forms

Throughout the chapter we will uncover more nuances in web forms programming but we already have enough information now to begin our first simple application.

Try It Out: Our First Web Form Project

We're going to use Visual C# Standard Edition to create a new ASP.NET Web Application. If you've installed a different version of Visual Studio .NET you may see a few things that differ from the screenshots below, but you'll be able to follow the examples as well without a problem.

We'll be adding functionality to this project through a series of examples in this chapter that will show us more about how ASP.NET can work with data. Let's start by creating the project.

1. Open Visual Studio .NET and create a new blank solution called `Chapter10_Examples`.

2. Add a new ASP.NET project to the solution by selecting File | Add Project | New Project... The by now familiar dialog will appear. Select the ASP.NET Web Application icon.

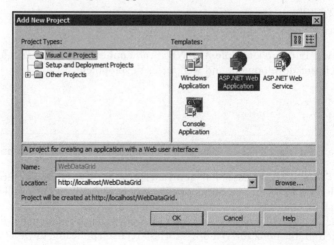

3. As shown in the screenshot, the dialog takes on a slightly different look when selecting a web application instead of a Windows application. Instead of finding a drive location for the new project, you need to enter an HTTP location. Microsoft's web server (IIS) will process and serve your ASP.NET web forms, so the form must be located in a directory managed by IIS. Visual Studio .NET will handle setting up the IIS side of our application for us. All we need to do is give it a name and make sure that IIS is running. In this example we create the project on the local machine, and Visual Studio .NET will configure IIS to accept the new project named WebDataGrid. All we need to make sure is that the location is http://localhost/WebDataGrid as shown above.

4. Once you click OK, your hard drive will get busy spinning, and eventually you'll have the basic building blocks of a web application ready to go.

How It Works

Let's take a look at what Visual Studio .NET has created for us. When Visual Studio .NET displays your new project, you might notice some file types you don't recognize in the Solution Explorer window:

These files are specific to web applications, and the list below describes the more important ones.

❑ Global.asax contains the code for responding to application-level events, for example, the Application_Start and Application_End events, which fire when a web application begins and ends.

❑ Web.config is an XML configuration file for the application. This file contains security, debugging, and other configuration information.

❑ WebForm1.aspx contains the **visual elements** of your web forms page, such as the controls and text to be rendered in HTML, XML, etc.

❑ WebForm1.aspx.cs is the **code-behind file** for the web form. You won't see this file appear

in the project list until you click the Show All Files button 🗐 on the Solution Explorer toolbar, then expand the tree node beside the ASPX file. The code-behind file contains the **application logic** to drive the ASPX file.

The rest of this chapter will be spent looking at the ASPX file and its associated code-behind file, but if you want to learn some more about ASP.NET, check out Beginning ASP.NET 1.0 with C# *(ISBN 1-86100-734-5) or* Professional ASP.NET 1.0 *(ISBN 1-86100-703-5) for more information.*

Technically, you can place both code and controls inside the same ASPX file, but the separation makes the ongoing development and maintenance of the web form that much easier. For example, it allows a web page designer to adjust the look and feel of a web page independently of the programmer who is writing the code to implement the page's functionality. The ASPX file contains the control tags, HTML, and script sent to the web browser, while the code-behind file contains C# code in a class.

Later in the chapter we will discuss how the ASP.NET runtime will bind these two pieces together when a client requests the form using a web browser. For now, let's move on and add some functionality to our application.

Try It Out: Designing the Web Form

Once Visual Studio has finished creating all the files in our project, it automatically opens the web form .aspx page and displays it in Design View which, by default, starts off in Grid Layout mode. This mode allows the very precise placement of the visual elements on your web form using X and Y coordinates in much the same way as controls are arranged in Windows Form development.

An alternative layout mode is Flow Layout mode in which controls are arranged top to bottom as you add them to the form. Instead of having precise control over the placement of controls, flow layout lets the client's web browser arrange the controls to match the user's environment as best it can; a good choice when if you are trying to reach as many different types of clients as possible.

1. We're going to work in Flow Layout mode so the first thing to do is switch over from Grid Layout mode. Right-click on the form and select Properties from the context menu. In the resulting dialog box (shown below), change the Page Layout option to FlowLayout and press OK.

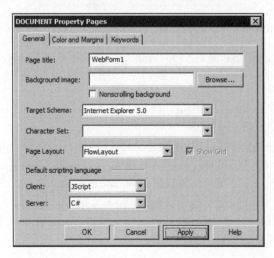

2. When we're working with web forms in design view, Visual Studio .NET adds two sections to the Toolbox window, called **Web Forms** and **HTML**, that contain the ASP.NET and HTML controls we can place on our web form.

We'll be using the `DataGrid` control from the Web Forms toolbox. Make sure the **Web Forms** horizontal divider is selected, and within that pop-up group, double-click on the `DataGrid` control. You'll see a `DataGrid` appear on the previously empty form.

3. Let's add some styling to our control. Right click on the `DataGrid` and select <u>A</u>uto Format... from the context menu to pick from a pre-designed list of color schemes. Choose the **Simple3** format and click **OK**.

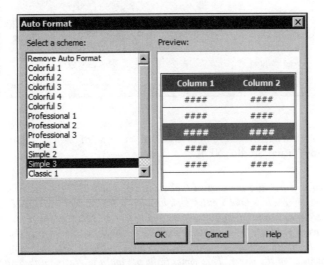

4. The only other control we'll put on our form for the time being is a `SqlConnection`. You'll find it under the **Data** tab of the **Toolbox** window. Double-click it to add it to the form and you'll notice it appears as a small box below our form. This is because the `SqlConnection` will not be visible to users who access our application.

5. Click on the `SqlConnection` and find the `ConnectionString` property in the **Properties** dialog. Select the blank box next to it and a drop-down list will appear containing a list of all the database connections you have defined in the Server Explorer window and an option to create a new connection. Back in Chapter 1, we created a connection to the Northwind database and it's this that we'll select from the list. If it doesn't appear, choose the **New Connection** option and follow the steps in Chapter 1 to create it.

6. So far our web form looks like the figure below. This is the design mode view of the web form. From here you can continue to tweak the design by setting properties and viewing the results in the WYSIWYG editor. To get to the underlying source for the ASPX page, click on the HTML button on the bottom of the design window.

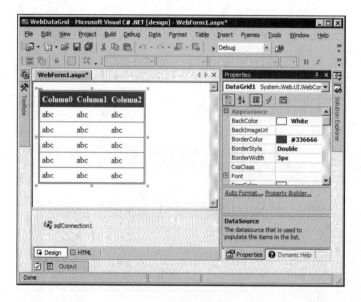

How It Works

Let's take a walk through what we've created, and look at some of the code that's generated automatically for us by Visual Studio .NET.

You may recall back in step two we learned that we can add both HTML controls and Web Forms controls to our web form – let's take a quick look at what we mean by that. **HTML controls** *are simple static controls, each control mapping to an equivalent HTML element. These controls are useful when you want to place, for example, a label on the page and not modify the contents when the page executes. By adding a* `Runat="Server"` *clause in the HTML of the page, though, we can interact with them on the server. This comes in handy when migrating a web application already in place to ASP.NET, replacing old HTML directly with the equivalent control.*

On the other hand, web form controls, also known as **server controls**, *are accessible by default from the C# code in the code-behind page, meaning you can change a server control's appearance and populate the control with data specific to each incoming request. These controls reside in the* `System.Web.UI.WebControls` *namespace.*

We've added two controls to our page – a `DataGrid` and a `SqlConnection`. However, the `SqlConnection` will not be displayed onscreen and so is dealt with only in the code-behind for the page and not the HTML determining how it looks onscreen. To see that this is so, we can click on the HTML tab at the bottom of our design window and look at the underlying ASPX source code.

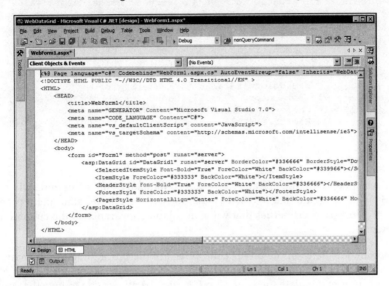

Let's walk through this code:

```
<%@ Page language="c#" Codebehind="WebForm1.aspx.cs"
  AutoEventWireup="false" Inherits="WebDataGrid.WebForm1" %>
```

The beginning of the file contains the **Page directive**. This gives the ASP.NET engine processing instructions for the ASPX file, including:

❑ The source `language` for this file (C#)

❑ Where to find the corresponding `Codebehind` file

❑ Whether we will manually assign event handlers for the page in our own code (`AutoEventWireup`)

❑ The name of the C# class (found in the code-behind file) with the logic for this page (`Inherits`).

Following the page directive, the `<HEAD>` section contains a few meta-tags declaring the server- and client-side languages being used and the application generating the code.

```
<HEAD>
  <title>WebForm1</title>
  <meta name="GENERATOR" Content="Microsoft Visual Studio 7.0">
  <meta name="CODE_LANGUAGE" Content="C#">
  <meta name="vs_defaultClientScript" content="JavaScript">
  <meta name="vs_targetSchema"
        content="http://schemas.microsoft.com/intellisense/ie5">
</HEAD>
```

It's the <body> of the HTML page that contains the code for the DataGrid control we've pulled onto our form.

```
<body>
   <form id="Form1" method="post" runat="server">
     <asp:DataGrid id="DataGrid1" runat="server" BorderColor="#336666"
                   BorderStyle="Double" BorderWidth="3px" BackColor="White"
                   CellPadding="4" GridLines="Horizontal">
        <SelectedItemStyle Font-Bold="True" ForeColor="White"
                   BackColor="#339966"></SelectedItemStyle>
        <ItemStyle ForeColor="#333333" BackColor="White"></ItemStyle>
        <HeaderStyle Font-Bold="True" ForeColor="White"
                   BackColor="#336666"></HeaderStyle>
        <FooterStyle ForeColor="#333333" BackColor="White"></FooterStyle>
        <PagerStyle HorizontalAlign="Center" ForeColor="White"
                   BackColor="#336666" Mode="NumericPages"></PagerStyle>
     </asp:DataGrid>
   </form>
</body>
```

Server control tags (like the <asp:DataGrid> tag) contain all of the color and style attributes for the control. The Simple3 template that we used to auto-format our grid set all of these properties for us. Notice there are also nested properties that will control the appearance of the column header, footer, and selected item.

The most important attributes in the server control tag are the runat and id attributes. Setting runat="server" tells ASP.NET to execute the control on the server, before the page goes to the client, allowing you to manipulate the control in C#, and id allows you to give the control a name with which we can access it from within our code. Let's have a look at the code itself now.

Viewing the Code Behind

The easiest way to view the code behind the form is to right-click on the form (in design view or in the Solution Explorer window), and select View Code from the context menu. Visual Studio has generated all of the code in this file, but we will be adding our own code throughout the rest of the chapter. At the top, you'll find a set of using directives allowing us to access the types inside the other namespaces common in web applications.

```
using System;
using System.Collections;
using System.ComponentModel;
using System.Data;
using System.Drawing;
using System.Web;
using System.Web.SessionState;
using System.Web.UI;
using System.Web.UI.WebControls;
using System.Web.UI.HtmlControls;
```

Of particular note in the next section of code are the two member variables: sqlConnection1 and DataGrid1. These represent the components we dropped on the form earlier. The ASP.NET runtime will initialize these variables to reference the form components when the user requests the page; more on this subject later. The class here is derived from the System.Web.UI.Page class. The Page class represents the ASPX form and provides a number of methods, properties, and events that we will use in the course of writing our data grid application.

```
namespace WebDataGrid
{
   /// <summary>
   /// Summary description for WebForm1.
   /// </summary>
   public class WebForm11 : System.Web.UI.Page
   {
      protected System.Web.UI.WebControls.DataGrid DataGrid1;
      protected System.Data.SqlClient.SqlConnection sqlConnection1;
```

The next method, the `Page_Load` method, is an event handler the runtime will call after the page is initialized and the member variables reference the controls. In later examples we will use this method to perform our data binding.

```
   private void Page_Load(object sender, System.EventArgs e)
   {
      // Put user code to initialize the page here
   }
```

The rest of the file, between the `#region` markers, is managed by the designer. The two methods here are responsible for initialization of variables and event handlers. We can see here the connection string we created back in Step 5 is given to the `sqlConnection1` member. We will not be changing any of the code in this section.

```
   #region Web Form Designer generated code
   override protected void OnInit(EventArgs e)
   {
      //
      // CODEGEN: This call is required by the ASP.NET Web Form Designer.
      //
      InitializeComponent();
      base.OnInit(e);
   }

   /// <summary>
   /// Required method for Designer support - do not modify
   /// the contents of this method with the code editor.
   /// </summary>
   private void InitializeComponent()
   {
      this.sqlConnection1 = new System.Data.SqlClient.SqlConnection();
      //
      // sqlConnection1
      //
      this.sqlConnection1.ConnectionString =
         "data source=(local)\\NETSdk;initial catalog=Northwind;" +
         "integrated security=SSPI;persist security info=False;" +
         "workstation id=LAPTOP;packet size=4096";
      this.Load += new System.EventHandler(this.Page_Load);

   }
   #endregion
   }
}
```

Binding Data to a DataGrid

The first task for us is to bind some data that we'll pull from the Northwind database to the `DataGrid` that we've added to our form. As we want to have the data onscreen when the page is loaded, we will tie this data binding into the `Page_Load` event, but it's perfectly possible to leave it until a user has clicked a button on the page first, as you require.

Try It Out: Binding Data

If you look back to the `InitializeComponent()` method generated by Visual Studio .NET, you'll see that it automatically sets up an event handler to call the `Page_Load()` method as the page is loaded. It's this method that lets us set up objects before the page generates any HTML output and this method in which we'll do our data binding.

We don't need to add any more controls to the form itself, so all we need do is add to the code-behind in `WebForm1.aspx.cs`.

1. Add a `using` statement for the `System.Data.SqlClient` namespace at the top of the file. This will give us access to the SQL Server .NET Provider methods we'll need.

2. The way to bind data to a `DataGrid` is straightforward but it's good practice to write it as a method that we may call more than once. Indeed we'll see later on in the chapter how this provides us with some flexibility when adding additional functionality. With the method written, all we need do then is call it from `Page_Load()`.

```
private void Page_Load(object sender, System.EventArgs e)
{
    // Put user code to initialize the page here
    BindDataGrid();
}
```

```
private void BindDataGrid()
{
    SqlCommand sqlCommand = new SqlCommand();
    sqlCommand.CommandText = "SELECT FirstName, LastName, " +
                             "Title, Extension FROM Employees";
    sqlConnection1.Open();
    sqlCommand.Connection = sqlConnection1;
    SqlDataReader sqlDataReader = sqlCommand.ExecuteReader();
    DataGrid1.DataSource = sqlDataReader;
    DataGrid1.DataBind();
    sqlConnection1.Close();
}
```

3. Save the code and execute the page by selecting **Start** from the **Debug** menu. The IDE will compile the code-behind file, launch Internet Explorer, and navigate the browser to the ASPX page, giving us the following display.

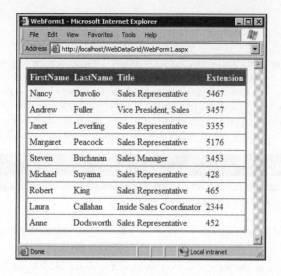

How It Works

If we look at `BindDataGrid()` again, we'll find that all bar the penultimate two lines of the method look decidedly familiar. All they're doing is creating a `DataReader` object that contains the data returned from the query we sent to Northwind. It's the following two calls to the `DataGrid` object that actually do all the hard work.

```
DataGrid1.DataSource = sqlDataReader;
DataGrid1.DataBind();
```

The first call sets the `DataSource` property of the `DataGrid` to our `DataReader`.

> *Note that a grid's `DataSource` could be a `DataView` object, an `Array`, or indeed any other object that implements the `IEnumerable` interface.*

The actual binding takes place when you invoke the `DataBind` method of the `DataGrid`. Just like a Windows form grid, the web-based `DataGrid` can display of all the query results using the field names as column headers.

Our first data grid example is very easy to get running, but there is not much functionality. Throughout the rest of the chapter we will add the ability to edit, delete, and sort records in the data grid, as well as look at some of the additional differences in web programming. The first feature we will add is the ability to page the results.

Paging in a DataGrid

If you've ever used a web-based search engine, then you've probably come across the scenario where your query has returned several million results, but rather than displaying all those results on one page, they are shown in groups of 10, 50, or 100 at a time. Chances are that you'll find what you're looking for in the first two or three pages anyway.

This act of breaking up a large set of results into groups that are easier to handle and adding controls for the user to navigate through these groups is known as **paging**.

Paging is important in web applications for two reasons. First, it is nice to present your users with manageable chunks of information. If the Employees table of Northwind contained 5,000 records, throwing all 5,000 items into the web browser would create a very long page of information. A second reason is the time needed to download the entire HTML for 5,000 records. Even as broadband usage continues to pick up, keeping your pages small increases the perceived performance of the application. Showing only 50 records at once is faster for the client than waiting for all 5,000 records to appear.

Try It Out: DataGrid Paging

Enabling paging on a DataGrid can be accomplished in several ways, but they all amount to setting the DataGrid's AllowPaging property to true.

❑   Right-click on the DataGrid and select **Properties** to bring up the properties dialog and set AllowPaging that way.

❑   Add the attribute to the @Page server control tag in the ASPX file (AllowPaging="True").

❑   If paging depends on some user preference setting (some users may want paged results, others may not), you could conditionally set the property in the Page_Load method using the C# code below.

```
DataGrid1.AllowPaging = FindThisUsersPagingPreference();
```

❑   Set the property using the DataGrid **Property Builder**.

In this example, we'll make use of the Property Builder. This tool categorizes the wide selection of properties for a DataGrid into functional tabs and it's very handy to know how to use it. We ourselves will use it a few more times in this chapter before we finish.

1.   Switch to the Design View for the form and right-click on the DataGrid. Select **Property Builder** from the context menu. When the dialog appears, click on the **Paging** icon in the left-hand column.

2.   As shown in the following dialog, set the AllowPaging property to true by selecting the **Allow paging** checkbox. Set the number of rows to display per page at **5**. We can leave the location and the type of page navigation controls (next and previous hyperlinks versus page numbered hyperlinks) for the grid at their defaults. However, if we wanted to provide our own custom navigation bar for moving among the pages, we would clear the **Show Navigation Buttons** checkbox.

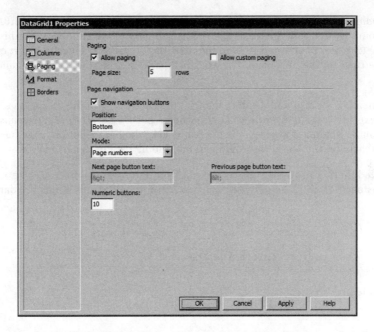

With our data now separated in pages, we have to teach the DataGrid what to do when someone chooses to change the page. We do this by creating an event handler for the PageIndexChanged event.

3. To assign an event handler, select the DataGrid in Design View and open the **Properties** dialog. Clicking on the lightning bolt at the top of the dialog will switch you to the event view for the DataGrid where you will find an empty listing for the PageIndexChanged event.

4. Double-click on the **PageIndexChanged** entry, and the IDE will open the code-behind file and insert an empty event handler for it. All we need to do is add the highlighted code.

```
public void DataGrid1_PageIndexChanged(object source,
    System.Web.UI.WebControls.DataGridPageChangedEventArgs e)
{
    DataGrid1.CurrentPageIndex = e.NewPageIndex;
    BindDataGrid();
}
```

5. Don't build and run this example yet. You might not see what you expect.

How It Works

So what will happen when we click on the grid to move to a different page? Well, the web form performs what's known as a **postback**. It's possibly the nicest piece of infrastructure provided by ASP.NET. A postback carries information from the client back to the web server and allows you to handle events inside the web form class; something that wouldn't happen automatically over the stateless HTTP protocol.

The event handler above takes a parameter of type `DataGridPageChangedEventArgs` containing the new page number to use in the `NewPageIndex` property. If we simply assign this value to the grid's `CurrentPageIndex` property and re-bind the data, the `DataGrid` object is smart enough to extract and display the rows for the new page. The grid then packages the rows as HTML and sends them back to the client.

You might remember we also had a call to the `BindDataGrid()` in the `Page_Load` method. Now we don't want to execute it again in `Page_Load()` when a postback event occurs because our event handler will handle binding if needed. We need to check whether or not the page has been loaded as a result of a postback for, if it were, we would end up binding data to the grid twice.

Fortunately, we inherit a property, `IsPostBack`, from the `System.Web.UI.Page` class to tell us if we are in a postback or not. The new `Page_Load` method below only binds the data on a fresh page request.

```
private void Page_Load(object sender, System.EventArgs e)
{
    // Put user code to initialize the page here
    if (!Page.IsPostBack)
    {
      BindDataGrid();
    }
}
```

Combining the DataGrid and DataSet

Although the `SqlDataReader` class is the best choice for performance, it now has a limitation. If we compile and execute the code we have so far, we will find the following error.

Although the `DataSource` property of the `DataGrid` accepts any object implementing `IEnumerable`, paging requires the data source object to implement `ICollection`, which `SqlDataReader` does not. Both `ICollection` and `IEnumerable` interfaces allow the grid to loop through each record in the resultset, but `ICollection` will provide a count of the total number if items in the resultset, while `IEnumerable` does not.

The grid uses this count to determine the total number of pages required. You could perform some custom paging calculations to replace the pieces of `ICollection` that would do this automatically, but we'll take an alternative route and replace the `SqlDataReader` with a `DataView`.

Try It Out: Binding to a DataView

All of the changes we need to switch from a `SqlDataReader` to a `DataView` are in the `BindDataGrid` method.

1. Replace the existing version of `BindDataGrid` with the following code. Notice we are using the same query as before, but we now populate a `DataSet` with the results of the query instead of a `SqlDataReader`.

```
private void BindDataGrid()
{
   string sqlQuery = "SELECT FirstName, LastName, Title, " +
                     "Extension FROM Employees";
   sqlConnection1.Open();
   SqlDataAdapter sqlDataAdapter =
     new SqlDataAdapter(sqlQuery, sqlConnection1);
   DataSet dataSet = new DataSet();
   sqlDataAdapter.Fill(dataSet, "Employees");
   DataGrid1.DataSource = dataSet.Tables["Employees"].DefaultView;
   DataGrid1.DataBind();
   sqlConnection1.Close();
}
```

How It Works

The reworked `BindDataGrid()` pulls the data from the Northwind database into a table stored in a `DataSet` object. The grid's `DataSource` property is then set to the `DefaultView` of that `DataTable`. Note that it's the `DefaultView` property (a `DataView`) of the `DataTable` rather than the `DataTable` itself that implements `ICollection` and will allow the grid to perform paging calculations for us.

Using a `DataSet` will turn out to have several other advantages for us, as we'll see later on, but right now, let's make sure it actually works. We should now be able to build and execute the form without errors. As shown below, the form will display five records with hyperlink page numbers to click on and see the rest.

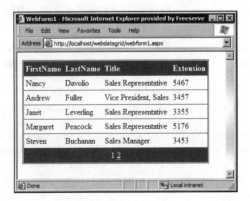

The next step in our application is to build in a small caching feature, but before we do it'll help a lot if we take a step back and take a quick look at how the ASP.NET runtime processes our page first. This background information will allow us to make some more improvements to the application besides the caching.

The ASP.NET Page Lifecycle

The first time a request arrives for an ASPX page, the ASP.NET runtime combines the ASPX page with the class in the code-behind file and creates a new class. The runtime dynamically compiles this new class and caches the result to service future requests. The lifecycle is demonstrated in the diagram below.

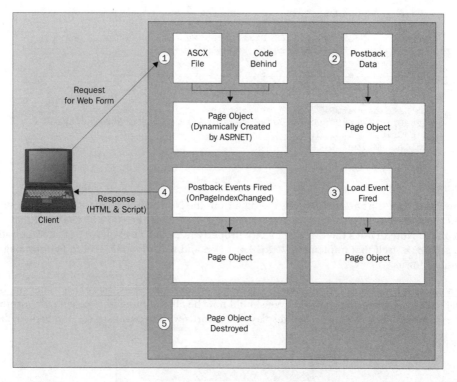

For each request, the runtime will instantiate a new instance of this class. This means when a user requests the paged data grid we built and then clicks on a new page number, a new instance of the dynamically generated class services the request – we do not have the same instance of the class we used for the initial request. This is a primary difference between web forms and Windows forms. In Windows forms, the same class can continue to handle events for a user during the entire life of the application.

To help cover up these seams, the ASP.NET runtime will repopulate the form's controls on postback with all of the properties just as they appeared on the client. So, for instance, a checkbox control marked checked on the client and then posted to the web server will have its Checked property set to true, instead of the default value of false. ASP.NET refers to this process as restoring the **view state**.

After restoring the view state, the runtime fires the `Load` event and our code can perform any initialization we need. Once this step is complete, any postback events are fired, such as the `OnPageIndexChanged` event we handle in the paged data grid. Finally, the page will render itself, and the result is a combination of HTML and script sent back over the network to the client. After rendering, the class is disposed of, freeing up resources to handle other incoming requests. Remember, in web applications, thousands of users may be requesting web forms at the same time.

Building for Scalability

Scalable software has the ability to perform well as the number of concurrent users increase. The ASP.NET runtime engine provides everything you need to write robust and scalable web applications, as long as you follow a few guidelines. Let's go through a few basic tips for scalability in database web applications.

First of all, we need to be conservative with server resources such as memory and database connections. In the sample code for this chapter, we try to close our database connection explicitly when we are finished with our queries. This immediately frees up a connection to use elsewhere. We could wait for the runtime to dispose of the page and let the garbage collector close the database connection, but doing so only holds a resource for longer than we need, and might prevent other requests from executing immediately.

Another guideline is to avoid trips to the database when possible. For example, we avoid binding our data grid during the `Page_Load` method during a postback. We know the postback event will re-bind the data if necessary. Try to avoid unnecessary queries and retrieve only the data you need for processing.

Caching

Like any programming guidelines however, one must often be traded against another and it's left to you to determine the balance for your own application. The balance between the two recommendations we've given for example is brought into focus when we start to think about caching data we've pulled from the database. Caching a query result in memory on the server uses more memory resources; on the other hand it also saves a trip to the database. Evaluating these types of tradeoffs correctly can help the performance of your application.

For example, once we query the `Employees` table and send the results to the client in a paged data grid, we can assume the client is probably going to examine more records. If we simply reload the `DataSet` from memory instead of the database, we can save a trip to the database. Caching the `DataSet` sounds like a good idea, particularly since we have a small number of rows in the table. If the `Employees` table contained thousands of records, we might use too much memory for caching and actually hurt our server performance. Evaluating these tradeoffs usually requires you to factor in the number of users you support, the hardware your application runs on, and even how your end users navigate through the application.

There are many techniques for caching available in ASP.NET. In this example we will use the `Session` object. The `Session` object allows you to store data specific to each client. ASP.NET creates a new `Session` when a client first navigates to your site. After a specified amount of inactivity (20 minutes is the default), ASP.NET will clear a user's `Session` contents to conserve resources.

You can configure ASP.NET to store session contents in memory (the default option, and also the fastest option) or even in a SQL Server database. Although storing the results of a database query in a database might sound strange, if the original query is particularly complicated, you still might see a performance gain. Also, remember you could store multiple queries in the same `DataSet`.

Try It Out: Using the Session Object

1. First, update the `BindDataGrid` method with the following code. Notice that the method takes a `bool` parameter to force a refresh of the `DataSet` from the database instead of the session cache.

```
private void BindDataGrid(bool refresh)
{
  DataSet dataSet = null;
  if(refresh == true || Session["Employees"] == null)
  {
    string sqlQuery = "SELECT FirstName, LastName, Title, " +
                      "Extension FROM Employees";
    sqlConnection1.Open();
    SqlDataAdapter sqlDataAdapter =
      new SqlDataAdapter(sqlQuery, sqlConnection1);
    dataSet = new DataSet();
    sqlDataAdapter.Fill(dataSet, "Employees");

    Session["Employees"] = dataSet;
    sqlConnection1.Close();
  }
  else
  {
    dataSet = (DataSet)Session["Employees"];
  }

  DataGrid1.DataSource = dataSet.Tables["Employees"].DefaultView;
  DataGrid1.DataBind();
  sqlConnection1.Close();
}
```

2. Add a second version of `BindDataGrid`. This version accepts no parameters and forwards the call to the `BindDataGrid` without requesting a refresh of the `DataSet` from the database. This will allow us to bind a grid without always specifying a refresh parameter.

```
private void BindDataGrid()
{
  BindDataGrid(false);
}
```

3. In the `Page_Load` method, add a `true` parameter to the call to `BindDataGrid`. This ensures that the most recent data is taken from the database when a page is first loaded. The `DataGrid1_PageIndexChanged` method can remain the same, and pull data from the `Session` cache.

```
private void Page_Load(object sender, System.EventArgs e)
{
  // Put user code to initialize the page here
  if (!this.IsPostBack)
  {
```

```
        BindDataGrid(true);
    }
}

private void DataGrid1_PageIndexChanged(object source,
    System.Web.UI.WebControls.DataGridPageChangedEventArgs e)
{
    DataGrid1.CurrentPageIndex = e.NewPageIndex;
    BindDataGrid();
}
```

How It Works

We've now overloaded the `BindDataGrid()` method, creating two versions with different signatures. The first now has a Boolean parameter (or '**flag**') to force a refresh of the `Session` contents, because one other big danger in caching data is showing your user out-of-date results when someone else has changed the underlying data. The best data to cache is static data; trying to cache rapidly changing information may show incorrect results.

Notice that we first test the `Session` collection (an instance of the `HttpSessionState` class) to see if an item named `Employees` exists. If this returns `null`, or if the refresh flag is set, we need to query the database and populate a new `DataSet` object to store in the `Session`. During `Page_Load`, we force a refresh to ensure that the user sees the most up to date data, but during processing of the `OnPageIndexChanged` event, we allow the page to use a cached copy of the data and save ourselves a trip to the database.

Selecting a Row

So far so good – the `DataGrid` has done everything we've asked of it so far, but it's not the be all and end all of simple data retrieval. Indeed, there are some types of data it's just not suited to displaying, be it for practical or aesthetic reasons. Take, for instance, the `Notes` field in Northwind's `Employees` table, which contains some additional facts and background information about the staff stored as free-form text.

Rather than displaying this text directly in the `DataGrid` which would clutter the screen up quite a bit, we're going to implement a more elegant solution and allow the user to select the row containing the employee the want to know more about. When they do select a row, the notes about that employee will appear in a separate area of the web form.

Adding a selection capability to the data grid is similar to the steps we just used in adding paging. First, we will adjust the data grid properties, and then add an event handler. We will also need to add some more user interface elements to display the employee's notes.

Try It Out: Adding a Detail Display

1. Return to the property builder once more by right-clicking on the `DataGrid` control in Design View and selecting **Property Builder**.

2. Select the **Columns** icon in the upper left list. Under the list of available columns, expand the **Button Column** node and move a **Select** node into the list of **Selected columns**. We will change the **Button Type** entry to **PushButton** and leave default values for all other settings. This will give us a column of buttons for the user to push when selecting a record.

3. Check the box marked **Create columns automatically at run time**. If we fail to do this, the grid will only display our columns of checkboxes. The property builder dialog should look like the figure shown below. Press **OK**.

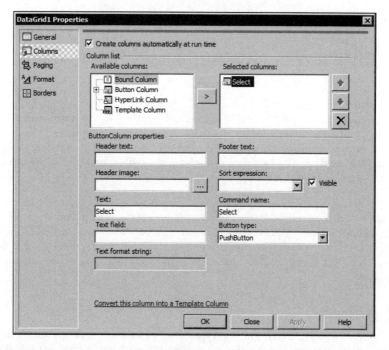

4. Drag a `Panel` web control from the Toolbox onto the form. A panel control is a container for other controls, which will come in handy when we want to show and hide the detail information display. Set the Panel's `Visible` property to `false`. Instead of hiding and displaying all the controls individually, we will just hide and display the panel control (and therefore all its contents as well) instead.

5. Widen the panel on the form to 250 x 50 pixels or thereabout and drag an HTML table into it. It should have one column and two rows.

6. Drag a `Label` control from the Web Forms section of the Toolbox to the second row of the table. We'll use it to display the notes. In keeping with our color scheme, we'll adjust the layout and color properties of our two new controls so the design view of the updated form looks like the following:

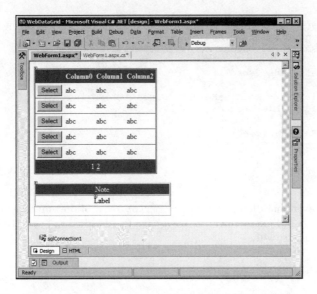

The ASPX for this section of the page should look like the following.

```
<asp:Panel id="Panel1" runat="server" HorizontalAlign="Center" Width="260px"
          Height="50px" Visible="False">
  <TABLE id="Table1" cellSpacing="1" cellPadding="1" width="300" border="1">
    <TR>
      <TD style="COLOR: white" align="middle" bgColor="#336666"
          colSpan="1" rowSpan="1">
      Note
      </TD>
    </TR>
    <TR>
      <TD align="middle">
        <asp:Label id="Label1" runat="server">Label</asp:Label></TD>
    </TR>
  </TABLE>
</asp:Panel>
```

7. The event we want to catch when a user has selected a record is the
SelectedIndexChanged event so we need to create a handler for it. Right-click on the
grid, select **Properties** from the context menu, and click the **Events** button (the lightning bolt)
in the **Properties** toolbar. Double-click on the SelectedIndexChange event and the IDE
will switch to the code-behind file with the focus on an empty event handler. Add the
following code to the empty method.

```
private void DataGrid1_SelectedIndexChanged(object sender,
    System.EventArgs e)
{
  string key = DataGrid1.DataKeys[DataGrid1.SelectedIndex].ToString();
  string sqlQuery = "SELECT Notes FROM Employees" +
                  " WHERE EmployeeId = @EmployeeID";

  sqlConnection1.Open();
```

```
    SqlCommand sqlCommand = new SqlCommand(sqlQuery, sqlConnection1);
    sqlCommand.Parameters.Add("@EmployeeID", key);
    SqlDataReader sqlDataReader = sqlCommand.ExecuteReader();

    if(sqlDataReader.Read())
    {
      Label1.Text = sqlDataReader["Notes"].ToString();
      Panel1.Visible = true;
    }
    sqlDataReader.Close();
    sqlConnection1.Close();
  }
```

How It Works

The first step in the event handler is finding the `EmployeeId` of the employee to detail. We haven't needed to access this in our example yet, so we'll have to add the `EmployeeId` field to the query in `BindDataGrid()` to start with.

```
private void BindDataGrid(bool refresh)
{
  DataSet dataSet = null;
  if(refresh == true || Session["Employees"] == null)
  {
    string sqlQuery = "SELECT EmployeeId, FirstName, LastName, " +
                      "Title, Extension FROM Employees";
    sqlConnection1.Open();
    ...
```

The `EmployeeId` field will now be bound to the grid with the other information, but how do we retrieve the ID of the selected employee from the grid? There are actually several ways to achieve this, but one of the safest approaches is to use the `DataKeys` collection of the data grid. This property is specifically designed to hold the primary key values for each record as they appear in the grid. All we need to do is to give the `DataGrid` the name of the field containing the key values, in this case `EmployeeId`. We add the following line of code to the `BindDataGrid` method, just after assigning the `DataSource` property.

```
  ...
  DataGrid1.DataSource = dataSet.Tables["Employees"].DefaultView;
  DataGrid1.DataKeyField = "EmployeeId";
  DataGrid1.DataBind();

  sqlConnection1.Close();
}
```

We can retrieve the correct ID to use from `DataKeys` by using the `SelectedIndex` property of the `DataGrid` object. Once we have retrieved the results of the query, we simply need to set the `Label` control's `Text` property to display the notes, and then unhide the `Panel` control. The grid will automatically highlight the selected row for us using the `SelectedItem` style property. The resulting display should look like the screen capture opposite.

Note that the `EmployeeId` is now also shown in the grid, even though it's of no real use to the user. Later in the chapter we'll look at keeping `EmployeeId` from being displayed in the `DataGrid` and using the column only to populate the `DataKeys` collection.

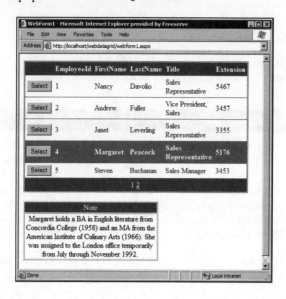

Tweaking the View State

If you build and run the page now, you'll see that everything seems to be working fine. However, there is a problem that's easy to recreate. Select a record on the first page (say, record number two) and then move to page two. Without some additional code, you'll see that the `DataGrid` will still think the second record on this new page is the one that has been selected, which it isn't. If we had selected the fifth record, this would have been even more awkward as page two doesn't have a fifth record to display.

The problem lies in that when ASP.NET rebuilds the grid as a form is posted back, it simply recreates the whole of a server control's view state unless told otherwise. Consider that when a row is selected, we don't call `BindDataGrid` in the respective event handler, because nothing in the `DataGrid` has changed. The grid can continue to use the same information we sent during the initial page request. The `DataGrid` saved the initial information in the view state, and the runtime restored this information during the initialization step of the postback request. During rendering the grid simply rewrote the HTML, with some slight adjustments to the formatting for the selected record.

What we need to do is reset the `SelectedIndex` property of the `DataGrid` to –1, meaning there is no selected row, and re-hide the detail panel. The updated event handler for the paging event is shown below.

```csharp
public void DataGrid1_PageIndexChanged(object source,
                        DataGridPageChangedEventArgs e)
{
  DataGrid1.CurrentPageIndex = e.NewPageIndex;
  DataGrid1.SelectedIndex = -1;
  Panel1.Visible = false;
  BindDataGrid();
}
```

We are starting to see a fairly functional database application emerge. However, there are still some cosmetic problems. For instance, the column names use the name of the database field instead of a friendly name. In the next section, we'll look at how to customize the columns of our `DataGrid`.

Using Bound Columns

Bound columns give you more control over the look of the columns in a `DataGrid`. Instead of letting the grid create, name, and format columns automatically, we can explicitly specify the columns for the grid to use.

Try It Out: Adding Bound Columns

1. We begin again with the **Property Builder** dialog for the grid by right-clicking the data grid and selecting **Property Builder**. Uncheck the **Create columns automatically at run time** checkbox.

2. From the **Available columns** list, move a **Bound column** node into the **Selected columns** list for each column we need to display. For each column we set the **Header text** to the text header we prefer (for instance, **First Name**), and the **Data Field** is set to the database column to bind to (`FirstName`). Move a bound column node over for **First Name, Last Name, Title, Phone**.

We're also going to add in the staff's hire dates to the grid to demonstrate how we can format a column automatically.

3. Add the `HireDate` file to the SQL query in the `BindDataGrid()` method.

```
private void BindDataGrid(bool refresh)
{
  DataSet dataSet = null;
  if(refresh == true || Session["Employees"] == null)
  {
    string sqlQuery = "SELECT EmployeeId, FirstName, LastName, Title," +
                      " Extension, HireDate FROM Employees";
    sqlConnection1.Open();
    ...
```

4. Back in the **Property Builder**, add another bound column for the Hire Date and set the **Data formatting expression** for the Hire Date column to `{0:d}`. This is the same format specifier as used in the `Format` method of the `String` class – it indicates a short date format and will exclude the time of day in the output. Check the **Read only** checkbox for the **Hire Date** column as well. We'll see why a bit later on.

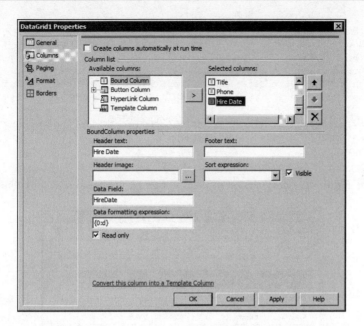

5. Last but not least, we'll alter the button column in our grid to use our own image rather than a button. Select the column in the Selected columns listbox and change Button type to LinkButton and Text to `<img border=0 src=images/magnify.gif>`. You'll find this image in the code download in the Chapter 10 solution.

Behind the scenes, the property builder has been turning our bound instructions into their corresponding code within the `<asp:datagrid>` controls tags.

```
<asp:datagrid id="DataGrid1" runat="server" AllowPaging="True" PageSize="5"
    BorderColor="#336666" BorderStyle="Double" BorderWidth="3px"
    BackColor="White" CellPadding="4" GridLines="Horizontal"
    AutoGenerateColumns="False" Width="163px">

  <SelectedItemStyle Font-Bold="True" ForeColor="White"
      BackColor="#339966"></SelectedItemStyle>
  <ItemStyle ForeColor="#333333" BackColor="White"></ItemStyle>
  <HeaderStyle Font-Bold="True" ForeColor="White" BackColor="#336666">
  </HeaderStyle>
  <FooterStyle ForeColor="#333333" BackColor="White"></FooterStyle>

  <Columns>
    <asp:ButtonColumn Text="<img border=0 src=images/magnify.gif>"
        ButtonType="LinkButton" CommandName="Select"></asp:ButtonColumn>

    <asp:BoundColumn DataField="FirstName" HeaderText="First Name">
    </asp:BoundColumn>
    <asp:BoundColumn DataField="LastName" HeaderText="Last Name">
    </asp:BoundColumn>
    <asp:BoundColumn DataField="Title" HeaderText="Title">
```

```
      </asp:BoundColumn>
      <asp:BoundColumn DataField="Extension" HeaderText="Phone">
      </asp:BoundColumn>
      <asp:BoundColumn DataField="HireDate" ReadOnly="True"
          HeaderText="Hire Date" DataFormatString="{0:d}"></asp:BoundColumn>
    </Columns>

    <PagerStyle HorizontalAlign="Center" ForeColor="White" BackColor="#336666"
        Mode="NumericPages"></PagerStyle>
  </asp:datagrid>
```

6. Rebuild and run the new version of `WebDataGrid`. It should now look like this:

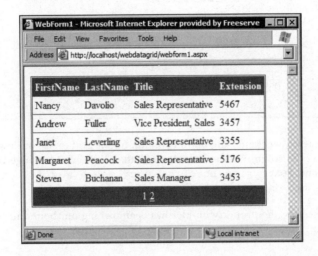

How It Works

There are two interesting items to note about this example. First, we did not specify a column for the `EmployeeId` field, but it is still a part of the query. We need the `EmployeeId` when a user clicks to see more details about an employee, so we still include this field in the `SELECT` statement and assign `EmployeeId` to the `DataKeyField` property of the grid. However, since we now have control over which columns from the `DataSet` appear, and since an internal identifier might not offer much value to the user, we simply do not provide a column to display the `EmployeeId`.

The second item to note is how we slightly changed the `ButtonColumn`. Instead of displaying a push button for selecting a row, we now display a link button. In addition, we changed the `Text` property of the column to write out an HTML image tag. This gave our grid a slightly fancier look with a custom icon (a magnifying glass).

Editing a DataGrid

So far, we've worked with the `DataGrid` control purely as a means to view the data already stored in a database, but we can use it to edit and update data as well.

Try It Out: Adding Editing Capability

In order to trigger its inline editing facilities, we'll add another button to the right of each row so users can indicate which row they want to alter.

1. Open the **Property Builder** dialog for the data grid once again. In the dialog go to the **Available columns** area and expand the **Button Column** node, then move an **Edit, Update, Cancel** button into the list of selected columns. We will place this new column at the end of the list so the buttons appear on the far right of the grid. We also change the **Button type** to a **PushButton** but leave all the other default values in place. The new column will give us three new events to handle. Press **OK**.

This new button column means that we now have to cater for the three possibilities we have given the user – to edit a row, update the data in the database, and to cancel any editing going on and reset back to read-only mode. Our next job then is to write the handlers for these three events.

2. First, we'll deal with a click of the `Edit` button. In Design view, select the `DataGrid` and bring up the Properties dialog. Switch to the Events view (click the lightning bolt in the dialog) and double-click on the **EditCommand** entry. Add the following code to the newly generated handler.

```
private void DataGrid1_EditCommand(object source,
    System.Web.UI.WebControls.DataGridCommandEventArgs e)
{
    DataGrid1.EditItemIndex = e.Item.ItemIndex;
    BindDataGrid();
}
```

3. Still in the Events view for the `DataGrid`, double-click `CancelCommand` in the event list, and add the following code to handle the **Cancel** button.

```
private void DataGrid1_CancelCommand(object source,
    System.Web.UI.WebControls.DataGridCommandEventArgs e)
{
    DataGrid1.EditItemIndex =-1;
    BindDataGrid();
}
```

4. Lastly we have the event handler for the **Update** event. We will need to construct an UPDATE statement for our grid, and then retrieve all of the values from the textbox controls in the edited row to use as the values in the command. Double-click on the **UpdateCommand** event in the **Properties** dialog for the grid and add the following code.

```
private void DataGrid1_UpdateCommand(object source,
    System.Web.UI.WebControls.DataGridCommandEventArgs e)
{
    string key = DataGrid1.DataKeys[DataGrid1.EditItemIndex].ToString();
    string sqlQuery =  "UPDATE Employees SET " +
            "FirstName = @FirstName, " +
        "LastName = @LastName, " +
```

```
                 "Title = @Title, " +
                 "Extension = @Extension " +
              "WHERE EmployeeId = @EmployeeID";

    sqlConnection1.Open();
    SqlCommand sqlCommand = new SqlCommand(sqlQuery, sqlConnection1);
    sqlCommand.Parameters.Add("@EmployeeID", key);
    sqlCommand.Parameters.Add("@FirstName",
                         ((TextBox)(e.Item.Cells[1].Controls[0])).Text);
    sqlCommand.Parameters.Add("@LastName",
                         ((TextBox)(e.Item.Cells[2].Controls[0])).Text);
    sqlCommand.Parameters.Add("@Title",
                         ((TextBox)(e.Item.Cells[3].Controls[0])).Text);
    sqlCommand.Parameters.Add("@Extension",
                         ((TextBox)(e.Item.Cells[4].Controls[0])).Text);

    sqlCommand.ExecuteNonQuery();
    sqlConnection1.Close();

    DataGrid1.EditItemIndex = -1;
    BindDataGrid(true);
}
```

5. Save, build, and run the web form.

How It Works

When we click the edit button, the `DataGrid1_EditCommand` method is invoked and we can find out which row is selected from the `DataGridCommandEventArgs` parameter. Making the row into a set of editable textboxes is then a matter of updating the grid's `EditItemIndex` property and rebinding the data to update the new edit controls. The grid will then provide an edit box for each field in the row, with the exception of the **Hire Date** column, because we marked this column as read-only in the last section.

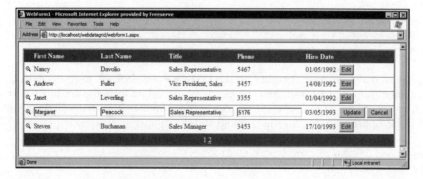

Once a row is in edit mode, the user can change the values in each textbox and press either **Cancel** or **Update**. These are the other two events we handle. For a cancel event, we just need to reset the grid's **EditItemIndex** property to –1, indicating no row is under edit, and rebind the data to ensure the grid reflects this.

To handle the update event, the first step is retrieving the `EmployeeID` to update from the `DataKeys` collection.

```
string key = DataGrid1.DataKeys[DataGrid1.EditItemIndex].ToString();
```

Then, to get the updated field values, we go to the `DataGridCommandEventArgs` parameter. As we have seen earlier, this parameter contains an `Item` property representing the currently selected row in the `DataGrid`. `Item` is a reference to a `DataGridItem` object. Previously we have used the `ItemIndex` property of `DataGridItem` to simply see which row the user clicked, but this time we need to dig a little deeper.

The `DataGridItem` contains a `Cells` collection, and there is one cell for each column in the grid. The first cell (`Cell[0]`) is the select column with the magnifying glass. The second cell (`Cell[1]`) is the first name column, and so on for each column. We must visit each cell containing a value we need and extract the contents of the edited textbox.

Each cell contains a property named `Controls`. This collection contains all of the child controls in the cell. For bound columns in a data grid, the textbox is always the only control in the collection, thus we use `Controls[0]` to retrieve a reference to the textbox. We cast the object returned from the `Controls` collection to a `TextBox` and then extract the `Text` property.

```
sqlCommand.Parameters.Add("@FirstName",
                          ((TextBox)(e.Item.Cells[1].Controls[0])).Text);
sqlCommand.Parameters.Add("@LastName",
                          ((TextBox)(e.Item.Cells[2].Controls[0])).Text);
sqlCommand.Parameters.Add("@Title",
                          ((TextBox)(e.Item.Cells[3].Controls[0])).Text);
sqlCommand.Parameters.Add("@Extension",
                          ((TextBox)(e.Item.Cells[4].Controls[0])).Text);
```

Before we leave the `DataGrid1_UpdateCommand` method we have to reset the `EditItemIndex` property to force the grid out of edit mode. Then we have to bind the data source again, forcing a refresh by passing `true` to `BindDataGrid` so the refresh will pick up the new values from the database and reset our cached `DataSet` in the `Session`.

One last point: we will need to modify the `DataGrid1_PageIndexChanged` event handler one more time. We need to ensure that edit mode is canceled if the user changes pages in the middle of an edit. This will prevent the same problem we discussed earlier when a record is selected and the page is changed. The following listing shows the updated method.

```
public void DataGrid1_PageIndexChanged(object source,
                DataGridPageChangedEventArgs e)
{
    DataGrid1.SelectedIndex = -1;
    Panel1.Visible = false;
    DataGrid1.EditItemIndex = -1;
    DataGrid1.CurrentPageIndex = e.NewPageIndex;
    BindDataGrid();
}
```

In the next section we will also allow the user to edit the hiring date, but with a new type of column: the template column.

Template Columns

A template column affords us the highest level of control in a grid column's appearance. It is completely up to us as developers to determine when and how to display data from the data source using a **data binding expression**. You could, for example, combine the first name and last name fields into a single column using a template column. To demonstrate, we will use a template column to display the hiring date.

Try It Out: Using a Template Column

1. Open the Property Builder for the grid again and navigate to the Hire Date column in the list of Selected columns. On the bottom of the dialog click the Convert this column into a Template Column link. Close the dialog and return to the design view.

2. We are going to modify the Template Column directly by switching to the HTML view. Visual Studio already has code for the static view of the date, but we're going to add the template for editing the date.

```
<asp:TemplateColumn HeaderText="Hire Date">
<ItemTemplate>
  <asp:Label runat="server"
    Text='<%# DataBinder.Eval(Container, "DataItem.HireDate", "{0:d}") %>'>
  </asp:Label>
</ItemTemplate>
<EditItemTemplate>
  <asp:Calendar ID="Calendar1" Runat="server" BorderColor="#336666"
    ShowGridLines="True" NextPrevFormat="ShortMonth"
    VisibleDate='<%# DataBinder.Eval(Container, "DataItem.HireDate") %>'
    SelectedDate='<%# DataBinder.Eval(Container, "DataItem.HireDate") %>'>
    <TitleStyle ForeColor="White" BackColor="#336666"></TitleStyle>
  </asp:Calendar>
</EditItemTemplate>
</asp:TemplateColumn>
```

3. The grid is now set up to edit the `HireDate`, but we need to adjust the event handler for the Update button so that it will update the `HireDate` field as well.

```
private void DataGrid1_UpdateCommand(object source,
    System.Web.UI.WebControls.DataGridCommandEventArgs e)
{
    string key = DataGrid1.DataKeys[DataGrid1.EditItemIndex].ToString();
    string sqlQuery =
      "UPDATE Employees SET FirstName = @FirstName, " +
      "LastName = @LastName, Title = @Title, Extension = @Extension, " +
      "HireDate = @HireDate WHERE EmployeeId = @EmployeeID";

    sqlConnection1.Open();
    SqlCommand sqlCommand = new SqlCommand(sqlQuery, sqlConnection1);
```

```
sqlCommand.Parameters.Add("@EmployeeID", key);
sqlCommand.Parameters.Add("@FirstName",
                    ((TextBox)(e.Item.Cells[1].Controls[0])).Text);
sqlCommand.Parameters.Add("@LastName",
                    ((TextBox)(e.Item.Cells[2].Controls[0])).Text);
sqlCommand.Parameters.Add("@Title",
                    ((TextBox)(e.Item.Cells[3].Controls[0])).Text);
sqlCommand.Parameters.Add("@Extension",
                    ((TextBox)(e.Item.Cells[4].Controls[0])).Text);
sqlCommand.Parameters.Add("@HireDate",
      ((Calendar)(e.Item.Cells[5].FindControl("Calendar1"))).
                                    SelectedDate.ToString());

sqlCommand.ExecuteNonQuery();
sqlConnection1.Close();

DataGrid1.EditItemIndex = -1;
BindDataGrid(true);
}
```

4. Build and run the page. When you try to edit a column, a calendar control will appear in place of the date originally there for you to choose another one.

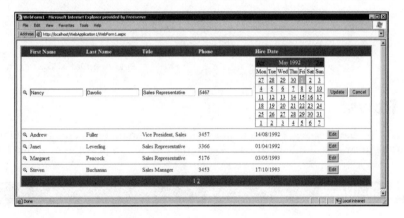

How It Works

Every template column is composed of one or more item templates. In this example, we use an `ItemTemplate` and an `EditItemTemplate`, but there are `HeaderTemplates` and `FooterTemplates` as well. The `ItemTemplate` controls the appearance of the data during normal viewing, while the `EditItemTemplate` controls the view when the item is in edit mode.

For the item template, we've used a simple `Label` control, and for the edit template, a `Calendar` control. While the regular display for the hiring date will look the same as when the column was a bound column, the edit display will look entirely different, albeit somewhat ungainly. As an exercise you may like to try and improve the aesthetics of this solution.

It is possible to insert any amount of text, HTML, and server-side controls into a template to achieve the desired result. When you are ready to display data from the data source, you'll need to use a data-binding expression.

As you can see from the ASPX code-snippet above, data bindings use a special expression format. You always place the expression between the delimiters <%# and %>.

```
<asp:Label runat="server"
    Text='<%# DataBinder.Eval(Container, "DataItem.HireDate", "{0:d}") %>'>
</asp:Label>
```

Inside these delimiters we use the static `Eval` method of the `DataBinder` class; this method was designed for just this purpose. There are two required parameters to `Eval`: first the container and then the expression to evaluate against the container. For a `DataGrid`, the container is always the `Container`. The expression is the field name to use, in this case `DataItem.HireDate`.

In the example above we set the `Label` control's `Text` property to the result of a data-binding expression. For the calendar control, we need to set both the `SelectedDate` and `VisibleDate` properties to make sure the hire date is both highlighted and visible in the monthly calendar.

Updating the employee hire date value uses the same basic logic to extract the date value from the `Calendar` control but with one slight difference – we cannot be exactly sure where the `Calendar` control actually appears in the cell's `Control` collection. To get a reference to the calendar then, we use the cell's `FindControl` method and pass it the id of the calendar control, as shown in the following expression:

```
sqlCommand.Parameters.Add("@HireDate",
    ((Calendar)(e.Item.Cells[5].FindControl("Calendar1"))).
                                    SelectedDate.ToString());
```

Deleting Rows

With everything we have learned to date in this chapter, we should find adding the ability to delete a row an almost familiar task, and indeed it is. Again, the `DataGrid` provides us with a lot of help to achieve this.

Try It Out: Deleting Rows

1. In design view, right-click the `DataGrid` and open the **Property Builder** again. Under the columns tab, expand the **Button Column** node and move a **Delete** button into the list of selected columns. Press **OK**.

2. Now open the **Properties** dialog for the `DataGrid` and switch to the events view. Double-click on the `DeleteCommand` entry in the event list and add the following code to the new event handler that is generated.

```
private void DataGrid1_DeleteCommand(object source,
    System.Web.UI.WebControls.DataGridCommandEventArgs e)
{
    DataGrid1.SelectedIndex = -1;
    Panel1.Visible = false;
    DataGrid1.EditItemIndex = -1;
```

```
      string key = DataGrid1.DataKeys[e.Item.ItemIndex].ToString();
      string sqlQuery = "DELETE FROM Employees " +
                        "WHERE EmployeeId = @EmployeeId";


    sqlConnection1.Open();
    SqlCommand sqlCommand = new SqlCommand(sqlQuery, sqlConnection1);
    sqlCommand.Parameters.Add("@EmployeeID", key);
    sqlCommand.ExecuteNonQuery();
    sqlConnection1.Close();
    BindDataGrid(true);
  }
```

3. Build and run the page. If the employee has made no orders you will be able to them from the `Employees` table. If they have, however, deleting them without first deleting their orders would violate the referential integrity of the database and you'll get an error message back saying as much.

How It Works

The event handler for the **Delete** button is quite straightforward. First we set the grid back to its original state by resetting `SelectedIndex` and `EditItemIndex`, and making the notes panel invisible again:

```
private void DataGrid1_DeleteCommand(object source,
    System.Web.UI.WebControls.DataGridCommandEventArgs e)
{
  DataGrid1.SelectedIndex = -1;
  Panel1.Visible = false;
  DataGrid1.EditItemIndex = -1;
```

Then we grab the `EmployeeID` of the record to be deleted from the `DataKeys` collection as we have done before and build a standard `DELETE` query:

```
    string key = DataGrid1.DataKeys[e.Item.ItemIndex].ToString();
    string sqlQuery = "DELETE FROM Employees WHERE EmployeeId = @EmployeeId";
```

Finally, we execute the query, and force a refresh while rebinding the `DataGrid`:

```
    sqlConnection1.Open();
    SqlCommand sqlCommand = new SqlCommand(sqlQuery, sqlConnection1);
    sqlCommand.Parameters.Add("@EmployeeID", key);
    sqlCommand.ExecuteNonQuery();
    sqlConnection1.Close();
    BindDataGrid(true);
  }
```

Sorting a DataGrid

The final feature to add to our `DataGrid` is the ability to sort the rows by any column.

Try It Out: Adding Sorting to a DataGrid

1. Adding the ability to sort begins with, as you might have guessed by now, the Property Builder dialog. On the General section of the dialog, select the Allow sorting checkbox. Doing this will change the column headings into hyperlinks that will raise the `OnSortCommand` when they are clicked on.

2. For each bound column representing a data field, specify a Sort expression matching the DataField name. For example, we set the sort expression for the First Name column to `FirstName`, the Last Name column to `LastName` and so on. When you've finished, press OK to leave property builder.

3. Now open the Properties dialog for the `DataGrid` and switch to the events view. Double-click on the `SortCommand` entry in the event list and add the following code to the new event handler that is generated. Notice we have modified the data-binding code to accept a sort expression, and simply forward the sort expression to this method for processing.

```
private void DataGrid1_SortCommand(object source,
                                   DataGridSortCommandEventArgs e)
{
  DataGrid1.SelectedIndex = -1;
  Panel1.Visible = false;
  DataGrid1.EditItemIndex = -1;
  BindDataGrid(e.SortExpression);
}
```

4. `BindDataGrid` won't accept a sort expression until we update it. As it turns out, we're going to overload it with two new versions as well. A caller will now be able to pass no parameters, just a refresh flag, just a sort expression, or both a refresh flag and a sort expression.

```
private void BindDataGrid()
{
  BindDataGrid(false, null);
}

private void BindDataGrid(bool refresh)
{
  BindDataGrid(refresh, null);
}

private void BindDataGrid(string sortExpression)
{
  BindDataGrid(false, sortExpression);
}

private void BindDataGrid(bool refresh, string sortExpression)
```

```
{
   DataSet dataSet = null;
   if(refresh == true || Session["Employees"] == null)
   {
      string sqlQuery = "SELECT EmployeeId, FirstName, LastName, Title," +
                         " Extension, HireDate FROM Employees";
      sqlConnection1.Open();
      SqlDataAdapter sqlDataAdapter =
                         new SqlDataAdapter(sqlQuery, sqlConnection1);
      dataSet = new DataSet();
      sqlDataAdapter.Fill(dataSet, "Employees");

      Session["Employees"] = dataSet;
      sqlConnection1.Close();
   }
   else
   {
      dataSet = (DataSet)Session["Employees"];
   }

   DataView dataView = dataSet.Tables["Employees"].DefaultView;
   if (sortExpression != null)
   {
      dataView.Sort = sortExpression;
   }
   DataGrid1.DataSource = dataView;
   DataGrid1.DataKeyField = "EmployeeId";
   DataGrid1.DataBind();
}
```

How It Works

When we click a column heading and raise a `SortCommand` event, its handler takes two parameters. One is the source and the other is of type `DataGridSortCommandEventArgs`. One of the properties we can read on this parameter is a string, the `SortExpression` property. We can specify a sort expression for each bound column and template column in our `DataGrid`. The sort expression passed in the event handler parameter is the sort expression given to the column. For example, we gave the **Last Name** column the sort expression `LastName`. When a user clicks on the **Last Name** header, this is the sort expression we will see in the event handler.

If you do not specify a sort expression for a bound column, the column does not display with a hyperlink and is not sortable. You can specify any string for the sort expression, however, to make the programming easier, we are going to use a sort expression compatible with the `DataView`'s `Sort` property. This property accepts a column name followed by `ASC` for an ascending sort, or `DESC` for a descending sort. If the sort order is not specified, ascending is used by default.

Summary

In this chapter we have demonstrated how powerful ASP.NET and in particular the web forms `DataGrid` control can be for online database-backed applications. Using just a small amount of code, we have written an application that lets us sort, edit, delete, select, and update rows in the grid. We have also seen how to take control of the rendering of the data in the grid using bound columns, and how to use data-binding expressions inside template columns. This is exciting, particularly considering the difficulties normally associated with web development before .NET came around.

Along the way to building this feature-complete grid application we have learned some of the differences in web versus windows programming. We can build on what we have learned in this chapter when we move to validation controls and ASP.NET data input in the next chapter.

Exercises

1. You have just received a request, asking you to add a new column to the employee report: `Country`. Take the steps necessary to pull this field from the database and display it in the report. The column will be sortable, but read only.

2. With the `Country` field now displaying and sorting in question one, give the user the ability to update the `Country` code during the edit process.

3. By default, the sort expression we gave to the new column ("`Country`") will sort the column in ascending order. Change the sort order to descending order.

4. Change the `Country` column from a bound column to a template column for additional flexibility, and update the code-behind page to use the template column (hint: the update logic will need to change).

5. Find a property to set on the textbox in the `EditItemTemplate` of the `Country` column to restrict the maximum length of the string the user can enter to a length of three characters.

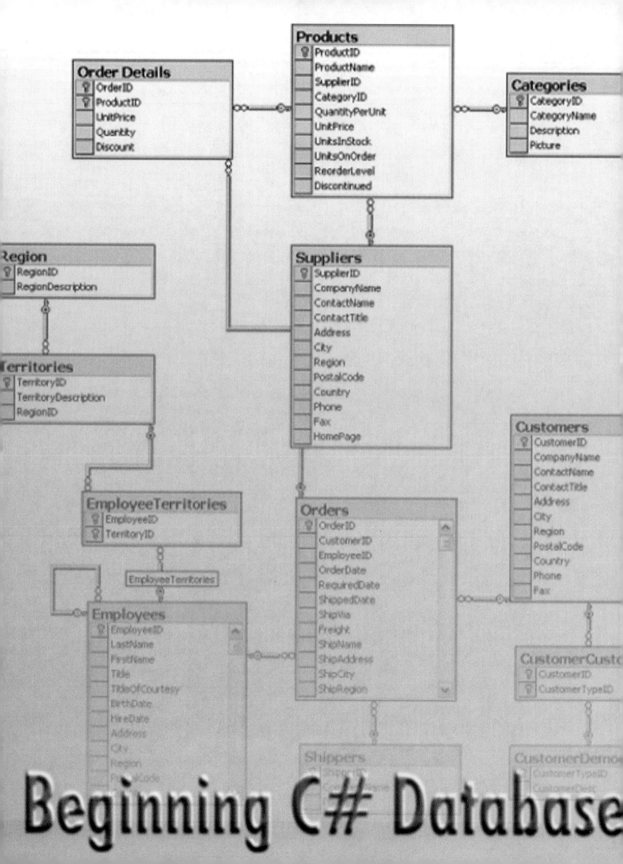

Order Details
- OrderID
- ProductID
- UnitPrice
- Quantity
- Discount

Products
- ProductID
- ProductName
- SupplierID
- CategoryID
- QuantityPerUnit
- UnitPrice
- UnitsInStock
- UnitsOnOrder
- ReorderLevel
- Discontinued

Categories
- CategoryID
- CategoryName
- Description
- Picture

Region
- RegionID
- RegionDescription

Suppliers
- SupplierID
- CompanyName
- ContactName
- ContactTitle
- Address
- City
- Region
- PostalCode
- Country
- Phone
- Fax
- HomePage

Customers
- CustomerID
- CompanyName
- ContactName
- ContactTitle
- Address
- City
- Region
- PostalCode
- Country
- Phone
- Fax

Territories
- TerritoryID
- TerritoryDescription
- RegionID

EmployeeTerritories
- EmployeeID
- TerritoryID

EmployeeTerritories

Orders
- OrderID
- CustomerID
- EmployeeID
- OrderDate
- RequiredDate
- ShippedDate
- ShipVia
- Freight
- ShipName
- ShipAddress
- ShipCity
- ShipRegion

Employees
- EmployeeID
- LastName
- FirstName
- Title
- TitleOfCourtesy
- BirthDate
- HireDate
- Address
- City
- Region
- PostalCode

CustomerCusto
- CustomerID
- CustomerTypeID

Shippers

CustomerDemo
- CustomerTypeID
- CustomerDesc

Beginning C# Database

Validating Web-Based User Input

Data validation is an important task in any database-backed application. Making sure the data conforms to the strictures imposed on it within a database is vital. If the data becomes corrupt, all sorts of problems will occur. Before inserting new information into a table you need to make sure the user has entered information in all required fields, make sure all the dates have a valid format, all the numbers are within the valid range, and carry out any other checks required to guarantee the data conforms to your database schema and business rules.

In web applications, data validation is no less important than it is for windows applications, but it has a different twist. Over the Internet, a user will enter information into a web form, and then post that to the server giving us a chance to validate their data twice: once on the client's web browser, and once more when the data reaches the server. This two step approach allows us a quick response when detecting an error on the client, while still preserving a high level of security on the server.

To help us on our way, ASP.NET provides a number of validation controls to ease the burden of performing validation on both sides of the network. These controls are the main focus of this chapter, which will touch the following topics:

❑ The ASP.NET validation controls: `RequiredFieldValidator`, `RangeValidator`, `CompareValidator`, and `RegularExpressionValidator`

❑ Creating custom client and server-side validations with the `CustomValidator`

❑ Showing validation error messages in detail and in summary

By the end of the chapter we will also have built a web form that enables us to validate and insert new employees into the Northwind database and along the way we will also learn some additional tips for data binding server controls. Before we get into any of the validation control details, however, we're going to build a quick application to demonstrate how the controls work.

Try It Out: A Validation Example

For our first example we will create an ASP.NET Web Application named WebDataValidation.

1. Open Visual Studio .NET and create a new blank solution called `Chapter11_Examples`.

2. Add a new ASP.NET project called WebDataValidation to the solution by selecting File | Add Project | New Project... As we saw in the last chapter, Visual Studio .NET will take care of configuring IIS to support the new application.

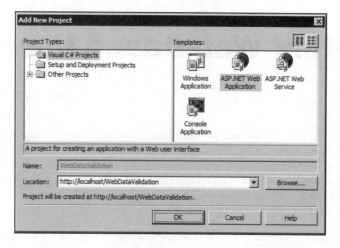

3. Once the new application is set up, switch the layout mode of `WebForm1.aspx` from `GridLayout` to `FlowLayout` by right-clicking on the empty form, selecting **Properties** from the context menu, and changing the `PageLayout` property.

4. We will begin by placing four controls from the **Web Forms** section of the **Toolbox** onto the form. First, place a `TextBox` control and give it an ID of `FirstNameTextBox`, then one `RequiredFieldValidator` (`FirstNameRequiredFieldValidator`), and two `Button` controls (`SubmitButton` and `CancelButton`).

5. For the `CancelButton`, find the `CausesValidation` property in the property dialog for the button and set it to `false`.

6. This `RequiredFieldValidator` forces the user to enter text into the control associated with the validator. In this case, it's the textbox. To link validator with textbox then, select the validator, find the `ControlToValidate` property in its **Properties** dialog and select `FirstNameTextBox` from the drop-down list. First name is now a required field in the form. Set the validator's `ErrorMessage` property to say `First Name Is Required` as well.

7. In design view, drag the controls around so the form looks similar to the following screenshot. Notice how we can see the `RequiredFieldValidator` error message displayed on the form. This is the exact position the error message will appear if validation fails.

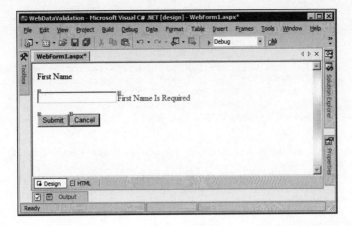

8. For this first example, we do not need to place much code into the code-behind file. Double-click on the `SubmitButton` control and add the following highlighted code to the event handler given by the IDE.

```
private void SubmitButton_Click(object sender,
                                    System.EventArgs e)
{
    if(Page.IsValid)
    {
        //process input here
    }
}
```

9. Switch back to the design view of the form and double-click on the `CancelButton`. Add the following highlighted code to the new event handler for the click event.

```
private void CancelButton_Click(object sender,
                                    System.EventArgs e)
{
    FirstNameTextBox.Text = "";
}
```

10. Build and run the web page. Type in a name and press Submit. Nothing will happen. Pressing Cancel meanwhile will remove the name from the textbox. Now press Submit again. This time our validator will pop up an error message telling us to type a first name in the box.

How It Works

So far, the page isn't doing very much, but we have already laid the foundations for an useful page. Switch to the HTML view and you'll see in the `<body>` of the page the new button validation property and validator control.

```
<body>
  <form id="Form1" method="post" runat="server">
    <P>First Name</P>
    <P>
      <asp:TextBox id="FirstNameTextBox" runat="server"></asp:TextBox>
      <asp:RequiredFieldValidator id="FirstNameRequiredFieldValidator"
          runat="server" ErrorMessage="First Name Is Required"
          ControlToValidate="FirstNameTextbox">
      </asp:RequiredFieldValidator>
    </P>
    <P>
      <asp:Button id="SubmitButton" runat="server" Text="Submit">
      </asp:Button>
      <asp:Button id="CancelButton" runat="server" Text="Cancel"
          CausesValidation="False">
      </asp:Button>
    </P>
    <P> </P>
  </form>
</body>
```

By default, whenever a button is pressed on a web form, it is validated, but by setting our **Cancel** button's `CausesValidation` property to `false`, we can override this. On our page, pressing **Cancel** will clear all of the fields on the form, so there's no need to validate any of the fields when the user presses this button. "All the fields on the form" means just the textbox at the moment, so when a user clicks the **Cancel** button we simply clear the control and allow the user to start over.

Although the event handler for the `SubmitButton` currently performs no activity in the database, pressing **Submit** will cause the form to validate its contents against whatever validation checks are in place. In this case, it's just the `RequiredFieldValidator`, so the textbox is checked for content. If something has been typed in, it will pass the page as valid; if not, it will raise the error given by its `ErrorMessage` property.

Before the end of the chapter, we'll be inserting the information in the form into Northwind in the `SubmitButton_Click` handler, but for now, notice that we check the `IsValid` property of the base class performing any action. If `IsValid` returns a value of `true`, you can be certain all of the validation checks were successful. Notice that this also means the form validation takes place before the code in the event handler.

Technically, the `RequiredFieldValidator` fails when the value in the associated control matches the value of the `InitialValue` property of the `RequiredFieldValidator`. If you want to make sure the user changes some default value placed into the control, set the control's `Text` value and the `InitialValue` property of the `RequiredFieldValidator` to the same value. In other words, the `ControlToValidate` does not need to be empty to fail a validation, it simply needs to contain the same value as the `InitialValue` of the `RequiredFieldValidator`, which in this example is empty.

As another example, suppose you wanted to make sure the first-name textbox first appeared on the form with the string "**No Name**" appearing inside. You could set the `InitialValue` of the `RequiredFieldValidator` and the `Text` property of the `TextBox` control to the string `No Name`. This will allow the string to appear on the form, but force the user to change the value in the textbox before the form will pass its validation checks.

Web Validation

With the first example of using an ASP.NET validation control under our belts, let's take a minute to discuss the use of validating data on both the client and server side, how ASP.NET controls work in both situations, and how to apply that knowledge to your web form applications.

Client-Side Validation

If a user's browser (or other web client) is capable and configured to execute client-side script – for example, JavaScript – validation will occur on the client before the browser posts the data to the server. Internet Explorer 4.0 and above can perform client-side validation if scripting is enabled.

Client-side validation provides the user with quick feedback since the validation code is executed on the client machine. By default, whenever the user presses a button on the form, the script executes the validation checks for each validation control on the form. If **any** of the validation controls on a form fails, the script cancels the postback to the server and displays error messages on the form. This behavior creates a quick turnaround time for a user since they do not wait on a server round trip to discover errors. It also helps save resources on the server since we won't waste time processing a request with invalid information. For these two reasons, client-side validations are a good feature to offer in a web application.

Disabling Client-Side Validation

Every good rule of thumb deserves an exception though, and there are times when you will want to avoid client-side validation checks. We have seen one such example in our first form. By setting the `CausesValidation` property of a `Button` to `false` you can disable all validation checks when a user presses that particular button. This is useful when you have a button control that does not require validation checks, such as a cancel button or a refresh button. Likewise, if a client-side check is likely to be unacceptably slow – for example, because the form requires checking against a long list on the server.

If you want to disable client-side validation for a specific validation control, you can set the control's `EnableClientScript` property to `false`.

Server-Side Validation

When a button is clicked by a user and a button-click event is fired, a postback is initiated. All data requiring validation is then validated by ASP.NET on the server side. It is possible, however, to completely disable a validation control by setting its `Enabled` property to `false`.

Of course, there are very good reasons why we should always perform validation checks on the server, even if the client supports validation. First, not executing server-side checks leaves your application code vulnerable to malicious users who might circumvent client-side validations in an effort to break into or damage your servers. For situations where we are verifying passwords or product activation codes, it's vital that we validate these items on the server. Simply put, we can never trust the data in an incoming request, and must always validate on the server.

Validation in the Page Lifecycle

In the last chapter we talked about the typical ASP.NET page lifecycle. After a request arrives, the server instantiates an object built from the code-behind logic and the ASPX file. The ASP.NET runtime then initializes this object, restores the viewstate of the server controls, and fires the Load event, which we typically handle with the Page_Load method. Once these steps are complete the runtime will execute all of the enabled server validation controls. It is possible to force validation again programmatically later on, but we'll leave this for the time being. If any of the controls fail, the IsValid Page property will test false. Finally, the engine fires the postback event (such as a button click event), then renders and disposes of the page. Validation is already complete by the time you reach a click event in your code-behind file.

> **When validation fails, the normal flow of execution continues. You need to check the IsValid property to know if a validation check failed.**

One of the great features of the built-in validation controls is how they will keep your server-side and client-side validation checks synchronized. When modifying an existing application it is sometimes easy to update one half of the validation code and not the other. The server validation controls keep this logic packaged into a single component.

So then, our validation controls take care of validation on both server and client unless we tell them otherwise. Except for a few occasions, this validation is a recommended good thing. In the next section, we'll take a look at the rest of the ASP.NET validation controls.

With a better understanding of the theory and mechanics behind validation controls, let's move on to an overview of the controls provided by the .NET Framework.

ASP.NET Validation Controls

There are six validation-related controls provided by ASP.NET and while they each check something different, they all work in much the same way as the RequiredFieldValidator control we saw earlier. They are:

Control Name	Description
RequiredFieldValidator	Seen earlier. Checks that the user changes the value of the field in the control from its InitialValue.
CompareValidator	Compares the value in a control against a constant value, the value in a second control, or a value in a database.

Control Name	Description
RangeValidator	Checks the value in a control against a minimum and maximum value.
RegularExpressionValidator	Compares the value in a control against a regular expression pattern.
CustomValidator	Performs user-defined validation against a control.
ValidationSummary	Summarizes error messages for a form in a single location on the web form.

All of these validation controls, with the exception of the ValidationSummary class, derive from the BaseValidator class, giving them common methods and properties. Indeed, we're already familiar with two key points concerning them that we must not forget.

❑ Validation controls execute when the user clicks a Button control, be it an HTML button server control or an <ASP:... button server control such as the LinkButton or ImageButton.

❑ Validation controls must have the ControlToValidate property set before rendering the page or the control throws a System.Web.HttpException. The one exclusion to this rule is the CustomValidator component, which does not need to be tied to a specific control to validate.

The standard controls you can associate a validator with are the TextBox, ListBox, DropDownList, and RadioButtonList controls. You can also validate some HTML controls, including HtmlInputText, HtmlInputFile, HtmlSelect, and HtmlTextArea.

We have seen the RequiredFieldValidator in our first sample program, so let's move on to examine the rest of the controls.

The RangeValidator Control

The next control we will use, the RangeValidator, ensures the value inside a control stays within a specified range. For example, we might need to restrict the value of an input box to between 0 and 100 to represent a percentage. Alternatively, in this example we will restrict input in a textbox to a range of dates. The date must be within one week (plus or minus) of the current date.

Try It Out: Using the Range Validator

1. Continuing to build on the first example web form, add an additional TextBox control and set the ID property to HireDateTextBox.

2. Drag a RangeValidator. control onto the form beside the HireDateTextBox. Set the ID property to HireDateValidator. Set the ControlToValidate property to HireDateTextBox, and set the Type property to Date. Set the ErrorMessage to The hire date must be within one week of today's date. The form should now look like this:

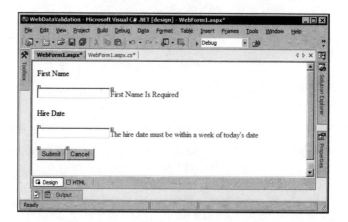

3. Change the `Display` property of the `RangeValidator` from `Static` to `Dynamic`.

4. Drag a `RequiredFieldValidator` control beside the `RangeValidator`. Set its ID property to `HireDateRequiredFieldValidator`, and set the `ControlToValidate` to the `HireDateTextBox`. The error message for this control is **Hire Date is required**.

5. Right-click on the form, select **View Code**, and add the following highlighted code to the form's `Page_Load` function.

```csharp
private void Page_Load(object sender, System.EventArgs e)
{
    // Put user code to initialize the page here
    if(!Page.IsPostBack)
    {
        DateTime nextWeek = DateTime.Today + TimeSpan.FromDays(7);
        DateTime lastWeek = DateTime.Today - TimeSpan.FromDays(7);

        HireDateValidator.MaximumValue = nextWeek.ToShortDateString();
        HireDateValidator.MinimumValue = lastWeek.ToShortDateString();
    }
}
```

6. We also need to add a line of code to clear the `HireDateTextBox` when the cancel button is pressed.

```csharp
private void CancelButton_Click(object sender, System.EventArgs e)
{
    FirstNameTextBox.Text="";
    HireDateTextBox.Text="";
}
```

7. Build and run the page. Try to raise the two possible errors for the `HireDateTextBox` on your own. Remember that validation will fail for a given input control if the value of the control does not convert into the `Type` property of the `RangeValidator`. For instance, an invalid (unconvertible) string will generate a validation error, like so:

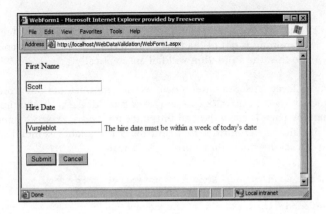

How It Works

In the above example we have created a textbox in which we require a date be added that is neither seven days more nor less than today's date. In order to enforce this, we have tied two validation controls to the form and tied them to the `HireDateTextBox`. Behind the scenes, the HTML looks like this:

```
<P>Hire date</P>
<P>
  <asp:TextBox
      id="HireDateTextBox" runat="server">
  </asp:TextBox>
  <asp:RangeValidator
      id="HireDateValidator"
      runat="server"
      ControlToValidate="HireDateTextBox"
      ErrorMessage="Hire date must be within one week of today's date"
      Type="Date"
      Display="Dynamic">
  </asp:RangeValidator>
  <asp:RequiredFieldValidator
      id="HireDateRequiredFieldValidator"
      runat="server"
      ControlToValidate="HireDateTextBox"
      ErrorMessage="Hire Date is required">
  </asp:RequiredFieldValidator>
</P>
```

Without the `RequiredFieldValidator`, the user does not have to type a value into the `HireDateTextBox` control, but if they do it must be in a proper date format and in the specified range. The `RangeValidator` will make this range check for us. Why not just use the `RangeValidator` by itself? Simply because this control will not validate the contents of an input control if the control is empty and thus we need the `RequiredFieldValidator`.

When multiple validation controls reference an input, all the validation checks must pass for the field to be valid. On the other hand, you need to be careful if you do use multiple `Validator` controls that they do not contradict each other. For example, two `RangeValidators` referencing a textbox with one specifying a range of 0 to 50, and the other a range of 100 to 150, will always fail that textbox and `IsValid` will return `false` for the page. By definition, the value in the textbox will always be outside the given range of at least one of the checks.

Remember also that the `RangeValidator` has a `Type` property. This property can take one of the following values: `String`, `Integer`, `Double`, `Date`, or `Currency`. If the value the `RangeValidator` is examining is not of the type expected, it will first try to convert the value into the correct type. If it can't do this, the validation will fail automatically.

Our requirement was to force a user to enter a date within one week of the current system time. Obviously we cannot enter a `MinimumValue` and `MaximumValue` at design time, so we need to set these properties when the page is executed and thus alter the `Page_Load()` handler. Fortunately, validation controls, like all the web form server controls, are available as member variables in the code-behind page and we can set the range limits programmatically.

```
private void Page_Load(object sender, System.EventArgs e)
{
    // Put user code to initialize the page here
    if(!Page.IsPostBack)
    {
        DateTime nextWeek = DateTime.Today + TimeSpan.FromDays(7);
        DateTime lastWeek = DateTime.Today - TimeSpan.FromDays(7);

        HireDateValidator.MaximumValue = nextWeek.ToShortDateString();
        HireDateValidator.MinimumValue = lastWeek.ToShortDateString();
    }
}
```

Displaying Error Messages

One last thing to mention before we move on to another control is why we set the `Display` property for the `RangeValidator`. The `Display` property can accept one of three values: `None`, `Static`, or `Dynamic`. If the `Display` property is set to `None`, no errors are displayed where the validation control is placed on the form. This may sound pointless, but we will see an example of setting `Display` to `None` later in the chapter when we look at the `ValidationSummary` control, which groups all error messages in one place on the form.

The `Static` and `Dynamic` settings both let error messages stay where they were placed but influence the layout of our page in a more subtle way.

❑ With the `Static` setting, the control reserves space to display an error message even when no error message is present. We can use this setting to ensure the appearance of our page stays exactly the same when an error message appears.

❑ With a `Dynamic` display, there is no space reserved for the error message. Instead, when validation fails and the control displays an error, the control adds space to the page for the error to appear, which can change the layout of the screen.

Note these two settings are only effective when we're using client-side validation. If the page validation is just on the server-side, the display is effectively dynamic. Back to our example then; if we had left the `Display` property of the `RangeValidator` as `statid`, our error message might display as shown in the screen capture opposite, out by itself to the right.

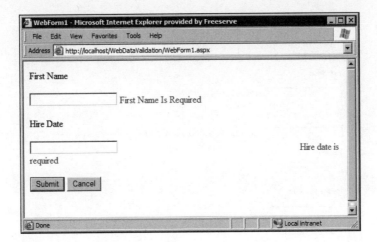

The CompareValidator Control

Our third control is the CompareValidator, which we use to compare the value of an input control to either a constant value (possibly from a database), or the value in another input control. If the former, we can specify the constant in the ValueToCompare property. If the latter, we specify the ID of the control containing the value we want for comparison in the ControlToCompare property.

> *Note you do not want to set both the ControlToCompare property and the ValueToCompare property. If this happens, however, the ControlToCompare property takes precedence and the only validation that will happen is that against the value in the second control.*

Like the RangeValidator, the CompareValidator has a Type property you can set to String, Integer, Double, Date, or Currency. The value in or pointed at by the ControlToValidate property must convert to this type for validation to succeed.

Try It Out: The CompareValidator

To demonstrate the CompareValidator, we'll use the scenario of setting a password. When the user types a password into the box the letters will display as asterisks. Since it is difficult for the user to know if they made a typing mistake, users are generally given two input controls: one to enter the password and another to confirm the password. These input values have to match for a valid password.

1. Drag two web forms TextBox controls onto the form. Set the ID properties to PasswordTextBox1 and PasswordTextBox2, and set the TextMode properties on both controls to Password.

2. Drag a CompareValidator onto the form. Set the ID property to PasswordCompareValidator. Set the ErrorMessage property to the string **Passwords do not match**. Set the ControlToValidate to PasswordTextBox2, and the ControlToCompare to PasswordTextBox1. The form should now look like this:

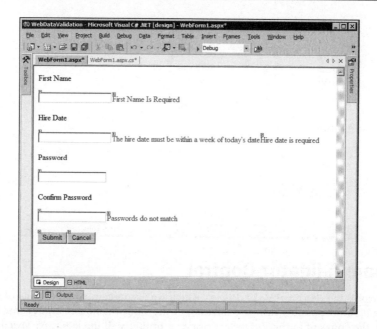

3. Build and run the page. Experiment with different strings to see what passes as valid.

How It Works

If you enter text into both of the password `TextBox` controls, the `CompareValidator` will perform a validation check. The validator will first try to convert the contents of the `TextBox` to the `Type` specified by the `Type` property of the validator. In this example we left the `Type` as the default of `String`, although you can also select `Integer`, `Double`, `Date`, and `Currency`.

The `CompareValidator` also has an `Operator` property to describe the type of comparison to perform. We have left this property at the default setting of `Equal`, although you can also perform greater than and less than comparisons.

Notice we have not placed a `RequiredFieldValidator` on either of the password input controls. This will allow the user to complete the form with an empty password. However, it also exposes the problem that the `CompareValidator` will compare an empty string with a non-empty string and not raise an error.

The RegularExpressionValidator Control

The last Validator control for which ASP.NET predetermines the functionality is the `RegularExpressionValidator`. This powerful control allows us to make sure the input of a certain control matches a certain pattern such as a phone number or e-mail address in the correct format. It also follows the same rules we've seen for the previous controls. For instance, it will not fail validation on an empty input control, and you specify the control to validate using the `ControlToValidate` property.

The pattern to check the input against must be given in the `ValidationExpression` property as a **regular expression** which, while powerful, uses a flexible but somewhat cryptic syntax. For example, the regular expression `*.cs` will match the strings `webform1.cs` and `myform.cs`, but not the string `myform.csx`. You might recognize this as one of the specifiers from a File Open or File Save dialog. You probably use regular expressions quite a few times a day without realizing it.

We won't work through the regular expression syntax here as it would take quite some time, but needless to say, if you want to go deep into it, there's a large section devoted to it in the .NET documentation.

We can't do justice to the full capabilities of regular expressions in this chapter, so instead of covering how to design your own regular expressions, we'll work with some of the expressions built into the `RegularExpressionValidator`.

Try It Out: The RegularExpressionValidator

For this example, we will add a control to the web form for a user to enter a web address and use a `RegularExpressionvalidator` to ensure the string entered by the user is a proper HTTP URL.

1. Reopen the WebDataValidation project if it is closed and drag a new `TextBox` control to the form. Give it an `ID` of `PhotoUrlTextBox`.

2. Drag a `RegularExpressionValidator` onto the form. Give it an `ID` of `PhotoURLRegularExpressionValidator` and the `ErrorMessage` "This is not a valid URL". Your form should now look like this.

3. We need to set a control to validate and an expression to validate it with. Right-click the new validator and open the **Properties** dialog. Choose the `PhotoUrlTextBox` from the drop-down for `ControlToValidate`. Find the `ValidationExpression` property, and click the ellipsis control (...) to enter the **Regular Expression Editor** dialog as shown below. The dialog contains a variety of predefined regular expressions to validate phone numbers, postal codes, and more. You can also enter a custom regular expression or build on one of the predefined items. Select **Internet URL**.

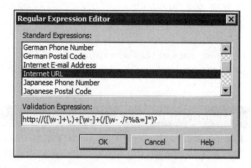

4. Build the page and run it. Try to enter some values into the new textbox and see what is valid. The predefined regular expression will force you to enter a URL in the form of http://computer.domain.

The CustomValidator Control

If none of the validation controls we have covered so far provides the check you need on your page, it is time to write your own validation logic in a `CustomValidator` control. A custom validation control is useful in a number of circumstances, including the following examples:

❑ The validation requires a database query

❑ The validation requires a mathematical expression beyond a simple comparison

❑ The validation requires the inspection of multiple input controls

`CustomValidator` objects obey most of the rules that govern the other validation controls, with the exception that the need to set the `ControlToValidate` property is optional. We have free reign in the validation code to gather and analyze any information required to declare the page valid.

Try It Out: The CustomValidator

As an example, let's assume that the image URL we introduced in the last example may only point to a JPG format file. Although this validation is also possible to achieve with a custom regular expression, we can demonstrate a straightforward `CustomValidator` for the same result.

1. Drag a `CustomValidator` from the toolbox onto the form next to the `RegularExpressionValidator` and set the `Id` to `PhotoUrlCustomValidator`. Set the `ControlToValidate` property to `PhotoUrlTextBox`, and the `ErrorMessage` property to the string "Unsupported file format".

2. Now set the `ClientValidationFunction` to `validate_photoformat`. This is the name of the function we'll write in the next step.

3. Switch to HTML view, and place the following JavaScript block at the top of the page's HTML `<body>`. This is the client-side validation routine for our `CustomValidator`.

```
<body>
<script language="javascript">
  function validate_photoformat(oSrc, args)
  {
    args.IsValid = false;
    if(args.Value)
    {
      var length = args.Value.length;
      var endsWidth = args.Value.substr(length - 3, 3);
      if(endsWidth == "jpg")
      {
        args.IsValid = true;
      }
    }
  }
</script>
<form id="Form1" method="post" runat="server">
...
```

4. Switch back to **Design** view, right-click the `CustomValidation` control, and bring up the event view of the **Properties** dialog. Double-click on the `ServerValidate` event and add the following code to the empty event handler that is generated for you.

```
private void PhotoUrlCustomValidator_ServerValidate(object source,
    System.Web.UI.WebControls.ServerValidateEventArgs args)
{
  args.IsValid = false;
  if(args.Value != null)
  {
    int length = args.Value.Length;
    string endsWidth = args.Value.Substring(length - 3);
    if(endsWidth == "jpg")
    {
      args.IsValid = true;
    }
  }
}
```

5. Build and run the page. You'll find that the URLs in the `PhotoURL` box must now end with `jpg`. It's not perfect however; both http://www.wrox.com/jpg and http://www.wrox.com/images/myjpg will be validated as true by our code. It's left as an exercise for you to tighten this up.

How It Works

When we use a `CustomValidator` we must supply code for both client- and server-side validation. The client-side code takes the shape of a Javascript function placed directly into our ASPX file between `<script>` and `</script>` tags, and sent directly to a client's web browser for execution as needed. The server-side code is housed inside the validator's `ServerValidate` event handler and is written in C#.

First, let's review the `ClientValidationFunction` property. This property is specific to the `CustomValidator`, and allows you to give the name of a function existing in client-side script to act as your client-side validation routine.

```
<asp:CustomValidator
    id="PhotoURLCustomValidator"
    runat="server"
    ControlToValidate="PhotoURLTextBox"
    ErrorMessage="Unsupported file format"
    ClientValidationFunction="validate_photoformat">
</asp:CustomValidator>
```

If this property is not set, you can still perform a server-side validation. We implemented this function in client-side script by adding code to the ASPX file inside of a `script` tag.

The name of the function must match the value of the `ClientValidationFunction` property and it must take two variable references.

```
function validate_photoformat(oSrc, args)
{
```

The second variable passed to the function (`args`) is the primary variable here. It is a collection with two members.

❑ The `IsValid` member (which we have to set) indicates if the validation has passed or failed.

❑ The `Value` member contains the text from the control we need to validate. If there was no control specified with the `ControlToValidate` property of the `CustomValidator`, the `Value` property contains an empty string.

The code here is quite simple to follow. We start by assuming that the control is not valid until we prove otherwise.

```
args.IsValid = false;
```

If there's no `Value` to check against, it remains invalid and we leave the function. If it does have a value, we just extract the last three characters and see if they are `jpg`. If so, we say the value in the control is valid. If not, then it isn't.

```
if(args.Value)
{
  var length = args.Value.length;
  var endsWidth = args.Value.substr(length - 3, 3);
  if(endsWidth == "jpg")
  {
    args.IsValid = true;
  }
}
}
```

The code in our server-side validation is not very different from the JavaScript version. The method accepts two parameters, with the second parameter of type `ServerValidateEventArgs` containing the important `IsValid` and `Value` properties.

Note that if you do want to write your own client-side routines, they need to be written in JavaScript, PerlScript, or some other scripting language that can be placed inside `<script>` tags.

ValidationSummary Control

The last control to cover here doesn't actually do any validation itself, but does interact with all the validation controls we've covered. The `ValidationSummary` control, then, lets us display all of our validation errors in a single location of the web form in a number of different formats.

There are only a few simple steps to achieve this behavior.

❑ Drop a `ValidationSummary` control onto a web form.

❑ Choose how to display the errors by setting the `DisplayMode` property of the control to `List`, `BulletList`, or `SingleParagraph`. You probably want to try each of these settings to see which looks best with your form layout.

❑ Set the `Display` property for each control to `None`, if you don't want the validation controls themselves to display errors on the form. This will force the `ErrorMessage` to display only inside the `ValidationSummary` control.

Try It Out: Our Validation Example in Full

In this final example, we've already prepared a new ASPX page for you to work with. You'll find it in the code download for this book in the Chapter 11 solution called `SummaryForm.aspx`. Open it up and you'll see that like the previous examples, it contains several `TextBox` controls and validators that check each of them.

Unlike the previous examples, however, each of the validator controls has had its `Display` property set to `None`, as indicated by their error messages being enclosed in braces (`[]`) on the form. You'll also see that we have placed a `ValidationSummary` control on the right side of the form with the `DisplayMode` property set to `List`.

```
<TD rowSpan="3">
<asp:validationsummary
    id="EmployeeValidationSummary"
    runat="server"
    DisplayMode="List">
</asp:validationsummary>
</TD>
```

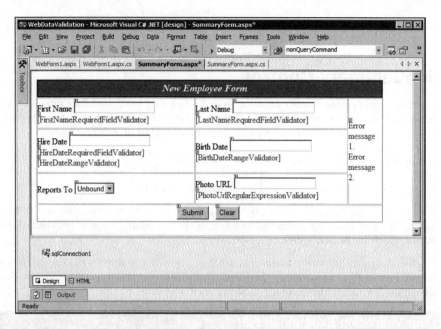

That's actually all the code we need to use the `ValidationSummary` control (the runtime will automatically place error messages inside the control for us), but before we can run the page, you'll need to make sure that `sqlConnection1` is pointing at your copy of the Northwind database. Alter its `ConnectionString` property accordingly. Underneath the form is some code to populate the new `DropDownList` and insert a valid set of data into the `Employees` database.

Now build and run the page. If we launch the form and click Submit without entering any values, we should see the following display. Notice all of the validation errors appear in the validation summary, but unfortunately there is no indication of which fields have produced the errors. This will place the burden on the user to find the input controls with the invalid values. In the next section we will try to improve the error feedback.

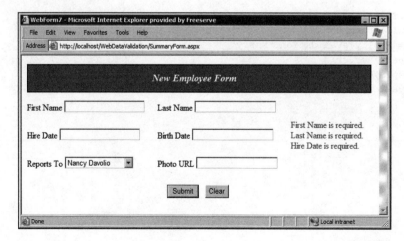

How It Works

The majority of `SummaryForm.aspx` is simply our previous example rearranged a bit so that the effect of the `ValidationSummary` control is a bit more obvious than it would be otherwise. Besides this control on the right of the form, you'll notice that we now have a drop-down control for the user to select the employee's manager in the bottom left corner of the form. To populate this, we'll call a method to create a list of employees from the `Employees` table in the Northwind database and copy those names into the control. We need this to occur before the page is rendered, so we'll call this method from within the `Page_Load` event handler.

```
private void Page_Load(object sender, System.EventArgs e)
{
    // Put user code to initialize the page here
    if(!Page.IsPostBack)
    {
        BindReportToDropDown();
        ...
    }
}
```

While this behavior seems unrelated to validation, it is a good example of the data binding capability of web form controls, and offers an example of how we can help the user avoid validation errors by forcing a selection from a list of good values. By not allowing the user to make a mistake, we have improved the quality of the user experience with our application.

The method to bind the data to the drop-down list is shown below.

```
private void BindReportToDropDown()
{
    SqlCommand sqlCommand = new SqlCommand();
    sqlCommand.CommandText = "SELECT EmployeeId, " +
        "Firstname + ' ' + Lastname As Name FROM Employees";

    sqlConnection1.Open();
    sqlCommand.Connection = sqlConnection1;
    SqlDataReader sqlDataReader = sqlCommand.ExecuteReader();

    ReportsToDropDownList.DataSource = sqlDataReader;
    ReportsToDropDownList.DataTextField = "Name";
    ReportsToDropDownList.DataValueField = "EmployeeId";
    ReportsToDropDownList.DataBind();

    sqlDataReader.Close();
    sqlConnection1.Close();
}
```

Note that we've retrieved both name and employee ID from the database. The list of names will be displayed in the `DropDownList` (as given by setting `DataTextField`) and the corresponding IDs will be the values returned by the list when a name is selected (as given by setting `DataValueField`). This distinction between display and value comes in handy when we examine the new code to insert an employee record into the database. The `ReportsTo` field in the `Employees` table holds the ID, rather than the name, of the new hire's boss, so the code will need to extract the `EmployeeId` of the selected manager to generate the correct `INSERT` statement for us. Thanks to our little trick, we can easily pull the `EmployeeId` using the value field of the selected item in the `DropDownList`.

293

The following code shows the updated event handler invoked when the user clicks the Submit button on the form.

```
private void SubmitButton_Click(object sender, System.EventArgs e)
{
    if(Page.IsValid)
    {
        SqlCommand sqlCommand  = new SqlCommand();
        sqlCommand.CommandText =
            "INSERT INTO Employees( " +
         "FirstName, LastName, HireDate, BirthDate, ReportsTo, " +
            "PhotoPath) " +
          "VALUES(@FirstName, @LastName, @HireDate, @BirthDate, " +
             "@ReportsTo, @PhotoURL)";

        sqlCommand.Parameters.Add("@FirstName", FirstNameTextBox.Text);
        sqlCommand.Parameters.Add("@LastName", LastNameTextBox.Text);
        sqlCommand.Parameters.Add("@HireDate", HireDateTextBox.Text);
        sqlCommand.Parameters.Add("@BirthDate", BirthDateTextBox.Text);
        sqlCommand.Parameters.Add("@ReportsTo",
                        ReportsToDropDownList.SelectedItem.Value);
        sqlCommand.Parameters.Add("@PhotoURL", PhotoURLTextBox.Text);

        sqlConnection1.Open();
        sqlCommand.Connection = sqlConnection1;
        sqlCommand.ExecuteNonQuery();
        sqlConnection1.Close();

        ClearFields();
    }
}
```

The last line of the handler makes a call to the new method `ClearFields()`. This short method simply clears each of the textboxes and the drop-down list in the form. It is also called when the Cancel button is clicked.

```
private void ClearButton_Click(object sender, System.EventArgs e)
{
    ClearFields();
}

private void ClearFields()
{
    FirstNameTextBox.Text = "";
    LastNameTextBox.Text = "";
    HireDateTextBox.Text = "";
    BirthDateTextBox.Text = "";
    PhotoURLTextBox.Text = "";
    ReportsToDropDownList.SelectedIndex = 0;
}
```

Using In-Line and Summary Errors

You may or may not have noticed during the chapter that all our validation controls have an additional property named Text. When there is no ValidationSummary control present on a Form, the runtime will use the Text property (if present) to display an error message on the form instead of the ErrorMessage property. However, when a ValidationSummary control is present on the form, the ErrorMessage text displays in the ValidationSummary area while the Text property still displays in-line where the validation control exists on the form. We can use this behavior to indicate the input controls failing validation.

Try It Out: Tweaking The Error Display

To demonstrate this behavior we will make a few final adjustments to our SummaryForm.aspx page.

1. For each of the validation controls on the form, change the Display property to Static and set the Text property to an asterisk (*). In design view, the form should now look like this.

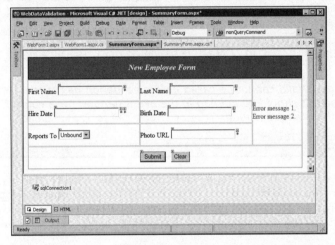

Now when we execute the form and validation errors occur, we have the following display. Each input control with an error is marked with an asterisk, which helps the user locate the problem data.

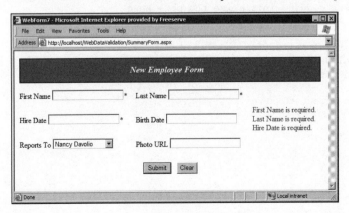

As you can see, the ValidationSummary control is useful for collecting validation errors into a single location on the WebForm. Remember to use the ErrorMessage and Text properties of your validation control to control the placement of your error messages while letting the user know where to correct the errors.

Programmatic Validation

If the need arises, we can force validation checks to occur in addition to those that run automatically. For example, we may want to pre-populate a form with information during initialization and need to check that it will validate. During the Page_Load handler, you might want to check the IsValid property of the page to see if the pre-populated data will validate. Without adding an additional step, however, a call to IsValid produces the following error.

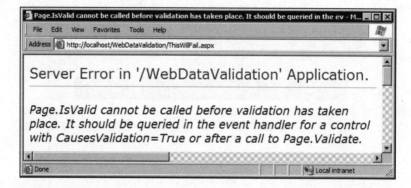

Calling the Validate method of the Page before checking the IsValid property will fix the exception shown above. This is the same method used by the ASP.NET runtime when a user presses a Button control with the CausesValidation property set to true. If we place this call in the Page_Load method as shown below, any validation errors will appear on the first page view for the user.

```
private void Page_Load(object sender, System.EventArgs e)
{
    // Put user code to initialize the page here
    if(!Page.IsPostBack)
    {
        // other initialization code
        Page.Validate();
        if(!Page.IsValid)
        {
            // we expect this to fail
        }
    }
}
```

Summary

Providing quality feedback to user data entry errors is an important feature for any type of application. We have seen how web applications are a special case, because you can perform validation logic on both the client and the server. The validation controls we covered is this chapter will give you the capability to perform these validations inside of a neatly designed framework where you can customize the validation logic if need be. During this chapter we saw how to perform the following:

❑ Use the `RequiredFieldValidator` to require a user to enter data into a field

❑ Use the `RangeValidator` to restrict data to a range of valid values

❑ Use the `CompareValidator` to compare the values of two input controls

❑ Use the `RegularExpressionValidator` to match input to a pattern

❑ Implement custom server-side and client-side validation logic in a `CustomValidator`

❑ Place error messages into a single location using the `ValidationSummary` control

The features we covered in this chapter are extremely useful for ASP.NET database applications. In Chapter 15, we will see how to use database constraints as another mechanism to ensure only valid data enters a database.

Exercises

1. Implement the web form shown in design view below. The form should give the user an error after the submit button is pressed while the string "**<none>**" still appears in the TextBox control. Hint: The RequiredFieldValidator control is used.

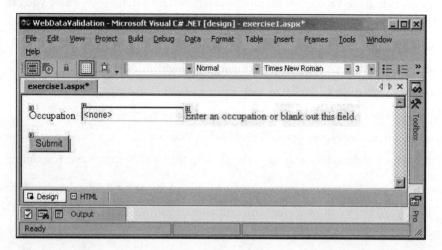

2. In the form shown running below, we are asking the user to pick a magic number between 1 and 10, allowing only whole numbers. Implement this form using one of the validation controls from the chapter.

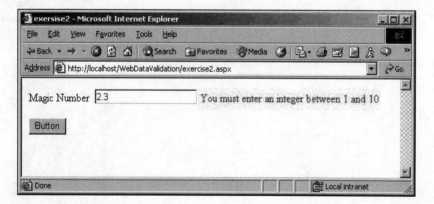

3. In the following form shown in design view, we are using a validation control to ensure the price a user enters is greater than 0. Implement this form using one of the validation controls from this chapter.

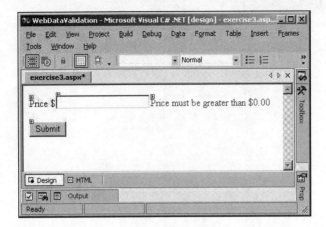

4. In the following form we ensure the user types a valid looking e-mail address into the `TextBox` control. Try to implement this form using a an ASP.NET validation control.

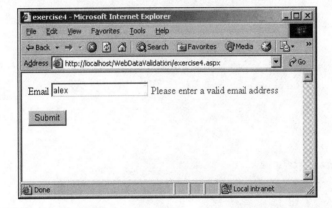

5. The form shown running below asks a user to enter their favorite number. This number must be evenly divisible by three. What sort of validation control can you use to perform this check? Implement the form shown below.

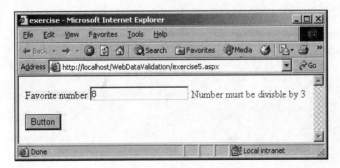

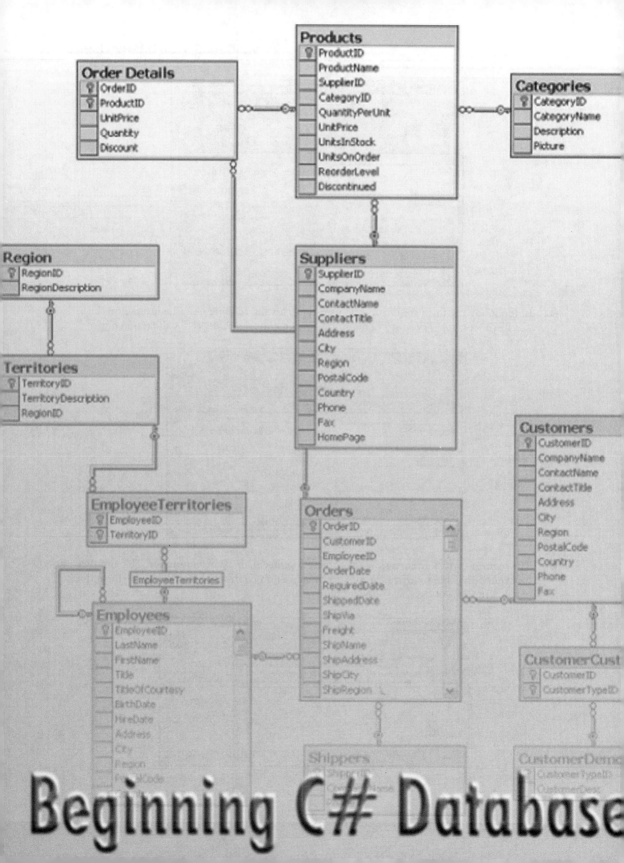

Tables and Relationships

In Chapter 1 we took a brief look at the structure of a database, and we know that a relational database provides the means to store and manage data in a very organized and related fashion. In this chapter, we will learn how to structure data in tables, and how to relate data in tables in order to maintain data integrity and manage relationships. The purpose of this chapter is to get an overview of how to create, modify and delete tables, as well as how to relate tables to each other and how to normalize their content. Specifically, the topics covered in this chapter are:

- ❑ Creating and deleting tables.
- ❑ Adding rows to a table.
- ❑ Keys and constraints – what primary keys and foreign keys are and how they are used to set relationships among tables. We will also learn about the different types of relationships and how to set them using database diagrams.
- ❑ Referential integrity.
- ❑ What normalization and de-normalization mean and their benefits.
- ❑ How to create tables and insert data into them from a simple C# application.

Tables

Let's now have a brief refresher on what we have learned about tables. As we know, tables are used to store data in a database. A database can have several tables. We can also design the tables in a database to share common data with each other thereby allowing us to create relationships between them. For example, a few rows and columns of the Employees table in the Northwind database are shown here:

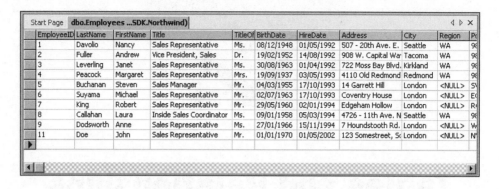

The columns of the table are listed on the top (EmployeeID, LastName, FirstName, etc.). These are the columns or the **field**s of the table. Each column represents a piece of information about an employee, for example, the second column in the table above holds the last name of each employee. A table can have one or more columns. The data pertaining to these columns appear directly underneath in the form of rows. Each row is an instance of an employee. In other words each row in the Employees table represents a distinct employee. A table can have zero or more rows but must have at least one column.

Of course, it is important to know what type of data we can enter or use in a given record, but as we'll see in the next section, each column created in a table is strongly-typed just like every variable in C#. Recall, however, that the types that MSDE and SQL server understand are different from those in C#, having been defined in the SQL92 standard. Refer to Chapters 3 and 7 for a list of the SQL server and .NET Framework types.

Without further ado, let's begin by creating a table with a few columns and rows. We'll do it using the server explorer in Visual Studio .NET, and then we'll show the equivalent SQL. Naturally, while creating our tables, we will also specify each column's data type.

Creating a Table

A table can be created in several ways, so let's look at the following two ways in some detail:

❑ Using the Server Explorer that is part of the VS.NET IDE. (Note that you can only add new tables with the full version of Visual Studio .NET, as Visual C# Standard has limited functionality, and only allows us to view existing databases and tables.)

❑ Directly using the CREATE TABLE statement in SQL.

In the following example we will create a table called test_Employees using the Server Explorer. We will specify the data type for three columns and save the table.

Try it Out: Creating a Table Using the Server Explorer

1. Open up the Server Explorer, open up the Northwind database tab, right-click on the **Tables** node and select **New Table**.

2. Now, let's specify three column names and their attributes: `EmployeeId` of type `int`, `LastName` of type `varchar(50)`, and `BirthDate` of type `datetime`. `varchar(50)` means that up to 50 characters can be stored in the `LastName` field. In order to choose which data type we want for each column, click in the **Data Type** column for each row, and pick the desired type from the available data types. Observe that in the following screenshot, the `BirthDate` field has the **Allow Nulls** attribute checked. This means that an employee record can be created in this table without a birth date. Think of `Null` as meaning that the value of the column is not known at the time the record is created.

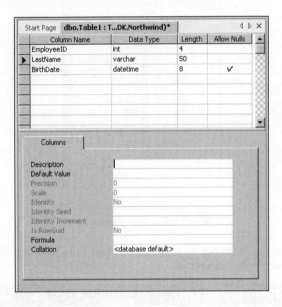

3. After specifying the column attributes, click on the save button on the toolbar. You will be prompted to provide a name for the table, so as mentioned earlier let's call it `test_Employees` and then click on **OK**.

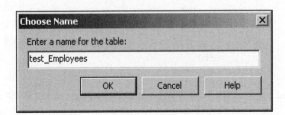

How It Works

If all has gone well, Visual Studio .NET has created a new database with one table. Now, to verify that the table was saved, expand the tables node in the server explorer. It should appear as follows, with the column names that we specified.

That should have refreshed our memory on how to create tables in a database using the server explorer. Now let's see how it is done using SQL statements.

Try It Out: Creating a Table Using SQL

We have already looked at how to create a database using SQL commands and our Wrox Tables can be created using the CREATE TABLE SQL statement. The simplest form of this statement is as follows

```
CREATE TABLE tablename
(
   column1 datatype1 nullspec1,
   column2 datatype2 nullspec2,
   ...,
   columnn datatypen nullspecn)
```

where tablename is the name of the table you want to create, column1 is the name of the column, datatype1 is the data type of column1 and nullspec1 is to specify whether the column should allow null values or not.

To create a similar table to the one we saw in the previous section using the CREATE TABLE statement, use the SQL command shown below to create a test_Employees2 table:

```
CREATE TABLE test_Employees2 (EmployeeId int NOT NULL, LastName varchar(50) NOT
NULL, BirthDate datetime NULL)
```

While most parts of this syntax are intuitive, notice that the nullability specification for columns is either NULL or NOT NULL. Also note that a database can have only one table with any one name, which is why we renamed the table in this example.

When a table is created using the Server Explorer, behind the scenes, a CREATE TABLE statement is issued against the database. We can also explicitly issue the CREATE TABLE statement from the following locations:

❑ A stored procedure (which we'll cover in Chapter 14)

❑ The SQL tool built in to Visual Studio .NET (as we saw in Chapter 3)

❑ An application like the one we'll build later in the chapter

❑ The SQL Query Analyzer, if you are using SQL Server database

❑ The OSQL.exe command-line tool (which we also met in Chapter 3)

Of course, we can also create tables using the design view in Access. This has a similar feel to the Server Explorer method, and is merely a case of clicking on **Create table in Design view** and assigning field names and data types. Now that we know how to create tables, let go on to see how we can add rows to our tables.

Adding Rows to a Table

After creating a table, we can add rows to it in several ways. We are going to explore two of these here, namely using:

❑ The Server Explorer

❑ A program written using the C# language.

For now, we are just going to show how we add rows using the Server Explorer since we will demonstrate this process using SQL statements in our example application at the end of the chapter.

Try It Out: Adding Rows to a Table from the Server Explorer

1. In the Server Explorer, right-click on the Employees table and select the **Retrieve data from table** option. This presents us with a grid where we can add rows as shown below:

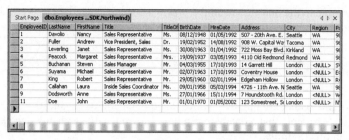

2. We can add a row by typing in values after the last employee. It isn't possible to specify the `EmployeeID` because it is an **identity** column. The values in identity columns are supplied by the database in sequence. This is to ensure that each row in the table is uniquely identified.

   You may have noticed that an `EmployeeID` of 11 was issued in the previous screenshot even though one would expect a 10. This is because the `EmployeeID` of 10 was in fact issued but that employee record was deleted from the table while testing on my machine. So the next time an employee was added, SQL issued the next unused number.

How It Works

When we type in values for a new row, the row is not actually added until all data has been entered and we actually move to another row. Then server explorer creates an `INSERT` statement in the background and runs that statement against the `Employees` table. If all the data entered is consistent with the data type, the row is inserted into the table.

To add a row to a table using SQL, you'd use the following syntax:

```
INSERT INTO test_Employees (EmployeeId, LastName, BirthDate)
    VALUES (1, 'Nathan', '12/28/1969')
```

Dropping a Table

Dropping a table from the database will completely remove it from the database and will lose all the data and dependency relationships. We can drop a table from the Server Explorer by right-clicking the table and selecting **Delete Table**. We can also drop a table by using the following SQL statement:

```
DROP TABLE tablename
```

The `tablename` is the name of the table to drop from the database.

Now we can create and drop tables with relative ease, and also create the columns and choose the data types we wish to use, we are going to move on to the really exciting and powerful techniques inherent in relational databases.

Table Relationships

In the first part of this chapter we learned how to create a single table. So far in this book, the information we've worked with in a table has been about a single entity, for example, a last name, a first name, a person, a phone number, and so on. But information is never isolated in our thoughts. We can easily move our thoughts from one thing to the next because it's all related in our heads. In a previous example in Chapter 7 we saw two tables together that contained related information – the employees in one table took the orders stored in the other table. Any table can be linked to another if there is a relationship between the two sets of information you wish to keep a track of.

We can have many tables in a relational database, all containing related data. If we relate loosely to the Northwind scenario, one sales rep in a company may have generated many orders, which have been placed by quite a few different companies. These companies may, however, have placed many different orders. The parts on the orders may have come from different suppliers, but the chances are that each supplier can supply more than one part to the Northwind company. Already we can see some groups of entities in our heads – our employees, their customers, orders, and suppliers. In the Northwind example, there are many more tables that help to relate our data, using different types of relationships.

There are three different types of relationship:

❑ One to one

❑ One to many

❑ Many to many

We'll look a bit more closely and discuss them in detail in the section about *Types of Relationships*.

If we have two tables related in a database then it is intuitive to think that we need rules in order to ensure that changes to one table won't make data in the second related table redundant, and that each row in each table is uniquely identified to avoid any confusion. This is where keys and constraints play a big role. In the next section of the chapter we are going to look in detail at keys and constraints and all the benefits and power they bring to relational databases.

Keys and Constraints

There are two main types of keys that are used in database, known as **primary keys** and **foreign keys**. In the next section we are going look at these in detail to learn how to use them to accurately describe the real-world situation that our databases are modeling.

Constraints are also important for keeping the data in our database useful. For example, if we were storing ages in a table, and had no constraints applied to the punitive Age field, then someone who accidentally hits the minus symbol before typing in their age could end up with all sorts of problems if, for example, we were using their age in an insurance calculation. Constraints will hopefully help us to avoid this sort of unfortunate incident.

Let's now begin this section by looking at keys!

Primary Keys

Let us take a closer look at the original `Employee` table in the Northwind database. The very first column is `EmployeeID`. The IDs range from 1-9 and each employee has a unique `EmployeeID` assigned to him or her. A column or a combination of columns that uniquely identify one row in the table is called the **Primary key**. Additionally, a primary key cannot have a null value. In the `Employees` table, the `EmployeeID` uniquely identifies each employee and is the primary key. On the other hand, the `LastName` column cannot be specified as the primary key since, there could be more than one employee with the same `LastName`. The primary key imposes some specific rules on the table as explained above.

To specify the primary key for a table using Visual Studio .NET, follow these steps:

❑ In the Server Explorer, right-click on the `test_Employee` table in the Northwind database, and select **Design Table**

❑ Select the column that you want to be the primary key, right-click, and select **Set Primary Key**, or select the column and click on the **Primary Key** button in the table's toolbar

Whichever method you choose, the column that now holds the primary key is marked with a key symbol as shown below in the `Employees` *table.*

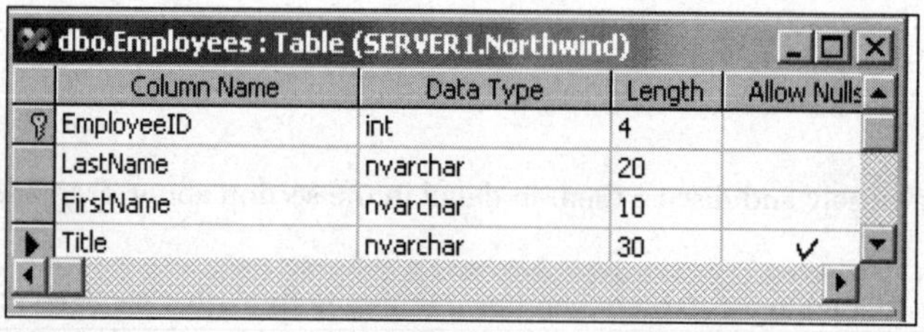

When using SQL statements, we can add a primary key at design time using the following statement:

```
CREATE TABLE test_Employees2
(EmployeeId int NOT NULL PRIMARY KEY,
 LastName varchar(50) NOT NULL,
 BirthDate datetime NULL)
```

We've simply added the words `PRIMARY KEY` against one of the column definitions.

Foreign Keys

The foreign key is a column or a combination of columns that references values of the primary key from another table. In order to better understand what this means, let's examine the `Orders`, `Order Details`, `Employees`, and `Products` tables. The tables are shown in the following diagram below with their columns:

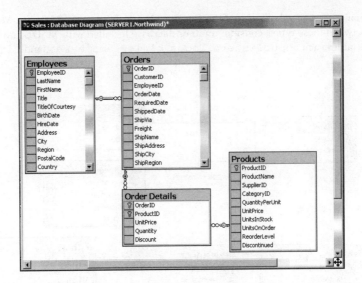

Say we want to determine which employee generated an order for Tofu. Here are the steps we follow:

1. First we find the `ProductID` for Tofu from the `Products` table, which is 14.

2. We look at the `Order Details` table and find that the `OrderID`s corresponding to the `ProductID` of 14 is 10249.

3. Then we scan the `Orders` table and find the `EmployeeID` corresponding to the `OrderID` of 10249 is 6.

4. Finally, we look at the `Employees` table and find that the `EmployeeID` of 6 belongs to Michael Suyama.

We have intuitively explained the concept of the foreign key in the preceding example. The `ProductID` column in the `Order Details` table references the `ProductID` primary key of the `Products` table. This guarantees that each `ProductID` in the `Order Details` table has a matching `ProductID` in the `Products` table. If we cannot find a matching `ProductID` in the `Products` table, we cannot figure out what the product is. Situations such as this are eliminated by constraining the `ProductID` column in the `Order Details` table with the foreign key. If an attempt is made to insert a 'bogus' row for which there is no corresponding `ProductID` in the `Products` table, then the database will produce an error. Foreign keys are also known as **Referential Integrity Constraints**.

Types of Relationships

Relations specify how a column of one table is related to a column of another table. Relationships ensure integrity and reduce the amount of redundancy of data in a database. Relationships are enforced by matching the primary key from one table with the foreign key in another table.

There are three main types of relationship: **One-to-One**, **One-to-Many**, and **Many-to-Many**. To understand the differences between these types, consider another database installed with MSDE and SQLServer called pubs, which has tables such as publishers, logos, titles, employees, and titleauthors as shown below:

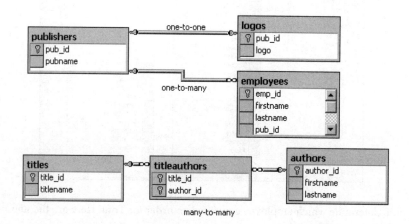

From the diagram we can see that:

❑   The publishers table contains a list of publishers

❑   The logos table contains a list of publishers and their logos

❑   The titles table contains a list of titles published

❑   The employees table has a list of all publishers and their employees

❑   The titleauthors table contains a list of titles and the authors who wrote them

The tables in the above diagram all have varying types of relationships to each other. Let's look at the different types to explain this more clearly:

❑   **One-to-One Relationships**: In a one-to-one relationship, a row in table A has exactly one matching row in table B, and vice versa. This type of relationship is created if both of the related columns are primary keys or have unique constraints. In the database represented by the above diagram, the relation between the publishers and the logos table is a one-to-one relationship – one publisher in the publishers table has one logo in the logos table. In the figure above, the one-to-one relationship is shown with a key on both sides of the relationship.

❑   **One-to-Many Relationships**: In a one-to-many relationship, one row in one table A can have many matching rows in table B. But any one row in table B can have only one matching row in table A. In our example database, the relation between the publishers table and the employees table is a one-to-many relationship. One publisher can have several employees.

Of course, it should not be ethically possible for one employee to work for several publishers, let us assume that this is a no-no! In the Northwind database, the relation between the `Orders` and `Order Details` tables is a one-to-many relationship. One order in the `Orders` table can have several details in the `Order Details` table. In a one-to-many relationship, the primary-key side is represented to the key symbol and the foreign-key side is represented by the infinity (∞) symbol as we can see from the previous diagram.

❑ **Many-to-Many Relationships**: In a many-to-many relationship, a row in table A can have many matching rows in table B, and vice versa. For example, in the database we represented previously, the relation between the `titles` table and the `authors` table is a many-to-many relationship. Several authors can write one title and one author can write several titles. A many-to-many relationship is created by defining a third table, called a **junction** table.

The primary key of this junction table consists of the foreign keys from both table A and table B. The many-to-many relationship is actually defined by a one-to-many relationship from the `titles` and `authors` tables to the `titleauthors` table. A many-to-many relationship between two tables is shown by means of two one-to-many relationships between the individual tables and the junction table as shown in the figure.

Now that we have an understanding of relationships and the different types of keys, let's look at what they mean in terms of what we can say about our relational databases.

Referential Integrity

When we set a relation between tables, we are enforcing **Referential Integrity** between the two tables. Referential integrity exists between two tables when all values in the foreign key column have corresponding primary key values.

This is important because it helps us to prevent inconsistent data from being entered into a database. Let's look at an example to demonstrate the point.

Try It Out: Demonstrating Referential Integrity

We can verify this by opening the `Order Details` table in the Northwind database, and inserting a row with `OrderID` of `20000` and `ProductID` of `77`. You can use the same method to do this as we saw in the *Adding Rows to a Table* section earlier in this chapter. An error message similar to the one following will appear:

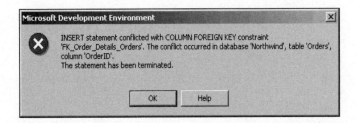

311

How It Works

When a row with `OrderID` of `20000` and `ProductID` of `77` was added to the `Order Details` table, the relationship that already exists between the `Orders` and `Order Details` tables was enforced. Since an `Order` with `OrderID` of `20000` does not exist, an error was raised by the database. Referential integrity is enforced easily among tables using database diagrams, which is the next topic of discussion.

Now that we have had a brief overview of the different types of relationships, let us now see how to set relationships using database diagrams.

Database Diagrams

Database diagrams are objects in a database that are used to show tables and their relationships. Relationships among tables can easily be specified and conceptualized in database diagrams. A large database with several tables can have several diagrams, for example a `Sales` diagram and an `Invoicing` diagram that show only the tables and the relationships relevant to `Sales` and `Invoicing` respectively. Database diagrams are objects in the MSDE/SQL-Server database just like tables and stored procedures are.

Let's try our hand at creating relationships using a database diagram by means of an example.

Try It Out: Creating Relationships Using a Database Diagram

Let's create a database diagram to show the `Orders`, `Order Details`, and `Products` tables in the Northwind database and the relationships between them.

> *This is another feature that you can't access in Visual C# Standard Edition, but Microsoft Access does have the ability to create custom diagrams, and the procedure for using Access is very similar to that for Visual Studio .NET.*

1. In Server Explorer, right-click on **Database Diagrams** and select **New Diagram**.

2. The screen that pops up will list all the tables in the database. Select **Order Details**, **Orders**, and **Products** as shown overleaf and click on the **Add** button.

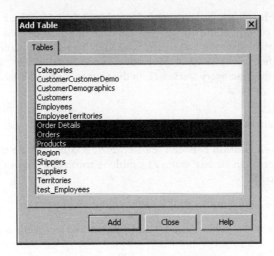

3. The tables will be added to the diagram and MSDE or SQL Server, depending on what you are using, will set up the relationships between the tables. Remove the relationship lines by selecting them, as we will learn how to reset these relationships ourselves. To remove the relationships, select a relationship, right-click on it, and pick **Delete Relationship from the database**.

4. Now let's set the relation between the `Order` and `Order Details` tables and the `Products` and `Order Details` table. Note that the `OrderID` column is a primary key in the `Orders` table and a foreign key in the `Order Details` table. Drag the `OrderID` column from the `Order Details` table to the `Orders` table. A window captioned **Create Relationship** pops up immediately as shown below:

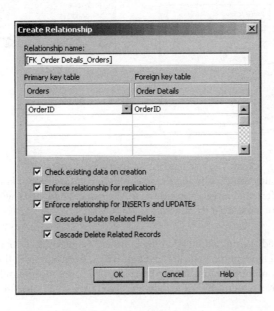

Note that the Orders table is listed as the primary key table and Order Details is listed as the foreign key table. The OrderID column of the primary key table (Orders) is listed in the left and the OrderId column of the foreign key table (Order Details) is listed in the right. A relation will be created between the tables based on these fields. The name of this relationship is [FK-Order Details_Orders]. The relation enforces the rule that that every OrderID in the Order Details table must also exist in the Orders table.

5. Click OK to create the relationship.

6. Similarly, set a relationship between the Products table and the Order Details table so that the ProductId in Order Details table is constrained by the values of ProductId in the Products table.

7. Click on the save button in the toolbar to save the relationship.

8. When the diagram window is closed, you will be asked to specify a name for the diagram. Name the diagram Sales.

9. We can access a saved diagram any time from the Server Explorer by selecting the diagram and choosing the **Design Database Diagram** menu option available from the right-click.

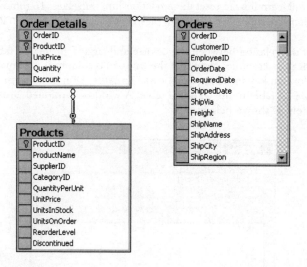

How It Works

In this exercise, relationships were set by linking the columns of the primary key table and foreign key tables. When a relation is set, referential integrity is enforced. We can change the relationships between the tables in the diagram and add more tables to it if we wish.

More importantly, we need to think about what the 'physical' relationship to our database is. It is no good just creating relationships that have no real-world meaning. Recall from earlier in the chapter how we could determine which person ordered the tofu simply by tracing back the meaningful relationships in the database. In terms of visualizing these relationships, the database diagram is a very useful tool.

The `Order Details` table has Primary Keys on `OrderID` and `ProductID` together. This is so that a given order can have a `ProductID` listed only once. For example, the following data will not be allowed to exist in the order details tables

OrderID	ProductID
1000	1
1000	1

If you think about it, this makes sense because in one single order we wouldn't ask for a single product a thousand times over, we would make an order for a thousand items in one go. Similarly, from the table above, we wouldn't need to make two orders of a thousand each; we simply make one order of two thousand.

Constraints

There are other rules that can be enforced on a table and its columns. Collectively, such rules are called **constraints**. When a table has constraints placed on it, all the rows in the column with constraints must satisfy them. Constraints are typically used for validation and integrity, and in Chapter 15 on *Indexes and Constraints*, we will look at constraints in detail, but here is a brief list of frequently used constraints:

❑ **NOT NULL**
   When a column is specified to be NOT NULL, null values cannot be assigned to that column. This means that either the column must have a default value or the user will be forced to enter a value for it before the row is inserted into the table.

❑ **UNIQUE**
   Unique constraint on a column insists that values for that column are unique. It is usually placed on columns that are not part of the primary key since primary keys are already unique.

❑ **DEFAULT**
   When a default constraint is specified on a column, a default value is generated if no value is supplied for that column.

❑ **CHECK**
   The check constraint checks if the value of the column satisfies a certain criterion.

Normalization

Normalization is the process of eliminating duplicate data and providing a fast, efficient search path to the data. A normalized database will have improved performance over a database that is not normalized because it will not have to spend time searching effectively redundant copies of data. Normalization will also help to make tables easier to maintain. For example, imagine we created a table with information on all of the CDs in our library. We could have more than one album by a single artist, or we could find that our entire collection could be categorized into four categories: Rock, Pop, Dance, and R&B. If we were to manually enter the genre of each CD, we'd be wasting time – why not just enter the four categories once, then refer to which one of the four each album belongs to? Indeed, this process is normalization, where we identify duplicate data that could be stored in separate tables.

Normalizing a logical database design involves a set of formal processes to separate the data into multiple, related tables. The result of each process is referred to as a **Normal Form**. There are three normal forms to a normalized database: first, second, and third normal form. Over-normalized databases will be normalized to the fourth and fifth forms, and they are rarely considered in practical relational database design so we will look at only the first three here:

❑ **First normal form**: This process eliminates repeating groups of data in a table. We create a separate table for each set of related data and identify each table with a primary key. An example of repeating groups of data would be if we had a table containing managers, and a manager had a block of columns for each employee. We would then move employees into a separate but related table.

❑ **Second normal form**: Creates separate tables for sets of values that apply to multiple records, and relates these tables with foreign keys. For example, in a table containing employees and their titles, since several employees can have the same title, we would create a separate `Titles` table with a `TitleId` column to hold the titles. Then we would relate the `Employees` table and the `Titles` table together by means of the `TitleId` column.

❑ **Third normal form** eliminates columns in a table that do not depend on the primary key. All the columns in a table should depend on the primary key of the table.

Normalization of a database will result in faster sorting and index creation. The database will have more compact indexes and fewer indexes in each table. This will improve the performance of INSERT, UPDATE, and DELETE statements. On the other hand, normalization can increase the complexity of joins required to retrieve the data. This, in some cases, might hinder performance. Sometimes, databases are de-normalized to reduce the complexity of joins and to get quicker query response times.

Now that we have had an overview of tables, constraints, and relationships, let us see how we can handle these in the context of a C# Windows Forms application.

Working with Tables in C#

Up till now we have seen how to manipulate tables and rows using the Server Explorer. In this section we are going to use SQL statements from a C# application that we will build in the next *Try It Out* section. This application takes a SQL statement that does not return any rows (a non-query statement), for example, a CREATE TABLE, INSERT, UPDATE, or DELETE statement, and executes the statement against the Northwind database.

Try It Out: Creating a Query Application

1. Create a chapter solution called `Chapter12_Examples`. Then, create a C# Windows Application project called `QueryApplication` within our solution.

2. Change the name of the form to `queries.cs`.

3. Add a textbox named `txtSQL` and a button named `cmdExecute`.

4. Add another textbox named `txtResult` to see the result of the execution.

5. Set the `MultiLine` property of the textboxes to `True`.

6. Add two labels and specify their text property as shown in the figure below:

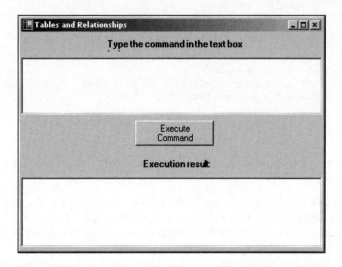

First add the following directive at the top of the `queries.cs` file. We need this since we will be using the `SqlClient` namespace.

```
using System.Data.SqlClient;
```

Double-click on the **Execute Command** button and type in the code as follows:

```
private void cmdExecute_Click(object sender, System.EventArgs e)
{
  try
  {
    //Create a SQL connection

    SqlConnection cn = new SqlConnection("Data Source=(local)\NETSDK;" +
      "Integrated Security=SSPI;database=Northwind");

    //Open the connection
    cn.Open();
    //Get the command from the text box
    string strSQL=txtSQL.Text;
    // Create the command object.
    SqlCommand cmd= new SqlCommand(strSQL, cn);
```

```
    //Execute the command
    cmd.ExecuteNonQuery();
    // close the connection.
    cn.Close();
    // Display the result message.
    txtResult.Text = "SQL Command Executed successfully.";
  }
catch ( System.Data.SqlClient.SqlException e1)
{
    // Display the error message.
    txtResult.Text = "There was an error in executing the SQL Command. " +
      "Error Message:" + e1.Message;
  }
}
```

7. Before running our application, delete the `test_Employees` table that we created earlier as we will be recreating it.

8. Now build and run the solution and in the textbox above, type in the CREATE TABLE statement as shown in the following screenshot and click on the **Execute** command button. After a pause you should see "**SQL Command executed successfully**" in the result textbox:

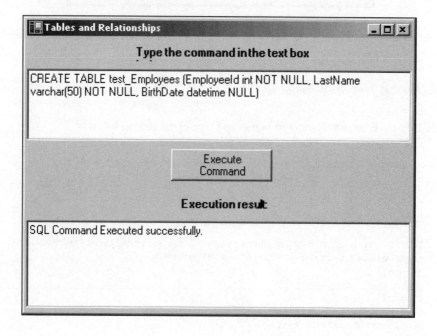

9. Verify whether the table exists in the Northwind database by right-clicking on the **Tables** node in the Server Explorer and selecting **Refresh**. You will see that the `test_Employees` table has been created with three column names as shown below.

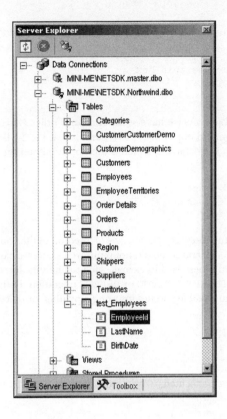

How It Works

We began by adding the following directive to the `queries.cs` file, since we will be using the `SqlClient` namespace.

```
using System.Data.SqlClient;
```

In the `cmdCreate_Click()` event we created a connection to the database like so:

```
//Create a sql connection
SqlConnection cn = new SqlConnection("Data Source=(local)\NETSDK;" +
    "Integrated Security=SSPI; database=Northwind");
```

Now that the connection object has been created, we opened it using the `Open()` method:

```
cn.Open();
```

Next, we got the SQL statement that was typed into a string variable `strSQL`:

```
//Get the command from the text box
string strSQL=txtSQL.Text;
```

Then we create a command object. As we have seen, `command` objects are used to execute SQL statements against the database. The command object needs two parameters, the SQL statement itself, which is stored in `strSQL` and the connection to the database, which is the object named `cn` created earlier.

```
// Create the command object.
SqlCommand cmd= new SqlCommand(strSQL, cn);
```

Following this we can execute the `ExecuteNonQuery()` method of the command object. Statements such as `CREATE TABLE`, `INSERT`, `UPDATE` and so on, do not return rows and are called non-query statements. The `ExecuteNonQuery()` method is best used to execute such statements. It returns an integer representing the number of rows affected in an `INSERT`, `UPDATE`, or `DELETE` operation. In this case, we choose not to catch the return value since we are creating a table and not inserting, updating, or deleting rows:

```
//Execute the command
cmd.ExecuteNonQuery();
```

Now that the command has been executed, we close the connection using the `Close()` method:

```
// close the connection.
cn.Close();
```

and then display a success message in the result textbox:

```
// Display the result message.
txtResult.Text = "SQL Command Executed successfully.";
```

If during the execution of the SQL statement, any error is encountered, this is trapped and shown in the result textbox.

```
catch ( System.Data.SqlClient.SqlException e1)
{
  // Display the error message.
  txtResult.Text = "There was an error in executing the SQL Command. Error
    Message:" + e1.Message;
}
```

That's it, nothing that should be new to us, but we have created a useful little tool for executing non-query SQL statements. Now let's see how we can add rows to our table using the app we have just built.

Try It Out: Adding Rows to a Table

In this example we will use a query analyzer to read our SQL, instead of using the built-in functionality of the Server Explorer. Again, all we have to do is to execute an INSERT INTO statement against the test_Employees table. To do this, follow the steps below

1. Verify if the test_Employees table exists in Server Explorer. Type in the statement to insert a row for an employee called Nathan as shown below:

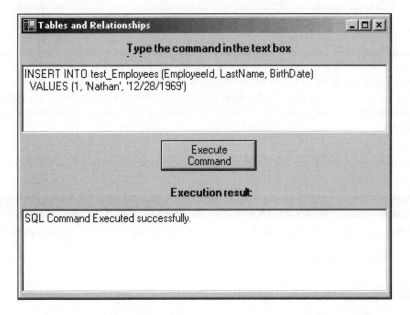

2. Verify that the record was added to the test_Employees table as we saw earlier.

3. Now let us try to add another row with the same EmployeeId. While it does not make sense for two different employees to have the same ID, the test_Employees table will at this time allow it as shown overleaf. Again, verify that there are two records in the test_Employees table with the same ID.

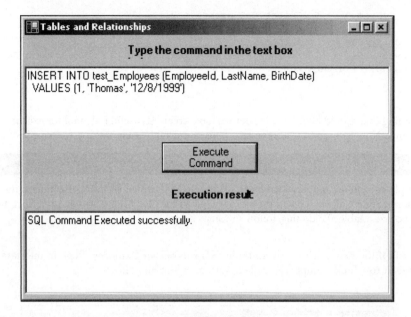

How It Works

At the moment, there is no integrity check on data in `test_Employees` table, which allows us to create two records with the same `EmployeeId`. This means that our table doesn't have any method to ensure that all records are uniquely identified. To prevent two records from having the same `EmployeeId`, we must set the primary key on `EmployeeId`. If we try to apply this to the table in its current state, we will receive an error message, because there are duplicate `EmployeeId`'s already in the table, and a primary key, as we know, must be unique.

Let's now go on to look at how we can test primary and foreign key constraints, as well as how we drop tables using SQL commands.

Try It Out: Testing the Primary Key Constraint

1. Delete all the rows in our table by issuing the following statement to our application:

```
TRUNCATE TABLE test_Employees
```

Recall that we first met this statement in Chapter 3.

2. Open the `test_Employees` table in design mode, click on the `EmployeeId` column and select the **Set Primary Key** menu item from the **Diagram** menu or by right-clicking and selecting the **Set Primary Key** menu item from the pop-up menu option. Note that the `CREATE TABLE` statement itself can be used to specify which columns are the primary key columns, as we saw earlier in the chapter.

3. Save the changes to the table design.

4. Add an employee to the table with `EmployeeId=1` using the following statement:

```
INSERT INTO test_Employees(EmployeeId, LastName, BirthDate) VALUES(1,'Nathan',
'12/28/1999')
```

5. Add another employee with a different last name and birth date, but the same `EmployeeId`.

If the constraint is being enforced then we will not be able to enter that data into the table, and we would expect some sort of error to be returned instead.

How It Works

As we expected, an error message will be given as shown overleaf. The error message indicates that the primary key constraint has been violated by attempting to insert a second employee with the `EmployeeId` of 1.

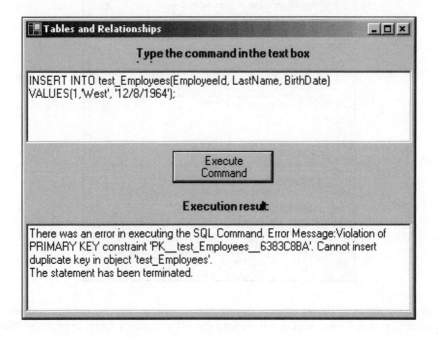

Now let us see an example where the foreign key constraint is violated.

Try It Out: Testing the Foreign Key Constraint (Referential Integrity)

Notice from our earlier example, involving the `Order Details` table in the Northwind database, that a relationship with the `Orders` table exists. This relationship specifies that if there is an order in the `Order Details` table, that order must exist in the `Orders` table as well. Let us try to violate this relationship and see what kind of error we will encounter:

1. In the Server Explorer, open the design view for the `Order Details` table.

2. Right-click in the design view (when the cursor is in any row) and select **Relationships**. You will see a screen similar to the following:

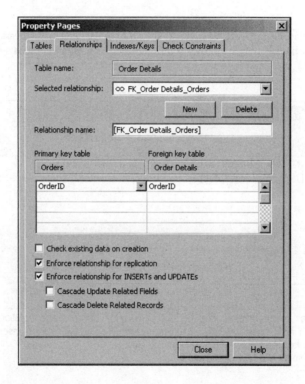

3. Close the **Property Pages** window shown above. Now let us try to add a record into the `Order Details` table for an order that does not exist in the `Orders` table. Type in the `INSERT` statement as shown in the following screenshot and notice the resulting error message:

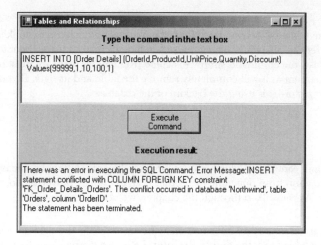

How It Works

As we can see, the message indicates that a foreign key constraint was violated, and so the INSERT statement was not executed against the table. Thus, the relationship prevented bad data from finding its way into the Order Details table. From this we can determine that referential integrity is being upheld by this relationship.

Let's now have one more example, and delete the table we added.

Try It Out: Dropping a Table

Let's now try to drop the test_Employees table, regardless of how many rows it may have.

1. Run the application and type in the DROP TABLE command and execute it as shown below:

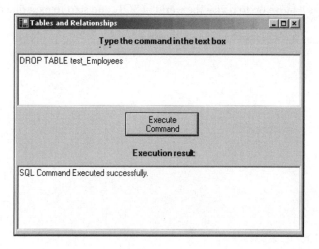

How It Works

We can verify that the table has been deleted from the Northwind database by looking in the Server Explorer. We didn't receive a single warning message telling us that we were about to make significant changes to our database, the command simply executed. Remember that care must be exercised while issuing the `DROP TABLE` statement as it will completely remove the table and its data. If you accidentally drop a table, the only way to restore it is using the backup of the database.

Summary

We've taken some significant steps to further our understanding of relational databases in this chapter. The ability to relate information from one table to another is an extremely powerful too, which gives us a lot of flexibility and power. As we walked through the chapter, we saw:

❑   How tables are used to store information, and how to create and drop tables. We also saw how to add rows to a table using the Server Explorer. Later, we learned how to do the same using C#.

❑   What primary keys and foreign keys are, and how they are used to set relationships among tables. We also learned about the different types of relationships and how to set them using database diagrams.

❑   How tables are refined to finer levels using the normalization process, and why normalization and de-normalization are important for database performance.

❑   How to trap the error messages that are generated when primary keys and relationships between tables are violated.

This chapter is intended to provide a quick overview of several issues that you will come across when designing a database. For a detailed discourse on database design please refer to the following Wrox Publication: *Professional SQL Server 2000 Database Design*, ISBN 1-86100-476-1.

In the next chapter we'll move on to revisit the world of SQL, and start to experiment with more of the tools it has to offer us.

Exercises

1. Write a SQL statement to create a table with the following information:

- ❑ Name of the table: tCustomers
- ❑ Columns:
  - ❑ cust_id , integer type, don't allow nulls
  - ❑ lastname, varchar, maximum of 25 characters, don't allow nulls
  - ❑ zip, char, 9 characters

2. Run the VC# application developed in this chapter and type in the CREATE statement developed in Exercise 1 and verify the result in the Server Explorer.

3. Construct a CREATE TABLE statement with the following information:

- ❑ Name of the table: tPurchaseOrders
- ❑ Columns:
  - ❑ pono_id , integer type, identity field, start the numbering from 10 and increment it by 1
  - ❑ vendorname, varchar, maximum of 25 characters, don't allow nulls
  - ❑ qty, int, don't allow null, default to 100

4. Insert a purchase order into tPurchaseOrders created in Exercise 4. Use the following values:

Vendor Name: Volcano Coroporation, Qty = 250

5. Construct a CREATE TABLE statement with the following information:

- ❑ Name of the table: tCustomers_1
- ❑ Columns:
  - ❑ cust_id , integer type, don't allow nulls, primary key
  - ❑ lastname, varchar, maximum of 25 characters, don't allow nulls
  - ❑ zip, char, 9 characters

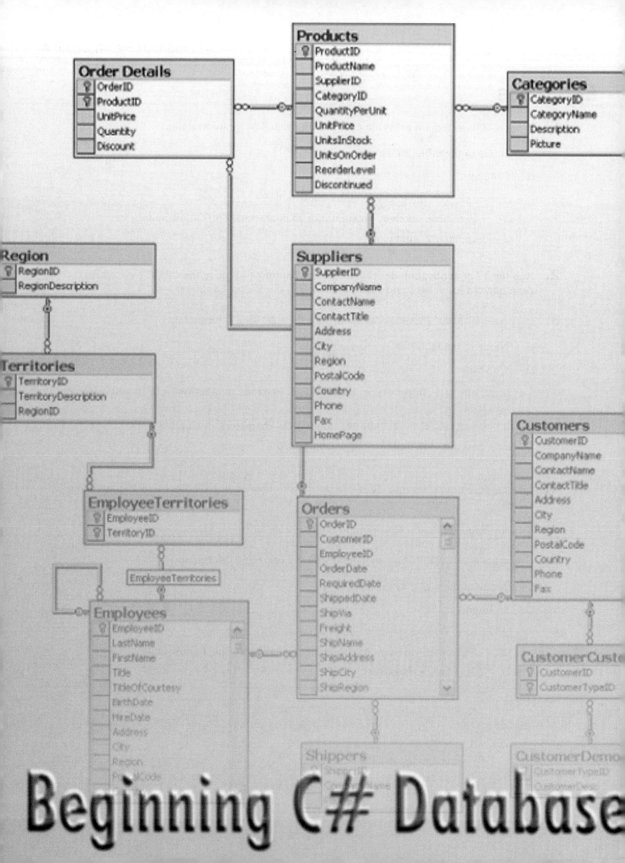

Beginning C# Database

SQL Queries

In Chapter 3, we learned about the SELECT, INSERT, UPDATE, and DELETE statements, and in Chapter 12 we saw how to create tables and set up relationships between them. Now we are going to look at a wider variety of SQL statements that are used to query the database and obtain information. The SQL language comes with numerous functions and constructs to query data, so while it is impossible to cover all permutations of the various functions in this chapter, we will look at the more frequently used statements.

Specifically, we will learn how to use the following functions and statements to query the database and obtain information:

❑   DISTINCT keyword

❑   Subqueries

❑   GROUP BY clause

❑   Aggregate functions

❑   CASE statement

❑   Date functions

❑   LIKE operator

Before we dive straight into these, we will first modify the C# application developed last chapter to run any SQL query and display the results. Then we will explore the various types of SQL queries in the context of the Northwind database.

Northwind Query Application, Part II

This application appears very similar to the one in Chapter 12, but is different in several ways in order to accommodate the data returned from our instructions. In Chapter 12, we used non-query SQL statements such as CREATE TABLE and INSERT INTO that did not return any rows back to us. As a result, in that application, we used the ExecuteNonQuery() method of the command object. In this application though, we may get no rows or several rows returned to us by our query. Also, depending on how we construct the statement, we may get one column of information or several columns of information. Let's see how this application is written to handle different numbers of rows and different numbers of columns.

Try It Out: Extending the Northwind Query Application

1. Create a solution for this chapter's examples, and call it Chapter13_Examples.

2. Create a C# Windows Application in the chapter solution, and call it Queries2.

3. Rename the main form to Queries2.cs and add a multi-line textbox, a command button, and a listview to it so that it appears as follows:

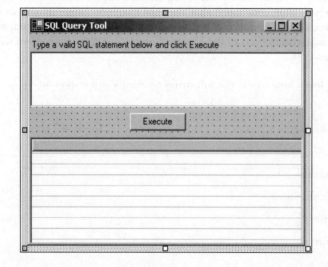

Name the textbox txtSQL, the **Execute** button as cmdExecute, and the listview as lvwDS (DS to indicate that this listview will display the resultset obtained by executing the query).

Set the View property of the listview to Details so that the results will be displayed with column headers.

Notice that we've also added a simple label to the top of the form to remind us how to use the tool.

4. Add the following directive at the top of the `queries2.cs` file. We need this since we will be using the `SqlClient` namespace.

```
using System.Data.SqlClient;
```

5. Return to Design view and double-click on the **Execute** button. In the `cmdExecute_Click()` event, type in the following code:

```
private void cmdExecute_Click(object sender, System.EventArgs e)
{
  try
  {
    //Clear the listview column header and items
    lvwDS.Columns.Clear() ;
    lvwDS.Items.Clear();

    //Create a connection
    SqlConnection cn = new SqlConnection(@"Data Source=(local)\NETSDK;" +
                       "Integrated Security=SSPI;database=Northwind");

    //Open the connection
    cn.Open();

    //Create a command object
    SqlCommand cmd= cn.CreateCommand();

    //Get the command typed by the user in a string
    string strSQL= txtSql.Text;

    //Specify the CommandText property of the command object
    cmd.CommandText = strSQL;

    //Create a datareader object
    SqlDataReader dr=cmd.ExecuteReader();

    //Get colummn names of the datareader and show in the listview's columns
    for (int i=0; i< dr.FieldCount; i++)
    {
      ColumnHeader ch = new ColumnHeader();
      ch.Text=dr.GetName(i);
      lvwDS.Columns.Add(ch);
    }

    //Get values of each row in the datareader and show them in the list view
    ListViewItem itmX;
    while (dr.Read())
    {
      //create the list view item
      itmX=new ListViewItem();

      //specify the text and subitems of the listview
```

```
      itmX.Text= dr.GetValue(0).ToString();
      for (int i=1 ; i< dr.FieldCount; i++)
      {
        itmX.SubItems.Add(dr.GetValue(i).ToString());
      }

      //Add the item to the list view's Items collection
      lvwDS.Items.Add(itmX);
    }

    //close the reader
    dr.Close();
    cn.Close();
  }
  catch ( System.Data.SqlClient.SqlException  e1)
  {
    // Display the error Message.
    MessageBox.Show ("There was an error in executing the SQL Command." +
                  "\nError Message:" + e1.Message, "SQL");
  }
  finally
  {
    // Close the connection
    cn.Close();
  }
}
```

6. Build the solution and run it. If you enter a simple query, you should see the following:

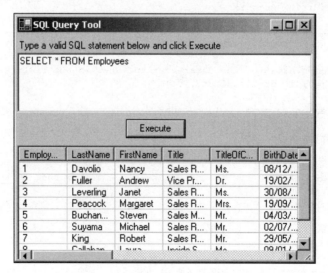

How It Works

Much of how we do things should be familiar to you now, but we will still run through the code for practice. We begin by using a `try` statement to catch exceptions and display them to the user. The next two lines are used to clear the column captions and the rows in the listview before anything else is done. These statements are needed because we will be using the application to execute several SQL statements and each statement will return different column names and different rows. We will therefore clear the listview completely before re-populating it with the results of the next SQL statement.

> *Remember that a listview has a columns collection and an items collection. The* `Columns` *collection contains* `ColumnHeader` *objects that represent the header of a listview and the* `Items` *collection contains* `ListViewItem` *objects that represent the rows.*

```
try
{
  //Clear the listview column header and items
  lvwDS.Columns.Clear() ;
  lvwDS.Items.Clear();
```

Then we establish a connection to the Northwind database with our familiar connection string, like so:

```
SqlConnection cn = new SqlConnection(@"Data Source=(local)\NETSDK;" +
                   "Integrated Security=SSPI;database=Northwind");
```

After creating the connection, we open it by explicitly calling the `Open()` method.

```
cn.Open();
```

Next we capture the command typed in by the user into a string variable:

```
string strSQL= txtSql.Text;
```

Now that we have a connection to the database, we need a command object that can be configured to execute our queries against the database. We do this by creating a command object and specifying the text in the textbox (which is now in `strSQL`) as the `CommandText` property of the command object, like this:

```
SqlCommand cmd = cn.CreateCommand();
cmd.CommandText = strSQL;
```

Now we call the `ExecuteReader` method of the command object. This will execute the SQL statement and return a `DataReader` object called `dr`:

```
SqlDataReader dr=cmd.ExecuteReader();
```

The next few lines of code are used to read the column names of the `DataReader` object and display them as columns of the list view. To do this, we iterate through the columns of the `DataReader` object until we reach the `FieldCount` value, which returns the number of columns in the `DataReader` object.

Then, each column of the listview is represented by a `ColumnHeader` object. For each column in the `DataReader` object, a corresponding `ColumnHeader` is created in the `listview`. The `DataReader`'s `GetName()` method returns the name of the column at a specified index. This name is assigned to the name of the listview's column. Finally the `ColumnHeader` object is added to the `Columns` collection of the listview as shown below, so that the listview will have a corresponding column for each column in the data reader

```
//get the colummn names of the datareader and show them in the listview's columns
for (int i=0; i< dr.FieldCount; i++)
  {
    ColumnHeader ch= new ColumnHeader();
    ch.Text=dr.GetName(i);
    lvwDS.Columns.Add(ch);
  }
```

Following this, we declared a `ListViewItem` object to represent each row that will be added to the listview. We called this item `itmX`:

```
    ListViewItem itmX;
```

Now we iterate through the rows of the `DataReader`. The `while (dr.Read())` line of code specifies that as long as there are rows in the `DataReader` object, we can iterate one row at a time.

```
while (dr.Read())
  {
```

Then we created a `ListViewItem` item and set its text value to the value of the first column of the `DataReader` object:

```
itmX=new ListViewItem();
itmX.Text= dr.GetValue(0).ToString();
```

The first column of the `ListView` has an index of 0. The second column of a `ListView` is called the first `SubItem`, the third column is the second `SubItem`, and so on. We now iterate from the second column of the `DataReader` object (index=1) and get the value of the row corresponding the second column and add it to the `SubItems` collection of the item object.

```
for (int i=1; i< dr.FieldCount; i++)
{
  itmX.SubItems.Add(dr.GetValue(i).ToString());
}
```

Then we add the item to the `Items` collection of the listview

```
    lvwDS.Items.Add(itmX);
```

After looping through and showing all the rows, we close the `DataReader` object and the connection using the `Close()` methods of the corresponding objects.

```
        //close the reader
        dr.Close();
        cn.Close();
    }
```

We simply show the error message should one occur due to incorrect syntax in the SQL statement.

```
catch ( System.Data.SqlClient.SqlException  el)
{
  // Display the error message.
  MessageBox.Show ("There was an error in executing the SQL Command." +
                   "\n Error Message:" + el.Message,"SQL");
}
```

Now that we have created an application that will execute and display the results nicely in the listview, we can proceed to learn about the queries that we can execute against the database.

SQL Commands

It is naturally important for any database programmer to master the fundamentals of SQL, and with this in mind we are going to expand our knowledge of SQL commands. For the rest of this chapter, we'll present scenarios with reference to the Northwind database where we need to query the database for specific information. Then we will construct the full query and execute it in the application we have just created in the previous section. This will provide us with a platform to discuss and demonstrate the use of the various commands we cover.

DISTINCT

The DISTINCT keyword is used in a SELECT statement to exclude duplicate values from the resultset. It can be used only once in the SELECT statement. If multiple columns are selected in the SELECT clause, DISTINCT eliminates rows where all the column values specified in the SELECT clause are identical.

Say we want to find the ProductIDs against which orders have been placed; DISTINCT can certainly help us in with this type of problem. Let's see how!

Try It Out: Query using DISTINCT

Run the application that we developed earlier in this chapter and type in the query as shown below:

```
SELECT DISTINCT ProductId
FROM [Order Details]
```

You should see the following result:

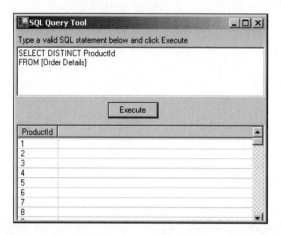

As we can see, all the IDs of products that have a order placed against them have been queried and displayed. Of course this list is not of much value without the product names. Later, when we learn about JOINs, we will see how to get the ProductName in the resultset too.

How It Works

We know that the Order Details table contains various ProductIds for various orders, and that the Products table has a list of products that are available for sale. Obviously, several orders can contain a specific ProductId, so the SELECT DISTINCT ProductId statement shows only the distinct product IDs in the Order Details table.

Note that whenever we use the table Order Details in our statements, we must enclose it with square brackets because the table name has a space in it. We would not have to do this if the table were named OrderDetails.

Subqueries

Subqueries use the result of one query as the input for another query. They are very helpful in reducing the number of steps it takes to retrieve the desired rows, but they should also be used carefully as they can get complex and unreadable. More often, we can use a JOIN to create equivalent queries as well. Joins will be discussed later in the chapter. Let's look at some subqueries now.

IN

The IN operator determines if any value in the rows you are querying matches a given value within a subquery or a list of values. This operator comes in handy when we have to find records with a specific value or a list of values in one or more columns, or when checking against a sub set of values returned in a subquery.

The syntax of the IN statement can take one of two forms:

```
SELECT column1, column2,…
FROM table1
WHERE columnN IN (1,10,14)
```

or:

```
SELECT column1, column2,…
FROM table1
WHERE column IN (SELECT columnB1 FROM table2 WHERE columnB3= table1.column1)
```

Both methods are essentially completing the same action in that you are testing one or more values on the right-hand side of the equals sign against a single column on the left-hand side. Don't worry too much about subqueries but essentially all that is happening is that you are completing another SELECT statement to return a set of values to be used against a single column for filtering.

We can use IN with other operators or functions, so we will present a series of *Try It Out here* sections to demonstrate each variation.

To begin with, let's look at IN by itself. As an example, we may want to get a list of all orders entered by the employees with IDs of 1 and 6.

Try It Out: Querying using the IN Operator

Type in the following query and execute it:

```
SELECT *
FROM Orders
WHERE EmployeeId IN (1,6)
ORDER BY EmployeeId
```

> *Recall that SELECT * is actually bad practice in real development scenarios. The better way is to specify explicitly which columns we'd like to look at to reduce load on the database server. We'll use * in this chapter for simplicity of reading, but don't forget to change this in your live applications.*

You should see the following output:

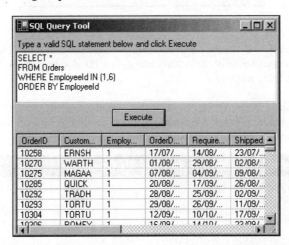

How It Works

Here, we use a list of values with the `IN` operator. The `WHERE` clause is used along with the `IN` operator. `WHERE EmployeeId IN (1,6)` specifies that only 1 and 6 must be retrieved.

The `NOT` operator, used in used in conjunction with the `IN` operator will determine all the values in a list that do not match a given value, or a list of values. Let's say that we need to get a list of all orders that have been entered by employees other than the ones with Employee IDs of 1 and 6.

Try It Out: Querying using the NOT and IN Operators

Execute the query as shown below:

```
SELECT *
FROM Orders
WHERE EmployeeId NOT IN (1,6)
ORDER BY EmployeeId
```

You should see the following results in the query application:

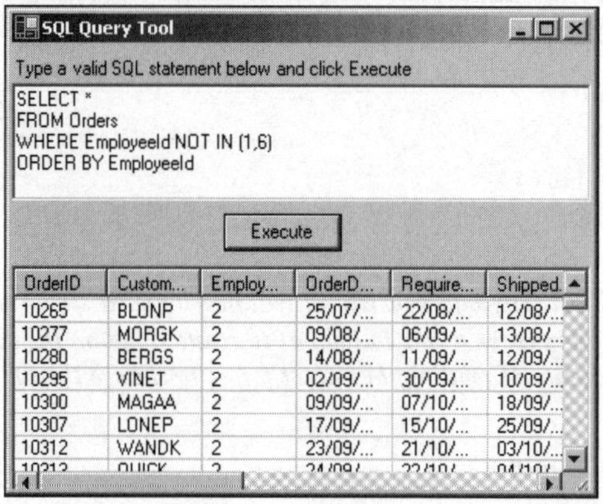

How It Works:

The `WHERE EmployeeId NOT IN (1,6)` clause removes employees with IDs of 1 and 6 from consideration and returns orders with any other employee ID. As we can see from the result, `EmployeeId` of 1 and 6 are not shown.

We can use functions along with the `IN` operator. For example, the `substring()` function returns a portion of a string. We could use this, for example, if we needed to find all the employees whose last name begins with a D or S.

Try It Out: Querying using a Function and the IN Operator

Run the following query as shown below:

```
SELECT *
FROM Employees
WHERE SUBSTRING(LastName,1,1) IN ('D', 'S')
```

You should see the following:

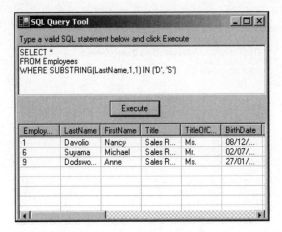

How It Works

We first use the SUBSTRING(LastName,1,1), which returns one character starting from the first position. The first argument to the function specifies the column name or expression from which we want to extract a substring. The second argument specifies the character position from where we want to begin extracting the substring. In this case, by specifying 1 as the argument, we are beginning the extract from the first character. The last argument specifies the number of characters we need to extract. In this case, by specifying 1 as the argument, we extract one character.

The net effect of this function is that the first character of the LastName column is extracted. Then we use the IN ('D','S') to see if that character belongs to the list specified in the IN operator. The resultset shows records from the three employees whose last name starts with a D or S.

GROUP BY

A GROUP BY clause is used to group together rows sharing a common column value, for the purpose of calculating an aggregate. Very often, we would want to generate reports from the database with summary figures for a particular column or a list of columns. For example, we may want to find out the total quantity ordered for each order from the Order Details table.

Try It Out: Querying using the GROUP BY Clause

The Order Details table contains the list of products in each order and the quantity of each product. We need to sum up the quantity of all products in each order.

Execute the following query:

```
SELECT OrderId, SUM(Quantity) [Total Quantity Ordered]
FROM [Order Details]
GROUP BY OrderId
```

You should see the following:

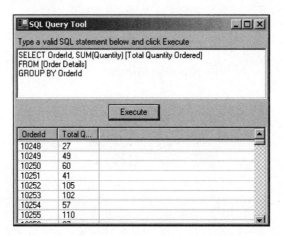

How It Works

We use the SUM() function to sum up the Quantity column of the Order Details table. The GROUP BY OrderId clause helps us to do this for each Order. The SUM(Quantity) function sums up the Quantity for each order. We give a new name to the calculated column as Total Quantity Ordered.

AGGREGATES

SQL has several functions to aggregate the values of a column. Aggregate functions return a single value. For example, we can use the aggregate functions to find the total number of orders taken by the sales personnel, or we can find the average value of the orders placed. We can find the order with the least value and the most expensive order. Aggregate functions, as their name indicates, work on a set of records and then calculate the appropriate aggregate value. SUM, MIN, MAX, AVG, and COUNT are the frequently used aggregate functions.

Let's take a look at an example of using an aggregate function. As an example, we will assume that the management of Northwind traders wants to find the total quantity ordered for all products put together.

Try It Out: Querying using the SUM Aggregate Function

Run the following query:

```
SELECT SUM (Quantity) [TotalOrdered]
FROM [Order Details]
```

The following results should be displayed:

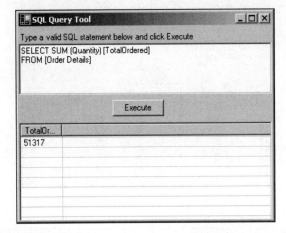

Naturally, the value you obtain here may differ from the one shown depending on whether you have changed the data in the database.

How It Works

The SUM function is used here without a GROUP BY clause, so it will return one number back. If we had wanted to group total quantity ordered by each order, we would use a GROUP BY OrderId clause as well.

There are other aggregate functions such as min(), which will calculate the minimum value in a column, max(), which will calculate the maximum value in a column, avg(), which will average the values of a column, and count(*), which will return the number of rows that were considered by the query.

Let's assume that we want to find the minimum, the maximum, the average, and the number of items of each product from the Order Details table.

Try It Out: Querying using the MAX, MIN, AVG Functions

Run the following query:

```
SELECT ProductId, MAX(Quantity)[Max],MIN(Quantity)[Min],
AVG (Quantity)[AVG], COUNT(*)[# of Items]
FROM [Order Details]
GROUP BY ProductId
ORDER BY ProductId
```

You should see the following output:

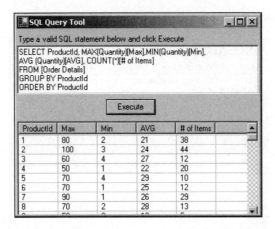

How It Works

We used the `min()` and `max()` functions to find the minimum and maximum values and the `avg()` function to calculate the average value. Since we want the results listed by each `ProductId`, we use the `GROUP BY ProductId` clause. From the resultset we can infer that 38 items were ordered for product ID =1, with a maximum order of 80, a minimum order of 2, and an average order of 21. Since we group by `ProductId`, the `count(*)` will give us the count for each product ID.

Date Functions

SQL provides date functions to deal with dates. The `datepart()` function can be used to extract a specific part of a date – such as the month or the year or the hour. Each specific part of a date has an abbreviation that is used while referring to it in date functions. The following table shows the different stipulations we can use to get parts of the date:

DatePart	Abbreviation	Example
Year	yy	2002
Month	mm	1-12
Day of month	dd	1-31
Day of year	dy	1-365 or 366 (leap year)
Week of year	wk	1-53
Day of week	dw	1-7 Sunday is 1
Quarter of year	qq	1, 2, 3, 4
Hour	hh	0-23, 0 is midnight
Minute	mi	0-59
Second	ss	0-59

A brief synopsis of the date functions is presented below. As an exercise, type in these statements in the application to see the results for yourself:

Problem statement	Query	Result
Get today's date and time.	SELECT getdate()	3/22/2002 6:08:08 AM
Get the month part of today's date.	SELECT datepart(mm,getdate())	3
Get the day part of today's date.	SELECT datepart(dd,getdate())	22
Get the quarter of the year in which today's date falls.	SELECT datepart(qq,getdate())	1
Find out how many days there are from now to Christmas. Note that if we change the datepart to mm, we can find the number of months to Christmas.	SELECT datediff(dd, getdate(), '12/25/2002')	283
Inform the customers when the invoice is due (30 days from today).	SELECT dateadd (dd,30,getdate())	4/22/2002 6:08:08 AM
Find today's month as a string instead of a number.	SELECT datename(mm, getdate())	March

CASE Statement

The CASE function allows an alternative value to be displayed depending on the value of a column. This change in data is temporary and permanent changes are not made to the data. For example, the CASE function can display Texas in a query resultset for rows that have the value TX in the state column.

First of all, let's take a look at the syntax for the CASE statement. There are two different ways you can use this function so let's split the syntax check in to those different styles.

```
CASE column to test against
WHEN value to test for
THEN true action
ELSE false action
END
```

or:

```
CASE
WHEN Boolean test
THEN true action
ELSE false action
END
```

In the first example, we can use the CASE function, which consists of a CASE keyword, the column or variable name that needs to be tested, the WHEN clauses specifying the values to test for, and then the THEN clauses specifying the result expression to action if the value is found, and optionally an ELSE clause if you wish to have an action to occur if the value is not found. You must complete this function with an END keyword.

In the second method of using the CASE function, a simple Boolean expression is placed in the WHEN clause, such as ISNULL(column1) or column3 > 102. If this expression is found to be true, then the THEN clause is executed, and if the expression is found to be false, then the ELSE clause. Again you need to complete this with an END keyword.

The CASE statement as described in this section is provided by T-SQL, which is Microsoft's version of SQL. Other database programs may or may not support CASE statements, and even if they do, their syntax may or may not be the same as that described here.

The Orders table has an OrderDate column, which holds the date when the order was placed. To verify the distinct years, run the following query:

```
SELECT DISTINCT datepart(yy,OrderDate) FROM Orders
```

and you will get 1996, 1997, and 1998 as the resultset. Now verify the number of orders in the database by running the following query:

```
SELECT count(*) FROM Orders
```

which returns 830 orders. If yours is different, note it because it will change the results of the next example in which we want to know how many Orders where entered in 1996, 1997, and 1998 respectively. We could write three queries separately and get the results. Using the CASE statement, we can find the result in one query.

Try It Out: Querying using the CASE Statement

Run the query shown below and observe the results:

```
SELECT SUM(CASE datepart(yy,OrderDate)
                    WHEN 1996 THEN 1 ELSE 0 END)[1996],
          SUM(CASE datepart(yy,OrderDate)
                    WHEN 1997 THEN 1 ELSE 0 END)[1997],
          SUM(CASE datepart(yy,OrderDate)
                    WHEN 1998 THEN 1 ELSE 0 END)[1998]
FROM Orders
```

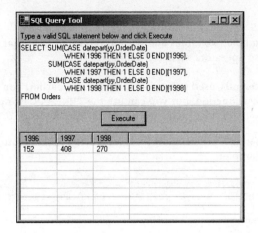

How It Works

Let us look at the first statement:

```
SUM(CASE datepart(yy,OrderDate) WHEN 1996 THEN 1 ELSE 0 END) [1996],
```

This statement finds the orders entered for 1996. The `datepart(yy,OrderDate)` is used to look at the year part of the `OrderDate` column. If it is 1996 we assign it a value of 1. If not 1996 then we assign it a value of 0. This is done for each row in the `Orders` table. Then we sum these numbers (1s and 0s) and get the number of orders entered for 1996. The result of this is displayed in a column captioned **1996** (`[1996]` represents this column). This is repeated for years 1997 and 1998.

JOINS

It's likely that we'll often need to query information that resides in more than one table. Queries that obtain data from more than one table are called multi-table queries. A `JOIN` is used to take data from two tables and then build a relationship between the two.

There are different types of joins – Cross Join, Self Join, Inner Join, Outer Join (left outer join, right outer join, and so on), and we will explain what these are in more detail a little later. Joining tables is a complex topic – this section will cover the basics of joins and demonstrate joins in the context of the Northwind database.

`JOIN`s performed using the `WHERE` clause are called Old-Style joins or ANSI-89 joins. Joins performed using the `JOIN` operator in the `FROM` clause are called new-style joins or ANSI-92 joins.

> **You should never use a WHERE statement to join two tables as this is an unsupported feature in SQL Server and could in fact, in future versions, not actually perform a join. Also, with a WHERE statement, you are limited to an inner join.**

INNER JOIN

An inner join is where you take two tables and wish to return all rows that match on the columns you are joining on. You can use operators such as >, <, or =.

INNER JOIN is a very frequently used type of join. As we said earlier, you should never use the WHERE clause as this is really a filter function, but you can use the INNER JOIN operator to specify the join. The use of the word INNER is optional – so we can simply use the word JOIN.

If we take a look at an inner join performed with the INNER JOIN operator you would code something similar to the following example:

```
SELECT ORD.OrderId, ORD.EmployeeId, EMP.LastName
FROM Orders ORD INNER JOIN Employees EMP ON ORD.EmployeeId = EMP.EmployeeId
WHERE Order.OrderId > 5000
ORDER BY EMP.LastName
```

The FROM clause with INNER JOIN operator and the ON keyword all define the join between the two tables. The FROM clause and the JOIN clause will name the two tables that form the basis of the query, with the ON clause defining the names of the columns that will form the join itself. The query above also uses a WHERE clause to filter out the records in the Orders table where the OrderId is less than 5,000. We will explore these in more detail in the following *Try It Out* exercises.

Let's start an example by saying that we want a list showing the OrderId, the EmployeeId, and the last name of the employees who placed an order.

Try It Out: Inner Join

1. To solve this, we will use the INNER JOIN clause and join the Orders and the Employees table based on the EmployeeId. Enter the following code in to the query tool:

```
SELECT ORD.OrderId, ORD.EmployeeId, EMP.LastName
FROM Orders ORD
INNER JOIN Employees EMP
ON ORD.EmployeeId=EMP.EmployeeId
ORDER BY EMP.LastName
```

2. If you execute this code you should see the following output:

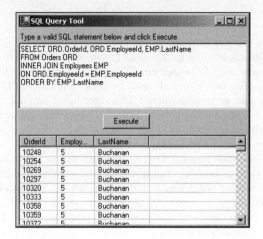

How It Works

Let's start with the SELECT statement:

```
SELECT ORD.OrderId, ORD.EmployeeID, EMP.LastName
```

This lists the desired column names – OrderId and EmployeeID from the Orders table and LastName from the Employees table.

The FROM clause:

```
FROM Orders ORD
```

lists one of the tables from which we are using to extract data. The INNER JOIN statement names the other table.

```
INNER JOIN Employees EMP
```

We then name the columns that we wish to join the tables with. In the example demonstrated we only named one column from each table but it is possible to name as many columns as you desire here. You can use brackets, AND, and OR to complete the actual join you wish to perform.

```
ON ORD.EmployeeId=EMP.EmployeeId
```

> *Aliases (*ORD *and* EMP*) are given for the* Orders *and* Employees *table to facilitate easy reference to the tables instead of writing out the entire name each time.*

The ORDER BY clause:

```
ORDER BY EMP.LastName
```

lists the resultset in the order of LastName. The default is in ascending sequence. If you wished to have the results in descending sequence you would then suffix those columns with DESC.

OUTER JOIN

Outer joins return all rows from at least one of the tables specified in the `join` clauses, as long as those rows meet any filter conditions detailed in the `WHERE` statement. There are three types of outer joins – left outer join, right outer join, and full outer join. The left and right refer to the tables on the left side and right side of a join. In a left outer join, all rows from the left table will be in the resultset regardless of whether they satisfy the join expression or not. In a right outer join, all rows from the right table will be in the resultset, regardless of whether they satisfy the comparison expression or not. In a full outer join, all rows from both tables are returned in the resultset.

You may be wondering when this is useful. One of these occasions might be when you are comparing your customer table with your order table and trying to find a list of all customers and whether they have placed an order with you or not. Using the inner join above, you would only see listed those customers that have in fact placed an order. Or perhaps, as we will see in a moment you would like to see a list of all employees including those that have yet to place an order. This would allow you to check on who is selling your goods and who is not.

To experiment with `OUTER JOIN`, add a few new employees to the `Employees` table. Retrieve data from the `Employees` table and type in the `LastName` and `FirstName` columns and a few other columns. Then when the cursor is moved away from the row, the row is saved and the `EmployeeID` is automatically assigned a new value. If we try to type a value in the `EmployeeID` field we will get a Cannot edit this cell message. This is because of the fact that the `EmployeeID` is an identity field, and is dispensed by the database automatically in sequence. My `Employees` table looks like this with two employees added:

Start Page	dbo.Employees ...SDK.Northwind)			◁ ▷ ×
EmployeeID	LastName	FirstName	Title	TitleOfCourtesy
1	Davolio	Nancy	Sales Representati	Ms.
2	Fuller	Andrew	Vice President, Sale	Dr.
3	Leverling	Janet	Sales Representati	Ms.
4	Peacock	Margaret	Sales Representati	Mrs.
5	Buchanan	Steven	Sales Manager	Mr.
6	Suyama	Michael	Sales Representati	Mr.
7	King	Robert	Sales Representati	Mr.
8	Callahan	Laura	Inside Sales Coordi	Ms.
9	Dodsworth	Anne	Sales Representati	Ms.
11	Doe	John	Sales Representati	Mr.
12	Nathan	Virek	VP	Mr.

Run the `INNER JOIN` query of the previous section again. We will see the same results, but this time, when a join is made between the `Orders` and `Employees` table, the employee IDs of 11 and 12 are not found in the resultset because there is no `Order` with `EmployeeID` of 11 or 12. Inner joins require a match between the joining tables.

Let's look at an example to demonstrate using an outer join and how to bring these employees into the results. Now, let's say we want a list of all orders placed by all employees – and this list must contain information about employees who have not placed any orders yet.

Try It Out: Querying using LEFT OUTER JOIN

Think of the Employees table on the left and Orders table on the right hand side. We want all the employees to be returned in the resultset along with their orders. If any of the employees have not placed an order, they too must be in the resultset with no orders listed against them. This is the correct place to use a LEFT OUTER JOIN. Run the query as follows:

```
SELECT EMP.LastName, ORD.OrderId
FROM Employees EMP LEFT OUTER JOIN ORDERS ORD
    ON EMP.EmployeeId=ORD.EmployeeId
ORDER BY EMP.LastName
```

You should see the following results:

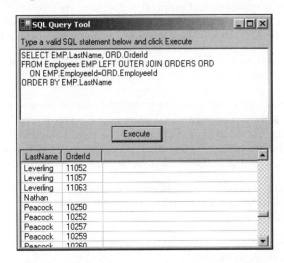

*We use the LEFT OUTER JOIN keyword because the Employees table is the left table and LEFT specifies that even though not all records of the Employees table may be found in the Orders table, they must still be returned. In the screenshot above, there is a record for **LastName** Nathan but no **OrderId** has been listed against him.*

It is possible to turn the query the so that the Employees table is on the right and the Orders table on the left and alter your join condition to a RIGHT OUTER JOIN. There is no right or wrong way when determining what goes on the left and what goes on the right except on how you then develop the query and any further joins.

Full Join

As the name suggests, this will join all rows from both tables in to the one resultset. If there is no actual join between the two tables, in other words there is a row in one table that has no join in the other, then the row will still be part of the resultset, but any columns named from the table where there is no join, will have a value of NULL in that column.

A FULL JOIN as follows would show any employees that had no territories attached, and also any territories that had no employees. Within Northwind this does not occur and so you will need to alter the database tables to achieve any results. We won't demonstrate this, but the code to complete this you would need to enter is the following. We are also going to show how to integrate different join conditions in one SELECT statement.

```
SELECT FirstName, LastName, TerritoryDescription
FROM Employees Emp
FULL JOIN EmployeeTerritories EmpTer
ON Emp.EmployeeId = EmpTer.EmployeeId
INNER JOIN Territories Ter
ON EmpTer.TerritoryId = Ter.TerritoryId
```

We are completing a full join between Employees and the EmployeeTerritories so that we know where there are uncovered territories and employees that have no territories. There should be a one-to-one relationship between EmployeeTerritories and Territories and we are building our query on the assumption that this link has not been broken. It is therefore possible to use an INNER JOIN for this condition.

Cross Join

A cross join is perhaps the most dangerous join to complete if you are unsure of how this works. By creating a CROSS JOIN within a SELECT statement, you are in fact saying "as you return each row in the left-hand table, I want it listed against every row in the right-hand table". So if you think about this, if in one table you had 1,000 rows and in the other table 500 rows, you would have returned 1,000 x 500 rows in the resultset, a total of 500,000! That's a large amount of processing and number of results.

Perhaps the smallest resultset to return from Northwind would be to use the following statement. Notice that there is no ON clause, as we are not actually joining two tables, we are simply listing all the rows from one table against all the rows in the other table.

```
SELECT TerritoryDescription, regionid
FROM EmployeeTerritories EmpTer
CROSS JOIN Territories Ter
```

This will return over 2,500 rows.

LIKE

The LIKE operator allows us to use wildcard characters to filter for rows. We can filter for all the rows where a particular column begins with a specific character or ends with a specific character. We can also filter for all rows where a particular column contains a specific string that we are searching for. For example, let's run through an example that gets a list of employees whose last name start with a D.

Try It Out: Querying using the LIKE Operator

We can use the LIKE operator as follows:

```
SELECT EmployeeID,LastName,FirstName,Title
FROM Employees
WHERE LastName LIKE 'D%'
```

This should produce the following result:

The:

```
WHERE LastName LIKE 'D%'
```

in the clause instructs SQL to retrieve all records that start with D and have any character to the right of D. If we want to find all employees whose last name ends with a D, we can use:

```
WHERE LastName LIKE '%D'.
```

If we want to find all employees whose last names have a D in them, regardless of whether the D is at the beginning or at the end of the LastName we can use:

```
WHERE LastName LIKE '%D%'
```

LIKE can also be used on date fields. For example, to find all the orders which where entered in the morning we can use:

```
WHERE OrderDate LIKE '%AM'
```

There are also other pattern matching wildcards that can be placed in a LIKE clause. These are detailed.

Wildcard	Explanation	Example code	Example results
_	Any single character at this position	SELECT Firstname FROM Employees WHERE Firstname LIKE 'Rob_n'	Roban Robin Robyn
[ ]	Any single character at this position within the defined range	SELECT Firstname FROM Employees WHERE Firstname LIKE 'Rob[a-1]n'	Roban Robin
[^]	Any single character at this position not within the defined range	SELECT Firstname FROM Employees WHERE Firstname LIKE 'Rob[^a-d]%'	Robin Robert Robson Robyn

That wraps up our discussion on SQL queries. We now have a broad knowledge base of SQL to draw upon when constructing our various queries and commands.

Summary

In this chapter we learned how to retrieve data using SQL Queries in the context of the Northwind database. We learned to construct several different queries as summarized below:

❑ The DISTINCT keyword was used to eliminate duplicate values from the resultset.

❑ Subqueries using IN and NOT IN were used to refine the search by providing a list of values.

❑ Aggregate functions such as MIN, MAX, SUM, and AVG were used to calculate aggregate values.

❑ The GROUP BY clause was used to group data by one or more columns and calculate values for new columns.

❑ The CASE statement was used to retrieve data based on the specific column values.

❑ Date functions retrieved data based on date values.

❑ JOINs were discussed and we learned how to perform CROSS JOINs, INNER JOINs, and OUTER JOINs.

❑ We also used the LIKE operator to do wildcard searches.

All the queries were executed from a C# application and the resultsets were displayed there too. There are several variations of these statements and several nuances to writing queries all of which cannot be covered in one single chapter. This chapter taught us how to use the basic SQL Query statements. You are strongly encouraged to read books on database design and T-SQL (Transact-SQL, which is Microsoft's version of SQL). Wrox has several books such as *Beginning SQL Server 2000 Programming,* ISBN 1-86100-523-7 or *Professional SQL Server 2000 Programming,* ISBN 1-86100-448-6, or for database design, *Professional SQL Server 2000 Database Design,* ISBN 1-86100-476-1.

In the next chapter, we will learn how to use two important elements of the database from C# code – Views and Stored procedures.

Exercises

1. Write a query to find the total quantity ordered of each product group (for instance, group by `ProductId`)

2. Write a query to find the total quantity ordered of each product group (for instance, group by `ProductId`) but show the best selling product first and then the next belling selling product.

3. Find how much would you have to pay to buy one piece of each product from Northwind Traders. Hint : Query the `Products` table to find the solution.

4. Write a query to find all employees whose last names have the string 'DA' in them

5. List the Product IDs, their names, and the total quantity ordered for these products.

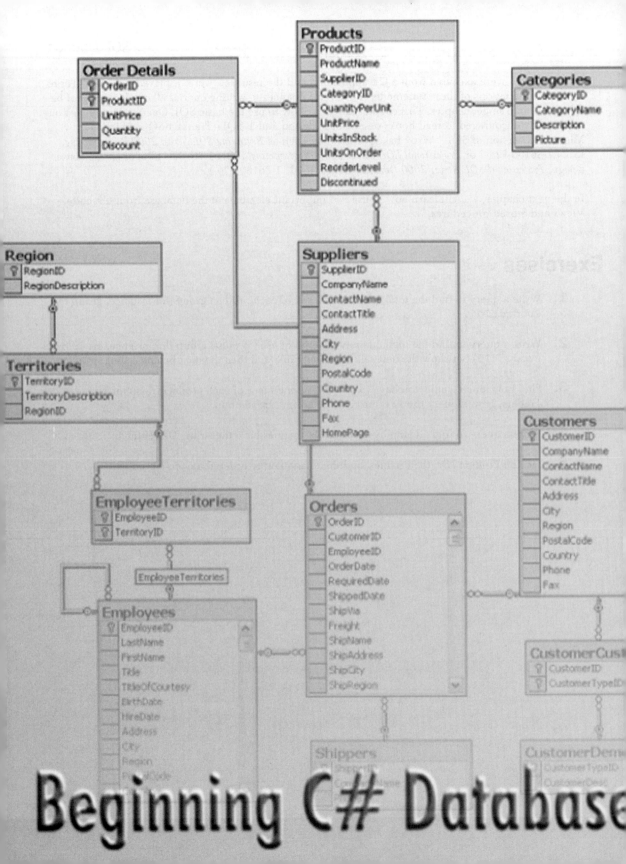

Views and Stored Procedures

In this chapter we will be learning about views and stored procedures. Views are used as security tools as well as giving developers a different outlook on the schematics of a database. We will be covering very early on in the chapter how these two statements can aid a database administrator as well as a developer.

Stored procedures on the other hand are chunks of code that are stored in a database and are mainly used when the same T-SQL needs to be executed several times, either in an overnight batch or as part of the overall online processing scenario of a development solution. We can do anything we want with stored procedures since they consist of SQL commands, so anything we can do in SQL we can achieve with a stored procedure.

There are many advantages to using both, and we will look at them in detail shortly. Specifically, in this chapter, we will look at:

❑   What a view is and how to create one

❑   How to use C# to retrieve data from a view

❑   What a stored procedure is and how to create one

❑   How to provide inputs to a stored procedure and handle the outputs

❑   How to use views and stored procedures from within C# applications

Views

When it comes to releasing your developed solution in to a production environment, it is crucial from a security stand point that you should not allow anyone into the raw tables themselves. This is for a number of reasons with perhaps the greatest being that you could be allowing developers to see crucial or sensitive corporate or employee information. Imagine if the whole development team could see your, or any employees salary? Or perhaps the details of your last appraisal? Something like that is not desirable. In this case you would create a view that was built on the HR table but would not contain those crucial columns or even rows of information.

Then there may be times that you allow users to query the data by entering their own T-SQL queries. No doubt they will have no concept of the underlying database structure whether it is tables, indexes or relationships. To aid them, and this also includes developers, you would create a view that would join the necessary tables together to provide a consistent view on the data and therefore keep any referential integrity intact and even ensure that the correct information was processed because all of the joins had been pre-determined and built.

A view is quite simply a logical table that has one or more physical tables defined as a SELECT statement query, and any join conditions required, that looks for all intents and purposes like an actual table. You can modify data, insert data or simply query data using a view contained within a database.

Views are queries that are saved and categorized under the **Views** node of the Server Explorer. The following is a list of frequent uses for view objects:

- ❑ **Join columns from multiple tables so that they look like a single table**: Views can be used in a similar way to tables, but in reality, the data that makes up the view is not stored in the database as a table since it may well actually be data from several tables which are stored on the database.

- ❑ **Restrict a user to specific rows in a table**: Say we had a table in our database that kept track of salaries of all employees including the CEO, CFOs, and the like – let us call them the "CXO" (where X these days could be anything from A-Z). If we wanted to restrict the non-CXO users from seeing the salary of CXOs, then we could create a view that would filter out the records of CXO employees and assign the non-CXO users permission to use this view only and deny permission to access the table.

- ❑ **Restrict a user to specific columns**: In the case of the CXOs as described above, we could create a view that shows the name, title and address of all the employees including the CXOs but does not show their salary information.

- ❑ **Aggregate information instead of supplying details**: Instead of showing all users all of the transaction details from a table containing sales information, we could create a view that summarizes the sales information for each year. Perhaps we could assign the auditors permission to view this summary view instead of letting them see all the transactions – or perhaps not!

Let us see the views that have already been created in the Northwind database. In the Server Explorer, expand the **Views** node. You will see the following views:

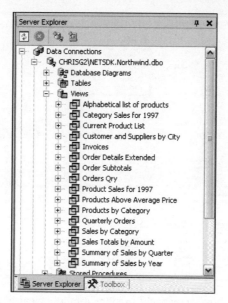

We can open the view by right-clicking it and selecting **Retrieve Data From View**. We can see the SQL statement behind the view by right-clicking the view and selecting **Design View**.

Views can be created in an MSDE database in two ways:

❑ Using the Server Explorer

❑ By executing the CREATE VIEW statement

If you are using a full SQL Server installation, you can use the query analyzer to execute the CREATE VIEW statement and also use the Enterprise Manager to create views; alternatively, we can write a C# script to execute the CREATE VIEW statement.

Since we're using MSDE, we'll look at using the Server Explorer first, before looking at the CREATE VIEW SQL statement.

Try It Out: Creating and Executing a View from Server Explorer

Let us create a simple view and execute it in the Server Explorer. Since, as explained before, a view is a saved query, we will define a query involving the Employees and the Orders table.

1. In the Server Explorer, right-click on the **View** node and select **New View**.

2. A dialog box will pop up listing all the tables in the database. Select the **Orders** and the **Employees** tables, and click **Add**. The tables that are selected will be placed in a diagram pane window. Check the boxes next to the **EmployeeId**, **LastName**, and **FirstName** columns in the **Employees** table and the **OrderId** column from the **Orders** table. As you check the columns, notice that they are added to the SQL statement in the third window. The screen should appear as shown below:

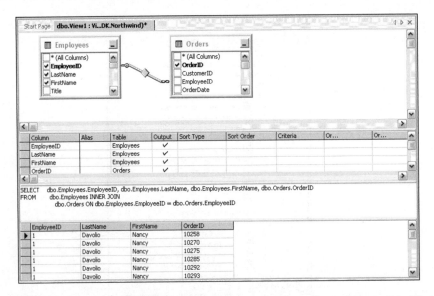

Let's quickly talk about the above screenshot to make it totally clear what is happening. The four windows shown together above are intended to help you create the view. The diagram pane shows the relationships between the tables. In this case, there is a one-to-many relation between the `Employees` table and the `Orders` table and this relationship is shown in the top pane.

The second pane is called the grid pane and it shows the columns selected in the query. Since we checked the boxes next to `EmployeeId`, `LastName`, and `FirstName` columns in the `Employees` table and the `OrderId` column from the `Orders` table, they also appear here in the column entitled Column and the column entitled Table. Notice that the column titled Output is checked – this means that the corresponding column in the table will be listed in the query output.

The third window is called the query pane. It shows a SQL statement that represents the query that we are trying to construct for the view. As we add or remove the tables that are used in the query, or the columns that need to show in the output of the query, this window will display the modified query accordingly. We can also directly modify the SQL statement in the query, and the diagram pane and the grid pane will change automatically to reflect the changes.

The fourth window is used to show the results of the query and is called the results pane. We can see the result of the view (or, the result of the SQL query behind the view) by right-clicking on any of the windows and selecting the Run option.

3. Save the view by clicking on the Save button. A window will pop up asking you to give a name to the view – call it `EmployeesAndOrders`. Actually, behind the scenes, a CREATE VIEW SQL statement is executed against the database to create the view. We will discuss the CREATE VIEW statement in more detail a little later.

4. To execute the view, right-click on it and select Retrieve Data from View. A list of all employees and their orders will be shown.

This view can be run any number of times and it will retrieve the data that is current at the time. But then, you might wonder, what is the real benefit of creating this view, other than the fact that it is saved in the database and can be reused.

How It Works

There's not really much more to this example as it was mainly explained in the screenshot, however, let's quickly answer the question posed a second ago and talk about why we use views.

The real benefit comes when constructing a query, which will need to utilize the result of this view. For example, say we want to get a list of all employees with EmployeeId greater than 5, and the orders entered by them. Instead of doing a join on the tables every time, we could directly query the view as follows:

```
SELECT EmployeeId, OrderId
FROM EmployeesAndOrders
WHERE EmployeeId> 5
```

Here, notice that the view itself is used as if it were a table in the FROM statement. This is a great convenience for querying the database. A database administrator can, for example, construct several views that summarize and group information by specifying parameters – say by year, state, or product category and so on. Other queries can use these views to filter information further – for example by a specific year or a specific state or a specific product.

Let us see how to use the EmployeesAndOrders view that we created earlier to obtain information about EmployeeId=1 only.

Try It Out: Creating a View using Another View

Expanding on the previous example, let's create a view that uses another view as though it were a table. We will use the EmployeesAndOrders view but filter the orders for EmployeeId=1

1. From the View node, select New View.

2. When a list of tables is presented, select Close – do not select any table.

3. In the Query pane type the following query:

```
SELECT *
FROM EmployeesAndOrders
WHERE EmployeeId=1
```

4. Right-click on the statement and select Run and notice the results. Only the orders of EmployeeId=1 are returned.

5. Save the view as EmployeesAndOrders_1. Now, we can open this view any number of times from now on. Right-click on it to retrieve the data and observe that the results are always displayed for EmployeeId=1.

How It Works

We reused the `EmployeesAndOrders` view that we created earlier to create another view. Whereas the `EmployeesAndOrders` view gets a list of all orders entered by all employees, the `EmployeesAndOrders_1` view further refines it down to select the orders entered by `EmployeeId` `=1` only. We can also create adhoc queries (that is, queries that are not saved as views) that use the `EmployeesAndOrders` view, to obtain information about other employees as well.

Creating a View using C#

When we create a query from the Server Explorer, behind-the-scenes a `CREATE VIEW` SQL statement is run to create the view. A simple form of this statement is as follows:

```
CREATE VIEW <view name>
AS
SELECT statement
```

For example, the `EmployeesAndOrders_1` view could have been created using the following command directly to the database:

```
CREATE VIEW EmployeesAndOrders-1
AS
SELECT EmployeeId,LastName,FirstName,OrderId
FROM EmployeesAndOrders
```

We could use Visual Studio .NET to run this statement by using the procedure described in Chapter 3, but we'll use a custom C# program to create views. We will also see how to open a view from C# and display the results.

Try It Out: Creating and Executing a View from C#

You can choose either to create this example by hand in this chapter, or you can download the finished application from the Wrox web site at http://www.wrox.com. We'll be building just the views functionality in this *Try It Out* section, and we'll be adding the Stored Procedure functionality later in this chapter. The downloaded application has both parts ready for you to use.

1. Create a new chapter solution called `Chapter14_Examples`.

2. Create a C# Windows Application project called `Views_and_SPs` in the chapter solution.

3. Add a `TabControl` control, and click the link in the Properties pane to create two tab pages.

4. In the views page add buttons, textboxes, and a listview as shown opposite. We will design the stored procedures page later in the chapter:

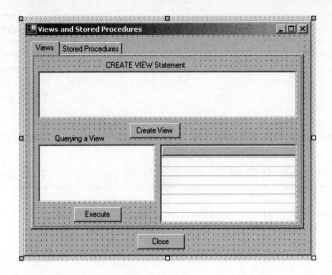

The controls are to be named and their properties set as follows:

Control	Name	Remarks
A `TabControl` control	`tabControl1`	Add two pages to the `TabPages Collection` property and specify the `text` property as `Views` and `Stored Procedures` respectively.
A `Label` captioned: **CREATE VIEW statement**	Default name	
A `TextBox` control positioned top center under the label.	`txtCreateView`	To type in the SQL statement to create a view. Set the `Multiline` property to `True`.
A `Button` control captioned: **Create View**	`cmdCreateView`	To execute the statement in `txtCreateView` and to actually create a view
A `TextBox` control	`txtSQL`	To type a query that references a view. Set the `Multiline` property to `True`.

Table continued on following page

Control	Name	Remarks
A `ListView` control	`lvwViewRS`	To show the data retrieved by the view. Set the `GridLines` property to `True` and `View` property to `Details`.
A `Button` control captioned **Execute**	`cmdExecuteView`	To execute the query typed in `txtSQL`.
A `Button` control captioned **Close**	`cmdClose`	To close the form.

5. Add a reference to `Sql.Data.SqlClient` by adding the following line to the `viewsandSPs.cs` file:

```
using System.Data.SqlClient;
```

Also, change the namespace in our code to the following:

```
Namespace Wrox.BeginningCSharpDatabases.Chapter14
```

6. Now double-click the **Create View** button and type in the following code for its click event:

```
private void cmdCreateView_Click(object sender, System.EventArgs e)
{
  try
  {
    //Create a SQL connection
    SqlConnection cn = new SqlConnection(@"Data Source=(local)\NETSDK;" +
      "Integrated Security=SSPI;database=Northwind");

    //Open the connection
    cn.Open();

    //Get the command from the text box
     string strSQL=txtCreateView.Text;

    // Create the command object.
    SqlCommand cmd= new SqlCommand(strSQL, cn);

    //Execute the command
    cmd.ExecuteNonQuery();

    // Once SQL command is executed, close the connection.
    cn.Close();

    // Display the result message.
    MessageBox.Show("View was created successfully");
```

```
    }
  catch ( System.Data.SqlClient.SqlException  e1)
  {
    // Display the error message.
    MessageBox.Show("Could not create the view. Error Message:" + e1.Message);
  }
}
```

7. In the `cmdExecuteView` button's click event, type in the following code:

```
private void cmdExecuteView_Click(object sender, System.EventArgs e)
{
  try
  {
    //Clear the listview column header and items
    lvwViewRS.Columns.Clear() ;
    lvwViewRS.Items.Clear();

    //Create a connection
    SqlConnection cn = new SqlConnection(@"Data Source=(local)\NETSDK;" +
      "Integrated Security=SSPI;database=Northwind");

    //Open the connection
    cn.Open();

    //Create a command object
    SqlCommand cmd= cn.CreateCommand();

    //Get the command typed by the user in a string
    string strSQL= txtSQL.Text;

    //Specify the CommandText property of the command object
    cmd.CommandText = strSQL;

    //Create a datareader object
    SqlDataReader dr=cmd.ExecuteReader();

    //Get the colummn names of the datareader and show in the listview's columns
    for (int i=0; i< dr.FieldCount; i++)
    {
      ColumnHeader c = new ColumnHeader();
      c.Text=dr.GetName(i);
      lvwViewRS.Columns.Add(c);
    }

    //Get the values of each row in the datareader and show them in the list view
    ListViewItem itmX;
    while (dr.Read())
    {

      //create the list view item
```

```
        itmX=new ListViewItem();

        //specify the text and subitems of the list view
        itmX.Text= dr.GetValue(0).ToString();
        for (int i=1 ; i< dr.FieldCount; i++)
        {
           itmX.SubItems.Add(dr.GetValue(i).ToString());
        }

        //Add the item to the list view's  Items collection
        lvwViewRS.Items.Add(itmX);
    }
    //close the reader
    dr.Close();

    cn.Close();
}
catch ( System.Data.SqlClient.SqlException  e1)
{
    // Display the error message.
    MessageBox.Show ("There was an error in executing the SQL Command. " +
        "Error Message:" + e1.Message);
}
}
```

8. Build and run the solution. Now in the textbox above where it says **CREATE VIEW statement**, type in the statement as shown below and click on the **Create View** button:

```
CREATE VIEW EmployeesAndOrders_2
AS
Select Employees.EmployeeId, Employees.LastName, Employees.FirstName,
Orders.OrderId
FROM Employees INNER JOIN
  Orders ON Employees.EmployeeId=Orders.EmployeeId
WHERE Employees.EmployeeId=2
```

You will get a confirmation message to say that the code executed successfully.

9. Go to the Server Explorer and refresh the **Views** node and notice the **EmployeesAndOrders_2** view listed there.

10. Now let's test the view itself. Recollect that the view is like a table and is used as such. In the textbox below the label captioned **Query using a View**, type in the SQL statement as shown below and click on the **Execute View** button:

```
SELECT * FROM
EmployeesAndOrders_2
```

You will see the result of the query displayed in the list view for `EmployeeId=2` as shown in the following screenshot:

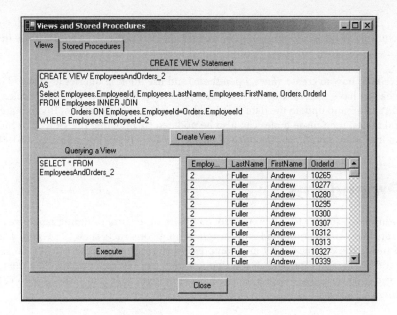

How It Works

Since most of the code should be familiar to us by now from discussion in previous chapters, we will go over only the main points here. Firstly, the CREATE VIEW statement was issued, which created a view showing the EmployeeId, LastName, FirstName, and the OrderId. Then when we clicked on the **Create View** button, the view was created. The command object was provided with this statement and we used the ExecuteNonQuery method to execute the command and create the view:

```
//Get the command from the text box
string strSQL=txtCreateView.Text;

// Create the command object.
SqlCommand cmd= new SqlCommand(strSQL, cn);

//Execute the command
cmd.ExecuteNonQuery();
```

After creating the view, we tested it by writing a SELECT statement on the view as though it were a table (SELECT * FROM EmployeesAndOrders_2) and executed the statement by clicking on the **Execute** button. Since views will return a resultset, we used the ExecuteReader() method to get the rows into a datareader, like so:

```
string strSQL= txtSQL.Text;

/Specify the CommandText property of the command object
cmd.CommandText = strSQL;

//Create a datareader object
SqlDataReader dr=cmd.ExecuteReader();
```

365

After creating the `DataReader`, we looped through the rows and columns and displayed them in the `ListView` control. In this case, since the `EmployeesAndOrders_2` view filters the information for `EmployeeId=2`, only rows for that employee are displayed.

So far we have seen how to create views, open them, and use them in queries as tables. There is more to views than what we have seen here so far. For example, views sometimes are updateable. We can get a view into a `DataSet` and update the data in it and have it saved in the tables. If views are created by joining several tables, then those tables can also be updated by updating the view. For more information on views, you may want to refer to *Beginning SQL Programming,* Wrox Press, ISBN 1-86100-180-0.

Stored Procedures

Stored procedures are similar to functions/procedures in other programming languages. They contain SQL statements that can be combined with programming constructs such as `IF` and `WHILE`, and so on, and are held inside the database itself in a compiled form so they execute quickly. Stored procedures can take several inputs and return several outputs, which can be scalar values (like the number of employees) or can be a resultset (like a list of all the employees). It is also possible to call and execute them from client programs.

In most real-world applications, stored procedures are the means of writing code to handle the transactions in a database. The following is a list of some important facts to remember regarding stored procedures:

- ❑ They can accept input parameters and return multiple values in the form of output parameters to the calling procedure.

- ❑ They can return a status value to a calling procedure or batch to indicate success or failure.

- ❑ They can call other stored procedures and execute them.

- ❑ They allow modular programming. That is, they can be created independently of the application and can be modified without recompiling the application.

- ❑ They allow faster execution. When a data-processing task is repeated several times, stored procedures can be faster than batches of SQL code submitted to the database from the application. Stored procedures are parsed and compiled when they are created, and an in-memory version of the procedure can be used after the procedure is executed the first time. This dramatically increases performance in client-server systems where several clients call and execute the same stored procedure.

    On the other hand SQL statements repeatedly sent from the client each time they run are compiled and optimized every time they are executed by the database engine and this can drastically affect the performance of the application.

- ❑ They can reduce network traffic significantly. Intense data manipulation tasks, when performed in a stored procedure and returned once only to the calling program will save much network traffic as opposed to sending several SQL statements several time over the network.

- ❑ They can be used as a security mechanism. User groups can be set up in such a way that only certain user groups can execute a certain stored procedure.

Now that we have a good general idea of what we can use stored procedures for, we will use the rest of this section to learn how to create different kinds of stored procedures using the server explorer, and how to use them in a C# application. We will begin by creating a stored procedure that does not take any input parameters. These kinds of stored procedures are useful when we want to execute pre-defined queries and get the results.

Try It Out: Creating and Executing a Stored Procedure with No Input Parameters

Suppose that we want a resultset showing the `EmployeeId` and `LastName` of all employees of Northwind traders by executing a stored procedure. We will refine this stored procedure later to take input parameters. Follow the steps outlined below:

Note that to successfully run this example, you must be running Visual Studio .NET Professional or higher. If you only have Visual C# Standard edition, you should follow the instructions that follow this example.

1. In the Server Explorer, right-click on the **Stored Procedures** node and select **New Stored Procedure**.

2. You will be presented with a window with the following code:

```
CREATE PROCEDURE dbo.StoredProcedure1
/*
(
  @parameter1 datatype = default value,
  @parameter2 datatype OUTPUT
)
*/
AS
    /* SET NOCOUNT ON */
RETURN
```

The `/*` and `*/` symbols are comments and code inside them is ignored by the database engine. They are used to comment out more than one line of code.

Modify the code above so that it looks like the code shown below.

```
CREATE PROCEDURE sp_Select_AllEmployees AS
  SELECT EmployeeId,LastName
  FROM
  Employees
RETURN
```

3. Save the stored procedure by clicking on the **Save** button in the toolbar. Notice that under the **Stored Procedures** node in the Server Explorer, we now have a entry for `sp_Select_AllEmployees`

4. Now let us execute the stored procedure. Right-Click on the `sp_Select_AllEmployees` item in the Server Explorer and select **Run Stored Procedure**. An output window, similar to the one shown below will appear showing the results of the stored procedure execution. Scroll down to the bottom and notice that the last line says `@RETURN_VALUE = 0`. Stored procedures return a value of 0 by default. But this can be changed, as we will see in the next *Try It Out*:

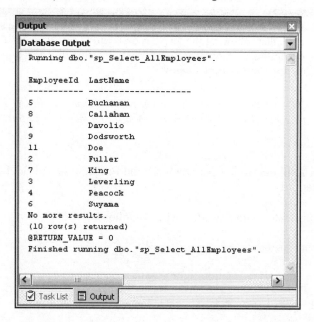

How It Works

This example shows a very simple stored procedure. The first line declares that a procedure by the name of `sp_Select_AllEmployees` is to be created and that it takes no parameters as input:

```
CREATE PROCEDURE sp_Select_AllEmployees AS
```

The `AS` is used to separate the signature of the stored procedure from the body of the stored procedure. After the `AS`, we simply write out a simple query that selects all columns and rows from the `Employees` table:

```
SELECT EmployeeID, LastName
FROM
Employees
RETURN
```

The `RETURN` is used to signify that the stored procedure has completed its work. That's it; after we saved the stored procedure, we executed it. Since it does not require us to supply any input parameters, it ran and produced a list of all employees.

To modify an existing stored procedure, right-click on it, select Edit stored procedure, and make changes in the editor window. Note that the code is now presented as:

```
ALTER PROCEDURE sp_Select_AllEmployees
```

This is because of the fact that we are 'altering' an existing stored procedure and ALTER PROCEDURE is the SQL statement that alters an existing stored procedure.

If you don't have a copy of Visual Studio .NET Professional, you won't be able to perform this example in the same way. If you're using Visual C# Standard Edition, you need to open up the query window as described in Chapter 3, enter the code into the query window, and hit the ! button. Let's walk through it briefly to recap the procedure. Note that although this is the only way to perform this task in Visual C#.NET Standard Edition, exactly the same procedure can be followed if you own the full version of Visual Studio, so we'll refer to Visual Studio .NET in this example in the inclusive context.

Try It Out: Creating a Stored Procedure from the Visual Studio .NET SQL Window

1. Open up the Server Explorer and open up a connection to our Northwind database.

2. Double-click on one of the tables, for example, the Employees table. Once the data grid of information is displayed, click the SQL button on the toolbar.

3. Enter our SQL code into the SQL pane:

```
CREATE PROCEDURE sp_Select_AllEmployees AS
   SELECT EmployeeId,LastName
   FROM
   Employees
RETURN
```

4. Click the ! button to execute the statement, and a new stored procedure is created. We get a small confirmation dialog to confirm this.

How It Works

Don't believe the dialog box? No problem – take a look at the Server Explorer. Our new Stored Procedure should appear within the tree as shown overleaf:

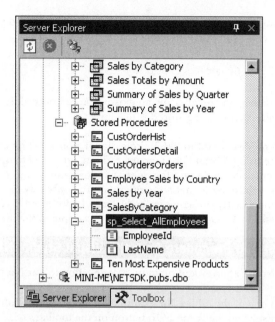

Notice that the two inputs to the stored procedure are shown as items within the Stored Procedure node in the Server Explorer.

For each of the other stored procedures we create in this chapter, if you don't have a full Visual Studio .NET installation, you will need to duplicate these steps for each SQL script to create our stored procedures, as the code in the later examples depends on them.

Let's move on to look at some more stored procedures.

Try It Out: Creating and Executing a Stored Procedure with RETURN values

In this example we will write a stored procedure that returns a value of 1 if the number of orders is greater than 100 and returns a value of 2 when the number of orders is less than 100. An application calling this stored procedure would then take the RETURN value and give out an appropriate message to the user. Follow the steps outlined below:

1. Create a stored procedure that looks like the one shown below:

```
CREATE PROCEDURE sp_Orders_MoreThan100 AS
  DECLARE @Orders int
  SELECT @Orders=count(*)
  FROM Orders

  IF @Orders > 100
    RETURN 1
  ELSE
    RETURN 2
```

2. Run the stored procedure and notice that, since there are 830 orders in the `Orders` table, the return value is 1, as shown below. If you are using Query Analyzer, you will need to use the following code:

```
DECLARE @Ret int
EXEC @Ret = sp_Orders_MoreThan100
SELECT @Ret
```

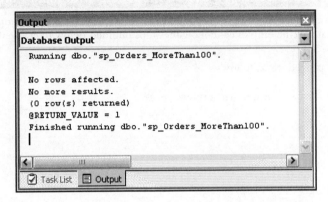

How It Works

We begin by creating a stored procedure called `sp_Orders_MoreThan100`:

```
CREATE PROCEDURE sp_Orders_MoreThan100 AS
```

As per the problem statement, this procedure will return 1 if the number of orders is greater than 100 and 2 otherwise. Then we declare a variable called `@Orders` to hold the number of orders. In T-SQL, which is the Microsoft version of SQL that is integrated into MSDE/SQL-Server, variables are declared beginning with an ampersand `'@'`:

```
DECLARE @Orders int
```

Then we assign a value to the `@Orders` variable by using the `count(*)` function:

```
SELECT @Orders=count(*)
FROM Orders
```

Finally we write a simple `IF` statement that will return 1 if the value of the variable `@Orders` is greater than 100 and will return 2 if the value is less than 100:

```
IF @Orders > 100
  RETURN 1
ELSE
  RETURN 2
```

When the stored procedure is executed, a value of 1 is returned as shown in the output. As we can see from this example, return values are very useful. A program written in C# can capture this return value and inform the user that there are more than 100 orders in the database.

Now let us now look at a stored procedure that accepts an input parameter. Stored procedures that take an input parameter are very useful to restrict the rows that are returned.

Try It Out: Creating and Executing a Stored Procedure with Input Parameters

In the following example, the stored procedure takes in an employee number as input and returns a list of orders placed by that specific employee. Follow the steps outlined below to create the stored procedure:

1. Create the procedure as follows:

```
CREATE PROCEDURE sp_Orders_ByEmployeeId
(
    @EmployeeID int
)
AS
    SELECT OrderId,OrderDate
    FROM Orders
    WHERE EmployeeId=@EmployeeID
RETURN
```

2. Save it and run the procedure. Since it requires an `EmployeeId` as the input parameter, it will prompt you for the input as shown below:

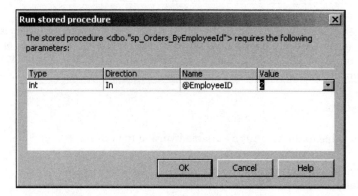

Observe the columns in the screenshot above. The name of the input parameter and its type are shown. The direction is shown as In meaning that the parameter is an input parameter. In the value column, type in a value of 2 and click OK

The stored procedure will run and return the following result.

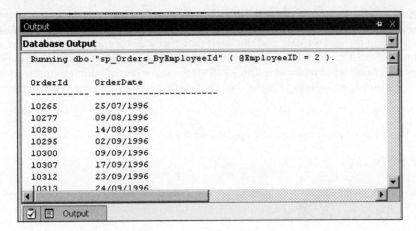

The screenshot above shows the name of the stored procedure we are executing and the input parameter we supplied, which is 2. Since we selected the `OrderId` and `OrderDate` columns, they are shown as well.

How It Works

When we create the stored procedure, this time, we specify the input parameter. The `@EmployeeId int` specifies that the name of the input parameter is `@EmployeeId` and its data type is `int`. By default, all parameters of a stored procedure are input parameters if they are not specified explicitly as output parameters:

```
CREATE PROCEDURE sp_Orders_ByEmployeeId
(
    @EmployeeID int
)
AS
```

In the body of the procedure, we simply use the `WHERE` clause to list all the orders placed by the employee whose ID was supplied to the procedure:

```
SELECT OrderId, OrderDate
FROM Orders
WHERE EmployeeId=@EmployeeID
RETURN
```

Several input parameters can be specified to a stored procedure. These inputs can be of any data type as long as they are valid.

Earlier, we used the `RETURN` statement to return a single numeric value. What if we want to return more than one value, or even return a numeric and a character value back? The `OUTPUT` parameter is used for this purpose. Stored procedures that return values using `OUTPUT` parameters are very useful in applications where several pieces of information need to be retrieved from the database but the information is not related, or obtaining the information in a resultset is an overkill.

Try It Out: Executing a Stored Procedure with Input and Output Parameters

Say we want to find the earliest date and the latest date that a given employee placed an order, as indicated by the `OrderDate` column in the `Orders` table. We could write a stored procedure that takes an `EmployeeId` as an input parameter and `RETURN` the dates in two output parameters in a `SELECT` statement. But instead, we will retrieve the dates in two `OUTPUT` parameters. Follow the steps outlined below:

1. Create a stored procedure called `sp_Dates_ByEmployeeId` as shown below:

```
CREATE PROCEDURE sp_Dates_ByEmployeeId
(
  @EmployeeID int ,
  @EDate datetime OUTPUT,
  @LDate datetime OUTPUT
)
AS
  SELECT @EDate=Min(OrderDate)
  FROM Orders
  WHERE EmployeeId=@EmployeeID

  SELECT @LDate=Max(OrderDate)
  FROM Orders
  WHERE EmployeeId=@EmployeeID
RETURN
```

2. Save and run the stored procedure. You will be prompted to supply the input parameter.

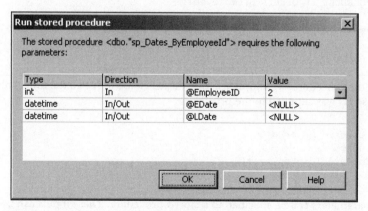

3. Type in 2 as the `EmployeeID` and set the other values to `<NULL>`. Click **OK** and the stored procedure will execute and return the earliest and the latest dates as shown:

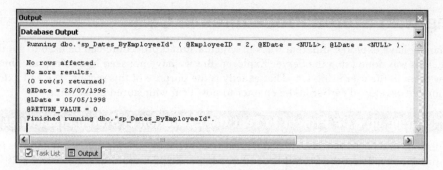

```
Output                                                                          ×
Database Output                                                                 ▼
  Running dbo."sp_Dates_ByEmployeeId" ( @EmployeeID = 2, @EDate = <NULL>, @LDate = <NULL> ). ▲

  No rows affected.
  No more results.
  (0 row(s) returned)
  @EDate = 25/07/1996
  @LDate = 05/05/1998
  @RETURN_VALUE = 0
  Finished running dbo."sp_Dates_ByEmployeeId".
  |
  ◄                          III                          ►                    ▼
  ☑ Task List  ▤ Output
```

Interestingly, the above screenshot shows the name of the stored procedure we are executing, which is sp_Dates_ByEmployeeId, and the value of the input parameter we supplied, which is 2. The @Edate and @Ldate output parameters were retrieved and their values are listed as 7/25/1996 and 5/5/1998 respectively.

How It Works

We created the stored procedure by specifying the @EmployeeId as the input parameter of type int. Then we specify the @Edate as a datetime parameter and qualify it with the OUTPUT keyword to indicate that this is an output parameter. This parameter will hold the order date of the earliest order that this employee has placed. Similarly, @LDate is specified as an output parameter to hold the order date of the latest order that this employee has placed.

```
CREATE PROCEDURE sp_Dates_ByEmployeeId
(
  @EmployeeID int,
  @EDate datetime OUTPUT,
  @LDate datetime OUTPUT
)
AS
```

In the body of the procedure, we assign values to the output parameters by using the Min and Max query functions on the OrderDate column. When we are done, we use the RETURN statement to return a value of 0 to the calling program.

```
SELECT @EDate=Min(OrderDate)
FROM Orders
WHERE EmployeeId=@EmployeeID

SELECT @LDate=Max(OrderDate)
FROM Orders
WHERE EmployeeId=@EmployeeID
RETURN
```

In this example, two output values were returned. In a more complex problem, several input parameters can be supplied to a stored procedure and several output parameters can be returned along with a RETURN value other than zero, and also a resultset.

375

Working with Stored Procedures in C#

OK, so far we have explored different ways in which a stored procedure can be used to get the data that we want. This was done using the Server Explorer. But we have not seen how to capture these results and show them to the user using C#. That exactly is the purpose of this section. We will extend the application we developed earlier in the chapter to now deal with stored procedures.

Try It Out: Setting up a C# Project to Test the Execution of Stored Procedures

1. Earlier in this chapter, we created a form with two tabs, one for views and another for stored procedures. Select the Stored Procedures tab and add buttons, textboxes and a listview as shown below.

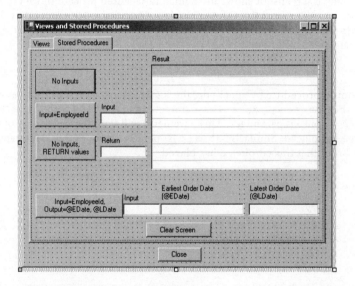

The controls are named as follows:

Control	Name	Remarks
A label captioned Result	Default name	
A listview	LvwRS	To display the results when some buttons in this tab are clicked. Set the GridLines property to True and View property to Details.
A command button captioned No-Inputs	cmdNoInput	To test the execution of a stored procedure without any input parameters.

Control	Name	Remarks
A command button captioned Input=EmployeeId	`cmdInput`	To test the execution of a stored procedure by supplying one input parameter.
A label captioned Input	Default name	
A textbox below the label	`txtEmpId1`	To supply the `EmployeeId` as input.
A command button captioned No-Inputs, RETURN values	`CmdReturn`	To test the execution of a stored procedure that returns values using the `RETURN` statement.
A label captioned Return	Default name	
A textbox below the label	`txtReturn`	To display the `RETURN` value.
A command button captioned Input=EmployeeId, Output= @Edate, @Ldate	`cmdOutput`	To test the execution of a stored procedure that takes in one input parameter and gives back our two output parameters.
A label captioned Input	Default name	
A textbox below the label	`txtEmpId2`	To supply the input.
A label captioned Earliest Order Date @EDate	Default name	
A textbox below the label	`txtEDate`	To display the output.
A label captioned Latest Order Date @Ldate	Default name	
A textbox below the label	`txtLDate`	To display the output.
A command button captioned Clear Screen	`cmdClear`	To clear the listview and textboxes to prepare for the next execution.
A command button captioned Close	`cmdClose`	To close the form.

2. Without any code behind the buttons, build and run the solution. Make sure all the controls are properly set up as per the table above.

Now let us try to execute the stored procedures one at a time and see how to handle each scenario.

Try It Out: Executing a Stored Procedure with No Input Parameters from C#

Previously in this chapter, we created a stored procedure called `sp_Select_AllEmployees`, which takes no input, and returns a list of all employees. We want to write code behind the `cmdNoInput` button to execute this stored procedure and display the results in the listview to the right.

1. Write code for the `cmdNoInput_Click()` event as follows:

```csharp
private void cmdNoInput_Click(object sender, System.EventArgs e)
{
  try
  {
    //Clear the listview column header and items
    lvwRS.Columns.Clear() ;
    lvwRS.Items.Clear();

    //Create a connection
    SqlConnection cn = new SqlConnection(@"Data Source=(local)\NETSDK;" +
      "Integrated Security=SSPI;database=Northwind");

    //Create a command object
    SqlCommand cmd= cn.CreateCommand();

    //Specify the stored procedure that is to be executed
    cmd.CommandType= CommandType.StoredProcedure;
    cmd.CommandText="sp_Select_AllEmployees";

    //Open the connection
    cn.Open();

    //Create a datareader object
    SqlDataReader dr=cmd.ExecuteReader();

    //Get colummn names of the datareader and show in the listview's columns

    for (int i=0; i< dr.FieldCount; i++)
    {
      ColumnHeader c = new ColumnHeader();
      c.Text=dr.GetName(i);
      lvwRS.Columns.Add(c);
    }

    //Get values of each row in the datareader and show them in the list view
    ListViewItem itmX;
    while (dr.Read())
    {
      //create the list view item
      itmX=new ListViewItem();

      //specify the text and subitems of listview
      itmX.Text= dr.GetValue(0).ToString();
      for (int i=1 ; i< dr.FieldCount; i++)
```

```
        {
          itmX.SubItems.Add(dr.GetValue(i).ToString());
        }

        //Add the item to the list view's Items collection
        lvwRS.Items.Add(itmX);
    }

    //close the reader and connection
    dr.Close();
    cn.Close();
}
catch ( System.Data.SqlClient.SqlException  e1)
{
    // Display the error message.
    MessageBox.Show ("There was an error in executing the SQL Command." +
        "Error Message:" + e1.Message);
}
}
```

2. Build and run the solution. Click on the **No-Inputs** button and see the results displayed in the listview as shown below:

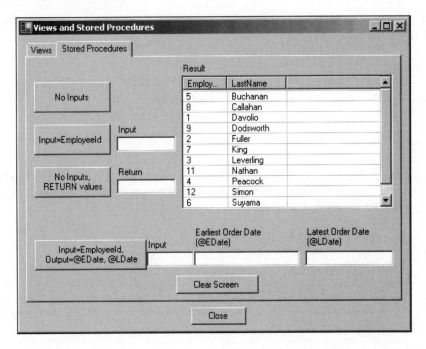

How It Works

The code shown above contains a portion where the rows of a `DataReader` object are read and displayed in a listview. This portion has already been described in Chapter 13 and so will not be described here. The section of code that is relevant to executing the stored procedure alone will be explained.

We establish a connection to the database using the following statement:

```
//Create a connection
SqlConnection cn = new SqlConnection("Data Source=(local)\NETSDK;" +
  "Integrated Security=SSPI;database=Northwind";
```

Then we create a command object using the `CreateCommand` method of the `Connection` object:

```
//Create a command object
SqlCommand cmd= cn.CreateCommand();
```

The command object's command type is given as a stored procedure by the following statement:

```
//Specify the stored procedure that is to be executed
cmd.CommandType= CommandType.StoredProcedure;
```

The actual stored procedure that is to be executed is specified in the `CommandText` property of the command object:

```
cmd.CommandText="sp_Select_AllEmployees";
```

The connection is then opened using the `Open()` method:

```
//Open the connection
cn.Open();
```

Finally we call the `ExecuteReader` method of the command object. This method will return a `DataReader` object that is stored in a variable called `dr`. Later in the code, the rows and columns in this `DataReader` are read and displayed:

```
//Create a datareader object
SqlDataReader dr=cmd.ExecuteReader();
```

Notice that we use the `ExecuteReader` method of the command object because we know that this stored procedure will return a resultset. Not all stored procedures will return a resultset – some will return just a return value or just one output value. In those cases, as we will see later, we must use other methods of the command object.

To demonstrate, let's see how to supply the `EmployeeId` as the parameter and get a list of `Orders` placed by this employee.

Try It Out: Executing a Stored Procedure with One Input Parameter from C#

We will use the sp_Orders_ByEmployeeId stored procedure that we created earlier by supplying the EmployeeId input from a textbox and display the results in the list view.

1. Write code for the cmdInput_Click() event as follows:

```
private void cmdInput_Click(object sender, System.EventArgs e)
{
  try
  {
    //clear the list view
    lvwRS.Columns.Clear();
    lvwRS.Items.Clear();

    //Create a connection
    SqlConnection cn = new SqlConnection(@"Data Source=(local)\NETSDK;" +
      "Integrated Security=SSPI;database=Northwind");

    //Create a command object
    SqlCommand cmd= cn.CreateCommand();

    //Specify the stored procedure that is to be executed
    cmd.CommandType= CommandType.StoredProcedure;
    cmd.CommandText="sp_Orders_ByEmployeeId";

    //Create a parameter object to provide the input
    SqlParameter parInput = cmd.Parameters.Add("@EmployeeId", SqlDbType.Int);
    parInput.Direction = ParameterDirection.Input;
    parInput.Value= Convert.ToInt32(txtEmpId1.Text);

    //Open the connection
    cn.Open();

    //execute the command and display the results
    //Create a datareader object
    SqlDataReader dr=cmd.ExecuteReader();

    //Get the column names of the datareader and show in the listview's columns

    for (int i=0; i< dr.FieldCount; i++)
    {
      ColumnHeader c = new ColumnHeader();
      c.Text=dr.GetName(i);
      lvwRS.Columns.Add(c);
    }
    //Get the values of each row in the datareader and show them in the list view
    ListViewItem itmX;
    while (dr.Read())
    {
      //create the list view item
```

```
        itmX=new ListViewItem();
        //specify the text and subitems of the list view
         itmX.Text= dr.GetValue(0).ToString();
        for (int i=1 ; i< dr.FieldCount; i++)
        {
           itmX.SubItems.Add(dr.GetValue(i).ToString());
        }
        //Add the item to the list view's Items collection
        lvwRS.Items.Add(itmX);

    }
    //close the reader
    dr.Close();
    cn.Close();
}
catch ( System.Data.SqlClient.SqlException  e1)
{
   // Display the error message.
   MessageBox.Show ("There was an error in executing the SQL Command." +
                  "Error Message:" + e1.Message);
}
}
```

2. Now, build and run the solution. In the Input textbox type in 2 to get the list of all orders placed by Employee with ID=2. Click on the button captioned Input=EmployeeId and observe the results as shown below:

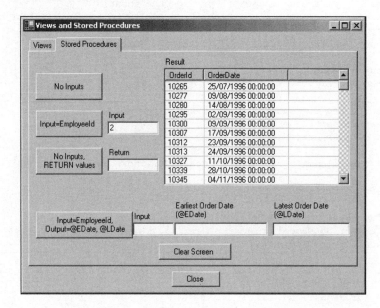

You can now experiment supplying different values for the employee IDs and observe the results.

How It Works

In this example, a `DataReader` object is returned much like in the one we saw before. The difference is that the `EmployeeId` is passed in as a parameter.

We create a command object as before using the `CreateCommand` method:

```
//Create a command object
SqlCommand cmd = cn.CreateCommand();
```

Then we specify the command type to be a stored procedure as well as the name of the stored procedure in the command text property:

```
//Specify the stored procedure that is to be executed
cmd.CommandType= CommandType.StoredProcedure;
cmd.CommandText="sp_Orders_ByEmployeeId";
```

Now we specify the `EmployeeId` as the input parameter. To do this we first create a variable called `parInput` that is of type `SqlParameter`. The command object has a collection called `Parameters`. Each parameter in this collection is of the `SqlParameter` type. We add a parameter to the collection using the following code:

```
cmd.Parameters.Add("@EmployeeId", SqlDbType.Int);
```

The input parameter of a stored procedure is given as the `Add` function's first argument and the type of the parameter is specified as the second argument. In this case `@EmployeeId` is the input parameter and the data type is specified as `SqlDbType.Int`. When this parameter is added to the collection, a `SqlParameter` object is returned:

```
SqlParameter parInput = cmd.Parameters.Add("@EmployeeId", SqlDbType.Int);
```

We have seen before that the arguments to a stored procedure can be input arguments or output arguments. We specify the direction of the `SqlParameter` object `parInput` by using one of the values of the `ParameterDirection` enum:

```
parInput.Direction = ParameterDirection.Input;
```

The `ParameterDirection` enum can take four values: `Input`, `Output`, `InputOutput`, and `ReturnValue`. The `Input` value is for specifying the input parameters, the `Output` value is for specifying output parameters, and the `ReturnValue` is for specifying `RETURN` values as is evident from their names. The `InputOutput` value of the `Direction` enum is used to specify parameters that can be used to feed in input parameters and at the same time are also used as output parameters.

Then we supply a value to the parameter. The `EmployeeID` typed in the `txtEmpId1` text box is taken and converted to an integer and then given to the `Value` property of the `SqlParameter` object:

```
parInput.Value= Convert.ToInt32(txtEmpId1.Text);
```

Finally, we open the connection and call the `ExecuteReader` method to get the resultset.

```
//Open the connection
cn.Open();

//execute the command and display the results
//Create a datareader object
SqlDataReader dr=cmd.ExecuteReader();
```

Let's summarize what we have done here briefly. To specify inputs to a stored procedure, we used the `SqlParameter` object, specified the direction as `Input`, and supplied a value to the parameter from the form. Then we called the `ExecuteReader()` method to get the resultset and displayed its contents in the listview.

Now let's see how to catch the `RETURN` value from stored procedures and handle it in C#. As mentioned before, these values are very useful in giving out messages to users so that they can take appropriate action.

Try It Out: Executing a Stored Procedure and Capturing its RETURN Value

Earlier in this chapter we created a stored procedure called `sp_Orders_MoreThan100` that returns a value using the `RETURN` statement. Let us capture this return value from C# and see how to use it.

1. Write code behind the `cmdReturn_Click()` event as follows:

```
private void cmdReturn_Click(object sender, System.EventArgs e)
{
  try
  {
    //Create a connection
    SqlConnection cn = new SqlConnection(@"Data Source=(local)\NETSDK;" +
      "Integrated Security=SSPI;database=Northwind");

    //Create a command object
    SqlCommand cmd= cn.CreateCommand();

    //Specify the stored procedure that is to be executed
    cmd.CommandType= CommandType.StoredProcedure;
    cmd.CommandText="sp_Orders_MoreThan100";

    //Create a parameter object to provide the input
    SqlParameter parReturn = cmd.Parameters.Add("ReturnValue", SqlDbType.Int);
    parReturn.Direction = ParameterDirection.ReturnValue ;

    //Open the connection
    cn.Open();

    //execute the command and display the results
    cmd.ExecuteScalar();
```

```
            txtReturn.Text= Convert.ToString(cmd.Parameters["ReturnValue"].Value);

            cn.Close();
    }
    catch ( System.Data.SqlClient.SqlException  e1)
    {
        // Display the error message.
        MessageBox.Show ("There was an error in executing the SQL Command. " +
            "Error Message:" + e1.Message);
    }
}
```

2. Build and run the solution. Click on the command button captioned No-Inputs, RETURN values and observe that a value of 1 is displayed in the textbox adjacent to the button as shown below. Remember that this stored procedure returns 1 if there are more than 100 orders placed.

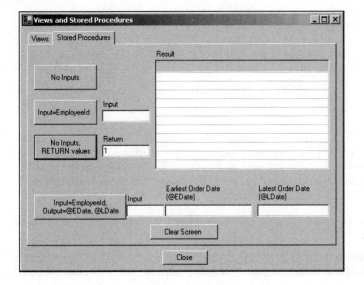

How It Works

In this case, since we are capturing the RETURN value from the stored procedure, our code will be different from the examples we have seen so far. We create the command object and specify the stored procedure name:

```
//Create a command object
SqlCommand cmd= cn.CreateCommand();

//Specify the stored procedure that is to be executed
cmd.CommandType= CommandType.StoredProcedure;
cmd.CommandText="sp_Orders_MoreThan100";
```

385

Then we create a parameter object called `parReturn` by adding an item to the `Parameter` collection. Returned values from stored procedures are considered as `ReturnValue` parameters – that is, they are neither input nor output parameters, but are identified as return value parameters by the `ReturnValue` argument of the `Add` method. The type of the return value is `int` (specified by `SqlDbType.Int`).

```
//Create a parameter object to provide the input
SqlParameter parReturn = cmd.Parameters.Add("ReturnValue", SqlDbType.Int);
```

The direction of the return value from a stored procedure is specified as `ReturnValue` of the `ParameterDirection` enumeration:

```
parReturn.Direction = ParameterDirection.ReturnValue;
```

Now that we have specified the parameter that will hold the return value, we can execute the stored procedure. Since this stored procedure will return only one value, we use the `ExecuteScalar()` method of the command object:

```
//execute the command and display the results
cmd.ExecuteScalar();
```

The return value from the stored procedure will be held in the value property of the `SqlParameter` object `parReturn`. This value is converted to a string and displayed in a textbox as well as a message box:

```
txtReturn.Text= Convert.ToString(parReturn.Value) ;
```

Stored procedures are commonly used to `INSERT`, `UPDATE`, or `DELETE` information. In these stored procedures we can check for a certain condition that would make it necessary to abort the inserts, updates, or deletes and inform the user of the reason for the failure to execute. In such cases we can use the `RETURN` statement in the stored procedure to inform the calling program of the reason, and the program can in turn give out specific messages based on the `RETURN` value.

Now let's look at a scenario where a stored procedure takes in an input, and outputs values back to the calling program.

Try It Out: Executing a Stored Procedure with Input and Output Parameters

Let us execute the `sp_Dates_ByEmployeeId` stored procedure that we developed earlier from C# and display the earliest and the latest dates of the orders placed by an employee.

1. Begin by writing code behind the `cmdOutput_Click()` event as follows:

```
private void cmdOutput_Click(object sender, System.EventArgs e)
{
  try
  {
    //Create a connection
    SqlConnection cn = new SqlConnection(@"Data Source=(local)\NETSDK;" +
      "Integrated Security=SSPI;database=Northwind");

    //Create a command object
```

```
SqlCommand cmd= cn.CreateCommand();

//Specify the stored procedure that is to be executed
cmd.CommandType= CommandType.StoredProcedure;
cmd.CommandText="sp_Dates_ByEmployeeId";

//Create a parameter object to provide the input
SqlParameter parInput = cmd.Parameters.Add("@EmployeeId", SqlDbType.Int);
parInput.Direction = ParameterDirection.Input;
parInput.Value= Convert.ToInt32(txtEmpId2.Text);

//Create two parameters to hold the outputs
SqlParameter parOutput1 = cmd.Parameters.Add("@EDate",SqlDbType.DateTime);
parOutput1.Direction = ParameterDirection.Output ;
SqlParameter parOutput2 = cmd.Parameters.Add("@LDate",SqlDbType.DateTime);
parOutput2.Direction = ParameterDirection.Output ;

//Open the connection
cn.Open();

//execute the command and display the results
cmd.ExecuteNonQuery() ;
txtEDate.Text= Convert.ToString(parOutput1.Value);
txtLDate.Text =Convert.ToString(parOutput2.Value);
cn.Close();
}
catch ( System.Data.SqlClient.SqlException  e1)
{
    // Display the error message.
    MessageBox.Show ("There was an error in executing the SQL Command. " +
      "Error Message:" + e1.Message);
}
}
```

2. Build and run the Solution. Specify an `EmployeeId` of 3 in the `Input` textbox and click on the button. Observe that the earliest date and latest date of orders entered by the employee are then displayed as shown below:

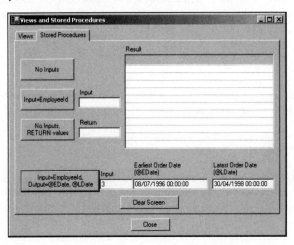

In order to play around a bit, you can specify a different `EmployeeId` and observe the results.

How It Works

We specify `sp_Dates_ByEmployeeId` as the stored procedure in the command object:

```
//Create a command object
SqlCommand cmd= cn.CreateCommand();

//Specify the stored procedure that is to be executed
cmd.CommandType= CommandType.StoredProcedure;
cmd.CommandText="sp_Dates_ByEmployeeId";
```

We create an input parameter object for `@EmployeeId` of type `Int` and specify its direction and value:

```
//Create a parameter object to provide the input
SqlParameter parInput = cmd.Parameters.Add("@EmployeeId", SqlDbType.Int);
parInput.Direction = ParameterDirection.Input;
parInput.Value= Convert.ToInt32(txtEmpId2.Text);
```

Then we create two output parameters to hold the earliest and latest dates. We call them `parOutput1` and `parOutput2` and specify their arguments as `@Edate` and `@Ldate` respectively (as in the stored procedure) and specify their direction as `Output`.

```
//Create two parameters to hold the outputs
SqlParameter parOutput1 = cmd.Parameters.Add("@EDate", SqlDbType.DateTime );
parOutput1.Direction = ParameterDirection.Output ;

SqlParameter parOutput2 = cmd.Parameters.Add("@LDate", SqlDbType.DateTime );
parOutput2.Direction = ParameterDirection.Output ;

//Open the connection
cn.Open();
```

Now that we have specified the input and output parameters, we can execute the stored procedure. But since this stored procedure does not return a resultset, we don't use the `ExecuteReader()` method, and since it does not return only one value, we don't use the `ExecuteScalar()` method either. We use the `ExecuteNonQuery` to execute the stored procedure, like this:

```
//execute the command and display the results
cmd.ExecuteNonQuery() ;
```

After the execution, the earliest dates and latest dates are retrieved from the `Value` property of the output parameters and shown in textboxes:

```
txtEDate.Text= Convert.ToString(parOutput1.Value);
txtLDate.Text =Convert.ToString(parOutput2.Value) ;
```

That's it as far as working with stored procedures goes. Of course, we could have spent hundreds of pages covering all the nuances involved in using stored procedures, but if you want to learn about them further, then you might want to read *Beginning SQL Programming,* Wrox Press, 1-86100-180-0.

Summary

In the first half of this chapter we learned about Views and Stored Procedures. First we discussed what views are and how they are useful in retrieving data based on a query without having to load up and execute the query. Then we learned how to create views from the Server Explorer as well as from C#. Following this, we saw how to write queries and use the view objects as tables.

In the second half, we learned how to create and execute different types of stored procedures (without parameters, with input parameters, with input and output parameters, and with return values). We also saw how and when to use the `ExecuteReader()`, `ExecuteScalar()`, and `ExecuteNonQuery()` methods when dealing with stored procedures. To finish off, we experimented with stored procedures in the context of the Northwind database with the help of the application developed at the beginning of the chapter.

Exercises

1. Write a SQL statement to create a view called `ProductsOrdered` that shows all the `OrderId`, `ProductId`, and `ProductName` for all the orders entered.

2. Run the application developed in this chapter and create the view constructed above. Then, write a query that will select all the records from the view for `ProductId=18` only.

3. Write a stored procedure called `sp_OrderValue` that does the following:

❑   Returns 1 if the value of all orders is less than 1,000

❑   Returns 2 if the value of all orders is between 1,000 and 5,000

❑   Returns 3 if the value of all orders is more than 5,000

Note: Value of an order is Qty*UnitPrice

4. Execute the stored procedure created in Exercise 3 in the application that was developed in this chapter. Capture the return value and show it to the user.

5. Create a stored procedure called `sp_ProductId` that accepts a `ProductId` as input and returns all the orders placed for this product. If no value is supplied to the stored procedure, it should output all the orders for `ProductId=17`.

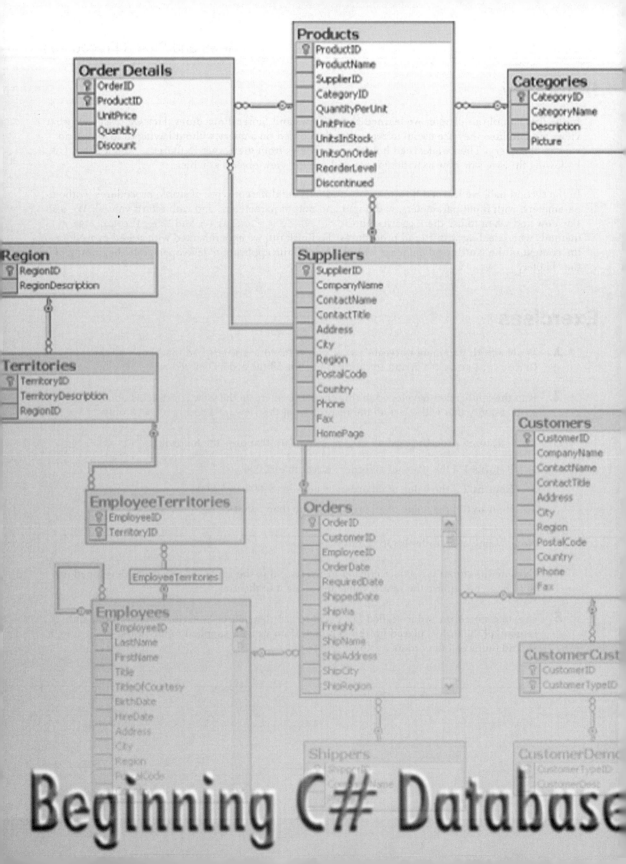

Order Details
- OrderID
- ProductID
- UnitPrice
- Quantity
- Discount

Products
- ProductID
- ProductName
- SupplierID
- CategoryID
- QuantityPerUnit
- UnitPrice
- UnitsInStock
- UnitsOnOrder
- ReorderLevel
- Discontinued

Categories
- CategoryID
- CategoryName
- Description
- Picture

Region
- RegionID
- RegionDescription

Suppliers
- SupplierID
- CompanyName
- ContactName
- ContactTitle
- Address
- City
- Region
- PostalCode
- Country
- Phone
- Fax
- HomePage

Customers
- CustomerID
- CompanyName
- ContactName
- ContactTitle
- Address
- City
- Region
- PostalCode
- Country
- Phone
- Fax

Territories
- TerritoryID
- TerritoryDescription
- RegionID

EmployeeTerritories
- EmployeeID
- TerritoryID

EmployeeTerritories

Orders
- OrderID
- CustomerID
- EmployeeID
- OrderDate
- RequiredDate
- ShippedDate
- ShipVia
- Freight
- ShipName
- ShipAddress
- ShipCity
- ShipRegion

Employees
- EmployeeID
- LastName
- FirstName
- Title
- TitleOfCourtesy
- BirthDate
- HireDate
- Address
- City
- Region
- PostalCode

CustomerCust
- CustomerID
- CustomerTypeID

Shippers
- ShipperID

CustomerDemo
- CustomerTypeID
- CustomerDesc

Beginning C# Database

Indexes and Constraints

Applying indexes and constraints to tables in a database has many advantages to offer. When used properly, indexes improve the performance of database queries, while constraints enforce rules during data modifications and help to ensure data integrity. Recall that we first worked with constraints in Chapter 12; we'll be building on that work here.

In particular, we'll be looking at the following areas in this chapter:

❑   The advantages and disadvantages of indexing

❑   Choosing the best columns and data types to index for various queries

❑   Clustered and non-clustered indexes

❑   Using constraints to maintain database integrity

❑   Understanding UNIQUE, CHECK, DEFAULT, and nullability constraints

Throughout the chapter, we will provide example scripts and screenshots to demonstrate the topics under discussion. The queries presented in this chapter can be executed inside the example application developed in Chapters 12 and 13.

Indexes

Relational databases use indexes to find data quickly when a query is processed. Although you may not have noticed it from the simple queries on the Northwind database in the previous chapter, each query takes some time for the database to run and return the correct results. This delay is more noticeable when running several complex queries against larger tables of data.

> **Creating and removing indexes from a database schema will rarely result in changes to an application's code; indexes operate 'behind the scenes' in support of the database engine. However, creating the proper index can drastically increase the performance of an application.**

A database engine uses a database index in much the same way as a reader uses a book index. For example, if we wanted to find all references to INSERT statements in this book, we could begin on page one and scan each page of the book, marking each time the word is found until we reach the end of the book. This approach is pretty time consuming and laborious. Alternately, we can also use the index in the back of the book to find a page number for each occurrence of an INSERT statement. This approach produces the same results as above, but with tremendous savings in time.

When a database has no index to use for searching, the result is similar to the reader who looks at every page in a book to find a word: the database engine needs to visit every row in a table. In database terminology, we call this behavior a **table scan,** or just a scan. A table scan is not always a problem, and is sometimes unavoidable. However, as a table grows to thousands or even millions of rows, scans become correspondingly slower and more expensive.

The following query on the Products table of the Northwind database retrieves products in a specific price range:

```
SELECT ProductID, ProductName, UnitPrice
FROM Products
WHERE (UnitPrice > 12.5) AND (UnitPrice < 14)
```

There is currently no index on the Product table to help this query, so the database engine performs a scan and examines each record to see if UnitPrice falls between 12.5 and 14. In the diagram below, the database search touches a total of 77 records to find just three matches:

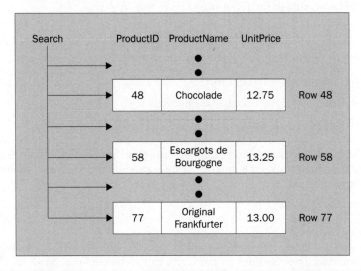

Suppose we created an index on the data in the UnitPrice column. Each index entry would contain a *copy of the UnitPrice value* for a row, and a *reference to the row* where the value originated (just like a page number). The database sorts these index entries into ascending order, creating an index that allows the database to quickly narrow in on the three rows to satisfy the query, and thus avoid scanning every row in the table.

In the Try It Out *sections of this chapter, we will introduce some of the features only available in the Architect and Professional versions of Visual Studio .NET. For owners of the Visual Studio .NET Standard Edition, we will also present the corresponding SQL statements that we can run to produce the same results.*

Try It Out: Creating a Simple Index

Having a data connection in the Server Explorer view of Visual Studio .NET allows us to easily create new indexes:

1. Navigate to the `Products` table of the Northwind database.

2. Right-click the table and select **Design Table** from the context menu.

3. With the design screen in focus, click the **Indexes/Keys** item on the **View** menu of the IDE. This should bring you to the following tabbed dialog box:

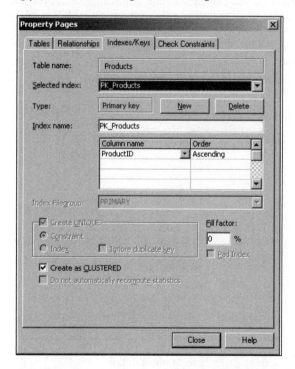

The dialog is currently displaying an existing index on the `Products` table: the **PK_Products** index. Later in this chapter, we'll see how primary key fields are automatically indexed to enforce the uniqueness of key values.

4. In the above dialog, click on the **New** button and in the **Index name** textbox, replace the existing entry with `IDX_UnitPrice`.

5. Beneath the textbox is a control where we set the columns to index. Pull down the entry with `ProductID` and select the `UnitPrice` column instead. Leave all of the other options with default settings.

6. Close the dialog and the table design view, making sure to save all changes when prompted to do so. The IDE will then issue the commands to create the new index.

We can create the same index using the application from Chapter 13 with the following SQL:

```
CREATE INDEX [IDX_UnitPrice] ON Products (UnitPrice)
```

The command specifies the name of the index (`IDX_UnitPrice`), the table name (`Products`), and the column to index (`UnitPrice`).

How It Works

To verify the index is created, you can execute the following stored procedure using the application from Chapter 13 to see a list of all indexes on the `Products` table:

```
EXEC sp_helpindex Products
```

The `IDX_UnitPrice` index should appear in the list as shown below:

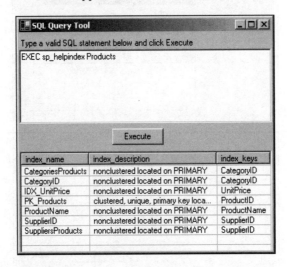

Let's take a look at what is happening here in more detail.

The database takes the columns specified in a `CREATE INDEX` command and sorts the values into a special data structure known as a **B-tree**. A B-tree structure supports fast searches with a minimum amount of disk reads, allowing the database engine to quickly find the starting and stopping points for the query we are using.

Conceptually, we may think of an index as shown in the diagram below. On the left, each index entry contains the **index key** (UnitPrice). Each entry also includes a reference, which points to the table rows that share the particular value. We can then can retrieve the required information from these rows.

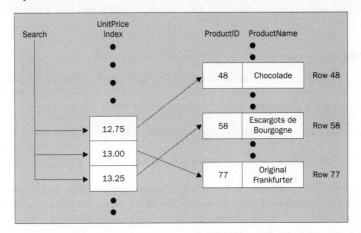

The database can quickly narrow down to a minimum the number of records it must examine using the sorted list of UnitPrice values stored in the index. This avoids a lengthy table scan to fetch the query results.

Given this sketch of how indexes work, let's now examine some of the scenarios where indexes can offer a benefit.

Taking Advantage of Indexes

The database engine can use indexes to boost performance in a number of different queries. Sometimes these performance improvements are dramatic. An important feature of SQL Server 2000 is a component known as the **query optimizer**. The query optimizer's job is to find the fastest and least resource-intensive means of executing incoming queries. An important part of this job is selecting the best index or indexes to perform the task. In the following sections, we will examine the types of queries that have the best chance of benefiting from an index.

Searching for Records

The most obvious use for an index is to find a record or set of records matching a WHERE clause. If we have an index ordered on the values in a particular column, then it can aid queries looking for results with values for this column inside of a range (as we demonstrated earlier), as well as queries looking for a specific value.

For example, the following queries can all benefit from an index on UnitPrice:

```
DELETE FROM Products WHERE UnitPrice = 1
```

```
UPDATE Products SET Discontinued = 1
WHERE UnitPrice > 15
```

```
SELECT * FROM PRODUCTS
WHERE UnitPrice BETWEEN 14 AND 16
```

Indexes work just as well when searching for a record in DELETE and UPDATE commands as they do for SELECT statements.

Sorting Records

When we ask for a sorted resultset, the database will try to find an index and avoid sorting the results during execution of the query. We control sorting of a resultset by specifying a field, or fields, in an ORDER BY clause, with the sort order as ASC (ascending) or DESC (descending).

For example, the following query returns all products sorted by price:

```
SELECT * FROM Products ORDER BY UnitPrice ASC
```

With no index, the database will scan the Products table and sort the rows to process the query. However, the index we created on UnitPrice in the *Try It Out* example above provides the database with a presorted list of prices. The database can now simply scan the index from the first entry to the last entry and retrieve the rows in sorted order.

The same index works equally well with the following query, simply by scanning the index in reverse:

```
SELECT * FROM Products ORDER BY UnitPrice DESC
```

Grouping Records

As we saw in Chapter 13, we can use a GROUP BY clause to group records and aggregate values, for example, counting the number of orders placed by a customer. To process a query with a GROUP BY clause, the database will often sort the results on the columns included in the GROUP BY.

The following query counts the number of products at each price by grouping together records with the same UnitPrice value:

```
SELECT Count(*), UnitPrice
FROM Products
GROUP BY UnitPrice
```

The database can use the IDX_UnitPrice index to retrieve the prices in order. Since matching prices appear in consecutive index entries, the database is able count the number of products at each price quickly. Indexing a field used in a GROUP BY clause can often speed up a query.

Maintaining a Unique Column

Columns requiring unique values (such as primary key columns) must have a unique index applied. There are several methods available to create a unique index. Marking a column as a primary key – as we discussed in Chapter 12 – will automatically create a unique index on the column. We could also create a UNIQUE constraint, which ultimately produces a unique index. Let's quickly look at an example to demonstrate this.

Try It Out: Creating a Unique Index

We can create a unique index by checking the **Create UNIQUE** checkbox in the **Index/Keys** dialog shown earlier. The screenshot of the dialog displayed the index used to enforce the primary key of the `Products` table. In this case, the **Create UNIQUE** checkbox is disabled, since an index to enforce a primary key *must* be a unique index. However, creating new indexes not used to enforce primary keys will allow us to select the **Create UNIQUE** checkbox – or not, as we choose.

Similarly, we can create a unique index using SQL, with the following command:

```
CREATE UNIQUE INDEX IDX_ProductName On Products (ProductName)
```

How It Works

The above SQL command will not allow any duplicate values in the `ProductName` column, and an index is the best tool for the database to use to enforce this rule. Each time an application adds or modifies a row in the table, the database needs to search all existing records to ensure the value in the new row does not duplicate any existing value. Indexes will improve this search time.

> *We'll see this technique again in the second half of this chapter, when we look at unique constraints in more detail.*

Index Drawbacks

There are tradeoffs to almost any feature in computer programming, and indexes are no exception. While indexes provide a substantial performance benefit to searches, there is also a downside to indexing, and we'll look at this now.

Indexes and Disk Space

The amount of space required to store an index will depend on the size of the table, and the number and types of columns used in the index. Disk space is generally cheap enough to trade for application performance, particularly when a database serves a large number of users. To see the space required for a table, use the `sp_spaceused` system stored procedure shown below in a query window (or in the query input of our sample application from Chapter 13):

```
EXEC sp_spaceused Orders
```

Given a table name – for example, `Orders` – the procedure will return the amount of space used by the data and all indexes associated with the table:

```
Name      rows      reserved      data      index_size   unused
-------   --------  -----------   ------    ----------   -------
Orders    830       504 KB        160 KB    320 KB       24 KB
```

According to the output above, the table data uses 160 kilobytes, while the table indexes use twice as much. The ratio of index size to table size can vary greatly, depending on the columns, data types, and number of indexes on a table.

Indexes and Data Modification

Another downside to using an index is the performance implication on data modification statements. Any time a query modifies the data in a table (INSERT, UPDATE, or DELETE), the database needs to update all of the indexes where data has changed, which could take a long time if we have many fields indexed or a very large number of changes.

As we discussed earlier, indexing can help the database during data modification statements by allowing the database to quickly locate the records to modify. However, an important caveat here is that providing too many indexes to update can actually hurt the performance of data modifications. This leads to a delicate balancing act when tuning the database for performance.

In decision-support systems and data warehouses, where information is stored for reporting purposes, data remains relatively static and report-generating queries outnumber data modification queries. In these types of environments, heavy indexing is commonplace in order to optimize the reports generated. In contrast, a database used for transaction processing will see many records added and updated. These types of databases will use fewer indexes to allow for higher throughput on inserts and updates.

So far, we've seen why indexes are useful and where they are best applied. Now let's look at the different options available when creating an index and then address some common rules-of-thumb to use when planning the indexes for your database.

Clustered Indexes

Earlier in the chapter we made an analogy between a database index and the index of a book. A book index stores words in order with a reference to the page numbers where the word is located. The corresponding type of index for a database is known as a **non-clustered index**: only the index key and a reference are stored.

In contrast, a common analogy for a **clustered index** is a phone book. A phone book still sorts entries into alphabetical order, but once we find a name in a phone book, we have also immediate access to the rest of the data for the name, such as the phone number and address. For a clustered index, the database will sort the table's records according to the column (or columns) specified by the index. A clustered index contains all of the data for a table in the index itself, sorted by the index key.

> **A clustered index determines the physical ordering of the rows in a table. For this reason, the database allows only one clustered index per table.**

In the following diagram, we have a search using a clustered index on the UnitPrice column of the Products table. Compare this diagram to the previous diagram with a regular index on UnitPrice. Although we are only showing three columns from the Products table, all of the columns are present. Note the rows are sorted into the order of the index and there is no reference to follow from the index back to the data:

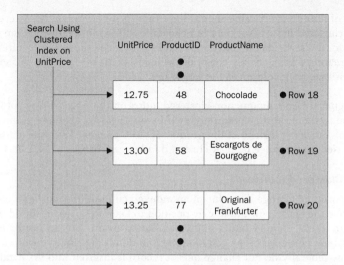

A clustered index is the most important index you can apply to a table. If the database engine can use a clustered index during a query, then it does not need to follow references back to the rest of the data, as would happen with a non-clustered index. The result is less work for the database and a better performance for a query using a clustered index.

To create a clustered index, simply select the **Create As CLUSTERED** checkbox in the dialog box we used at the beginning of the chapter. The corresponding SQL syntax for a clustered index adds a new keyword to the CREATE INDEX command:

```
CREATE CLUSTERED INDEX IDX_SupplierID ON Products(SupplierID)
```

Most of the tables in the Northwind database already have a clustered index defined. Since we can only have one clustered index per table, and the Products table already has a clustered index (PK_Products) on the primary key (ProductId), the above command should generate the following error:

Cannot create more than one clustered index on table 'Products'. Drop the existing clustered index 'PK_Products' before creating another.

Likewise, Visual Studio .NET will give the following error message if you attempt to add a second clustered index to the Products table using the interface:

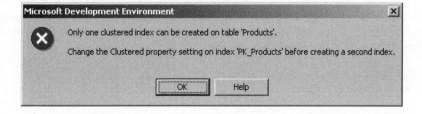

As a general rule of thumb, every table should have one clustered index. If you create only one index for a table, use a clustered index. Not only is a clustered index more efficient than other indexes for retrieval operations, it also helps the database efficiently manage the space required to store the table. In SQL Server, creating a primary key constraint will automatically create a clustered index (if none exists) using the primary key column as the index key.

Sometimes it is better to use a unique non-clustered index on the primary key column, and place the clustered index on a column more commonly used by queries. For example, if the majority of searches are for the price of a product instead of the product ID (the primary key), the clustered index could be more effective if used on the price field. A clustered index can also be a UNIQUE index.

A Disadvantage to Clustered Indexes

If we update a record and change the value of an indexed column in a clustered index, the database might need to move the entire row into a new position to keep the rows in sorted order. This behavior essentially turns an UPDATE query into a DELETE followed by an INSERT, with an obvious decrease in performance. A table's clustered index can often be found on the primary key or a foreign key column, because key values generally do not change once a record is inserted into the database.

> **Don't use a clustered index on values that are subject to frequent change.**

Composite Indexes

A composite index is an index on two or more columns from a table. Both clustered and non-clustered indexes can be composite indexes. Composite indexes are especially useful in two different circumstances:

- ❑ To **cover** a query – we'll see what this means in a moment
- ❑ To help match the search criteria of specific queries

We will go into more detail and give examples of these two areas in the following sections.

Covering Queries with an Index

Earlier in the chapter, we saw how a non-clustered index contains only the key values and a reference to the associated row of data. However, if the key value contained all of the information needed to process a query, then the database would never have to follow the reference and find the row; it could simply retrieve the information from the index and save processing time.

Consider the index we created on the Products table for UnitPrice. The database copied the values from the UnitPrice column and sorted them into an index. If we execute the following query, the database can retrieve all of the information for the query from the index itself:

```
SELECT UnitPrice FROM Products
ORDER BY UnitPrice
```

We call these types of queries **covered queries**, because all of the columns requested in the output are contained in the index itself.

> *A clustered index, if selected for use by the query optimizer, always covers a query, since it contains all of the data in a table.*

For the following query, there are no covering indexes on the `Products` table:

```
SELECT ProductName, UnitPrice FROM Products
ORDER BY UnitPrice
```

Although the database will use the index on `UnitPrice` to avoid sorting records, it will need to follow the reference in each index entry to find the associated row and retrieve the `ProductName`. On the other hand, a composite index on two columns – `ProductName` and `UnitPrice` – can cover this query.

Matching Complex Search Criteria

For another way to use composite indexes, let's take a look at the `OrderDetails` table of Northwind. There are two key values in the table, `OrderID` and `ProductID`, which are foreign keys, referencing the `Orders` and `Products` tables respectively. There is no column dedicated for use as a primary key; instead, the primary key is the combination of the two columns, `OrderID` and `ProductID`. We should see only unique combinations of these two keys in the table. In other words, an application cannot enter a row with an `OrderID` and `ProductID` matching another row with the same `OrderID` and `ProductID` combination.

The primary constraint on these columns will generate a composite index that is unique. Here is the command the database can use to create the index:

```
CREATE UNIQUE CLUSTERED INDEX PK_Order_Details
ON [Order Details] (OrderID, ProductID)
```

The order in which columns appear in a `CREATE INDEX` statement is significant. The primary sort order for this index is `OrderID`. When the `OrderID` is the same for two or more records, then the database will sort this subset of records on `ProductID`.

This has an effect on how useful the index is for a query. For example, the phone book is sorted by last name, then first name, which makes it easy to find all of the listings with a last name of Smith, or all of the listings with a last name of Jones and a first name of Lisa. Suppose you wanted to find all listings with a first name of Gary, however. In this case, you'd need to scan the book page by page.

Likewise, the composite index on `Order Details` is useful in the following two queries:

```
SELECT * FROM [Order Details] WHERE OrderID = 11077
```

```
SELECT * FROM [Order Details] WHERE OrderID = 11077 AND ProductID = 13
```

However, it is of no help to the query shown below, since `ProductID` is the second part of the index key, just like the first name field in a phone book:

```
SELECT * FROM [Order Details] WHERE ProductID = 13
```

Try It Out: Creating a Composite Index

Suppose the following query is the most popular query executed by our application, and we need to tune the database to support it:

```
SELECT ProductName, UnitPrice
FROM Products
ORDER BY UnitPrice
```

We could create the following index to cover the query. Notice we have specified two columns for the index: `UnitPrice` and `ProductName` (making the index a composite index):

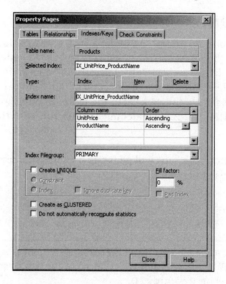

The equivalent SQL command is shown here:

```
CREATE INDEX IX_UnitPrice_ProductName ON Products(UnitPrice, ProductName)
```

The index is primarily sorted by `UnitPrice`, but when the `UnitPrice` is equal for two records, they are sorted by `ProductName`.

How It Works

There are now two columns in the index. The query outlined earlier can now retrieve the data needed from the index without following references to the rest of the data in the table. The following diagram provides a graphical illustration of the new index. Data from the two columns – `UnitPrice` and `ProductName` – make up the index, but if we need further data, such as the `ProductID`, then we must follow the reference to the relevant row in the database.

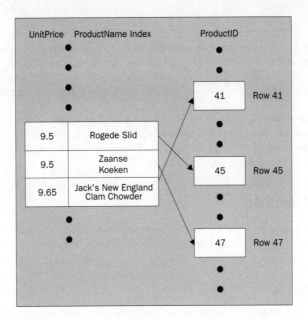

While covered queries can provide a performance benefit, remember there is a price to pay for each index we add to a table, and you can never cover every query in a non-trivial application. You need to ensure that such indexes are used only for the most common queries.

Additional Index Guidelines

Choosing the correct columns and types for an index is only the first step in creating an effective index. In this section, we will talk about the other two main factors that help to maintain the performance of your index:

❑   Short index keys

❑   Selective indexes

Keep Index Keys Short

The larger an index key is, the harder a database has to work to use the index. There are several approaches to keeping an index key short. First, try to limit the index to as few columns as possible. While composite indexes are useful and can sometimes optimize a query, they are also larger and cause more disk reads for the database. Second, try to choose a compact data type for an index column, based on the number of bytes required for each data type. Integer keys are small and easy for the database to compare. In contrast, strings require a character-by-character comparison.

> **As a rule of thumb, avoid using character columns in an index, particularly primary key indexes. Integer columns will always have an advantage over character fields in ability to boost the performance of a query.**

Distinct Index Keys

The most effective indexes are those with a small percentage of duplicated values. Think of having a phone book for a city where 75% of the population has the last name of Smith. A phone book in this area might be easier to use if the entries were sorted by the resident's first names instead. A good index will allow the database to disregard as many records as possible during a search.

An index with a high percentage of unique values is a **selective** index. Obviously, a `unique` index is the most selective index of all, because there are no duplicate values. SQL Server will track statistics for indexes and will know how selective each index is. The query optimizer utilizes these statistics when selecting the best index to use for a query.

Maintaining Indexes

In addition to creating an index, we'll need to view existing indexes, and sometimes delete or rename them. This is part of the ongoing maintenance cycle of a database as the schema changes, or even naming conventions change.

View Existing Indexes

A list of all indexes on a table is available in the dialog box we used to create an index. Click on the Selected index drop-down control and scroll through the available indexes, as shown below.

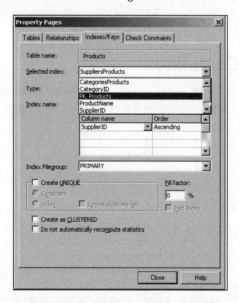

There is also a stored procedure named `sp_helpindex`. This stored procedure gives all of the indexes for a table, along with all of the relevant attributes. The only input parameter to the procedure is the name of the table:

```
EXEC sp_helpindex Products
```

Recall that you can execute stored procedures using the sample application developed in Chapter 13.

Rename an Index

To rename an index, type the new name of the index in the Index name textbox of the dialog shown earlier. After closing the design view and saving all changes, the IDE will issue the correct commands to alter the name of the index. Remember, the ability to manage indexes from Visual Studio .NET is not provided in the Standard Edition.

We can also rename indexes (and any user created object) with the sp_rename stored procedure, which takes the current name of the object and the new name for the object. For indexes, the current name must include the name of the table, a dot separator, and the name of the index:

```
EXEC sp_rename 'Products.IX_UnitPrice', 'IX_Price'
```

This will change the name of the IX_UnitPrice index to IX_Price.

Delete an Index

It is a good idea to remove an index from the database if it is not providing any benefit. For instance, if we know the queries in an application are no longer searching for records on a particular column, we can remove the index on that column. Unneeded indexes only take up storage space and diminish the performance of modifications. You can remove most indexes with the Delete button on the index dialog box, which we saw earlier. The equivalent SQL command is shown below:

```
DROP INDEX Products.IX_Price
```

Again, we need to use the name of the table and the name of the index, with a dot separator.

We can't delete any index supporting a unique or primary key constraint. For example, the following command tries to drop the PK_Products index of the Products table:

```
DROP INDEX Products.PK_Products
```

Since the database uses PK_Products to enforce a primary key constraint on the Products table, the above command will produce the following error message:

An explicit DROP INDEX is not allowed on index 'Products.PK_Products'. It is being used for PRIMARY KEY constraint enforcement.

Removing a primary key constraint from a table is a redesign of the table, and requires careful thought. The only way to achieve this task is to either drop the table and use a CREATE TABLE command to recreate the table without the index, or to use the ALTER TABLE command. These types of tasks fall more under constraint management, which we're going to look at next.

Constraints

The primary job of a **constraint** is to enforce a rule in the database. Together, the constraints in a database maintain its **integrity**. For instance, we have foreign key constraints to ensure that all orders reference existing products; we cannot enter an order for a product that the database does not know about.

Maintaining integrity is of utmost importance for a database, so much so that we cannot trust users and applications to enforce these rules by themselves; we must build these rules into the database. Once integrity is lost, we may find customers are double-billed, payments to the supplier are missing, and everyone loses faith in our application.

Data Integrity

Data integrity rules fall into one of three categories:

❑   Entity integrity – ensures each row in a table is uniquely identifiable

❑   Referential integrity – ensures the relationships between tables remain preserved as data is inserted, deleted, and modified

❑   Domain integrity – ensures the data values inside a database follow defined rules for values, range, and format

You can apply **entity integrity** to a table by specifying a primary key constraint – each table must specify a primary key. For example, the ProductID column of the Products table is a primary key for the table. A primary key constraint builds a unique index on the column to prevent duplicate values. Entity integrity is invaluable to the overall integrity of our data and software. Suppose the database allowed us to enter two product rows with the same ProductID. When we go to query the Order Details table and find two products assigned to a single identifier, how can we trust the result of the query? Did the customer actually place an order for both products, or just one of them? Which unit price do we assign for the order? Protecting the identity of our entities will avoid questions about the quality of the data.

Referential integrity, as we saw in Chapter 12, can be applied using a foreign key constraint. The ProductID column of the Order Details table has a foreign key constraint applied referencing the Products table. This constraint prevents an Order Detail record from using a ProductID that does not exist in the database. Also, we cannot remove a row from the Products table if an order detail references the ProductID of the row.

Entity and referential integrity together form **key integrity**. Since we have already covered primary and foreign key relationships in this book, we'll spend the rest of this chapter focusing on the constraints that allow us to maintain domain integrity.

A database can enforce **domain integrity** using a variety of techniques, including check constraints, unique constraints, and default constraints. These are the techniques we will cover in this chapter, but you should be aware that there are other options available to enforce domain integrity. Even the selection of the data type for a column enforces domain integrity to some extent. For instance, the selection of datetime for a column data type is more restrictive than a free format varchar field.

The following list gives a sample of domain integrity constraints that we could apply to the `Product` and `Orders` tables:

❑ A product name cannot be `NULL`

❑ A product name must be unique

❑ The date of an order must not be in the future

❑ The product quantity in an order must be greater than zero

❑ The discount percentage must be greater than 0% and less than 40%

❑ The default price for a product is $0.00

Unique Constraints

A **unique constraint** uses an index to ensure a column (or set of columns) contains no duplicate values. By creating a unique constraint – instead of just a unique index – we are telling the database we really want to enforce a rule, and are not just providing an index for query optimization. The database will then not allow someone to drop the index without first dropping the constraint.

We can create a unique constraint using Visual Studio .NET from the same Indexes/Keys tab we have used before. There are times when we might need a unique column, but do not want to make the column a primary key. For example, we might want the `ProductName` to contain unique values, but because string fields are more difficult for the database to compare, we wouldn't want to use this for our primary key.

Try It Out: Creating a Unique Constraint

To create a unique constraint on the `ProductName` column of the `Products` table:

1. Open the `Products` table in design view and select Indexes/Keys from the View menu.

2. Press the New command button on the resulting dialog and change the Index name to `IX_ProductName`.

3. As shown in the dialog below, select `ProductName` as the column to index, and check the Create UNIQUE checkbox. Note that the Constraint radio button is selected by default, we are creating a constraint rather than a regular index.

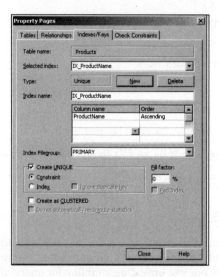

From a SQL point of view, there are three methods available to add a unique constraint to a table:

4. Create the constraint inside a CREATE TABLE command as a **column constraint**. The following SQL will create a unique constraint on a new table, Products_2:

```
CREATE TABLE Products_2
(
  ProductID int PRIMARY KEY,
  ProductName nvarchar (40) Constraint IX_ProductName UNIQUE
)
```

Note that the constraint name here is optional.

5. A different syntax allows us to create a **table constraint**. Notice there is now a comma after the ProductName column definition:

```
CREATE TABLE Products_2
(
  ProductID int PRIMARY KEY,
  ProductName nvarchar (40),
  CONSTRAINT IX_ProductName UNIQUE(ProductName)
)
```

6. Add a constraint to an existing table using the ALTER TABLE command:

```
CREATE TABLE Products_2
(
  ProductID int PRIMARY KEY,
  ProductName nvarchar (40)
)
```

```
ALTER TABLE Products_2
  ADD CONSTRAINT IX_ProductName UNIQUE (ProductName)
```

How It Works

In our first SQL method above, the command will actually create two unique indexes. One is the unique, clustered index given by default to the primary key of a table. The second is the unique index using the `ProductName` column as a key and enforcing our constraint. A column constraint applies to only a single column.

The second method – a table constraint – is able to enforce a rule across multiple columns. A table constraint is a separate element in the `CREATE TABLE` command.

Our final method shows how to add a constraint to an existing database. To check to see if our `UNIQUE` constraint is working correctly, we could, for example, insert two rows into our table between the `CREATE TABLE` and `ALTER TABLE` commands. If both rows used a product name of `'Hamburger'`, then running the `ALTER TABLE` command gives us an error message like this one:

Server: Msg 1505, Level 16, State 1, Line 1
CREATE UNIQUE INDEX terminated because a duplicate key was found for index ID 2. Most significant primary key is 'Hamburger'.

Server: Msg 1750, Level 16, State 1, Line 1
Could not create constraint. See previous errors.
The statement has been terminated.

Check Constraints

We use **check constraints** to narrow the range of allowed values and formats for a particular column. They are extremely useful for enforcing rules in the database. Check constraints contain an expression, which the database will evaluate when we modify or insert a row. If the expression evaluates to `false`, the database will not save the row.

Building a check constraint is similar to building a `WHERE` clause. We can use many of the same operators (>, <, <=, >=, <>, =) in addition to `BETWEEN`, `IN`, `LIKE`, and `NULL`, and also build expressions around the `AND` and `OR` operators.

> **Check constraints have a performance implication since the constraint is executed during data modifications. Too many constraints can slow down performance.**

Try It Out: Check Constraints

A check constraint is built in Visual Studio .NET Architect and Professional versions by opening a table in design view and selecting **Check Constraints** from the **View** menu. In the dialog shown below, we can see an existing constraint on the `Products` table, `CK_Products_UnitPrice`. In the **Constraint expression** textbox, we can see this ensures that the `UnitPrice` value for any row is greater than or equal to 0:

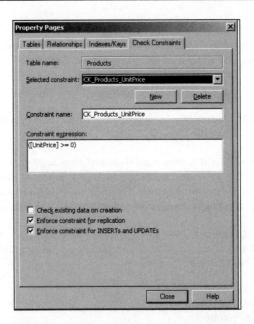

We can use the same three techniques we saw earlier to create a check constraint using SQL. The first technique places the constraint after the column definition, as shown below. As with unique constraints, the constraint name is optional:

```
CREATE TABLE Products_3
(
    ProductID int PRIMARY KEY,
    UnitPrice money CHECK(UnitPrice > 0 AND UnitPrice < 100)
)
```

How It Works

In the above example we are restricting values in the UnitPrice column to between 0 and 100. Let's try to insert a value outside of this range with the following SQL statement to see what happens:

```
INSERT INTO Products_3 VALUES(1, 101)
```

The database will not save the values and instead will respond with the following error message:

```
Server: Msg 547, Level 16, State 1, Line 1
INSERT statement conflicted with COLUMN CHECK constraint
'CK__Products___UnitP__2739D489'. The conflict occurred in database 'Northwind', table
'Products_3', column 'UnitPrice'.
The statement has been terminated.
```

Check Constraint Examples

Let's get some practice by looking at some additional ways to create constraints. The following SQL creates as a table constraint, separate from the column definitions:

```
CREATE TABLE Products_3
(
    ProductID int PRIMARY KEY,
    UnitPrice money,
    CONSTRAINT CK_UnitPrice2 CHECK(UnitPrice > 0 AND UnitPrice < 100)
)
```

Remember, with a table constraint we can reference multiple columns. The constraint in the following SQL will ensure that we have either a telephone number *or* a fax number for every customer:

```
CREATE TABLE Customers_3
(
    CustomerID int,
    Phone varchar(24),
    Fax varchar(24),
    CONSTRAINT CK_PhoneOrFax CHECK(Fax IS NOT NULL OR PHONE IS NOT NULL)
)
```

We can also add check constraints to a table once it exists using the ALTER TABLE syntax. The following constraint will ensure an employee date of hire is always today or in the past by using the system function GETDATE():

```
CREATE TABLE Employees_2
(
    EmployeeID int,
    HireDate datetime)

    ALTER TABLE Employees_2
    ADD CONSTRAINT CK_HireDate CHECK(hiredate < GETDATE()
)
```

Check Constraints and Existing Values

As with unique constraints, if you add a check constraint to a populated table, then you run a chance of failure, because the database will check existing data to see if it complies with the constraint. This is not optional behavior with a unique constraint – all the data must comply. However, it is possible to avoid the conformance test when adding a check constraint. In the design view, the default behavior is *not* to check existing data, but you can change this by selecting the Check existing data on creation checkbox:

The following sequence of commands would typically fail because the existing data in the table does not meet the constraint requirements, but is OK if since we have disabled data checking using WITH NOCHECK syntax in SQL:

```
CREATE TABLE Employees_2
(
    EmployeeID int,
    Salary money
)

INSERT INTO Employees_2 VALUES(1, -1)

ALTER TABLE Employees_2 WITH NOCHECK
ADD CONSTRAINT CK_Salary CHECK(Salary > 0)
```

Check Constraints and NULL Values

Earlier in this section, we mentioned how the database will only stop a data modification when a check constraint returns `false`. We did not mention, however, how the database allows the modification to take place if the expression is **logically unknown**. This is an expression the database *cannot* evaluate because a NULL value is present. For example, suppose we use the following INSERT statement on the last table we created:

```
INSERT INTO Employees_2 (EmployeeID, Salary) VALUES(2, NULL)
```

Even with the constraint on salary (`Salary > 0`) in place, the INSERT is successful. A NULL value doesn't allow the database to evaluate the expression as `true` or `false`, making the expression logically unknown.

> A **CHECK** constraint will only fail an **INSERT** or **UPDATE** if the expression in the constraint explicitly returns **false**. Expressions that either return **true** or are logically unknown will allow the command to succeed.

Restrictions on Check Constraints

Although check constraints are by far the easiest way to enforce domain integrity in a database, they do have some limitations, namely:

❑ A check constraint cannot reference a different row in a table
❑ A check constraint cannot reference a column in a different table

For example, you cannot create a check constraint on the Products table to test if a product name is unique, since a check constraint cannot examine values in rows other than the row currently under examination. For this situation you could use a unique constraint. Likewise, you could not create a check constraint on the Products table to test if a product's CategoryId is present in the Categories table, as a check constraint cannot examine values in other tables. For this scenario, use a foreign key constraint.

You can, however, create a check constraint that references more than one column within the same row.

NULL Constraints

Although not a constraint in the strictest definition, the decision over whether or not to allow NULL values in a column is a type of rule enforcement for domain integrity. This decision is made in the table design view by checking or unchecking in the column named Allow Nulls:

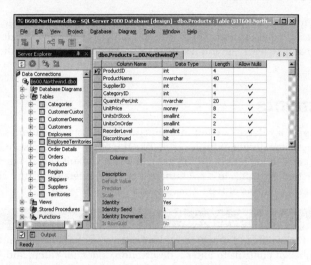

Using SQL you can use NULL or NOT NULL on a column definition to explicitly set the **nullability** of a column. In the following table, the FirstName column will accept NULL values while LastName always requires a non-NULL value:

```
CREATE TABLE Employees_2
(
  EmployeeID int PRIMARY KEY,
  FirstName varchar(50) NULL,
  LastName varchar(50) NOT NULL
)
```

Primary key columns **require** a NOT NULL setting, and default to this setting if not specified.

If we do not explicitly set a column to allow or disallow NULL values, the database uses a number of rules to determine the nullability of the column, including current configuration settings on the server.

> *We recommended you always define a column explicitly as NULL or NOT NULL in your scripts to avoid problems when moving between different server environments. This also makes the scripts you write self-documenting, is helpful in avoiding bugs, and improves maintainability.*

Given the above table definition, the first two INSERT statements shown below can succeed:

```
INSERT INTO Employees_2 VALUES(1, 'Geddy', 'Lee')
INSERT INTO Employees_2 VALUES(2, NULL, 'Lifeson')
INSERT INTO Employees_2 VALUES(3, 'Neil', NULL)
```

413

However, the third INSERT statement will fail with this error message:

Server: Msg 515, Level 16, State 2, Line 3
Cannot insert the value NULL into column 'LastName', table 'Northwind.dbo.Employees_2'; column does not allow nulls. INSERT fails.
The statement has been terminated.

We can declare columns in a unique constraint to allow NULL values. However, the constraint checking considers NULL values as equal, so on a single column unique constraint, the database allows only one row to have a NULL value. Clearly, if you are using a unique constraint then allowing NULL values is not a good idea.

Default Constraints

Default constraints apply a value to a column when an INSERT statement does not specify the value. Although default constraints do not enforce a rule like the other constraints we have seen, they do provide the proper values to keep domain integrity intact. A default can assign a constant value, the value of a system function, or NULL to a column. We can use a default on any column except IDENTITY columns and columns of type timestamp.

Try It Out: Creating a Default Constraint

In Visual Studio .NET, defaults are specified in the design view for a table. Underneath the column definitions are a number of controls to enter a description, a default value, and more. In this example, we'll see how to create a default constraint with SQL, placing the default value inline with the column definition. We also mix in some of the other constraints we have seen in this chapter to show how everything can be put together:

```
CREATE TABLE Orders_2
(
   OrderID int IDENTITY NOT NULL ,
   EmployeeID int NOT NULL ,
   OrderDate datetime NULL DEFAULT(GETDATE()),
   Freight money NULL DEFAULT (0) CHECK(Freight >= 0),
   ShipAddress nvarchar (60) NULL DEFAULT('NO SHIPPING ADDRESS'),
   EnteredBy nvarchar (60)  NOT NULL DEFAULT(SUSER_SNAME())
)
```

If no values are specified for the columns with a default, OrderDate receives the system date, Freight will receive a 0, ShipAddress will receive a string value indicating no shipping address, and EnteredBy receives the username of the current database user. The username is retrieved using the SQL Server system function SUSER_SNAME(). This demonstrates how to use a system function inside a constraint.

How It Works

We can examine the behavior of the defaults with the following INSERT statement, placing values only in the EmployeeID and Freight fields:

```
INSERT INTO Orders_2 (EmployeeID, Freight) VALUES(1, NULL)
```

If we then query the table to view the row we just inserted, we see the following results:

```
OrderID EmployeeID OrderDate  Freight  ShipAddress          EnteredBy
------- ---------- ---------- -------- -------------------- ---------
1       1          2002-03-23 NULL     NO SHIPPING ADDRESS  sa
```

Note that the `Freight` column did not receive the default value of 0. Specifying a `NULL` value is not the equivalent of leaving the column value unspecified. The database does not use the default and `NULL` is placed in the column instead.

Maintaining Constraints

In this section we will examine how to delete an existing constraint. We will also take a look at a special capability to temporarily disable constraints for special processing scenarios.

Dropping Constraints

Using Visual Studio .NET, we can easily delete unique and check constraints with the **Delete** buttons on the index and constraint design tabs respectively. We can also remove constraints with the DROP CONSTRAINT clause of the ALTER TABLE statement in SQL.

Let's remove the check on `UnitPrice` in the `Products` table:

```
ALTER TABLE Products DROP CONSTRAINT CK_Products_UnitPrice
```

If all we need to do is drop a constraint to allow a one-time circumvention of the rule's enforcement, a better solution is to temporarily disable the constraint, which we'll see how to do in the next section.

Disabling Constraints

Special situations often arise in database development where it is convenient to temporarily relax the rules. For example, it is often easier to load initial values into a database one table at a time, without worrying about foreign key constraints and checks until *all* of the tables have finished loading. After the import is complete, we can turn constraint checking back on and know the database is once again protecting the integrity of the data.

> *The only constraints we can disable are foreign key and check constraints. Primary key, unique, and default constraints are always active.*

We can disable foreign key constraints from the **Relationships** tab of a table's property pages. Simply uncheck the **Enforce relationship for INSERT's and UPDATEs** checkbox:

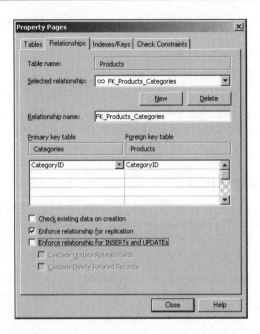

Check constraints can be disabled in the same fashion on the **Check Constraints** tab. Simply remove the check from the **Enforce constraint for INSERTS and UPDATEs** checkbox.

Disabling a constraint using SQL is done through the ALTER TABLE command. The following statements disable the check constraint on the UnitsOnOrder column, and the foreign key constraint on the CategoryID column respectively:

```
ALTER TABLE Products NOCHECK CONSTRAINT CK_UnitsOnOrder
ALTER TABLE Products NOCHECK CONSTRAINT FK_Products_Categories
```

Manually navigating through the interface or writing a SQL command for each constraint to disable it can be a laborious process. Fortunately, there is an easy alternative: the ALL keyword:

```
ALTER TABLE Products NOCHECK CONSTRAINT ALL
```

To re-enable just the CK_UnitsOnOrder constraint, for example, we can use the following statement:

```
ALTER TABLE Products CHECK CONSTRAINT CK_UnitsOnOrder
```

Bear in mind that when a disabled constraint is re-enabled, the database does not check to ensure any of the existing data meets the constraints. To turn on all constraints for the Products table, use the following command:

```
ALTER TABLE Products CHECK CONSTRAINT ALL
```

Summary

We started off this chapter with an in-depth examination of indexes, looking at what they are, and at the advantages and disadvantages of using them. While indexes can increase the performance of some queries, they can slow down the overall process of updating the database. Consequently, we need to use careful thought when deciding how and where to apply an index, and which are the most appropriate queries to index for. We also looked at the difference between clustered and non-clustered indexes, and the strengths and disadvantages of using them.

In the second part of the chapter, we learned how to use various constraints to ensure the data in our database stays intact and matches our expectations. There are several ways of doing this, and we looked at the three most important:

❑   Unique constraints, which ensure the uniqueness of a value in a column and are used mainly in the primary key column

❑   Check constraints, which allow us to ensure that the data lies within a certain range, for example

❑   Default constraints, which allow us to specify a default value for a column

Understanding of all of these areas will help you to build solid and optimized database applications. For more advanced information on designing a database, try reading *Professional SQL Server 2000 Database Design* published by Wrox Press, ISBN 1-86100-476-1.

Exercises

1. After analyzing some application code for the Northwind database, you discover the most popular query on the involving the `Territories` table is the following:

```
SELECT TerritoryDescription, RegionDescription
FROM Region, Territories
WHERE Region.RegionID = Territories.RegionID
```

Is there an index you can apply to the `Territories` table to improve the query?

2. The `PostalCode` column of the `Suppliers` table in the Northwind database is indexed. Let's imagine we have done an examination of an application and determined the database never needs to use this index for a query. Drop the index to conserve database resources.

3. The `Shippers` table of the Northwind database has a `CompanyName` column. Let's imagine we have decided to enforce a rule saying all the company names must be unique. Modify the `Shippers` table to add a unique constraint on the `CompanyName` column.

4. The `RequiredDate` column of the `Orders` table in the Northwind table indicates the time when a customer must receive an order. To prevent data entry mistakes, we want to enforce a rule that the `RequiredDate` must always be a date in the future. Alter the `Orders` table to add such a constraint, but do not check existing data for conformance.

5. If you have added the `RequiredDate` constraint in the previous exercise, try to modify the `Orders` table again to remove the constraint.

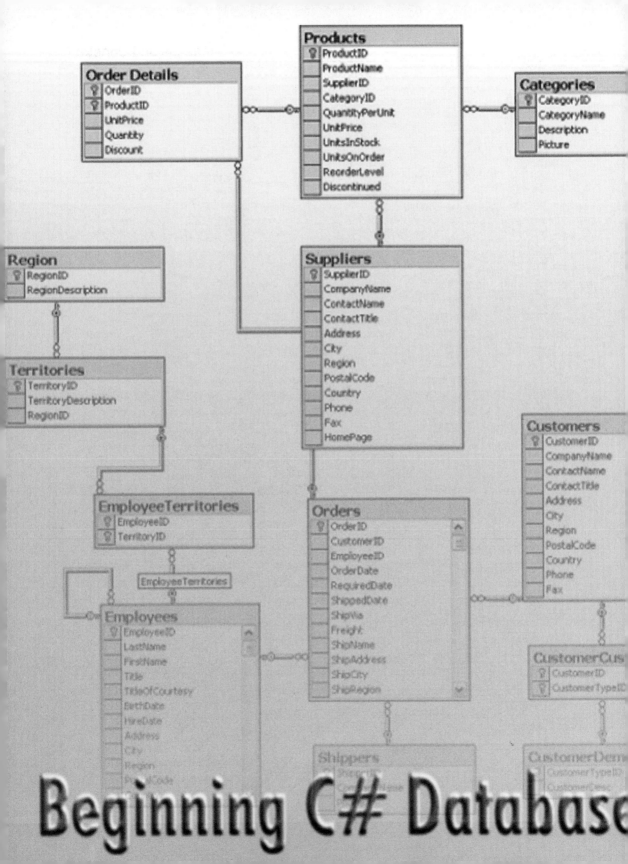

Authentication and Authorization

Two of the most critical questions you need to answer when thinking about database security are:

- ❑ **Who** will you grant access to?
- ❑ **What** operations will you allow them to perform?

The first step in answering these questions is determining the identity of the person trying to access the database; we call this process **authentication**. A classic authentication mechanism requires a person to provide a username and password to prove their identity. The next step in the process is **authorization**. Given the identity of a person, the database can evaluate what actions to allow the user to perform, for example, whether they are allowed to change the schema by creating or altering tables. We can achieve this by setting different **permissions** for users or groups of users.

Although there are additional subtleties involved in security topics, authentication and authorization are the primary topics for this chapter. Specifically, we will cover the following areas:

- ❑ Using Windows and Mixed Authentication Modes
- ❑ Managing logins and users
- ❑ Managing and using database roles
- ❑ Granting, revoking, and denying permissions to database objects and statements

By the end of the chapter, you will have a solid understanding of the basic security mechanisms offered by MSDE.

Included in the code download for this chapter is a Windows Forms-based utility named AdminHelp. This utility will allow us to view security-related settings inside the database. So, before we get started with the topics outlined above, we'll take a moment to introduce the application.

The AdminHelp Utility

To be able to view and set the various security settings – such as logins and permissions – in SQL Server or MSDE, the database engines use a number of built-in system stored procedures. While SQL Server provides a useful GUI for you to use to administer security, MSDE does not. For that reason, we'll use our own little utility, AdminHelp, which will act as a forms-based interface making the use of the more common stored procedures a little easier. Here is the main screen for the utility:

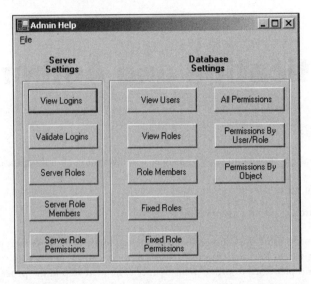

The source code for this utility is available with the code download for this chapter from http://www.wrox.com. You just need to build and execute the code to see the form shown above. Note that before you can view any of the settings, you need to connect to the database, which you can do from the File menu. Here's the code for the connection:

```
protected void GetNewConnection()
{
    string connectionString = @"server=(local)\NetSDK;" +
                             "Integrated Security=SSPI;database=Northwind";
    sqlConnection = new SqlConnection(connectionString);
    sqlConnection.Open();
}
```

If you want to use this utility to work with a different database, then it's simply a question of changing the parameters in the connection string.

Introduction to Database Security

Before we dive into the details of database security, let's first look at a quick overview of the whole security process and how it works.

When dealing with Windows security, a system administrator typically places users into one or more groups to ease system management. In addition to built-in groups, such as `Administrators` and `Guests`, an administrator can create new groups.

For example, Joy, Tim, and Amy all work in human resources. All three employees will probably need access to the same resources on a machine or network, such as a spreadsheet of employee salaries. An administrator could create a new group named `HR` and add each user to the group. The administrator then grants permissions for the salary spreadsheet to the group, instead of each individual user. As employees join or leave the HR department it is easier to add them to or remove them from the `HR` group than to comb through each resource and grant or deny privileges at the user level.

Now, suppose Joy needs to access an employee database to run a report. The first stage is to log into the database server. As we will see shortly, the login may be authenticated by either the SQL Server instance itself or managed separately by the Windows security system (if Joy has already been authenticated by a Windows domain server). Once the login is authenticated, she is logged into the database server, but can't actually do anything. To be able to access a particular database, the login needs to be mapped to one of the user accounts managed by that database. The database then grants certain permissions to each user, which describe whether they can, for example, view a table or run a stored procedure. This process is known as authorization.

As with Windows, it can be difficult to manage all these permissions at the level of the individual user. For a database administrator, groups work equally well. It's likely that everyone in the human resources department will need to run reports, so rather than add map Joy, Tim, and Amy to individual database user accounts, we can just add the `HR` group as a whole. As employees join and leave the HR group there is no work required to grant and deny the employees access.

Furthermore, the database includes the concept of roles, which work at both the server and the individual database level. Rather than apply permissions to individual users, you can add or remove users from roles. We'll see how all this works later on.

> *If you're logged into Windows as an Administrator, a lot of this is sorted out under the hood for you, and you will automatically have full administrative rights over any of the databases in the database server.*

Throughout the rest of this chapter, we'll be taking a closer look at how all this works, and at the various stored procedures that are provided for you by SQL Server / MSDE that allow you to view and alter the security settings.

Authentication

The SQL Server database engine (which powers MSDE) operates in one of two authentication modes. In **Windows Authentication mode,** the engine relies on the operating system to authenticate users. This is the mode that we've been using throughout the book, specified by the `Integrated Security=SSPI` clause in the connection string.

In **Mixed Mode**, the database engine can still use Windows Authentication, but can also perform authentication itself by verifying a user's login and password credentials, using **SQL Server Authentication**. We will examine both of these modes in more detail in the following sections.

Windows Authentication Mode

Windows Authentication mode is the preferred authentication mode for SQL Server 2000 and MSDE database servers, because of the tight integration with the more robust and manageable security features of the Windows security system. Unless you are installing the engine on a Windows 98-based system, Windows Authentication mode is the default option during installation.

> *Windows 98 doesn't have the strong security system of the Windows NT, 2000, and XP Operating Systems, so Windows Authentication Mode is not available in this case. For the rest of this discussion, when we use the term "Windows security" we are referring to Windows NT 4 or later.*

In a typical forms-based data access application using Windows Authentication, a user will first log into a Windows machine. The local machine or a domain controller on the network will validate the username and password combination supplied by the user. At this point, the user launches the application to connect to an MSDE or SQL Server instance. The connection string in the application might look something like this:

```
Integrated Security=SSPI;Initial Catalog=Northwind;Data Source=CompName
```

This connection string instructs the client-side database software to establish a **trusted connection**. This term simply indicates that the SQL Server instance is relying on Windows to authenticate the user who is connecting to the database. The client establishes the connection using a layer of Microsoft software known as the **Security Support Provider Interface** (**SSPI**).

The engine will retrieve the account information from the trusted connection to compare with entries for valid database logins – the list of users who can connect to the instance of the database server.

> *A successful authentication allows a client to connect to an instance of the database engine, but does not yet grant access to a database managed by the instance. We'll see how this works later when we look at how we can map database user accounts to server logins.*

Windows Authentication Mode allows a database administrator to take advantage of the built-in security features of Windows. These features include (but are not limited to) the following:

❑ **Password expiration** forces users to change passwords after a set amount of time.

❑ **Account lock out** helps prevent malicious users from guessing a password by disabling an account after a set number of failed login attempts.

❑ **Strong passwords** protection also prevents password guessing by enforcing a minimum length for passwords and preventing the use of common words as passwords.

In addition to providing a robust security infrastructure, using Windows Authentication allows your clients to use the same login and password combinations to access resources on the local machine, resources on the network, and the database server.

Mixed Mode Authentication

In Mixed Mode, the database engine can still perform Windows Authentication over trusted connections, but it also adds a second type of authentication, namely **SQL Server Authentication**.

In a typical Mixed Mode Authentication scenario, a user logs into a machine and launches a form-based application connecting to a database. The connection string in this case may look like the following:

```
User ID=poonam;
Password=picnic;Initial
Catalog=Northwind;Data
Source=CompName
```

This connection string explicitly specifies a username and password. The client will connect on a **non-trusted connection**, because there are no Windows credentials associated with the connection. The database engine will extract the parameters to see if the user ID exists, and then see if the password for the user ID matches the given password. It is the database server that carries out the authentication process.

Mixed Mode Authentication puts more of a burden on the both the database and the database administrator to manage users and passwords. In addition, the security features are not as robust. For these reasons, Windows Authentication mode is the preferred authentication setting.

Managing Users

Both of the authentication techniques described above require valid login entries in the database server. In order to gain access to an individual database, however, a login must map to a database-specific user account. Authorization in MSDE revolves around **database users** and **database roles**, which are similar to the users and groups of Microsoft Windows, but are specific to each database in the engine.

In this section, we'll be examining how to manage these user accounts and roles, but first we'll take a look at how to view server login information, and also how to add or remove users from the list of available logins.

Database Logins

We can view the list of logins using the `sp_helplogins` stored procedure. When you execute this it returns two sets of records:

❑   One resultset contains the list of available logins

❑   A second resultset contains detailed information for each login and details of the databases to which they can connect

Although many query windows will only show one resultset, you can use the AdminHelp application included with this chapter to view both sets of results. You need to make sure you have established a connection, and then click the View Logins button. Example output is shown overleaf:

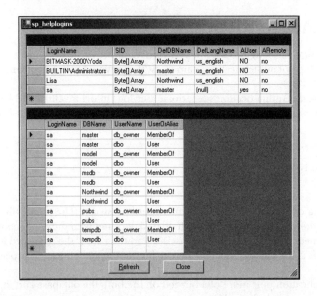

Many of the queries in this chapter will return a column with a security identification number (SID). We will not make any special use of SIDs in this chapter. The database uses a SID internally to uniquely identify each login name.

For now we want to concentrate on the first column (**LoginName**) of the top set of results. The results include four valid logins for the database engine. The first entry is a Windows account name. Windows logins are always qualified with a computer name (`ComputerName\Username`) or a domain name (`DomainName\Username`).

The second row is an entry for a Windows group. Users placed into the `Administrators` group have additional privileges to perform administrative tasks on a machine. Adding a group as a SQL Server or MSDE login allows any of the users who are a member of the group to log in. When adding a local built-in group such as `Administrators`, a special prefix (`BUILTIN`) is used instead of the computer or domain name.

> **The default installation for MSDE and SQL Server 2000 will add `BUILTIN\Administrators` as an available login.**

With Windows Authentication, we recommend you manage database logins with groups instead of by individual Windows accounts. As you create database objects (tables, views, and stored procedures), think about how the groups in your organization should be able to access these objects.

The third row is a SQL Server login. A client accessing the database using Mixed Mode Authentication can use this login name as the user ID property in the connection string. The last entry is also a SQL Server login. The `sa` login is a special account: the System Administrator login. This all-powerful login is used to perform administrative tasks within SQL Server (members of `BUILTIN\Administrators` have the same power). The `sa` login is created by default for use with mixed mode authentication.

Note that the availability of this default login (with a default password of an empty string) can be a potential security hole, and is particularly dangerous since it has administrative privileges. You need to be very careful of this if you are using Mixed Mode Authentication.

Adding and Removing Login Entries

The stored procedure `sp_grantlogin` will allow add a Windows user or group as a login entry to the database engine. Only a single argument is required: the user name or group name to add. As shown in the `sp_helplogins` output earlier, you must precede the Windows user or group name with a computer name or domain name (or `BUILTIN` if the name is a local built-in group) and a backslash. For example, suppose we really do have a Windows group for human resources named `HR`. The following command will allow members of the HR group to login:

```
EXEC sp_grantlogin 'ComputerName\HR'
```

You can execute this stored procedure using the application provided with Chapter 14.

You can grant a login to an individual user with the same stored procedure:

```
EXEC sp_grantlogin 'ComputerName\Joy'
```

To remove a Windows user or group, use the `sp_revokelogin` stored procedure. This procedure also requires a user or group name in the same format as above. For example, executing the following in a query window will remove the HR group from the list of available logins:

```
EXEC sp_revokelogin 'ComputerName\HR'
```

Joy may still login to the database engine, since she was added as an individual user with `sp_grantlogin`. Revoking login permissions for a group will not revoke login permissions for users within the group if they already have individual logins. Individual security specifications override those for a group.

As the time passes, an administrator may remove users and groups from Windows, but the login permission remains in the database server. You should use the `sp_validatelogins` stored procedure to see a list of logins granted on the database server with no corresponding entry in Windows. You can also view this list in AdminHelp with the **Validate Logins** button. These logins will be unusable, so you should revoke them.

SQL Server Logins

Managing logins for SQL Server Authentication requires a different set of stored procedures. To add a SQL Server login use the `sp_addlogin` stored procedure. While the only required parameter is a login name, we also recommend you supply a password as the second parameter. The following command adds the login name Juan:

```
EXEC sp_addlogin 'Juan', 'secretword'
```

With Windows Authentication, when a user changes their password in the operating system there is no additional work required to synchronize a database password. The database relies on the operating system to validate the identity. With SQL Server Authentication, the password is stored in the database, not in Windows. To change a password for a SQL Server login, use the sp_password stored procedure. The parameters are the existing password, the new password, and the login name:

```
EXEC sp_password 'secretword', 'goterps', 'Juan'
```

The stored procedure sp_droplogin is used to remove a SQL Server login. The only parameter for this procedure is the login name. The next command will remove Juan from the list of available logins:

```
EXEC sp_droplogin 'Juan'
```

SQL Server will never confuse a Windows group or user name with a SQL Server login name. Windows groups and usernames always have a backslash (after the computer or domain name). The backslash is an illegal character for SQL Server login names.

It does not matter which particular database you are currently using when executing the stored procedures above. You might be currently using the Northwind database, or the master database. In either case, logins apply to the server instance, not a specific database.

As we mentioned earlier in the chapter, a successful login does not give a user access to any particular database on the server. For instance, we could apply security settings in the Northwind database restricting access to administrators only. Other users could still login to the database server, and perhaps use other databases. However, only members of the BUILTIN\Administrators group, or users logging in as sa, would have the ability to retrieve information from Northwind.

Special Users

There are two special users in MSDE/SQL Server:

❑　The **dbo user** – present in every database. This user is the **database owner** and has permissions to perform any activity in a database. You cannot delete the dbo user. Note that both the SQL Server sa login and the BUILTIN\Administrators group map to the dbo user in all databases.

❑　The **guest user** – by default, not present when you create a new database. You can remove the guest user from a database (except the master and tempdb databases). The guest account allows a person to access the database if they have a valid login to the database server, but don't have a user account for a database.

Shown opposite is a diagram that illustrates conceptually the process of mapping logins to user accounts using Windows Authentication. Here we have our three members of the HR group, Joy, Tim, and Amy, who are using the guest user account:

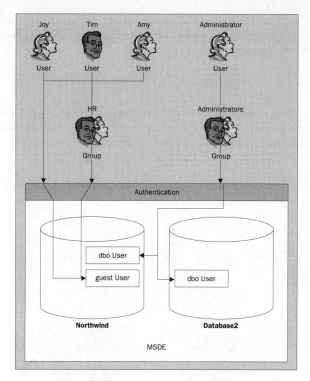

In this diagram, we have logins available for the user Joy, the group HR, and the BUILTIN\Administrators group. The engine maps administrators to the dbo user implicitly. Joy, Tim, and Amy will all log into the Northwind database as a guest user since there is no user account explicitly created for them. In the second database, there is no explicit user for Joy, Tim, and Amy, nor is a guest account present. The second database is not available to the members of HR, but is available to administrators.

User Accounts

You must map server-level logins to user accounts in each database. Although you could use the guest account to allow access to a database from any login (as shown above), this is not recommended practice. Instead, you should add a user account into each database for every user with a server login that needs to access it. A login can map to different user accounts in different databases; the names do not need to be the same. In the following section we will discuss how to add, delete, and view user accounts.

Adding a User Account

You can map a login to a user account in the current database using the sp_grantdbaccess stored procedure. The first parameter to the stored procedure is the login name and the second parameter is the name of the user account to create and associate with the login. Assuming we are in the Northwind database as an administrator, we can map the human resources login to a user account named HR with the following command:

```
EXEC sp_grantdbaccess 'ComputerName\HR', 'hr'
```

The user account name does not need to reflect the login name. For example, we could have also named the user account 'humanresources'. One member of the human resources group has her own login: Joy. We can associate Joy with a specific user account as shown below:

```
EXEC sp_grantdbaccess 'ComputerName\Joy', 'joy'
```

When Joy logs in, she will map to the user account specified for her login (joy), even though she is a member of the human resources group and can gain access via the hr user. The engine will always try to match an individual account first, before looking for a group the user is a member of. We can use this behavior to assign the user different permissions from the groups they are in.

After applying these new changes we can re-examine the conceptual diagram from earlier. The result looks like this:

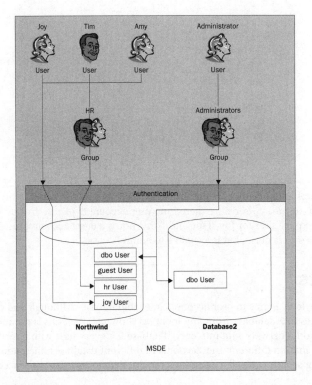

Viewing User Accounts

You can view all of the user accounts in a database using the system stored procedure sp_helpuser. The AdminHelp application executes this stored procedure when you click on the View Users button of the main form. The output for our Northwind database looks like this:

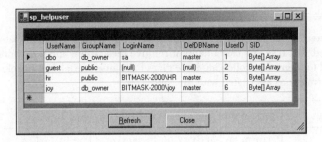

Removing a User Account

You can remove a user account from a database using the system stored procedure `sp_revokedbaccess`. The only parameter to this procedure is the user name. To remove the user `joy`, we would issue the following command:

```
EXEC sp_revokedbaccess 'joy'
```

In this case, however, Joy may still be able to login to the database if she is still a member of the HR group under Windows.

As you can see, it makes more sense to handle user authorization at the group level rather than the level of the individual user. If you make changes to a group, then you are not left with the problem of 'dangling users'.

Note that you cannot remove the dbo user, and you cannot remove a user who owns an object in the current database. If you need to revoke access for a user with objects in a database, you can use the `sp_changeobjectowner` stored procedure to change ownership.

Managing Roles

Database roles are similar to groups in Windows. You can use groups to collect users into a single entity and manage permissions using the collection instead of a single entity. If you are already creating logins based on Windows groups, you are already achieving this behavior. However, database roles add an extra degree of flexibility.

There are two different types of role:

❑ Fixed server roles: these apply at the server level and are in built in the database server. They cannot be deleted or changed.

❑ Database roles: these are applicable at the level of the individual database. Again, there is a set of fixed database roles that are defined for you, but you can also write your own custom roles.

You'll see later on in this section how to create your own application-specific roles. It's worth taking a look at the built-in roles first, however, to see if they might fit your needs.

In this section, we'll also begin to touch upon specific database permissions; for example, is a given user allowed to create a table or query a table? Once we have a better understanding of the roles, we will then tackle specific permissions in a database in the next section.

Fixed Server Roles

Adding a user to a fixed server role will grant the user all of the permissions associated with the server role. Server roles are "fixed" because you cannot add or remove these roles, and you cannot modify the permissions assigned to them. The following table gives the name of each server role and a general description of the permissions associated with the role:

Fixed Server Role	Users in this role are allowed to:
sysadmin	Perform any activity on the server. (The BUILTIN\Administrator group is a member of this role by default. This is the administrative role.)
serveradmin	Modify configuration settings on the server and shut the server down.
setupadmin	Add and remove remote (linked) servers.
securityadmin	Manage logins and change passwords.
processadmin	Manage processes in the engine, and could, for example, kill a connection.
dbcreator	Add, modify, and remove databases.
diskadmin	Manage the physical disk files used by the server for data storage.
bulkadmin	Perform bulk inserts to the database.

To view the specific permissions assigned to each fixed server role, execute the sp_srvrolepermission stored procedure. Alternatively, you can use the **Server Role Permissions** button in AdminHelp to display the results of the stored procedure. The utility will first ask you to select the name of the server role to display. As an example, permissions for the dbcreator role are shown below:

You can add database users to a fixed server role with the sp_addsrvrolemember stored procedure. Since these are server-level roles, not database roles, you must add a login name, not a user name from a specific database. For example, if Joy still has a valid login we could make Joy a member of the sysadmin group with the following command:

```
EXEC sp_addsrvrolemember 'ComputerName\Joy', 'sysadmin'
```

You can view members in each server role by executing `sp_helpsrvrolemember`. This query is also available from AdminHelp by clicking the **Server Role Members** button. The procedure returns a record for each member in each server role. Shown below is the output from the above command:

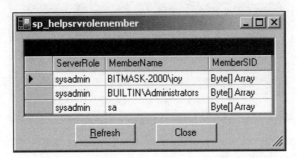

To remove a user from the `sysadmin` server role, execute the `sp_dropsrvrolemember` procedure, using the login and the role name as parameters:

```
EXEC sp_dropsrvrolemember 'ComputerName\Joy', 'sysadmin'
```

Fixed Database Roles

Adding a user to a fixed database role will grant to the user all of the permissions associated with the database role for the given database. These roles are "fixed" because you cannot add or remove these roles from a database or modify the permissions assigned to them. The table below summarizes the fixed database roles:

Fixed Database Role	Description
db_owner	Users can perform any activity in the database.
db_accessadmin	Users can add or remove users in the database.
db_securityadmin	Manages all permissions, roles, and role memberships.
db_ddladmin	Users can issue data definition language commands to create, drop, and alter objects.
db_backupoperator	Users can perform backup and diagnostic operations.
db_datareader	Users can issues SELECT queries on any user table in the database.
db_datawriter	Users can modify the data in any user table (using INSERT, UPDATE, DELETE SQL statements).
db_denydatareader	Denies permissions to select data to any members of the role.
db_denydatawriter	Denies modification permissions to any member of the role.

To uncover the specific permissions assigned to a fixed database role, use the
`sp_dbfixedrolepermission` stored procedure, or click the **Fixed Role Permissions** button in
AdminHelp. Sample output for the `db_datawriter` role is below:

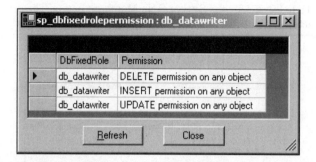

A member placed into `db_datawriter` role will be able to perform `INSERT`, `UPDATE`, and `DELETE`
commands on any table in the database.

If an existing database role already has the required permission set for a user, the best solution is to use the
fixed database role instead of creating a new role. To add a user into a role, execute the
`sp_addrolemember` stored procedure, passing the database role and the user name:

```
EXEC sp_addrolemember 'db_owner', 'joy'
```

You can view a list of the roles with and their members using the `sp_helprolemember` procedure. You
can view these in AdminHelp by clicking the **Role Members** command button.

Removing a user from a role is accomplished with the `sp_droprolemember` procedure:

```
EXEC sp_droprolemember 'db_owner', 'joy'
```

The Public Role

Every database also contains a fixed role named **public**. Every user in a database is a member of the `public`
role. You cannot remove the `public` role, nor can you add or remove users from it. The permissions
assigned to the public role become the default permissions for the database.

Let's now take a look at permissions after we see how to create our own custom roles.

Creating Roles

You can create a custom role using the `sp_addrole` stored procedure, passing the role name as shown
below:

```
EXEC sp_addrole 'customrole'
```

You can only create roles at the database level. The only server roles available are the fixed server roles created by default. Adding a user to a custom role uses the same `sp_addrolemember` procedure we have seen earlier:

```
EXEC sp_addrolemember 'customrole', 'hr'
```

If we now take a look at the available roles and users for the database through AdminHelp (with the **Role Members** button), we should find the following results:

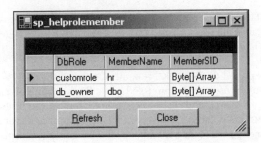

Notice the dialog only shows the roles currently populated with users. Even though other fixed database roles exist in Northwind, they do not have any members. The stored procedure will also not show the members of the `public` group, since all users (and even the other groups) are members of the this group.

To remove a role, execute the `sp_droprole` stored procedure, passing the name of the role as a parameter. However, you need to remove all members of a role before the procedure returns success. You can remove a member from a role with the `sp_droprolemember` stored procedure:

```
EXEC sp_droprolemember 'customrole', 'hr'
EXEC sp_droprole 'customrole'
```

With all of our users and roles in place, we can finally begin to look at how to assign specific permissions to our users, and our roles.

Applying Permissions

The ability to adjust permissions comes in three flavors: you can **grant**, **deny**, or **revoke** permissions. You give these permissions to database users, or roles, and permissions are granted, revoked, or denied on database objects (such as tables and stored procedures), and even at a finer-granularity on a limited number of statements (such as CREATE TABLE).

The ability to adjust the permissions in a database is restricted to a limited number of roles. You need to be in the sysadmin server role, or the db_owner or db_securityadmin database roles. The owner of a database object (the creator) is also allowed to adjust permissions for their own objects.

First, we will review the differences between grant, deny, and revoke using a simple example. In the following sections we will change the ability for users to SELECT data from the Employees table of the Northwind database.

Revoke a Permission

In the Northwind database, the `public` role has the ability to `SELECT` from the `Employees` table. Recall that every database user is a member of the `public` group, so any user has the ability to `SELECT` from the `Employees` table. In order to start imposing restrictions in Northwind, we will first need to remove this permission from the `public` role. You can remove a permission with the `REVOKE` command:

```
REVOKE SELECT ON Employees TO public
```

The revoke syntax for a database object (such as a table) requires you to specify the privilege(s) (such as `SELECT`), the object name, and the user or role you are removing the privilege from. We will take a closer look at available privileges later in this section.

After an administrator has applied this `REVOKE` statement, none of the users will be able to retrieve data from the table – with the exception of users in certain fixed roles. Remember, you can never adjust the permissions of fixed roles, such as the `sysadmin` and `db_owner` roles. Users placed in these roles will always have unrestricted access to objects in a database. However, our `hr` group has a user account in the database but belongs to no roles other than `public`. If a member of the `hr` group performs a `SELECT` on `Employees`, they will receive the following error:

Server: Msg 229, Level 14, State 5, Line 1
SELECT permission denied on object 'Employees', database 'Northwind', owner 'dbo'.

> *Remember, we mapped the database user* hr *to the Windows group* HR *earlier in the chapter with* `sp_grantdbaccess`, *so the database user* hr *is an alias for the Windows group* HR.

Grant a Permission

Granting a permission will allow a user or role to perform some activity. In the example below, we grant permission to the `hr` users to `SELECT` from the employee table. The syntax is similar to `REVOKE`:

```
GRANT SELECT ON Employees TO hr
```

Here, we allow all three members of the `hr` group (Joy, Tim, and Amy) to `SELECT` from the `Employees` table once more.

Deny a Permission

Denying a permission explicitly prohibits a user or role from obtaining a permission, even through inheritance. While `REVOKE` will remove a previous permission, `DENY` simply insures the permission cannot be gained. Remember, a user may be a member of multiple groups or roles, and each collection might grant different permissions. The only way to ensure a user or role never has a specific permission is to explicitly `DENY` the permission.

As an example, let's first add Tim as an explicit user to the database:

```
EXEC sp_grantdbaccess 'ComputerName\Tim', 'tim'
```

When Tim accesses the Northwind database, he will now do so as the user `tim`, instead of the user `hr`. Remember, the database engine is as selective as possible when mapping a login to a database user. Now we will explicitly DENY Tim's SELECT access to the `Employees` table:

```
DENY SELECT On Employees TO tim
```

Although Tim has been explicitly granted the permission to SELECT from `Employees` earlier as a member of the Windows group HR, we have now specifically denied this privilege to `tim`, so he will no longer have this permission.

> A **DENY** takes precedence over any permissions a user, group, or role has been given with a **GRANT**. Explicitly denying a permission ensures the permission is never inherited from another role or group. However, a **DENY** will not work against a fixed server role.

We can see a specific example of DENY in action in the following section.

Resolving Permission Conflicts

We've changed a few of the permissions on the database now, so let's quickly review the actions on the `Employee` table to this point:

- ❑   Revoked SELECT to the `public`
- ❑   Granted SELECT to the group `hr`
- ❑   Denied SELECT to the user `tim`

Now let's explicitly add Amy (the third member of the HR group) to the database with the following command:

```
EXEC sp_grantdbaccess 'ComputerName\Amy', 'amy'
```

and revoke Joy's permission to select from the `Employees` table:

```
REVOKE SELECT ON Employees TO joy
```

At this point we have conflicting permissions. Amy is a member of the HR group, and since we granted this group SELECT permissions, Amy can still SELECT from `Employees`. In the next line, we have revoked the permission for Joy. However, she is still a member of the HR group and inherits the permissions of HR. The permissions allow Joy to SELECT from `Employees`. A REVOKE (unlike a DENY) will not take away permissions granted to a user from another role or group. To Tim, on the other hand, we explicitly denied SELECT permission, and the database will not allow him to inherit this permission from the HR group he is a member of. The following diagram illustrates the behavior:

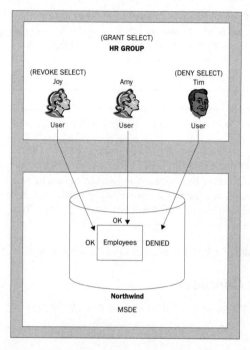

With a better understanding of GRANT, DENY, and REVOKE, let's move on and take a look at the other permissions we can adjust with these statements.

Object Permissions

Object permissions are the permissions you can apply to objects, such as tables or stored procedures. So far, we've been looking at how to work with the SELECT permission in our examples. For tables and views we can grant, deny, or revoke the following permissions:

- ❏ SELECT
- ❏ INSERT
- ❏ DELETE
- ❏ UPDATE
- ❏ REFERENCES
- ❏ EXECUTE

The first four items in the list above control the ability to execute SELECT, INSERT, DELETE, and UPDATE commands respectively. You can place more than one permission in a GRANT, DENY, or REVOKE statement in a comma-separated list. For example, if we wanted to allow the hr group to retrieve rows, insert rows, and update row from the employee table (but not delete rows), we could use the following command:

```
GRANT SELECT, INSERT, UPDATE ON Employees TO hr
```

For `SELECT` and `UPDATE` statements, you can include a column list to grant, deny, or revoke permissions on specific columns, instead of the entire table. For example, if we wanted to remove Joy's ability to see the `BirthDate` and `HireDate` columns, we could use the following command:

```
DENY SELECT (BirthDate, HireDate) ON Employees TO Joy
```

Notice we need to use a `DENY` statement instead of a `REVOKE`, because `REVOKE` will not take away the `GRANT` we gave to the `HR` group, which Joy is a member of. Joy can still update the table with the previous grant, but if Joy tries to retrieve all columns from the database table the following errors will occur:

```
Server: Msg 230, Level 14, State 1, Line 1
SELECT permission denied on column 'HireDate' of object 'Employees', database 'Northwind', owner 'dbo'.
Server: Msg 230, Level 14, State 1, Line 1
SELECT permission denied on column 'BirthDate' of object 'Employees', database 'Northwind', owner 'dbo'.
```

You can use the `REFERENCES` permission to control the placement of foreign key constraints on a table. Foreign key constraints have an obvious impact on `INSERT`, `UPDATE`, and `DELETE` logic for a table, as well as performance implications. We could remove the permission from the `public` role like this:

```
REVOKE REFERENCES ON Employees TO public
```

Stored procedures have only one permission to regulate: `EXECUTE`. This permission controls the ability to invoke a stored procedure. We can revoke the ability to execute the customer order history procedure (`CustOrderHist`) from the public role like this:

```
REVOKE EXECUTE ON CustOrderHist TO public
```

Finally, there is a shortcut to modify all permissions for a given object at once. This uses the `ALL` keyword:

```
REVOKE ALL ON Employees TO public
```

The command removes any permissions the `public` role has on the `Employees` table.

Statement Permissions

You also have the ability to grant, deny, or revoke permissions on a select list of statements at the database level. These permissions relate to the kinds of things you can do in terms of the actual structure of the database rather than simply the data it contains. The statements include:

- ❑   CREATE DATABASE
- ❑   CREATE DEFAULT
- ❑   CREATE FUNCTION

- ❏ CREATE PROCEDURE
- ❏ CREATE RULE
- ❏ CREATE TABLE
- ❏ CREATE VIEW
- ❏ BACKUP DATABASE
- ❏ BACKUP LOG

By default, only members of the sysadmin, db_owner, and ddl_admin roles have the ability to create a table. We can give Joy the permission to create tables in the Northwind database with the following command:

```
GRANT CREATE TABLE TO Joy
```

Notice some statements are not present in the list, for example, DROP TABLE and ALTER TABLE. Permissions for these statements are implicitly given to the owner of a database object (and of course system administrators and database owners, who have full control). If Joy has permission to create a table, then she will have the ability to change or delete any table she has created.

Viewing Permissions

You can view permissions using the stored procedure sp_helprotect. This procedure allows you to view all the permission settings in the database, or to view just the settings regarding a specific object and/or user.

The AdminHelp utility provides an interface to the sp_helprotect procedure. The **All Permissions** button will list all of the permission settings in the current database. As you can see by the scroll bar in the screenshot below, listing all of the permission settings in a database can produce many output records:

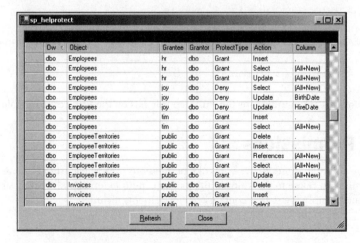

You can also view the permissions assigned to a specific user or role by clicking the **Permissions By User / Role** button. A dialog will pop up asking you to select the user or role to view in a combo box. The following screenshot shows the permissions given to Joy:

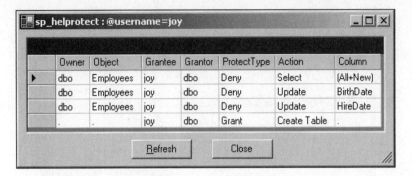

Finally, you can view the permissions assigned to a specific object using the **Permissions By Object** button. You can then select one of the user tables, stored procedures, views, or statements to see the permissions for the given object. The following screenshot shows a sample report for the Employees table:

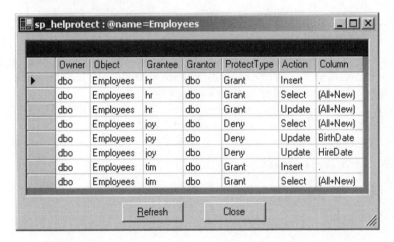

The sp_helprotect stored procedure only provides output for explicit permissions. The permissions given to fixed roles (such as sysadmin or db_owner) are implicit, unchangeable, and not listed in the output.

AdminHelp and Viewing Object Permissions

We have seen a few examples now of using AdminHelp when a parameter is required for the query. In these cases, AdminHelp uses a form named PickOne to allow the user to select a parameter from a ComboBox, shown in the design view overleaf:

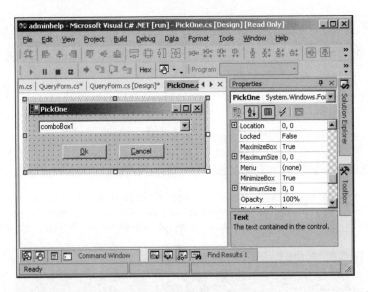

The `ComboBox` is populated with one of the two methods of the `PickOne` form shown below. The `PickOne` form maintains an `ArrayList` as a data source for the combo box. Items are added to the `ArrayList` from a `SqlDataReader` or from a string array:

```
public void AppendListContents(SqlDataReader sqlDataReader,
                               string fieldName)
{
    while(sqlDataReader.Read())
    {
        list.Add(sqlDataReader[fieldName]);
    }
    PickList.DataSource = list;
}

public void AppendListContents(string [] items)
{
    for(int i = 0; i < items.Length; i++)
    {
        list.Add(items[i]);
    }
    PickList.DataSource = list;
}
```

The reason we have two methods to populate the `ComboBox` is that some of our queries build the parameter list from hard-coded values as well as from a database query. For example, the last query we demonstrated was calling `sp_helpprotect` to view the permissions on a database object. We want to populate the list with the names of the tables, stored procedures, and views in the database (excluding the system, as well as a list of the statement permissions, which we can keep in an array.

```
private void PermissionObject_Click(object sender, System.EventArgs e)
{
    CheckConnection();
    if(sqlConnection != null)
    {
        PickOne pickOne = new PickOne("Select an object or statement");

        SqlCommand sqlCommand = GetUserObjectsCommand();
        SqlDataReader sqlDataReader = sqlCommand.ExecuteReader();

        pickOne.AppendListContents(sqlDataReader, "name");

        sqlDataReader.Close();

        string [] statementPermissions =
            {
                "CREATE DATABASE",  "CREATE DEFAULT",   "CREATE FUNCTION",
                "CREATE PROCEDURE", "CREATE RULE",      "CREATE TABLE",
                "CREATE VIEW",      "BACKUP DATABASE",  "BACKUP LOG"
            };

        pickOne.AppendListContents(statementPermissions);

        if(pickOne.ShowDialog() == DialogResult.OK)
        {
            sqlCommand = GetPermissionsCommand();
            SqlParameter sqlParameter = new SqlParameter("@name",
                                                    pickOne.Selected);
            sqlCommand.Parameters.Add(sqlParameter);

            QueryForm queryForm = new QueryForm(sqlCommand);
            queryForm.ShowDialog();
        }
    }
}
```

If the user successfully picks one of the objects or statements from the PickOne dialog, we can add a parameter to the command's Parameter collection and pass the command to QueryForm for execution and display.

Implementing Security

Implementing a security design requires you to analyze all of your users and how they are going to use your application. Typically, the users will fall into one of the following groups, although larger applications and larger organizations might well require more fine-grained control:

❑ Users who require full control of the database application

❑ Users who perform a handful of administrative tasks, such as backing up the database

❑ Typical application users, who can query a majority of the tables, but might have restrictions placed on certain objects

❑ Special application users, who have the all of the abilities of a typical application user, plus additional rights

Remember, first you will need to grant login rights to the server for any users or Windows groups who require access. For a concrete example, let's image we are writing a customer service forms-based application and have the following Windows users and groups:

Account	Description
WROX\dbas	Database administrator group
WROX\netoperations	Network operations, responsible for backups and other maintenance duties
WROX\customerservice	Customer service employees, who require read and update permission on all of the tables with the exception of a few tables and fields with sensitive information
WROX\Jill	A customer service manager, who will have all of the permissions of the customer service group, and the additional capability to view and modify sensitive information

You could add the WROX\dbas group to the sysadmin fixed server role, giving members control over each database on the server. Recall there is also the fixed database role, db_owner, if you wish to restrict the highest level of control to a single database, instead of all databases on the server.

By adding the Wrox\netoperations group to the db_backupoperator fixed role in the database, we can allow the network operations group to perform backups of the database.

You can GRANT permissions to the non-sensitive database objects directly to the customerservice group, and then GRANT additional permissions to Jill. Ideally, Jill would belong to Windows group identifying her as a customer service manager. However, if she does not, instead of granting access to sensitive areas of the database directly to Jill, we could create a new role in the database, called managers for example, assign Jill to the role, and give the additional GRANTs to this role. This provides an extra layer of indirection, in case we need to re-assign or assign new privileges to others.

This is just one example of an application with simple security requirements. More complex applications will require additional planning with additional custom roles.

Summary

In this chapter we have presented the basic security concepts for MSDE and SQL Server.

❑ Using Windows and Mixed Mode Authentication

❑ Mapping server logins to database accounts

❑ Grouping users into custom roles, fixed server roles, and fixed database roles

❑ GRANT, REVOKE, and DENY permissions on database objects and statements

Taking advantage of these features will help you to create a secure and flexible database application.

Exercises

1. If your database is configured for Windows authentication, add an additional login to the database from the list of users on your machine. If you are using mixed-mode authentication, add a login for the user 'Bart', with a password of 'chips'.

2. In Exercise 1, you added a new login to the database server. Now give the login access to the Northwind database.

3. Try adding a custom role to the Northwind database named 'readers'.

4. Given the user created in Step 1, give the user read-only access to objects in the Northwind database. Hint: You can use a fixed database role.

5. Given the custom role 'reader' created in Exercise 3, make sure members in this role can never DELETE records from the Employees table.

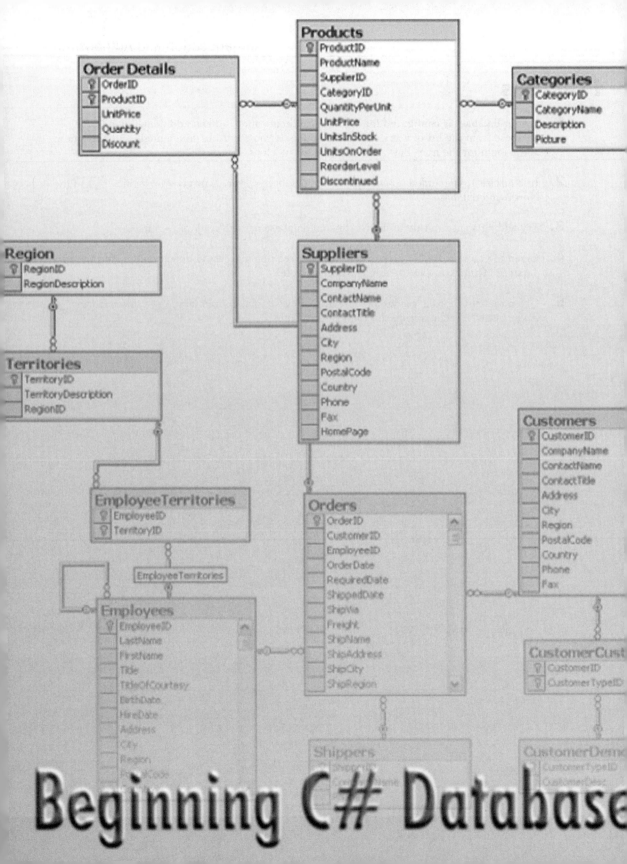

Beginning C# Database

XML and ADO.NET

XML (eXtensible Markup Language) is a means of storing data in simple, structured, text-based format. The self-describing nature of XML makes it very convenient for exchanging information between systems.

The use of XML today is so widespread that there is very extensive support for it in .NET and, thus, in Visual Studio .NET and C# too. While the intent of this chapter is not to delve deeply into XML, we will discuss the basics and how XML can be used in C# applications. Specifically, we will explore the following topics:

❑ Advantages and disadvantages of XML

❑ The structure of an XML document

❑ ADO.NET support for XML

❑ *Try It Out* exercises to experiment with XML from C#

XML is a very big topic and it can be put to use in many ways. In this chapter, we will cover only the very basic features of XML. To get up to speed with XML, there's an XML primer in Appendix B that you can refer to. However, if you want to know more about XML than this, you should refer to *Beginning XML 2nd Edition*, Wrox Press (ISBN 1-86100-559-8).

The Pros and Cons of XML

XML is becoming the defacto standard for data exchange in the industry. It is very easy to use and very flexible in that it allows you to make up your own tag elements. A snippet of XML looks like this:

```
<book>
  <title>Title1</title>
  <author>Author1</author>
</book>
```

You can see that this document contains three elements. There is a `title` element, delimited by an opening tag `<title>` and a closing tag `<title/>`, which contains the data `Title1`. There is a similar `author` element, and both the `title` and `author` elements are contained within a `book` element. This hierarchical structure is typical of XML.

We'll examine the structure more later on. For now, here's a list of the important advantages to using the XML format.

❑ XML is a text-based format containing data and a semantic description of that data. This makes the format very human-readable. Its hierarchical, structured nature makes it effective for storing series of records, for example addresses or purchase orders.

❑ XML is a platform-independent standard. This makes it an excellent format for exchanging data between applications, even when they are running on different operating systems. The popularity and strength of the standard is such that XML has been very deeply integrated into the .NET Framework and C#.

❑ XML is at the heart of web services – a way of programmatically accessing functionality over the Internet. Discovery documents used to locate available web services are stored in the XML format.

❑ XML parsing is well defined and widely implemented, making it possible to retrieve information from XML documents in a variety of environments. Using schemas (themselves a specialized form of XML document), the structure of the XML data can be validated before acceptance.

❑ XML is built on a Unicode foundation, making it easy to create internationalized documents.

❑ The resultset of a query from a relational database can be obtained in XML using the XML support in SQL Server 2000 and MSDE.

❑ C# code can be documented with XML and, using VS.NET, we can compile all the documentation into an HTML file.

❑ XML documents can use the HTTP protocol and can be transferred across firewalls more easily than binary data.

Of course, there are a few drawbacks to using XML as well. Its text-based format means that:

❑ Data stored as XML will be more verbose than the binary representation of the same data

❑ XML data takes up more network bandwidth and storage space

❑ XML parsing can be slower than parsing highly optimized binary formats and can require more memory

The flexibility, human-readability, and open standard of XML mean that its advantages far outweigh the disadvantages. Almost all software these days comes with some support for XML. Let us now look at the basic structure of an XML document in more detail and create one in VS.NET.

The Structure of an XML Document

An XML document can be a file in the disk or a string in memory. Here's our simple XML document again:

```
<xml version="1.0" encoding="utf-8" ?>
<book>
  <title>Title1</title>
  <author>Author1</author>
</book>
```

The document begins with an XML **declaration**, as follows:

```
<xml version="1.0" encoding="utf-8" ?>
```

The XML standard itself and those standards that complement it (for searching, presenting, and transporting XML) are all designed by the Internet standards body called the World Wide Web Commission, or W3C for short (www.w3c.org). XML itself is still at version 1.0. Hence this line, which appears in the beginning of most XML documents.

Next, the XML document is made up of one or more **elements**. As we saw before, each element consists of an opening tag with the name for the element, the data within the element, and a closing tag. In addition, elements can contain other elements – in our code snippet, the <title> and <author> elements are part of the <book> element.

Each element can also have **attributes**. For example, in the following element called author, id is an attribute with a **value** of 1234. The value of the author element itself is Ranga.

```
<author id="1234">Ranga</author>
```

You can make up your own tags, as long as they are constructed properly. Properly constructed XML files are classified as **well-formed**. How do you know if an XML document is well-formed? There are many rules but the main ones are

❑ Every document must start with an XML declaration.

❑ Every document must have a single top-level element, known as the **root** element (in our example, this is <book>).

❑ Elements are case sensitive, so <title> and <Title> are different elements.

❑ Elements must be closed in the reverse order that they were opened. So <title>Title1<author>Author1</title></author> is illegal.

While an XML document is stored in a file or in a string variable in memory, there is a Document Object Model (DOM) available to access the different parts of the document. This object model is referred to as the **XML-DOM**. The XML-DOM refers to elements, attributes, and textual content as the **nodes** of the document. The .NET Framework provides a namespace called System.Xml that contains classes that implement the XML-DOM.

Let's jump in and create a simple XML document using Visual Studio. In this file, we will represent two books, their titles, the authors of those titles, and their ages. After constructing the file, we will view it and then modify it.

Try It Out: Creating an XML Document from Visual Studio .NET

1. Create a new chapter solution, and call it `Chapter17_Examples`.

2. Create a C# Windows Application project within our solution and call it `Chapter17`.

3. Right-click on the newly-created project node in Solution Explorer and select **Add** and **Add New Item**. Select the **XML File** template item (as shown below), and make sure the file name is `XMLFile1.xml`. Then press **Open**.

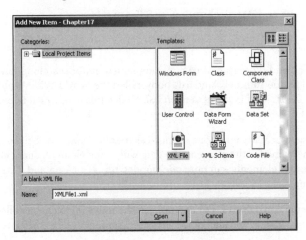

4. Edit the file so that it reads as follows:

```xml
<?xml version="1.0" encoding="utf-8" ?>
<books>
  <book>
    <title>Title1</title>
    <author>
      <name>Author1</name>
      <age>34</age>
    </author>
  </book>
  <book>
    <title>Title2</title>
    <author>
      <name>Author2</name>
      <age>24</age>
    </author>
  </book>
</books>
```

5. Right-click in the editor and select **View Data**. Even though the XML file is in a hierarchical text format, it can be shown in the familiar grid format. You will see the data in the XML file rendered as follows:

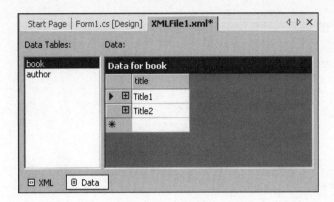

6. Expand the plus signs next to Title1 and Title2 and click on the book author link to see the author information for each title. As you can see, even though the data was described in XML using tags, VS.NET shows it to you in a relational manner. Notice that you can see the XML file in either the data format or XML format by clicking on the XML and Data buttons at the bottom left of the window.

7. Now, let us try to add a new title in the data view and see if the XML file changes to reflect this. Click on the row marked with an asterisk below Title2 and type Title3. Then expand the node, click on the book author link, and enter Author3 and 54 for age:

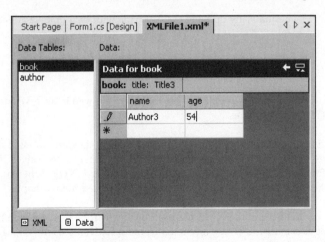

8. Click on the XML button on the bottom left corner of the window. You will now see the new XML document listed as follows:

```
<?xml version="1.0" encoding="utf-8" ?>
<books>
  <book>
    <title>Title1</title>
    <author>
      <name>Author1 </name>
      <age>34</age>
    </author>
  </book>
  <book>
    <title>Title2</title>
    <author>
      <name>Author2</name>
      <age>24</age>
    </author>
  </book>
  <book>
    <title>Title3</title>
    <author>
      <name>Author3</name>
      <age>54</age>
    </author>
  </book>
</books>
```

As you can see, VS.NET automatically updated the XML file with data that we added in the data view.

Schemas

There are two ways to define what elements and attributes are allowed in an XML document – Document Type Definitions (DTDs) and Schemas.

DTDs were invented first but, because they use non-XML syntax, they are not used much in the .NET Framework. Schemas, on the other hand, are actually XML documents themselves. .NET supports two types – XML Schema Definition (XSD) schemas and XML-Data Reduced (XDR) schemas. XDR schemas are a Microsoft-specific format; XSD is more widely used and will be used in this chapter.

Schemas can either be included in the XML file itself or they can be in a separate file, which is referenced by the XML file. Let us see how to create a schema from an XML file using VS.NET. Follow the steps outlined.

Try It Out: Creating an XSD Schema from VS.NET

1. In the VS.NET IDE, open the `XMLFile1.xml` file that we created in the previous exercise and right-click on it. In the popup menu, select **Create Schema** as shown:

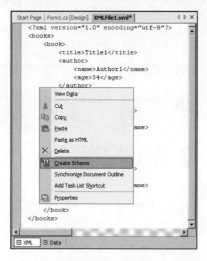

2. A file called `XMLFile1.xsd` is immediately created and added to the project.

In `XMLFile1.xml`, notice that the new XSD file has been referenced now, as follows:

```
<books xmlns="http://tempuri.org/XMLFile1.xsd">
```

By doing this, the XML file has now been restricted to only allow elements that are defined in the XSD file. We will try to violate this schema and see what happens in the next step. http://tempuri.org is a temporary link. When you deploy your application, you will need to replace this with your company's website so that the parsers can identify the location of your XSD file – for example, http://www.yourcompany.com/XMLFile1.xsd.

3. In the `XMLFile1.xml` file, add a new element to `Author1` called `<salary>`, as follows:

4. Notice that the editor marks it with a red wavy underline and the tool tip says that the active schema does not support the `salary` element. This warning shows us that the schema specified in the XSD file is keeping our XML document in clean shape. Observe that the `salary` element is ignored in the data view.

5. Now open the `XMLFile1.xsd` file in the editor. You will be presented with the following view of the schema:

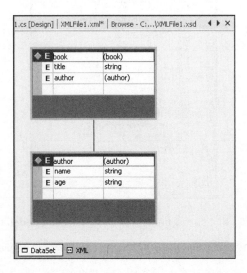

6. Observe that the presentation looks like a relational database. The book element has title and author properties and the author element in turn has name and age properties. This view is only a graphical representation. The actual code in the XSD file can be seen by clicking the **XML** button in the lower left corner. The `XMLFile1.xsd` file has been created by VS.NET, based on the elements in `XMLFile1.xml` as follows:

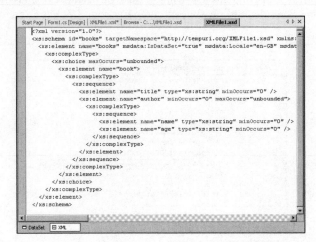

As you can see, the elements in this file are quite complex. There is a whole set of elements and rules required for an XSD schema. We will not cover this topic any further; it is sufficient for our purposes to know how to create an XSD file from an XML file in VS.NET.

Valid XML

An XML file that has an associated schema is considered **valid** when the structure and content of the XML file is consistent with the schema. The elements in the XML document must appear in the structure defined in the schema and the content of the individual elements must conform to the data types specified in the schema.

Note that XML documents can be both well-formed *and* valid. A document that is not well-formed will raise errors with a parser. A document that *is* well-formed can be parsed properly whether it has an associated schema or not.

The XML Designer can be used to verify that XML files are both well-formed and valid. Let's work through this now.

Try It Out: Using VS.NET to Test if an XML Document is Well-Formed and Valid

1. Load the XML file you want to check into the XML Designer. When an XML file is in the editor, the XML menu is shown in the main menu bar along the top. Select XML | Validate XML Data.

2. The status bar will indicate if errors were found in the XML file. If errors *were* found – that is, the document is not well-formed – they will be listed in the Task List window. In this case, we have loaded an XML document that is not well-formed and does not have an associated schema either:

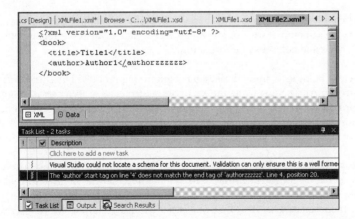

The top error message in the Task List says, "Visual Studio could not locate a schema for this document. Validation can only ensure this is a well formed XML document and cannot validate the data against a schema."

3. If a schema is specified but the XML file does not conform to the schema, then you will get the following types of messages in the Task List window. These indicate that the file is not valid.

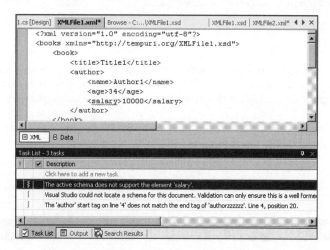

4. If the file is valid – it obeys the schema – then the Task List window will be empty.

With the basic knowledge of XML and XSD that we have gained so far, we can jump in to learn how ADO.NET incorporates XML in its classes and how to use them from C# applications.

ADO.NET and XML

We have seen that data formatted using XML appears in a hierarchical format as opposed to a rows-and-columns format. At the same time, we also know that ADO.NET is all about relational database management, with rows and columns of information.

The .NET architecture helps us to unify these two programming models. The DataSet class represents a relational data source in ADO.NET, while the XmlDocument class in System.Xml implements the XML-DOM, letting us programmatically access the elements of an XML document. The unifies ADO.NET and XML by representing relational data from a DataSet and synchronizing it with the XML-DOM. In other words, the XmlDataDocument maps XML to relational data in an ADO.NET DataSet.

ADO.NET objects such as the SqlCommand object and the DataSet object support XML. The SqlCommand object has an ExecuteXMLReader() method that can be used to get an XML document from the tables and present the data in a hierarchical view by navigating the document using the classes in the System.Xml namespace. The DataSet object has extensive support for XML; the data in a DataSet is stored internally in XML format. We can read data from an XML document into a DataSet and write a DataSet into an XML document. Let's go ahead and see how to do this.

Try It Out: Reading an XML Document into a DataSet

1. In `Form1.cs`, add three buttons and datagrid as follows. Name the buttons `btnReadXML`, `btnWriteXML`, and `btnConfigXML`, and the datagrid `dataGrid1`.

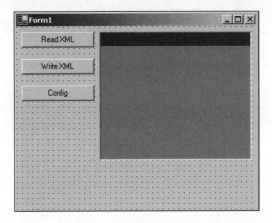

2. In the `Click` event of the `btnReadXML` button, type in the following lines of code:

```
private void btnReadXML_Click(object sender, System.EventArgs e)
{
  DataSet ds = new DataSet();
  ds.ReadXml("c:\\BegCSharpDb\\Chapter17\\XMLFile1.xml",
          XmlReadMode.InferSchema);
  dataGrid1.SetDataBinding(ds,"book");
}
```

3. Build and run the solution. When the form pops up, click on the Read XML button. You will see that the XML file has been read and the datagrid has been populated, as shown next. You can click on the book author links to see the name and age.

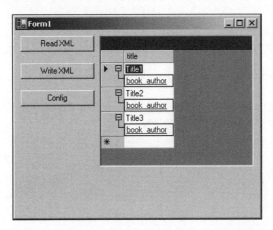

How It Works

First we create a `DataSet` object as follows:

```
DataSet ds = new DataSet();
```

Then we use the `ReadXML()` method of the `DataSet` object and specify the name and location of the file.

```
ds.ReadXml("c:\\BegCSharpDB\\Chapter17\\XMLFile1.xml",XmlReadMode.InferSchema);
```

The `ReadXML()` method takes the mode that is used to read the XML document file as a parameter. XML documents can be read in several modes and these modes are listed as `XMLReadMode` enumerations. We use `InferSchema` to tell the `ReadXML()` method that the schema for this document must be inferred from the XML document itself and not from the XSD file.

Finally, we bind the table in the `DataSet` to the datagrid – here `book` is the name of the `DataTable` and `ds` is the `DataSet` that contains it. We bind this to the datagrid using the `SetDataBinding()` method of the datagrid control.

```
dataGrid1.SetDataBinding(ds,"book");
```

Now let us try to change the `DataSet` and write back the changes to the XML file.

Try It Out: Writing a DataSet to an XML File

1. In the **Write XML** button's `Click` event, write code as follows:

```
private void btnWriteXML_Click(object sender, System.EventArgs e)
{
  DataSet ds;
  ds=(DataSet) dataGrid1.DataSource;
  ds.WriteXml(C:\\BegCSharpDB\\Chapter17\\XMLFileOut.xml",
              XmlWriteMode.IgnoreSchema);
}
```

2. Build the solution and run it.

3. Click on the **ReadXML** button and populate the datagrid with the contents of the XML file.

4. Now click on the **book author** link in the row for **Title2**. You will be taken to the screen shown next. Change the age of the author to 44.

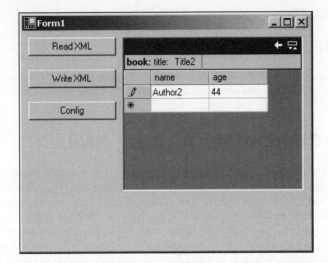

5. Now click on the **WriteXML** button. The `XMLFileOut.xml` file will be created in the `Chapter17` folder. Close the application and add the `XMLFileOut.xml` file to the project by using the **Add | Add Existing Item** context menu option in Solution Explorer.

6. Open the `XMLFileOut.xml` file, right-click on it, and **View Data**. Drill-down to see the age of **Author2**. It will be 44. Now see the XML source of this file and observe again that the age is listed as 44.

7. Experiment by reading the `XMLFile1.xml` file into the datagrid, changing the values in the datagrid, and writing the changes to the `XMLFileOut.xml` file.

How It Works

We first create a `DataSet` object:

```
DataSet ds = new DataSet( );
```

Then the change to the author's age is made in the datagrid. The data source of the datagrid is cast to the `DataSet` type as follows:

```
ds=(DataSet) dataGrid1.DataSource;
```

Now we use the `WriteXML()` method of the `DataSet` object to write the contents of the `DataSet` to the `XMLFileOut.xml` file. `XMLWriteMode.IgnoreSchema` instructs the method to write the contents of the `DataSet` to the XML file specified without regard to any schema.

```
ds.WriteXml("C:\\BegCSharpDB\\Chapter17\\XMLFileOut.xml",
            XmlWriteMode.IgnoreSchema);
```

If you experiment with reading the `XMLFile1.xml` file – changing its values in the datagrid and then writing it back to `XMLFileOut.xml` – since you have already added the `XMLFileOut.xml` file into the project, you simply have to open the file to see the change.

As you can see, reading and writing XML files is very easy thanks to the XML support in ADO.NET. Now let us see another use of XML in database applications, through Application Configuration files.

Application Configuration Using XML

An application may need some startup values when it is started. For example, database applications need a connection string to connect to the database. Instead of hard-coding this string into the application, if we can store it in a file and read it at runtime, then we can change the connection string to perhaps point to a backup database should the primary database go down. We can store the connection string in an XML file. The application can interrogate the specific section of the XML file where the connection string is stored and use it. In the past, connection strings and startup information were generally located via an entry in the registry, but this method is not so easily readable or editable. XML files give us a more robust way of handling initial values that are needed by applications.

The .NET Framework supports configuration of applications, machine, security settings, and so on using the `System.Configuration` namespace. Configuration is a large topic and a detailed discussion is beyond the scope of this book. But we will learn how to access the connection string stored in an XML file.

Configuration files are XML files that have the `.config` extension, and they must have the same name as the assembly. For example, if `chapter17.exe` is the name of the executable assembly, then the name of the configuration file must be `chapter17.exe.config`. The config file must be in the same folder as the assembly or in the Global Assembly Cache. Depending on what we are trying to configure, the config file can implement one of several schemas available – for example, a Startup Settings schema, a Network Setting schema, or a Configuration Sections schema. Each schema has a specific set of elements. The Configuration Sections schema provides XML elements that can be used to specify custom application settings, such as the connection string. So, let us now create an XML file called `chapter17.exe.config` and access the connection string therein from a C# application.

Try It Out – Creating an Application Configuration File

1. Right-click on the **Chapter17** project node and select **Add | Add New Item**. Create an XML file called `chapter17.exe.config`.

2. Edit it to add elements as follows:

```
<?xml version="1.0" encoding="utf-8" ?>
<configuration>
  <appSettings>
    <add key="cnNorthWind" value="Data Source=(local)\NETSDK;
       Integrated Security=SSPI;database=Northwind"/>
  </appSettings>
</configuration>
```

3. Notice that a schema file is not referenced here. It is not necessary to do so as the .NET Framework recognizes the elements that we used.

4. In the form, add the following directives (for ADO.NET, for accessing the config file, and for working with XML, respectively):

```
using System.Data.SqlClient;
using System.Configuration;
using System.Xml;
```

5. Write event code for the `btnConfigXML_Click()` event as follows:

```
private void btnConfigXML_Click(object sender, System.EventArgs e)
{
  // Get the connection string from the .config file
  string strConn= ConfigurationSettings.AppSettings["cnNorthWind"];

  // Create a new connection object based on the connection string
  SqlConnection cn=new SqlConnection( strConn);

  // Create a command object
  SqlCommand cmd=new SqlCommand();

  // Retrieve all the employees in XML format
  cmd.CommandText="SELECT EmployeeId,LastName FROM Employees FOR XML AUTO";

  // Set the connection property
  cmd.Connection=cn;

  try
  {
    // Open the connection
    cn.Open();

    // Get the XML formatted resultset into an XML reader object
    XmlReader xmlrdr= cmd.ExecuteXmlReader();

    // Create a dataset object
    DataSet ds = new DataSet();

    // Read the XmlReader object into the dataset
    ds.ReadXml(xmlrdr,XmlReadMode.InferSchema);

    // Bind the dataset to the datagrid
    dataGrid1.DataSource=ds;
  }

  catch (SqlException e1)
  {
    MessageBox.Show (e1.Message);
  }

  finally
  {
    cn.Close();
  }
}
```

6. Build the solution but don't run it yet. Copy the `chapter17.exe.config` file to the `Chapter17\bin\Debug` folder where the `chapter17.exe` file is placed by the compiler.

7. Now run the solution. When the form loads, click on the **Config** button. Expand the plus button inside the datagrid and click on the **Employees** link. You will see the grid open up as shown here.

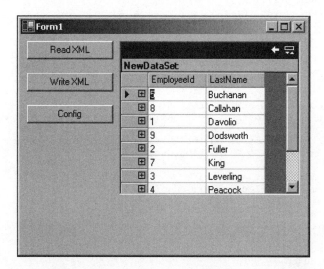

So, in this example, we placed the connection string in an XML file and the C# program accessed it using the `System.Configuration.ConfigurationSettings` class. After getting the connection string, a query was executed on the database. The XML document that the query returned was read into a `DataSet`, and the `DataSet` was bound to the datagrid.

How It Works

When creating the `chapter17.exe.config` file, we started by specifying the XML declaration and then the `<configuration>` root element.

```
<?xml version="1.0" encoding="utf-8" ?>
<configuration>
```

Then we used the `<appSettings>` element to specify the application-specific custom settings that we want:

```
<appSettings>
  <add key="cnNorthWind" value="Data Source=(local)\NETSDK;
    Integrated Security=SSPI;database=Northwind"/>
</appSettings>
```

Within the `<appSettings>` element, we added another element called `<add>` that is used to specify the key-value pair. Finally, the closing `</configuration>` element signifies the end of configurations in this file.

Next, we added the necessary `using` directives to our C# program. Then, in the `Click` event, the `AppSettings` collection of the `ConfigurationSettings` class was used to retrieve the connection string with the key `"cnNorthWind"`.

```
string strConn= ConfigurationSettings.AppSettings["cnNorthWind"];
```

A `config` file can have several keys and they can all be accessed in the same manner.

Next, we created a `SqlConnection` object using the retrieved string, and we created and initialized a `SqlCommand` object:

```
// Create a new connection object based on the connection string
SqlConnection cn=new SqlConnection(strConn);

// Create a command object
SqlCommand cmd=new SqlCommand();

// Retrieve all the employees in XML format
cmd.CommandText="SELECT EmployeeId,LastName FROM Employees FOR XML AUTO";

// Set the connection property
cmd.Connection=cn;
```

Notice that the query has some extra pieces to it. The `FOR XML AUTO` instructs the database to return the results in XML format and not in the usual rows-and-columns result set format. SQL Server 2000 and MSDE support XML, and the `SELECT` statement with `FOR XML AUTO` is one instance of this support in action. It is also possible to insert, update, and delete records in a database using XML with the `OPENXML` T-SQL statement. Refer to SQL Server Books Online or to *Professional SQL Server 2000 XML* (ISBN 1-86100-546-6) for more information about this.

Now we execute the command. Since the query will return an XML document, we cannot store it in a `SqlDataReader` object as we have done so far throughout the book. Instead, we use the `ExecuteXmlReader()` method of the `Command` object and store the XML document in an `XmlReader` object called `xmlrdr`. The `XmlReader` class belongs to the `System.Xml` namespace. This namespace contains several classes that support XML data processing.

```
try
{
  // Open the connection
  cn.Open();

  // Get the XML formatted resultset into an XML reader object
  XmlReader xmlrdr= cmd.ExecuteXmlReader();
```

Now we create a `DataSet` object and use the `ReadXml()` method to read the contents of the `xmlrdr` object. Note that the `ReadXml()` method takes the `xmlrdr` object as the argument. This is different from the previous example where a physical XML file on the disk was used to read in the data.

```
// Create a dataset object
DataSet ds = new DataSet();

// Read the XmlReader object into the dataset
ds.ReadXml(xmlrdr,XmlReadMode.InferSchema);
```

Finally, we bind the `DataSet` to the datagrid:

```
//bind the dataset to the datagrid
    dataGrid1.DataSource=ds;
```

Try changing the value properties in the config file to an incorrect machine name or database and click on the buttons to see what error message results.

Where to Go from Here

There is much to learn about XML. This section will provide you with some sources of further information.

The major thrust of .NET is around a concept called **web services**. Web services are based on XML and allow businesses to expose their services over the Web. This was possible without .NET but was more difficult due the variety of protocols, such as DCOM, RMI, CORBA, and so on. Moreover, accessing business logic through a firewall was very cumbersome. This can be achieved easily with web services, through the union of XML and HTTP in a communication protocol called the Simple Object Access Protocol, or **SOAP**. As XML and SOAP are open standards, web services can be hosted on any platform and they are becoming very powerful tools for business to business commerce and enterprise application integration.

> *For more on web services, consult* Professional ASP.NET Web Services *published by Wrox Press (ISBN 1-86100-545-8).*

You may also wish to learn about other XML-related technologies such as XPATH and XSLT. XPATH provides a mechanism to query XML documents. An XSLT style sheet is used to transform the content of a source XML document into a presentation that is tailored specifically to a particular user, media, or client.

> *For more on XPATH and XSLT, consult* Beginning XML 2nd Edition *published by Wrox Press (ISBN 1-86100-559-8).*

Summary

This chapter began with a quick overview of XML, and its advantages and disadvantages. Then, after analyzing the basic elements of an XML document, we used Visual Studio .NET to construct an XML document and generate its schema automatically. Next, support for XML in ADO.NET was discussed; we read an XML document into a `DataSet` and wrote an XML document from a `DataSet`. Finally, we looked at application configuration files, an important application of XML in database programs.

XML is a huge topic and we've just skimmed the surface here. Hopefully, this chapter will be a good foundation from which you can develop your experience with this new standard for describing and storing data.

In the next chapter, we will look at handling errors arising from our ADO.NET code and the database itself.

Exercises

1. What is wrong with the following XML document?

```
<?xml version="1.0" encoding="utf-8" ?>
<Product>
  <name>Toshiba TV</name>
  <year> 2002 </year>
</Product>
<Book>
  <Title>Beginning C# Databases </Title>
</Book>
```

2. Correct the XML above to make it well-formed.

3. Write an XML document to represent two sales orders with order numbers 101 and 102 respectively.

4. Create a XSD schema for the XML file created in Exercise 3, using VS.NET.

5. True or False? An XML file need not have a schema associated with it to be valid.

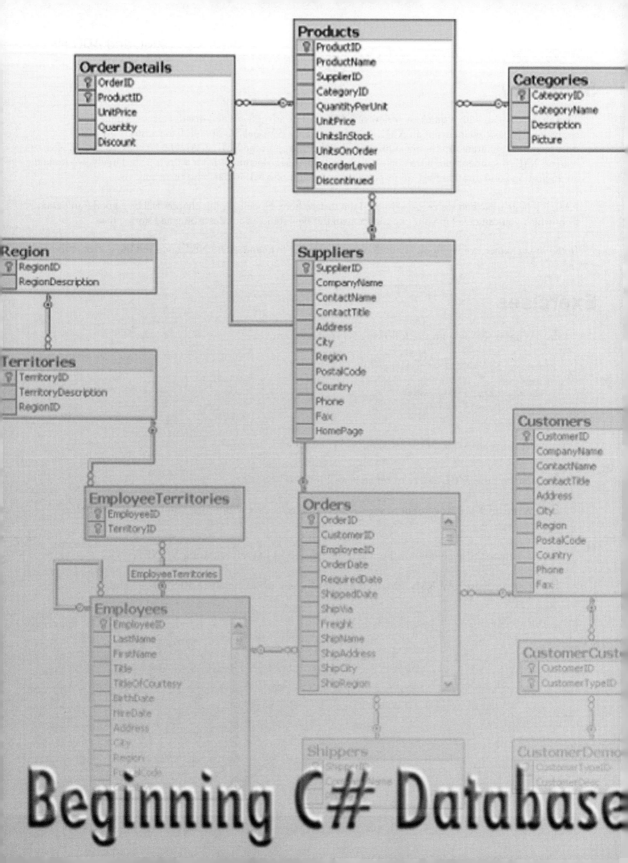

Handling ADO.NET and Database Exceptions

Before we start, we should note a terminology change that has been introduced with .NET. When something goes wrong within any .NET application, it is known as an **exception**. In .NET, the term **error** is reserved for catastrophic exceptions that your application does not usually recover from. The term exception covers these kinds of errors, along with unusual situations or problems, or even cases where sections of code generate results outside of pre-defined sets of parameters. Therefore, an exception doesn't always mean that an error has occurred.

When database-based applications generate exceptions, they mainly come from two sources – either from the ADO.NET code or from the database itself. ADO.NET exceptions can be caused by non-database sources such as network connections or the file system. It is important to handle these exceptions and recover from them in a timely and orderly fashion, and we will demonstrate basic techniques for doing this in this chapter. We will focus specifically on the `SqlClient` data provider, as this is the ADO.NET provider we've been using to connect to MDSE throughout this book. However, the ADO.NET exceptions experienced with ODBC, Oracle, or any other data providers that are around for .NET will follow a similar pattern to that which you will observe in the following pages.

Specifically, we will cover the following topics:

❑   A review of the general C# exception handling principles

❑   Understanding the difference between ADO.NET exceptions and database exceptions

❑   Handling exceptions

General Exception Handling in C#

C# supports structured exception handling using `try...catch...finally` code blocks. The syntax is as follows:

```
try
{
  // code that may throw an exception
}

catch (<ExceptionType> e)
{
```
...code that will address a specific exception...
```
}

catch (<ExceptionType> e2)
{
  // code that will address a specific exception that is different to the
  // exception caught above
}

catch
{
  // code that will address any exception not caught by any other catch code
  // defined prior to this point
}

finally
{
  // cleanup code that always executes, whether there has been an exception or not
}
```

All code should, in essence, be covered by a `try...catch...finally` block so that it can deal with any exception that may occur in an efficient, user-friendly fashion. Some developers believe that not all code does require exception blocks, but you can never guarantee that any particular line of code is 100% tolerant.

There will be times when you may wish to handle an exception that is thrown internally by executing code that records the exception and then moves forward. Alternatively, you may wish to display a useful message to the user. Otherwise, any code not surrounded by a `try...catch...finally` code block that could be prone to an exception will probably present the user with a horrible gray box of unintelligible error details at some point in the future. We will see this happening in a moment.

If no exception occurs in the code in the `try` block, then the control will move to the `finally` block if it exists. It is not mandatory to provide a `finally` block. However they are useful places for closing any temporary connections and other cleanup code.

The code in the `finally` block will always be executed, regardless of whether the `catch` block was entered or not. If several `catch` blocks are provided, type-specific `catch` blocks are listed first and the generic `catch` block is listed last.

> **If a `finally` block is defined, this code will always execute whether an exception has occurred or not.**

You can also nest one `try` block within another. In this scenario, `catch` blocks only relate to the `try` block that they are defined within.

As you saw in the syntax definition above, you can cater for many specific exception conditions that may exist, or let the exception fall in to the generic `catch` block. To expand on this and to clarify, you may be executing a section of code that has been defined to connect to a SQL Server database. You may have an incorrect argument for the connection that throws an `ArgumentException`. If a `catch` block defined specifically for this exception is detailed, then the code within this block executes. If you do not have this `catch` block defined, then the program will look for a `catch` block that has no defined exception detailed and execute that one. If there is no specific `catch` block that is relevant, and no generic `catch` block either, then you will find the ugly gray exception message box appearing.

It is possible to not have a `try...catch` block around a piece of code and yet still have exception handling in place. If the code that generates an exception is in a called section of code like a method, and the calling code has a `try...catch` around it, then you will find that .NET will check the calling stack and move up through that stack, constantly checking the calling code until it finds a `try...catch` block.

At the uppermost level of code, it is imperative that all code is surrounded by a `try...catch` so that no users see a totally unhelpful message (like that shown next) or, if it is a batch process, then you can have the error logged in a relevant location.

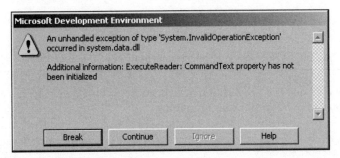

The Generic Exception Class

All exceptions that can occur derive from a basic generic `Exception` class that exposes methods and properties that all exception classes will also expose.

Properties of the Exception Class

Property	Description
HelpLink	Used to define a link to a help file that will give more details of the exception
InnerException	Returns the exception instance that caused the current exception
Message	Gives a full description of the exception that has just occurred
Source	You can either set this to the source of the exception or you can retrieve the source of the exception
StackTrace	A string of the call stack defining the top-down route the code took to the point of the exception
TargetSite	Names the method that has thrown the exception

Methods of the Exception Class

Method	Description
Equals	Used when trying to determine if two exceptions are exactly equal.
GetBaseException	When overridden in a derived class, returns the exception that is the root cause of one or more subsequent exceptions.
GetHashCode	Hash function. Used in hashing algorithms.
GetObjectData	When overridden in a derived class, sets the SerializationInfo with information about the exception.
GetType	Returns the type of the current instance (for example, ArgumentException).
ToString	Returns a string representation of the exception.

You will see these methods and properties in use throughout this chapter. Here's a simple example of how to retrieve some of an Exception's properties:

```
// Specific exception catch block. This catch block will catch exceptions of
// type SqlException only
catch (System.Data.SqlClient.SqlException e1)
{
  string strEx;
  strEx = "Source:"+ e1.Source;
  strEx = strEx + "\n"+ "Exception Message:"+ e1.Message;
  MessageBox.Show (strEx,"Database Exception");
}

// Generic exception catch block
```

```
catch (System.Exception e2)
{
  string strEx;
  strEx = "Source:"+ e2.Source;
  strEx = strEx+ "\n"+ "Exception Message:"+ e2.Message;
  MessageBox.Show (strEx,"ADO.NET Exception");
}

catch
{
  MessageBox.Show ("Unhandled exception has occurred","Unhandled Exception");
}
```

It is possible that there is no generic `catch` block but several specific `catch` blocks. In that case, if the exception thrown is not caught by any specific `catch` block, then the CLR's default exception handler will come into play. It will inform the user that an exception has been encountered and provide two choices – either to quit the application or to ignore the exception and continue. Obviously, exceptions should be caught and fixed by the application, rather than relying on the CLR to catch them.

The throw Statement

Exceptions can be forcibly thrown by means of a `throw` statement. Any type of exception can be explicitly thrown in this way. For example, if a string has a `null` value assigned to it, then we can throw a `System.ArgumentNullException` exception. The syntax of the `throw` statement is as follows:

```
throw <exception object>
```

Here's an example of a valid `throw` statement:

```
throw new System.ArgumentNullException
```

When this statement is used, the corresponding `catch` block (if it exists) or a generic `catch` block will come into play and handle the exception.

This structured exception handling is robust and helps us to take corrective action and clean up resources before proceeding further. With this structure in mind, let us explore the `SqlException` class.

ADO.NET Exceptions and Database Exceptions

As we noted before, when you write a C# application that accesses a database, you can expect to generally encounter exceptions from two different sources – ADO.NET or the database itself:

Exceptions in C# code that uses the ADO.NET namespace are handled just like any other C# exception. There are very few specific ADO.NET exceptions themselves and they usually come about when you are building database relationships within your code. The actual exception thrown will be a CLR runtime exception and this can be handled with the `try...catch...finally` mechanism.

With good design and validation, it should be rare that you actually have an exception thrown in a database application due to problems within the database itself. Within the `try...catch...finally` mechanism, the `System.Data.SqlClient` namespace provides us with the `SqlException` class that can be queried to find more information about the exception. Bear in mind though that you may often want to "force" exceptions in order to divert control into various `catch` blocks depending on specific stored procedure return codes.

Note that, if an exception comes from the database itself, it will have to come through ADO.NET. Therefore, there seems to be no apparent way of distinguishing between exceptions originating in the database and those from the ADO.NET code. To clarify this gray area of terminology, in the rest of this chapter, the CLR runtime-generated exceptions in C# code are referred to as "ADO.NET exceptions" and exceptions raised strictly by the database are referred to as "database exceptions".

Exception Classes

The .NET Framework provides a hierarchy of classes that we can use to catch exceptions in our code, whether the source of the exception is in the ADO.NET code or the database. The hierarchy of exceptions classes can be summarized as follows:

❑   `System.Object`

   ❑   `System.Exception`

      ❑   `System.SystemException`

         ❑   `System.Data.SqlClient.SqlException`

         ❑   `System.InvalidOperationException`

         ❑   `System.IndexOutOfRangeException`

         ❑   Other classes derived from `System.Exception`

      ❑   `System.ApplicationException`

         ❑   `System.Reflection.TargetException`

         ❑   `System.Reflection.InvalidFilterCriteriaException`

         ❑   Other classes derived from `System.ApplicationException`

As you can see, there are two categories of exceptions listed under the base class `System.Exception`. They are:

❑   `System.SystemException`, which is the base of a set of pre-defined CLR exception classes. The classes derived from this include `System.Data.SqlClient.SqlException`, which is used to catch exceptions from the database (referred to as database exceptions in this chapter) and other non-database-related exceptions (referred to as ADO.NET exceptions in this chapter), such as `System.InvalidOperationException`. We will explore `System.Data.SqlClient.SqlException` and `System.InvalidOperationException` later in the chapter.

❑ `System.ApplicationException`, which is the base of user-defined application exception classes such as `System.Reflection.TargetException`. Application exceptions are thrown by a user program only and not by the CLR. We will not be discussing this type of exception in this chapter.

ADO.NET Exceptions

Let us first see how to handle exceptions caused by faulty ADO.NET code. We will pretend that we forgot to specify the `CommandText` property and try to execute a stored procedure to see what kind of exception is thrown. First of all, we will not surround any code with a `try...catch` block so as to see a raw ADO.NET exception. We will then surround the code with a `try...catch` block to demonstrate effective error handling practice. Follow the steps outlined here:

Try It Out: Handling an Exception in ADO.NET Code – Part 1

1. Create a new chapter solution called `Chapter18_Examples`.

2. Create a C# Windows Application project in our solution called `Chapter18`.

3. In the default `Form1`, add the following controls:

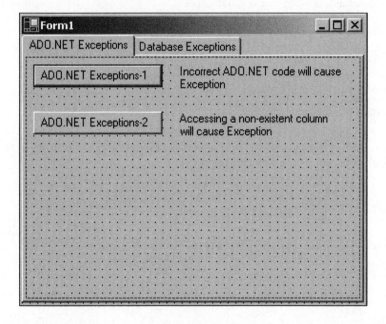

Control	Name	Remarks
Tab Control	`tabControl1` with `TabPages` called `tabPage1` and `tabPage2`	Add two tabs and set their `Text` properties to **ADO.NET Exceptions** and **Database Exceptions**.
Button	`btnADOEx1`	Set `Text` property to **ADO.NET Exceptions-1**. Clicking on the button will execute ADO.NET code that will throw an exception.
Button	`btnADOEx2`	Set `Text` property to **ADO.NET Exceptions-2**. Clicking on the button will execute ADO.NET code that will throw an exception.
Label	`label1`	Set `Text` property to **Incorrect ADO.NET code will cause Exception.**
Label	`label2`	Set `Text` property to **Accessing a non-existent column will cause Exception.**

4. At the very top of the program, you need to include the namespace to connect to a SQL Server database, the `SqlClient` namespace:

```
using System;
using System.Drawing;
using System.Collections;
using System.ComponentModel;
using System.Windows.Forms;
using System.Data;
using System.Data.SqlClient;
```

5. Enter the following code in the `Click` event of the `btnADOEx1` Button. This will provide you with your first unhandled exception.

```
private void btnADOEx1_Click(object sender, System.EventArgs e)
{
  // Create a connection
  SqlConnection cn = new
  SqlConnection(@"Data Source=(local)\NetSDK;" +
              "Integrated Security=SSPI;database=northwind");

  // Create a command object
  SqlCommand cmd = cn.CreateCommand();

  // Specify the stored procedure that is to be executed
  cmd.CommandType = CommandType.StoredProcedure;

  // Deliberately comment out the following line
  // cmd.CommandText = "sp_Select_AllEmployees";
```

```
{
  // Open the connection
  cn.Open();
  // Create a DataReader object
  SqlDataReader drdr = cmd.ExecuteReader();
  // Close the reader
  drdr.Close();
  cn.Close();
}

if (cn.State == ConnectionState.Open)
{
  MessageBox.Show ("Finally closing the connection","Finally block");
  cn.Close();
}
}
```

6. When you build and execute the project, and click the **ADO.NET Exceptions-1** button, you will see the following exception:

Within the `Click` event of the `Button` named `btnADOEx1`, modify the code as shown below. We are now going to add the `try...catch` block

```
private void btnADOEx1_Click(object sender, System.EventArgs e)
{
  // Create a connection
  SqlConnection cn = new
  SqlConnection("Data Source=(local)\\NetSDK;" +
               "Integrated Security=SSPI;database=northwind");

  // Create a command object
  SqlCommand cmd = cn.CreateCommand();

  // Specify the stored procedure that is to be executed
  cmd.CommandType = CommandType.StoredProcedure;

  // Deliberately comment out the following line
  // cmd.CommandText = "sp_Select_AllEmployees";
```

```
try
{
  // Open the connection
  cn.Open();
  // Create a DataReader object
  SqlDataReader drdr = cmd.ExecuteReader();
  // Close the reader
  drdr.Close();
  cn.Close();
}

catch (System.Data.SqlClient.SqlException e2)
{
  string strEx;
  strEx = "Source:"+ e2.Source;
  strEx = strEx + "\n"+ "Exception Message:"+ e2.Message;
  MessageBox.Show (strEx,"Database Exception");
}

catch (System.Exception e3)
{
  string strEx;
  strEx = "Source:"+ e3.Source;
  strEx = strEx+ "\n"+ "Exception Message:"+ e3.Message;
  MessageBox.Show (strEx,"Non-Database Exception");
}

finally
{
  if (cn.State == ConnectionState.Open)
  {
    MessageBox.Show ("Finally closing the connection","Finally block");
    cn.Close();
  }
}
}
```

7. Build and run the solution again and click on the button captioned **ADO.NET Exceptions-1**. This time, you will see an error message displayed as shown here:

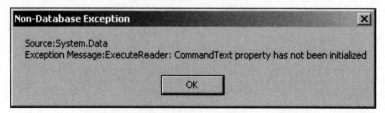

The source of the message indicates that the exception was thrown from the `System.Data` namespace and the message is clear – the `CommandText` property was not supplied.

How It Works

Our goal with this section was to demonstrate an exception using `try...catch...finally` blocks. It would be unusual to miss the `CommandText` property. However, this is a quick way of creating an exception. When we tried to call the `ExecuteReader` method, we got an exception as there had been no call to the database to retrieve data.

```
// Deliberately comment out the following line
// cmd.CommandText = "sp_Select_AllEmployees";

// Create a DataReader object
SqlDataReader dr = cmd.ExecuteReader();
```

To catch the exception and prevent the program from crashing, we specified two `catch` blocks as follows:

```
catch (System.Data.SqlClient.SqlException e2)
{
    string strEx;
    strEx = "Source:"+ e2.Source;
    strEx = strEx + "\n"+ "Exception Message:"+ e2.Message;
    MessageBox.Show (strEx,"Database Exception");
}

catch (System.Exception e3)
{
    string strEx;
    strEx = "Source:"+ e3.Source;
    strEx = strEx+ "\n"+ "Exception Message:"+ e3.Message;
    MessageBox.Show (strEx,"Non-Database Exception");
}
```

In the first `catch` block, we specified a specific exception type called `SqlException`. We touched on this earlier in the chapter when demonstrating the hierarchy of exceptions. But note the caption of the message box in this `catch` block. It says **Non-Database Exception**. The second `catch` block, which produced this message box, is a generic block that catches all types of exceptions. Although you may think that what we have received is a database exception, it is more of a client-side exception – in other words, this error is trapped before it gets to the database server itself.

When the button was clicked, since the `CommandText` property was not specified, an exception was thrown and caught in the generic `catch` block. Even though a `catch` block for `SqlException` was provided, the type of exception thrown was `System.InvalidOperationException`. This is a common exception thrown by the CLR and is not a database exception. Referring to the exception classes hierarchy presented earlier in the chapter, you can see that there are several other CLR exceptions that could be trapped.

The exception message shown indicates where the problem occurred – in the `ExecuteReader` method. The `finally` block checks if the connection is open and, if it is, closes it and gives a message.

```
finally
{
  if (cn.State == ConnectionState.Open)
  {
    MessageBox.Show ("Finally closing the connection","Finally block");
    cn.Close();
  }
}
```

Let us try to see another example of an ADO.NET Exception. We will execute a stored procedure and then reference a non-existent column in the `DataSet`. This will raise an ADO.NET exception. Initially, we will fall into the same error as before but, this time, there will be a specific `catch` block to trap the error.

Try It Out: Handling an Exception in ADO.NET Code – Part 2

1. First, the stored procedure. We will use the `sp_Select_AllEmployees` stored procedure that we created in Chapter 14. If you haven't already created it, please go to Chapter 14 and follow through the steps listed there in the *Try It Out: Creating a Stored Procedure from the Visual Studio .NET SQL Window* section.

2. In the `Click` event of the `Button` named `btnADOEx2`, write code as follows:

```
private void btnADOEx2_Click(object sender, System.EventArgs e)
{
  // Create a connection
  SqlConnection cn = new SqlConnection(@"Data Source=(local)\NetSDK;" +
    "Integrated Security=SSPI;database=Northwind");

  // Create a command object
  SqlCommand cmd = cn.CreateCommand();

  // Specify the stored procedure that is to be executed
  cmd.CommandType = CommandType.StoredProcedure;
  cmd.CommandText = "sp_Select_AllEmployees";

  try
  {
    // Open the connection
    cn.Open();

    // Create a DataReader object
    SqlDataReader dr = cmd.ExecuteReader();

    // Access a column that does not exist
    string strName = dr.GetValue(20).ToString();

    // Close the reader
    dr.Close();
  }
```

```
catch (System.InvalidOperationException e1)
{
  string strEx;
  strEx = "Source:"+ e1.Source;
  strEx = strEx+ "\n"+ "Message:"+ e1.Message;
  strEx = strEx+"\n"+ "\n";
  strEx = strEx+ "\n"+ "Stack Trace :"+ e1.StackTrace;
  MessageBox.Show (strEx,"Specific Exception");
}

catch (System.Data.SqlClient.SqlException e2)
{
  string strEx;
  strEx = "Source:"+ e2.Source;
  strEx = strEx+ "\n"+ "Message:"+ e2.Message;
  MessageBox.Show (strEx,"Database Exception");
}

catch (System.Exception e3)
{
  string strEx;
  strEx = "Source:"+ e3.Source;
  strEx = strEx+ "\n"+ "Message:"+ e3.Message;
  MessageBox.Show (strEx,"Generic Exception");
}

finally
{
  if( cn.State == ConnectionState.Open)
  {
    MessageBox.Show ("Finally closing the connection","Finally block");
    cn.Close();
  }
}
}
```

3. Build and run the solution. Click on the ADO.NET Exception-2 button. You will see a message box like this:

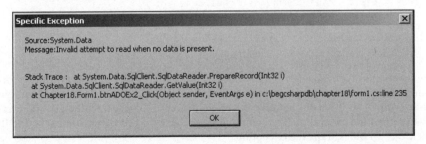

479

4. For a quick comparison, let's now demonstrate a SQL client error – in other words, an error that occurs *within* the database. Alter the name of the stored procedure to a name that doesn't exist within the Northwind database, like so:

```
// Specify the stored procedure that is to be executed
cmd.CommandType = CommandType.StoredProcedure;
cmd.CommandText = "sp_IDontExist";
```

5. If you now build and execute this code, you will find that the program drops into the SqlClient.Exception as this error comes directly from the database.

How It Works

When we create the DataReader object and try to access an invalid column, an exception is thrown:

```
// Create a DataReader object
SqlDataReader dr = cmd.ExecuteReader();

// Access a column that does not exist
string strName = dr.GetValue(20).ToString();
```

Here we tried to get the value of column 20, which does not exist. There are three catch blocks to trap this exception, and we saw two of them in the previous example. In *this* example, we added a new catch block as follows:

```
catch (System.InvalidOperationException e1)
    {
    string strEx;
    strEx = "Source:"+ e1.Source;
    strEx = strEx+ "\n"+ "Message:"+ e1.Message;
    strEx = strEx+"\n"+ "\n";
    strEx = strEx+ "\n"+ "Stack Trace :"+ e1.StackTrace;
    MessageBox.Show (strEx,"Specific Exception");
    }
```

When an exception of type System.InvalidOperationException is thrown, this catch block will execute, displaying the source, message, and trace of the exception. This is an example of trapping errors of a specific type. If we did not give this specific catch block, then the generic catch block would have trapped the exception. Try commenting out this catch block and executing the code, so as to see which catch block traps the exception.

Let's now look in detail at handling exceptions caused by the database itself.

Database Exceptions

An exception of type `SqlException` is thrown when the SQL Server database returns a warning or error, just as we saw at the end of the previous *Try It Out*. This `SqlException` class cannot be inherited, but it has several useful members that can be interrogated to obtain valuable information about the exception. The derivation hierarchy of this class, which was shown earlier in the chapter, is as follows:

- ❑ `System.Object`
  - ❑ `System.Exception`
    - ❑ `System.SystemException`
      - ❑ `System.Data.SqlClient.SqlException`

An object of the `SqlException` class is created whenever the SQL Server .NET Data Provider encounters an exception generated by the database. The properties of this class that provide information about the exception are listed next, along with brief descriptions.

This class also has methods that you can use to get more information about the object. For more detailed information on these, refer to the ADO.NET documentation.

Property Name	Description
Class	Gets the severity level of the error returned from the `SqlClient` data provider. The severity level is a numeric code that is used to indicate the nature of the error. Levels 1 to 10 are informational errors, 11 to 16 are user-level errors, and 17 to 25 are software or hardware errors. A level of 20 or more and the connection is usually closed.
Errors	Contains one or more `SqlError` objects that have detailed information about the exception. This is a collection that can be iterated through.
HelpLink	The help file associated with this exception.
InnerException	Gets the exception instance that caused the current exception.
LineNumber	Gets the line number within the Transact-SQL command batch or stored procedure that generated the exception.
Message	The text describing the exception.
Number	The number that identifies the type of exception.
Procedure	The name of the stored procedure that generated the exception.
Server	The name of the computer running an instance of SQL Server that generated the exception.
Source	The name of the provider that generated the exception.
State	Numeric error code from SQL Server that represents an exception, warning, or "no data found" message. For more information, see SQL Server Books Online.

When an error occurs within MSDE or SQL Server, it will use a RAISERROR statement to raise an error back to the calling program. A typical error message looks like the one shown below:

```
Server: Msg 2812, Level 16, State 62, Line 1
Could not find stored procedure 'sp_DoesNotExist'
```

In this message, 2812 represents the error number, 16 represents the severity level, and 62 represents the state of the error.

We can also use the RAISERROR statement to display specific messages within a stored procedure. The RAISERROR statement in its simplest form takes three parameters. The first parameter is the message itself that needs to be shown. The second parameter is the severity level of the error. Severity levels 11 through 16 can be used by any user. They represent messages that can be categorized as information, software, or hardware problems. The third parameter is an arbitrary integer from 1 through 127 that represents information about the state or source of the error.

Let us see how a SQL error, raised from a stored procedure using a RAISERROR statement, is handled in C#. We will use this to raise an error when the number of orders in the Orders table exceeds ten:

```
IF @OrdersCount > 10
RAISERROR ('Orders Count is greater than 10- Notify the Business Manager',
           16,1)
```

Note that, in this RAISERROR statement, we use a severity level of 16, an arbitrary state number of 1, and we provide a message string. When a RAISERROR statement that we write contains a message string, the error number is automatically given as 50000. When SQL Server raises errors using RAISERROR, it uses a pre-defined dictionary of messages to give out the corresponding error numbers. Please consult SQL Books Online (search for RAISERROR) to determine how to incorporate your own messages along with SQL Server's pre-defined messages.

Follow the steps outlined here to try out the RAISERROR statement.

Try It Out: Handling an Exception in the Database – Part 1: RAISERROR

1. In Form1, in the **Database Exceptions** tab, add buttons and labels as shown here:

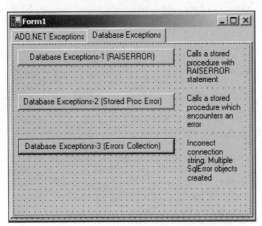

Control	Name	Remarks
Button	btnDBEx1	Set Text property to **Database Exceptions-1 (RAISERROR)**. Clicking on the button will execute a stored procedure that will throw an exception.
Button	btnDBEx2	Set Text property to **Database Exceptions-2 (Stored Proc Error)**. Clicking on the button will execute a stored procedure that will throw an exception.
Button	btnDBEx3	Set Text property to **Database Exceptions-3 (Errors Collection)**. Clicking on the button will execute code that creates several errors.
Label	Label3	Set Text property to **Calls a stored procedure with RAISERROR statement.**
Label	Label4	Set Text property to **Calls a stored procedure which encounters an error.**
Label	Label5	Set Text property to **Incorrect connection string. Multiple SqlError objects created.**

2. Create a stored procedure using the VS.NET Server Explorer called sp_DBException_1, as follows:

```
CREATE PROCEDURE sp_DBException_1
AS
  SET NOCOUNT ON
  DECLARE @OrdersCount int
  SELECT @OrdersCount=count(*)
  FROM Orders

IF @OrdersCount > 10
  RAISERROR ('Orders Count is greater than 10- Notify the Business Manager',
            16,1)
RETURN
```

3. In the Click event of the button named btnDBEx1, write code as follows:

```
private void btnDBEx1_Click(object sender, System.EventArgs e)
{
  // Create a connection
  SqlConnection cn = new SqlConnection(@"Data Source=(local)\NetSDK;" +
    "Integrated Security=SSPI;database=Northwind");

  // Create a command object
  SqlCommand cmd = cn.CreateCommand();

  // Specify the stored procedure that is to be executed
  cmd.CommandType = CommandType.StoredProcedure;
```

```
cmd.CommandText = "sp_DBException_1";

try
{
  // Open the connection
  cn.Open();

  // Execute the stored procedure
  cmd.ExecuteNonQuery();
}

catch (System.Data.SqlClient.SqlException e2)
{
  string strEx;
  strEx = "Source:"+ e2.Source;
  strEx = strEx+ "\n"+ "Number:"+ e2.Number.ToString();
  strEx = strEx+ "\n"+ "Message:"+ e2.Message;
  strEx = strEx+ "\n"+ "Class:"+ e2.Class.ToString ();
  strEx = strEx+ "\n"+ "Procedure:"+ e2.Procedure.ToString();
  strEx = strEx+ "\n"+ "Line Number:"+e2.LineNumber.ToString();
  strEx = strEx+ "\n"+ "Server:"+ e2.Server.ToString();

  MessageBox.Show (strEx,"Database Exception");
}

catch (System.Exception e3)
{
  string strEx;
  strEx = "Source:"+ e3.Source;
  strEx = strEx+ "\n"+ "Error Message:"+ e3.Message;
  MessageBox.Show (strEx,"General Exception");
}

finally
{
  if (cn.State == ConnectionState.Open)
  {
    MessageBox.Show ("Finally closing the connection", "Finally block");
    cn.Close();
  }
}
}
```

4. Build and run the solution, then click on the RAISERROR button. You will see a message box as follows:

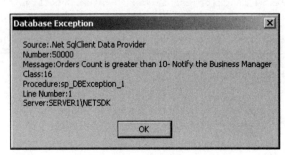

Observe the caption and contents of the message box. The source, the message, the name of the stored procedure, the exact line number where the error was found, and the name of the machine are all listed. We are able to obtain this detailed information about the exception by using the `SqlException` object.

How It Works

In the `sp_DBException_1` stored procedure, we first find the number of orders in the `Orders` table and store it in a variable called `@OrdersCount`. Then, if `@OrdersCount` is greater than 10, we raise an error using the `RAISERROR` statement.

```
    DECLARE @OrdersCount int
    SELECT @OrdersCount=count(*)
    FROM Orders

IF @OrdersCount > 10
    RAISERROR ('Orders Count is greater than 10- Notify the Business Manager',
               16,1)
    RETURN
```

Then we execute the stored procedure using the `ExecuteNonQuery()` method of the `Command` object.

```
    try
    {
      // Open the connection
      cn.Open();

      // Execute the stored procedure
      cmd.ExecuteNonQuery();
    }
```

When the stored procedure is executed, the `RAISERROR` statement raises an error. This is trapped by the `catch` block shown here:

```
    catch (System.Data.SqlClient.SqlException e2)
    {
      string strEx;
      strEx = "Source:"+ e2.Source;
      strEx = strEx+ "\n"+ "Number:"+ e2.Number.ToString();
      strEx = strEx+ "\n"+ "Message:"+ e2.Message;
      strEx = strEx+ "\n"+ "Class:"+ e2.Class.ToString ();
      strEx = strEx+ "\n"+ "Procedure:"+ e2.Procedure.ToString();
      strEx = strEx+ "\n"+ "Line Number:"+e2.LineNumber.ToString();
      strEx = strEx+ "\n"+ "Server:"+ e2.Server.ToString();

      MessageBox.Show (strEx,"Database Exception");
    }
```

As you can see, a lot of information about the exception can be obtained by accessing the properties of the exception object. This is extremely useful for debugging the problem at hand.

Now let us see what happens when a statement in a stored procedure encounters an error. We will create a stored procedure that will do an illegal INSERT and then we will extract information from the SqlException object.

Try It Out: Handling an Exception in the Database – Part 2: Stored Procedure

1. Create a stored procedure called sp_DBException_2 as follows:

```
CREATE PROCEDURE sp_DBException_2
AS
  SET NOCOUNT ON
  INSERT INTO Employees(EmployeeId,FirstName) VALUES(50,'Cinderella')
RETURN
```

2. In the Click event of the button named btnDBEx2, write code as follows:

```csharp
private void btnDBEx2_Click(object sender, System.EventArgs e)
{
  // Create a connection
  SqlConnection cn = new SqlConnection("Data Source=(local)\\NetSDK;" +
    "Integrated Security=SSPI;database=Northwind");

  // Create a command object
  SqlCommand cmd = cn.CreateCommand();

  // Specify the stored procedure that is to be executed
  cmd.CommandType = CommandType.StoredProcedure;
  cmd.CommandText = "sp_DBException_2";

  try
  {
    // Open the connection
    cn.Open();

    // Execute the stored procedure
    cmd.ExecuteNonQuery();
  }

  catch (System.Data.SqlClient.SqlException e2)
  {
    string strEx;
    strEx = "Source:"+ e2.Source;
    strEx = strEx+ "\n"+ "Error Number:"+ e2.Number.ToString();
    strEx = strEx+ "\n"+ "Message:"+ e2.Message;
    strEx = strEx+ "\n"+ "Class:"+ e2.Class.ToString ();
    strEx = strEx+ "\n"+ "Procedure:"+ e2.Procedure.ToString();
    strEx = strEx+ "\n"+ "Line Number:"+e2.LineNumber.ToString();
    strEx = strEx+ "\n"+ "Server:"+ e2.Server.ToString();
    MessageBox.Show (strEx,"Database Exception");
  }
```

```
catch (System.Exception e3)
{
  string strEx;
  strEx = "Source:"+ e3.Source;
  strEx = strEx+ "\n"+ "Error Message:"+ e3.Message;
  MessageBox.Show (strEx,"ADO.NET Exception");
}

finally
{
  if (cn.State == ConnectionState.Open)
  {
    MessageBox.Show ("Finally closing the Connection","Finally block");
    cn.Close();
  }
}
}
```

3. Build and run the solution, then click on the second button captioned **Stored Proc Error**. You will see a message box as shown here:

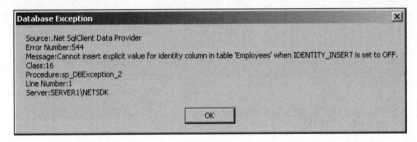

How It Works

The stored procedure tried to insert a new employee into the `Employees` table:

```
INSERT INTO Employees(EmployeeId,FirstName) VALUES(50,'Cinderella')
```

However, since the `EmployeeId` column in the `Employees` table is an Identity field, we cannot explicitly assign a value to the `EmployeeId`.

Actually, we can – as the message indicates – if we SET IDENTITY_INSERT OFF in the stored procedure before we do the INSERT, but identity fields are not normally turned off.

When this SQL error occurs, the specific `SqlException catch` block traps the exception and displays the information. The `finally` block checks and closes the connection.

It is common for stored procedures to encounter several errors, either due to invalid arguments being supplied or data integrity constraints. These can be captured and debugged using the `SqlException` object, as we will see next.

The `SqlException` object contains an `Errors` collection. Each item of the `Errors` collection is an object of type `SqlError`. When a database exception occurs, this `Errors` collection is populated. For the example, let us try to establish a connection to a non-existent database, and investigate the `SqlException` object's `Errors` collection.

Try It Out: Handling an Exception in the Database – Part 3: Errors Collection

1. In the `Click` event of the button named `btnDBEx3`, write code as follows:

```
private void btnDBEx3_Click(object sender, System.EventArgs e)
{
  // Create a connection with a non-existent database called Northwnd
  SqlConnection cn = new SqlConnection(@"Data Source=(local)\NetSDK;" +
    "Integrated Security=SSPI;database=Northwnd");

  // Create a command object
  SqlCommand cmd = cn.CreateCommand();

  // Specify the stored procedure that is to be executed
  cmd.CommandType = CommandType.StoredProcedure;
  cmd.CommandText = "sp_DBException_2";

  try
  {
    // Open the connection
    cn.Open();

    // Execute the stored procedure
    cmd.ExecuteNonQuery();
  }

  catch (System.Data.SqlClient.SqlException e2)
  {
    string strEx = "";
    for (int i=0; i < e2.Errors.Count; i++)
      {
      strEx = strEx+ "\n"+ "Index #" + i + "\n" +
                "Exception : " + e2.Errors[i].ToString() + "\n" +"Number:" +
                e2.Errors[i].Number.ToString()+ "\n" ;
      }
    MessageBox.Show(strEx,"Database Exception");
  }

  catch (System.Exception e3)
  {
    string strEx;
    strEx = "Source:"+ e3.Source;
    strEx = strEx+ "\n"+ "Error Message:"+ e3.Message;
    MessageBox.Show (strEx,"ADO.NET Exception");
  }
```

```
  finally
  {
    if (cn.State == ConnectionState.Open)
    {
      MessageBox.Show ("Finally closing the connection","Finally block");
      cn.Close();
    }
  }
}
```

2. Build and run the solution, and click on the button captioned Errors Collection. You will see a message box like this:

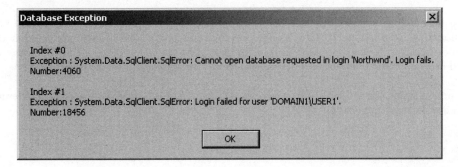

Observe that two items are found in the `Errors` collection, and their error numbers are different.

How It Works

In the `Connection`, we specified a database name that does not exist on the server – we misspelled Northwind as Northwnd:

```
// Create a connection with a non-existent database called Northwnd
SqlConnection cn = new SqlConnection(@"Data Source=(local)\NetSDK;" +
  "Integrated Security=SSPI;database=Northwnd");
```

Then, when we tried to open the connection, an exception of type `SqlException` was thrown:

```
catch (System.Data.SqlClient.SqlException e2)
{
  string strEx = "";
  for (int i=0; i < e2.Errors.Count; i++)
    {
    strEx = strEx+ "\n"+ "Index #" + i + "\n" +
            "Exception : " + e2.Errors[i].ToString() + "\n" +"Number:" +
            e2.Errors[i].Number.ToString()+ "\n" ;
    }
  MessageBox.Show(strEx,"Database Exception");
}
```

We then looped through the items of the `Errors` collection and got each `Error` object using the `Errors[I]` syntax.

This example shows that the `SqlException` object carries detailed information about each and every SQL error in its `Errors` collection.

Summary

We began this chapter by reviewing the `try...catch...finally` structured error handling construct. Then we discussed the two most probable sources of exceptions in database applications – namely ADO.NET and the database itself.

We saw how coding mistakes in the ADO.NET portion of our C# program can cause "ADO.NET exceptions", which are basically CLR exceptions, and we saw how to handle them. We then tried out several exercises with the database as the source of errors – we called these "database exceptions" – and learned how to handle them using the `System.Data.SqlClient.SqlException` class.

In the next chapter, we will look at transactions – an area that is critical for maintaining the integrity of data in our database applications.

Exercises

1. Which `catch` block will catch the exception thrown in the following code?

```
try
{
  f();
}

catch (System.ArgumentNullException e1)
{
  MessageBox.Show (e1.Message);
}

catch (System.Exception e2)
{
  MessageBox.Show (e2.Message);
}

private void f()
{
  throw new System.ArgumentNullException();
}
```

2. What changes must be made to make the generic `catch` block handle the exception?

3. What type of object represents an error in the `Errors` collection property of `SqlException`?

4. Write a statement that would raise a suitable message to the client if the value of a sales order (`@Value`) entered is less than 100 dollars. Assign a severity level of `15` and state value of `5`. What would be the error number returned to the calling program?

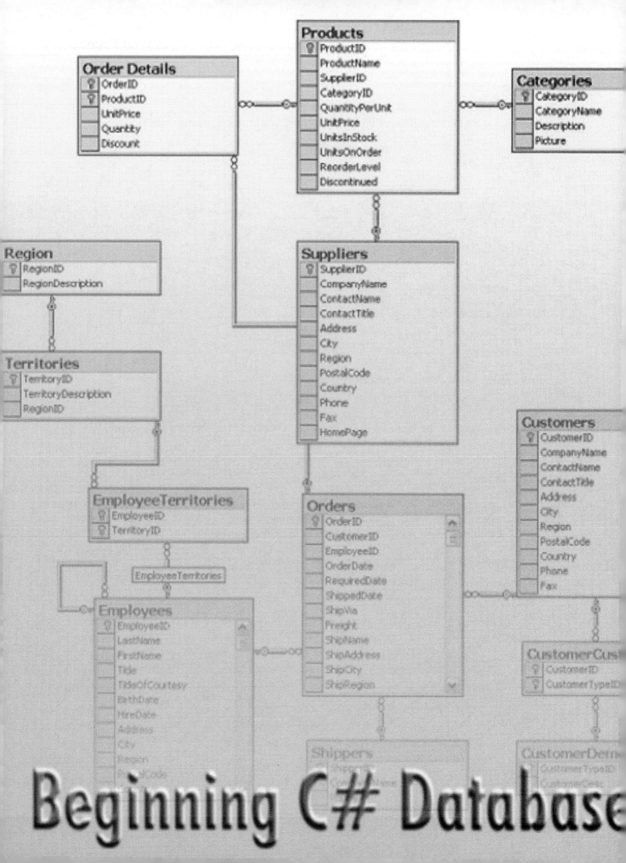

Order Details
- OrderID
- ProductID
- UnitPrice
- Quantity
- Discount

Products
- ProductID
- ProductName
- SupplierID
- CategoryID
- QuantityPerUnit
- UnitPrice
- UnitsInStock
- UnitsOnOrder
- ReorderLevel
- Discontinued

Categories
- CategoryID
- CategoryName
- Description
- Picture

Region
- RegionID
- RegionDescription

Territories
- TerritoryID
- TerritoryDescription
- RegionID

Suppliers
- SupplierID
- CompanyName
- ContactName
- ContactTitle
- Address
- City
- Region
- PostalCode
- Country
- Phone
- Fax
- HomePage

Customers
- CustomerID
- CompanyName
- ContactName
- ContactTitle
- Address
- City
- Region
- PostalCode
- Country
- Phone
- Fax

EmployeeTerritories
- EmployeeID
- TerritoryID

EmployeeTerritories

Orders
- OrderID
- CustomerID
- EmployeeID
- OrderDate
- RequiredDate
- ShippedDate
- ShipVia
- Freight
- ShipName
- ShipAddress
- ShipCity
- ShipRegion

Employees
- EmployeeID
- LastName
- FirstName
- Title
- TitleOfCourtesy
- BirthDate
- HireDate
- Address
- City
- Region
- PostalCode

CustomerCust
- CustomerID
- CustomerTypeID

Shippers

CustomerDem

Beginning C# Database

Transactions

A transaction is a set of tasks that are performed in such a manner that they are either all guaranteed to succeed or they are all guaranteed not to succeed.

A common example of a simple transaction is the case of transferring money from a checking account to a savings account. This involves two tasks – deducting money from the checking account and adding the money to the savings account. Both must succeed together and be **committed** to the accounts or they must fail together and be **rolled back** so that the accounts are in the same state as they were before the transaction was attempted. They should not be in a state where money has been deducted from the checking account but not added to savings or vice versa. By using transactions, both these tasks can be guaranteed to pass or fail and not be in limbo.

Transactions may comprise many individual tasks and even other transactions. By making use of transactions to ensure that related pieces of information are kept and updated together without being separated, we have another means to ensure the integrity of the data in our database.

So then, in this chapter we will cover the following topics:

❑   When and when not to use transactions

❑   The ACID properties of a transaction

❑   How to write Manual Transactions

❑   What Automatic Transactions are

❑   Try It Out sections to explore the transaction features of ADO.NET

As we'll discover, pieces of the Northwind database use transactions to maintain their integrity as well. The examples for this chapter then will look at its Order Entry System in which the header information for an order is inserted into the Orders table and the detail information is inserted into the Order Details table. It is necessary to ensure that there is no detail in the Order Details table without a corresponding header in the Orders table. When the order is authorized, transactional statements can be written to ensure that an order is saved completely with header and details together or not saved at all.

When to Use/ When Not To Use Transactions

Transactions must be used when several tasks have to succeed or fail as a batch. Some of the frequently used scenarios where transactions must be used are as follows:

❑   When there is a need to INSERT\UPDATE\DELETE several rows into one table, using transactions will ensure that they are either all committed or all rolled back.

❑   When trying to modify data in two or more tables, or even two or more databases simultaneously, transactions must be used to maintain data integrity.

❑   In distributed transactions, wherein the data is written to several databases on different machines, transactions are absolutely necessary.

❑   We can also use transactions when we want to test that a T-SQL statement or indeed several T-SQL statements that update a table or several tables will modify the correct set of rows before actually committing those changes.

To clarify this last scenario, let's say we need to update the prices for all the products in a particular category by 10%. We would create a SELECT statement with the necessary joins and filters to ensure the correct rows are selected and then set them into an appropriate UPDATE statement. However, rather than just executing this UPDATE, we can make it a transaction that will rollback if something goes awry. In this way, we have double checked that the data we want to update matches that of the SELECT statement. Look out for this later on in the chapter.

When transactions are used, locks are placed on the data so that the transaction can be protected and executed correctly. No other operations can be carried out on the data until the lock is lifted. Depending on what is happening, we could be locking anything from a single row up to the whole database. The issue then is one of concurrency – that is, how many queries the database can handle at once.

In our bank example, a lock would ensure that two transactions don't access a current account at the same time and use the same value in the account as the basis for their deposits. If they did, one deposit would be lost in the system when they each update the account's balance with different values.

> **It is therefore crucial that we keep a transaction in progress for the shortest period of time. While we have a lock on any piece of information we will be stopping any other person from accessing that. As noted, we could be locking a whole database, and having a whole organization grind to a halt as a result.**

Putting a lock on any piece of the database also uses up a few resources in order to maintain it until it's released. As you can imagine then, there is a trade-off to be made between using transactions and maintaining data integrity against consuming resources and reducing the efficiency (concurrency) of the application, especially in enterprise-level database applications. Considering that we're only starting to work with databases however, this issue is one to note rather than to act on.

❑   The only scenario where transactions are not necessary are when rows are selected from a database. Every data modification should be surrounded by a transaction, whether it is one row or many rows.

Let's move on to the basic properties of a transaction.

ACID Properties

A transaction is characterized by four properties, often referred to as the ACID properties: Atomicity, Consistency, Isolation, and Durability.

❑ **Atomicity**: A transaction is atomic if it is regarded as a single action rather than a collection of separate tasks. So then, only when all the separate tasks succeed does a transaction succeed and is it committed to the database. Only the other hand, if a single task fails during the transaction, everything is considered to have failed and must be undone (rolled back) if it has already taken place. In the case of the Order Entry System of Northwind database, when we enter an order into the Orders and Order Details tables, data will be saved together in both tables or will not be saved at all.

❑ **Consistency**: The transaction should leave the database in a consistent state – whether it completed successfully or not. The data modified by the transaction must comply with all the constraints placed on the columns in order to maintain data integrity. In the case of Northwind, when an order is saved, it must have a set of details associated with it – in no case can we have records in Order Details table without a corresponding record in the Orders table, as this will leave the data in an inconsistent state.

❑ **Isolation**: Every transaction has a well defined boundary. One transaction should not affect other transactions running at the same time. Data modifications made by one transaction must be isolated from the data modifications made by any other transaction. A transaction either sees data in the state it was in before another concurrent transaction modified it, or it sees the data after the second transaction has completed, but it does not see an intermediate state. (Note that we are not covering Isolation levels in this chapter.)

❑ **Durability**: Data modifications that occur within a successful transaction will be kept permanently within the system regardless of what then occurs. Transaction logs are maintained so that should a failure occur, the database can be restored back to its original state before the failure occurred. As each transaction is completed, a record is made within the database transaction log. If we have a major system failure that requires the database to be restored from a backup, we would then use this transaction log to insert any successful transactions that had taken place.

Every database server that offers support for transactions ensures these four properties are enforced automatically when we start to make use of that functionality. There's no onus on us as programmers to build in ACID support for our transactions. All we need do is create the transactions in the first place, which is what we'll look at next.

Transaction Statements

Transaction statements are written either inside a stored procedure or surrounding a set of adhoc SQL code. There are three important statements that we need to be familiar with when working with MSDE or SQL Server:

❑   BEGIN TRANSACTION – marks the beginning of a transaction.

❑   COMMIT TRANSACTION – marks the end of a successful transaction. It gives the go-ahead to the database to commit the work.

❑   ROLLBACK TRANSACTION – denotes that a transaction has not been successful and instructs the database not to save the work but roll back to the state it was in prior to beginning the transaction.

> *A fourth statement, SAVE TRANSACTION, also exists but its use is outside the scope of this book. Check out* Professional SQL Server 2000 *by Robert Vieira, ISBN 1-86100-448-6, if you want to learn more.*

Once written, transactions will be performed either as stored procedures, or, if written as adhoc SQL, within any tool that will execute that particular dialect of SQL. For example, adhoc T-SQL may be executed by osql, SQL Server Query Analyzer, the SQL window in VS.NET, or one of our own applications that we've written with C# and ADO.NET.

Later on we'll see that it's also possible to make calls in C# that begin, commit, and rollback a transaction rather than relying on a stored procedure or piece of adhoc SQL to do it for us. We'll refer to these as **ADO.NET transactions** and those that are defined in just the SQL and run as suggested in the last paragraph as **SQL transactions**.

Working with SQL Transactions

In the next two *Try-It-Out* sections, we'll get our feet wet with two SQL transactions – one that fails and rolls back and one that succeeds and commits its actions to the database. In the course of these exercises, we will learn how ADO.NET supports transactions.

Try It Out: Rolling Back a SQL Transaction

Our first example looks at how to go about safely deleting a sales order in the Northwind database. As we know, an order will have a header record in the Orders table and detail records in the Order Details table. When we delete an order, we need to delete either both header and details or neither. There are several ways to achieve this but for the purposes of this example, we'll do it with a stored procedure. We could use cascading deletes or triggers instead but these actions are outside the scope of this book.

1.   Let's start by building our stored procedure in the SQL window of VC# Standard Edition. In the **Server Explorer** window, expand your link to the Northwind database and double-click on the Orders table. Double-click the now active SQL panel icon, ▣, to bring up the SQL query notepad.

Note that we could also use the tool in the appendix at the rear of this book, osql, or the SQL Server management console to create the stored procedure as well. Feel free to use one of these if you like.

2. Now create a stored procedure called sp_TransTest1_SQL on the Northwind database by typing the following code into the SQL panel and running it:

```
CREATE PROCEDURE sp_TransTest1_SQL(@OrderId as integer)
AS
DECLARE @Err int

BEGIN TRANSACTION
-- Delete the Order from the Orders table first
-- this will cause an error due to violation of referential integrity

DELETE Orders
WHERE OrderId=@OrderId

-- save the @@ERROR number in a local variable @Err
SET @Err=@@ERROR

-- if error number is not zero, then rollback
-- PRINT and RAISERROR are shown for test purpose

IF @Err <>0
BEGIN
ROLLBACK TRANSACTION
    PRINT 'TRANSACTION ROLLED BACK -Orders'
    RAISERROR('TRANSACTION ROLLED BACK -Orders',10,1)
    RETURN @Err
END

-- Delete the order from the Order Details table
-- since the table name has a space in it, we enclose it within [braces]

DELETE [Order Details]
WHERE OrderId=@OrderId

 -- save the new @@ERROR number in a local variable @Err
SET @Err=@@ERROR

-- if error number is not zero, then rollback
-- PRINT and RAISERROR are shown for test purpose

IF @Err<> 0
 BEGIN
   ROLLBACK TRANSACTION
   PRINT 'TRANSACTION ROLLED BACK -Order Details'
   RAISERROR('TRANSACTION ROLLED BACK -Order Details',10,1)
   RETURN @Err
 END
```

```
-- if no error has been encountered till this point,
-- then go ahead and commit the transaction and return 0
COMMIT TRANSACTION
PRINT 'TRANSACTION COMMITTED'
RETURN
```

All being well, you'll see sp_TransTest1_SQL appear under Northwind's **Stored Procedures** node in Server Explorer once you've refreshed it.

3. Before running the stored procedure, we need to make sure that the relationship between the Orders and Order Details tables does not enforce the cascaded deletions of related records. We can't check this directly from VC# Standard Edition, as we know from Chapter 12, but we can manage it from Access, SQL Server Enterprise Manager or larger versions of VS.NET. The method is largely the same in all three.

In Access, open the Northwind database, and choose **View | Relationships** from the menu. When the relationship diagram appears, double-click on the relationship line between the Orders and Order Details tables. If checked, uncheck the **Cascade Delete Related Records** box in the **Edit Relationship** dialog box that appears.

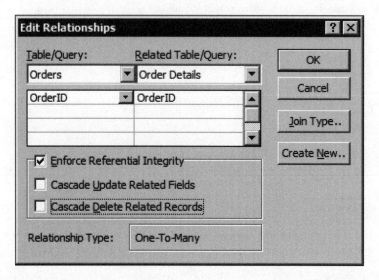

In Enterprise Manager or VS.NET, open the Database Diagram for Northwind and right-click on the relationship line between the Orders and Order Details and select **Properties** from the context menu. Again, make sure the checkbox labeled **Cascade Delete Related Records** is unchecked.

4. Run the new stored procedure in VC# by right-clicking on it in Server Explorer and choosing **Run Stored Procedure** from the context menu. When asked, enter **10260** as the OrderId. You'll see the following error message in the output window:

Running dbo."sp_TransTest1_SQL" (@OrderId = 10260).

DELETE statement conflicted with COLUMN REFERENCE constraint
'FK_Order_Details_Orders'. The conflict occurred in database 'Northwind', table 'Order
Details', column 'OrderID'.
The statement has been terminated.
No rows affected.
(0 row(s) returned)
@RETURN_VALUE = 547
Finished running dbo."sp_TransTest1_SQL".

Interesting. Apparently 0 rows were affected, but this conflict can only have occurred when
we tried to delete a record from the database. Has our transaction worked and the records for
Order with ID 10260 been restored?

5. Go to the Server Explorer window and double-click the Northwind **Orders** table. Sure enough,
Order 10260 is still in the database and so are its details in the Order Details table if you
look there too. Thanks to the transaction statements, the integrity of data has been maintained.

How It Works

Before we see why our stored procedure went off the rails, let's see what it does in full. We need to
delete the records for a given OrderId from the Orders and Order Details table and we want to
do this in a transaction. We begin by declaring the OrderId as an input parameter for the stored
procedure and a local variable @Err which we'll use to check if an error has occurred and hold the
error number should one occur.

```
CREATE PROCEDURE sp_TransTest1_SQL(@OrderId as integer)
AS
DECLARE @Err int
```

We begin the transaction with the BEGIN TRANSACTION statement. Note that we can also write this as
BEGIN TRAN and similarly, we can use COMMIT TRAN and ROLLBACK TRAN as appropriate.

```
BEGIN TRANSACTION
```

Next we try to delete the record for the nominated Order from the Orders table.

```
DELETE Orders
WHERE OrderId=@OrderId
```

Error handling is very important at all times in SQL Server, and never more so than inside transactional
code. When we issue the DELETE statement, there is a possibility that it may not succeed for whatever
reason. If an error does occur, a variable built into SQL Server called @@ERROR will store the error's
number. If an error doesn't occur, the value of @@ERROR will be 0.

Now @@ERROR is reset to 0 after every T-SQL statement is executed so before it's reset we store its
current value for the DELETE statement in @Err for checking. Unlike C#, T-SQL has no try...catch
statement or exceptions, so we need to write our own error handling routines.

```
-- save the @@ERROR number in a local variable @Err
SET @Err=@@ERROR
```

So then, if `@Err` is any value other than 0, an error has occurred and we must rollback the transaction. We also include `PRINT` and `RAISERROR` statements to tell us that a rollback has occurred.

```
-- if error number is not zero, then rollback
-- PRINT and RAISERROR are shown for test purpose
IF @Err <>0
BEGIN
ROLLBACK TRANSACTION
    PRINT 'TRANSACTION ROLLED BACK -Orders'
    RAISERROR('TRANSACTION ROLLED BACK -Orders',10,1)
    RETURN @Err
END
```

If all's gone well so far, we now try to `DELETE` the corresponding details from the `Order Details` table for this `@OrderId`. As before, we save the error returned by `@@ERROR` in the local variable `@Err` and use it to determine if we should rollback the transaction or not.

Note that we place the name of the `Order Details` table within braces `[]`, because the table name has a space in it, which will cause a syntax problem in the SQL statement. `SELECT * FROM Order Details` will confuse the database and hence we use `SELECT * FROM [Order Details]`.

```
DELETE [Order Details]
WHERE OrderId=@OrderId

 -- save the new @@ERROR number in a local variable @Err
SET @Err=@@ERROR

-- if error number is not zero, then rollback
-- PRINT and RAISERROR are shown for test purpose

IF @Err<> 0
 BEGIN
    ROLLBACK TRANSACTION
    PRINT 'TRANSACTION ROLLED BACK -Order Details'
    RAISERROR('TRANSACTION ROLLED BACK -Order Details',10,1)
    RETURN @Err
 END
```

If the stored procedure still hasn't caused any errors, we can issue the `COMMIT TRANSACTION` statement to commit the transaction and return back to the calling program. By default, if no parameter is set after the `RETURN` statement, a value of 0 is sent to the calling program.

```
-- if no error has been encountered till this point,
-- then go ahead and commit the transaction and return 0
COMMIT TRANSACTION
PRINT 'TRANSACTION COMMITTED'
RETURN
```

Now we're clear on what the stored procedure does, we've two things to discover: what went wrong and why none of the error messages we so diligently included showed up when something did go wrong.

When we executed the stored procedure and provided 10260 as the OrderId, the stored procedure began a transaction and tried to delete the OrderId from the Orders table. However, records from the Orders table cannot be deleted before deleting the detail records because if we could, then the detail records would be orphaned without a corresponding order record. This constraint is enforced by the relationship between the two tables we altered in Step 3. So, when we encountered the error, @@Err<> 0 became true and the ROLLBACK TRANSACTION statement was issued to rollback the transaction. The code did not execute the second DELETE statement since we told the stored procedure to RETURN immediately after the rollback.

So why did we alter the tables' relationship in Step 3? The reason is simple: if we had left the **Cascade Delete Related Records** switch on, when our stored procedure deleted the entry from the Orders table, the database would have automatically deleted any related records in other tables. In this case, this would mean the details record for the order in the Order Details table and there wouldn't have been a problem with the DELETE statement and we wouldn't have got our error and the rollback we wanted to see.

This is a good example of why cascaded deletes and cascaded updates must be carefully used – if they are not used at all, then records from all related tables must be explicitly deleted in a stored procedure, as we are doing in **sp_TransTest1_SQL**.

Now a little confession: Our stored procedure did indeed return both the rollback messages to VC#, but it just didn't know what to do with them. If we had had a copy of SQL Query Analyzer and ran sp_TransTest1_SQL there, we'd get a somewhat more gratifying error message. It shows not only the error raised because of the foreign key constraint violation, but it also shows the output of the PRINT and RAISERROR messages.

```
Server: Msg 547, Level 16, State 1, Procedure sp_TransTest1_SQL, Line 8
DELETE statement conflicted with COLUMN REFERENCE constraint
'FK_Order_Details_Orders'. The conflict occurred in database 'Northwind', table 'Order
Details', column 'OrderID'.
The statement has been terminated.
TRANSACTION ROLLED BACK -Orders
TRANSACTION ROLLED BACK -Orders
```

The client program running the stored procedure must know how to catch and process these messages and the procedure's return value as necessary. We'll see how PRINT and RAISERROR messages show up in the client side of a C# application later, but it's worth noting that in real-life situations, we'll most likely end up using a RAISERROR statement to display the message to the user.

Alternatively, by returning the value of @@ERROR from the stored procedure, we could simply assign it to a variable in the parent C# program and if that variable is non-zero, we'll know that an error has occurred as well. We don't need to use both RAISERROR and RETURN to determine if there has been a problem, but by doing so, we can give the calling program a bit more flexibility to deal with errors in its own way.

Try It Out: Committing a SQL Transaction

In this second SQL transaction example, we'll create a fixed version of the stored procedure in the first one by switching the DELETE statements so that the record in the Order Details table is deleted first followed by the one in the Orders table. When we run the stored procedure this time, the transaction will be COMMITted. Later on in this chapter, we'll write a C# application that will call both.

1. Create a new stored procedure called sp_TransTest2_SQL with the following code. The changes between this and the code for sp_TransTest1_SQL are highlighted.

```
CREATE PROCEDURE sp_TransTest2_SQL(@OrderId AS Integer)
AS
DECLARE @Err int

BEGIN TRANSACTION

DELETE [Order Details]
WHERE OrderId=@OrderId

SET @Err=@@ERROR

IF @Err<> 0
 BEGIN
    ROLLBACK TRANSACTION
    PRINT 'TRANSACTION ROLLED BACK -Order Details'
    RAISERROR('TRANSACTION ROLLED BACK -Order Details',10,1)
    RETURN @Err
  END

DELETE Orders
WHERE OrderId=@OrderId

SET @Err=@@ERROR

IF @Err <>0
BEGIN
    ROLLBACK TRANSACTION
    PRINT 'TRANSACTION ROLLED BACK -Orders'
    RAISERROR('TRANSACTION ROLLED BACK -Orders',10,1)
    RETURN @Err
END

COMMIT TRANSACTION
PRINT 'TRANSACTION COMMITTED'
RETURN
```

2. Now run the new stored procedure from VC# and provide 10260 as the input. We'll get the following unhelpful message in the output window.

Running dbo."sp_TransTest2_SQL" (@OrderId = 10260).

3. Go back to the `Orders` and `Order Details` tables and verify if the Order 10260 exists. We will notice that they have been deleted.

How It Works

The new stored procedure differs from the first only in the order of the `DELETE` statements, which has been reversed. When we execute the stored procedure, a transaction begins and the order record is deleted from the `Order Details` table first and then the `Orders` table. This ensures that the foreign key constraint is not violated and no error is generated. With both deletions having been successfully carried out, we then call `COMMIT TRANSACTION`.

So far we have seen how to write transaction code within a stored procedure. But, as we saw from the chapter on Stored Procedures (Chapter 14), in order to call this stored procedure from a C# application, we will be writing code using ADO.NET. In the following *Try It Out* section, we will see how to call a stored procedure which has transactional code in it from C# and test the rollback and commit features.

Try It Out: Executing a Stored Procedure with SQL-Transaction from C#

Let's get our hands dirty with some C# and write a C# ADO.NET application that will call our two stored procedures. We'll take our cue from the application in Chapter 14 but add a few more things to make sure we can handle any error messages the stored procedures kick up and test our transaction has done what we expected.

1. Create a new blank solution in Visual C# called `Chapter19_Examples` and add a new C# Windows Application called `Transactions` to it.

2. Bring up the Properties dialog for `form1`. Set `FormBorderStyle` to **Fixed Single** and `Text` to **Transactions**.

3. Add a `TabControl` to the form and create two tab pages for it within its `TabPages` collection property. Caption the first **SQL-Transactions** and the second, **ADO.NET Transactions** – this second page we'll use later.

4. Add six controls as shown below to the SQL-Transactions tab page.

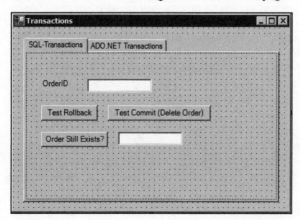

From left to right, top to bottom, the controls are as follows:

Control	Name	Properties to Change
Label	label1	Text : OrderID
Textbox	txtOrderId	None
Button	cmdRollbackSQL	Text : Test Rollback
Button	cmdCommitSQL	Text : Test Commit (Delete Order)
Button	cmdOrderStillExists	Text : Order Still Exists?
Textbox	txtResult	None

5. Double-click on the Test Rollback button and add the following code to its click event handler:

```
private void cmdRollbackSQL_Click(object sender, System.EventArgs e)
{
    //code calls sp_TransTest1_SQL to delete the order
    //but because of error, transaction will be rolled back

    //Create a connection
    SqlConnection cn =
        new SqlConnection(@"Data Source=(local)\NETSDK;" +
                            "Integrated Security=SSPI;database=Northwind");

    //Create a command object
    SqlCommand cmd = cn.CreateCommand();
    try
    {
        //Specify the stored procedure that is to be executed
        cmd.CommandType = CommandType.StoredProcedure;
        cmd.CommandText = "sp_TransTest1_SQL";

        //Create a parameter object to provide the input
        SqlParameter parInput = cmd.Parameters.Add("@OrderId", SqlDbType.Int);
        parInput.Direction = ParameterDirection.Input;
        parInput.Value= Convert.ToInt32(txtOrderId.Text);

        //Open the connection
        cn.Open();

        //execute the command and display the results
        cmd.ExecuteNonQuery();
    }

    catch ( System.Data.SqlClient.SqlException  e1)
    {
        // Display the error message.
```

```
      MessageBox.Show (e1.Message, "Rollback Transaction");
    }

    catch ( System.Exception  e2)
    {
      // Display the error message.
      MessageBox.Show ("System Error " + "\n"+  e2.Message,"Error");
    }

    finally
    {
      //close the connection
      cn.Close();
    }
  }
```

6. Switch back to the form and double-click on the **Test Commit** button. Add the following code to its `click` event handler:

```
private void cmdCommitSQL_Click(object sender, System.EventArgs e)
{
  //code calls sp_TransTest2_SQL to delete the order

  //Create a connection
  SqlConnection cn =
      new SqlConnection(@"Data Source=(local)\NETSDK;" +
                          "Integrated Security=SSPI;database=Northwind");

  //Create a command object
  SqlCommand cmd= cn.CreateCommand();
  try
  {
    //Specify the stored procedure that is to be executed
    cmd.CommandType= CommandType.StoredProcedure;
    cmd.CommandText="sp_TransTest2_SQL";

    //Create a parameter object to provide the input
    SqlParameter parInput = cmd.Parameters.Add("@OrderId", SqlDbType.Int);
    parInput.Direction = ParameterDirection.Input;
    parInput.Value = Convert.ToInt32(txtOrderId.Text);

    //Open the connection
    cn.Open();

    //execute the command and display the results
    cmd.ExecuteNonQuery();
    MessageBox.Show ("Transaction Committed"+ "\n" +
                    "Order and Order Details have been successfully deleted",
                    "Commit Transaction");
```

```
      }

      catch ( System.Data.SqlClient.SqlException  e1)
      {
        // Display the error message.
        MessageBox.Show ("Error " + "\n" + e1.Message,"Commit Transaction");
      }

      catch ( System.Exception  e2)
      {
        // Display the error message.
        MessageBox.Show ("System Error " + "\n" + e2.Message,"Error");
      }

      finally
      {
        //close the connection
        cn.Close();
      }
    }
```

7. Switch back to the form and double-click on the **Order Still Exists?** button. Add the following code to its `click` event handler:

```
    private void cmdOrderStillExists_Click(object sender, System.EventArgs e)
    {
      //Create a connection
      SqlConnection cn =
          new SqlConnection(@"Data Source=(local)\NETSDK;" +
                             "Integrated Security=SSPI;database=Northwind");

      //Create a command object
      SqlCommand cmd = cn.CreateCommand();
      try
      {
        //Specify the stored procedure that is to be executed
        cmd.CommandType = CommandType.Text;
        cmd.CommandText = "SELECT count(OrderId) FROM Orders WHERE OrderId=" +
                          txtOrderId.Text;

        //Open the connection
        cn.Open();

        //execute the command and display the results
        Int32 intRes = (Int32) cmd.ExecuteScalar();

        if (intRes==1)
          txtResult.Text = "Yes";
        else
          txtResult.Text = "No";
```

```
        }

        catch ( System.Data.SqlClient.SqlException  e1)
        {
          // Display the error message.
          MessageBox.Show ("Error " + "\n"+  e1.Message,"Error");
        }

        catch ( System.Exception  e2)
        {
          // Display the error message.
          MessageBox.Show ("System Error " + "\n"+  e2.Message,"Error");
        }

        finally
        {
          //close the connection
          cn.Close();
        }
      }
```

8. Still in code view, add `System.Data.SqlClient` to the list of `using` statements at the top of the code and change the namespace to that of the book's code.

```
using System;
using System.Drawing;
using System.Collections;
using System.ComponentModel;
using System.Windows.Forms;
using System.Data;
using System.Data.SqlClient;

namespace Wrox.BeginningCSharpDatabases.Chapter19
{
  /// <summary>
  /// Summary description for Form1.
  /// </summary>
  public class Form1 : System.Windows.Forms.Form
  {
```

9. Now build and run the solution. When the form loads, type 10248 into the OrderId textbox and click on the OrderStillExists? button. We will see a Yes in the textbox next to it as shown below, indicating that particular order exists in the database.

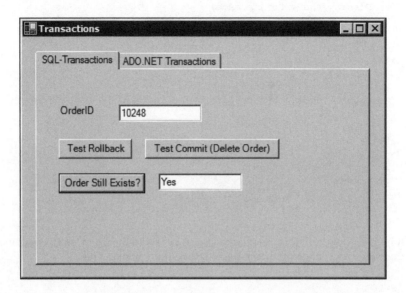

10. Now that we have confirmed that the order exists, we can click on the Test Rollback button and check that sp_TransTest1_SQL doesn't work, as expected. An error message will pop up as follows:

11. Now click on the OrderStillExists? button and verify that the textbox still says Yes. This proves that the transaction was rolled back and that the data is in a consistent state.

12. Now click on the Test Commit button and check that sp_TransTest2_Sql does work as expected. We will see a confirmation message as follows:

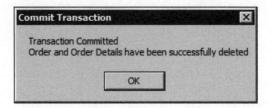

13. Now click on the OrderStillExists? button and we will see No in the textbox. This proves that the transaction was committed successfully.

How It Works

The idea behind this half of the application is simple. When we run the application, we can check an order still exists by typing in its ID and clicking on Order Still Exists? The textbox txtResult will display Yes or No accordingly. To test sp_TransTest1_SQL, and catch and display the rollback error messages, we click Test Rollback. To verify the transaction has been rolled back, we can click Order Still Exists? to check the order entries are still there. Finally, to test sp_TransTest2_SQL which will commit its transaction and delete an order and its details, we press Test Commit. Clicking on the Order Still Exists? button will check that the order has definitely been deleted.

The code listed above for the buttons is pretty straightforward. The Test Rollback button creates all the necessary objects (connection,command etc) and takes in the input from the textbox. When the transaction gets rolled back from the stored procedure, an error is encountered and the message of the error is displayed. In the Test Commit button, no error is encountered and the confirmation message is shown. In the OrderStillExists? button, the count(*) SQL function is used to find if an order still exists or not and the ExecuteScalar() method of the command object is used to stored this value and display the result as Yes or No.

Notice a few things about the screenshots shown above. In the screenshot showing the message box raised after pressing Test Rollback, the first line shows the error raised when the foreign key constraint was violated. This causes the rollback to occur – when it does, the PRINT and RAISERROR statements are executed and they are also carried forward to the application and shown. We can access the Errors collection property of the SqlException object and find out the error numbers corresponding to any messages that are raised from the database.

In the message box raised after clicking Test Commit, since no error was encountered, a message is displayed indicating that the transaction was committed successfully.

Nested Transactions

So far we have seen how a C# program can call a stored procedure with transaction statements. We began, committed, and rolled back only one transaction. It is quite possible to encounter situations where we may have to begin several transactions and commit or roll them back at different points in the stored procedure. In the code below for example, two transactions are executed in sequence.

```
-- begin first transaction
BEGIN TRAN
  <code>
  IF @Err > 0
    ROLLBACK TRAN -- rollback first transaction

COMMIT TRAN -- commit first transaction

-- begin second transaction
BEGIN TRAN
  <code>
```

```
    IF @Err > 0
       ROLLBACK TRAN -- rollback second transacton

    COMMIT TRAN -commit second transaction
```

We may also come across a situation where we may have to begin, roll back, and commit one transaction within another transaction. For example:

```
BEGIN TRAN -- begin outer transaction
   <code>

   BEGIN TRAN  -- begin inner transaction
     <code>
     IF @Err > 0
        ROLLBACK TRAN -- rollback inner transaction

   COMMIT TRAN -- commit inner transaction

   <code>
COMMIT TRAN -- commit outer transaction
```

These kinds of transactions are called **nested transactions**. As we can see, the outer transaction was started first and then an inner transaction was started. This could be because we needed to complete a sub-section of updates that will fail or succeed no matter whether the outer transaction succeeds or not. Let's take the example of a customer trying to use their credit card for a purchase. Their purchase transaction fails as they have exceeded their credit limit. The outer transaction would be the purchase but the inner transaction would be a log of credit card usage.

Transaction handling is always better completed within stored procedures. After all, we may not always be calling the stored procedure from a program, we may be running it directly from a query tool or the database itself. There will be times though that we will be executing raw T-SQL from a C# application. In these cases, transaction support provided by ADO.NET comes in handy. Using ADO.NET, we can enlist several command objects within the same transaction and execute all the command objects and achieve transactional results. We'll learn more about these ADO.NET transactions in the next section.

ADO.NET Transactions

As we know from earlier chapters, three .NET data providers have been released – OleDB, SqlClient, and ODBC – with a fourth, for Oracle, currently in beta. Each of these providers has an implementation of a transaction class that helps perform ADO.NET transactions.

❑ The OleDB data provider has the OleDbTransaction class in the System.Data.OleDb namespace.

❑ The SQLClient data provider has the SqlTransaction class in the System.Data.SqlClient namespace.

❑ The ODBC provider has the OdbcTransaction class in the System.Data.Odbc namespace.

Earlier chapters have taught us that there is often little difference between the workings of equivalent classes across the three data provider namespaces and the same is true here. For the rest of the chapter, we'll be working with `SqlTransaction`, but if you fancy following along using `OleDbTransaction` say, it won't be too difficult.

The SqlTransaction class

A `SqlTransaction` object is created when an application calls a `Connection` object's `BeginTransaction()` method:

```
SqlTransaction objTrans = cn.BeginTransaction(); //cn=connection object
```

The `SqlTransaction` class has two member properties.

❑   `Connection` returns the `Connection` object associated with the transaction.

❑   `IsolationLevel` allows us to specify one (or a combination) of six possible locking behaviors for the transaction. What they each do is beyond the scope of the book, but the most common is `Serializable`. This lock prevents other users from inserting or modifying the data being used by the transaction, until the transaction has finished.

There are also several public methods exposed by this class mostly inherited from parent classes. The most frequently used ones, however, are the three unique to the class – `Commit`, `Save`, and `Rollback`. As you might have guessed, these correspond to their SQL counterparts and have the same purpose. Like `SAVE TRANSACTION`, the use of `Save()` is left for another book, but we will use `Commit()` and `Rollback()` in the next set of examples to demonstrate how to perform ADO.NET transactions.

ADO.NET Transaction Code Guidelines

Here are the general steps we should take while writing ADO.NET transaction code.

1. Establish a connection to the database and `Open()` it as follows, where cn is the `Connection` object:

```
cn.Open()
```

2. Begin a transaction using the `BeginTransaction()` method of the connection object. The method will return a reference to an object belonging to the `Transaction` class (`OleDbTransaction`, `ODBCTransaction`, or `SqlTransaction` as the case may be).

```
SqlTransaction objTrans = cn.BeginTransaction()
```

3. Create one or more `Command` objects as required and set their `Connection` and `Transaction` properties to the `Connection` and `Transaction` objects we've created:

```
SqlCommand objCmd1=new SqlCommand();
objCmd1.Connection=cn;
objCmd1.Transaction= objTrans;
```

4. Execute a SQL command using the `Command` object in a `try` block. We can use one command object repeatedly for different queries or use several command objects each with a different query. Remember that if we do use several `Command` objects, the `Transaction` property for each should be set the same `Transaction` object that we want them to be part of.

```
try
{
  cmd.CommandText=strSql1; (or a stored procedure and its input parameters)
  cmd.ExecuteNonQuery();
```

5. If the SQL command runs successfully, call the `Transaction` object's `Commit()` method to commit the transaction.

```
  objTrans.Commit();
}
```

6. If the SQL command results in an error, this will be picked up as an exception by our C# code, so we place a call to the `Transaction` object's `Rollback()` method inside the `catch` block for that exception.

```
catch ( System.Data.SqlClient.SqlException  e1)
{
  objTrans.Rollback;
}
```

Note the subtle difference here between SQL Transactions and ADO.NET Transactions. In SQL Transactions, we first look for the error and then if there is an error we roll back and if there is no error we commit the transaction. In ADO.NET Transactions, after we have prepared the command object with all the required information, we commit the transaction. If there is any exception thrown, then we trap that exception in a `catch` block and then roll back the transaction.

7. Last but not least, we `Close()` the connection in a `finally` block

```
finally
{
  cn.Close()
}
```

To reiterate then, our stored procedures should contain the SQL statements we want to execute transactionally. The statements are then run within an ADO.NET `Transaction` object with which we can begin, commit, and roll back the transaction as appropriate.

Try It Out: Working with ADO.NET Transactions

In this example, we're going to fill in the rest of our C# application from the previous example and use it to perform the ADO.NET Transaction equivalents of the two SQL transactions, `sp_TransTest1_SQL` and `sp_TransTest2_SQL`.

1. Reopen our `Transactions` project if it isn't already.

2. Add the controls to the tab marked ADO.NET Transactions in our form as shown below.

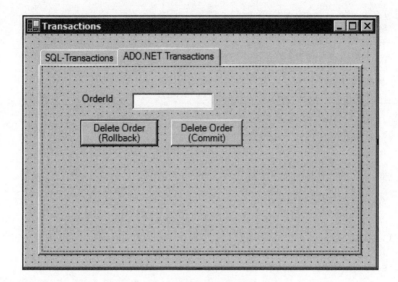

From left to right, top to bottom, the controls are as follows:

Control	Name	Properties to Change
Label	`label2`	Text : OrderId
Textbox	`txtOrderId2`	None
Button	`cmdRollbackADONET`	Text : Delete Order (Rollback)
Button	`cmdCommitADONET`	Text : Delete Order (Commit)

3. Double-click on the Delete Order (Rollback) button and add the following code to its `Click` event handler:

```
private void cmdRollbackADONET_Click(object sender, System.EventArgs e)
{
   //Create a connection
   SqlConnection cn =
```

```
          new SqlConnection(@"Data Source=(local)\NETSDK;" +
                       "Integrated Security=SSPI;database=Northwind");

     //Open the connection
     cn.Open();

     //Begin the transaction
     SqlTransaction objTrans= cn.BeginTransaction();

     try
     {
        //Create a command object
        SqlCommand cmd = cn.CreateCommand();

        //supply values to the command's properties
        cmd.CommandType = CommandType.Text;
        cmd.CommandText = "DELETE Orders WHERE OrderId=" +
          Convert.ToString(txtOrderId2.Text);

        //set the Transaction property of the command object
        cmd.Transaction = objTrans;

        //Delete the order
        cmd.ExecuteNonQuery();

        //Commit the Transaction
        objTrans.Commit();

        //If no exception has been raised,
        //transaction has been committed - give message
        MessageBox.Show ("Transaction Committed"+ "\n"+
                       "Order and Order Details have been successfully deleted",
                       "Commit Transaction");
     }

     catch ( System.Data.SqlClient.SqlException  e1)
     {
        //Rollback the transaction
        objTrans.Rollback();

        // Display Error Message.
        MessageBox.Show ("Error-TRANSACTION ROLLED BACK " + "\n"+
                       e1.Message, "Rollback Transaction");
     }

     catch ( System.Exception  e2)
     {
        // Display Error Message.
        MessageBox.Show ("System Error " + "\n"+  e2.Message,"Error");
     }

     finally
```

```
    {
      //Close the connection
      cn.Close();
    }
  }
```

4. Switch back to the form and double-click on the **Delete Order (Commit)** button. Add the following code to its `Click` event handler:

```
private void cmdCommitADONET_Click(object sender, System.EventArgs e)
{
  //Create a connection
  SqlConnection cn =
    new SqlConnection(@"Data Source=(local)\NETSDK;" +
                      "Integrated Security=SSPI;database=Northwind");

  //Open the connection
  cn.Open();

  //Begin the transaction
  SqlTransaction objTrans = cn.BeginTransaction();

  try
  {
    //Create a command object
    SqlCommand cmd = cn.CreateCommand();

    //supply values to the command's properties
    cmd.CommandType = CommandType.Text;
    cmd.CommandText = "DELETE [Order Details] WHERE OrderId = " +
      Convert.ToString(txtOrderId2.Text);

    //set the Transaction property of the command object
    cmd.Transaction = objTrans;

    //Delete the order
    cmd.ExecuteNonQuery();
    cmd.CommandText="DELETE Orders WHERE OrderId = " +
      Convert.ToString(txtOrderId2.Text);

    //Delete the order
    cmd.ExecuteNonQuery();

    //Commit the Transaction
    objTrans.Commit();

    //If code comes here, transaction has been committed - give message
    MessageBox.Show ("Transaction Committed"+ "\n"+
                     "Order and Order Details have been successfully deleted",
                     "Commit Transaction");
  }
```

```
    catch ( System.Data.SqlClient.SqlException  e1)
    {
      //Rollback the transaction
      objTrans.Rollback();

      // Display Error Message.
      MessageBox.Show ("Error-TRANSACTION ROLLED BACK " + "\n" +
                       e1.Message,"Rollback Transaction");
    }

    catch ( System.Exception  e2)
    {
      // Display Error Message.
      MessageBox.Show ("System Error " + "\n" + e2.Message,"Error");
    }

    finally
    {
      //Close the connection
      cn.Close();
    }
  }
```

5. Build and run the solution. When the form pops up, switch to the **ADO.NET Transactions** tab and enter **10249** for **OrderId** and click the **Delete Order (Rollback)** button. As expected, an error message box appears.

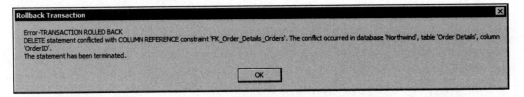

6. Now click on the **Delete Order (Commit)** button. As expected, we'll get a message box confirming that our transaction has been successful.

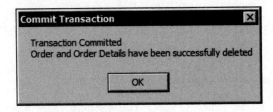

How It Works

The code behind the form follows the guidelines for creating ADO.NET transactions that we saw earlier. In `Click` handler for `cmdRollbackADONET` for example, we create and open a `Connection` object and then call `BeginTransaction` to return a reference to a `SqlTransaction` object which we store in `objTrans`.

```
private void cmdRollbackADONET_Click(object sender, System.EventArgs e)
{
  //Create a connection
  SqlConnection cn =
    new SqlConnection(@"Data Source=(local)\NETSDK;" +
                      "Integrated Security=SSPI;database=Northwind");

  //Open the connection
  cn.Open();

  //Begin the transaction
  SqlTransaction objTrans= cn.BeginTransaction();
```

Note that **transactions are connection specific**. We cannot start a second transaction on the same connection without committing or rolling back the first before we do so. Only one transaction can be active at any one time.

Back to the code; with our transaction object initialized, we create a `Command` object and assign it a SQL command. As this is the rollback button, we'll take the cue of `sp_TransTest1_SQL` and try to delete the entry in the `Orders` table. This will cause an error as required when we try to execute it.

```
try
{
  //Create a command object
  SqlCommand cmd = cn.CreateCommand();

  //supply values to the command's properties
  cmd.CommandType = CommandType.Text;
  cmd.CommandText = "DELETE Orders WHERE OrderId=" +
    Convert.ToString(txtOrderId2.Text);
```

With the `Command` object set up, we need only assign it the transaction object to make sure it is executed as transaction and then execute it. Since a `DELETE` statement isn't a query, we can use the `ExecuteNonQuery()` method. If it doesn't encounter any errors, we'll `Commit()` the transaction.

```
  //set the Transaction property of the command object
  cmd.Transaction = objTrans;

  //Delete the order
  cmd.ExecuteNonQuery();

  //Commit the Transaction
  objTrans.Commit();
```

Then we give out a message that the transaction has been committed and that the order and its details have been deleted. We use the \n escape sequence to separate the error message.

```
MessageBox.Show ("Transaction Committed"+ "\n"+
                "Order and Order Details have been successfully deleted",
                "Commit Transaction");
}
```

If an error is encountered (which it will be), the catch block contains the code to Rollback() the transaction and display an error message.

```
catch ( System.Data.SqlClient.SqlException  e1)
{
  //Rollback the transaction
  objTrans.Rollback();

  // Display Error Message.
  MessageBox.Show ("Error-TRANSACTION ROLLED BACK " + "\n"+
                  e1.Message, "Rollback Transaction");
}
```

The code for the cmdCommitADONET_Click() event is similar, but we need to take the lead from sp_TransTest2_SQL and execute two DELETE statements to successfully remove the order and its details. As we need both DELETE statements to succeed within the one transaction, the SQL code for both actions has to be defined and executed before we tell the handler to Commit() (or roll back) the transaction.

What Next?

We've really only touched the tip of the transaction iceberg in this chapter. There's a great deal more to learn beyond this basic knowledge we've learned here. Indeed, we've already noted three important topics during the course of our examples.

❑ **Nested Transactions**. There are a lot of subtleties to nested transactions we haven't covered here.

❑ **Isolation Levels**. We noted that ADO.NET defines six levels of isolation for a transaction. The next step would be to discover what they are and under what circumstances we would use each of them. We didn't look at isolation in too much detail in this chapter, so if you want to take your knowledge further, you may want to learn more about this.

❑ **Save Points**. These work much like save points in a computer game. Defined by the SAVE TRANSACTION statement we saw earlier, they define points the code in a transaction can return to when it is rolled back rather than all the way back to the beginning. For example:

```
BEGIN TRANSACTION
  <statement1>
  <statement2>
```

```
SAVE TRANSACTION savepoint1

<statement3>
<statement4>

IF @Err>0
    ROLLBACK TRANSACTION savepoint1

COMMIT TRANSACTION
```

Here we issue a `SAVE TRANSACTION` statement after `statement2` and give it the name `savepoint1`. If an error has occurred after `statement4`, the transaction will roll back, but only up to `savepoint1`. That is, any changes to data done by `statement3` and `statement4` are rolled back. Then the `COMMIT TRANSACTION` will commit the changes done by `statement1` and `statement2`.

Then there are several other techniques, such as how to handle transactions when one stored procedure calls another, and handy built-in features, such as the `@@TRANCOUNT` variable, which keeps track of the transactions that are active in a connection, which we haven't covered at all here.

As we have seen in this chapter, anything we can do in SQL Transactions, we can also do as ADO.NET Transactions. This applies equally to these new topics we've just mentioned. If you want to work more with ADO.NET transactions, *Professional ADO.NET Programming ISBN 1-86100-527-X* and the *ADO.NET Programmer's Reference ISBN 1-86100-558-X* will both be able to help you advance your knowledge. You'll also find a section of Visual C#'s help files on transactions by searching for transaction processing.

Summary

In this chapter we learned what transactions are and when to use them. We learned about the ACID properties that characterize transactions, and the difference between SQL Transactions and ADO.NET Transactions. We then learned how to write code using both. Specifically we learned that:

❑ SQL- Transactions are usually written in stored procedures and use the `@@ERROR` system variable to test if an error has occurred. If an error is encountered, it is raised to the client. We can also use the `PRINT` or `RAISERROR` statements to raise adhoc messages. The statements `BEGIN TRAN`, `COMMIT TRAN`, and `ROLLBACK TRAN` are used to begin, commit, and roll back transactions respectively.

❑ ADO.NET Transactions are written using the classes in `System.Data.SqlClient` namespace as well as the `SqlTransaction` class. The `SqlTransaction` class supports methods such as `Commit()` and `Rollback()` that are used to commit and roll back transactions. When a transaction errors out, a `SqlException` is thrown which is trapped by a `catch` block. It is in this `catch` block that we `Rollback()` the transaction.

❑ We tried out exercises using both SQL Transactions and ADO.NET Transactions and achieved the same results in both cases. In exercises where a transaction was rolled back, we verified that the data integrity was maintained.

❑ We learned that features such as Save Points, Isolation Levels and nested transactions will provide us more control and flexibility in writing transaction code and these can be implemented using either SQL-Transactions or using ADO.NET Transactions.

This chapter provides the basic concepts and orientation required to get started in writing transactional applications. If we are ever called upon to write transactional applications, we will very much be using the techniques described in this chapter.

Exercises

1. Write a stored procedure that will execute the following statements as transactions:

```
INSERT INTO table1 VALUES(1,2,3)
DELETE table2 WHERE c1='Apples'
UPDATE table3 SET c1='x' WHERE c1='y'
```

2. When an error occurs in the INSERT statement, will the transaction be rolled back in the following code?

```
DECLARE @Err int
BEGIN TRANSACTION
  INSERT table1 VALUES (x,y,z)
  IF @@ERRROR<>0
    @Err=@ERROR
  IF @Err<>0
    BEGIN
      ROLLBACK TRANSACTION
      RETURN @Err
    END
COMMIT TRANSACTION
```

3. Write a stored procedure that takes two orders as inputs and then deletes them both transactionally.

4. Write a method in C# called EnlistTransaction that executes the following statements transactionally against the Northwind database. Observe the instructions regarding the Command objects.

A command object called cmdOne must execute the following two statements:

Statement1 – INSERT INTO Products(ProductName) VALUES('Spicy Tofu')
Statement2 – UPDATE Shippers SET Phone='503-888-9999' WHERE ShipperId=1

A command object called cmdTwo must execute the following two statements:

Statement3 – INSERT INTO Products(ProductName) VALUES('Spicy Mutton')
Statement4 – UPDATE Shippers SET Phone='503-999-8888' WHERE ShipperId=2

All the four statements must be executed within the same transaction.

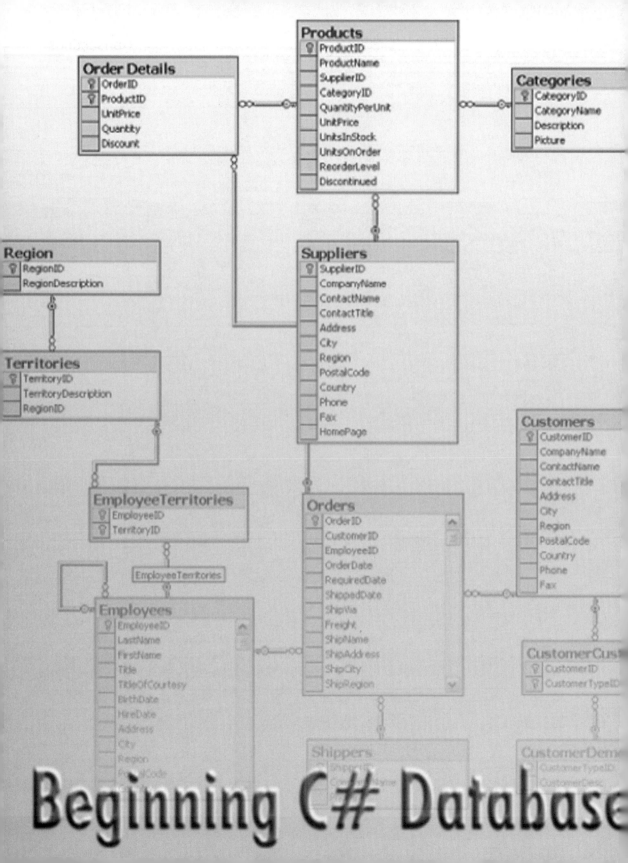

ADO.NET Events

ADO.NET objects (such as the `connection` and `DataSet` objects) can fire events when a certain property has changed. For example, a `Connection` object can be made to notify us when it is opened or closed. Similarly, a `DataSet` object can be made to notify us when a column value is changed or when a row is deleted. In this chapter we will discuss the following topics about events:

❑ What events and delegates are and how they are useful

❑ How to add and remove event handlers

❑ Different types of events supported by ADO.NET objects

❑ Try It Out sections to demonstrate event handling

Events and Delegates

An event is a message sent by an object to signal the occurrence of an action. The action could be caused by user interaction, such as a mouse click, or it could be triggered by program logic. The object that raises (triggers) the event is called the **event sender**. The object that captures the event and responds to it is called the **event receiver**. The method that handles the event is called the **event handler**.

The event sender does not know if any object or method will receive (handle) the events it raises. The .NET Framework provides a special type of class called a **Delegate** that maps an event to a method that will handle the event. It's worth remembering the following chain to describe the process:

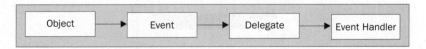

Delegates can be bound to a single method or to multiple methods, referred to as multicasting. A multicast delegate maintains an invocation list of the methods it is bound to. The multicast delegate supports a Combine method to add a method to the invocation list and a Remove method to remove it. We will not be covering multicast delegates in this chapter, but for further reading on this topic, you might want to look at *Professional C# Second Edition*, ISBN: 1-86100-704-3.

Delegates can also allow multiple events to be bound to the same method, allowing a many-to-one notification. For example, a button-click event and a menu-command–click event can both invoke the same delegate, which then calls a single method to handle these separate events the same way. For example, imagine a web browser application. You could initiate a "browse" method by either clicking a "Go" button, by pressing *Enter* after an address is entered in an address bar, or by hitting a link in a Favorites menu. Each event – the clicking of a button, the pressing of a key, and the selecting of a menu option – is handled by the same "browse" method.

The binding mechanism used with delegates is dynamic – a delegate can be bound at run time to any method whose signature matches that of the event handler. This feature allows you to set up or change the bound method depending on a condition and to dynamically attach an event handler to a control.

When an event is raised, the code within the event handler is executed. Each event handler provides two parameters that help in handling the event correctly. The first parameter, sender, provides a reference to the object that raised the event. The second parameter is an object specific to the event that is being handled. By referencing the object's properties (and, sometimes, its methods), you can obtain detailed information about the event. Typically each event has an event handler with a different event-object type for the second parameter.

The event handling process described above applies to events raised by all objects in the .NET Framework. Consequently, ADO.NET objects, such as the connection object and the SqlAdapter and DataSet objects, also raise events that can be handled using the same process. We will discuss the events raised by ADO.NET objects in detail in later sections, but for now, let us quickly get a feel for how all the different pieces of this process look.

The database connection object supports two events – InfoMessage and StateChange. These are shown by a yellow lightning bolt icon in the Visual Studio .NET IntelliSense pop-up menu, as shown below:

The declaration of the delegate that binds the `StateChange` event to an event handler looks like this:

```
public delegate void StateChangeEventHandler(object sender,
                                             StateChangeEventArgs e);
```

The code to bind the `StateChange` event to the `CnStateChange` event handler looks like this (note the += operator):

```
cn.StateChange+=new StateChangeEventHandler(CnStateChange);
```

The event handler itself, which will execute after the event is raised, looks like this:

```
private void CnStateChange(object sender, StateChangeEventArgs ev)
{
// Event handler CODE for the StateChange Event
}
```

Note the parameters of the event handler, which are the same as the parameters of the delegate declaration. All these will be covered in more detail in the following sections. We will now look at the syntax of adding and removing event handlers.

Adding and Removing Event Handlers

In C#, a delegate is specified by using the += operator. For example, we can bind the `StateChange` event of the connection object called `cn` to the `CnStateChange` method (which you write yourself) by activating a delegate called `StateChangeEventHandler` (that is provided for you by .NET). The `StateChange` event of the connection object fires whenever its connection state changes to open or closed.

```
cn.StateChange+=new StateChangeEventHandler(CnStateChange);
```

Similarly, we can deactivate a delegate by removing it with the -= operator as follows:

```
cn.StateChange-=new StateChangeEventHandler(CnStateChange);
```

Once deactivated, when the `StateChange` event fires, it will not be handled by the `CnStateChange` event handler. This process of activating a delegate into service and deactivating it can be done as needed in code.

In this chapter we will be discussing the events raised by ADO.NET objects and how to handle them. While events can be raised and handled by non-ADO.NET objects as well, our focus in this chapter only pertains to the ADO.NET objects.

ADO.NET Events

The events raised by ADO.NET objects can be handled using appropriate delegates. These events are raised when a certain property of the object changes. While there are several events that are raised by these objects, we will discuss a few and others can be handled in the same fashion. Again, we will limit our discussion to the `System.Data.SqlClient` .NET data provider. Other data providers handle events the same way and information about them can be found in the MSDN Library.

Connection Object Events

The connection object has two events – the `StateChange` event and the `InfoMessage` event. Let's look at these in more detail.

The StateChange Event

The `StateChange` event is raised by the connection object when the state of the connection itself changes. The event handler receives a `StateChangeEventArgs` object, which can be investigated for more information about the event itself. For example, this object has an `OriginalState` and a `CurrentState` property that can be queried to find out the state of the connection object before and after the status change.

Let us see how this event is handled by trying it out in the following example. We will open a connection to the Northwind database, retrieve one row from the `Customers` table, and close the connection. Then we will write an event handler to notify us when the connection state changes.

Try It Out: Connection.StateChange Event

1. Create a new chapter solution called `Chapter20_Examples`.

2. Create a new C# Windows Application within the solution and name the project `Chapter20`.

3. In `Form1`, add buttons and a listbox as follows. A screenshot of how the form should look is also shown.

Object	Name	Remarks
Form1	Form1	Set `MaximizeBox` property to `false` and `Text` property to "ADO.NET Events"
Button	cmdCnStateChange	On clicking this button, we'll try out the `StateChange` event
Button	cmdCnInfoMsg	On clicking this button, we'll try out the `InfoMessage` event
Button	cmdSqlDARowUpdating	On clicking this button, we'll try out the `RowUpdating` and `RowUpdated` events
Button	cmdMultHandler	On clicking this button, we'll try out handing the same event by many handlers
Label	label1	Set its text to "Event Log"
ListBox	lbResult	To display results

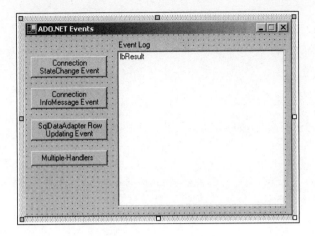

4. Import the `System.Data.SqlClient` namespace.

5. We will now connect to the database and retrieve one row of data from the `Customers` table. In the click event of the `cmdCnStateChange` button write code as follows:

```
private void cmdCnStateChange_Click(object sender, System.EventArgs e)
{
  //create a connection
  SqlConnection cn = new SqlConnection(@"Data Source=(local)\NETSDK;" +
    "Integrated Security=SSPI;database=Northwind");

  //create a command object and initialize it
  SqlCommand cmd = new SqlCommand();
  cmd.CommandText="SELECT TOP 1 CustomerId, CompanyName FROM Customers";
  cmd.Connection=cn;

  //delegate the StateChange event to the CnStateChange function
  cn.StateChange+=new StateChangeEventHandler(CnStateChange);

  try
  {
    lbResult.Items.Clear();

    //Open the connection

    cn.Open();

    //create a data reader to hold the results
    SqlDataReader dr=cmd.ExecuteReader();

    //Display the row in the listbox
    while(dr.Read())
    {
      lbResult.Items.Add(dr.GetString(0) + "-" + dr.GetString(1));
```

```
        }

    //Close the connection - CnStateChange event will be fired

    }

  catch(SqlException e1)
  {
    MessageBox.Show (e1.Message);
  }
  finally
  {
    //Close the connection - CnStateChange event will be fired
    cn.Close();
  }
}
```

6. Write the `EventHandler` for the `StateChange` event as follows:

```
private void CnStateChange(object sender, StateChangeEventArgs ev)
{
    // Event handler for the StateChange Event
    lbResult.Items.Add("----------------------------");
    lbResult.Items.Add("Entering StateChange EventHandler");
    lbResult.Items.Add("Sender="+ sender.ToString());
    lbResult.Items.Add("Original State="+ ev.OriginalState.ToString());
    lbResult.Items.Add("Current State="+ ev.CurrentState.ToString());
    lbResult.Items.Add("Exiting StateChange EventHandler");
    lbResult.Items.Add("----------------------------");
}
```

7. Build and run the solution. When the window loads up, click on the button captioned **Connection StateChange event**. You will see the results displayed in the listbox as follows:

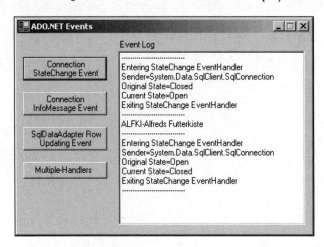

Notice the values of the Original State and Current State Properties before and after the data is displayed. This example shows that as the connection state changes the event handler takes over and handles the event.

How It Works

First we begin by creating and initializing the connection object.

```
SqlConnection cn = new SqlConnection(@"Data Source=(local)\NETSDK;" +
        "Integrated Security=SSPI;database=Northwind");
```

Then we create and initialize the command object. We provide a SQL statement that will select one row from the Customers table.

```
//create a command object and initalize it
SqlCommand cmd = new SqlCommand();
cmd.CommandText="SELECT TOP 1 CustomerId, CompanyName FROM Customers";
cmd.Connection=cn;
```

Next, we specify the event handler for the StateChange event using the += operator that we discussed earlier.

```
//delegate the StateChange event to the CnStateChange function
cn.StateChange+=new StateChangeEventHandler(CnStateChange);
```

In the IDE, when you type the dot after the cn object, you will be presented with an IntelliSense window shown below, where you can find the StateChange event; events are listed using a yellow lightning bolt icon.

On the right-hand side, after you type += new, the IntelliSense window will open up as follows. Select the StateChangeEventHandler delegate. Delegates are marked by a lock icon. Notice also the tooltip information. Even though it mentions the OleDb provider, this is applicable to the SqlClient provider as well. Then for the delegate's argument, we specify a name of a function that we will be writing that will handle the event.

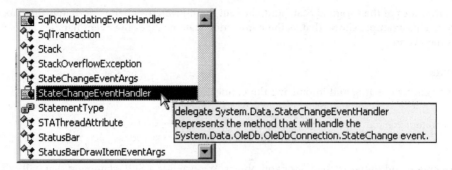

The location in your code where the event handler is specified is important. In this case, since we want to capture the `StateChange` event, we have specified it before we actually open the connection.

Next, we clear the listbox, open the connection, create a `DataReader` object to hold the row that will be retrieved, and display the data in the row in the listbox. Finally, we close the connection. The code for these actions is enclosed in a `try` block.

```
try
{
  //Clear the listbox

  lbResult.Items.Clear();

  //Open the connection - CnStateChange event will be fired

  cn.Open();

  //create a data reader to hold the results
  SqlDataReader dr=cmd.ExecuteReader();

  //Display the row in the listbox
  while(dr.Read())
  {
    lbResult.Items.Add(dr.GetString(0) + "-" + dr.GetString(1));
  }
}

//If any exception is thrown in the try block
//the catch block will display the message
catch(SqlException e1)
{
  MessageBox.Show (e1.Message);
}


finally
{
  //Close the connection - CnStateChange event will be fired
  cn.Close();
}
}
```

We then write the EventHandler method. Earlier, we specified CnStateChange as the name of our function that will handle the event. The StateChangeEventHandler delegate provides objects with information about the event – the sender object and the StateChangeEventArgs object. The declaration of our event handler must have the same parameters as the StateChangeEventHandler delegate declaration. In the C# documentation, if you search for StateChangeEventHandler, you will see the following declaration for the delegate:

```
public delegate void StateChangeEventHandler(
    object sender,
    StateChangeEventArgs e
);
```

As you can see, the two parameters are sender and StateChangeEventArgs. The StateChange event provides the delegate with these objects and the delegate gives the EventHandler these objects, so the EventHandler could handle the event appropriately. That is why the CnStateChange event handler has the same parameters as the StateChangeEventHandler delegate described above. We also capture the sender object's identity in the sender.ToString() statement.

```
private void CnStateChange(object sender, StateChangeEventArgs ev)
{
    // Event handler for the StateChange Event
    lbResult.Items.Add("----------------------------");
    lbResult.Items.Add("Entering StateChange EventHandler");
    lbResult.Items.Add("Sender="+ sender.ToString());
    lbResult.Items.Add("Original State="+ ev.OriginalState.ToString());
    lbResult.Items.Add("Current State="+ ev.CurrentState.ToString());
     lbResult.Items.Add("Exiting StateChange EventHandler");
    lbResult.Items.Add("----------------------------");
}
```

This makes it clear when the execution enters and leaves the event handler. You can also see that the sender object is the SqlConnection object. When the connection is opened, its current state is Open and its original state is closed. When the connection is closed, the current state is Closed and the original state is Open.

So, our example runs pretty well, and we can see what's happening, but, in a real-life-application, why would the user care to be notified if a connection is open or closed? All they need is to see the data. One way to use the StateChange event is to keep track of how many times connections are established and keep a running total. Based on this the user can be charged a fee per connection. Of course this is a rudimentary way of charging a fee and other factors will have to be figured in. Another way to use this event would be to keep track of how much time a user has had a connection open and charge them a fee based on this fact.

The InfoMessage event

The InfoMessage event is raised by the connection object when the database gives out information messages. Information messages are not error messages from the database. They are warning messages issued by the database and also the output of PRINT SQL statements, which you might find in a stored procedure that is being debugged. In the case of Microsoft SQL Server, and MSDE, which we have been using throughout this book, any message with a severity of 10 or less is considered informational and would be captured using the InfoMessage event.

The `InfoMessage` event handler receives an `InfoMessageEventArgs` object that contains a collection of the messages from the data source in its `Errors` collection property. The `Error` objects in this collection are of type `SqlError` and can be queried for information such as the number, source, message, and the exact line number in the stored procedure where this message originated from, among others. Let's run a couple of SQL statements against the Northwind database, one of which is a `PRINT` statement. We will capture this event and query the information in the `Errors` collection.

Try It Out: Connection.InfoMessage Event

1. Return to the design view of our form, and double-click the button captioned **Connection InfoMessage Event**. Enter the following code for the `Click` event:

```
private void cmdCnInfoMsg_Click(object sender, System.EventArgs e)
{
  //create a connection
  SqlConnection cn = new SqlConnection(@"Data Source=(local)\NETSDK;" +
    "Integrated Security=SSPI;database=Northwind");

  //delegate the StateChange event to the CnStateChange function
  cn.InfoMessage +=new SqlInfoMessageEventHandler(CnInfoMessage);

  //delegate the StateChange event to the CnStateChange function
  cn.StateChange+=new StateChangeEventHandler(CnStateChange);

  //create a command object and initalize it
  SqlCommand cmd = new SqlCommand();
  cmd.CommandText="SELECT TOP 2 CustomerId FROM Customers";
  cmd.Connection=cn;

  try
  {
    //clear the listbox
    lbResult.Items.Clear();

    //Open the connection
    cn.Open();

    //create a data reader to hold the results
    SqlDataReader dr=cmd.ExecuteReader();

    while(dr.Read())
    {
      lbResult.Items.Add(dr.GetString(0) );
    }

    dr.Close();

    // execute a print statement against the database
    cmd.CommandText="PRINT 'Get CustomerId for all customers ' ";
    cmd.ExecuteNonQuery();
```

```
        }

    catch(SqlException el)
    {
      MessageBox.Show (el.Message);
    }
    finally
    {
      //Close the connection
      cn.Close();
    }
}
```

2. Write an `EventHandler` method as follows. We will discuss it later.

```
private void CnInfoMessage(object sender, SqlInfoMessageEventArgs ev)
{
  foreach (SqlError err in ev.Errors)
  {
    lbResult.Items.Add("----------------------------");
    lbResult.Items.Add("Entering InfoMessage Event Handler");
    lbResult.Items.Add("Source-"+ err.Source);
    lbResult.Items.Add("State-"+ err.State);
    lbResult.Items.Add("Number-"+ err.Number);
    lbResult.Items.Add("Procedure-"+ err.Procedure);
    lbResult.Items.Add("Server-"+ err.Server);
       lbResult.Items.Add("Message-"+ err.Message);
    lbResult.Items.Add("Exiting InfoMessage Event Handler");
    lbResult.Items.Add("----------------------------");
  }
}
```

3. Build and run the solution. The results are displayed as shown below. Observe the section of the `InfoMessage EventHandler`.

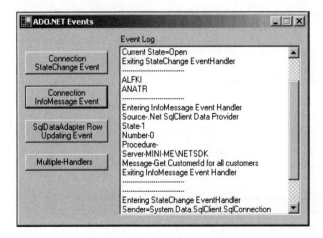

As you can see in the **InfoMessage Event Handler** section, the message of the PRINT statement is shown and since we did not place this statement in a stored procedure, the **Procedure** property is blank. Other pieces of information such as the state and the server name are shown.

How It Works

After creating a connection object, we specify the CnInfoMessage function as the EventHandler for the InfoMessage event.

```
//delegate the StateChange event to the CnStateChange function
cn.InfoMessage +=new SqlInfoMessageEventHandler(CnInfoMessage);
```

We also capture the StateChange event by the same EventHandler that we used before.

```
//delegate the StateChange event to the CnStateChange function
cn.StateChange+=new StateChangeEventHandler(CnStateChange);
```

Then we execute a query and get the CustomerIds of two employees and add them to the listbox.

```
//create a command object and initalize it
SqlCommand cmd = new SqlCommand();
cmd.CommandText="SELECT TOP 2 CustomerId FROM Customers";
cmd.Connection=cn;

try
{
  //clear the listbox
  lbResult.Items.Clear();

  //Open the connection
  cn.Open();

  //create a data reader to hold the results
  SqlDataReader dr=cmd.ExecuteReader();

  while(dr.Read())
  {
  lbResult.Items.Add(dr.GetString(0) );
  }

  dr.Close();
```

Now, we execute a PRINT statement against the database. We use the ExecuteNonQuery() method of the command object since the PRINT statement does not return any rows.

```
// execute a print statement against the database
cmd.CommandText="PRINT 'Get CustomerId for all customers ' ";
cmd.ExecuteNonQuery();

}
```

The `EventHandler` method `cnInfoMessage` is then written with the same signature as the delegate `SqlInfoMessageEventHandler`. The two arguments are the `sender` object and the `SqlInfoMessageEventArgs` object, which contains information about the event. We then loop through the `Errors` collection of the object and list several pieces of information about the message itself:

```
private void CnInfoMessage(object sender, SqlInfoMessageEventArgs ev)
{
  foreach (SqlError err in ev.Errors)
  {
    lbResult.Items.Add("-----------------------------");
    lbResult.Items.Add("Entering InfoMessage Event Handler");
    lbResult.Items.Add("Source-"+ err.Source);
    lbResult.Items.Add("State-"+ err.State);
    lbResult.Items.Add("Number-"+ err.Number);
    lbResult.Items.Add("Procedure-"+ err.Procedure);
    lbResult.Items.Add("Server-"+ err.Server);
    lbResult.Items.Add("Message-"+ err.Message);
    lbResult.Items.Add("Exiting InfoMessage Event Handler");
    lbResult.Items.Add("-----------------------------");
  }
}
```

The `InfoMessage` event can be used to log all the messages from a database in a log file for reference by the user during a application session.

Row Update Events

So far we have seen the connection object's events. There are a wide variety of other events supported by ADO.NET for the purpose of aiding in data validation. As discussed earlier in the book, the `SqlDataAdapter` object serves as a bridge between the `DataSet` object and the database. When the `SqlDataAdapter` object is ready to do an update using the changes in the `DataSet`, pre-defined events are raised. We can code handlers for these events to find more information about the status of the update. Some of the common events raised when data is manipulated in ADO.NET objects are listed below. The object that raises the event, the event name, the name of the delegate, and the `EventArgs` object received by the event handler are presented in the table. The object received by the event handler itself has several properties that can be used to take appropriate action. This can be found in the documentation or using IntelliSense in the VS.NET IDE.

Object	Event	Delegate	Remarks
SqlDataAdapter	RowUpdating	SqlRowUpdatingEvent Handler	Raised before the row is updated at the database. The event handler receives a `SqlRowUpdatingEvent Args` object.
SqlDataAdapter	RowUpdated	SqlRowUpdatedEvent Handler	Raised after a row is updated in the database. The event handler receives a `SqlRowUpdatedEvent Args` object.

Table continued on following page

Object	Event	Delegate	Remarks
SqlDataAdapter	FillError	FillErrorEvent Handler	Raised when the Fill method is called. The event handler receives a FillErrorEventArgs object.
DataTable	Column Changing	DataColumnChange EventHandler	Raised when the data in a DataColumn is changing. The handler receives a DataColumnChanging EventArgs object.
DataTable	Column Changed	DataColumnChange EventHandler	Raised after value has been changed for the specified DataColumn in a DataRow. The handler receives a DataColumnChanged EventArgs object.
DataTable	RowChanging	DataRowChangeEvent Handler	Raised when a DataRow is changing. The event handler receives a DataChangeEventArgs object.
DataTable	RowChanged	DataRowChangeEvent Handler	Raised after a DataRow has changed. The event handler receives a DataChangeEventArgs object.
DataTable	RowDeleting	DataRowChangeEvent Handler	Raised before a DataRow is deleted. The event handler receives a DataRowChangeEvent Args object.
DataTable	RowDeleted	DataRowChangeEvent Handler	Raised after a DataRow is deleted. The event handler receives a DataRowchangeEvnet Args objects.

Let us try experimenting with the SqlDataAdapter's RowUpdating and RowUpdated events and see how they are fired and handled when a value in a DataSet changes.

Try It Out: DataAdapter.RowUpdating/RowUpdated Events

1. In the `cmdSqlDARowUpdating` button's click event write code as follows:

```
private void cmdSqlDARowUpdating_Click(object sender,System.EventArgs e)
{

  //clear the listbox
  lbResult.Items.Clear();

  //create a connection
  SqlConnection cn = new SqlConnection(@"Data Source=(local)\NETSDK;" +
    "Integrated Security=SSPI;database=Northwind");

  try
  {

    //Open the connection
    cn.Open();

    // create the SqlDataAdapter object
    SqlDataAdapter daSql = new SqlDataAdapter("SELECT * FROM Customers" ,cn);

    SqlCommandBuilder cb = new SqlCommandBuilder(daSql);

    // Create and fill dataset (select only first 1 row)
    DataSet ds = new DataSet();
    daSql.Fill(ds, 0, 1, "Customers");


    // add handlers
    daSql.RowUpdating += new SqlRowUpdatingEventHandler( OnRowUpdating );
    daSql.RowUpdated += new SqlRowUpdatedEventHandler ( OnRowUpdated );


    // Modify the dataSet
    DataTable dTable = ds.Tables["Customers"];
    dTable.Rows[0][1] = "The Volcano Corporation";

    // update, this operation fires two events (RowUpdating/RowUpdated)
    daSql.Update(ds, "Customers");

    // remove handlers
    daSql.RowUpdating -= new SqlRowUpdatingEventHandler( OnRowUpdating );
    daSql.RowUpdated -= new SqlRowUpdatedEventHandler( OnRowUpdated );

  }

  catch (SqlException e1)
  {
    MessageBox.Show(e1.Message);
  }
  finally
  {
    //Close the connection
    cn.Close();
  }
}
```

2. Write an event handler for the `RowUpdating` event as follows. Note that the name of the EventHandler is `OnRowUpdating`.

```
// Event Handler for RowUpdating event
private void OnRowUpdating(object sender, SqlRowUpdatingEventArgs e)
{
  DisplayEventArgs(e);
}
```

3. Write an event handler for the `RowUpdated` event as follows. Note that the name of the EventHandler is `OnRowUpdated`.

```
// Event Handler for RowUpdated event
private void OnRowUpdated(object sender, SqlRowUpdatedEventArgs e)
{
  DisplayEventArgs(e);
}
```

4. Write code for the `DisplayEventArgs` function as follows. Note that there are two overloaded functions with different argument types.

```
private void DisplayEventArgs(SqlRowUpdatingEventArgs args)
{
  lbResult.Items.Add("OnRowUpdating event");
  if (args.Status !=UpdateStatus.Continue)
    lbResult.Items.Add("RowStatus="+args.Status.ToString());
}

private void DisplayEventArgs(SqlRowUpdatedEventArgs args)
{
  lbResult.Items.Add("OnRowUpdated event");
  lbResult.Items.Add("Records Affected="+ args.RecordsAffected);
}
```

5. Build and run the solution. Click on the **Row Updating** event button. You will see the results displayed as shown below.

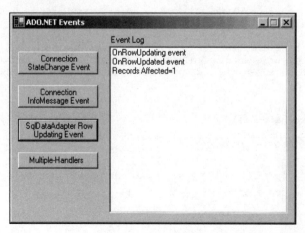

6. Click on the button again. You will see the results displayed as shown below.

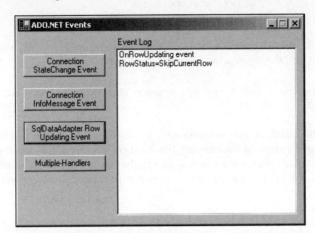

How It Works

Note that the first time the button was clicked, the RowUpdating and RowUpdated events were fired. But the second time, the RowUpdated event was not fired and the RowStatus has been shown as SkipCurrentRow.

What we have essentially done in this example is to retrieve one row from the customer table, update it and have the RowUpdating and RowUpdated events fire and handle the events. We create and initialize the SqlDataAdapter object and a SqlCommandBuilder object as follows:

```
// create the SqlDataAdapter object
SqlDataAdapter daSql = new SqlDataAdapter("SELECT * FROM Customers" ,cn);

SqlCommandBuilder cb = new SqlCommandBuilder(daSql);
```

Then we create a DataSet and use the Fill method to fill the DataSet with one row of data.

```
// Create and fill dataset (select only first 1 row)
DataSet ds = new DataSet();
daSql.Fill(ds, 0,  1,  "Customers");
```

Then we add handlers to the RowUpdating and RowUpdated events using the += operators as follows.

```
// add handlers
daSql.RowUpdating += new SqlRowUpdatingEventHandler( OnRowUpdating );
daSql.RowUpdated += new SqlRowUpdatedEventHandler ( OnRowUpdated );
```

We now begin to modify the DataSet. We change the name of the company to "The Volcano Corporation".

```
// Modify the dataSet
DataTable dTable = ds.Tables["Customers"];
dTable.Rows[0][1] = "The Volcano Corporation";
```

We now update the database by sending the `DataSet` changes to it. At this moment, the `RowUpdating` event and the `RowUpdated` event are fired.

```
// update, this operation fires two events (RowUpdating/RowUpdated)
daSql.Update(ds, "Customers");
```

Finally we remove the handlers. It is not necessary in this example, but shown here for demonstration purposes. As mentioned earlier in the chapter, the location in code where handlers are added and removed is important, and will have a bearing on whether events are handled or not, even if event handlers are present. Notice that we use the `-=` operator to remove the handlers.

```
// remove handlers
daSql.RowUpdating -= new SqlRowUpdatingEventHandler( OnRowUpdating );
daSql.RowUpdated -= new SqlRowUpdatedEventHandler( OnRowUpdated );
```

Both the `OnRowUpdating` and `OnRowUpdated` event handlers call another function called `DisplayEventArgs`. The `OnRowUpdating` event handler receives the `SqlRowUpdatingEventArgs` objects and the `OnRowUpdated` event handler receives the `SqlRowUpdatedEventArgs` object. As these two events are different, the delegates of these events pass slightly different information to the handler:

```
// Event Handler for RowUpdating event
private void OnRowUpdating(object sender, SqlRowUpdatingEventArgs e)
{
    DisplayEventArgs(e);
}

// Event Handler for RowUpdated event
private void OnRowUpdated(object sender, SqlRowUpdatedEventArgs e)
{
   DisplayEventArgs(e);
}
```

The overloaded `DisplayEventArgs` function adds an item to the listbox indicating that the executing code has entered it. It also uses the argument passed to it and checks the `Status`. The `Status` is an enumeration of type `UpdateStatus`. If the `Status` is not `UpdateStatus.Continue`, the status is written to the listbox. When a row is in the process of being updated, if a change has been made to the row, the status of the row will be marked as `Continue` and the `RowUpdated` event will fire for the row. If the status is not `UpdateStatus.Continue`, then the `RowUpdated` event will not fire.

```
private void DisplayEventArgs(SqlRowUpdatingEventArgs args)
{
   lbResult.Items.Add("OnRowUpdating event");
   if (args.Status !=UpdateStatus.Continue)
     lbResult.Items.Add("RowStatus="+args.Status.ToString());
}
```

If the row can be updated, the `RowUpdated` event will fire, which will be handled by the `OnRowUpdated` event handler, which in turn will pass the execution to the version of `DisplayEventArgs` function that takes the `SqlRowUpdatedEventArgs` object as the parameter. This object carries with it information about how many rows were updated in the `RecordsAffected` property, which is displayed in the listbox:

```
private void DisplayEventArgs(SqlRowUpdatedEventArgs args)
{
  lbResult.Items.Add("OnRowUpdated event"
lbResult.Items.Add("Records Affected="+ args.RecordsAffected);
}
```

The first time the button is clicked, the company name is changed to "The Volcano Corporation". This raises both the `RowUpdating` and the `RowUpdated` events. The second time the button is clicked, since the Company name is already "The Volcano Corporation", only the `RowUpdating` event is raised and the row's Update Status is marked as `SkipCurrentRow`. So the `RowUpdated` event does not fire.

Working with Multiple Handlers

It is also possible to have the same event call multiple handlers. This can be done in two ways. In the first alternative, we just bind the event to two different event handlers separately. In the second alternative, we can use a multicast-delegate where we can specify a list of event handlers to the delegate and when the event is fired, all the enlisted handlers will be invoked successively. We will see how the first alternative works. We'll not be looking at multicast-delegates in this book, so for more information, you may want to refer to the MSDN Library documentation.

In this *Try It Out*, we will bind the `StateChange` event of the connection object to two different event handlers. When the event is raised, we will verify that both the event handlers are called and executed.

Try It Out: Multiple Handlers for the Same Event

1. In the click event of the `cmdMultHandler` button write code as follows:

```
private void cmdMultHandler_Click(object sender, System.EventArgs e)
{
  //create a connection
  SqlConnection cn = new SqlConnection(@"Data Source=(local)\NETSDK;" +
    "Integrated Security=SSPI;database=Northwind");

  //delegate the StateChange event to the CnStateChange function
  cn.StateChange+=new StateChangeEventHandler(CnStateChange);
  cn.StateChange+=new StateChangeEventHandler(CnStateChange2);

  //create a command object and initalize it
  SqlCommand cmd = new SqlCommand();
  cmd.CommandText="SELECT TOP 1 CustomerId, CompanyName FROM Customers";
  cmd.Connection=cn;
  try
  {
    lbResult.Items.Clear();
    //Open the connection
    cn.Open();
    //create a data reader to hold the results
```

```
    SqlDataReader dr=cmd.ExecuteReader();

    while(dr.Read())
    {
      lbResult.Items.Add(dr.GetString(0) + "-" +
        dr.GetString(1));
    }

  }

  catch(SqlException e1)
  {
    MessageBox.Show (e1.Message);
  }
  finally
  {
    //Close the connection
    cn.Close();
  }
}
```

2. Write a second event handler for the `StateChange` event as follows. Note that the signature of this function is the same as the signature of the `StateChangeEventHandler` function.

```
private void CnStateChange2(object sender, StateChangeEventArgs ev)
{
  // Second Event handler for the StateChange Event
  lbResult.Items.Add("-----------------------------");
  lbResult.Items.Add("Entering Second Statechange EventHandler");
  lbResult.Items.Add("Sender="+ sender.ToString());
  lbResult.Items.Add("Original State="+ ev.OriginalState.ToString());
  lbResult.Items.Add("Current State="+ ev.CurrentState.ToString());
  lbResult.Items.Add("Exiting Second StateChange EventHandler");
  lbResult.Items.Add("-----------------------------");
}
```

3. Build and run the solution. The following results are displayed:

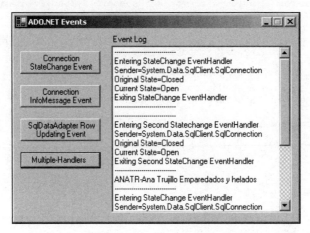

Observe that the event log in the screenshot shows that first the StateChange event handler was invoked and then the second StateChange event handler was invoked. These two handlers, of course, can be coded to do different things.

How It Works

We bind the StateChange event to two different handlers separately:

```
//delegate the StateChange event to the CnStateChange function
cn.StateChange+=new StateChangeEventHandler(CnStateChange);
cn.StateChange+=new StateChangeEventHandler(CnStateChange2);
```

Notice that in the second instance, we bind it to the CnStateChange2 function, which we write as follows, similar to the CnStatechange function with a minor change to mark the entrance into and exit from the handler.

```
private void CnStateChange2(object sender, StateChangeEventArgs ev)
{
   // Second Event handler for the StateChange Event
   lbResult.Items.Add("----------------------------");
   lbResult.Items.Add("Entering Second Statechange EventHandler");
   lbResult.Items.Add("Sender="+ sender.ToString());
   lbResult.Items.Add("Original State="+ ev.OriginalState.ToString());
   lbResult.Items.Add("Current State="+ ev.CurrentState.ToString());
   lbResult.Items.Add("Exiting Second StateChange EventHandler");
   lbResult.Items.Add("----------------------------");
}
```

When the program is run, we can observe that both the handlers are invoked when the connection state is opened and closed.

Summary

This chapter discusses the concepts behind ADO.NET events. We saw what events are and how to use delegates to bind them with their event handlers. Specifically we learned and tried out the following features:

❑ We learned that the StateChange event of the connection object fires when the state changes from Open to Closed or Closed to Open. We wrote an event handler for this event by using the StateChangeEventHandler delegate. In the process, we learned that the signature of the event handler must be the same as the signature of the delegate.

❑ We learned that the InfoMessage event of the connection object fires when the database returns informational messages that are not errors. We also learned that we can bind any number of events to their respective event handlers from within the same function.

❑ We then saw how to use the RowUpdating and RowUpdated events of the SqlDataAdapter object to find out the status of a row before and after it is updated.

❑ We also saw how to bind the same event to more than one event handler. This resulted in each event handler being called and executed.

In the next chapter we will learn how to handle irregular data – that is, how to insert and retrieve BLOBs (Binary Large Objects) from the database.

Exercises

1. While using the RowUpdating event of the SqlDataAdapter object, how would you find what type of statement is being executed against the data source?

2. Write an event handler called OnRowUpdated, for the RowUpdated event of the SqlDataAdapter object.

3. Use the table provided in the chapter to find the type of parameters needed for the event handler. While updating a record in the database, if an error occurs, this event handler must contain instructions to skip the current row and continue.

4. While using the InfoMessage event of the Connection object, if more than one information message is returned by the database, how will you access each of these messages?

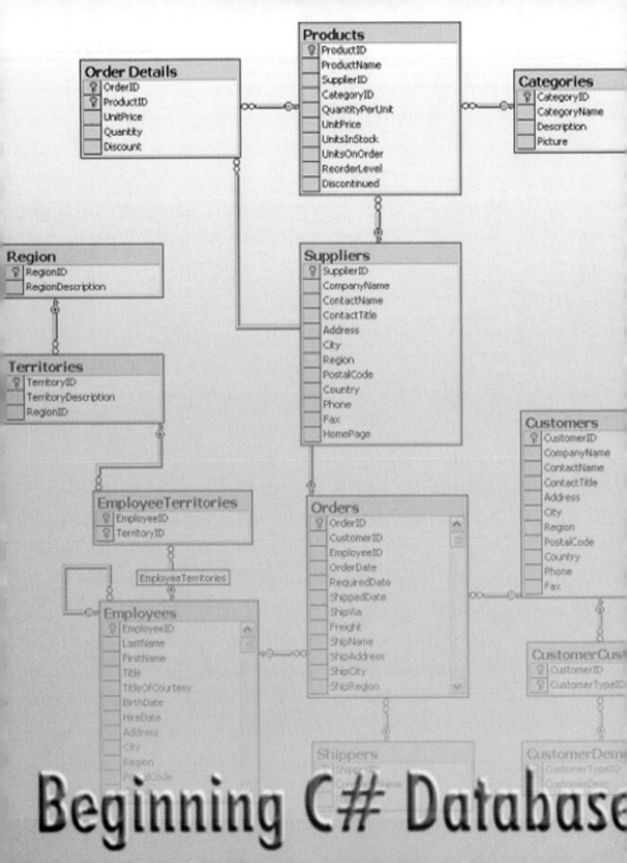

Irregular Data

Well, we're down to the final chapter of the book. Congratulations on making it this far! In this chapter, we're going to learn how to work with **irregular data** in ADO.NET. But before we do, we need to figure out what we mean by irregular data.

Well, first let's try to define **regular** data. When you picture the data in a relational database, you probably think of a spreadsheet or grid with neat rows and columns containing numbers or short character strings such as first name, last name, address, and so on. Alphanumeric data that fits neatly into a data entry field or into rows and columns on a grid control is "regular" data.

Irregular data does not fit neatly into rows and columns, at least not the kinds of rows and columns that you can see and edit in a grid control. One example of irregular data is **binary data**, such as a picture, sound, video, or other special format, which requires special handling to display the data.

Another aspect of irregular data is its size. The binary data for a single picture, sound, or especially a video may be very large, containing megabytes of data. Large binary data items are often called **BLOBs**, where BLOB is an acronym standing for Binary Large OBject. Processing and storing such a large amount of data in a single field in a database requires some special handling, which is another reason we characterize it as "irregular". The size may also vary greatly from one instance to the next; one picture may be 50 megabytes in size while the next is 200 megabytes.

Text data can also be large and varying in size, requiring special handling. Imagine, for example, a column in a database containing the entire text of this chapter. Text data of this size isn't easy to manipulate in the normal way we handle short text fields.

So, to summarize, irregular data may have a special format, be very large, and vary greatly in size. In this chapter we'll learn techniques for working with all these kinds of irregular data including:

- ❑ What data types can be used for irregular data, with their advantages and disadvantages
- ❑ How to load and retrieve binary image data and display it on the screen
- ❑ How to work with headers on binary data
- ❑ How to work with data too large to fit easily into memory
- ❑ How to retrieve and store large text data
- ❑ How irregular data is handled in different ADO.NET data providers

We're going to use the `SqlClient` .NET data provider for SQL Server or MSDE in the following irregular data examples. The concepts are basically the same in other .NET data providers and we'll touch on their similarities and differences towards the end of this chapter.

Let's get started by examining what data types can be used for irregular data.

SQL Server Data Types for Irregular Data

SQL Server provides the standard data types CHAR, NCHAR, VARCHAR, NVARCHAR, BINARY, and VARBINARY for working with character and binary data. These can be used with regular and small irregular data up to a maximum data size of 8,000 bytes.

For larger irregular data, SQL Server provides the TEXT, NTEXT, and IMAGE data types. TEXT and NTEXT are for large character text data (NTEXT is for 2-byte Unicode characters, corresponding to the NCHAR and NVARCHAR data types), while IMAGE can used to store anything else. The SQL Server designers must have decided IMAGE was more intuitive than BLOB, as the most common use for large binary data is pictures. However, IMAGE is applicable to any type of binary data; video, sound, word processing documents, or anything else you might store in a file.

> Note: Oracle, MySQL, and other databases actually call their large binary data type a BLOB or some variation of that name.

Within your C# program, binary data types map to an array of bytes (`byte[]`) and character data types map to strings or character arrays (`char[]`). This table summarizes the characteristics of these data types:

SQL Server Data Type	C# Data Type	Maximum Size
CHAR, VARCHAR	string, char[]	8,000 characters
NCHAR, NVARCHAR	string, char[]	4,000 2-byte (Unicode) characters
BINARY, VARBINARY	byte[]	8,000 bytes
TEXT	string, char[]	2,147,483,647 characters
NTEXT	string, char[]	1,073,741,823 2-byte (Unicode) characters
IMAGE	byte[]	2,147,483,647 bytes

Advantages/Disadvantages of Irregular Data Types

Before getting into the advantages of these types, I should point out that one alternative to using them is not to store irregular data in the database, but instead define a column containing a path and filename pointing to where the irregular data is stored. While not as neat as storing the data directly in the database, it can be faster especially for large amounts of data and saves resources on the database server (essentially by transferring it to your file server). The disadvantage is that it is less centralized and always contains the potential for your database and the files to be out of sync (that is, the file gets moved to another directory but the reference to it in the database does not get updated).

Assuming you've decided you want to directly store the irregular data in the database, IMAGE is almost always going to be the best choice for binary data, because it is very rare that you can guarantee that the size of a binary data item is always going to be less than 8,000 bytes. Even small pictures or sound files often exceed this size.

IMAGE is stored as a "pointer" within the table that points to another location within the SQL Server database that stores the data, so there is some slight overhead for IMAGE data compared to BINARY and VARBINARY, but for binary data the savings for the overhead consideration is rarely worth the price of living with the length limitation.

NTEXT and TEXT are implemented in a similar way to IMAGE, as a pointer to the data. In this case however, the overhead consideration is worth thinking about more in choosing between these types and NVARCHAR or VARCHAR; it depends on your application needs. Many applications have a "notes " column or other similar field for text notation that can be "long", but even several pages of text can be accommodated in 8,000 characters (the rule of thumb is 2,000 characters per page).

The choice between the NTEXT and TEXT depends on whether you want text to be stored as Unicode 2-byte characters or 1-byte ASCII/ANSI characters. The native character type in C# and the .NET Framework is Unicode, so the text will be converted to 2-byte characters when loaded into memory. If your application will be used internationally with different languages and character sets then it makes sense to use Unicode storage. However, if this is not the case then it may not be worthwhile to double the storage requirement (a large text containing 3,000,000 characters would require 6 megabytes of storage as 2-byte Unicode characters but only 3 megabytes of storage as 1-byte characters). Storage is always getting cheaper so flexibility may outweigh the overhead consideration, but with multi-megabyte data it is worth thinking about.

CHAR, NCHAR, and BINARY are fixed-length data types directly stored in the database tables; they always take up the size specified when creating the table, even if the actual size of the data stored in each column is less. You would want to use this only if the data in each row was exactly the same length and was never null. For example, if your table stored program icons where the binary size was small and every icon was exactly same size, then BINARY might be an appropriate data type. Most character data larger than a few hundred characters or so varies in length, so I can't think of an "irregular data" situation where fixed-length CHAR or NCHAR would be appropriate.

NVARCHAR, VARCHAR, and VARBINARY accommodate varying-length data and so do not waste space in the database. Very small bitmaps or sound files that will always be less than 8,000 bytes are appropriate for VARBINARY. As we said above, VARCHAR or NVARCHAR are good choices for text data a few paragraphs or pages in length, always guaranteed to be less than 8,000 bytes in total.

Storing Images in a Database

Let's start by creating a database table for storing images, and then loading some images into it. We need some image data to work with. There are some suitable examples included with Visual Studio .NET. Let's use the product images in the "GrocerToGo" sample in the ASP.NET QuickStart, located in the following path:

```
C:\Program Files\Microsoft Visual Studio .NET\FrameworkSDK\Samples\
                                    QuickStart\aspplus\images
```

We'll start by using the "milk carton" images `milk1.gif`, `milk2.gif`, etc. as shown here:

These are small images that can actually fit in any of the data types we just discussed.

Try It Out: Loading Binary Data from Files

In this example, we'll write a program that creates a database table and then stores the milk carton images in it. To make the code easier to follow, we'll create the skeleton of the application first and then the functions that it calls in the next section. As we don't need a graphical interface for this program, we'll also create it as a console application for some extra clarity.

1. Open Visual Studio .NET and create a new blank solution called `Chapter21_Examples`.

2. Within the new solution, create a new C# Console Application project called `LoadImagesExample`. Rename `Class1.cs` to `LoadImagesExample.cs`.

3. Edit the code to match the following:

```
using System;
using System.Data;              // use ADO.NET namespace
using System.Data.SqlClient;    // use SQL Server .NET data provider namespace
using System.IO;                // used for file I/O
```

```
namespace Wrox.BeginningCSharpDatabases.Chapter21
{
  class LoadImagesExample
  {
    string imageFileLocation =
        @"C:\Program Files\Microsoft Visual Studio .NET\"  +
        @"FrameworkSDK\Samples\QuickStart\aspplus\images\";

    string imageFilePrefix = "milk";
    int numberImageFiles = 8;
    string imageFileType = ".gif";
    int maxImageSize = 10000;
    SqlConnection imageConnection = null;
    SqlCommand imageCommand = null;

    static void Main()
    {
      LoadImagesExample loader = new LoadImagesExample();

      try
      {
        // open connection to database
        loader.openConnection();
        // create command object
        loader.createCommand();
        // create table
        loader.createImageTable();
        // prepare insert command
        loader.prepareInsertImages();

        int i;
        for (i = 1; i<=loader.numberImageFiles; i++)
        {
          loader.executeInsertImages(i);
        }
      }
      // catch exception if database error
      catch (SqlException ex)
      {
        // display details of error
        Console.WriteLine(ex.ToString());
      }
      finally
      {
        loader.closeConnection();
      }
    }

    // insert remaining methods following this comment
  }
}
```

Much of this program should be familiar to you from previous examples in this book, especially from Chapter 5 and 6 since it is essentially a framework for connecting to the database and issuing some SQL commands. The `Main()` function shows the basic flow of the program logic; first we will open a database connection using `loader.openConnection`, then create a `Command` object for passing commands to SQL Server. The path name where the sample image files are located, and the type and number of files are indicated in the initial values for the `imageFileLocation`, `imageFileType`, and `numberImageFiles` variables. We'll create a table for storing the images, prepare an insertion command for inserting images, and execute the insertion command for each one of the image files.

How it Works

Let's fill in the missing methods and explore the workings as we go along. First let's open the database connection:

```
void openConnection()
{
  // create SqlConnection object
  imageConnection = new SqlConnection(
    @"Server=(local)\NetSDK;"    +    // server instance name
    "Integrated Security=SSPI;" +    // use Windows login
    "Connection Timeout=5;"      +    // wait only 5 seconds
    "Database=tempdb"                 // use tempdb to create table
    );
  // Open connection
  imageConnection.Open();
}
```

Note that we create the table in `tempdb`, the temporary database that is always created when SQL Server or MSDE is installed. The tables in this database are temporary; that is, they are always deleted when SQL Server is restarted. That's good for our examples that are temporary in nature, but remember not to use `tempdb` for any actual application data that needs to be persistent.

The next three methods are essentially "housekeeping" that execute the obligatory ADO.NET functions for closing the database, creating the `SqlCommand` object, and executing a non-query command. These are exactly the same as the example from Chapter 6:

```
void closeConnection()
{
  // close connection
  imageConnection.Close();
  // close was successful
  Console.WriteLine("Connection Successfully Closed!");
}

void createCommand()
{
  imageCommand = new SqlCommand();
  imageCommand.Connection = imageConnection;
}

void executeCommand(string commandText)
```

```
{
  int commandResult;
  imageCommand.CommandText = commandText;
  Console.WriteLine("Executing command:");
  Console.WriteLine(imageCommand.CommandText);
  commandResult = imageCommand.ExecuteNonQuery();
  Console.WriteLine("ExecuteNonQuery returns {0}.", commandResult);
}
```

Now let's create some methods that are actually specific to this application. First we create the table itself, a very simple table containing the image and the file name that the image will be loaded from, using a SQL DDL CREATE TABLE statement (I've split the SQL commands into multiple lines for clarity):

```
void createImageTable()
{
  executeCommand(
    "CREATE TABLE imagetable ( " +
    " imagefile NVARCHAR(20),  " +
    " imagedata IMAGE)"
  );
}
```

Note we use an IMAGE data type for the image data. Now we will prepare an INSERT statement using parameters as described in Chapter 6:

```
void prepareInsertImages()
{
  imageCommand.CommandText =
    "INSERT INTO imagetable VALUES (@ImageFile, @ImageData)";
  imageCommand.Parameters.Add("@ImageFile", SqlDbType.NVarChar);
  imageCommand.Parameters.Add("@ImageData", SqlDbType.Image);
}
```

We use the SqlDbType enumerations when binding to ensure an exact match when the parameters are converted from our C# program variables.

Now let's add the executeInsertImages method to execute the INSERT statement for each image. Recall that we pass the file number to this method from the for loop in our Main() function; here we assemble the file name from the prefix, file number, and file type to get the full file name (for example, "milk" + "1" + ".gif" = "milk1.gif").

We also call the loadImageFile() method (shown in just a minute) to do the actual reading of the file into the imageImageData byte array, and then set the INSERT command parameter values to the imageFileName and imageImageData to get ready to insert the data into the table:

```
void executeInsertImages(int imageFileNumber)
{
  string imageFileName = null;
  byte[] imageImageData = null;
  imageFileName =
    imageFilePrefix + imageFileNumber.ToString()+ imageFileType;
  imageImageData =
    loadImageFile(imageFileName, imageFileLocation, maxImageSize);

  imageCommand.Parameters["@ImageFile"].Value = imageFileName;
```

```
            imageCommand.Parameters["@ImageData"].Value = imageImageData;

            executeCommand(imageCommand.CommandText);
        }
```

Finally, we create the `loadImageFile` method to read the file. This returns a `byte[]` array, which is the C# data type that maps to an `IMAGE` column, as you'll recall from earlier in this chapter. The full path location is added here; we open the file as a `FileStream` and read it using a `BinaryReader`:

```
byte[] loadImageFile(string fileName, string fileLocation, int maxImageSize)
{
    byte[] imagebytes = null;
    string fullpath = fileLocation + fileName;
    Console.WriteLine("Loading File:");
    Console.WriteLine(fullpath);
    FileStream fs = new FileStream(fullpath, FileMode.Open);
    BinaryReader br = new BinaryReader(fs);
    imagebytes = br.ReadBytes(maxImageSize);

    Console.WriteLine("Imagebytes has length {0} bytes.",
                                    imagebytes.GetLength(0));
    return imagebytes;
}
```

The `maxImageSize` variable is passed to the `BinaryReader ReadBytes()` method simply because `ReadBytes()` requires a maximum number of bytes to read and as we specified a `maxImageSize` (10000) larger than any of our target files, it will always read the entire file into the `byte[]` array. A bit later in this chapter we will see how to handle the case where we do not want to read the whole file in one operation.

As this is the last method we need to add, let's compile and run the program we've just created. You can use Debug | Start without Debugging (*ctrl-F5*) to compile and run in one step. The output is not exactly as shown here – we've cheated a little to show you its beginning and end:

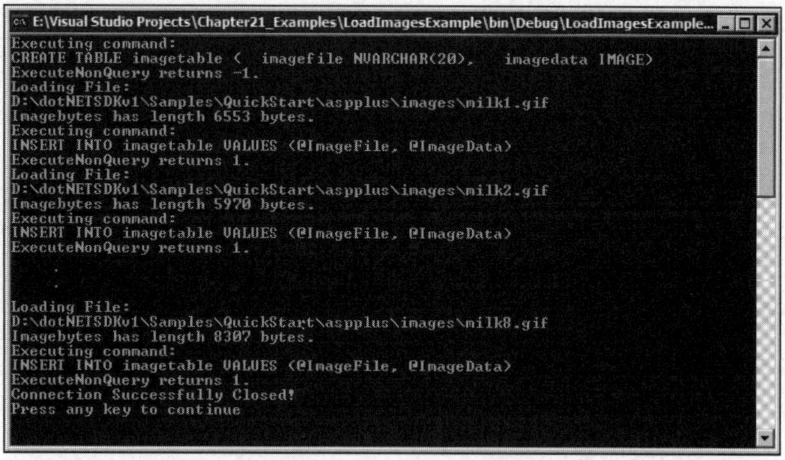

We can see that the `CREATE TABLE` statement was executed, followed by the load file and `INSERT` statements for each of the image files. Finally, the connection was closed.

Recreating the Table

If you have to run this program more than a couple of times to get it work the first time (as I have) you may get an error message back saying that `imagetable` already exists in the database because we've already created it during a previous attempt to get it working. To correct this, add a check to DROP the image table if it exists already:

```
void createImageTable()
{
    executeCommand(
        "IF EXISTS ( " +
        " SELECT TABLE_NAME " +
        " FROM INFORMATION_SCHEMA.TABLES  " +
        " WHERE TABLE_NAME = 'imagetable' " +
        ")       DROP TABLE imagetable "
    );

    executeCommand(
        "CREATE TABLE imagetable ( " +
        " imagefile NVARCHAR(20),  " +
        " imagedata IMAGE" +
        ")"
    );
}
```

That sets the program up for multiple runs, and lets us add some variations to it as well.

Using a Different SQL Data Type

Just to illustrate what happens when you specify a data type with small length restrictions, modify the CREATE TABLE statement in `createImageTable()` to specify a VARBINARY(8000) as follows:

```
executeCommand(
    "CREATE TABLE imagetable ( " +
    " imagefile NVARCHAR(20),  " +
    " imagedata VARBINARY(8000))"
);
```

This works for the first three or four images, and then this exception appears:

```
E:\Visual Studio Projects\Chapter21_Examples\LoadImagesExample\bin\Debug\LoadImagesExample...
Loading File:
D:\dotNETSDKv1\Samples\QuickStart\aspplus\images\milk5.gif
Imagebytes has length 8664 bytes.
Executing command:
INSERT INTO imagetable VALUES (@ImageFile, @ImageData)
System.Data.SqlClient.SqlException: String or binary data would be truncated.
The statement has been terminated.
```

So you can see it is not easy to live within the size restrictions of BINARY/VARBINARY even when working with small images like these.

Try It Out: Displaying Stored Images

Now that we've discovered how to store our images into the database, let's see how to pull them back out and display them. Of course, in order to see them, we'll have to move away from the command prompt and switch to a Window Forms application.

1. Add a new C# Windows Application project called `DisplayImages` to our open solution, `Chapter21_Examples`. Rename `Form1.cs` to `DisplayImages.cs`.

2. Add the following three controls from the Toolbox to `Form1` as follows:

- ❑ A `TextBox`, `textBox1`, in the upper left of the main form.
- ❑ A `Button`, `button1`, in the upper right.
- ❑ A `PictureBox`, `pictureBox1`, filling the lower part of the form.

The `PictureBox` will display our images, and the textbox will show which image file was used to load the image. The button lets us navigate to the next image row. Modify the properties of the button (`button1`) so that the text on the button (`Text` property) reads "**Next**". If you like, modify the `TextBox` default text to be blank. The form should now look like the following screen (the `PictureBox` is highlighted to make it stand out):

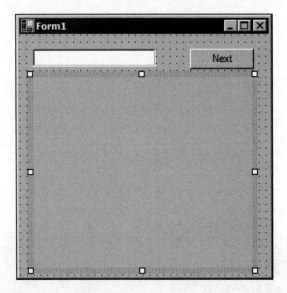

3. To activate the **Next** button, double-click on the button and fill in the `button1_Click` event handler as shown here:

```
    private void button1_Click(object sender, System.EventArgs e)
    {
      if (img_query.get_row())
      {
        this.textBox1.Text = img_query.get_filename();
        this.pictureBox1.Image = (Image) img_query.get_image();
      }
      else
      {
        this.textBox1.Text = "DONE";        // reached last row
        this.pictureBox1.Image = null;
      }
    }
```

We'll create a new object, called image_query, to perform the database queries. However, we'll add that to the project as a separate file in just a minute. It will have the get_filename and get_image methods, as shown, to update the form.

4. While we are editing Form1.cs, let's add an instance variable for our image_query class and modify the namespace for Form1 as shown here:

```
namespace Wrox.BeginningCSharpDatabases.Chapter21
{
  /// <summary>
  /// Summary description for Form1.
  /// </summary>
  public class Form1 : System.Windows.Forms.Form
  {
    image_query img_query;
```

5. Add this code to the Form1() constructor after the call to InitializeComponent():

```
    public Form1()
    {
      //
      // Required for Windows Form Designer support
      //
      InitializeComponent();
      //
      // TODO: Add any constructor code after InitializeComponent call
      //
      img_query = new image_query();

      if (img_query.get_row())
      {
        this.textBox1.Text = img_query.get_filename();
        this.pictureBox1.Image = (Image) img_query.get_image();
      }
      else
      {
        this.textBox1.Text = "DONE";
        this.pictureBox1.Image = null;
      }
```

6. Just to be complete, let's also clean up after ourselves in the `Dispose` method:

```csharp
/// <summary>
/// Clean up any resources being used.
/// </summary>
protected override void Dispose( bool disposing )
{
    img_query.end_query();
```

7. Now add a new class to the project; name the class file `getdata.cs` and create its code as shown here:

```csharp
using System;
using System.Data;
using System.Data.SqlClient;
using System.Drawing;
using System.IO;

namespace Wrox.BeginningCSharpDatabases.Chapter21
{
  public class image_query
  {
    string image_filename = null;
    byte[] image_bytes = null;

    SqlConnection image_connection = null;
    SqlCommand image_command = null;
    SqlDataReader image_reader = null;

    // constructor initializes connection,
    // command, and reader objects

    public image_query()            // constructor; initialize queries
    {
      image_connection = new SqlConnection(
        @"Data Source=(local)\NetSDK;" +
        "Integrated Security=SSPI;"     +
        "Initial Catalog=tempdb;"       +
        "Connect Timeout=3");
      image_command = new SqlCommand(
        @"SELECT imagefile, imagedata FROM imagetable",
        image_connection);

      // Open the connection and read data into the DataReader.
      image_connection.Open();
      image_reader = image_command.ExecuteReader();
    }

    public Bitmap get_image()
    {
      MemoryStream ms = new MemoryStream(image_bytes);
```

```
      Bitmap bmap = new Bitmap(ms);
      return bmap;
    }

    public string get_filename()
    {
      return image_filename;
    }

    public bool get_row()
    {
      if (image_reader.Read())
      {
        image_filename = (string) image_reader.GetValue(0);
        image_bytes = (byte[]) image_reader.GetValue(1);
        return true;
      }
      else
      {
        return false;
      }
    }

    public void end_query()
    {
      // Close the reader and the connection.
      image_reader.Close();
      image_connection.Close();
    }
  }
}
```

8. Compile and run this program. The images from the database will appear as shown here:

Click on **Next** to see all the milk bottle images; when the end of the table is reached **DONE** will appear in the textbox. Since we didn't put in an exit button, just click on the window close button (**x**) to exit.

How It Works

Most of the operation of this program has been covered in previous chapters. What we will concentrate on here is the retrieval of the image data itself and how it is transformed into a nice pretty picture on your form.

As we showed in the data type table at the beginning of the chapter, table columns containing binary data are mapped into a byte array in C# (`byte[]`) and we do so here. When we retrieve a row of data from the table with the `get_row()` method, we do so by calling `GetValue()` on each column in the row. We learned in Chapter 7 that this method returns an `object` containing the value for that column, but the actual object type returned for the "imagedata" column within this row is a byte array (`byte[]`) so we need to cast the `object` into a byte array as we assign it to `image_bytes`:

```
public bool get_row()
{
    if (image_reader.Read())
    {
        image_filename = (strjng) image_reader.GetValue(0);
        image_bytes = (byte[]) image_reader.GetValue(1);
        return true;
    }
    else
    {
        return false;
    }
}
```

You may wonder whether there isn't some type-specific `Getxxxx` routine for the byte array. We could have called `GetString(0)` for the file name column, so isn't there some equivalent for binary data? Yes, there is a `GetBytes()` method that we could have used to return the byte array; it works differently and has more parameters. In fact, we'll explain how `GetBytes()` works in the next example following this one, where we have a use for its extra parameters.

Back to this example; once we have the byte array how do we turn it into a displayable image? Well, there are a few hoops to jump through, but it's actually fairly simple. In the `button1_Click()` method in `DisplayImages.cs`, we assign the `PictureBox` control's image through the `get_image()` method in `getdata.cs`:

```
private void button1_Click(object sender, System.EventArgs e)
{
    if (img_query.get_row())
    {
        this.textBox1.Text = img_query.get_filename();
        this.pictureBox1.Image = (Image) img_query.get_image();
    }
    else
    {
        this.textBox1.Text = "DONE";        // reached last row
        this.pictureBox1.Image = null;
    }
}
```

The PictureBox control Image property can be a Bitmap, Icon, or Metafile (all subclasses of Image). Bitmap supports a variety of formats including Windows bitmap (BMP), GIF, and JPG. The get_image() method, shown here, returns a Bitmap object:

```
public Bitmap get_image()
{
    MemoryStream ms = new MemoryStream(image_bytes);
    Bitmap bmap = new Bitmap(ms);
    return bmap;
}
```

Bitmap does not take a byte array directly in any of its constructors, but it will take a MemoryStream, which is in effect an in-memory representation of a file. MemoryStream has a constructor that takes a byte array. So, the path from the binary data column to the picture displayed on our form is:

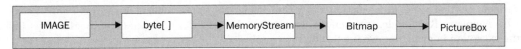

Does this result in a lot of extra memory usage? A bit, though it can be minimized by calling the Dispose() method on each object as soon as that stage of the conversion is complete. We'll look at a technique that helps minimize memory usage even further when reading large binary or text objects a bit later on in this chapter.

Displaying Images with Headers

Let's modify our DisplayImages program to show images from a different database. This will give us a chance to revise what we've just learned and introduce an interesting little conundrum that you may encounter when working with images – what happens if the image file contains more than just the image?

To demonstrate, we'll use the Northwind sample database included with SQL Server and MSDE rather than loading the images into a table ourselves to start with. The Employees table in Northwind actually contains pictures of the employees; we've been working with them throughout the book so let's finally see what they look like.

Create a new Windows Application project called DisplayImagesWithHeaders in our Chapter21_Examples solution, delete form1.cs, and copy DisplayImages.cs and getdata.cs into the project. Rename DisplayImages.cs to DisplayImagesWithHeaders.cs.

Theoretically, the only things we need to modify are the connection string in the image_query constructor used when creating the SqlConnection and the SQL query used to initialize the SqlCommand, like so:

```
public image_query()           // constructor; initialize queries
{
    image_connection = new SqlConnection(
      @"Data Source=(local)\NetSDK;" +
        "Integrated Security=SSPI;" +
        "Initial Catalog=Northwind;" +
```

```
                             "Connect Timeout=3");
               image_command = new SqlCommand(
                   @"SELECT firstname+' '+lastname, photo FROM Employees",
                                              image_connection);
               // Open the connection and read data into the DataReader.
               image_connection.Open();
               image_reader = image_command.ExecuteReader();
           }
```

Because our Windows Form is only expecting to display one string rather than two, we've concatenated the `firstname` and `lastname` fields in the `Employees` table in our SQL command. The query now creates and returns a single character string that contains the first and last name separated by a space. Note that the quotation marks around the space are single quotes (' '), not double quotes.

That's all the source changes we seem to need, isn't it? We could rename the `image_filename` variable to `employee_name` or something similar but who cares, a string is a string, right? Let's see what happens! Recompile, run, and we see: an exception. Click on **Yes** to enter the debugger and see the exception information; we see this dialog:

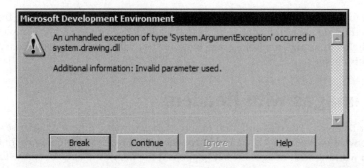

Where is this exception occurring? The debugger is pointing to the `Bitmap` assignment in `get_image()`:

```
    public Bitmap get_image()
    {
        MemoryStream ms = new MemoryStream(image_bytes)
        Bitmap bmap = new Bitmap(ms);
        return bmap;
    }
```

Something is going wrong at the point where the raw stream of bytes is converted into an actual image format. `Bitmap()` does not like the stream of bytes it is being given as input. What is going on?

The problem is that the Northwind images have a **header** attached to the beginning of the image and the extra information in the header causes the data in the stream not to be in the true bitmap format. The header in this case is an OLE (Object Linking and Embedding) header appended when the employee bitmap images were loaded with Microsoft Access. We need to skip over this header to get to the true graphics image and fortunately, there's a fairly painless way to do this.

Try It Out: Using the GetBytes() Method to Skip Image Headers

We could skip over the image header in one of several ways, such as when converting from the byte array to the MemoryStream, or when going from MemoryStream to the Bitmap, but because this is a database book, we're going to skip over the header when retrieving the image data from the database using the GetBytes() method we made a note of earlier.

GetBytes() is one of the retrieval methods provided by the DataReader object. It is analogous to GetString() or GetInt32() but retrieves a byte array for a binary data item rather than a string or integer. Unlike these other retrieval methods, however, it does not return its target data type (a byte array). Instead the byte array is one of the five parameters you pass to GetBytes(), which is declared as follows:

```
long SqlDataReader.GetBytes(
    int column, long dataIndex, byte[] buffer, long bufferIndex, int length)
```

The five parameters are as follows:

- ❑ int column: the index number of the column in the row you're retrieving the byte array from. Like the int parameter for the other GetXxxx() methods, the value of column starts at 0 (zero) for the first column in the DataReader, 1 is the next column, and so on.

- ❑ long dataIndex: the offset within the binary data of the column where you want to start retrieving the data from. 0 (zero) starts at the first byte, 1 would skip the first byte and start retrieving at the second byte, 10 would skip the first 10 bytes and start retrieving the eleventh byte, and so on.

- ❑ byte[] buffer: the byte array you want the retrieved bytes to be stored in.

- ❑ long bufferIndex: the offset within the byte array given by buffer after which the retrieved data should be stored.

- ❑ int length: the number of bytes of data we want to retrieve.

The return type of this method is a long containing the number of bytes actually read by GetBytes(). Alternately, if you specify null for the buffer parameter, GetBytes() will return the total size (number of bytes) contained in the column (the combined size of image and header in our particular case here) before you retrieve it, so you know how much memory to allocate for the byte array. This handy little trick works with the other .NET data providers and not just SqlDataReader.

> *Maybe you can see now why I prefer to use GetValue() for the simple case of retrieving the entire contents of the binary column!*

Of course, the problem we are currently solving is not the simple case. We need to retrieve only that part of the binary column data which is the actual bitmap image. Now the key to our whole problem here is that the OLE header for the Northwind images is 78 bytes long, so if we skip the first 78 bytes we'll get the actual bitmap.

Let's try this using GetBytes(). Change the logic in the if clause in the get_row() method to this:

```
public bool get_row()
{
  if (image_reader.Read())
  {
    image_filename = (string) image_reader.GetValue(0);
    //image_bytes = (byte[]) image_reader.GetValue(1);

    long bytes_in_column = image_reader.GetBytes(1, 0, null, 0, 0);
    image_bytes = new Byte[bytes_in_column-78];

    long bytesread =
     image_reader.GetBytes(1, 78, image_bytes, 0, (int) bytes_in_column-78);
    return true;
  }
  else
  {
    return false;
  }
}
```

OK, let's compile and run this version; now we see Nancy Davolio's smiling face:

Click on **Next** to see the other employees, until **DONE** appears in the textbox.

How It Works

Let's look again at those lines of code we added to get_row():

```
// image_bytes = (byte[]) image_reader.GetValue(1);
long bytes_in_column = image_reader.GetBytes(1, 0, null, 0, 0);
```

We commented out the call to GetValue(1) and replaced it with a call to GetBytes(1,...). We've passed null to the buffer parameter in the first call, so we get back the size of the data to be retrieved from the column. Using this information, we then initialize the image_bytes byte array not forgetting to subtract the 78 bytes of header that we're going to skip.

```
image_bytes = new Byte[bytes_in_column-78];
```

Next we call `GetBytes()` again, passing 78 as the `dataIndex` to start reading after the 78th byte. We pass our newly allocated `image_bytes` array, 0 for the `bufferIndex` since we want to copy the data to the start of `image_bytes`, and finally for the `length` we ask for all the bytes in the column save the 78 we are skipping. Note: It would be better style to define a constant instead of using 78 everywhere.

```
long bytesread =
   image_reader.GetBytes(1, 78, image_bytes, 0, (int) bytes_in_column-78);
```

OK, come on, really, how did we know to skip 78 bytes? Well to be honest I looked it up on the Internet: http://homepages.borland.com/efg2lab/Library/Delphi/ADO/ Northwind/#Hack.

While this link indicates the 78-byte size, another link to a Microsoft Knowledge Base article gives much more detail about the internal structure of the OLE header for the Northwind data: http://support.microsoft.com/default.aspx?scid=kb;EN-US; q147727.

The sample code for this chapter includes an additional sample program, `DisplayOleHeaderSize.cs`, that goes through the full calculation of the OLE header size using the information from this Knowledge Base article; it also shows some more advanced topics than we have space to detail here, such as using a binary reader to extract structures embedded within the binary data.

The header size used here is specific to bitmap files encoded as OLE objects. A different type of binary file might have a different header size or other format; there is no general method that works for all binary types. If you encounter a situation like this, you'll have to research the format and come up with a solution unique to your particular encoding problem. `GetBytes()` gives you a way to skip the part of the binary you don't need or to extract the part of the binary you want to examine.

Let's look at another use for `GetBytes()`; conserving memory by retrieving data in small chunks.

Extracting Binary Data to Files

Now that we've seen how to pull irregular data from a file and put it into a database, it probably won't surprise you to learn that doing the reverse – getting data from the database and putting it into a file – is just as common a task and the next one for us to tackle. As mentioned, we'll also look at another technique using `GetBytes()` to conserve memory while extracting the file.

Try It Out: ExtractToFile Program

1. Add a new C# Console Application project called `ExtractToFile` to our open solution, `Chapter21_Examples`. Rename `Class1.cs` to `ExtractToFile.cs`.

2. Copy and paste the code from `getdata.cs` in our last project, `DisplayImagesWithHeaders`, into `ExtractToFile.cs`, replacing all the code already there. Edit it to look like the following:

```
using System;
using System.Data;
using System.Data.SqlClient;
using System.IO;        // Delete reference to System.Drawing

namespace Wrox.BeginningCSharpDatabases.Chapter21
{
  public class image_query
  {
    string image_filename = null;
    byte[] image_bytes = null;

    SqlConnection image_connection = null;
    SqlCommand image_command = null;
    SqlDataReader image_reader = null;

    // constructor initializes connection,
    // command, and reader objects
    public image_query()
    {
      image_connection = new SqlConnection(
        @"Data Source=(local)\NetSDK;" +
        "Integrated Security=SSPI;"     +
        "Initial Catalog=Northwind;"       +
        "Connect Timeout=3");
      image_command = new SqlCommand(
        @"SELECT firstname+' '+lastname, photo FROM Employees",
        image_connection);

      // Open the connection and read data into the DataReader.
      image_connection.Open();
      image_reader =
        image_command.ExecuteReader(CommandBehavior.SequentialAccess);
    }
```

The `CommandBehavior.SequentialAccess` argument to `ExecuteReader()` is particularly important; this is what makes the memory conservation work by preventing ADO.NET's normal behavior of reading the entire row and caching it in memory before you ask for it.

3. Delete the `get_image()` and `get_filename()` methods.

4. Rewrite `get_row()` to create a file and copy the data from the image column to the file, as follows:

```
public bool get_row()
{
  FileStream fs;
  BinaryWriter bw;
  long readOffset;                       // place to start reading from BLOB
  int bufferSize = 1000;                 // Size of the BLOB buffer.
  long bytesread, byteswritten;            // bytes read, total bytes written
  image_bytes = new Byte[bufferSize]; // initialize buffer
```

```
    if (image_reader.Read())
    {
      image_filename = image_reader.GetString(0)+ ".bmp";

      // Create file for this bitmap
      fs = new FileStream(image_filename ,
        FileMode.OpenOrCreate, FileAccess.Write);
      Console.WriteLine("Created file: " + image_filename);
      bw = new BinaryWriter(fs);

      // Set the starting read offset to skip over the OLE header.
      readOffset = 78;
      byteswritten=0;
      bytesread=0;

      // Read one buffer's worth of bytes into imagebytes.
      bytesread = image_reader.GetBytes(1,
        readOffset, image_bytes, 0, bufferSize);
      Console.WriteLine("read {0} bytes into buffer of size {1}",
        bytesread, bufferSize);

      // read and write in a loop until we reach the last "chunk"
      while (bytesread == bufferSize)
      {
        bw.Write(image_bytes);          // write this "chunk" to the file
        byteswritten +=bytesread;
        Console.WriteLine("Wrote {0} bytes to file {1};" +
          "total written so far {2} bytes.",
          bytesread, image_filename, byteswritten);

        // Reposition the offset to the next chunk of bytes to read.
        readOffset += bufferSize;
        bytesread = image_reader.GetBytes(1,
          readOffset, image_bytes, 0, bufferSize);
      }

      bw.Write(image_bytes, 0, (int) bytesread);
      byteswritten +=bytesread;
      Console.WriteLine("Wrote final {0} bytes to file {1};" +
        "total written {2} bytes.",
        bytesread, image_filename, byteswritten);
      bw.Close();
      fs.Close();
      return true;
    }
    else
    {
      return false;
    }
  }
```

Quite a lot of code, isn't it? We'll explain it just ahead, but I want you to see it run first as that helps the explanation.

5. Now, last set of changes. Leave the end_query() method in place, and add a Main() function (this is a console program, after all):

```
public void end_query()
{
  // Close the reader and the connection.
  image_reader.Close();
  image_connection.Close();
}
```

```
    static void Main()
    {
      image_query iq = null;

      try
      {
        iq = new image_query();
        while (iq.get_row()==true)
        {
          Console.WriteLine("Finished processing file {0}",
            iq.image_filename);
        }
      }
      catch (SqlException ex)        // catch exception if database error
      {                             // display details of error
        Console.WriteLine(ex.ToString());
      }
      finally
      {
        iq.end_query();             // close connection
      }
    }
  }
}
```

6. Compile and run. The (abridged) output looks like the following:

And so on for all the employees in the table. We didn't specify an output directory, so the files are created in the same directory as the `ExtractToFile.exe` executable, located in the `Debug\bin` directory of your project as shown here:

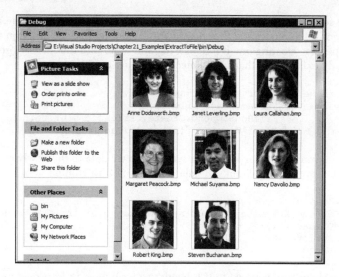

We can see that the files we created are perfectly valid bitmap files from the thumbnail image of the selected file. If we double-click on the file, Paint opens it correctly. If we had not skipped over the OLE image header, Paint would complain about an invalid format. If our copying logic was somehow incorrect, we might get an invalid format error or else the picture would not display correctly.

How It Works

Let's go back to the code in the `get_row()` method. We are going to write the binary data in each row to a file, so we create `FileStream` and `BinaryWriter` objects to do this:

```
public bool get_row()
{
  FileStream fs;
  BinaryWriter bw;
```

We're limiting our memory use while copying the file, so we allocate a buffer only 1,000 bytes in size:

```
int bufferSize = 1000;       // Size of the BLOB buffer.
image_bytes = new Byte[bufferSize];   // initialize buffer
```

We declare some numeric variables to keep track of where we are as we do the copy:

```
long readOffset;               // place to start reading from BLOB
long bytesread, byteswritten;    // bytes read, total bytes written
```

Now we're ready to read the row and create the empty file to put the image into. We generate the filename by taking the employee's full name and adding the bitmap file extension (`.bmp`) to it.

569

```
if (image_reader.Read())
{
    image_filename = image_reader.GetString(0)+ ".bmp";
```

With the filename sorted out, we just create the file and tell the world we've done so. Notice that we specify `OpenOrCreate` in our call to the constructor; by doing this, the program will create the file if it doesn't exist, or open the existing one if it does exist and write into that instead (stomping over any contents that already existed, but that's OK since we created the file):

```
// Create file for this bitmap
fs = new FileStream(image_filename ,
            FileMode.OpenOrCreate, FileAccess.Write);
Console.WriteLine("Created file: " + image_filename);
```

We now create the `BinaryWriter` object for writing binary data to the newly created file and initialize our counter variables for reading chunks of data from the `image` column:

```
bw = new BinaryWriter(fs);
// Set the starting read offset to skip over the OLE header.
readOffset = 78;
byteswritten=0;
bytesread=0;
```

The images in Northwind still have that OLE header so we'll need to start reading the first chunk of data at byte 78 again in order to get just the image. This time then, the arguments to `GetBytes()` are 1 for column 1 (actually the second column since the number is zero-based), `readOffset=78` since this is the first `GetBytes()` operation, `image_bytes` is the name of our buffer (byte array), 0 for the `bufferIndex` parameter since we want to write at the start of our `image_bytes` buffer, and `bufferSize=1000` for the length of the data we wish to retrieve:

```
// Read one buffer's worth of bytes into imagebytes.
bytesread = image_reader.GetBytes(
    1, readOffset, image_bytes, 0, bufferSize);
Console.WriteLine("read {0} bytes into buffer of size {1}",
    bytesread, bufferSize);
```

Now if we have read a full buffer (1000 bytes) of data, we perform a `while` loop to read each chunk in succession:

```
// read and write in a loop until we reach the last "chunk"
while (bytesread == bufferSize)
{
    bw.Write(image_bytes);        // write this "chunk" to the file
    byteswritten +=bytesread;
    Console.WriteLine("Wrote {0} bytes to file {1};" +
        "total written so far {2} bytes.",
        bytesread, image_filename, byteswritten);

    // Reposition the offset to the next chunk of bytes to read.
    readOffset += bufferSize;
    bytesread = image_reader.GetBytes(1,
        readOffset, image_bytes, 0, bufferSize);
}
```

You might ask, shouldn't the test for the while loop be (bytesread >= bufferSize)? Well, no, this should "never happen" since we pass bufferSize to GetBytes() as the length parameter.

Instead of silently continuing if that is true, perhaps we should have an assertion preceding the while loop to test that assumption:

```
System.Diagnostics.Debug.Assert(bytesread <= bufferSize,
  "ERROR: bytesread > buffersize");
```

An assertion is a mechanism for inserting a test into your code that makes sure an assumption made by the code is really true. The Debug form of assertion is included only in debug builds, so you can check your assumptions during development and testing but then skip the extra checks in a more streamlined version of the code in release builds. For more details see the "Debug.Assert" topic in the .NET Framework Class Library section of the C# online documentation, or look out for Beginning Visual C# from Wrox Press (ISBN: 1-86100-758-2).

Now at the end of the while loop we write the final bytes from the buffer. We use a slightly different form of the BinaryWriter Write() method that lets us specify how many bytes to write (the Write() inside the while loop writes the entire byte array):

```
            bw.Write(image_bytes, 0, (int) bytesread);
            byteswritten +=bytesread;
            Console.WriteLine("Wrote final {0} bytes to file {1};" +
              "total written {2} bytes.",
              bytesread, image_filename, byteswritten);
```

Note that this final Write() also works correctly for the case where the while loop never executes because the image was less than 1,000 bytes in size. Finally, we close the binary reader and file stream:

```
            bw.Close();
            fs.Close();
```

That was a lot of work; what did we accomplish with it? Well, we wrote the file out but never used more 1000 bytes of memory for the byte array. We could have saved all the extra code from the while loop if we wrote this code instead:

```
// Create file for this bitmap
fs = new FileStream( . . . ;
bw = new BinaryWriter(fs);
image_bytes = (byte[]) image_reader.GetValue(1);
bw.Write(image_bytes, 78, image_bytes.GetLength(0)-78);
bw.Close();
fs.Close();
```

If we didn't have that pesky OLE file header to deal with, it could be even shorter:

```
// Create file for this bitmap
fs = new FileStream( . . . ;
bw = new BinaryWriter(fs);
bw.Write((byte[]) image_reader.GetValue(1));    // watch memory use here
bw.Close();
fs.Close();
```

Both of these code fragments allocate a byte array as big as the entire image; for the Northwind employee images this is only about 21,000 bytes so the difference is not worth dealing with, but some images or multimedia files could be megabytes or even gigabytes in size. For these very large files saving memory is worth some consideration. In that last code fragment where we cast the return from GetValue() into a byte array, it is not at all obvious from looking at the line of code that a multi-megabyte chunk of memory may be allocated at that point; a comment like the one inserted is good to put in to point out to others who may miss that subtle point.

Now don't get me wrong, using memory to make your code faster and simpler is a good thing, not a bad thing. But it something to be aware of when working with irregular data, and we've offered some techniques to deal with it if the memory use is excessive.

Working with Large Text Files

Hands up all those who think we need a rest from working with images? Thought so: time to move on.

We described the TEXT data type at the beginning of the chapter, but haven't shown any examples of working with large text files yet. Let's do so now.

First, we need some large text files to work with. Visual Studio .NET has dozens of README.TXT files, most of which I've never read yet; let's put these in a database so we can track and browse through them.

First we need a list of README.TXT files to work with; we can make one easily enough using the DIR /B /S command at a command prompt:

The /b option to DIR suppresses all detail information except for the file name. The /s option tells DIR to do a recursive search through all subdirectories. The redirection with the greater-than sign (>) directs the output to a file (readmes.txt) instead of the console window.

The contents of the readmes.txt file we just created has the full path of each file listed on a separate line. The files listed will vary according to what exactly you've installed:

C:\Program Files\Microsoft Visual Studio .NET\Common7\IDE\PrivateAssemblies\readme.txt
C:\Program Files\Microsoft Visual Studio .NET\Common7\IDE\PublicAssemblies\readme.txt
C:\Program Files\Microsoft Visual Studio .NET\Vb7\VB Samples\WebForms-DHTMLSample\
DHTMLSample\Readme.txt
C:\Program Files\Microsoft Visual Studio .NET\Vb7\VB Samples\WebServices-WinFormClient-
AsyncWebService\AsynchWebService\ReadMe.txt

C:\Program Files\Microsoft Visual Studio .NET\Vb7\VB Samples\WinForms-Calc \Calc\readme.txt
C:\Program Files\Microsoft Visual Studio .NET\Vb7\VB Samples\WinForms-Framework-Implements-LoggingSample\WinLogger\Readme.txt
C:\Program Files\Microsoft Visual Studio .NET\Vb7\VB Samples\WinForms-Localization-VBMultilingualForm\VBMultilingualForm\readme.txt
C:\Program Files\Microsoft Visual Studio .NET\VC#\VC#Wizards\CSharpConsoleWiz \Templates\1033\readme.txt

We'll read this file in our program to get the list of `readme.txt` files to put in our database.

Try It Out: Loading Large Text Data from Files

This program is largely similar to the one we did for loading binary images into a database table except of course we're dealing with text files instead.

1. We start, as ever, by adding a new C# Console Application project, called LoadTextExample, to our open solution, Chapter21_Examples.

2. Rename Class1.cs to LoadTextExample.cs and edit the code within as follows:

```csharp
using System;
using System.Data;               // use ADO.NET namespace
using System.Data.SqlClient;     // use SQL Server .NET data provider namespace
using System.Data.SqlTypes;      // use SQL data type definitions
using System.IO;                 // used for file I/O
using System.Collections.Specialized; // used to get dynamic list of files
```

We've declared the `System.Collections.Specialized` namespace here so we can use a `StringCollection` to store the filenames loaded from the list we've just created. We chose `StringCollection` so the list could grow dynamically without our having to size it explicitly. Depending on what you installed, there could anything from five to fifty readme files in your list so the dynamic nature of `StringCollection` suits us well.

```csharp
namespace Wrox.BeginningCSharpDatabases.Chapter21
{
  class LoadTextExample
  {
    string FileName_ListOfFiles =
      @"C:\Program Files\Microsoft Visual Studio .NET\readmes.txt";

    // dynamic array of file names that grows as needed
    StringCollection ListOfFiles = new StringCollection();
```

The `FileName_ListOfFiles` string holds the name of the file containing the list of readme files. We specify it as located in `C:\Program Files\Microsoft Visual Studio .NET\` since that is where we created it earlier; if you created it in a different directory be sure to change this path name here to match what you created. The function to load the list is shown immediately following the standard `Connection` and `Command` objects we have seen before:

```
        SqlConnection textConnection = null;
        SqlCommand textCommand = null;

        void loadListOfFiles()
        {
          // open list of files to read
          FileStream fs = new FileStream(
            FileName_ListOfFiles, FileMode.Open);
          StreamReader sr = new StreamReader(fs);
          string thisFileName = sr.ReadLine();

          while (thisFileName != null)
          {
            ListOfFiles.Add(thisFileName);
            Console.WriteLine("Added file name : "+thisFileName);
            thisFileName = sr.ReadLine();
          }

          Console.WriteLine("{0} files in list.", ListOfFiles.Count);
          sr.Close();
          fs.Close();
        }
```

The `Main()` function as before shows the general flow of the program:

```
        static void Main()
        {
          LoadTextExample loader = new LoadTextExample();
          try
          {
            // initialize list of files to load
            loader.loadListOfFiles();
            // open connection to database
            loader.openConnection();
            // create command object
            loader.createCommand();
            // create table
            loader.createTextTable();
            // prepare insert command
            loader.prepareInsertTextFiles();

            foreach (string thisFileName in loader.ListOfFiles)
            {
              loader.executeInsertTextFile(thisFileName);
            }

            Console.WriteLine("Loaded {0} files into texttable.",
              loader.ListOfFiles.Count);
          }
          catch (SqlException ex)                 // catch exception if db error
          {
```

```
        Console.WriteLine(ex.ToString());    // display details of error
    }
    finally
    {
        loader.closeConnection();             // close connection
    }
}
```

The `createTextTable()` function shows where we change the table design slightly from our `imagetable`. We need to make the `textfile` column larger than in our images example because we store a full path name, and of course we declare the `textdata` column as a TEXT type instead of an IMAGE because it will hold a large text column.

```
void createTextTable()
{
    executeCommand(
        "IF EXISTS ( " +
        " SELECT TABLE_NAME " +
        " FROM INFORMATION_SCHEMA.TABLES  " +
        " WHERE TABLE_NAME = 'texttable' " +
        ")      DROP TABLE texttable "
        );

    executeCommand(
        "CREATE TABLE texttable ( " +
        " textfile VARCHAR(255),   " +
        " textdata TEXT" +
        ")"
        );
}
```

The "housekeeping" methods are exactly the same as in previous examples:

```
void openConnection()
{
    // create SqlConnection object
    textConnection = new SqlConnection(
        @"Server=(local)\NetSDK;" +        // server instance name
        "Integrated Security=SSPI;" +   // use Windows login
        "Connection Timeout=5;" +        // wait only 5 seconds
        "Database=tempdb"                // use temp db to create table
        );
    // Open connection
    textConnection.Open();
}

void closeConnection()
{
    // close connection
    textConnection.Close();
```

```
    // close was successful
    Console.WriteLine("Connection Successfully Closed!");
}

void createCommand()
{
    textCommand = new SqlCommand();
    textCommand.Connection = textConnection;
}

void executeCommand(string commandText)
{
    int commandResult;
    textCommand.CommandText = commandText;
    Console.WriteLine("Executing command:");
    Console.WriteLine(textCommand.CommandText);
    commandResult = textCommand.ExecuteNonQuery();
    Console.WriteLine("ExecuteNonQuery returns {0}.", commandResult);
}
```

Here we prepare and execute the INSERT statements. These are similar to previous examples except for the data column being of TEXT type and the parameters a little simpler because of the full path name:

```
void prepareInsertTextFiles()
{
    textCommand.CommandText =
        "INSERT INTO texttable VALUES (@TextFile, @TextData)";
    textCommand.Parameters.Add("@TextFile", SqlDbType.NVarChar);
    textCommand.Parameters.Add("@TextData", SqlDbType.Text);
}

void executeInsertTextFile(string textFileName)
{
    string textTextData = null;
    textTextData = loadTextFile(textFileName);
    textCommand.Parameters["@TextFile"].Value = textFileName;
    textCommand.Parameters["@TextData"].Value = textTextData;
    executeCommand(textCommand.CommandText);
}
```

Last but not least, the loadTextFile method is where we actually open one of the readme.txt files in our list and load its contents into the database:

```
string loadTextFile(string textFileName)
{
    string textbytes = null;
    Console.WriteLine("Loading File: "+textFileName);

    FileStream fs = new FileStream(textFileName, FileMode.Open);
    StreamReader sr = new StreamReader(fs);
    textbytes = sr.ReadToEnd();
```

```
        Console.WriteLine("Textbytes has length {0} bytes.",
            textbytes.Length);
        return textbytes;
    }
  }
}
```

3. That finishes the program. Compile and run it. The output is similar to our previous loader program. Here is the tail end of it:

How It Works

The way to work with text in a file is basically the same irrespective of whether the destination column type is TEXT, CHAR, or VARCHAR. Instead of a `BinaryReader` we use a `StreamReader` (which is a subclass of `TextReader` in the .NET Framework) and we read the contents of the file into either a character array (`char[]`) or a `string`. Strings are easier to deal with so that's what we use here:

```
string loadTextFile(string textFileName)
{
    string textbytes = null;
    Console.WriteLine("Loading File: "+textFileName);

    FileStream fs = new FileStream(textFileName, FileMode.Open);
    StreamReader sr = new StreamReader(fs);
    textbytes = sr.ReadToEnd();

    Console.WriteLine("Textbytes has length {0} bytes.",
        textbytes.Length);
    return textbytes;
}
```

The `ReadToEnd()` method of the `StreamReader` reads the entire contents of the file in one gulp and returns it as a string. Again this is one of those innocuous looking lines of code that look so simple but are actually consuming a lot of resources, in this case creating a monster string if the file is very large. It's fine to do this as long as you are aware of what you are doing and how many resources it might take up.

Within `executeInsertTextFile()` again the variable assigned to the `TextData` parameter is a string:

```
void executeInsertTextFile(string textFileName)
{
    string textTextData = null;
    textTextData = loadTextFile(textFileName);
    textCommand.Parameters["@TextFile"].Value = textFileName;
    textCommand.Parameters["@TextData"].Value = textTextData;
    executeCommand(textCommand.CommandText);
}
```

And these are the keys to working with text. The way to retrieve information from a TEXT column is similar, as we'll see next.

Retrieving Data from Large Text Columns

We'll make a simple console mode program to show how this works. Retrieving data from TEXT columns is just like retrieving from the smaller character types. If you want to retrieve the entire text, just use the GetString() method in the DataReader. However, you do have an alternative if you want to get just part of the data out of a large text column – the GetChars() method, which we'll use in this example.

Try It Out: Using GetChars() to Retrieve Large Text Columns

1. Add a new C# Console Application project, called RetrieveLargeText, to our open solution, Chapter21_Examples.

2. Rename class1.cs to RetrieveLargeText.cs and edit the code as follows:

```
using System;
using System.Data;          // ADO.NET
using System.Data.SqlClient; // SQL Server .NET Data Provider

namespace Wrox.BeginningCSharpDatabases.Chapter21
{
  public class text_query
  {
    string text_filename = null;
    char[] text_chars = null;
    SqlConnection text_connection = null;
    SqlCommand text_command = null;
    SqlDataReader text_reader = null;

    public text_query()            // constructor; initialize queries
    {
      text_connection = new SqlConnection(
        @"Data Source=(local)\NetSDK;" +
        "Integrated Security=SSPI;" +
        "Initial Catalog=tempdb;" +
        "Connect Timeout=3");
      text_command = new SqlCommand(
```

```
        @"SELECT textfile, textdata FROM texttable",
        text_connection);
    // Open the connection and read data into the DataReader.
    text_connection.Open();
    text_reader =
        text_command.ExecuteReader();
}

public bool get_row()
{
    long size_of_text;                // size of text file
    int bufferSize = 100;             // size of the text buffer.
    long charsread;      // chars read, total chars written
    text_chars = new Char[bufferSize];    // initialize buffer

    if (text_reader.Read())
    {
        // get the file name
        text_filename = text_reader.GetString(0);
        Console.WriteLine("------ start of file:");
        Console.WriteLine(text_filename);
        size_of_text = text_reader.GetChars(1, 0, null, 0, 0);
        Console.WriteLine("--- size of text: {0} characters -----",
            size_of_text);
        Console.WriteLine("--- first 100 characters in text -----");
        charsread = text_reader.GetChars(1, 0, text_chars, 0, 100);
        Console.WriteLine(new String(text_chars));
        Console.WriteLine("--- last 100 characters in text -----");
        charsread = text_reader.GetChars(1,
            size_of_text-100, text_chars, 0, 100);
        Console.WriteLine(new String(text_chars));
        return true;
    }
    else
    {
        return false;
    }
}

public void end_query()
{
    // Close the reader and the connection.
    text_reader.Close();
    text_connection.Close();
}

static void Main()
{
    text_query tq = null;
    try
    {
        tq = new text_query();
```

579

```
      while (tq.get_row()==true)
      {
        Console.WriteLine("----- end of file:");
        Console.WriteLine(tq.text_filename);
        Console.WriteLine("======================================");
      }
    }
    catch (SqlException ex)          // catch exception if database error
    {
      Console.WriteLine(ex.ToString());    // display details of error
    }
    finally
    {
      tq.end_query();                // close connection
    }
  }
}
```

3. Compile the code and run it. The program queries the database and displays the file name, file size, and first and last parts of each text stored within the database, like so:

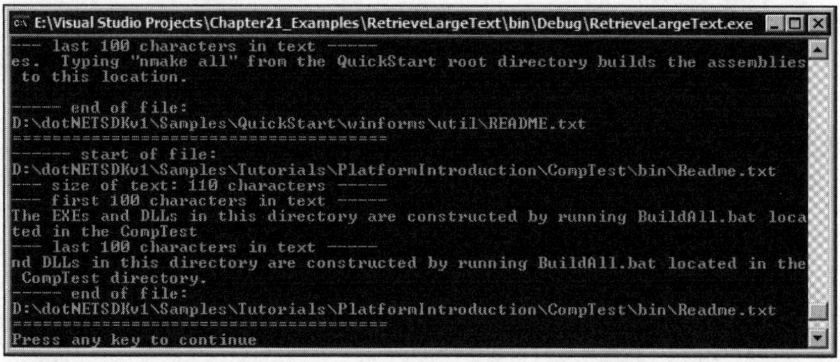

Note that the output shown here may be different on your system depending on what version of C# you have and what options you specified when you installed it.

How It Works

The core of this program is within the `if` statement inside `get_row()`:

```
if (text_reader.Read())
{
```

We start by getting the filename from the table with `GetString()` and printing it out to show which of the `readme.txt` files we are displaying. Then we call `GetChars()` with a null character array to get the size of the `TEXT` column, just as we did with `GetBytes()` in the earlier example with images:

```
            // get the file name
            text_filename = text_reader.GetString(0);
            Console.WriteLine("------ start of file:");
            Console.WriteLine(text_filename);
            size_of_text = text_reader.GetChars(1, 0, null, 0, 0);
            Console.WriteLine("--- size of text: {0} characters -----",
               size_of_text);
```

Rather than print out the whole readme file, we're going to sample the first 100 bytes of the file, using `GetChars()` ability to pull a subset of the column data into memory. This will present us with a character array, which we'll have to convert to a string before we can display it with `Console.WriteLine()`; we'll do this with the `String` constructor that takes a character array as a parameter:

```
            Console.WriteLine("--- first 100 characters in text -----");
            charsread = text_reader.GetChars(1, 0, text_chars, 0, 100);
            Console.WriteLine(new String(text_chars));
```

We do the same thing with the last 100 characters in the text, again using `GetChars()` to extract just the part we want:

```
            Console.WriteLine("--- last 100 characters in text -----");
            charsread = text_reader.GetChars(1,
               size_of_text-100, text_chars, 0, 100);
            Console.WriteLine(new String(text_chars));
            return true;
         }
```

Again, if we wanted the entire contents of the text in one large buffer in memory we would dispense with this more complex code and just call `text_reader.GetString(1)` to obtain the full text as a `String`.

Irregular Data in Other ADO.NET Data Providers

The use of irregular data with the other ADO.NET data providers (OLE DB and ODBC) is very similar to the SQL Server `SqlClient` data provider examples we have shown so far. Indeed, the actual irregular data handling code is exactly the same in many examples, with differences occurring in the other operations of connecting to the database, setting parameters, and so on as shown in Chapters 5 and 6.

To demonstrate, let's return to the Northwind employee images again but let's use the OLE DB .NET data provider (`System.Data.OleDb`) and the Microsoft Access (Jet) database (`Northwind.mdb`) to see them. You'll find the database underneath the main `Office` directory in `C:\Program Files \Microsoft Office\Office10\Samples\Northwind.mdb` or alternatively, if you do not have Office, a copy of `Northwind.mdb` is included in the code download for this chapter.

Try It Out: Display Images with OLE DB from a Microsoft Access (.mdb) File

1. Add a new C# Windows Application project called `DisplayImagesOLEDB` to our open solution, `Chapter21_Examples`.

2. Copy and paste `getdata.cs` and `DisplayImagesWithHeaders.cs` from the `DisplayImagesWithHeaders` project into this new project. Rename `DisplayImagesWithHeaders.cs` to `DisplayImagesOLEDB.cs`.

3. Rename `getdata.cs` to `getdataOLEDB.cs` and make the following changes to it:

```
using System;
using System.Data;
using System.Data.OleDb;      // Use Ole DB Provider
using System.Drawing;
using System.IO;

namespace Wrox.BeginningCSharpDatabases.Chapter21
{
  public class image_query
  {
    string image_filename = null;
    byte[] image_bytes = null;

    OleDbConnection image_connection = null;
    OleDbCommand image_command = null;
    OleDbDataReader image_reader = null;
```

Note that the `OleDb` versions of the connection, command, and data reader objects are specified instead of the SQL versions.

```
    // constructor initializes connection,
    // command, and reader objects

    public image_query()            // constructor; initialize queries
    {
```

Here where the connection object is initialized, the Microsoft Access (Jet) OLE DB provider is specified in the `Provider=` clause of the connection string, and the full path name to the `.mdb` file is set in the `Data Source=` clause of the connection string.

Note that there are several possible locations for the `Northwind.mdb` file, so it's up to you to modify the path name according to the location of `Northwind.mdb` on your machine; if you have multiple copies of `Northwind.mdb` any one will do.

```
        image_connection = new OleDbConnection(
          @"Provider=Microsoft.Jet.OLEDB.4.0;" +
          @"Data Source=E:\Visual Studio Projects\Chapter21_Examples" +
          @"\DisplayImagesOLEDB\Northwind.mdb");
```

Next the `OleDbCommand` constructor is used instead of the `SqlCommand` constructor to initialize `image_command`, but the SQL query itself remains exactly the same as in `DisplayImagesWithHeaders`:

```
image_command = new OleDbCommand(
    @"SELECT firstname+' '+lastname, photo FROM Employees",
    image_connection);

// Open the connection and read data into the DataReader.
image_connection.Open();
image_reader = image_command.ExecuteReader();
}
```

The remaining methods from the `SqlClient` version of `DisplayImageswithHeaders.cs`, namely `get_image()`, `get_filename()`, `get_row()`, and `end_query()`, are exactly the same as the originals. Leave these methods alone. That is all the changes we need to make, as no changes are needed in the code for `Form1` (`DisplayImagesOLEDB.cs`) at all.

Build the example and run without debugging (*Ctrl-F5*). You'll see the same form with Nancy Davolio's name and picture as with the SQL example, though you'll notice that Nancy doesn't look exactly like herself – the photo bitmaps used in the `Northwind.mdb` file included with Microsoft Access 2000 & XP are different (higher-resolution) from the ones included with SQL Server or the MSDE samples.

How It Works

Overall, the `OleDb` .NET data provider is very similar to `SqlClient`; very little had to change in this program to switch to a different data source, and nothing in the code that deals with the irregular data.

If you get an `OleDbException` error on running the program, the most likely cause is that the program is not finding the file `Northwind.mdb` at the path name specified; if you debug the exception the location will be shown as at or immediately following the call to the `image_connection.Open()` method. If this happens, double-check the path name to the `Northwind.mdb` file in the program; make sure the correct path is specified and that it is not commented out. Browse to the directory specified in path to make sure `Northwind.mdb` really exists at that location; do a search on your system to locate `Northwind.mdb` or download the copy from the sample code.

Irregular Data Type Enumeration Differences Between Providers

There is one case where you can expect a difference between .NET data providers in their handling of irregular data, and that is in the names of the irregular data types used for defining parameters. Recall that in the `LoadImagesExample` with `SqlClient` and SQL Server/MSDE, we used the `SqlDbType` enumeration when preparing the insert command for adding binary data to the database:

```
void prepareInsertImages()
{
    imageCommand.CommandText =
      "INSERT INTO imagetable VALUES (@ImageFile, @ImageData)";
    imageCommand.Parameters.Add("@ImageFile", SqlDbType.NVarChar);
    imageCommand.Parameters.Add("@ImageData", SqlDbType.Image);
}
```

Each .NET data provider has its own data type enumeration, and the names of the data types within each enumeration are usually quite different. For OLE DB, the name of the type enumeration is `OleDbType`, and the irregular data type names are shown in this table with the equivalent `SqlClient` names as we have seen in previous programs:

SqlDbType	OleDbType
Image	LongVarBinary
Text	LongVarChar
NText	LongVarWChar

The `SqlDbType` names are the same as the names of these data types within SQL Server's SQL language dialect (Transact-SQL); this can be exact because the `SqlClient` .NET data provider supports only one back-end database, SQL Server and its close relatives such as MSDE. The `OleDb` provider supports many different backends, and the irregular data type names may be different in each, so its names are more "generic" in a sense. They still map to the closest equivalent type in the back-end database or data format, however, if an equivalent type exists (not all databases support irregular data types). As an example of this, let's look an OLE DB version of our `LoadImagesExample` program that uses the OLE DB provider but still targets the SQL Server database.

Try It Out: Load Images using OLE DB with SQL Server/MSDE

The aim of this example is to do the same thing as `LoadImagesExample` – load some images into a newly created table in `tempdb` – but do it using the OLE DB .NET provider.

1. Add a new C# Console Application project called `LoadImagesOLEDB` to our open solution, `Chapter21_Examples`.

2. Copy and paste the contents of `LoadImagesExample.cs` into `class1.cs` and rename it `LoadImagesOLEDB.cs`. Modify the copied code as shown below:

```
using System;
using System.Data;           // use ADO.NET namespace
using System.Data.OleDb;     // use OLE DB .NET data provider namespace
using System.IO;             // used for file I/O

namespace Wrox.BeginningCSharpDatabases.Chapter21
{
    class LoadImagesOLEDB
    {
```

The code that initializes the image file location and name and number of files remains the same. Just for fun, change the `imageFilePrefix` to `soda` instead of `milk` so that we can see that different data is loaded into the database:

```
        string imageFilePrefix = "soda";
```

The connection and command objects are changed to be `OleDbConnection` and `OleDbCommand`, respectively:

```
OleDbConnection imageConnection = null;
OleDbCommand imageCommand = null;
```

The `Main()` function stays mostly the same, except that our class loader is now of type `LoadImagesOLEDB` and the name of the exception object in the `catch` clauses changes to `OleDbException`:

```
static void Main()
{
   LoadImagesOLEDB loader = new LoadImagesOLEDB();

   try
   {
      ...
   }
   catch (OleDbException ex)        // catch exception if database error
   {
      Console.WriteLine(ex.ToString());      // display details of error
   }
   finally
   {
      loader.closeConnection();                  // close connection
   }
}
```

In the `openConnection()` method, we add the `Provider=SQLOLEDB` clause to the connection string to state we're using the SQL Server OLE DB provider, and use the `Data Source=` clause to specify the server instance name as the OLE DB data provider does not support the `Server=` clause. Similarly we must specify `SSPI` (System Security Provider Interface) in the `Integrated Security=` clause as the SQL OLE DB provider requires that exact phrasing:

```
void openConnection()
{
   // create OleDbConnection object
   imageConnection = new OleDbConnection(
      "Provider=SQLOLEDB;"             +
      @"Data Source=(local)\NetSDK;" +  // server instance name
      "Integrated Security=SSPI;"      +  // use Windows login
      "Connection Timeout=5;"          +  // wait only 5 seconds
      "Database=tempdb"                   // use temp db to create table
      );
   // Open connection
   imageConnection.Open();
}
```

In `createCommand()` too, we must remember to create a new `OleDbCommand` object rather than a `SqlCommand` object.

```
void createCommand()
{
  imageCommand = new OleDbCommand();
  imageCommand.Connection = imageConnection;
}
```

The `closeConnection()`, `executeCommand()`, and `createImageTable()` methods remain exactly the same. Note that the CREATE TABLE syntax in `createImageTable()` stays exactly the same and uses the Transact-SQL names for the irregular data types. When we execute a command, we are passing a SQL command to the back-end database and the syntax of this command depends on the backend, not on the .NET data provider.

One place we do need to use the enumerated OLE DB data types, however, is in `prepareInsertImages()`. Besides the use of the `OleDbType.LongVarBinary` enumeration in place of `SqlDbType.Image`, we also use `OleDbType.VarWChar` instead of `SqlDbType.NVarChar` as the name of the "wide" (2-byte Unicode) character type is different in OLE DB also. The regular data type names in these enumeration types also differ between the .NET data providers.

Fianlly, we must remember to change the parameter specifiers in the INSERT command to question marks (?) as described in Chapter 6 as OLE DB does not support the named parameters in the way `SqlClient` and SQL Server do.

```
void prepareInsertImages()
{
  imageCommand.CommandText =
    "INSERT INTO imagetable VALUES (?, ?)";
  imageCommand.Parameters.Add("@ImageFile", OleDbType.VarWChar);
  imageCommand.Parameters.Add("@ImageData", OleDbType.LongVarBinary);
}
```

The remaining methods, `executeInsertImages()` and `loadImageFile()`, are the same as in the `SqlClient` version of `LoadImageExample`.

3. Build the project and run without debugging (*Ctrl-F5*). The output is the same as the `SqlClient` example of this program, except that the echoed INSERT commands show the ? specifiers:

4. You can display the results with the original `SqlClient DisplayImages` example, without any changes as we loaded into the very sample SQL Server instance and database. Open the `DisplayImages` example and run without debugging (*Ctrl-F5*), or locate the `DisplayImages.exe` executable and execute directly. You will see that the `imagetable` now contains the images of the different soda varieties from the GrocerToGo data.

Irregular Data in the ODBC .NET Data Provider

The sample download code for this chapter also includes a pair of programs showing both `LoadImagesExample` and `DisplayImages` for the ODBC .NET data provider with the MySQL open-source SQL database as the backend, using the MyODBC ODBC driver for MySQL. These programs are located in the directories labeled `LoadImagesExampleODBC` and `DisplayImagesODBC`.

The code for these examples is so similar to the `SqlClient` and OLE DB provider examples that we're not going to list every line of code in both programs. However, we will highlight the differences here, most of which occur in `LoadImagesExampleODBC`.

As described in detail in Chapter 5, the ODBC .NET data provider (`Microsoft.Data.Odbc`) is not included with the .NET Framework and must be downloaded separately from Microsoft's web site.

> *MySQL and MyODBC are also separate downloads available from* http://www.mysql.com. *Licensing information is detailed on this web site as well. The MySQL database server must be installed and running on the local machine (localhost), and the MyODBC ODBC Driver version 3.51 must also be installed.*

Also as shown in Chapter 5, you must also explicitly include a reference to the downloaded `Microsoft.Data.Odbc.dll` in your C# project, and reference the `Microsoft.Data.Odbc` namespace. The .NET data provider connection and command objects have the `Odbc` prefix as shown here at the start of `LoadImagesDataODBC`:

```
OdbcConnection imageConnection = null;
OdbcCommand imageCommand = null;
```

as does the `OdbcException` object used in the `catch` clause in `Main()`:

```
catch (OdbcException ex)        // catch exception if database error
```

The `Connection` object is initialized using the ODBC connection string for MyODBC as described in Chapter 5 and `createCommand()` creates an `OdbcCommand` object:

```
void openConnection()
{
    // create OdbcConnection object
    imageConnection = new OdbcConnection(
      "DRIVER={MySQL ODBC 3.51 Driver};" +
      "SERVER=localhost;" +
      "DATABASE=test;" +
      "UID=root;" +
      "PASSWORD=;"          );

void createCommand()
{
    imageCommand = new OdbcCommand();
    imageCommand.Connection = imageConnection;
}
```

The `closeConnection()` and `executeCommand()` methods remain exactly the same as in the previous examples for `SqlClient` and `OleDb` but the SQL command given in `createImageTable()` differs since the backend is now different and SQL databases have differences in SQL syntax, especially for the `CREATE TABLE` statement. MySQL (also Oracle) uses the `BLOB` keyword to define a column for a large binary object:

```
void createImageTable()
{
    executeCommand(
      "CREATE TABLE imagetable ( " +
      " imagefile VARCHAR(20),   " +
      " imagedata BLOB)"
    );
}
```

Note also that we used `VARCHAR` instead of `NVARCHAR` because MySQL does not support the `NVARCHAR` type. Maximum size for a given column type may differ as well; for example in MySQL, `BLOB`s may be defined as `TINYBLOB`, `BLOB`, `MEDIUMBLOB`, or `LARGEBLOB` with different maximum sizes on each. See the documentation for your back-end database for exact information on details such as these.

In the last method to change, `prepareInsertImages()`, we see the `OdbcType` names for the irregular data type enumerations actually match the `SqlClient` `SqlDbType` names more closely than the `OleDb` data provider:

```
void prepareInsertImages()
{
  imageCommand.CommandText =
    "INSERT INTO imagetable VALUES (?, ?)";
  imageCommand.Parameters.Add("@ImageFile", OdbcType.VarChar);
  imageCommand.Parameters.Add("@ImageData", OdbcType.Image);
}
```

The OdbcType enumeration also supports NVarChar, Text, and NText in its list of types. However, as with the OleDb provider, these types are dependent on the back-end database support, and not all ODBC backends will support all these types.

Well, that pretty much covers the differences between .NET data providers in their support of irregular data, and also ends our chapter on irregular data as well. Let's summarize what we have learned.

Summary

In this chapter we've learned exactly what irregular data and BLOBs (Binary Large OBjects) are. We've also learned what database data types can be used to store irregular data.

We learned how to store and retrieve large text and binary data items. We showed how to deal with data items that are too large to fit into memory. We saved retrieved data items to a file, and then read the data back from a file to store in the database.

We saw how some binary data can have extra headers that interfere with other programs working with them, and how to bypass those headers for some common cases. We then discussed the issues with irregular data in other ADO.NET data providers including both the OLE DB and ODBC data providers.

That about wraps it up for this book. There's plenty more out there to learn about ADO.NET beyond what's covered here, but consider consolidating what you've learned here with your own projects before you continue on to more advanced topics. If you do feel you're ready to learn more, check out *Professional ADO.NET* (Wrox Press, ISBN: 1-86100-527-X) for the complete lowdown on this topic.

Exercises

1. What are the three SQL Server data types that support large irregular data?

2. Are there any sets of images in the GrocerToGo sample that will fit into a VARBINARY column type? If so, modify LoadImagesExample to use these.

3. Modify the program that displays photos from the Employees table in the Northwind sample database to instead display the category names and pictures in the Categories table, also in Northwind. Does the same OLE header offset work for these images as well?

4. Modify the ExtractToFile program to make the initial readOffset equal to zero. What happens when you try to open the generated files with Paint?

5. Undo the change made to ExtractToFile in the previous exercise, then change the GetBytes() call to copy one byte less than it is supposed to (hint: bufferSize-1). What happens to the images?

6. Convert LoadImagesExample to use another ADO.NET data provider such as OlE DB or ODBC.

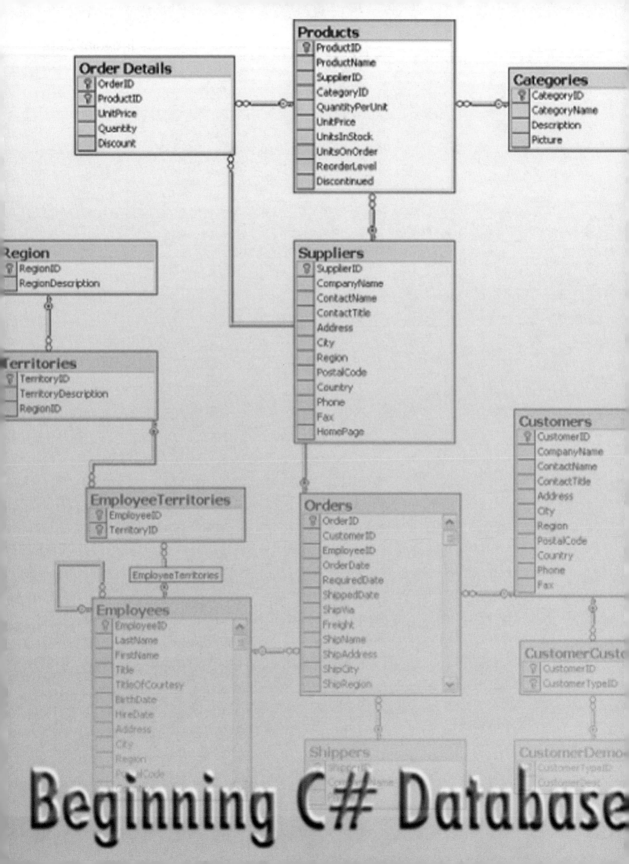

The Custom Query Tool Application

In Chapter 3, we discussed various methods for working with SQL statements, including every tool from osql, through the Visual Studio .NET SQL tool, up to the SQL Server Query Analyzer. However, throughout that chapter, we used our own custom application to demonstrate simple SQL queries. Because this tool is a simple C# project that uses data access, we are including the full instructions for how to create this tool in this appendix.

The utility is not as powerful as ISQL/w that comes with SQL Server or as other graphical tools in the marketplace, but this is free and also it can be easily expanded and modified to suit your own particular needs.

Let's now build the tool for use.

Try It Out: A Custom Query Tool

The application is a standard C# Windows Application, so you will want to fire up Visual Studio.NET and follow the steps below.

1. Create a new solution called AppendixA_Examples.

2. Create a new C# project within this solution by right-clicking on the solution, selecting Add | New Project... and creating a new Windows Form application called SqlTool.

3. Click on the form, and set the following properties using the Properties panel:

Property	Value
Text	SQL Tool
Name	frmSql
WindowState	Maximized

4. Drag and drop a `RichTextBox` control from the toolbox to the form.

5. Using the Properties panel, set the following properties for the control. Set the font by clicking the (…) button to the right of the Font property in the panel and select the font name and size from the dialog:

Property	Value
Name	rtfSql
Dock	Top
Text	(Clear this property)
Font	Courier New
FontSize	10

6. Drag and drop a `Splitter` control from the toolbox to the window. This handy control latches on to the last control placed on a form with a specific value set for the Dock property. We want to be able to change the size of the Textbox, so we just need to change a single property on the `Splitter` control.

Property	Value
Dock	Top

Your form should now look something like this:

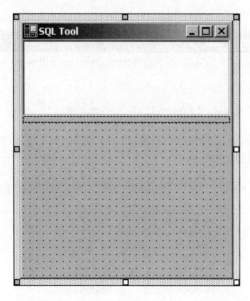

7. Drag and drop a `ListView` control from the toolbox on to the empty part of the form.

8. Using the Properties panel, set the following properties on the `ListView`:

Property	Value
Name	listViewResult
Dock	Fill
GridLines	True
View	Details

9. Double-click a `MainMenu` control in the toolbox. This will add a `MainMenu1` control to the form and allow you to edit the menu items themselves at the top left of the form.

10. Create five menu items by clicking the topmost item, and entering the text in the value column below in the box, and after completing that, selecting the item just below it. In the order from top to bottom, enter the following values:

Property	Value
Text	&Actions
Text	&Execute
Text	&Format statements
Text	-
Text	E&xit

11. Three of the above menu items need to have a few more properties set. Select the item with the text **&Execute**. In the Properties panel set the following properties:

Property	Value
Name	menuItemExecute
Shortcut	F5

12. Select the menu item with the text **&Format statements** and set the following properties:

Property	Value
Name	menuItemFormat
Shortcut	F12

595

13. Select the menu item with the text **E&xit** and set the following properties:

Property	Value
Name	menuItemExit

14. The form should now look something like this:

15. Right-click the form and select **View Code**.

16. Add this `using` statement to the top of the code:

```
using System.Data.SqlClient;
```

17. Add the following fields at the top of the `frmSql` class (the `menuItemExit` statement should already be there):

```
private System.Windows.Forms.MenuItem menuItemExit;
private SqlConnection mConnection;
private SqlCommand mCommand;
private string[] mSqlKeyWords = new string[] {"select",
                                              "update",
                                              "insert",
                                              "into",
                                              "delete",
                                              "from",
                                              "values",
                                              "truncate",
                                              "table",
                                              "join",
```

```
                                             "on",
                                             "where",
                                             "create",
                                             "drop",
                                             "set",
                                             "in",
                                             "between",
                                             "is",
                                             "null",
                                             "not",
                                             "Order by",
                                             "asc",
                                             "desc"};
```

18. Add the following code to the form's constructor:

```
public frmSql()
{
    InitializeComponent();

        mConnection = new SqlConnection(@"data source=(local)\NetSDK;" +
                        "database=Northwind;" +
                        "integrated security=SSPI;");
}
```

19. Return to the design view, and double-click the menu item with the text **&Execute**. Enter the code below:

```
private void menuItemExecute_Click(object sender, System.EventArgs e)
{
    string selectedText = rtfSql.SelectedText;

    // First get the text to use. If the user has selected part of the text,
    // we use only the selection
    if (selectedText.Length == 0)
    selectedText = rtfSql.Text;

    // Check to see if the select keyword exists in the text. If it does we
    // treat all the text as a query. If this isn't a select, execute the
    // command
    if (selectedText.ToLower().IndexOf("select", 0) >= 0)
      ExecuteSelect(selectedText);
    else
      ExecuteNonQuery(selectedText);
}

private void ExecuteSelect(string pText)
{
  try
  {
    bool first = true;
```

```
      ListViewItem lvi = null;

      // Create a command object. Pass to its constructor the command (pText)
      // and the connection (mConnection)
      mCommand = new SqlCommand(pText, mConnection);

      // Open the connection
      mConnection.Open();

      // Execute the query and get a SqlDataReader returned
      SqlDataReader dr = mCommand.ExecuteReader();

      // Check to see if the DataReader was returned
      if (dr == null)
        return;

      // We've got a valid DataReader, use it
      while (dr.Read())
      {
        // If this is the first loop, we want to create column headers in the
        // listview.
        if (first)
        {
          listViewResult.Items.Clear();
          listViewResult.Columns.Clear();
          for (int i = 0; i < dr.FieldCount; i++)
            listViewResult.Columns.Add(dr.GetName(i).ToString(), 100,
                                                HorizontalAlignment.Left);
          first = false;
        }
        // Add the row to the listview
        for (int i = 0; i < dr.FieldCount; i++)
        {
          if (i == 0)
            lvi = listViewResult.Items.Add(dr.GetValue(i).ToString());
          else
            lvi.SubItems.Add(dr.GetValue(i).ToString());
        }
      }
    }
    catch (System.Exception err)
    {
      // If an error is caught, display it to the user
      MessageBox.Show(err.Message);
    }
    finally
    {
      // This ensures that the SqlConnection object is always closed when we
      // leave this method.
      mConnection.Close();
    }
}
```

```
private void ExecuteNonQuery(string pText)
{
  try
  {
    int rowsAffected = 0;

    // Create the command. pText is the text to use and mConnection is the
    // connection object.
    mCommand = new SqlCommand(pText, mConnection);

    // Open the connection
    mConnection.Open();

    // Execute the command
    rowsAffected = mCommand.ExecuteNonQuery();

    // Clear the listview
    listViewResult.Columns.Clear();
    listViewResult.Items.Clear();

    // Display the number of rows affected.
    MessageBox.Show(rowsAffected + " row(s) affected");
  }
  catch (System.Exception err)
  {
    // If an error is caught, display it to the user.
    MessageBox.Show(err.Message);
  }
  finally
  {
    // The ensures that the connection is closed when we leave this method
    mConnection.Close();
  }
}
```

20. Return to the design view, and double-click the menu item with the text Format statements. Insert the code below

```
private void menuItemFormat_Click(object sender, System.EventArgs e)
{
  for (int i = 0; i < 23; i++)
  {
    int index = 0;
    while ((index = rtfSql.Find(mSqlKeyWords[i],index,
                                    RichTextBoxFinds.WholeWord)) >= 0)
    {
      index++;
      rtfSql.SelectionColor = Color.Blue;
      rtfSql.SelectedText = mSqlKeyWords[i].ToUpper();
    }
  }
```

```
    }
```

21. Return to the design view, and double-click the menu item with the text **E&xit**. Enter the following code:

```
private void menuItemExit_Click(object sender, System.EventArgs e)
{
    Application.Exit();
}
```

22. Run the application. You should get a window that looks something like this:

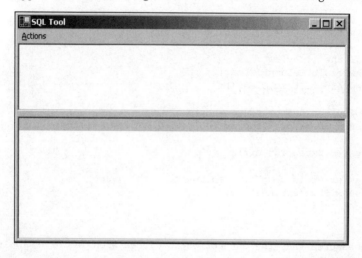

How It Works

We have created a simple application that allows you to enter SQL statements and send them to a database. You enter the statements in the RichTextBox at the top of the dialog and get the result back in the ListView below. You can change the size of the RichTextBox and ListView by clicking the splitter bar between them, and dragging it to your desired position.

Let's look briefly at the code. The first interesting place in the code is the constructor, where we create the connection and initialize it with a connection string:

```
mConnection = new SqlConnection(@"data source=(local)\NetSDK;" +
            "database=Northwind;" +
            "integrated security=SSPI;");
```

If you are using a different database instance, or are accessing a different server for your database, you need to change the `data source` statement appropriately.

The next interesting place in the code is the `ExecuteSelect` method. This method is called whenever the text we want to execute contains the word "SELECT". The code that retrieves the data from the database is as follows:

```
// Create a command object. Pass to its constructor the command (pText)
// and the connection (mConnection)
mCommand = new SqlCommand(pText, mConnection);

// Open the connection
mConnection.Open();

// Execute the query and get a SqlDataReader returned
SqlDataReader dr = mCommand.ExecuteReader();
```

We first create a command object and instantiate it with the text (the SQL statement) that we want to send to the database, as well as the connection object we created in the constructor. We then open the connection and call the `ExecuteReader` method on the command object. This method returns another object, a `SqlDataReader` that allows us to read the data from the database.

The following lines of code, all the way down to the `catch` statement, concern themselves with inserting the data in the `ListView`. The `catch` statements are interesting, because we use them to perform two critical tasks: to inform the user of errors and to make absolutely sure that the connection object is closed when we leave the method:

```
catch (System.Exception err)
{
    // If an error is caught, display it to the user.
    MessageBox.Show(err.Message);
}
finally
{
    // The ensures that the connection is closed when we leave this method
    mConnection.Close();
}
```

Remember that the finally section of the `try...catch...finally` structure is always run before the structure is left, no matter how the structure is left. This means that the code in the `finally` section is run even after the return statement is called if no data was returned!

The other method that is used to call the database is named `ExecuteNonQuery`. The reason for this is that the commands this method will send to the database don't return any rows. The method is therefore somewhat less complex than the `ExecuteSelect` method. The three lines of code that speak with the database are almost identical to the ones we saw in the `ExecuteSelect` method above:

```
int rowsAffected = 0;

// Create the command. pText is the text to use and mConnection is the
// connection object.
mCommand = new SqlCommand(pText, mConnection);

// Open the connection
mConnection.Open();

// Execute the command
rowsAffected = mCommand.ExecuteNonQuery();
```

Note the final line. Instead of calling the `ExecuteReader` method on the command object, we call the `ExecuteNonQuery` method instead. We do so because we know that no rows will be returned to us anyway. The `ExecuteNonQuery` returns a number that indicates how many rows were affected by the command.

The final method of interest doesn't actually do anything on the database. The `menuItemFormat_Click` method simply runs through the text in the `RichTextBox` and adds a bit of color to the keywords and changes them all to upper case. This is entirely cosmetic, and there are many, many SQL keywords that are not included in the list, but for the purpose of this chapter, you should be OK with the keywords here.

Summary

Of course, this application has massive amounts of room for expansion if so desired, but all that is required from it is to execute T-SQL code. Our small, simple application is fast, simple, easy to use, and can be expanded to cover any needs that you desire. In fact you could use this as a method for progressing your C# database programming with more complex code to enhance the project further.

This tool will only point to the database that is detailed within the connection. It would be possible to expand this utility so that you could select other databases for example, or allow output to be saved to an external file. You may even want to stretch yourself to allow for most of the options within the `osql` command. The only limitation is time and your needs.

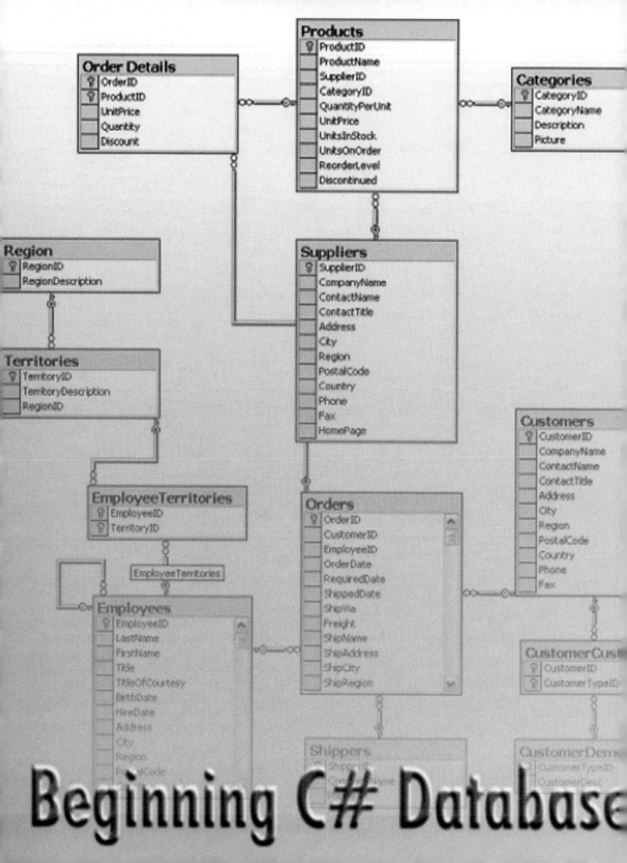

XML Primer

XML

Throughout this book, we've mentioned XML from time to time. XML stands for **Extensible Markup Language** and is a way of storing data in a simple text format, which means that it can be read by any computer. As we see in some of the later chapters about web programming, this makes it a perfect format for transferring data over the Internet. It's even not too difficult for humans to read!

The ins and outs of XML can be very complicated, so we won't look at every single detail here. The basic format is very simple, however, and most of the time you won't require a detailed knowledge of XML, as VS will normally take care of most of the work for you – you will rarely have to write an XML document by hand. Having said that, XML is hugely important in the .NET world, as it's used as the default format for transferring data, so it's vital to understand the basics.

> *If you need a fuller understanding of XML, please check out* Beginning XML, *ISBN 1-86100-341-2, also published by Wrox Press.*

XML Documents

A complete set of data in XML is known as an **XML document**. An XML document could be a physical file on your computer, or just a string in memory. It has to be complete in itself, however, and must obey certain rules (we'll see what these are shortly). An XML document is made up of a number of different parts. The most important of these are **XML elements**, which contain the actual data of the document.

XML Elements

XML elements consist of an opening tag (the name of the element enclosed in angled brackets, such as `<myElement>`), the data within the element, and a closing tag (the same as the opening tag, but with a forward slash after the opening bracket: `</myElement>`).

For example, we might define an element to hold the title of a book such as this:

```
<book>Tristram Shandy</book>
```

If you already know some HTML, you might be thinking that this looks very similar – and you'd be right! In fact, HTML and XML share much of the same syntax. The big difference, is that XML doesn't have any predefined elements – we choose the names of own elements, so there's no limit to the number of elements we can have. The most important point to remember is that XML – despite its name – isn't actually a language at all. Rather, it's a standard for defining languages (known as **XML applications**). Each of these languages has its own distinct vocabulary – a specific set of elements that can be used in the document and the structure that the elements are allowed to take. As we'll see shortly, we can explicitly limit the elements allowed in our XML document. Alternatively, we can allow any elements, and allow the program using the document to work out for itself what the structure is.

Element names are case-sensitive, so <book> and <Book> are counted as different elements. This means, that if you attempt to close a <book> element using a closing tag that doesn't have identical casing (for example, </BOOK>), your XML document won't be legal. The programs that read XML documents and analyze them into their individual elements, are known as **XML parsers**, and they will reject any document that contains illegal XML.

Elements can also contain other elements, so we could modify this <book> element to include the author, as well as the title by adding two sub-elements:

```
<book>
   <title>Tristram Shandy</title>
   <author>Lawrence Sterne</author>
</book>
```

Overlapping elements aren't allowed, however, so we *must* close all sub-elements before the closing tag of the parent element. This means, for example, that we can't do this:

```
<book>
   <title>Tristram Shandy
   <author>Lawrence Sterne
   </title></author>
</book>
```

This is illegal, because the <author> element is opened within the <title> element, but the closing </title> tag comes before the closing </author> tag.

There's one exception to the rule that all elements must have a closing element. It's possible to have 'empty' elements, with no nested data or text. In this case, we can simply add the closing tag straight after the opening element, as above, or we can use a short-hand syntax, adding the slash of the closing element to the end of the opening element:

```
<book />
```

This is identical to the full syntax:

```
<book></book>
```

Attributes

As well as storing data within the body of the element, we can also store data within attributes, which are added within the opening tag of an element. Attributes are in the form:

```
name="value"
```

Where the value of the attribute must be enclosed in either single or double quotes. For example:

```
<book title="Tristram Shandy"></book>
```

or:

```
<book title='Tristram Shandy'></book>
```

These are both legal, but this is not:

```
<book title=Tristram Shandy></book>
```

At this point, you may be wondering why we need both these ways of storing data in XML. What's the difference between:

```
<book>
    <title>Tristram Shandy</title>
</book>
```

and:

```
<book title="Tristram Shandy"></book>
```

The honest answer is that there isn't any earth-shatteringly fundamental difference between the two. There isn't really any big advantage in using either. Elements are a better choice if there's a possibility that you'll need to add more information about that piece of data later – you can always add a sub-element or an attribute to an element, but you can't do that for attributes. Arguably, elements are more readable and more elegant (but that's really a matter of personal taste). On the other hand, attributes consume less bandwidth if the document is sent over a network without compression (with compression there's not much difference), and are convenient for holding information that isn't essential to every user of the document. Probably the best advice is to use both, using whichever you're most comfortable with storing a particular item of data in. There really are no hard and fast rules, however.

The XML Declaration

Besides elements and attributes, XML documents can contain a number of constituent parts (the individual parts of an XML document are known as **nodes** – so elements, the text within elements, and attributes, are all nodes of the XML document). Many of these are only important if you really want to delve deeply into XML. There's one type of node, however, that occurs in almost every XML document. This is the **XML Declaration**, and, if we include it, it *must* occur as the first node of the document. The XML declaration is similar in format to an element, but has question marks inside the angled brackets. It always has the name xml, and it always has an attribute named version; currently, the only possible value for this is "1.0". The simplest possible form of the XML declaration is, therefore, like this:

```
<?xml version="1.0"?>
```

Optionally, it can also contain the attributes `encoding` (with a value indicating the character set that should be used to read the document, such as `"UTF-16"` to indicate that the document uses the 16-bit Unicode character set) and `standalone` (with the value `"yes"` or `"no"` to indicate whether or not the XML document depends on any other files). These attributes are not required, however, and you will probably normally include only the `version` attribute in your own XML files.

Structure of an XML Document

One of the most important things about XML is that it offers a way of structuring data that is very different from relational databases. As we've seen, most modern database systems store data in tables that are related to each other through values in individual columns. Each table stores data in rows and columns – each row represents a single record, and each column a particular item of data about that record. In contrast, XML data is structured hierarchically, a little like the folders and files in Windows Explorer. Each document *must* have a single **root element**, within which all elements and text data are contained. If there is more than one element at the top level of the document, the document will not be legal XML. We *can* include other XML nodes at the top level, however – notably the XML declaration. So this is a legal XML document:

```
<?xml version="1.0"?>
<books>
    <book>Tristram Shandy</book>
    <book>Moby Dick</book>
    <book>Ulysses</book>
</books>
```

This, however, isn't:

```
<?xml version="1.0"?>
<book>Tristram Shandy</book>
<book>Moby Dick</book>
<book>Ulysses</book>
```

Under this root element, we have a great deal of flexibility about how we structure the data. Unlike relational data, in which every row has the same number of columns, there's no restriction on the number of sub-elements an element can have. Although XML documents are often structured in a similar way to relational data, with an element for each record, XML documents don't actually have to have any predefined structure at all. This makes XML far better suited than relational databases to store irregular data. For example, XML can be used to mark up a text document. The web markup language, HTML, although not strictly an XML application, is very closely related.

XML Namespaces

Just as everyone can define their own C# classes, everyone can define their own XML elements; and this gives rise to exactly the same problem – how do we know which elements belong to which vocabulary? If you noticed the title of this section, you will already have realized that this question is answered in a similar way. Just as we define namespaces to organize our C# types, we use XML namespaces to define our XML vocabularies. This allows us to include elements from a number of different vocabularies within a single XML document, without the risk of misinterpreting elements, because (for example) two different vocabularies define a `<customer>` element.

XML namespaces can be quite complex, so we won't go into great detail here, but the basic syntax is simple. We associate specific elements or attributes with a specific namespace using a prefix, followed by a colon. For example, `<wrox:book>` represents a `<book>` element that resides in the `wrox` namespace. But how do we know what namespace `wrox` represents? For this approach to work, we need to be able to guarantee that every namespace is unique. The easiest way to do this, is to map the prefixes to something that's already known to be unique. This is exactly what happens: somewhere in our XML document, we need to associate any namespace prefixes we use with a **Uniform Resource Identifier** (URI). URIs come in several flavors, but the most common type is simply a web address, such as `"http://www.wrox.com"`.

To identify a prefix with a specific namespace, we use the `xmlns:<prefix>` attribute within an element, setting its value to the unique URI that identifies that namespace. The prefix can then be used anywhere within that element, including any nested child elements. For example:

```
<?xml version="1.0"?>
<books>
    <book xmlns:wrox="http://www.wrox.com">
        <wrox:title>Beginning C#</wrox:title>
        <wrox:author>Karli Watson</wrox:author>
    </book>
</books>
```

Here we can use the `wrox:` prefix with the `<title>` and `<author>` elements, because they are within the `<book>` element, where the prefix is defined. If we tried to add this prefix to the `<books>` element, however, the XML would be illegal, as the prefix isn't defined for this element.

We can also define a default namespace for an element using the `xmlns` attribute:

```
<?xml version="1.0"?>
<books>
    <book xmlns="http://www.wrox.com">
        <title>Beginning C#</title>
        <author>Karli Watson</author>
        <html:img src="begcsharp.gif"
                  xmlns:html="http://www.w3.org/1999/xhtml" />
    </book>
</books>
```

Here, we define the default namespace for our `<book>` element as `"http://www.wrox.com"`. Everything within this element will, therefore, belong to this namespace, unless we explicitly request otherwise by adding a different namespace prefix, as we do for the `<img>` element (we set it to the namespace used by XML-compatible HTML documents).

Well-formed and Valid XML

We've been talking up till now about "legal" XML. In fact, XML distinguishes between two forms of "legality". Documents that obey all the rules required by the XML standard itself are said to be **well-formed**. If an XML document is not well-formed, parsers will be unable to interpret it correctly, and will reject the document. In order to be well-formed, a document must:

❑ Have one and only one root element

❑ Have closing tags for every element (except for the shorthand syntax mentioned above)

❑ Not have any overlapping elements – all child elements must be fully nested within the parent

❑ Have all attributes enclosed in quotes

This isn't a complete list by any means, but it does highlight the most common errors made by programmers who are new to XML.

XML documents can obey all these rules, however, and still not be **valid**. Remember that we said earlier that XML is not itself a language, but a standard for defining XML applications. Well-formed XML documents simply comply with the XML standard; in order to be valid, they also need to conform to any rules specified for the XML application. Not all parsers check whether documents are valid; those that do are said to be **validating parsers**. In order to check whether a document adheres to the rules of the application, however, we first need a way of specifying what those are.

Validating XML Documents

XML supports two ways of defining which elements and attributes can be placed in a document and in what order – **Document Type Definitions** and **Schemas**. DTDs use a non-XML syntax inherited from the parent of XML, and are gradually being replaced by schemas. DTDs don't allow us to specify the data types of our elements and attributes, and so are relatively inflexible and not used that much in the context of the .NET Framework. Schemas, on the other hand, are flexible – they do allow us to specify data types, and are written in an XML-compatible syntax. However, unfortunately schemas are very complex, and there are different formats for defining them – even within the .NET world!

Schemas

There are two separate formats for schemas supported by .NET – XML Schema Definition language (XSD), and XML-Data Reduced schemas (XDR). Schemas can be either included within our XML document, or kept in a separate file. These formats are mutually incompatible, and you really need to be very familiar with XML before you attempt to write one, so we won't go into great detail here. It is, however, useful to be able to recognize the main elements in a schema, so we will explain the basic principles. To do this, we'll look at sample XSD and XDR schemas for this simple XML document, which contains basic details about a couple of Wrox's C# books:

```xml
<?xml version="1.0"?>
<books>
    <book>
        <title>Beginning C#</title>
        <author>Karli Watson</author>
        <code>4982</code>
    </book>
    <book>
        <title>Professional C#</title>
        <author>Simon Robinson</author>
        <code>4990</code>
    </book>
</books>
```

XSD Schemas

Elements in XSD schemas must belong to the namespace
`"http://www.w3.org/2001/XMLSchema"`. If this namespace isn't included, the schema elements won't be recognized.

In order to associate our XML document with an XSD schema in another file, we need to add a `schemalocation` element to the root element:

```
<?xml version="1.0"?>
<books schemalocation="file://C:\BegCSharpDB\XML\books.xsd">
    ...
</books>
```

Let's have a quick look at an example XSD schema:

```
<schema xmlns="http://www.w3.org/2001/XMLSchema">
    <element name="books">
        <complexType>
            <choice maxOccurs="unbounded">
                <element name="book">
                    <complexType>
                        <sequence>
                            <element name="title" />
                            <element name="author" />
                            <element name="code" />
                        </sequence>
                    </complexType>
                </element>
            </choice>
            <attribute name="schemalocation" />
        </complexType>
    </element>
</schema>
```

The first thing to notice here, is that we set the default namespace to the XSD namespace. This tells the parser that all the elements in the document belong to the schema. If we don't specify this namespace, the parser will think that the elements are just normal XML elements, and won't realize it needs to use them for validation.

The entire schema is contained within an element called `<schema>` (with a lower-case 's' – remember, that case is important!). Each element that can occur within the document must be represented by an `<element>` element. This element has a `name` attribute, which indicates the name of the element. If the element is to contain nested child elements, we must include the `<element>` tags for these within a `<complexType>` element. Inside this, we specify how the child elements must occur. For example, we use a `<choice>` element to specify that any selection of the child elements can occur, or `<sequence>` to specify that the child elements must appear in the same order as they are listed in the schema. If an element may appear more than once (as our `<book>` element does), we need to include a `maxOccurs` attribute within its parent element. Setting this to `"unbounded"`, means that the element can occur as often as we like. Finally, any attributes must be represented by `<attribute>` elements, including our `schemalocation` attribute that tells the parser where to find the schema. We place this after the end of the list of child elements.

XDR Schemas

To attach an external XDR schema to an XML document, we specify a namespace for the document with the value `"x-schema:<schema_filename>"`:

```
<?xml version="1.0"?>
<books xmlns="x-schema:books.xdr">
    ...
</books>
```

The schema below is the XDR equivalent of the XSD schema we've just looked at. As you can see, it is very different:

```
<Schema xmlns="urn:schemas-microsoft-com:xml-data">
    <ElementType name="title" content="textOnly" />
    <ElementType name="author" content="textOnly" />
    <ElementType name="code" content="textOnly" />
    <ElementType name="book" content="eltOnly">
        <group order="seq">
            <element type="title" />
            <element type="author" />
            <element type="code" />
        </group>
    </ElementType>
    <ElementType name="books" content="eltOnly">
        <element type="book" />
    </ElementType>
</Schema>
```

Again, we set the default namespace to tell the parser that all the elements in the document belong to the schema definition; this time to `"urn:schemas-microsoft-com:xml-data"`. Notice, that (unlike XSD schemas), this is a proprietary format, so won't work at all with non-Microsoft products. In fact, XDR schemas are particularly useful when working with SQL Server, Microsoft's database server, as this has in-built support for XDR.

This time our root element is `<Schema>` with a *capital* 'S'. This root element again contains the entire schema definition (remember that XML documents must have a single root element). After this, though, there's a big difference – the elements that will appear in our document are defined *in reverse order*! The reason for this, is that each element in the document is represented in the schema by an `<ElementType>` element, and this contains an `<element>` element (note the lower-case 'e' here) for each child element. Within the `<element>` tags, we set the `type` attribute to point to an `<ElementType>` element – and this must already have been defined. If we want to restrict how child elements can appear, we can use a `<group>` element within the `<ElementType>`, and set its `order` attribute. In this case, we set it to `"seq"`, to specify that the elements occur in the same sequence as in the schema – just like the `<sequence>` tag in the XSD schema!

Try It Out: Creating an XML Document in Visual Studio .NET

Now we've covered the basic theory behind XML, we can have a go at creating XML documents. Fortunately, VS does a lot of the hard work for us, and will even create an XSD schema based on our XML document, without us having to write a single line of code!

1. Open up Visual Studio and create a new solution called `AppendixB_Examples`. Right-click on our solution and select **Add | Add New Item...** from the menu:

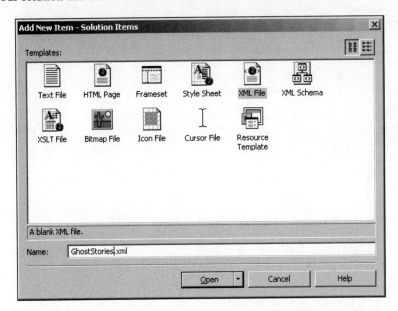

2. Select **XML File**, name it `GhostStories.xml` and click on **Open**. Visual Studio will create a new XML document for us. Notice how Visual Studio adds the XML declaration, complete with an `encoding` attribute (it also colors the attributes and elements, but this won't show up very well in black and white print):

```
<?xml version="1.0" encoding="utf-8" ?>
```

3. Move the cursor to the line underneath the XML declaration, and type the text `<stories>`. Notice, how VS automatically puts the end tag in as soon as we type the greater than sign to close the opening tag:

```
<?xml version="1.0" encoding="utf-8" ?>
<stories></stories>
```

4. Type in this XML file:

```xml
<?xml version="1.0" encoding="utf-8" ?>
<stories>
   <story>
      <title>A House in Aungier Street</title>
      <author>
         <name>Sheridan Le Fanu</name>
         <nationality>Irish</nationality>
      </author>
      <rating>eerie</rating>
   </story>
   <story>
      <title>The Signalman</title>
      <author>
         <name>Charles Dickens</name>
         <nationality>English</nationality>
      </author>
      <rating>atmospheric</rating>
   </story>
   <story>
      <title>The Turn of the Screw</title>
      <author>
         <name>Henry James</name>
         <nationality>American</nationality>
      </author>
      <rating>a bit dull</rating>
   </story>
</stories>
```

5. Click the Data tab at the bottom of the code window and you should see the following:

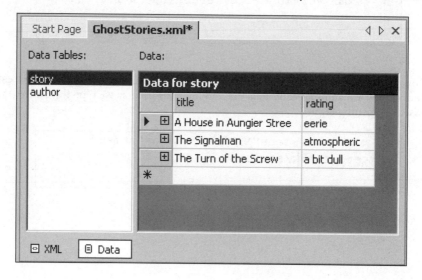

6. We can actually edit the data in this table, so we can modify our XML document here without even having to type the tags. Click on the box for the title column in the empty row at the bottom of the grid, and type **Number 13**. Now, move to the rating box beside it, and type **mysterious**. This enters a new story, but we still need to enter the author. To do this, click on the plus sign next to the new row. This will bring up a link for the `<author>` element:

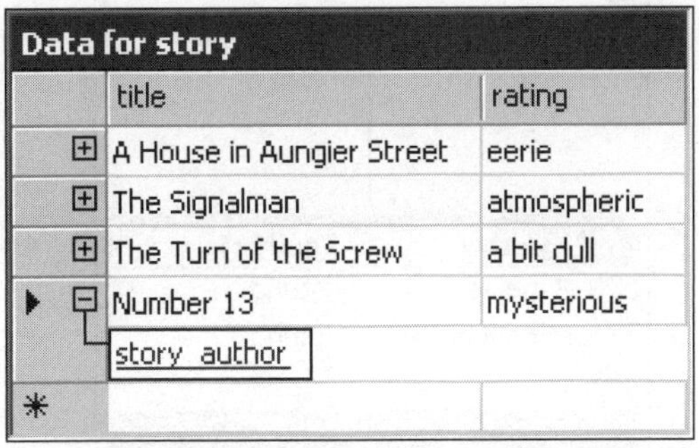

		title	rating
	⊞	A House in Aungier Street	eerie
	⊞	The Signalman	atmospheric
	⊞	The Turn of the Screw	a bit dull
▶	⊟	Number 13	mysterious
		story author	
✳			

Data for story

7. Click on this link, and another table will be displayed, where we can enter the name and nationality of the author. Enter **MR James** and **English** in the two columns (make sure you press *Enter* after typing the nationality, or the data will be lost):

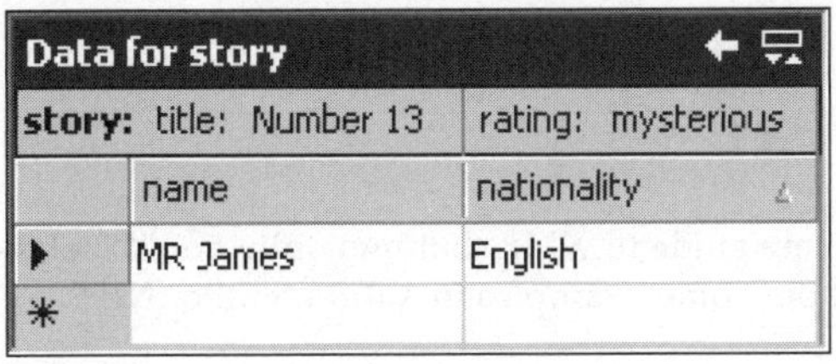

Data for story

story:	title: Number 13	rating: mysterious
	name	nationality
▶	MR James	English
✳		

8. Now click on the **XML** tab at the bottom of the window to view the XML source again. A new `<story>` element should have been added just before the closing `</stories>` tag:

```
<story>
   <title>Number 13</title>
   <rating>mysterious</rating>
   <author>
      <name>MR James</name>
      <nationality>English</nationality>
   </author>
</story>
```

9. As its final party trick, we'll get Visual Studio to create an XSD schema for this XML document. Go back to **Data** view by clicking on the **Data** tab at the bottom of the window. Right-click on the grid and select **Create Schema**. Visual Studio will create an XSD schema, but it also creates a diagram to visually represent the schema:

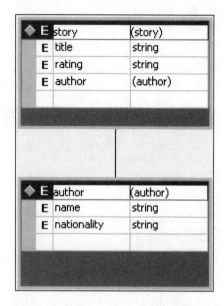

10. To view the actual schema, right-click on the diagram, and select View XML Source.

Summary

This appendix isn't a complete guide to XML, but hopefully you'll feel more confident about using and creating XML having tried out some examples in Visual Studio .NET.

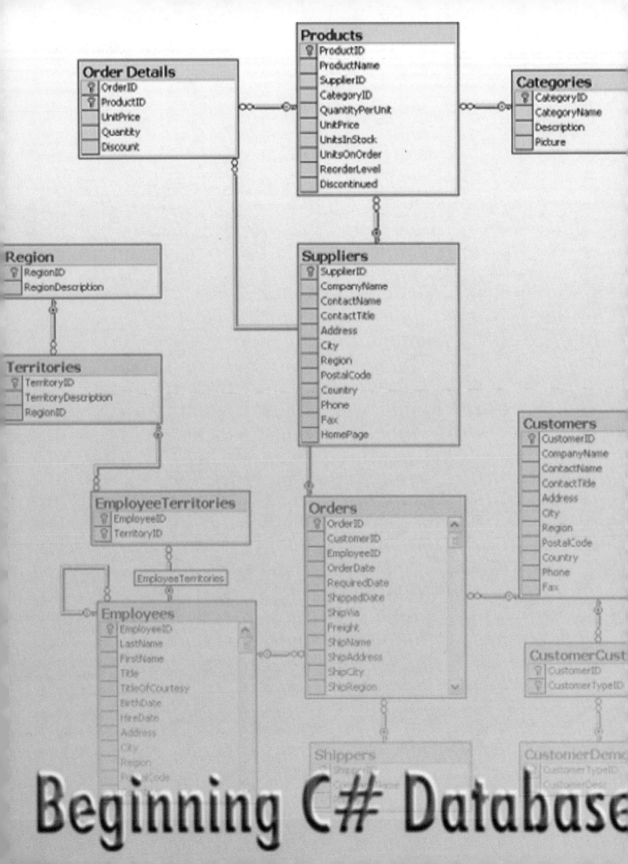

Index

O

R

X

wrox

Programmer to Programmer™

Registration Code: | 6098039QAN35DR01 |

Wrox writes books for you. Any suggestions, or ideas about how you want
information given in your ideal book will be studied by our team.
Your comments are always valued at Wrox.

Free phone in USA 800-USE-WROX
Fax (312) 893 8001

UK Tel.: (0121) 687 4100   Fax: (0121) 687 4101

Beginning C# Databases – Registration Card

Name _____

Address _____

_____

_____

City _____ State/Region _____

Country _____ Postcode/Zip_____

E-Mail _____

Occupation _____

How did you hear about this book?

❏ Book review (name) _____

❏ Advertisement (name) _____

❏ Recommendation _____

❏ Catalog _____

❏ Other _____

Where did you buy this book?

❏ Bookstore (name) _____ City_____

❏ Computer store (name) _____

❏ Mail order_____

❏ Other _____

What influenced you in the purchase of this book?

❏ Cover Design   ❏ Contents   ❏ Other (please specify):

_____

How did you rate the overall content of this book?

❏ Excellent   ❏ Good   ❏ Average   ❏ Poor

What did you find most useful about this book? _____

_____

_____

What did you find least useful about this book? _____

_____

Please add any additional comments. _____

_____

What other subjects will you buy a computer book on soon?

_____

What is the best computer book you have used this year?

_____

Note: This information will only be used to keep you updated
about new Wrox Press titles and will not be used for
any other purpose or passed to any other third party.

wrox

Programmer to Programmer™

Note: If you post the bounce back card below in the UK, please send it to:

Wrox Press Limited, Arden House, 1102 Warwick Road,
Acocks Green, Birmingham B27 6HB. UK.

Computer Book Publishers